BUILD YOUR HARVEST KITCHEN

Editor: William H. Hylton

Art Director: Barbara Field
Assistant Editor: John Blackford

Editorial Assistants: Nancy Arobone
**   Susan Scharadin**
Proofreaders: Noreen Parker
**   Felicia Knerr**

Principal Text by John Blackford   *Text Contributions by* *Peter Beidler*
                   Marjorie Hunt   *Mitch Brown*
                   William H. Hylton   *Bill Keough*
                                                                    Rich Kline
                                                                    Glenn Kranzley
                                                                    Earl Lehman
                                                                    John Ravage

Illustrations by Keith Heberling   *Additional Illustrations by Tom Evert*
                  Linda Heberling   *Barbara Field*
                  John Hoover   *Andy Hall*
                  Gene Mater   *Ted Niemczyk*
                  David Purcell   *Terry Pierce*
                  Mark Schultz   *Ken Raniere*
                  Tom Walz   *Chris Tackacs*
                                                                     Roger Taylor

Photographs by Mitchell T. Mandel
Cabinets and Projects Designed and Built by Jim Eldon
                                             Philip Gehret
                                             Fred Matlack

BUILD YOUR YOUR HARVEST KITCHEN

 Rodale Press Emmaus, Pennsylvania

Printed in the United States of America on recycled paper containing a high percentage of de-inked fiber.

Library of Congress Cataloging in Publication Data

Main entry under title:
Build your harvest kitchen.
   Includes index.
   1. Kitchens—Design and construction.   I. Hylton, William H.
TX653.B82   643′.3   80-14889
ISBN 0-87857-316-X hardcover

2 4 6 8 10 9 7 5 3 1 hardcover

Contents

Contents _____

Part V Building Projects for the Harvest Kitchen

Part IV Cabinets and Storage

Part V Building Projects for the Harvest Kitchen

Acknowledgments

For help in creating the black and white photos for this book, the editors would like to thank the folks at the following firms: The Chestnut Greenery, Emmaus Nutrition Center and Wentz Hardware, all of Emmaus, Pennsylvania; Silversmith Shop, Kitchens by Wieland, Ann Ar Book Shoppe, Ace Hotel and Bar Supply and the Anna Rodale Gourmet Center, all of Allentown, Pennsylvania; and Owen M. Bastian, Inc., of Trexlertown, Pennsylvania. General Electric appliances were provided by Harwick Appliances of Emmaus. Fine cookware was provided by La Belle Cuisine, 36 South Ninth Street, Allentown, Pennsylvania 18102.

Part I

Planning the Kitchen You Want

Your harvest kitchen won't just happen. It can't be dreamed into being. Dreaming about it *is* clearly the first step. But to have a harvest kitchen in which to work and live, you've got to put those dreams on paper, work with them, modify them, give them substance and dimension. The planning process is one of research and contemplation, of talking and thinking. It is building on paper. Only when you've got a blueprint of your harvest kitchen, whether a formal architect's blueprint, a draftsman's measured drawing or your own sketch marked with dimensions, can you get down to work, wiring, building, finishing.

Gathering Information

Somewhere in the back of your mind there's an image of an ideal kitchen. Your ideal is probably compounded partly of nostalgia for the cozy kitchen of your childhood, envy for the efficient kitchen of friends, and wistfulness for the spacious kitchens you've seen in magazines. Negative thoughts, as well, may have gone into your

kitchen fantasy—memories of the awkward cabinet door you bumped your head on in your first apartment, a loathing for your present undependable stove, boredom with the run-of-the-mill linoleum or kitchen lighting fixtures.

As you have developed your own patterns of cooking and preserving food, you've had a chance to learn about the kind of kitchen you need. You've probably imagined one with plenty of space for cooking and preserving food, possibly even with special areas set aside for baking, canning, and cold storage. That imagined kitchen can form the basis for your new kitchen plan.

Fantasies, however, are only the first step. You will also need hard information in order to make sound judgments. Before you do any work on your present kitchen, take some time to gather facts and ideas. Even in a big project, gathering the information and developing the plan can take longer than the work itself.

Background Information

Before you actually start planning a new kitchen, collect as much information as you can. You might even start a file and put everything you acquire into it. Talk to friends who have recently done their kitchens. Find out about building codes. Call up supply houses and ask for information. Write to manufacturers for brochures. Ask plumbers, electricians and carpenters to make estimates, and pump them for information. This doesn't mean you're going to take them for a ride under the pretext of hiring out the work. Until you learn what a certain job would cost in the trade as against the cost in time and money for you to do it yourself, you won't know whether you should do it yourself. You may very well decide to contract out part of the work, if your skills are weak in some area, or if your available time is short.

As you talk to people about kitchens, jot down the main points they make—dollar amounts, quantities of material, problems to avoid. When you look over these notes a few months later, you'll probably be surprised at all you've forgotten of those memorable talks. But gradually, you will get a feel for the amount of work required for different projects, the cost in materials and labor to have them done professionally, and the elements of design that you want.

During the preliminary stages of information gathering, don't worry much about exactly how much renovation you will have done by others or how much you'll do yourself. Just fill in the background as much as you can. Spend as much as a couple of months on this stage. If you plan to do the work in the summer, the fall is a reasonable time to begin gathering information.

What You Need to Know

With the background information you've acquired to guide you, begin thinking about the specific work you may require. Start with your present kitchen. Measure the length of the walls, the width of the windows and doors, and the height and width of the cabinets and counters. Later on, when you draw up plans for your new kitchen, whether it will be in the same location as your present kitchen or in some other room, you can use these measurements to help in the design. If 36-inch-high counters are too high for you, you'll never know it more clearly than if your present counters are that high. What you need to do now is to translate vague feelings like "too high" into inches, types of wood, and brand names, into the specifics you'll need to build your harvest kitchen.

The things you'll need to learn will obviously depend on the changes you are going to make. But you need to know enough about each aspect of the kitchen to be able to decide. Whether you depend on contractors or on yourself for expertise, any kitchen project has common aspects. You'll need to examine the wiring, if only to decide that the present wiring is adequate. But if you are moving or adding large electric appliances, you'll probably need at least one new circuit.

You'll need to know about your plumbing, and if you move the sink or add a dishwasher,

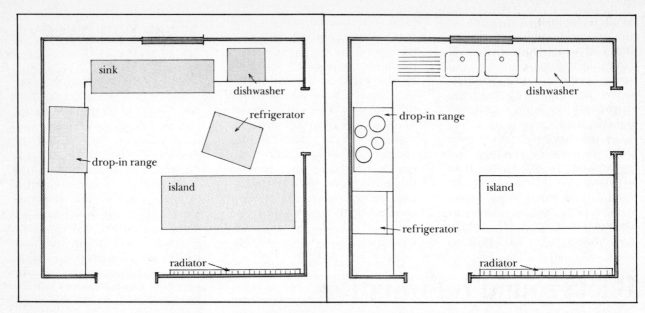

Start planning your new harvest kitchen by measuring the present kitchen. Lay it out to scale on graph paper. Using paper cutouts representing the major appliances, start playing around with kitchen arrangements.

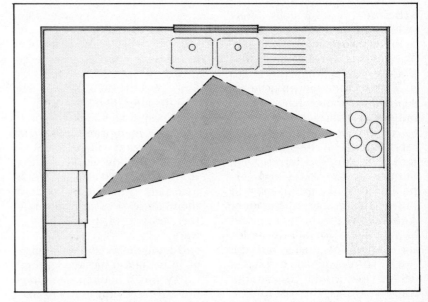

The ideal is to arrange the refrigerator, stove and sink, each with an accompanying work center, in a triangle.

you will probably do some plumbing, too. You should be familiar with not only the dimensions of your present kitchen, but with the underlying structure as well. Before you commit yourself to a particular design, you'll want to know what kinds of materials are available for floors, walls and ceilings, and whether the present surfaces can be repaired rather than replaced.

You should check the market for cabinets and counters. If you have enough free time, consider making your own cabinets. However, for this you'd have to be able to work wood to closer tolerances than for general carpentry, and you might have to buy some new tools.

Find out about appliances, how much they cost, which ones are energy efficient, and whether they are really needed

4

in a harvest kitchen. In addition to reading about the appliances, you'll want to shop around at different suppliers, paying particular attention to such things as power ratings of various models, guarantees, apparent durability and quality of design and workmanship.

You must learn about the design elements that go into an efficient kitchen, the particular relation between appliances and work centers that make the work easier. In this effort, you'll have to give a lot of weight to your own experience, because the standard information is inadequate for the person who does much canning, butchering or baking. You'll need extra work and storage space for these activities.

Before you get too far along, learn about the building codes in your area. The nearest township or municipal authority can acquaint you with these regulations. There are building codes, electrical and plumbing codes, and often zoning regulations. Call the building inspector first. He will be able to direct you to the other pertinent agencies.

Finally, inventory your resources. Estimate the time required for various projects to see whether you have enough time to do them. Decide whether you can acquire the necessary skills. Learn how much materials will cost and whether you can afford them. Find out how much professional help you can afford. You may discover that a bank loan is the only way to do justice to your kitchen requirements. Better now than when the work has already begun. If that turns out to be the case, examine financing, and shop around at different banks.

Design for a Special Kitchen

Harvest kitchens differ from ordinary kitchens because they must accommodate large quantities of garden and homestead produce in an orderly and efficient manner. A harvest kitchen needs plenty of counter and storage space. Each appliance should have some adjacent counter space. If possible, the kitchen should be provided with work centers where the tools for different jobs are located. This keeps footwork to a minimum. The ideal relation between sink, stove and refrigerator is a triangle. These three elements form the basic kitchen, and each should be set up as a work center. Other possible centers include space for bread making, small-scale butchering, canning (possibly located in another room), baking, and food freezing. Many of these functions overlap, and all kitchens present unique opportunities and limitations. But even at this stage, it's useful to give some thought to the eventual organization of the kitchen.

How Much Change Is Necessary?

With some idea of basic harvest kitchen design in mind, you can begin to shape your list of needs. Start with a careful examination of your present work habits. Are you frustrated by lack of room or poorly organized space when there is a large quantity of harvest produce to deal with or when there are several tasks that need doing at the same time? Try to pinpoint your frustrations and then ask yourself what it would take to relieve them.

There are many degrees of change possible, each with particular requirements. In approximate order of complexity, they are:

- Sprucing up.
- Rearranging and remodeling.
- Enlarging the present kitchen.
- Moving to a new room.
- Building on a new room.
- Starting from scratch by designing a kitchen as part of a new house.

Sprucing Up

Return from your vacation, and you find that the murky green kitchen wallpaper pops out at you as it never did before. You've isolated and identified a nagging problem. Or you may realize that there isn't enough light—you've been squinting over recipes and avoiding the kitchen in the evening. Maybe,

5

Before

After

looking with new eyes, you'll see that the drab linoleum casts a dreary spell over the whole kitchen.

Stripping wallpaper and adding a coat of fresh paint, building in a recycling center, installing a bank of good lights, laying a new floor, or even buying a new stove will cost a fraction of what a new kitchen would. You can call your renewal project "sprucing up," and you'll be amazed at the difference it can make in your kitchen.

Sprucing up may involve anything short of rearranging the work areas and major renovation of the kitchen. It will typically include such things as painting and patching walls or ceilings, replacing an old linoleum floor, refinishing cabinets, replacing an old sink, and running electrical cable for new receptacles or fixtures. You will probably not be concerned with the structural frame of the kitchen, except perhaps to run cable through it. More drastic changes, like adding a new window or installing a heavy tile floor that requires extra support for the floor joists, would be remodeling.

You may have decided to add a large light panel to brighten a gloomy room. You won't need a thorough knowledge of all the components in your kitchen to

Sprucing up a drab kitchen may include installing new light fixtures, overhead and at work centers, replacing a worn-out stove, adding a new cabinet and ventilation hood, or simply changing the window treatment.

do the job, but you must be able to answer a few questions. Which way do the ceiling joists run? Where is the nearest electrical cable, and can the circuit safely take additional load? What is the best way to run the cable to the projected fixture? Each job has its own set of questions. Find the answers, and make sure you understand the steps that will be required. Before you start the job, gather all the tools and materials you'll need.

Rearranging and Remodeling

For people who process harvest food, rearranging and redesigning must be preceded by patient self-observation. You alone know, or can learn, the motions you and your crew go through when preparing broccoli for the freezer, making apple butter, or canning peaches.

You know whether you spend more time over the sink or over the stove, and therefore can judge which area should be centrally located and which should be given more elbow room. Is reaching easier than bending for you? Then allow yourself more over-the-counter storage. Do you work better alone or with others? Do you like to sit down for long jobs, or do you always seem to stay on your feet however many comfortable stools are provided? Answering such questions will help you determine just where extra space is needed, and rearrangement is often the key to useful space.

There are several common

kitchen problems that rearranging can solve, among them: awkward relationships among appliances, lack of convenient preparation centers near appliances, traffic-flow problems.

Maybe one appliance, say the refrigerator, seems miles away from anything else, so that getting an egg for a recipe can mean a major trip. Rearranging will allow you to move appliances in closer to make a tighter and more efficient appliance triangle.

Even if the appliance triangle is balanced, your kitchen may frustrate you because appliances stand alone with no rationally organized working space attached to them. When you come in with a big basket of refrigerator-bound vegetables with no place to set it, you wind up carrying vegetables piecemeal across the room. Rearranging can organize appliances into their own interrelated centers and allow adequate work space.

Probably the most common major flaw in kitchen design is an inconvenient traffic pattern. If someone removes hot bread from the oven is he apt to collide with someone else removing carrots from the refrigerator? Will better appliance placement correct this hazard?

What areas adjoin the kitchen? The garden? The dining room? The parlor? Do you mind traffic or does it cheer you? Is tracking a problem after rain or snow? What proportion of total kitchen floor space goes into throughways? A solution to the rush hour confusion may be as simple as blocking off the back stairway, or making part of

the kitchen into a pantry.

You'll have to think about problems like how to keep a free passage to the herb and kitchen gardens while discouraging its use by small, dripping snowball makers or stray door-to-door insurance salesmen. Moving the door may be a solution.

When rearranging your kitchen you'll probably have to get down to the basic supporting structure. Moving a window or door will certainly require that you close up the old opening and cut a new one through the wall studs. If you move the sink or add a dishwasher, you must run plumbing to the new location. If you have to run the pipes through joists or studs, you must do it without weakening them. The sink must remain close to the vent stack. If the sink is farther from the stack than the critical distance defined by the plumbing code, you'll need a new stack, and that will require even more changes in the structure.

If you move the stove, you'll have to allow for ventilation ducts from the hood to the outside, or endure a moist kitchen. The heavy electrical cable will have to be rerouted for an electric range; for a gas or propane range, it will be the gas pipes. Heating pipes or ducts, possibly a flue for a wood stove, will all have to run safely through the structural portion of the kitchen without interfering with one another and without weakening the structure. This will require careful planning of each aspect of the kitchen, thorough knowledge of the procedures, and familiarity with pertinent codes.

7

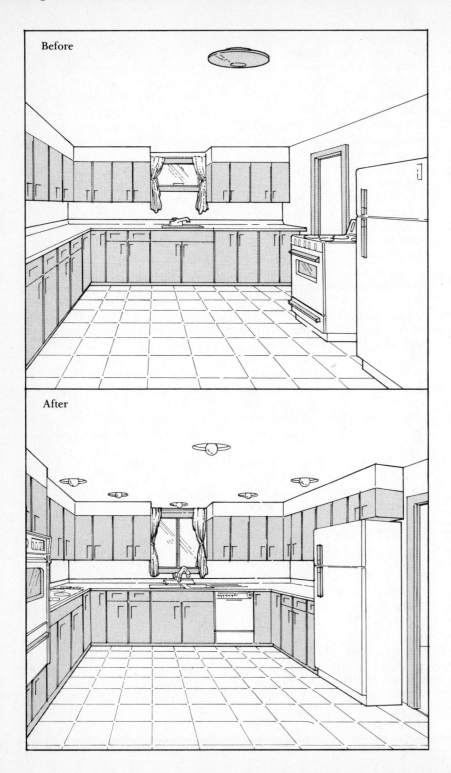

Before

After

Enlarging

It may well be that when you return from that vacation, something occurs to you as suddenly as if you had been slapped— your kitchen is simply too small. If, whenever you try to can a bushel of tomatoes, you trip over your own feet, fight with people who try to help you, bruise your elbows and wind up feeling as if you'd spent the day in a phone booth, you'll appreciate what more space can do for you.

Remember, though, that the space we use is not only the space we move through. Visual space is as important psychologically as floor space is physically. Many a kitchen has been "enlarged" into spaciousness by the addition of a good window or the removal of half of the wall that separated it from a breakfast area.

After you've played about with visual-space possibilities, however, you may decide you will need more "moving-around" space to ease congestion in your appliance triangle, to allow for counter working areas between appliances, to rectify a bad traffic pattern, or just to allow for broader motions and deeper breaths.

Is there a wall or two you can move back or take down to gain the space? Maybe it's the wall of

Analyze your own needs when considering rearranging your kitchen. Here, the traffic pattern was improved by moving the doorway and major appliances. Additional lighting was added, as well as much-needed counter and cabinet space.

a seldom-used and therefore contractible dining room, or the wall between the kitchen and the back porch. It may be that you can make an antiquated butler's pantry into part of the kitchen.

If you're thinking of taking out or moving a wall to gain space, stand in the newly projected space and pretend the wall's not there. Move things around in your mind. Reckon the space gained and figure out how best to use it for your freezing, canning, drying and other harvest chores.

You'll have to be certain that you can move an unwanted wall without danger. As a practical matter, the outside walls of a house are considered load bearing. That means they support the weight of the house. But even interior walls can be load bearing. And if you would like to knock out a wall to incorporate a porch or back room, be sure that the wall between the kitchen and the porch isn't the bearing wall. The porch may have been added after the house was built.

The question of load can be tricky. If you can't be sure whether or not a wall carries load, you'll have to call in a builder or architect to find out. If the wall does bear load, you can still remove a portion of it as long as you support it during construction and install a beam of the proper size at the top of the opening. The beam must rest on vertical posts thick enough to carry the load above the opening, and these posts may have to run all the way to footings in the basement. Per-

missible spans for beams and the required size of supporting posts are standard. If you decide to tackle this kind of project, your work will have to be inspected by a building inspector. You may be able to get the pertinent information from him, from a carpentry textbook or possibly even from a friendly architect or builder. Just make sure you have the correct information.

Moving to a New Room

There is another option when your kitchen is too small, or when it's awkward or poorly situated. You can move the whole kitchen to another room. Attached garages, outgrown or little-used dining or family rooms, screened porches, parlors, downstairs bedrooms or dens often make fine kitchens if properly converted. Then, after you've moved out of the present kitchen, you can turn the vacant space into a pantry, a storage room or a sitting room. This may be an expensive option, but it's often a sensible one.

Moving to a new room means you must decommission your old kitchen. You will have to cap off plumbing and tie off wiring. In the new room, you'll have to provide the necessary plumbing, heating, ventilation and wiring. The work is much the same as in rearranging a kitchen.

Building On

An even more ambitious way

of getting more kitchen space is to build a new kitchen onto your existing house. When you do this, you can almost start from scratch in your design of appliance relationships and traffic patterns. You will, however, have to maintain the structural and design integrity of the whole house.

You have to match the exterior of the addition with that of your house, or use complementary materials. You'll also have to decide where to situate the new addition so that as a family center it will fit into the overall organization of the living area and that as a kitchen it will function separately.

It's not always easy to match exterior siding, roofing materials, or window and door frames. You may have cringed at the sight of shoddy patchwork houses with mismatched shingles, window frames and siding, and you may have admired rambling old farmhouses that have obviously grown outward over many years, but grown gracefully. Try for the latter.

Perhaps you'll want to consult an architect to make sure that your planned addition will add to the appearance and effectiveness of your home. Also, ask advice of building contractors and suppliers. They may be able to suggest materials that will blend, or pleasantly contrast, with those on your home.

In building on, you will have to tie into the existing house in a structurally sound manner. Your new roof must connect with the old one without disrupting the drainage. You'll have to be sure that your foun-

9

dation extends well below the frost line. Here again, your building inspector can probably tell you how deep to make the foundation, since it's part of his job to know.

Building an addition presents some of the same problems as rearranging the kitchen, and offers many of the advantages of building a new house. Once you've tapped into the service lines, you are working from scratch. This gives you real flexibility in locating appliances where you want them. There's also more work involved, and careful planning is essential.

Examine your heating system to find out if it has the capacity to heat another room. Where the heater doesn't have enough reserve capacity (not very likely), a separate heating unit may be necessary in the new room, possibly a wood heater or some kind of built-in electric unit.

Starting from Scratch

Building a kitchen as part of a new house is easier in some ways and more difficult in others than renovation. In renovation, you must protect parts of the kitchen from damage during the construction. You must tear out walls to get at wires and pipes, then patch them up again. But in a new house, you start with nothing. Like an artist facing a blank canvas you'll ask the question, "Where to begin?"

Soon enough, however, external constraints will begin to shape the project—cost of ma-

terials, size and layout of the building lot, perhaps desire for a southern exposure in the kitchen, need for proximity to the dining area.

Consider how the sun will shine into the kitchen. Do you want sun in the morning, the evening or throughout the day? Consider the view from the sink—you'll be seeing a lot of that view in all seasons of the year. You may want to consider how the kitchen door leads to the driveway and the garden. Which family functions would serve as a pleasant, convivial background for the harvest cook, and which wouldn't?

In general, it is wise to let the member of the household who is to use the kitchen most have most say in its planning. In harvesting households, the kitchen is probably the most important room in the house; the layout of the other rooms may have to be arranged to make the kitchen work to its best advantage.

Growing and Changing

By now you have an idea how extensive the changes you'll

make will be—from sprucing up to totally new. You also have a rough idea of what you can afford to undertake. Knowing where you are going will help you to ask the right questions and gather the most useful information.

Don't forget that people and their patterns change too. Family size increases and then diminishes. Harvesting ambition waxes and wanes. An enlarged, rearranged or new kitchen may be designed to grow as resources and needs grow—say by leaving room for an island work center, leaving part of one wall free for expanded counter and cabinet space, or designing in an alcove where something you haven't thought of yet will someday fit. Your kitchen can keep changing as you do.

If you haven't enough money to renovate all at once, design the project so that you can do it step by step. Allow enough room for the cabinets you will have. If you adopt this approach, finish each step completely so that the kitchen remains functional and attractive. You don't want it to look like a five-year construction project, even if it is.

Codes, Ordinances and Inspectors

You've probably heard stories about people who went ahead and built additions, or even whole houses, without ever submitting a plan to an authority—and without catch-

ing sight of a building inspector. You may decide to follow their example, and if you live in the country or in a sparsely populated and loosely governed area, or if you only make minor changes, you may have no problems.

In some localities, however, zoning or building code infractions can cost you a stiff fine, require you to abandon your plans, or even force you to remove what you have built. If you are going to ignore or defy the law, you are taking a very real risk; be prepared to accept the consequences.

Codes and inspections and inspectors can drive you batty. Instead of specifying only that a structure must be sound and safe, some codes specify exactly what materials and types of construction are to be permitted. Some permit only licensed professionals to do certain tasks. Many have become so detailed, technical and conservative that only an expert can read and interpret them. These codes seem designed to offend and frustrate the do-it-yourselfer.

But carefully drawn codes protect you and others from dangerous, unsound structures. They do have a rational purpose and can be a genuine benefit. Avoid problems by finding out what's required.

Gathering Information about Codes and Zoning

Before you begin any but a small kitchen-renewal project, find out what the situation is in your locality:

- Learn what, if any, national and local building codes are in effect in your area by calling the local municipal or township building inspector.

- Obtain a copy of the code from the building inspector and read it thoroughly. He can help you interpret it. Ask the advice of friends who've obtained permits for their own work.

- If building permits are required, find out from the inspector how much they cost and what additional material must accompany the permit form, such as specifications, drawings or value estimates.

- If you live in an uncrowded area, you may be able to find out who will do your building inspection. Learn what kind of person he is (how finicky, how open to new methods), how others have found it best to deal with him, and what his own background and interests are. If he's a former heating contractor, for example, he may be more interested in and critical of your heating ducts than your carpentry.

- Find out when in the building process inspection is made and how many inspections are required.

- Learn about the mechanism for appeal over the building inspector—who his superiors are and how to deal with them. Most codes spell out appeal procedures.

- Find out how your property is zoned and, if necessary, how to obtain variances.

- If your project comes under building codes or is affected by zoning ordinances, arrange formal or informal discussion with the people

who issue permits, enforce zoning restrictions, or do inspections, so that you can tailor your plans to their concerns and anticipate points of friction. Be prepared with cogent arguments to show why your proposed construction and materials are safe. Remember that public safety is the "bottom line" of any code.

Building Codes

Codes specify how buildings may be constructed and of what materials. They mandate permits for certain projects, and provide for inspections during the building process. They also impose penalties for failure to comply.

In most states, each municipality may:

- Decide to adopt no code at all.
- Draft its own code.
- Adopt an entire model code drafted by an organization.
- Adopt the model code, providing sections of its own.

Find out which course your municipal governing body has taken, and which, if any, national model code is in use. There are four major codes:

- The National Building Code (NBC) was developed by a group of insurance companies as a means of reducing losses by fire.
- The Uniform Building Code (UBC) is widely used in the West.

11

- The Basic Building Code (BBC), often used in the Midwest and East, was written by the Building Officials and Code Administrators International (BOCA).
- The Standard Building Code (SBC) was written by the Southern Building Code Conference; used for much of the South, it includes provisions for regional problems like termite control.

In addition, all four model-code organizations collaborated to produce the One- and Two-Family Dwelling Code, a simply organized, easy-to-follow manual that is available from any of the four organizations. Your local governing authority, usually located at a city hall or county courthouse, will have a copy of the code it requires. There you also will find permit applications.

The Kitchen Builder and the Codes

Probably the first thing you need to determine is whether or not your project comes under the jurisdiction of the local code. Under some codes, it is the cost of the project or the amount it adds to the value of the house that determines whether a permit is required. To apply for a permit, you must place monetary value on the work you propose to do. Here are some ways in which building codes may affect your project:

- Some codes stipulate that no structural, plumbing or electrical changes may be made, nor any repairs costing over $100 undertaken, without a permit.
- Others specify that if a certain percentage (usually 50 percent) of the value of a structure is spent for an alteration, the entire structure must conform to the code. Older homes can remain after a new code is in effect, provided they are not altered. The materials or techniques used in an older home may no longer pass code requirements. Codes have been made stiffer recently, especially in their requirements for light, ventilation and fire safety.
- The value of your project determines the price you must pay for a permit, according to some codes. The code may require the inspector to place a value on alterations. The SBC requires a plan-checking fee of half the cost of the building permit for construction over $1,000.
- If you are adding a room or building a new house, you'll have to learn what types of foundations are permitted under the local code. Some require masonry, while others (NBC and SBS) permit a variety of foundation systems, including wood frame of specified standard that resists decay. Most codes stipulate that foundations must extend below the frost line, must support a load and distribute it within the load-bearing value of the soil, and must be as thick as the walls they support.
- When you add on or build a new room, you'll be doing framing, and codes stipulate permissible framing methods as well as, in some cases, the materials to be used. Check to see if post and beam framing is permitted. It is economical and sound but often frowned upon by conservative building authorities, so you may have to defend its use. Older, more detailed codes may set forth the length of lumber spans and bracing requirements. Other codes put emphasis on function—for example, framing above an opening (window or door) must transfer all superimposed load to the nearest vertical member.
- Some codes require that only grade-stamped lumber be used for framing. If you are providing lumber from your own woodlot or are using salvaged lumber, you may have to convince the person who issues the permit, and the building inspector, that it is the equivalent of graded lumber.
- There are minimum requirements for room size (usually 50 square feet) in most codes, but a harvest kitchen will almost certainly exceed them. The ceiling will also certainly exceed the minimum 7-foot height requirement.
- The Dwelling Code states that a kitchen, like any other habitable room, must have an area equal to one-tenth of the floor area, but at least 10 square feet, in windows or window-doors, half of which can open. Exceptions can be

made for kitchens where the ventilation system changes the air every 30 minutes. Some of the model codes permit skylights and venting systems as alternatives or supplements to windows. Most kitchens would be dreary and stuffy indeed if they didn't meet these minimal requirements.

- Under the Dwelling Code, kitchens sinks must be connected to a municipal sewer or an approved private sewer system and to an approved water supply with capacity for hot and cold water. Sewer requirements can be a problem in some areas for people who wish to install a composting toilet and a small grey-water leach field. You have to convince the inspector. Health and safety codes usually require inspection of drain fields and pipes before they are covered; if your kitchen project involves extensive plumbing or enlarging the septic system, be prepared to obtain a permit and undergo inspection.
- If you're installing a fireplace or wood range, check what your code says about chimneys and flues.
- Many codes require a certain amount of insulation for new additions. The requirements are not unreasonable, and they result in savings of fuel. Newer provisions, often added to local codes under state mandate, dictate that passive solar techniques, like placing windows in south-facing walls, must be used.

Other Codes

Fire prevention codes are enforced by local fire departments. These are enforced where there are no building codes.

Sanitary and health codes are used in many rural areas that do not have building codes, to govern the installation of septic tanks and leach field disposal systems; they require percolation tests for new installations.

Electrical codes have been consolidated into the National Electrical Code, which is widely used. You do not need to read over this extensive document to do electrical work, but be aware of it, and learn the basic rules that govern residential installations as outlined in the wiring chapter of this book. Learn any changes from the National Code that have been adopted by your local authority. These are usually available from the electrical inspector.

The National Plumbing Code is less widely used than the National Electrical Code but, adopted in its most restrictive form, it can require that your work be done only by a licensed plumber. Check with your local authority.

Zoning Ordinances

Some city, township or county authorities classify all the property within their jurisdiction into land-use categories—for example, single dwelling, multi-family dwelling, city center, watershed, agricultural, industrial, commercial. Zoning ordinances are intended to promote orderly growth and to protect natural resources and property values.

No one wants a fish market, poorly designed trailer park or an oil refinery plunked down next to his or her property after he has worked hard and spent heavily to make the home a pleasant place to live. That is why zoning ordinances restrict such facilities.

Some zoning ordinances also try to control the overall appearance of a locality by keeping new building out of certain historic areas, stipulating how a house is to be placed on a lot, and in a few cases, defining permissible housing styles.

You can purchase a copy of the zoning ordinance from your city or township authority.

When It Matters

Here are a few sample situations in which someone building or redesigning a kitchen might have trouble with zoning regulations:

- If zoning regulations have been established or changed in your locality within the past few years, your present home may be nonconforming. Under some ordinances, it has been granted what amounts to a temporary stay of execution. You'll be all right as long as you live in it as it is, but the minute you sell it, or more importantly, the day you make any substantial alterations, it is in violation of the ordinance. It is possible to get variances **13** and extensions of immunity, but you must apply for them before starting your project.

- Suppose you are building on a new kitchen and find that the most sensible way to join it to your house is to extend an ell that will reduce the size of your front and side yards. Check to be sure your addition won't be closer to a street or another building than allowed.

- You've designed the kitchen as part of a new family activity center. In fact, you're nearly doubling the floor space of your home. If your lot is small, check to see that your extended structure won't occupy more of your lot than the zoning law permits.

Other Legal Pitfalls

You work within the requirements of codes and zoning ordinances to avoid legal complications, but there are other pitfalls to avoid when planning to remodel:

- Check your home insurance coverage to make sure the space you add will come under your present coverage.
- If you are adding a kitchen fireplace, see whether that will affect your fire insurance.
- Make sure you will not be liable if someone is hurt while working on your kitchen. You may have to take out temporary insur-

ance to protect yourself from injury suits.

- If you use a contractor, make sure you'll not be held accountable for money owed by him to his suppliers in the event that he goes bankrupt before finishing your job.
- Look over your house mortgage to be sure you can remodel without getting permission from the mortgage holder. Permission is given readily by most banks, but failure to obtain it can get you into legal trouble.

An Inventory of Resources

By the time you've spent a couple of months gathering information and thinking about your kitchen, you should have a fairly clear idea of what appliances and materials are available. You should have some idea what they cost and what the going rate is for plumbers, electricians and carpenters. But, before you sit down to draw up a detailed plan, make a list of your resources.

Such an inventory will give you a clear view of the cost of renovation and of the amount of work you can expect to do yourself. It will enable you to draw your plan realistically. If you find that the time you have to spend on the project is short, you may have to reconsider your intention to make your own cabinets or do the plumbing. If required changes will cost more than you can afford, you may be able to plan the work in stages. Or you may begin your search for financing. Remember, though, that material costs and time spent usually turn out to be greater than they were estimated to be. It may take you three times as long to do a job for the first time as it

would an experienced worker. Be generous in your estimates.

Materials and Appliances

While you should be aware of the prices of materials and equipment, just as you should be of the cost of professional help, you may not always have to buy new. Weathered barn siding has a beauty all its own, yet you might find a farmer who will let you have all you want if you'll just haul it away.

When a building is being torn down, it is not at all uncommon for cabinets and paneling to be ripped out and sold for scrap lumber, or even junked. Houses that have been abandoned for years sometimes yield usable items, if you can track down the owner. Look for paneling, wooden cabinets that can be salvaged, possibly even flooring. If you do salvage a floor, allow for damage during removal and waste during installation. The floor you remove must be larger than the one you install.

When you gather information on materials and equipment,

make lists of sources—manufacturers, retailers of new products, even antique and secondhand dealers. Since your final plan will be influenced by the available materials, find out as much as you can now; when you draw up your plan, it will be based on actual measurements and specifications.

You'll need building supplies for a large-scale renovation. If you can salvage some of this material, fine. For the rest, visit lumberyards and other suppliers. Check prices and ask if they stock the materials you'll need. Find out what it will cost to have them deliver. Often there is no charge if you order more than a minimum amount. For cabinets and finishing materials, visit kitchen supply stores and hardware stores. Building suppliers and some lumberyards carry sinks, cabinets and other kitchen supplies, as do some of the large department store chains. For specialized supplies, see also plumbing and heating stores or electrical and lighting retailers.

Find out about appliances and equipment at many of the suppliers mentioned above and at appliance stores and restaurant supply houses. At the latter, you'll find products designed for professional use that are durable and unadorned, just what you need for harvest processing.

When you make your rounds, collect brochures and manufacturers' product descriptions. These often contain important specifications hidden among the glowing descriptions and color pictures. You can use these specifications to help decide which products really fit your needs.

In addition, write to manufacturers for literature on their products. Look through magazines, both for articles and advertisements. Sometimes an article will mention a new product without naming it. Write to the author of the article, in care of the magazine, for the name and address of the manufacturer. You'll usually find the addresses of advertisers somewhere in the magazine.

Tools

The next time you see a plumber or electrician, ask him how much of an investment he has in what he carries around in his truck. You'll probably be astonished at the high figure. Of course, you don't need everything he has by any means.

It's as important to assemble tools for a job as it is to secure materials, but supplying yourself with new tools can take a bite out of the capital you've set aside for your project. Buying secondhand tools saves money, but requires care, experience, and all kinds of time. You can also rent specialized, expensive tools that you aren't likely to use more than once. Borrowing tools may be the most economical solution as long as you don't wear out your welcome. It helps to have tools or skills to offer in return. A skilled helper may supply his own tools.

Skills

How much of the work on your project will you be able to do yourself? Will you be unwilling to tackle the job of building cabinets, doing the wiring and plumbing, framing a wall? If you are unsure of your ability, carefully read up on how to do the job. After you've finished, if you still aren't confident you can meet the challlenge, look for alternatives. An excellent means of acquiring a skill at the same time you're getting the job done, is to work alongside a more skilled person.

If you decide to take on an unfamiliar task yourself, arrange for assistance in case of problems. Despite their jokes about amateur workers, most tradespeople are sympathetic toward someone who makes an honest effort. There was a time when each one of them knew less than you do. Unless you really botch up a job, you can usually get assistance for a modest fee. In looking for skilled labor, don't neglect the retired tradesman, the moonlighting professional or the vocational-technical student who needs experience.

You may want to hire a general contractor, but do some of the work yourself under his direction. He can help you set up a schedule, secure materials, deal with subcontractors for jobs you don't want to tackle yourself, and handle permits and inspectors. Such assistance may be worth the money the contractor will charge you. If you adopt this method, make sure the contractor sympathizes with your plans and is somewhat flexible. You can run into problems deciding who is in charge **15** of whom and where his responsibility ends and yours begins.

For a building project that involves structural changes affecting your whole house, consider hiring an architect. An architect can help you with the design, draw plans, check specifications and lists of materials, secure a contractor if you need one, oversee the work, obtain permits, deal with inspectors, and make a final assessment of the finished job. Or he can simply review your plans and give you suggestions.

Time

One of the most important considerations is one that is often overlooked: How long will the job take? The danger of frayed nerves and family tension caused when a building deadline is not met is reason enough for an honest and realistic assessment of how much you can do and how quickly you can do it. Nothing can turn the project sour faster than a half-finished kitchen, unsightly, difficult or impossible to use, with no clear prospect for completion. Make your schedule carefully, and allow a generous margin of error for your own time, up to three times what you think the job will take. Allow for delays caused when materials are delivered late or workers don't start on time.

Make sure all preliminaries are taken care of by the day you've scheduled the work to start. This means that weeks and months prior to that day you will begin to assemble materials, tools, people and detailed plans. Schedule carefully and, if you're working with others, have a clear understanding about who is to do what and when they will do it.

Money

The amount of money you can spend or borrow will determine the extent of the changes you make. Carefully add up the prices of all the items you will need for the job. Allow at least 10 percent waste for materials such as lumber and wallboard, more for items like sheet flooring. Make allowances for the hidden costs, price changes and oversights that will invariably increase the final bill.

If you hire people to help, add in their salaries. Labor costs may come to 50 percent of materials costs for skilled help. Save all bills and invoices for materials and labor. Doing so will help you keep track of costs and can help save money in tax deductions. Energy-saving improvements such as storm windows or insulation earn a deduction. Records of money spent on home improvement will also reduce capital gains taxes when you sell the house.

If you haven't got the capital for the improvements you need, consider breaking the improvements into affordable steps spread over a year or more. Some building suppliers offer short-term payment plans, usually up to 90 days. But you may have to apply for a home improvement loan. There are several types, and the one you choose will depend on the amount you need, the equity you have in your home, the value of the home, and the value of the improvement.

Home improvement loans are generally available for projects ranging from redecorating to building an addition, and they can be obtained through banks, savings and loan associations, credit unions, and finance companies. In general, loans are easier to obtain from savings and loan associations than from banks. Members of credit unions may sometimes borrow money for home improvements at advantageous interest rates. Loans from finance companies are comparatively easy to secure, but interest rates are high.

Installment Loans. By far the most common for home improvement, these loans are secured by a signature only, or by collateral from a lien on the house, on other property or on securities. These loans allow up to ten years for repayment and are usually limited by law to $15,000, though ceilings vary from state to state.

Mortgage Extensions. Your current mortgage can be increased in amount. You receive the difference between the old and new mortgage value and pay an increased monthly rate. The worth of the improvement and the amount you have already paid on your mortgage give the lender security on the loan. Banks often place ceilings on mortgage extensions and if you exceed the ceiling you must remortgage your home. There may be a clause in your mortgage that allows these extensions.

Remortgage. If you remortgage, you may have to pay settlement costs, but if the current interest rate is lower than the rate on your mortgage—an unlikely situation—you may reduce your interest payments significantly. Whether the monthly payments are higher or lower than your present ones depends on the amount you increase the mortgage. The amount you receive in cash is the difference between the value of the old mortgage and the value of the new one, less any settlement costs.

Before you apply for a loan from a bank or savings and loan association, you must discuss your plans with a loan officer. Be prepared to:

- Give information on the value of your home and on any liens attached to it.
- Produce your home mortgage.
- Establish the value of the improvement you wish to make. In some cases, especially for savings and loan associations, this will require documented prices from the suppliers for the materials you plan to use.
- Give evidence that you have had sufficient experience in building to be able to complete the project satisfactorily (especially required for large projects). Banks, especially when the house is to be used as collateral, are more apt than savings and loan associations to question your ability to improve the value of your house if you do your own work.

- Have your credit rating checked.
- Have an appraiser inspect your house to determine its value. Factors which determine whether or not a bank will require that its appraisers evaluate your house are the value of the house, the extent of the mortgage, and the amount of money still due. Savings and loans are less apt to require appraisal than banks.
- Ask the lending institution if you qualify for a federally guaranteed loan under FHA or VA.
- Produce a sketch or plan of your improvement and a list of specifications.

Design

While you are looking for materials at building supply stores and restaurant suppliers, learn as much as you can about design. Note the arrangement in sample kitchens—how the work areas relate to each other, how the storage space fits into the plan, how the work gets done. Make note of arrangements that you might find useful, perhaps by drawing a simple sketch of the layout.

By the time you've learned what you need to about materials, you should recognize the most common kitchen floor plans. Many of these designs would not be useful for a harvest kitchen, but you may be able to extract elements that you can use in your kitchen. Set out to make lists of specific features you want and of problems you want to avoid.

It may help to keep a file on each element of design you are gathering ideas about—work centers, traffic flow, appliance arrangement, floor plans and storage. Drop sketches, clippings and notes into the appropriate folders. Later on, go back and remove the material that doesn't seem useful and, store it in some out-of-the-way place. You may have to dig out an address or two at some other time.

Continue to gather ideas on design by visiting and carefully observing friends' kitchens. Visit some kitchens that do quantity food preparation. A small restaurant kitchen can be a revelation, especially if the chef has had a hand in the design. It is amazing how much work you can get done in a small kitchen if it is well designed.

Don't overlook libraries and bookstores as sources for ideas. You can size up many books fairly quickly. Skim through the text looking for ideas and information you haven't seen before. In the library, take notes on salient points and make photocopies of drawings, pictures or even pages of text.

At first, you'll be gathering information, collecting ideas, just getting a feel for the subject. But over a period of some months, your understanding of design will grow. As that happens, you will be more and more able to combine general principles with your particular harvest needs. Then you will be ready for the next step, drawing the plan for your own kitchen.

17

Designing Your Harvest Kitchen

In a well-designed kitchen, the work gets done efficiently, without a lot of extra steps. The work areas are well lit and storage space is ample. The areas are arranged so that tasks progress from one to the other, more or less in the order they are performed. Temperature is moderate throughout. The kitchen is attractive, neither too cluttered nor too spacious. It

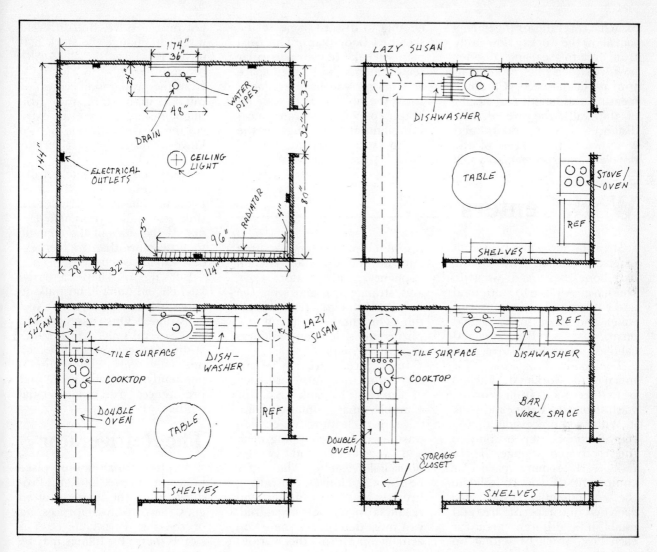

Planning begins with a scaled sketch of the room and carries through a variety of layouts. Perseverance is a key element: don't quit when you've got one layout. Keep trying to improve it.

strikes a balance, in other words, between a number of seemingly irreconcilable factors—and does it within the budget and in the space you have available.

To perform this minor miracle with your harvest kitchen, you'll need a clear understanding of each job you'll be doing in the kitchen, what equipment is needed, and how the job fits into the entire kitchen operation. Take out your folders and notes and go over them with a view toward the overall design. Think carefully how your own style of cooking and preserving will affect the plan. Identify problems, whether they result from lack of space, difficulty in moving vents or plumbing, or poor arrangement of work areas. Relate possible solutions to the rest of the design.

Before you draw a detailed plan, consider how each part of the kitchen fits into the whole. **19**

Sketch several arrangements that allow the work to flow easily from area to area, and consider how well each one responds to your particular needs. Carefully measure the length and height of the walls, the size of, and distance between, doors and windows. On the basis of the detailed measurements, you'll be able to discard some of the sketched floor plans. The final plan will balance your particular requirements with the space and money you have available. Draw the final plans to scale on graph paper. Accurate measurements and drawings are the key to a successful plan.

Work Centers

Strip the most luxurious and extensive kitchen down to the bare-bones basics and what do you have? A place to store food and equipment, and a source of water and heat. In household terms, that's a refrigerator and cabinets, a sink and a stove.

The basic progression for much of the work in the kitchen is to take food from storage, wash it or add water, and cook it. With food processing, there's the additional step of putting the food into storage. These tasks each require particular equipment. If you consolidate the equipment necessary for each task into a specific area and establish a different area for each task, you'll be setting up work centers.

Work centers save steps and make the work easier. Ideally, you shouldn't need to cross the kitchen just for a single item, and if the utensils are arranged by function, you won't have to. An effective work center has plenty of working space and storage. If you don't have room to work, having the tools in one place won't help. The tools must be out of the way but ac-cessible. Work centers are often built around the main kitchen appliances: refrigerator, stove and, strange as it may seen, the sink. (Although few people think of the sink as an appliance, most kitchen designers regard it as one.)

In practice, there may be several work centers at each appliance. The sink area, for example, may contain equipment for cleaning vegetables, washing dishes, chopping meat and vegetables, and general household cleaning. There may be pots, knives, scouring brushes and bowls. If the end result is to be well organized, you must determine where you actually perform the various tasks, and store the equipment there.

Also important in good design is how the work proceeds from one center to another. The work flows naturally from refrigerator to sink to stove, so the most natural place to have the main preparation center is between the sink and the stove. Vegetables, for instance, can then be washed, diced and dropped directly into the soup pot on the stove. But different tasks can change the work pattern. For salads, which are brought straight to the table from the preparation center, or put back in the refrigerator, you might decide to have an extra cutting board with one or two knives between the refrigerator and the sink.

Many cooks and kitchen designers prefer to have the three kitchen basics—refrigerator, sink, stove—in a triangular layout. If the sides of the triangle total no more than 22 feet, excess walking is reduced.

But if you have a large kitchen and don't mind walking between work areas, don't feel constrained. One possibility is to have several small refrigerators at different centers so that each one functions almost independently. Your own needs and preferences are the essential guide.

The Refrigerator

A refrigerator is a busy place in a productive kitchen. Produce from the garden often goes there to await processing or cooking. Perishable food is stored there. Pie fillings may be chilled, salad stored until time for serving, and batches of food from a large freezer may remain temporarily in the freezer compartment.

Equip the refrigerator area with plenty of containers for leftovers and garden produce. Rolls of aluminum foil and waxed paper for wrapping food are handy to have there, as are small and large plastic bags.

Position your refrigerator so

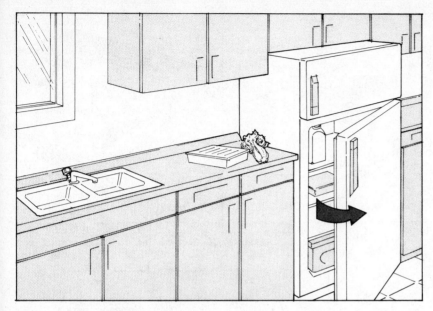

The refrigerator door should open away from the sink.

teakettle may end up on the stove, but it first must be filled with water. The best storage place is thus near the sink. While you don't need to think this out in complete detail as you plan the arrangements of work centers, you do have to allot sufficient storage and work space for each task.

A wide variety of sinks is available. You can get a "standard" kitchen sink that you set into a hole cut in the counter top. But you can also get double- and triple-compartmented sinks, deep sinks, shallow sinks. You may want to save an old cast-iron kitchen sink with integral drainboards. Or a slate sink. You may find an enormous utility sink useful in a food processing area, especially if the area doubles as a laundry and mudroom.

The Stove

The standard stove has four burners and an oven, but many cooks prefer a counter-mounted cooktop and a separate wall oven or two.

Whatever your preference, you need lots of counter and storage space on both sides of the stove. Especially during the summer canning season, a stove will make you cry out for breathing space. Make sure at least one of the counter tops adjacent to the stovetop is heat resistant so that hot pans won't mar it.

A built-in cooktop and a separate wall oven take up more wall and floor space than the conventional all-in-one setup, but separating the oven from the

that the door opens away from the sink. That way, the door won't come between you and the sink. The refrigerator door must be able to open completely so that racks and drawers may be removed for cleaning. Its door should not cross passage with any other door.

You will need a surface near the refrigerator on which to set the groceries and produce when you put them into or take them out of the refrigerator. A nearby kitchen table can serve this purpose, but an adjacent counter surface is easier to use.

The Sink

The sink is a focal point for the kitchen. It's where most food is washed and prepared, and it may be where dishes, utensils and pots are cleaned. Food is carried from the re-

frigerator, pantry or root cellar to the sink, then to the stove. Position the sink to fit that sequence, preferably in a triangular relation to the refrigerator and stove. The sink, with its plumbing, is also the most difficult part of the kitchen to situate. Choose its location first, then arrange the other work centers in relation to it.

You are also likely to spend much of your time near the sink, so it makes sense to have an interesting view. Sinks are often placed under windows. They can also be set in kitchen islands, peninsulas or divider-units that overlook a family room or children's play area.

If you think you'll want to sit by the sink to do some jobs, be sure to design space for your knees into the sink cabinet.

Put the equipment you'll use within reach of the sink. A

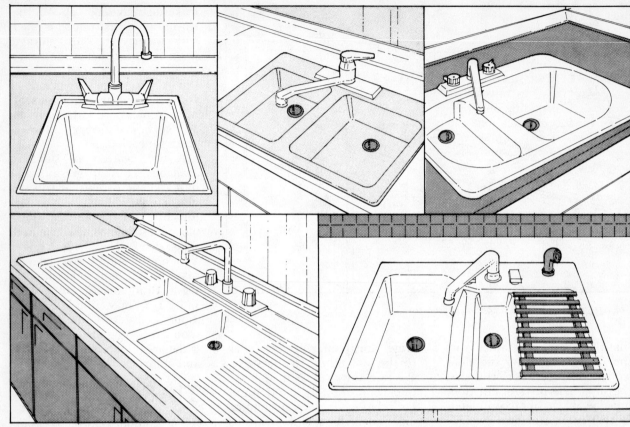

Consider your food-processing needs when choosing from the wide variety of available sinks. Do you want a deep sink, a double-compartmented sink, a sink with integral drainboards?

cooktop has certain advantages. It allows you to store equipment under the cooktop. And it allows you to adjust the height of the cooking surface by building your counter tops either higher or lower than the standard 36 inches. By the 36-inch standard, all cooks are the same height. That isn't the case, obviously, and even for people of average height, mixing, kneading and chopping are more easily done

Tiles set into the counter top beside the stove provide a place to set hot pots and pans, protecting the counter surface.

at a height of about 30 inches. Before building the cabinets and counter next to a cooktop, experiment to find a comfortable working height for the mixing and kneading you do.

If you have a conventional stove, or plan to buy one, build counter tops the right height for you even though the cooktop will be 36 inches high. Remember that it is at the preparation center, not the stovetop, that most of your work will be done. Build a small heat-resistant counter top at the standard height on each side of the stove, then step your counter up or down to the main preparation area. If you are tall, you can raise a stove to a comfortable height by building a platform for it. If you are short, consider mounting a cook-top unit in a counter built to your height.

Additional Work Centers

Any area that is set up for a particular task is a work center. To make it worthwhile to set up a special area, the task done there should be one that you perform often. A job that's done infrequently—such as cleaning, cutting and wrapping small game—may just as easily be done where you normally cut up your vegetables. But if the job is done regularly, or, as is true with canning, it takes place seasonally over weeks or months, a work center will speed the work while keeping the rest of the kitchen functioning normally.

If you are tall, you may want to raise the stove to a comfortable working height by setting it on a wooden platform.

Preparation Center. Somewhere between the refrigerator and the stove, you'll have to slice, chop, grate and grind ingredients. Put the appropriate tools near a large cutting board for a preparation center. This center is an integral part of the kitchen and should be in the triangle formed by the refrigerator, sink and stove.

There is no single correct way to equip it. The essentials are knives, graters, mixing bowls, beaters, whisks, and measuring cups and spoons. If you locate the center between the refrigerator and the sink, you may want to keep the mixing tools nearer the stove area, in effect creating two preparation areas, one for chopping, the other for mixing. You may add baking materials—grain mills, flour, sifter, pie pans and the like—to the mixing preparation area if you don't have a separate baking center.

Baking Center. If you do much bread and pastry making, consolidate everything you need for baking into one area. It need

The preparation center provides a central location for all your mixing and chopping tools, so they are at hand when you need them.

A baking center, near the oven, has a recessed marble slab for easier kneading and rolling. All the equipment and supplies needed for baking are located there.

not be in the kitchen triangle, but proximity to the oven helps. This is one case where a separate cooktop and oven would be more effective than the standard stove. One person using the sink and cooktop could cook an entire meal without ever crossing paths with someone else using the baking area.

A marble slab is ideal for kneading and rolling out dough. Mount one about 6 inches lower than the normal height for counter tops; you will find kneading dough and rolling out pastry easier than on the counter. Put all your baking equipment and ingredients, including flour and cake pans, near the marble slab. Things like measuring cups and spoons and mixing bowls can be either in the baking center or the preparation center, or in both if you can afford duplicates. You'll probably use a big electric mixer in the baking center more than in the preparation center. A small hand-held electric mixer would be very handy in the preparation center for jobs like mashing potatoes or beating eggs.

Canning and Freezing Area. Full-scale food processing can take over your kitchen. Getting the jars, kettles and equipment cleaned up and put away in time to cook a meal can be a bother. Leaving them out may be worse. You'll be using the sink, the stove and plenty of counter space, and it can continue all summer.

A separate room devoted to preserving is an ideal solution. Or you might use a porch or a shed near the house for a summer kitchen. You can set up a wood range there; with plenty of screened-in windows to let the breeze through, the heat from the range will be tolerable.

If you can't afford the luxury of a separate room, try to arrange the kitchen so that a canning operation won't totally prevent cooking. Try to locate the preserving equipment where you will use it. The most likely spot is between the sink and the stove. This may conflict with your preparation center. If so, store the essentials of a mini-preparation center between the refrigerator and the sink.

Trash Recycling Center. Trash and garbage accumulates in the kitchen before it goes to the compost pile or the recycling center. A cabinet or a set of bins can keep this material out of the way of kitchen activities and keep the organic waste separate from the trash. You can also have special containers for glass and metal.

Family Center. A cook spends much time in the kitchen and should feel at home there. Indeed, in many households, the kitchen is the center of the home, the place where the family gathers to eat, talk, play or work.

A built-in or freestanding desk in a corner of the kitchen would be ideal for family record keeping, letter writing and homework. Built-in shelves can hold cookbooks, gardening reference books, do-it-yourself books, story books or whatever else you like. You can plan your garden a little at a time over the table with your family, work out

The ideal canning and freezing center occupies a separate room so normal kitchen routines aren't disrupted. It has its own sink and stove and storage space for food-processing equipment and supplies.

A trash recycling center has individual containers to separate items for recycling and for composting.

The family center provides a central location for home business and planning.

plans for a new building project, or fill out a nursery order together.

Utility Sink. A special sink for big or dirty jobs can spare the the main sink. It need not be in the work triangle, and can, in fact, be near the garden, on a porch, in a utility room or in the food-processing area. Here you could get the worst mud off carrots or beets before storing them or hauling them to the main sink.

(Left) A utility sink in a porch or garage off the kitchen is handy for washing off garden-fresh produce.

Space and Storage

It's nice to have everything stored neatly behind cabinet doors, but if not a single utensil is visible, the kitchen might end up looking a bit remote. There are many ways to give it a friendly look while preserving an open feeling. For example, you could hang pots on hooks over the stove or arrange bowls and containers on open shelves. A combination of storage methods is more interesting than the boxed-in look of cabinets alone.

Probably the most essential place for harvest processing is the counter top. You'll need plenty of uncluttered space. As far as possible, avoid storing things on the counter. Counters nowadays usually cap floor cabinets. These units, which you can build, purchase in kits, or buy ready-made, are useful for storing large bowls or pots. If you build your own, make open shelves for some of the units.

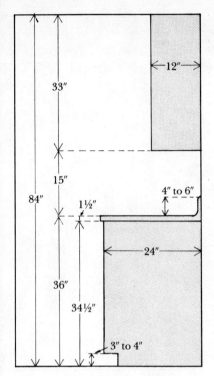

Conventional kitchen cabinet dimensions.

only freestanding furniture: a table and chairs, workbenches for counters, cupboards, hutches and shelves for storage. You can use new furniture or old. Hoosier cabinets, corner cupboards, old hutches and jelly cupboards are all in great demand because, in the correct setting, they look good and are functional.

Plan the storage space around your inventory. Bins may be more convenient than cupboards for grains, nuts, flour and other items stored loose. To organize baking pans and cookie sheets, try using slotted file holders like those used in

offices. A pegboard pullout on a track in a cabinet will hold a variety of small tools and make them far more accessible than they would be in a drawer. Examine both your ingredients and your utensils for their decorative potential and, as long as they will not interfere with the work, hang them where they can be appreciated.

Kitchen islands are useful in making a large room more efficient. By locating an island between two walls that are far apart, you can make the work area more effective and save footsteps. Islands can be designed with a cooktop, a sink or

The average height of counter tops is 36 inches.

Mount wall-hung cabinets above counter tops at a convenient height for the person who uses the kitchen most often. The distance between the counter tops and the bottom of the wall cabinets should be between 15 and 20 inches. The cabinets themselves are usually between 30 and 33 inches high, and, as a rule of thumb, the tops of the cabinets should be 84 inches above the floor.

Don't feel compelled to have built-in cabinets. Most people do expect kitchens to have ranks of cabinets, but some very lovely and functional kitchens have

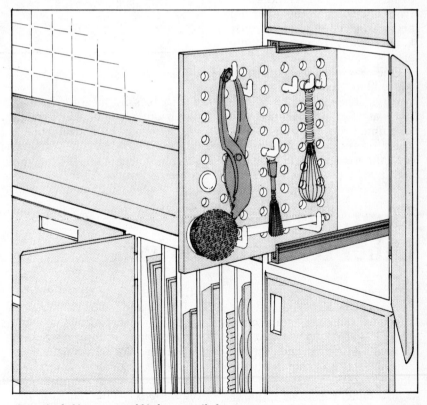

Organize baking pans and kitchen utensils for easy access.

A kitchen island can tighten up the work triangle in a large kitchen, provide more storage and additional work surfaces and help channel traffic through the kitchen away from work areas.

simply a preparation space. You can place a ventilating hood, shelves or cabinets above the island, but keep the area open at least to eye level. This will help preserve a sense of the kitchen as one large room. Of course, you can also divide a room by locating cabinets low over an island counter. Such an arrangement may be ideal between the kitchen and a dining area, because it allows food and dishes to be transferred easily from one room to the other but keeps the clutter of a busy kitchen away from the dining area.

One way to save space is to consolidate food storage in a pantry. The rationale is the same as for work areas: You'll save time by saving steps. To be really useful, a pantry must be near the work triangle. You can use it as a cool room to store perishables by locating it on a north outside wall and providing a vent to the outside. A pantry is also nice if you buy food in bulk—it keeps the large containers out of sight.

the outside to reduce the moisture content of the room. The kitchen must be maintained at a comfortable temperature. This may require hot-air ducts or hot water pipes that run to registers or radiators. If there is to be a wood stove or a wood range, the flue must be installed safely, usually straight up through the house to the roof. Light fixtures and windows must be arranged to make the most of available light and to ensure that work areas remain well lit at all times.

Heat, Light and Other Kitchen Services

Proper arrangement of appliances is important in the kitchen, but the appliances won't do anything without the proper plumbing and wiring. Supplying the kitchen with the things necessary to make it a comfortable workplace requires as much detailed planning as drawing the floor plan.

Pipes and electrical cable must be inconspicuous yet supply electricity and water where it is needed. Wastewater must be drained and the drainpipes vented according to plumbing regulations. The air in the kitchen should also be vented to

Plumbing and Wiring

Water has countless uses in the kitchen, from cleaning vegetables to filling a coffeepot. In many kitchens, hot and cold water goes to the sink and nowhere else. This may be completely adequate. But you may also install a utility sink for messy jobs, an island sink between the kitchen and the dining area, even a sink in the baking area or where you clean fish and fowl.

Wherever you run water, you must drain it away. The National Plumbing Code requires that each drain be vented to the outside within a certain distance, called the critical distance. The critical distance is 48 pipe diameters. For standard sink drainpipe 1½ inches in diameter, that's 72 inches. If the existing vent stack in your kitchen is farther from the sink's drain than that, you must either run a separate vent stack or put in an additional vent within the critical distance: straight up to a point 6 inches higher than the overflow point of the highest fixture in the house, then horizontally to the existing vent stack. Your floor plan is not complete until you know how each sink will be vented and where the supply pipes will run.

The National Electrical Code stipulates that, in addition to lighting circuits, a kitchen be supplied with two special 20-amp circuits called small-appliance circuits. You may not connect any lights to the small-appliance circuits. The reason for the requirement is that toasters, mixers and other electric equipment use a lot of electricity; the appliance circuits will supply it—and without dim-

ming your lights when an appliance starts up. Electric heaters and electric stoves also require their own circuits.

If your present kitchen does not meet these requirements, you should add the necessary circuits. To do this safely, you'll need to compute the present capacity of your electrical service and be certain that any added circuits will not overload your system. You'll need to install the circuits in an approved manner and run the cable where it will not accidentally be damaged.

Light

In planning kitchen lighting, take full advantage of possibilities for natural light from windows, glass doors or skylights. The sunniest location for a kitchen is on the south side of a house. Eastern exposure receives pleasant morning sunlight. Western exposure is less desirable because the afternoon sun may be too hot.

The quality of lighting is affected by the colors and textures you use in your kitchen furnishings and decorations. Light colors and smooth, glossy surfaces reflect light and make rooms seem brighter and more spacious. A kitchen that is too bright can cause discomfort, however. Dark colors make the kitchen seem smaller but are restful to the eye.

General light should be adequate without being harsh. It should illuminate corners and work areas without making the room too bright. A central ceiling light will often throw

shadows on counters if light immediately above them is not sufficient. Many cooks therefore prefer luminous ceilings to a single ceiling light.

In addition to general lighting, a kitchen needs adequate and well-placed local or task lights near every working surface. Plan lighting when you plan work centers. Ceiling or wall-mounted spot lights, under-the-cabinet strip lights and recessed panels over work areas all give concentrated light where it is needed. Pull-down or flexible lamps used at various heights, track-mounted spot lamps and rheostat switches can also be used to adjust lighting according to the demands of individual tasks.

Heat

The kitchen is usually an easy room to heat. Leakage from stove surfaces, cooking pots and ovens, exhaust from refrigerators, and just the fact that people in a kitchen are always in motion all contribute warmth.

If you plan to have a wood stove or range, you may not need another heat source. If you do require additional heat, your home's central heat is generally the best source, even for a new addition. Make sure your furnace has the necessary capacity, though. If your present heating system seriously limits your options, for example by requiring a radiator at an awkward place, you may heat the kitchen separately with electric baseboard units controlled by individual thermostats. These are inexpensive to install, **29** but expensive to operate.

You may be able to capture solar heat by placing windows where they will be unobstructed by trees or buildings on the south side of the kitchen, or by adding a solar greenhouse next to the kitchen. To make the most of the energy coming through the windows, try to arrange to have exposed stone or masonry facing them. The masonry stores the sunlight as heat. The more light that falls on the storage medium, the more heat will be released at night.

Ventilation

Kettles put out a lot of vapor during canning season. Cooking in general releases moisture too. You'll need adequate ventilation. Mount an exhaust fan over your stove, and run exhaust ducts to the outside. Figure how you'll run the ducts before you fix the stove's location.

An Attractive Kitchen

Your kitchen, if it is to enhance your harvest-processing ability and make you happy, must be a pleasant place to live and work in. Many people would say that the aesthetic side of kitchen designing cannot be taught—it is a matter of taste, a flair that some people have and others don't. To some extent this is true. There are nevertheless, some basic principles of design that apply to kitchens and that make one kitchen look better than another.

Unity. A kitchen, even if it is part of an open-style house, should be seen as one environment. Interruptions of pattern, texture, line, style or color will disturb the unity. There will be a jarring interruption in the way you perceive a room if, for example, the cabinets on one wall are dark wood with elaborate carved trim, and the cabinets on the adjacent wall are stark white metal. A kitchen should make one unified and

definite impression on the eye. This can be achieved by a color scheme that emphasizes one color only or by a combination of several harmonious colors of varying hues and strengths. It can be brought about by repeating colors, textures, materials and design elements in a flowing arrangement or at pleasing intervals so that they seem to pull the room together.

Simplicity. The human nervous system has its limits. It is distressed by too much noise, too much light, too much of almost anything. The eye can take in and fully see only a few objects at one time.

The kitchen is not, first and foremost, a place to look at. It's a working place. But if the kitchen is well designed, it will be attractive because it is simple, and because the decor is subordinate to utility.

Balance and Repetition. Though the human nervous system cannot perceive an un-

limited number of stimuli at once, it does have a mechanism that groups similar elements. The eye moves from one patch of blue to another, from material to similar material (stainless steel sink to stainless steel stove), from one curve to a similar curve. You will achieve harmony, unity and simplicity if you help the eye by grouping colors and textures throughout the kitchen.

One of the easiest groupings to appreciate is the triad—three objects perceived together. The triangle of appliances is also the most functional arrangement for making kitchens work smoothly. Bring visual and functional triangles together, emphasizing the visual similarities in your sink, refrigerator and stove. When you do this, your kitchen can hardly help but show an internal balance.

Consistency of Style. If your house is rustic and antique, you can have simple, modern fixtures, but take care to preserve and highlight a few rustic or antique elements in the kitchen. Leave the oak mantel of a fireplace of earlier days and hang your pans from it. Keep the old stone floor. Set a rocking chair in your chimney corner or retain one large antique cupboard, finishing the functional cabinets in the rest of the room to be in harmony with it.

Use pine plank floors if you live near pine forests or slate ones if you're in a slate-quarrying area. An adobe and dark wood beam kitchen may set the style of a Spanish house in the Southwest, but it would only contribute disharmony if tacked onto a New England farmhouse.

Don't be overly impressed by the style-names given to cabinets by kitchen designers: Mediterranean, French Provin-cial, American Colonial. Style doesn't come in a package; it's something you create yourself. Look for consistency of material, line and detail, and forget about the brand name.

Drawing the Plan

After you have collected all the information you can absorb and have looked at all the appliances and kitchens you can stand, you are ready to draw the plan. You know roughly how much renovation you will do, what work centers are essential for you, and you have some sketches. Now you need a detailed plan, accurate to within ⅛ inch, to show exactly where the appliances and cabinets will be located. You should also make drawings that show where pipes, ventilation or heating ducts and electrical cable will run.

Floor Plans

The first step in making a detailed floor plan is to group appliances and their preparation centers, along with any extra centers, into carefully related arrangements. Try drawing up graph paper representations of the appliances to scale, then add on, also in scale, the preparation spaces you'd like to have near them. Or use scaled paper cutouts to represent the appliances and cabinets. If you're in the market for new appliances, determine the dimensions of those you want. Be precise in your mea-surements. Being an inch off may mean the difference between an appliance that fits its spot and one that doesn't.

Start your drawing with the structural "givens" of the room. Draw in radiators, ducts, wall switches, electrical outlets, doors, windows, pipe entrances and all the existing features you plan to retain. Indicate where doors and passageways lead and consider how areas outside the kitchen (garden, garage, porch) will affect kitchen activities. Move your paper appliances around on the graph paper to see how many sensible variations you can come up with. Work toward the one that fills your needs best.

When you've finished the floor plan, make an elevation drawing of each kitchen wall, showing the exact placement of windows, doors, shelves, electrical outlets, plumbing and all other wall features.

One-Wall Kitchens

If you are building a kitchen for a very small house or cabin, a one-wall kitchen may be the only feasible design. There is no real triangle when only one wall is used for appliances, and walking back and forth along a single line may become tedious.

One advantage of a one-wall kitchen is that it goes well in an open-style house, allowing many household activities to be carried on in a room without having kitchen activities dominate. One-wall kitchens are favored in apartments and places where space is limited.

Corridor Kitchens

Corridor or galley kitchens are usually the least tiring to use because they have a compact work triangle. Appliances are located with one on one wall and two on the opposite wall. The arrangement is convenient provided that at least 4 feet is left free for passage. There are space-saving advantages to the plan, because there are no corners where space is wasted.

In a blind-corner kitchen, the far end of the corridor can be used for storage or a wall oven. An open-corridor plan is usually less successful because it is open to distracting traffic, but if the far opening leads to a pantry or greenhouse, the plan has a better chance of success.

Very large rooms are often designed with a galley on one side. In this way, general traffic is channeled to one side of the working area, and spaces between appliances are reduced. If one side of the corridor is a counter rather than a wall, the cook will be able to participate in household conversation without sacrificing privacy. Corridor kitchens often open to adjoining dining areas.

L-Shaped Kitchens

An L-shaped kitchen occupies two adjoining walls, forming its **31**

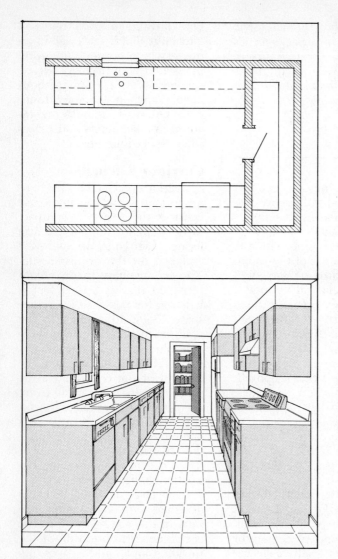

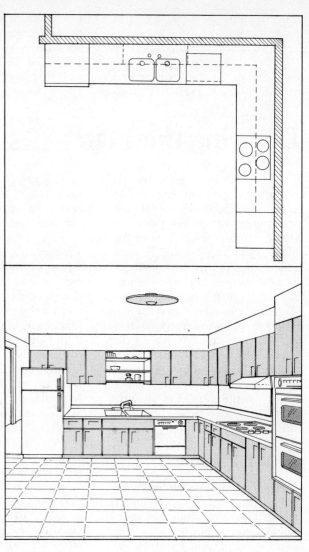

The corridor kitchen (left) provides a compact work triangle that saves time and energy. The arrangement works best if the counters are about 4 feet apart and if the corridor is not a main traffic route in the house. Having a pantry at the end of the corridor is ideal. The L-shaped kitchen (right) is a very common arrangement. It can combine a fairly tight, efficient work triangle with lots of storage, so long as a doorway doesn't interrupt the run of counters.

triangle with one appliance on one wall and two on the adjacent one. This placement leaves the rest of the room free for other activities. An L shape can also be achieved by extending a peninsula out from a wall to split a large space into smaller areas. There are corner cabinets with lazy Susan shelves to ease access to all the storage space.

A common problem with L-shaped kitchens is that they tend to crowd appliances toward the interior corner. Try to avoid this tendency as you plan your layout.

The plan is very flexible and has numerous applications. In this kind of kitchen, a large table can play an important role by providing extra islandlike

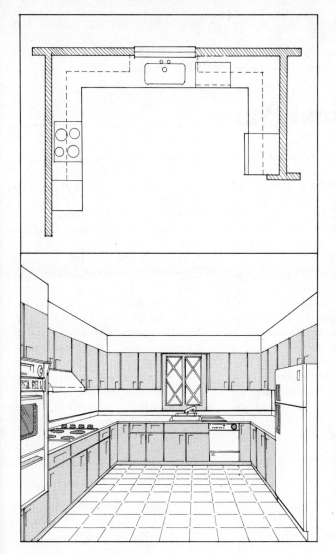

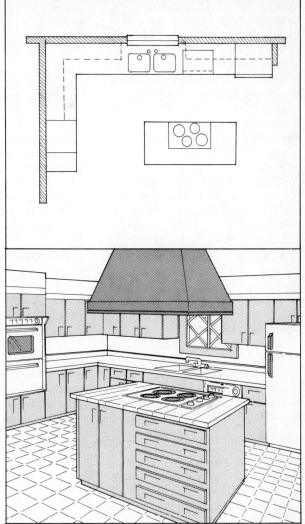

working space and doubling for use in family activities.

U-Shaped Kitchens

The most popular, and often the most spacious and efficient kitchen is the U shape. This type puts each work center on a different wall and reduces traffic flow by eliminating doors that break the continuity of counter tops and interrupt the work triangle. U-shaped designs work best when the room width at the base of the U is at least 9 feet. If the width is less, the central working area will seem cramped.

The two extensions of the U may be of unequal length; in large rooms where the U occupies only a portion of the

The U-shaped kitchen (left) may very well be the ideal arrangement, keeping the work triangle tight and at the same time providing a great deal of counter space and storage. Adding an island to a kitchen (right) can transform it by creating more storage space and an extra work surface, by tightening the work triangle, by separating the general area of a kitchen from the work area.

room, the U may actually be composed of a peninsula and two walls or two peninsulas and one wall. One arm can serve as a divider between the kitchen and a living area. Arms can function as eating counters. An advantage of the U-shaped over the L-shaped design is that the cooking area can more easily be separated from the living or eating area.

If many doors open into your present kitchen or if it contains isolated appliances, rearranging it into a U shape may increase its efficiency. Remember, however, that with a U you have two corners to turn and you'll have to minimize wasted space in both of them.

Island Kitchens

The so-called island kitchen is achieved by simply adding an island to a one-wall, L-shaped or U-shaped layout. The island can serve as a divider between the work area and another part of the room, or it can simply provide more work and storage space. An island will change a one-wall kitchen into a modified corridor kitchen or an L-shaped one into a modified U. In either case, it will make the work triangle more compact. An island can also house a surface cooking unit or a sink. If used in this manner, the island should be a yard or more wide.

To function efficiently, an island should be at least 4 feet long and 2 feet wide. Allow about 4 feet of space on all sides of it, and don't put it where it will interrupt a triangle of appliance centers. If you can't walk in a straight line between the stove and the sink or between the sink and the refrigerator without bumping into your island, then the island won't be effective. Racks for hanging storage often complement an island work area better than overhead cabinets.

The Final Plan

Just imagining solutions or simply being knowledgeable about principles of design are not enough to guarantee a successful kitchen. It is precision of plan and exactness of measurement that are most important.

Put your floor plan out of sight and give it the test of time. Then go over it carefully. Get out your old sketches and clippings to see if earlier ideas were either incorporated in the plan or rejected for good reason. Determine the final dimensions of work centers with great care; go over each measurement and aspect of design one more time. Although the interiors of cabinets can be rearranged later, space relationships and external dimensions are hard to change.

With exact dimensions, you can begin to draw up specifications and to list the materials you will need in construction. Estimate quantities carefully, and allow for waste. Planning tends to continue right up to, and sometimes beyond, the building stage. But when you've made the plan as complete as it can be on paper—and you're sure the measurements are correct—you will be ready to order the materials and schedule the work.

Scheduling the Work

Should you really bother with a detailed work schedule? Or could you spend your time more profitably wielding a hammer? After all, you may have been planning and shopping for months now, yet the work hasn't even begun. Just jot down some notes, and figure it out as you go, right? That may be okay on a small job, but you

will run into problems if you try it on any sizable project.

For one thing, the sequence is important in enabling you to avoid damage to finished work. You don't want to complete a wall only to realize you must rip out part of it to run some pipes. Or to resurface the kitchen floor before you tear out a plaster ceiling. You might grind chunks of plaster into the new floor.

For another thing, a careful work sequence can save time. You'll obviously lose time ripping out or repairing new work, but you may have to do that if you don't schedule carefully. You may also waste time if you do one small plumbing job, put in some insulation, run a single electrical circuit, then go back to do more plumbing. The tools for each job are different, and assembling them takes time. Besides, jumping from one job to another leads to mistakes. Try to group jobs by type: Remove everything that must go before you do the framing work; complete all the rough wiring and plumbing before you put up the wall surfaces. As far as possible, complete each stage before you go on. Consider how each job may be affected by others. Wiring, for example, will be easier if wall surfaces are removed, but you can't install the final switch covers until they are up again. Work out a logical sequence for the project. On occasion, your sequence may differ from the standard one that builders use. Let the particulars of your job determine the order.

There's another reason why scheduling is important. Remodeling is going to disrupt your household. It's hard to cook a meal with scrap lumber all over the place or when the plumbing is disconnected. You may have to set up a temporary kitchen in another room. Food preserving should definitely be done elsewhere. If the work drags on too long, even the temporary kitchen will seem unworkable. You need a schedule to get a clear idea of how long the project will take and to give others an idea of when they can expect to live normally again.

With a schedule, you'll be able to arrange your vacation or other free time to coincide with the most demanding work. You'll know when materials must be delivered, and you will be able to line up professional help for when you need it.

Scheduling is just a formal way of deciding when to do each step of your project. The hardest part of scheduling is to estimate time realistically. It's difficult to know how long an unfamiliar job will take and impossible to anticipate some of the problems that will crop up. Be generous in your estimates, and allow extra time for the problems. Adhere to your basic work sequence, but be flexible about it. If a plumber, electrician or cabinetmaker is delayed, work on something that can be done out of sequence.

The Work Sequence

Your schedule should include everything from permits and inspections to last-minute arrangements before the work begins. Make sure you have the necessary building, wiring or plumbing permits, and arrange timely inspections to keep the work flowing smoothly. Schedule the order of each job, starting with any framing work and proceeding through wiring, plumbing, heating and ventilation to windows, walls, ceilings, cabinets and floors. Allow time for painting, papering and interior trim, and remember that installation of electrical switches and cover plates, heating grates, and the sink and faucets is usually done last.

Your renovation may not be so drastic as to require gutting the kitchen. The walls may only need a coat of paint. Or you might remove one wall while retaining another. The sequence remains the same: Do all the rough work of one job before going to the next. If you have to run pipes and cable through finished walls, try to minimize the damage, and plan carefully. Even if your plan is good, there's always the chance that an obstruction hidden inside a wall will force you to change it as the work proceeds. Save the patching until all the rough work is done, and do it at the same time you prepare the walls for painting or papering.

Once you have determined the sequence of the work, you can set about making a week-by-week calendar of jobs and fitting into it the schedule of any outside help that you hire. You'll want to make sure that materials are delivered on time, but, unless you have lots of storage space, don't be so cautious that you have stacks of wallboard sitting around for months on end. Finally, your schedule should reflect the time you'll spend arranging temporary cooking facilities while your kitchen is out of commission, and it should provide a clear accounting of your own time. If it is carefully done, the schedule will help you finish all the preliminaries before you are due to start work. When the work does get under way, the schedule will keep it moving ahead steadily.

Permits and Inspections

The first thing to decide is when to secure the required permits and arrange inspections of your work. The essential ones are naturally the ones that allow you to get started. But there can be delays even after you have begun. You may find that the wiring must be inspected before the walls are put up so the inspector can see all parts of the job. If he is delayed, work may be stalled. Let the inspector know as far in advance as possible when to come, and make sure the work is done when he gets there.

The Kitchen's Framework

Unless your renovation is extensive, you may never see the stud frame that supports the walls of your kitchen. But if you do remove the walls, you'll have an easier time with any wiring, plumbing or heating work that you do. Start your project by removing all the parts you will replace. Then make any required changes in the frame. These include creating an opening for a new window or door, closing off such an opening, perhaps even removing or adding a wall.

If you must keep your kitchen functioning during the renovation, planning and scheduling become even more important. Instead of tearing out every wall and all the cabinets, you might have to remove one wall, add the necessary plumbing and wiring, replace the wall, and move certain appliances over to it. Later, you might add cabinets to another wall and, only then, remove the old cabinets and the wall behind them. You are better off avoiding this little-by-little approach, but if your situation requires it, schedule each step with care.

Demolition

Do as much of the demolition as you can before anything else. The work is incredibly messy and dirty. If you take out walls or ceilings, the dust will get all over the place. Seal the kitchen by closing the doors to other parts of the house and stuffing damp towels in the cracks.

Demolition is fun. This may be your favorite part of the job. It doesn't take very long, though. Destruction is much faster than construction. In a full-scale renovation, you first shut off electricity and water to the entire kitchen. Disconnect appliances and move them away from the walls or into another room. Cabinets and counters come out next, followed by the ceiling, the walls and, finally, the finish floor.

Anything you don't remove must be well protected. Clean up as you go to give yourself room to work and to keep nail-studded lumber off the floor. By the end of this phase, the kitchen will look like the rough-framed shell of a new room.

If you've correctly located studs, pipes and wiring, there should be few surprises as you work. However, you may discover architectural features that will change your plans—a stone wall behind the plaster or a rough-hewn beam hidden by the ceiling. Stay somewhat flexible to allow for unexpected opportunities.

Framing

Framing goes fairly quickly compared with other building jobs. You can probably build the stud frame for a wall in an afternoon. Cutting an opening for a new door or window on the other hand, can take just as long if you have trouble cutting through the sheathing and exterior siding. And if you should happen to find pipes and electrical cable where you plan your new door, you'll have to stop and do a little plumbing and wiring before you can frame it in. That's the kind of thing that throws off your schedule and thwarts a rigid job sequence.

As long as you are doing all the work yourself, such a situation would only be an inconvenience. But if you are depending on professional help and the plumbers and electricians have already come and gone before you get around to the door, you could be in for a long delay. Making the opening for a window or door or removing part of a wall can easily require changes in the heating or ventilation as well as in the plumbing and wiring. Find out about such complications before you start working and in enough time to make the extra work part of the regular schedule for each type of job.

You may be required to have your framing work inspected; whether you are depends on local regulations and on the extent of your changes. If an inspection is required, you'll have to wait until it's done before you put up the walls. Try to arrange the inspection well ahead of time.

Rough Wiring, Plumbing, Heating and Ventilation

These jobs are easiest when the rough frame of the kitchen is exposed to view. You've got better access to the work, and you can see what you're doing.

Sometimes you'll have to run several things close together; then do the most difficult installation first. That may require some juggling of the sequence of jobs, but it's still best to do the rough work of one job completely before starting another. Finishing each comes later.

A likely sequence for the work is to locate and install electrical boxes for switches, receptacles and light fixtures and to run cable to them. Next do your plumbing, starting with the drain pipes. Since these are larger than supply pipes and must be pitched correctly, it is easier to get them done first. Then run the supply pipes to where they will leave the walls.

After this rough wiring and plumbing is complete, make any required changes in the heating, then the ventilation. Hot-air ducts, ventilation ducts, or insulated stovepipe may run inside or through the walls and may require framing alterations. If you have confidence in your measurements and have an accurate plan, you'll have made these framing changes when you did the rest of the framing.

The last step before installing wall surfaces over the rough frame is to place insulation in exterior walls. The reason for doing this last is that it is easier to cut pieces of insulation to fit around pipes or ducts than the other way around. After the insulation is in place, staple sheets of plastic to the studs as a vapor barrier.

Finishing

The finishing stage covers a lot of ground, from installing windows and doors to placing light fixtures and nailing up the last strips of molding. Keep in mind that you want to follow a sequence that will minimize damage to completed parts. The exact order will depend on the nature and extent of your work.

Windows and Doors

Windows and doors are usually mounted in their frames while the room is still stripped down to the frame, but they can also be mounted with the walls in place. If you are adding a window or exterior door, in effect opening a hole in your wall, you'll want to get the unit in place as soon as possible. Installing interior doors, as well as replacing existing ones, can be done before or after the walls are in place, whichever is more convenient.

Walls and Ceilings

Start with the ceiling, whether you're merely doing some patching or tearing out the entire ceiling. That way you won't run the risk of damaging a recently completed wall. Of course, if you are ripping out the ceiling, do that during the demolition. Install a dropped ceiling after any new walls have been installed. The frame of it fastens to the wall. Plastering, whether of the wall or the ceiling, requires curing time before the finish is applied. For example, you should wait roughly 90 days before you use oil-base paint. Plastering is one thing you should probably leave to professionals. If you must have a plaster surface, you'll need to schedule outside help and allow for curing.

Gypsum wallboard is most often used in place of plaster and it is especially good for the do-it-yourselfer. Other possible wall surfaces include paneling, planks, tongue-and-groove board, and exposed brick or stone. Install or repair your walls before you add any cabinets or shelves. Generally paint, wallpaper or ceramic tile is added before the cabinets are installed. That reduces the risk that you'll accidentally damage the cabinets while doing paneling.

Cabinets and Shelves

Mount cabinets or shelves on the finished, painted walls. Cabinets may be purchased finished or unfinished, prefabricated in the home shop or built in place. The order of installation remains the same. You may find it easier to finish cabinets in a separate workshop and install them when they are dry, although there is a slightly greater risk of scratching the finish this way. Obviously, if you build in the cabinets, you'll have to finish them in place. Once the cabinets are finished, install the counter top.

If you are stripping existing cabinets, do so before you paint the walls since the procedure is messy, and splattering is common. Then paint the walls, and finally finish the cabinets. Add molding, and paint or varnish it after the cabinets are installed. If the molding is to match the cabinets, put the finish on the molding at the same time as on the cabinets.

Floors

A resilient floor covering is usually installed after the walls have been painted and the cabinets installed. It may extend to the base of cabinets, rather than under them, because it is not hard to cut such a floor covering. More exotic floors, like slate and ceramic tile, are also installed after the cabinets. A finished hardwood floor, on the other hand, generally runs under cabinets and is thus installed before the cabinets. Finish such a floor as soon as it is down to help protect the wood. Paint dripped on unfinished wood can be very hard to remove.

Finish Wiring, Plumbing, Heating and Ventilation

The final work in the kitchen is to complete the service to it. Then you have running water, light and heat—a functioning kitchen. The electrical work involves mounting light fixtures and heating units, putting switches and receptacles in the

electrical boxes, making the final electrical connections, and screwing on the cover plates. The wiring should be connected to the main panel and tested after all the units have been wired up but before the cover plates are mounted.

Finish plumbing involves installing the sink in the counter, adding faucets and drains, and attaching them to the supply and drainage stub-outs. Since this work usually involves compression fittings that do not require soldering or plastic welds, it shouldn't take a great deal of time, as long as everything is correctly positioned.

Finishing a hot-air heating system and the kitchen ventilation both require installation of registers. A ventilation hood over the stove usually has the register already built in. Complete a hot-water or steam system by adding convectors or radiators. Radiators use friction fittings, while convectors are often soldered.

Completing the Schedule_____

Once you have decided the sequence you'll follow in renovating your harvest kitchen, complete the schedule by estimating how long each stage will take. Find out when you can get outside help. Work out a week-by-week calendar and arrange for inspectors to visit at the appropriate times. Be certain you will have the necessary tools on hand, and arrange for delivery and storage of materi-

als. Finally, set up a temporary kitchen or other cooking arrangements. Make sure you and any helpers have the necessary free time, and you will be ready to begin.

Calendar of Events

Make a calendar for your project, assigning dates for the completion of each step. Some people don't like this sort of scheduling; it seems unnecessary to them. Besides, it is difficult to estimate accurately the time a job will take. Your own skill may vary considerably from one task to another, and the time required will vary accordingly. But if you have other commitments and can't spend all your time on the kitchen, if the job is large or if outside help will be involved, scheduling is essential.

Make the schedule carefully, and leave yourself plenty of extra time to allow for delays. Observe yourself at work; make a record of the time it takes you to finish various small jobs, and use the information to gauge your speed. If you take the time to do a professional-quality job, it can take you three to five times as long as it takes someone who does the same thing week in and week out. And it will take more hours of work to complete a project working part-time than it would full-time.

Above all, be realistic about the schedule. Don't have yourself slaving every night and weekend. Give yourself some time to relax. Rest assured that most of the so-called extra time you allow will be used.

Scheduling Outside Help

The larger the project and the more people involved in it, the more important the schedule becomes. If you hire an electrician to do rough wiring at one time and finish wiring later, you've got to give him an accurate account of how your project will proceed. If an inspector must visit at the end of one stage before the next can begin, a schedule is even more important.

Work out estimates for the various parts of your project. First, consider your own time: when you can get the most free time; when you can count on helpers. Then get estimates for jobs you plan to contract out, both of the cost to you and of the time each will take. It doesn't hurt to get a couple of estimates for each job. Try to contact people whose work is recommended by those you trust. Find out when these people can start, how flexible they are in their own schedules. Will they be able to begin when you're ready?

Once you have found the right people to do the work, get firm commitments from them to do it on schedule, and make it clear that you expect the work to be done on time. Don't sour the deal with threats, though. If someone does a job well but is late, you really don't have much recourse except to pay him, perhaps a little more slowly than usual. In a grievous case, you might recover some of the cost in small-claims court if you could demonstrate that you suffered actual monetary loss because the job was not done on time. But tradespeople do depend on reputation. In the final analysis, you depend on mutual goodwill and understanding to get the job done satisfactorily. You can help by being clear about your own requirements and by doing your part of the project when you say you will.

Materials, Delivery and Storage

One aspect of scheduling that can easily be overlooked is the need to have all materials on hand for each part of the project before work begins on that part. You can't solder copper pipe without a can of flux, and you certainly won't get far with your new walls if the wallboard fails to arrive as promised. As a matter of fact, the wallboard should sit in the room where it will be used for at least two days before installation to allow the temperature and humidity to be equalized, so it must be delivered days ahead.

That leads to a second consideration: storage. You may not have enough storage space to order all the materials at one time. Instead, arrange delivery of things like windows, doors, wallboard, cabinets and flooring a week before you will need them. Know your supplier to be sure he will deliver on time. When you receive a shipment, immediately check everything for damage and make sure the order is complete.

Store materials that won't be used immediately in a safe place. The location should be weatherproof—in the house, if possible. If you use a garage or basement, keep it locked. Stack materials carefully away from well-trafficked areas to avoid accidental damage. Store them off the floor if the area is damp or subject to flooding.

Final Preparations

Before you begin work, assemble all the specialized tools you'll need. Be certain you actually have everything you think you do. Check that power tools are operating properly, that you have the nails, screws and hardware you will need, and generally do everything possible in advance to assure that you can start work on time. A couple of unexpected trips to the hardware store can blow a good part of a workday.

When you are sure you have the tools ready and the materials scheduled for delivery, confirm that inspectors and tradesmen will arrive as planned. Make sure you have the proper permits. It will help to have a final checklist on hand for the last-minute frenzy that seems to accompany the start of a large project.

Your temporary cooking arrangements should be complete, or as ready as possible, if you are moving the appliances to another location once the work begins. If the project is large, or if you have scheduled it over a long period, the temporary kitchen should be fully able to function as a tolerable kitchen for the person doing the cooking.

Finally, clear your own time. Starting the job during a vacation is a good way to get it well under way from the beginning. Much of the success depends on your attitude, and spending at least a few solid days on the job and seeing some immediate results will help to establish momentum for the work. Having the project well organized also helps, as does the support of a few experienced friends willing to help if things bog down. Keep the work moving steadily, even if the pace is slow. If you've prepared well, this challenge is one you will be able to meet successfully, and enjoy.

Part II

The Basics

In the ideal construction project, you will begin with a bare room. You'll have four walls, a floor and a ceiling. You doubtless will have at least one door, and hopefully a window or two. This is the space you have to deal with, to turn into your harvest kitchen. A lot of work must go into the room before it even begins to look like the kitchen you envision. You may want to add or eliminate a door or a window. Surely you'll do plumbing and electrical work, installing outlets and lights, faucets and drains. The floor and walls and ceiling must be spruced up with plaster, paneling, tiles or paint, all to make the room that will be a harvest kitchen a functional and attractive place. This is the basic work that lays the foundation for the cabinets and appliances that dominate the harvest kitchen.

Preparing the Shell

The physical work of building your harvest kitchen begins with the shell. You've got a design, a plan, a schedule, the tools and materials, and the time and money. If you are an experienced home handyman, the next step is taken boldly and with enthusiasm: the real work is finally beginning. If you are a novice, this step is taken with

44

trepidation and sweaty palms: you hope you don't get in over your head and botch up the job.

The nature of the work you perform at this stage depends totally on the nature of your kitchen project and the state of the room that is eventually to be your harvest kitchen. In a new house, the shell will have been prepared in the course of framing the whole house and you'll undoubtedly have a rough-framed room, probably with sheathing nailed up, windows and doors installed, subfloor in place. You escape the razing that your fellow traveler who's remodeling an old kitchen must perform. If you are that fellow traveler, and you are looking at an old kitchen, your construction project must begin with a destruction project. How much you will have to do in the way of removing old cabinets, flooring, wall coverings and perhaps walls themselves depends upon how far your remodeling plan is going to take you. If your plan requires reconstruction, perhaps involving the installation of new windows or a kitchen greenhouse, or removal of a partition to expand the room, then you'll need to strip out the old interior finishings to the point where your kitchen looks like the rough-framed shell of the new one.

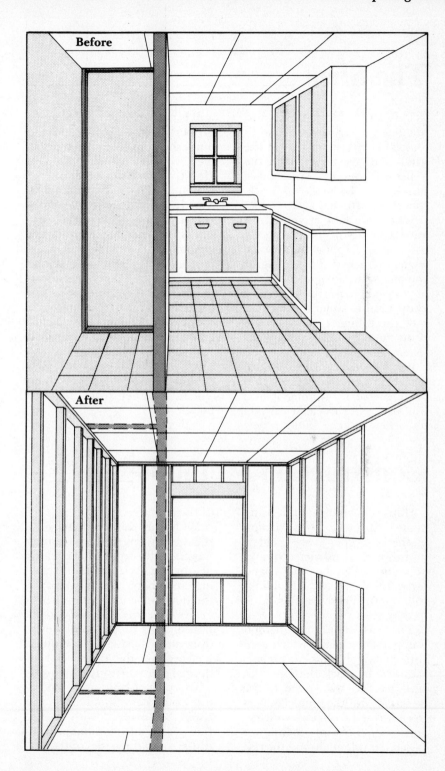

To renovate your kitchen completely, you may have to take everything out except the supporting frame. Here, the window opening has been enlarged and an unneeded closet removed. The floor tiles have been stripped away, revealing a sound subfloor.

45

The Shell

This shell is the frame you will hang your kitchen on. In most kitchens, it consists of the studs and joists that form the structural support of the house. But it may be made of brick, concrete or stone walls.

When you look at your present kitchen, you see surfaces—counter tops, cabinets and walls, perhaps cracked and peeling. If you are doing a major renovation of the kitchen, you need to know what is under the surface, how the cabinets and walls are supported, how everything fits together.

Ask yourself where, once you've gotten the best of that peeling wall by ripping it out, will you put the electrical box for a new switch? When a new wall is up, will the cover plate fit properly? How far should the pipes stick out from the studs so they will link up with the sink after the finish work is done?

Details! That's what will make a successful kitchen. The problem for many a home craftsperson is that many techniques are unfamiliar. Yet each step must be thought out as part of the whole effort. You should already have acquainted yourself with the various techniques, if only through books. You should know which jobs you want to do yourself and which you want to hire out. Your working plan should show how everything will fit together from the shell out.

Construction Methods

Houses have been built using many different construction methods. The very oldest houses were constructed of logs or stone or adobe bricks, and some of these early buildings still stand. These houses don't have frames.

The earliest framing method was post and beam, which consists of widely spaced timbers spanned by thick floor planks. This method was suited to the technology of the time. Timbers were formed from logs with axe and adz. Lots of manpower raised the ridgepole and the rest of the frame too.

With the development of a reliable sawmill, lighter framing members became more easily obtainable. With lighter framing members, albeit more of them, fewer construction workers were needed to build a given house. This most recent development, called stud framing, has become the standard residential construction technique.

In constructing or remodeling your harvest kitchen, you could be involved with any of these systems. It's helpful to understand the basics of them.

Stud Construction

Probably the best way to visualize the stud frame is to understand it as it was constructed. The frame supports the weight of the house, provides a place to attach walls and fixtures, and separates areas. The supporting frame of most houses is made of framing lumber, 2×4s for the walls, 2×8s, 2×10s and 2×12s for the joists and rafters.

There are two basic types of stud construction, platform framing and balloon framing. Platform framing is seen almost without exception in current development housing. Balloon framing is passé, although carpentry texts still include it. It's passé because platform framing is easier, and the building industry always does what's easy. But if you have an old house, especially a stuccoed house, it just may be balloon framed.

Platform Framing

Platform framing is so called because the framework is erected upon a series of floor platforms. Builders lay sills of 2×8 lumber atop the foundation and fasten them down with bolts mortared into the foundation. Joists of 2×10 or 2×12 lumber are set on edge upon the sills, spaced 16 inches apart, and boxed in with a header joist. Finally, a subfloor of plywood or particle board is nailed to the joists.

The stud walls are erected atop the floor platform. The 2×4 framework for a complete wall is laid out on the platform, nailed together, then erected

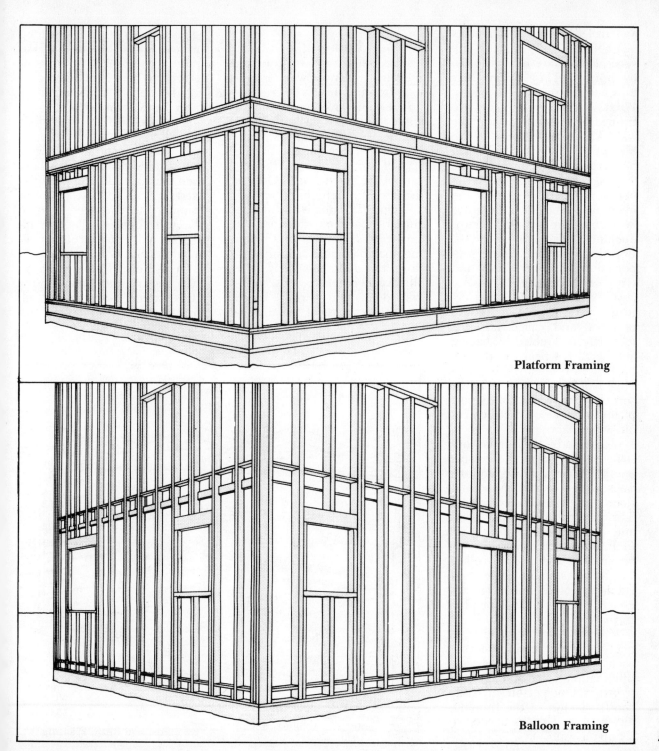

Platform Framing

Balloon Framing

and nailed to the floor and its neighboring wall frames. The vertical studs are held in place by horizontal 2 × 4s at their tops and bottoms, called plates. Window and door openings are framed as integral parts of the wall. Above these openings are horizontal supports called headers, fabricated of 2 × 6s, 2 × 8s, 2 × 10s or 2 × 12s, depending upon the span of the opening. Rough sills, the lower horizontal supports in window openings, are made of 2 × 4s. Both headers and sills are supported by trimmer studs and cripples, also made of 2 × 4s.

When all the walls of a structure are framed, erected, plumbed and nailed fast, the top plate is doubled by having another 2 × 4 nailed to the top of the wall framework, overlapping from unit to unit at the corners. The sections of the sole plates in doorways are then cut out with a handsaw.

If a second floor is to be constructed, the builders construct another floor platform atop the walls, then construct the second floor's walls and erect them. This pattern of floor platforms and wall sections continues up to the attic. There the joists may be smaller, since they have less weight to support. The roof frame of rafters and ridge are erected on this final floor platform.

The whole works is sturdy. It goes together easily because each section forms a complete unit that is erected and attached to others. One person can easily construct most of the framing, although a helper is needed to set up the walls.

Balloon Framing

The other type of framing used in residential work is balloon framing. Instead of resting on the subfloor, the vertical wall studs rest on the sill and extend all the way up to the rafters. Because of limitations on the size of studs, balloon framing cannot be used for buildings over two stories high.

Balloon framing is useful with stucco exteriors because it shrinks less than platform framing, making cracks around windows and doors less likely. The shrinkage is less because lumber does not shrink much lengthwise; most of the shrinkage is in cross section. The long vertical studs of the balloon frame are unbroken by horizontal top and bottom plates, reducing the pull of the studs away from the exterior surface.

Non-load-bearing partitions are always platform framed. Any partition you are likely to put up remodeling the kitchen, even one extending beyond the exterior wall, will use platform framing. All you need is to be able to recognize balloon framing should you encounter it. Windows and doors are framed as in platform framing, except that the trimmer and cripple studs extend down to the sill, instead of the bottom plate, and

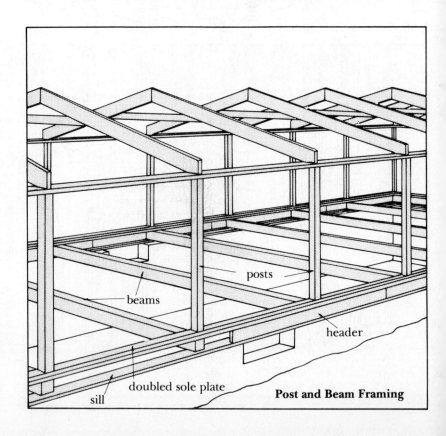

posts

beams

header

doubled sole plate

sill

Post and Beam Framing

48

headers extend to regular studs. A doubled trimmer frames one side of the rough opening.

Post and Beam Construction

In post and beam construction, the house is supported by larger structural elements than in stud construction. This allows greater flexibility in design than conventional methods. Post and beam is sometimes used with stud framing. For example, the walls might be framed with studs while the roof would be built of beams covered with planks, which are 2-inch-or-more-thick boards. Planks are often used with post and beam framing, so that a single thickness of material serves as subfloor, floor and ceiling.

In remodeling, you are more likely to use standard stud framing, but there are a few things to know about post and beam if you should encounter it. The load is carried by the posts and beams. Any framing between the posts is for support of walls, siding, windows and doors. Because stud framing is often used with post and beam to provide lateral support, it is not uncommon to find studs between posts. This is one case where an outside stud wall is not load bearing.

Because load is carried by the posts and beams, windows and doors do not need headers. This makes framing of openings simpler and allows large windows and sliding doors to be framed easily.

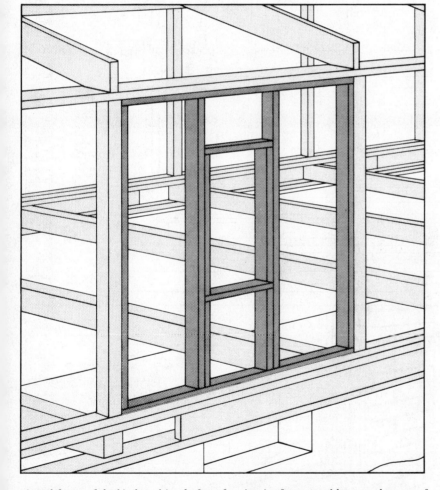

A stud frame of the kind used in platform framing is often erected between the posts of post and beam construction to support the walls. This frame does not carry the load of the house. No special support is required if you alter the frame.

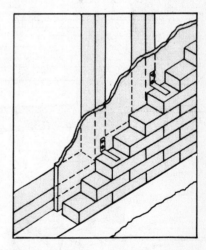

Brick veneer forms the exterior of some stud-frame houses. Most of the load of the structure is supported by the studs, not the brick.

49

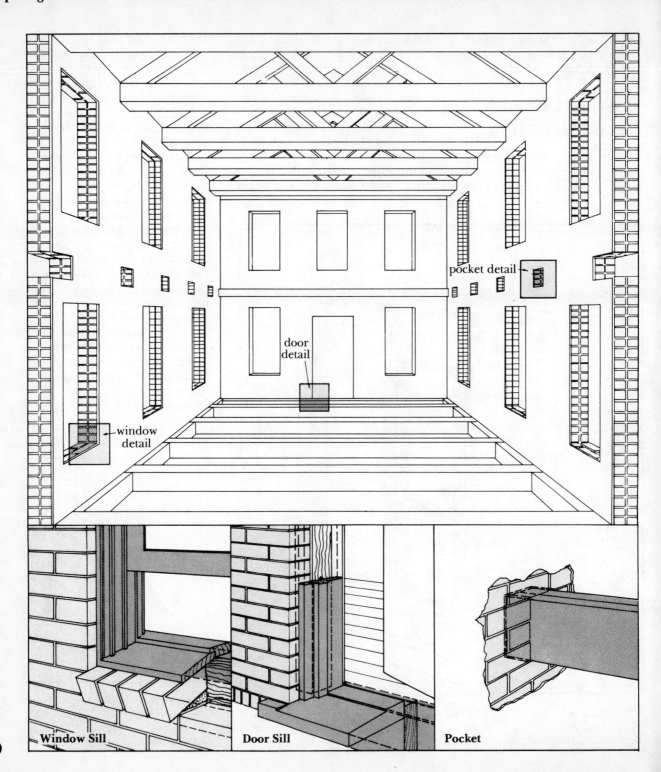

pocket detail

door
detail

window
detail

Window Sill

Door Sill

Pocket

Masonry

Most brick houses built nowadays are actually frame construction with a brick veneer. The brick itself has nothing to do with the support of the house, only the appearance.

But it was not always so. If your brick home is 50 or more years old, it's entirely likely that the bricks are what's holding the house up. Same with a stone house. These houses were built as much nonresidential construction is still built, with a shell of masonry and a wood frame interior construction. Joists are set in pockets in the masonry walls. Interior partition walls are stud frame construction. Exterior walls are raw masonry. Urban America's old rowhouses were built this way, as were thousands of stone and brick farmhouses.

Doing any remodeling of exterior walls in a kitchen with masonry walls, whether solid masonry or veneer, will require a mason's skills, practiced by you or by a mason. A veneer is easier to deal with, since it is only a single course thick, but altering any masonry is hard physical labor.

A solid brick house has walls two bricks thick. The load of the house rests on these walls. The interior plaster wall is applied directly to the inner layer of bricks. Joists rest in pockets built into the walls. Sometimes metal plates under the joists help distribute the load. The frame for doors and windows must be carefully built into the wall.

Load

Load and load-bearing wall are terms used frequently by builders that may be a bit mysterious to you. If your remodeling is not sprucing up but *is* reconstruction, you should get to understand load before beginning work. Opening up new windows or doors, ripping out a partition, closing in a porch or adding a pantry wing, or any other kitchen reconstruction that affects the basic construction of your house is going to affect the way the house holds itself and its contents.

Load is the amount of weight a structure supports. All buildings must conform to certain specifications that ensure that the frame is able to carry the weight of the building and everything in it or on it, including snow. In residential construction, the standard methods exceed these requirements.

But local building codes vary. And in special cases, where a very heavy object is to be located in one spot or a beam is to be used to span a wide opening, you must consult local codes and possibly an architect to be sure that what you have in mind is safe and legal.

The main load of a house falls on the studs directly under the ends of floor and ceiling joists. Most of the load is thus carried by the two outside walls perpendicular to the joists. In addition, if the span of the joists from one side of the house to the other is great, the joists may be supported in the middle. Sometimes two joists meet above the middle support. Sometimes

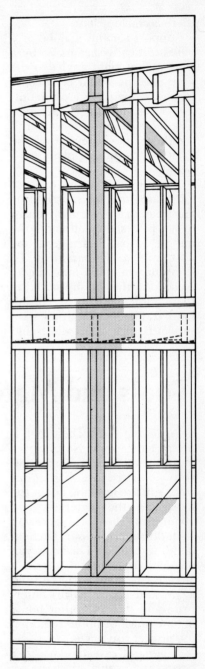

A stud in an outside wall supports the joist and flooring above it, halfway to the studs on each side of it, and halfway to the stud supporting the other end of the joist.

51

there is one long joist.

Support for this may be provided either by beams or by a stud wall at right angles to the joists. Beams would be used to create an open effect, or, in outside walls, for large openings. The joists support the weight of the floor and whatever is on the floor—furniture, appliances or people.

All walls under the ends of joists are load bearing. If the joists have a long span or consist of two pieces, the wall under the middle is load bearing, all the way down to the basement. To find out whether a long single-piece joist must be supported in the middle, you must consult local codes on maximum span for joists of a given width and thickness. Any load-bearing wall continues all the way to the foundation. There is no such thing as load from above being transferred from one side of the house to another.

But the joists in the attic may run one way while those in floors run another. In that case, all the outside walls are bearing load from either the floors or the roof. Outside walls are generally considered load bearing, anyway, even when they run parallel to the joists.

Sometimes the joists in the attic run in two directions, with one group of joists ending at and being supported by the first joist of the other group. Under the supporting joist is a load-bearing wall.

Tools and Materials

Preparing the kitchen shell is pretty basic work. Not surprisingly, the tools and the materials you will need are basic. But what you are learning about the tools and the materials, and about using them, will serve you well throughout your kitchen-building project. The tools you buy to do this work, if you don't already own them, will be used again and again in this enterprise and in every other home maintenance or home remodeling project you tackle.

A general caveat is in order here, and you'll find it repeatedly throughout this book. *Don't cheat yourself by buying cheap.* Do shop for the best price, but always get good-quality tools and materials. Purchasing a well-designed, well-made tool is as good an investment as you can make these days. It will serve you throughout your lifetime. And top-quality materials will make your work easier and make your finished product more durable and better looking. Shop wisely.

If you think your construction work will be a once-in-a-lifetime proposition, you might try renting as many of the tools as you can. The most likely rental items are power tools like the circular saw and the reciprocating saw. It's doubtful that you'll be able to rent the hand tools you'll need. But perhaps you have a friend who's well equipped with tools and trusting. Certainly an effort to borrow one-use tools is in order.

Tools

Prying, striking and cutting will be your principal actions in preparing the kitchen shell. Basic hand tools, which already are in your possession if you've done any repair work around the house, are required.

Hammers. Buy a good hammer first. A good all-around hammer to get is a 16-ounce claw hammer. Every carpenter has one, as it is the basic tool for driving nails, pulling nails, striking other tools like chisels and exercising general persuasion. A 16-ounce hammer is a bit large for driving brads or tacks, it's a bit small for exercising brute persuasion, and it's not the best tool for striking large cold chisels or wood-handled chisels, so at a later stage of your work in the kitchen, you may want to add other hammers to your collection.

If you anticipate doing a lot of framing work, buy a 22-ounce ripping hammer now. Its slightly longer handle combined with its slightly greater weight will enable you to drive 16d or 20d nails with more authority. Its less sharply curved claws will make the hammer a more useful prying tool.

Removing masonry should not be done with a claw hammer. Instead, equip yourself with a 3-pound hand sledge and a cold chisel. If you also have masonry to lay up, you may want to invest in a bricklayer's hammer for working with bricks

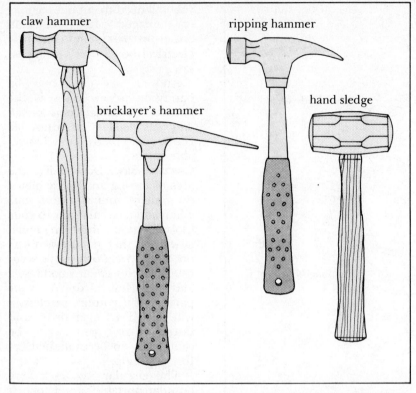

claw hammer

ripping hammer

bricklayer's hammer

hand sledge

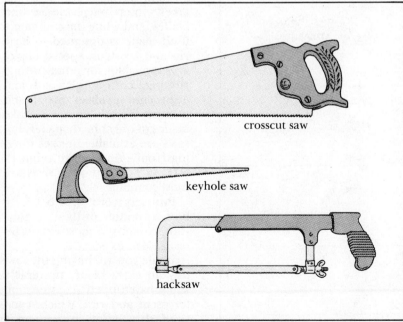

crosscut saw

keyhole saw

hacksaw

or a stonemason's sledge hammer for stonework. For a masonry project of modest size, these hammers may get little use, and thus not be worth the cost.

In shopping for any metal-headed hammer, look for a drop-forged head rather than a brittle cast-iron one.

Hand-Powered Saws. Buy a good handsaw of the crosscut variety. Handsaws are about 26 inches long and taper from their broadest point at the handle to a blunted tip. The handles are wooden on good saws, plastic on cheap ones. Handsaws with Teflon-coated blades are available; the coating is supposed to slide the saw through its cut more easily, but a sharp, rust-free blade will serve for most of the cutting you'll be doing.

Handsaws are available with varying numbers of cutting teeth. The number of teeth per inch—referred to as points—ranges from 6 through 12. The greater the number of teeth per inch, the finer the cut and the slower it is made. An 8 point handsaw is the general-purpose saw.

Another saw that could come in handy, depending upon the nature of your shell preparations, is a compass or keyhole saw. This is a small saw with a foot-long blade that tapers to a point from a width of about 1 inch. It's used to cut rounded shapes and holes, tasks it does well because of its pointed, narrow blade. To cut a hole, you first bore a hole with a drill, then insert the tip of the compass saw and start stroking. If

53

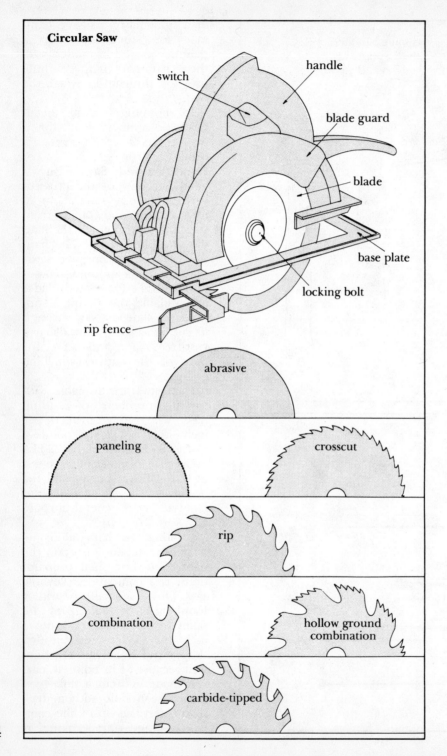

Circular Saw

switch

handle

blade guard

blade

base plate

locking bolt

rip fence

abrasive

paneling

crosscut

rip

combination

hollow ground combination

carbide-tipped

you will need to cut out sections of damaged plaster or wallboard or cut holes for new electrical boxes, get a compass saw.

Another saw that may be handy in a few cases is the hacksaw. This saw cuts metal. The saw itself is an adjustable frame that holds interchangeable blades.

Circular Saw. Do you like the idea of having an electric motor do some of your work for you? Then add a circular saw to your tool collection. There isn't much it will do that handsaws won't do; it won't cut any more accurately, but it will cut wood faster and with less effort on your part. And if you are careless, it will rip off a finger or a hand faster than you can be cautioned. So be cautioned before you shop.

The circular saw is a very popular portable power tool. It takes interchangeable round blades, and while the commonly used blade is designed to both rip and crosscut, special blades are available for crosscutting, ripping, cutting plywood and even cutting sheet metal and masonry. Each saw will take blades of only one diameter, but saws are available in sizes ranging from 4½ inches through 12 inches; 7- to 7½-inch sizes are most common.

Probably your best bet is to buy a middle-of-the-line saw, rather than the most expensive or the least expensive.

While you are buying the saw, buy an extra blade, preferably a carbide-tipped combination (crosscut and rip), which won't need sharpening as frequently

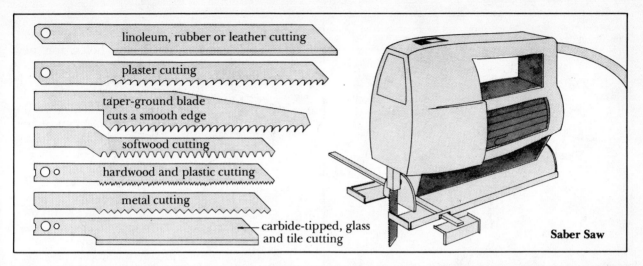

linoleum, rubber or leather cutting

plaster cutting

taper-ground blade
cuts a smooth edge

softwood cutting

hardwood and plastic cutting

metal cutting

carbide-tipped, glass
and tile cutting

Saber Saw

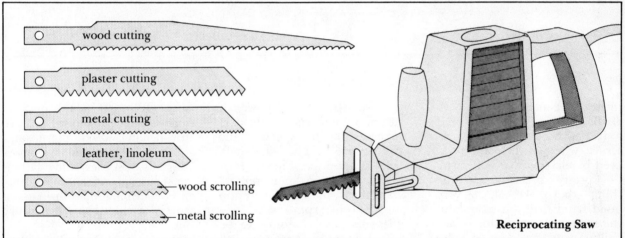

wood cutting

plaster cutting

metal cutting

leather, linoleum

wood scrolling

metal scrolling

Reciprocating Saw

as a regular blade. And get a heavy-duty extension cord.

Saber Saw. The saber saw is a portable jigsaw. It makes the sort of cuts that a compass saw makes, but, because it has an electric motor, it makes them with less effort on your part. You don't *need* a saber saw any more than you *need* a circular saw. You still have to exercise skill to get quality work, but it makes it easier.

The saber saw has interchangeable blades, with blades available for all sorts of special applications, including cutting glass and ceramics.

Reciprocating Saw. The reciprocating saw has a lot in common with the saber saw; it's bigger and does big jobs better than a saber saw, but because it's bigger, it's a bit clumsy for finer work. At this stage of your kitchen project, however, the

reciprocating saw is probably a better choice than a saber saw.

The most obvious difference between the two saws is that the reciprocating saw moves its blade in a horizontal plane, while the saber saw moves its blade in a vertical plane. But the reciprocating saw has a blade that's stockier too. The blades come in the same one-for-every-job variety as the saber saw's. The sizes range from 2½

55

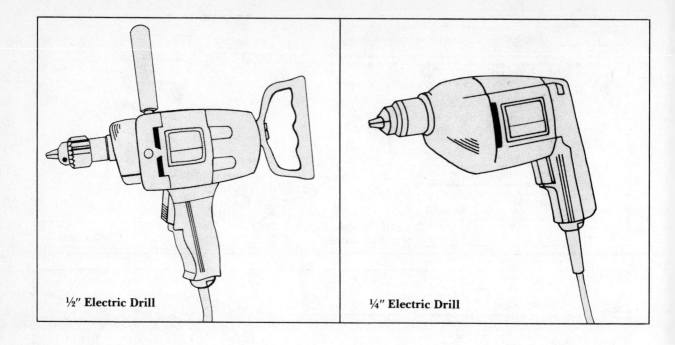

½″ **Electric Drill**   ¼″ **Electric Drill**

inches to 12 inches long.

Drills. You may or may not need a drill at this stage of the work. Drills, whether they are powered by electricity or your arm, do pretty much the same thing—they make holes. A very good hand drill will cost about the same as a serviceable power drill; if you have a lot of holes to make, the hand drill will make your arm tired; the power drill won't.

Hand drills usually have a chuck capacity ranging from ¼ inch to ⅜ inch.

Power drills come in ¼-inch, ⅜-inch and ½-inch sizes. The size refers to the capacity of the chuck, which holds the interchangeable drill bits that actually make the holes. A ¼-inch drill has a chuck that will accept bits with shanks up to ¼ inch in diameter. As the chuck capacity

increases, the size and power of the motor and the whole drill increases, but the speed of the drill decreases. Thus, a ¼-inch drill has a top speed in excess of 2,000 revolutions per minute, while the ½-inch drill may top out at only 600 rpm.

If you have masonry to be drilled, a special hammer drill may be a worthwhile investment. The hammer drill has a percussive action that helps break up masonry as the bit turns. A special bit is made for use in such a tool, and you *should* use it. This may be a tool you'll rent for special jobs. A regular drill *can* be used with a masonry bit to drill in masonry, but it does put an unusual strain on the tool.

All sorts of interchangeable drill bits are available. A small set ranging in ¹/₃₂ -inch incre-

ments from ¹/₁₆ inch through ¼ inch is fine. *Carbon steel* bits are for drilling wood, plastic and other soft materials. *High-speed steel* bits drill everything carbon steel bits will and metal besides.

For drilling masonry, use a special carbide-tipped masonry bit.

For drilling larger holes than drill bits produce, use spade bits. These bits range from ¾ inch through 1½ inch, but all have ¼-inch shanks. Spade bits need the rpms delivered by a ¼-inch drill to work effectively.

Pry Bars. For ripping apart an old kitchen, you'll need a variety of crowbars and pry bars. The most common type is the familiar crowbar or J bar, which is a length of bar stock shaped into a J. The ends are flattened and shaped so the bar can be forced into seams and joints. The

56

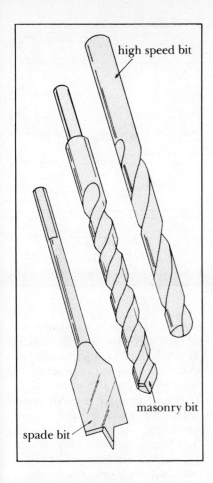

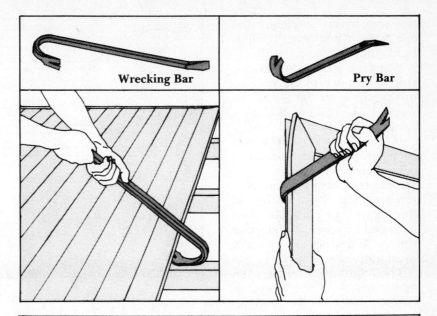

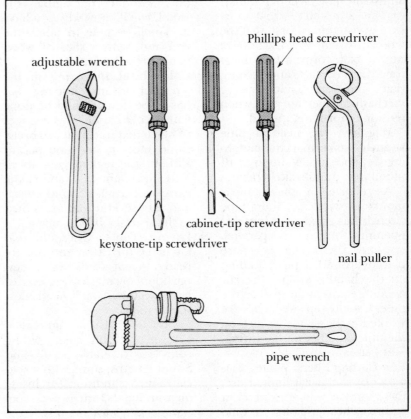

goose-necked end is split for hooking and pulling nails. The J configuration gives leverage for ripping things apart. Hence, the larger the bar, the more leverage. If you've a lot of ripping to do, get a big crowbar. Or two of them.

A fairly new style of pry bar is a flat bar. Though small, it is still J shaped. Its extremely thin tips make it an excellent tool for breaking into tight joints and cracks.

Screwdrivers. There will be screws to be removed in your old kitchen. There are many types

57

of screwdrivers available, the two basic types being Phillips head and plain head.

When using screwdrivers, one rule of thumb is to use a screwdriver which fits the slot of the screw. If the blade is too big or small it will tear the screwhead.

If you plan to do the wiring later, buy plastic-handled screwdrivers now.

Wrenches. There may not be a repeated call for wrenches in this stage of the work, but when you need a wrench, nothing else will do. Wrenches are available in astonishing variety.

The adjustable wrench is the most versatile. These wrenches have a stationary jaw and an adjustable jaw. When purchasing an adjustable wrench, be sure of two things: first, that the wrench, when closed around a nut or bolt, forms a hex shape for a firm contact; and second, that the adjustable spring mechanism does not slip when tension or torque is applied.

Whether you need a pipe wrench to take apart the plumbing depends upon the kind of plumbing your old kitchen has.

A relative of the familiar monkey wrench, the pipe wrench has a loosely adjustable opening with nearly parallel, serrated jaws. The jaws are placed around a pipe; pulling on the handle toward the jaw opening tightens the grip on the pipe. Usually pipe wrenches are worked in pairs, one wrench on the pipe, another on the fitting. Many sizes are available.

End-Cutting Pliers. While this is a tool of somewhat limited use, the moment you encounter a nail, sans head, that has to come

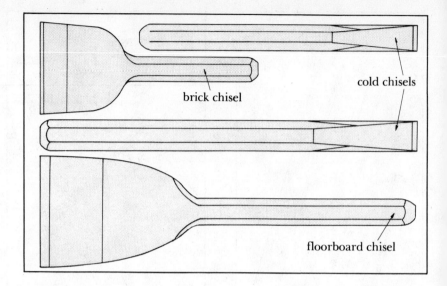

brick chisel

cold chisels

floorboard chisel

out without damaging the wood, you'll know why you have it. You'll be able to pinch the nail and, with a slice of wood beneath the jaws, rock it out.

Cold Chisel. In tearing out the old kitchen, any chiseling that has to be done should be done with a cold chisel. This is a tool of hardened steel that can break stone, mortar, steel and plaster without undue damage to itself. You may want to examine the variety of available cold chisels and buy several that are suited to the special jobs you have.

Layout Tools. Once the old kitchen is torn away and you are ready to cut studs for a new partition or mark locations of new windows, you'll need measuring tools.

The most basic is a tape measure or a folding rule. Folding rules are available in 6- and 8-foot lengths, some with a special 6-inch extension for inside measurements, others with special markings for masons. Tape

measures come in an assortment of tape widths—¼ inch, ½ inch, ¾ inch and 1 inch—and an even greater assortment of lengths—from 6 feet up to 25 feet and even more. All come with tape locking devices and belt clips.

When it comes to laying out plates and studs, you'll need a try square or combination square or framing square—all different—to guide your pencil across the lumber.

The framing square is the framing carpenter's primary layout tool, used to mark plates and joists, as well as rafters and stairs. It's an L-shaped tool, with one leg 24 inches long and 2 inches wide, and the other leg 16 inches long and 1½ inches wide.

The combination square has a calibrated blade 12 inches long which can be adjusted to different lengths through the head for gauging. The head has one edge at right angles (90 degrees)

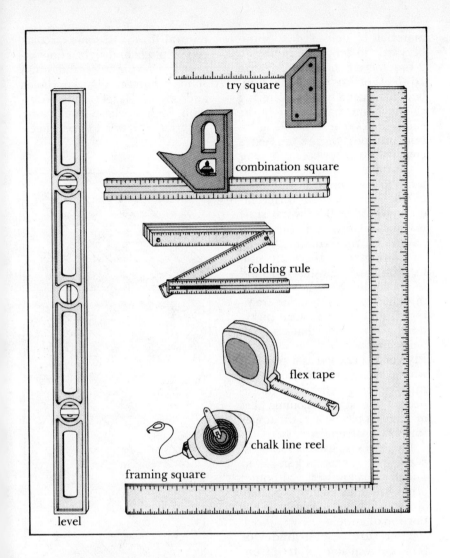

try square

combination square

folding rule

flex tape

chalk line reel

framing square

level

lines on walls or floors, use a chalk line. There are many types of chalk lines; some are self-chalking, others are not. The basic principle is that a cord is dusted with chalk and tensed over the area to be marked. The cord is then plucked and a straight mark is left on the surface from the chalk.

Some chalk lines can double as plumb lines. A plumb line has a conical weight that is suspended on the end of a string to establish or test vertical lines. Any weight so suspended will drop at an angle of 90 degrees to the horizontal, which is known as plumb.

Levels are also valuable tools for layout and setting up work. A level is an instrument for determining a true horizontal, vertical or angular direction by centering a bubble in a glass tube filled with alcohol or ether. There are many types of levels from a couple of inches in length to over 6 feet. Some have only horizontal and vertical vials, while others have 45-degree vials or 360-degree protractor vials.

Carpenters generally use aluminum levels. Masons use levels that are wood with brass edges. A good mason's level will cost two or three times what a carpenter's level costs. In practice, the two are interchangeable.

In the course of your work, you may find other tools that are necessary or simply helpful. You must consider your own ultimate plans, your financial resources and your network of trusting and helpful friends (who might lend you tools) be-

to the blade and the other at 45 degrees. In addition, the combination square has a spirit level and a scriber built into the head. While the square can perform the functions of a try square including measuring or laying out 45-degree miters, it can also be used as a marking gauge and level, and the steel blade can be removed from the head and used as a straightedge.

The try square is an L-shaped measuring tool most commonly used for laying out or checking right (90 degree) angles. The tool generally has a scale on its steel blade and certain types can also be used for measuring or laying out 45-degree miters or angles. The handles of the try square are made from either wood, metal or plastic.

For marking long straight

fore actually buying all the tools listed here. Besides, your particular project may be completed with only a few of them.

Materials

The array of materials used in preparing the kitchen shell is limited indeed. You'll be using framing lumber, mostly 2 × 4s, perhaps some 2 × 6s and 2 × 8s, maybe 2 × 10s and 2 × 12s. You may need a sheet of plywood to sheath the spot where you've closed up a window or door opening. And you'll use lots of nails. Big ones, of 8 through 20 penny weights. Every lumberyard stocks these materials.

Lumber. For the uninitiated, measuring that first lumber purchase can be something of a surprise. Your new 2 × 4s don't measure 2 × 4, they measure 1½ × 3½. You've discovered nominal measurements.

Dimension lumber, which is the softwood stuff every lumberyard stocks, is sold in nominal measurements for thickness and width; only the length is an actual measurement. The reason for the disparity between the nominal measure and the actual measure is that the wood is planed and dried after it leaves the saw mill. It measures 2 × 4 coming off the saw, but drying shrinks the wood, and planing to eliminate splintery roughness removes a fraction of an inch from each surface.

Nevertheless, the wood retains its nominal-dimension name.

Ordinarily, framing material is sold by the running foot. The material is delivered to lumberyards in lengths ranging in 2-foot increments from 8 feet to 16 feet or more. Some lumberyards, usually those catering to the home handyman trade, will sell wood in other lengths, but ofttimes there's an extra charge for the service.

Grading systems for wood tend to be obscure. But even 2 × 4s do come in different-quality grades. The worst stuff is what's advertised in the newspaper; it's the economy grade. Ascending from there are utility, standard, construction and select grades. You don't need to buy the highest grade for framing. But do be somewhat picky; don't accept wood that's bowed, twisted or crooked.

Plywood. Plywood is a piece of wood made from an odd number of glued layers of veneer. The grain of adjoining plies or layers is placed at right angles for greater strength.

Plywood is usually sold in 4 × 8-foot sheets and in ¼- to 1-inch thicknesses, although other sheet sizes are available. Some lumberyards will sell a portion of a sheet.

There are several grades of plywood available: N, free from defects, suitable for a natural finish; A, smooth and free from defects, suitable for painting or

The nominal size that you use to order a piece of lumber is not the same as its actual dimensions. The familiar 2 x 4 actually measures 1½ by 3½ inches. The nominal measurement refers to the width and depth of the stock. The length is an actual dimension.

natural finish; B, some circular repair plugs and tight knots allowed; C, knotholes and small splits common; D, knotholes and slightly larger splits common. Each side has a letter rating. Exterior plywood has been

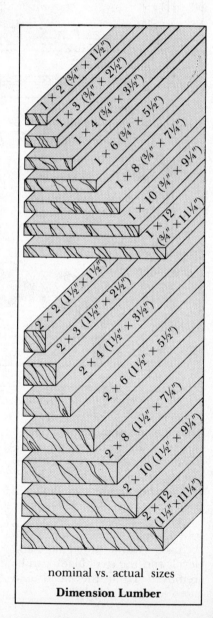

nominal vs. actual sizes

Dimension Lumber

bonded with waterproof glue and is suitable for use outside; interior ply is bonded with water-resistant glue, and should not be used outdoors.

In common parlance, the grading system is usually reduced to a choice between sheathing, which has knotholes and unsanded surfaces, and panels good on one or both sides. "Good" means with knotholes filled and surface sanded.

Nails. Nail sizes are indicated by pennyweights. Originally, these designations indicated the price per hundred, and the abbreviation for penny, d, derives from the Roman penny, the de-

Nailing techniques: a. Use nails 2½ to 3 times as long as the thickness of the lighter piece to ensure that the nails will hold, and nail the lighter piece of wood to the heavier one. b. Toenail from opposing directions to keep the piece from working loose, and offset the nails to be sure they will pass each other. c. Don't put more than one nail along the grain line or the wood will split. d. Blunt the point of nails to avoid splitting the wood when you are nailing near the end of a piece.

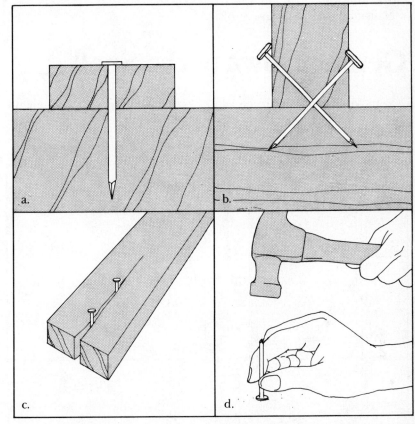

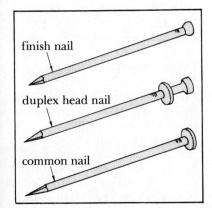

finish nail

duplex head nail

common nail

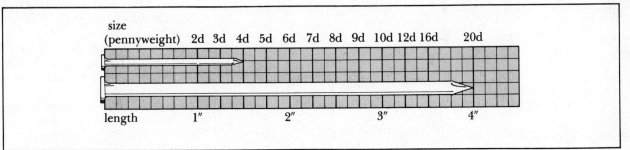

Nails are sold by pennyweight, abbreviated "d." The larger the nail, the greater the pennyweight. Each pennyweight corresponds to a specific length, no matter what the nail type. An 8d finishing nail is the same length as an 8d common nail, although you'll get more finishing nails per pound.

61

narius. Now the pennyweights designate the nail length, and since the diameter of the nail increases with the length, the thickness. A 10d nail is 3 inches long, for example, a 16d nail 3½ inches long.

Nails are sold in a variety of styles. The common nail, which is used in framing, has a head. The finishing nail, used in finishing work, has no head to speak of.

Nails are now sold by the pound.

Getting Down to the Shell

Removing surfaces can be as easy as letting yourself loose with a crowbar and sledgehammer. It's best to resist this temptation, especially in the kitchen where there are so many hidden pipes and wires.

If you are doing something less than gutting the entire kitchen, protect all finished surfaces that will remain. It is very easy to cause damage at this stage. Cabinets and counters are best protected with cardboard taped over them, floors with a heavy tarpaulin, frequently emptied. If you are only removing a portion of the wall, to enlarge a window or door, cut the wall in a straight line to make patching easier. It is often easier to remove entire sections of 4 × 8-foot wallboard than to fit in little patchwork squares later, although it is more costly.

Before cutting any walls or ceilings, make a careful inspection to locate any electric circuits or pipes in the wall. Shut off any circuits near the areas to be cut. If you are at all unsure about the circuits in the wall (one might run up to the next floor and have no outlets in the kitchen) shut off the power to the entire house at the main breaker or pullout. Naturally, this will prevent the use of power tools, but hand tools work fine for this type of job. If water pipes are located in the wall, it's not a bad idea to shut off the water, too. Part of kitchen planning involves locating new doors and windows to avoid disruption of service lines. But sometimes there is no way around making a new opening

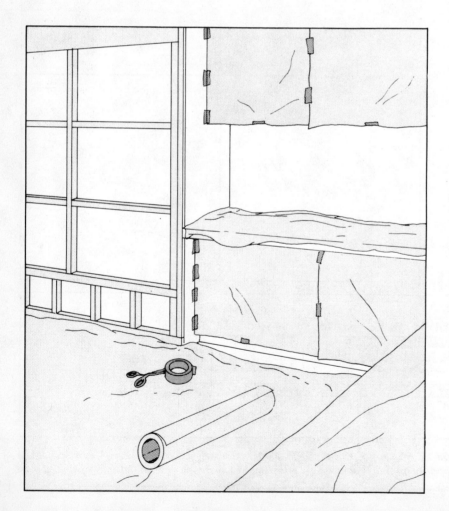

Protect usable surfaces with cardboard, sheets of kraft paper or drop cloths during demolition.

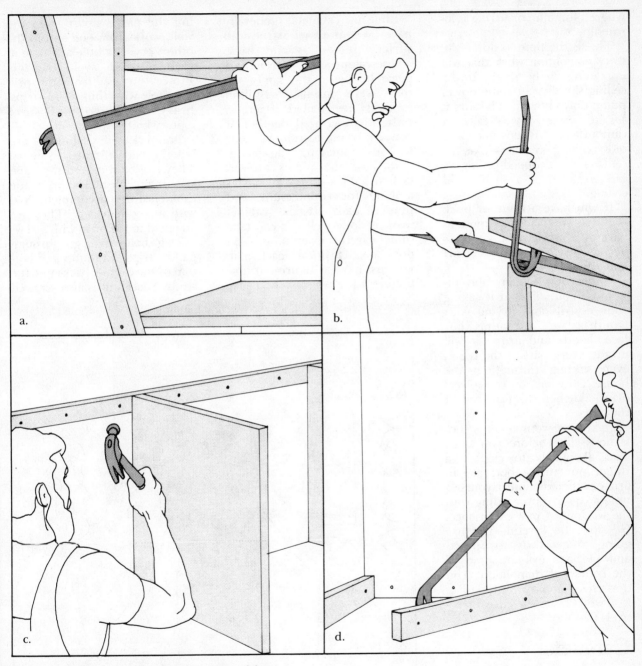

Remove built-in cabinets in roughly the reverse of the order that they were built: First pry away the facing, then the counter top, using a pry bar; knock out the sides with a hammer or mallet; finally pry the supporting pieces away from the wall.

where plumbing or wiring is located.

This is the time to do all the dirty demolition work that will ever have to be done. If the ceiling simply *must* come down, pull it down now. Just be sure it *has* to come down. Lots of camouflaging is possible, and most ceiling systems—like tile ceilings and dropped ceilings—can go on over a shabby old ceiling.

If you have a stone or brick wall that you want to expose as part of your harvest kitchen's decor, chisel the old plaster off it now.

Plaster dust is incredibly insidious. You will find it caking your nostrils and drying your mouth as well as coating your face, hands and arms. It will invade every part of the room, even settling throughout the house. Do what you can to seal off the kitchen from the rest of the house.

Make sure your tetanus shot is up-to-date before you start. You are likely to clobber a finger, puncture a foot, rake an arm or otherwise injure yourself unless you are proceeding with the wisdom of past experience. Go slow. Be careful. You are going to get dirty, frustrated and perhaps evil-tempered in the course of demolition. You don't need lockjaw on top of it. You won't be able to curse effectively that way.

Cabinets

Cabinets are the first thing removed, if you are removing them at all. Start with the floor units.

Built-in cabinets generally have no rear panel as the wall surface serves as the back. These cabinets can be removed piece by piece, the same way they were installed. Built-in cabinets are nailed together, rather than screwed together. If you are trying to remove units without damaging the wood, note how the pieces are attached. This usually means looking for countersunk and puttied nails. If the cabinet work is done well this can take some careful examining. You don't need to locate each nail, you just have to figure out how they join the wood. When pry-

ing the pieces apart from the wall, work from one end to the other, prying a little at a time in each place to avoid damage. Protect surfaces from the prying tools with thin wood strips, heavy cardboard or the blade of a putty knife.

Prefabricated cabinets are bought and installed in units. They can be removed the same way, in one piece. Factory-made cabinets form a complete box, with a wooden back. They are attached to the walls with screws or lag bolts that go through nailer strips at the top and bottom of the cabinet backs into the studs. Each unit is also screwed

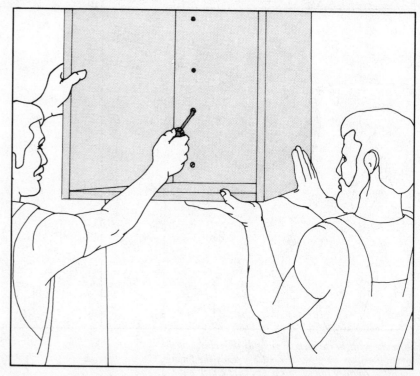

Remove prefab cabinets one by one, first by unscrewing a unit from those on each side, then—with someone holding it—by unscrewing it from the wall.

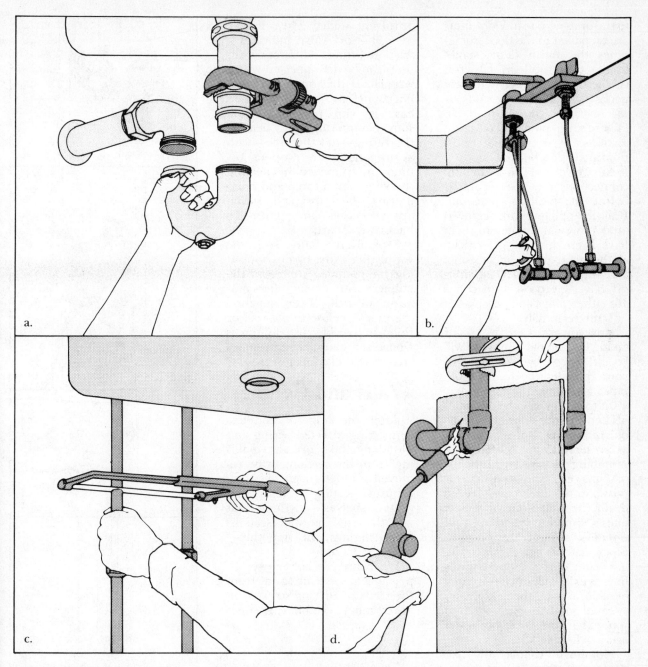

Before you remove the sink, you've got to disconnect the drainage and supply pipes: a. Drains can be disconnected with a pipe wrench. b. Use a basin wrench to disconnect the faucet. c. Any supply line can be cut with a hacksaw. d. Copper lines can be unsweated.

to the ones next to it. Floor units are toenailed to the floor, sometimes the finish floor, sometimes the subfloor. Built-in cabinets, on the other hand, are generally built over the subfloor to save on finish material. (There's no point in covering sections of expensive finish flooring with cabinets.)

Any electrical or plumbing connections must be separated before the cabinets come out. Built-in appliances are removed after power and water to them have been shut off—electricity at the main panel or subpanel and water at the nearest shut-off valve. Electrical connections are either plugs and receptacles or screw terminals.

How you approach the task of taking out the old plumbing will be influenced by the extent of your remodeling. If *all* the old pipes are coming out, you may want to simply saw the old pipes off beneath the sink and cart the old relic away. But if you want to preserve as much of the old plumbing as possible, unscrew or "unsweat" fittings wherever possible. In any case, try to drain the water out of supply lines so you don't suddenly find a puddle around your knees as pipes and fittings part. (Draining water out of copper supply lines is essential, since you won't be able to melt the solder in a sweated joint to get it apart if water is in the lines; the water acts as a heat sink.)

Plumbing connections for waste are usually friction fittings, although they can be soldered or solvent-welded (with plastic pipe) fittings. Supply fittings may be threaded, soldered

or solvent welded. The presence of a shut-off valve indicates a friction fitting. All friction fittings can be disconnected with a wrench. If the union is a stubborn one, you may be able to ease it with penetrating oil, some hammering, or by heating the fitting—not the pipe—with a propane torch. Copper fittings are removed by heating the joint with a torch and hammering the pipe and fitting apart. Plastic lines must be hacksawed apart.

Separate the faucet from the supply lines first by disconnecting the coupling nut from the tailpiece with locking pliers or a basin wrench. Then separate the pipes as close to the wall or floor as possible; usually this is where the shiny chrome pipes change to dull copper or iron.

Walls and Ceilings

After checking for and disconnecting affected wiring and plumbing, take off any molding from the sections to be removed. Outlet covers, lighting fixtures, heating or ventilating grates, shelves—anything that will prevent the wall sections from coming out smoothly—must also be removed.

Wallboard can be removed by prying it at the seams away from the studs or furring strips. You are certain to crumble the edges

Remove wallboard in sections: Cut out the area to be removed with a reciprocating saw, a circular saw, or a utility knife, and force it away from the stud frame with a pry bar.

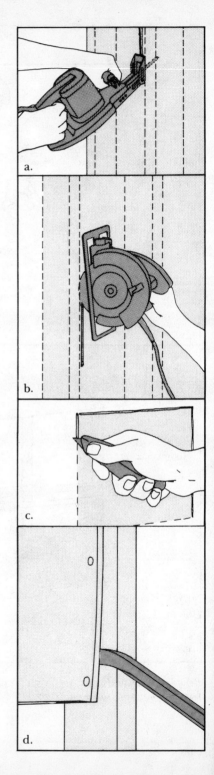
a.
b.
c.
d.

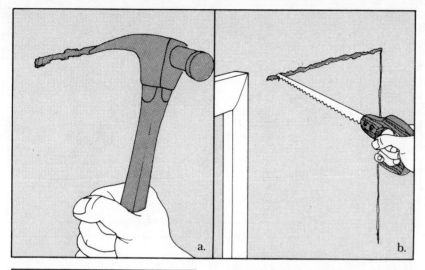

Take out a section of plaster by chopping around the area with the claw of a rip hammer—or by cutting the perimeter with a keyhole saw—and ripping out the plaster bit by bit.

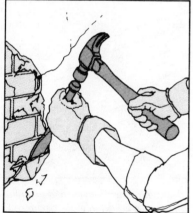

Chip plaster away from masonry or brick with a hammer and cold chisel.

baseboard molding

wedge

shoe molding

Pry molding loose with a pry bar or wrecking bar, prying a little bit at a time. You may need to stick thin wedges between the molding and the wall to hold it out as you go.

of the sheets in prying them away from the wall, but if large sections can be removed intact, they can be used for patching. Smaller sections can be cut out with a keyhole saw or a reciprocating saw. Either approach risks cutting electrical cable. With the power saw, at least one circuit has to be on to run the tool. Whatever kind of saw you use, you won't believe how fast drywall dulls the blade. Use only replaceable blade saws.

Plaster is removed by chopping horizontal lines between the lath, either with a chisel (a cold chisel, not a wood chisel), a crowbar, or the claw end of a ripping hammer. The plaster inside the vertical lines is cut out for a couple of inches to allow the lath to be cut. Cutting the lath prevents damage to the remaining sections of wall. Pulling off plaster without cutting the lath would cause the lath to pull with the plaster, cracking the remaining surfaces.

If the ceiling must go, cover everything that will not be replaced, or even that will remain in use for a while, because there will be a mess. Make sure power is off in any circuits running in the ceiling. Check for pipes. Any molding must be off, and it will be if you have removed the walls.

Floors

Generally, flooring is only removed to the subfloor. If the subfloor is damaged or wildly out of level, it must be repaired, of course. But for most purposes, a new kitchen floor

67

Remove resilient flooring tile by tile or section by section with a stiff-bladed scraper. If the floor is in large sheets, cut it into strips 1 or 2 feet wide before using the scraper. Heat hard-to-remove patches with an electric iron to loosen the adhesive.

Take out wooden flooring by cutting across the floor with a circular saw and prying up the planks with a pry bar or the claw of a rip hammer. Set the depth of the circular saw so that it will not cut into the subfloor.

means a new surface, whether it is linoleum, tile, quarry tile or wood. After removing all molding, sheet or tile flooring is removed with a pry bar. Get up as much of the old adhesive as possible to provide a level surface for the new floor. Tongue-and-groove flooring—if it can't be restored—is removed with a pry bar or crowbar and a ripping hammer. If the surface of a wooden floor is even, you can lay linoleum or vinyl tile right over it.

Altering the Framing

At this point, it's time to tackle the framing if your remodeling affects partitions, doors and windows.

Kitchen remodeling seems most likely to involve only adding or removing an interior partition or opening or closing a window or doorway. If you've planned properly, you know what you are getting into. You know that what you are ripping out is non-load-bearing, or that you will install headers or beams to accept the load. You know the sizes of the windows or doors that you intend to install, and how large to frame the rough openings. You know how much framing material you're going to need.

Building a whole new wing to expand the kitchen is beyond the scope of this book, but closing in a porch or a garage to

To remove a wall, first shut off the electricity and water to any cables or pipes that run through the wall. a. Knock apart the kitchen wall and remove it. b. Then, without leaving the kitchen, knock out the wall surface on the other side of the studs by knocking it into the other room. c. Cut all the studs except the end studs in half and pull them apart. d. Cut out a 3-inch section from the middle of each end stud, then pry out the pieces. Finally, pry out the top plate.

69

expand the kitchen is just a larger-scale version of partitioning and closing in doors and windows.

The first step in these reframing projects is to analyze your house's framing. Is it stud framed or masonry? Balloon framed or post and beam? Then you've got to adjust your plans accordingly. Masonry construction means you've got heavy labor ahead of you, pounding a cold chisel with a hand sledge. Frame construction is easier, but requires no less care.

Removing a Partition

A non-load-bearing partition is easy to remove. Tear off all the wall surface—paneling, wainscotting, plaster—and expose the studs. Then carefully tear out the studs. Perhaps the easiest method is to saw the studs in half and wrench the halves akimbo. Then pry the top halves off the top plate and the bottom halves off the sole plate. With all the studs removed, pry up the plates.

It's dirty, sweaty work, but not difficult.

Adding a Partition

A chance to actually build, rather than wreck, should be welcome at this point. Not every kitchen project will offer the opportunity at the shell stage, but if your project does, here's what to do.

The first step is to locate exactly where the partition will go. With chalk or some other marker that will show up, mark where the sole and top plates will go and where the new partition will tie into existing walls.

Tying into the Wall

There are two means of at-taching a partition at right angles to a wall. Both these methods provide a nailing base at the corners for wall surfaces. The first method requires two extra studs. One is placed at right angles to the regular stud nearest where the walls and partition will meet. The second extra stud is placed against the first, but at right angles. The three are nailed together with 16d nails spaced 12 inches apart. The second extra rests in the frame in the same position as any other stud, with the first sandwiched between it and the regular stud. The partition is nailed to the middle stud with 10d nails.

The other method of attaching a partition allows a little more flexibility because the par-

Two ways to anchor partitions to other walls: a. Partition meets wall at a stud. b. Partition meets wall between studs.

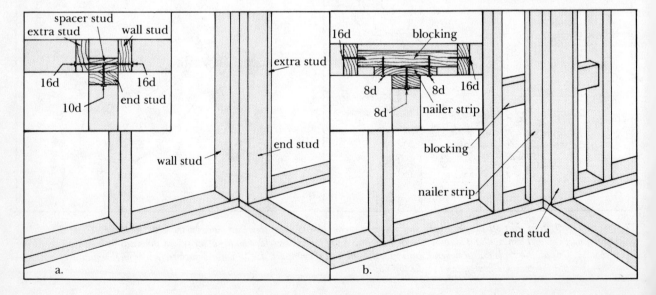

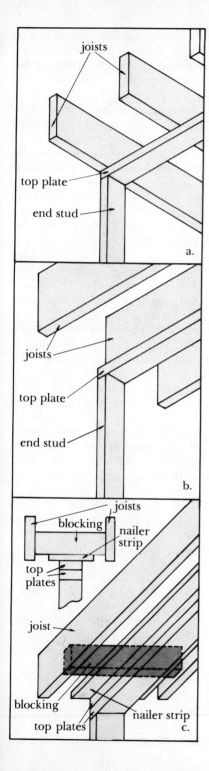

joists

top plate

end stud

a.

joists

top plate

end stud

b.

joists

blocking

nailer strip

top plates

joist

blocking

top plates

nailer strip

c.

Three ways to anchor partitions to the ceiling frame: a. Partition is perpendicular to the joists. b. Partition is parallel to the joists. c. Partition is parallel to the joists but must be located between them.

tition doesn't have to be right next to a regular stud. In this method, stud blocking is nailed between two regular studs with 16d nails through the face of the studs. The blocking is placed every two feet and is located so that 1 × 8-inch backing nailed to it on the inside of the frame will be flush with the inside edges of the frame. The backing board is attached to the blocking with 8d nails. The partition is placed against the backing, plumbed, and nailed to it with 10d nails.

Tying into the Ceiling

Inside partitions should be nailed to the joists. If the partition runs perpendicular to the joists, just nail up through the top plate. Occasionally you will miss the joist. The nail will enter with no resistance. Try again, it won't show. If the partition runs parallel to the joists, blocking must be nailed between the joists. Use pieces of 2 × 4 for this. A nailer is attached to the blocking with 10d nails. The nailer should be flush with the bottom of the joists and wider than the studs to provide a surface to support the ceiling material. The nailer strip is then nailed down into the top plate or plates with 8d nails for single plate or 10d for double plate. This method requires that you

uncover the ceiling material on both sides of the two joists to allow room for nailing.

Nailing to Floor Joists

Locating the joists may present a challenge if the nails through the subfloor are not visible. To secure the partition to a finished surface such as linoleum or a tongue-and-groove floor, you may have to drill holes through the floor (where the partition will cover them up) and stick heavy wire through to locate the joists. Then mark the spot with chalk. Once you have established the distance between the joists, you can lay out a tape measure and mark off the location of all the joists. Don't use a short ruler and proceed from joist to joist, because this method can lead to cumulative error.

Building the Stud Wall

The construction of the stud wall is fairly standardized.

Before any studs are nailed together, the top and bottom plates are cut to size and placed on the floor next to each other. The regular distance between studs is marked on each plate—either 16 or 24 inches on center. In practice, the distance from the outside edge of the end stud to the center of the second is 16 or 24 inches, while the distance from the center of the second to the center of all following studs is 16 or 24. The first distance is thus half the thickness of a stud less than the standard distance. For the rest of the studs, from the second on, it is simpler and just as accurate to measure from edge to

71

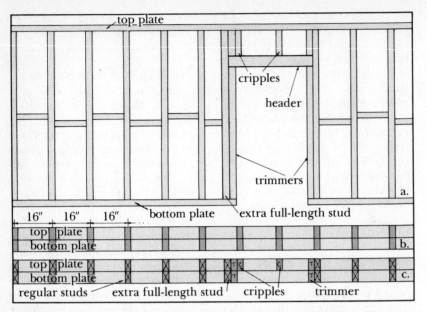

Laying out the plates: a. A stud wall with the door framed in. b. The layout of a top and bottom plate showing where studs will be in a regular wall with no openings. c. Top and bottom plate layout showing regular, trimmer and cripple studs for a wall with a door opening.

edge instead of middle to middle.

Each locating mark is the full size of the stud. You can use a scrap of framing stock and mark a line on each side of it. When stud layouts are marked on paper, the regular studs are indicated with an X inside the stud marks, cripple studs with a C, and trimmer studs with a T. Use the same method on the top and bottom plates. There will be no confusion about the use of the studs. Cripple studs are part of the regular 16- or 24-inch spacing, while trimmer studs are in addition to it. The trimmers are placed inside the regular studs. The distance between them is the width of the rough opening. See "Window and Door Framing" for details.

If your partition plans call for a doorway, you've got to fabricate a header, although since you're dealing with a non-load-bearing wall, the header can be a 2 × 4 and you can eliminate trimmer studs that would ordinarily be a part of the doorway framing. If you are framing a closet or a pantry, and you are actually framing two (or more) walls, you'll have to make corner posts.

Corners

Wall frames form corners where the end studs meet at right angles. To ensure that the frames can be nailed together securely, the frame of one wall must contain an extra stud.

There are two ways this is done. The simplest is to nail the extra stud at right angles to the end stud, flush with the inside of the frame. The other is to place the extra stud in the frame just as any other stud, one stud width from the end. The extra stud is first nailed through the face (the 4-inch side of a 2 × 4) into three or four short pieces of stud blocking. The blocking separates the extra stud from the end stud by the proper distance. Then the extra stud is secured by driving 20d nails through the plate into its butt end.

In both methods, the sections are nailed together with 10d nails through the face of the end wall frame. These nails are spaced about 12 inches apart and staggered, first on the outside edge, then the inside. Both methods leave a surface facing towards the room on both the end frame and the side frame. These surfaces are to allow the interior wall surface to be nailed at the corners of the room.

Setting Up the Wall

If you were framing a house or working on an addition, you'd next separate the plates and lay out the studs between them. You'd nail the studs to the plates by driving 16d common nails through the plates into the butt ends of the studs. Then you'd nail in blocking, sometimes called firestopping, in the stud spaces midway between the sole plate and top plate. The blocking can be staggered up and down to make it easier to nail into place. The blocking serves as a nailing surface, but

72

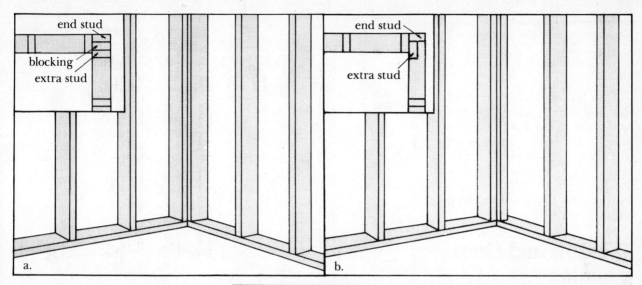

a.

b.

Two methods of forming a corner: a. With 2 x 4 blocking and an extra stud. b. With an extra stud nailed at right angles to the end stud.

as firestopping it prevents a fire from leaping unchecked from floor to ceiling through the stud space "chimney." Finally, you'd erect the partition.

Because you are working indoors, you won't be able to set up a full-size wall frame unit since its diagonal cross section is longer than its vertical cross section.

You have two options. One is to trim 1½ inches, the thickness of a 2 × 4, from each stud, then nail the unit together. The unit can then be tipped up into an erect position. The gap between top plate and ceiling is filled by doubling the top plate (or the sole plate). Whether you choose to double the plate at the ceiling or the floor, nail the extra plate in exact position with 16d nails.

Then slide the stud wall unit into place, plumb it up using a level, preferably a 4-footer, and nail it fast.

Positioning the frame: First nail one of the top plates to the ceiling joists; then slide the stud frame into place under it and nail the two plates together.

73

Make a temporary support if you plan to cut an opening in a load-bearing wall.

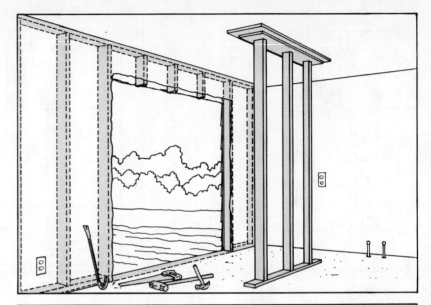

Your second option is to build the stud wall in place. Nail the sole plate to the floor, the top plate to the ceiling, and toenail the studs in between. This may not be the easiest way to frame the partition, but it's an option to consider if you are working alone.

Window and Door Framing

The last alteration to the kitchen shell to consider is adding or removing windows and doors.

In a frame house, these changes aren't all that difficult. In a masonry house, the work is harder but not significantly more difficult.

Window work will clearly involve changes to exterior, load-bearing walls. Doors could too, but they could also involve non-load-bearing interior partitions. Suffice it to say about doors in interior walls that the basic framing techniques are the same, *but* you won't have to set up temporary framing to support the load while the work is being done, and you can use a single 2 × 4 for a header and eliminate the trimmers.

Assume the outside wall is load bearing—that the studs you will cut out are supporting the floors and ceilings above. This load must be supported until the header and trimmer studs are in place. This is usu-

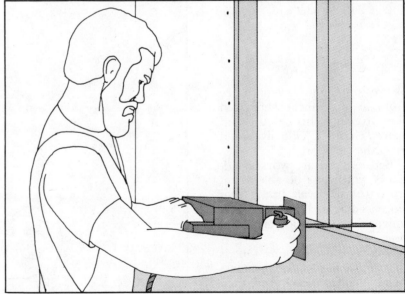

Making an opening: Cut out the studs with a handsaw or a reciprocating saw after removing the exterior sheathing. When you cut the studs, remember to allow for the header and rough sill that will frame the top and bottom of the opening.

ally done by constructing a rectangle of 2 × 4s and forcing it into place close to the wall. It stands like a miniature partition about two feet into the room, the top and bottom resting

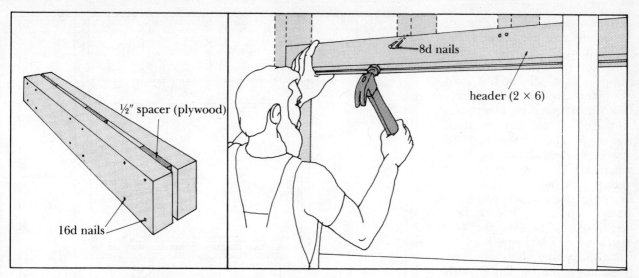

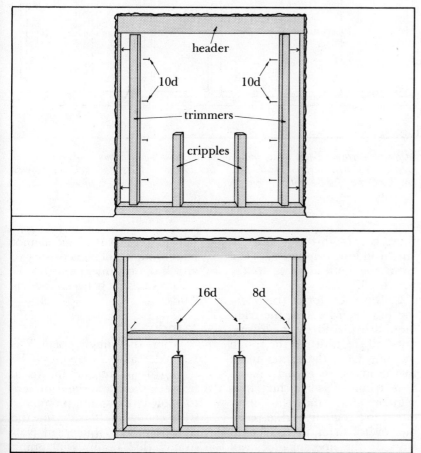

Make a header of two 2 x 6s with ½-inch plywood spacers between them, and nail them together. Toenail the header into the side studs and cut-off studs above the opening.

against the ceiling and the floor. It should be slightly wider than the rough opening. You can tap it into place with your foot or a hammer. The ceiling can be protected by placing paper over the top of the support.

This method of support is only effective when the ceiling joists are perpendicular to the wall to be cut. If the joists are parallel to the wall, any support provided must be under the top plate. When the wall is parallel to the ceiling joists, there is a joist directly above the top plate. Even though the wall may be bearing load, this joist can tem-

Placing the trimmers and sill after the header is in place.

75

porarily support extra load. When the wall in a one- or two-story house is parallel to the joists in the ceiling, no extra support is needed if less than four studs are to be cut.

With the temporary supports in place, you are ready to attack the wall. The first step, is to mark the location of the new opening. Then strip away the interior surface to expose the framing. How much you strip away is up to you. It is possible to make the hole in the wall surface only a bit larger than the rough opening, but you may want to make the hole much larger to ease access to the framing, especially if the wall has to be extensively repaired anyway.

In a load-bearing wall (see the previous discussion of load), the studs that are cut to make space for the opening must be supported. This is done with two boards placed on edge above the opening. They form the header. The header can be made of anything from 2 × 4 on up to 2 × 12 lumber, depending on the span of the opening. Several spacers of ½-inch plywood placed between the pieces bring them flush with the stud wall.

Framing an opening requires at least two studs in addition to the regularly spaced ones. On each side of the opening, a trimmer stud supports the header. The inside face of the trimmers form the rough opening width. When regular studs are cut for the opening, the shortened studs that remain or are put in, are called cripples. The cripples run from the top plate to the header—assuming

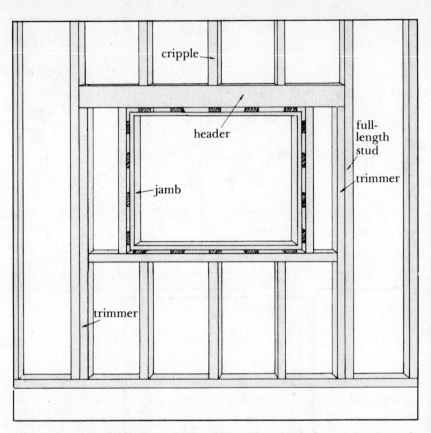

In an ideal framing job, the opening looks like this: The trimmer studs support the header. Cripples above the header add to the stability of the installation and provide nailing surface for the walls.

there is enough room above it. In a window, cripples also run from the bottom plate to the rough sill.

Once the center of the opening has been located, the trimmers are placed by measuring one-half the width of the rough opening from the center mark to the inside of each trimmer. One trimmer is attached to a regular stud and the other either to a regular stud, if possible, or to an extra full-length stud. If the opening does not

fall at a regular stud and cannot be moved, it will be necessary to attach the trimmers to two full-length studs set between regular studs.

Windows

When the rough opening is framed, allowance must be made for jambs and for space between them and the trimmers to allow leveling and plumbing, with enough left over for the window units to squeeze in. Naturally, this requires planning

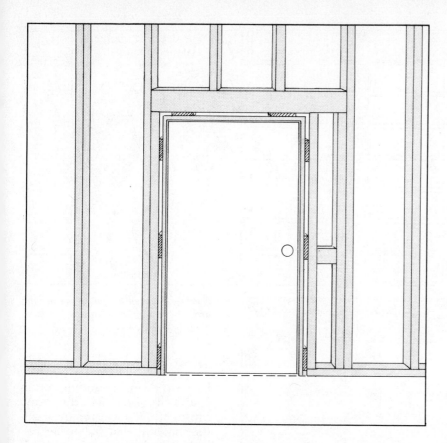

information on size from the manufacturer's data, but if that is not available, leave 2 ½ inches more than the door width and height for the rough opening.

In exterior door frames, the sill rests on joists and headers that support the subfloor. The sill, which is the bottom member of the door frame, must be placed so that the finished floor is even with it. This usually requires removal of some of the subfloor and trimming the top edge of the sill header. This will be explained in the chapter "Finishing." Interior doors do not require a wood sill at this stage.

Your task is to cut out the studs to be removed, fabricate a header of a suitable size, cut trimmers and a sill—if it's a window you are framing—and nail them in place. With the new framing in place, you must next cut away the outer skin of the house. In each of the four corners of your newly framed window or door, drive a nail through the sheathing and siding. Using the nails as reference points, you'll be able to delineate the perimeter of the required opening on the outside wall so that you can cut away only the siding and sheathing that needs to be removed.

Obviously, adding a window or door to a masonry house won't follow this pattern. Instead, you'll have to lay out the rough opening on the wall.

ahead. If you are going to install prebuilt windows, you can get information on the size of the window from the manufacturer. But note: The unit dimension is actually larger than the rough opening. In a prefabricated window, the casing marks the outer dimension of the unit. Since the casing laps over supporting studs, the unit dimension is larger than the rough opening. Most manufacturers' specifications include information on the rough opening and sash size. If this information is not listed, but you have the windows, measure the distances between the outside face of the side jambs and the outside faces of the sill and the head. Allow one-half inch for each side jamb and three-fourths of an inch above the head for plumbing and leveling. The rough opening then will be one inch wider than the outside of the jambs and three-fourths of an inch longer than the head-to-sill measurement.

Doors

As with windows, the rough frame opening for a door must allow room for the door, the jambs and space between the jambs and the studs for leveling and plumbing. It is best to get

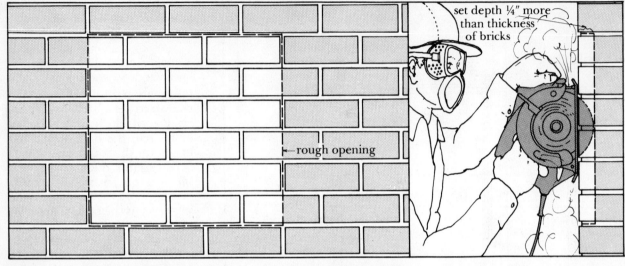

←rough opening

set depth ¼" more
than thickness
of bricks

Cutting an opening for a window in brick by using an abrasive masonry blade in a circular saw.

mortar in full-size bricks

To brick up an old window opening, dig out the half bricks around the perimeter of the opening. Mortar full-size bricks into these spaces to tie the new bricks to the old ones.

have to keep pounding until you've broken all the way through and have removed all the material that has to be removed. A lot of heavy physical work it is.

Working with a house that's got a masonry veneer is going to combine the two methods. You'll have to strip away the interior, frame the opening, then pound away the veneer.

Closing Up a Window or Door

The job of removing a door or window that's not where you want it is a lot easier than adding one. Especially if your house is masonry, for then you merely remove the window or door and close up the opening with brick or stone. You may want to have a

Then, starting in the center of the area to be opened and using a cold chisel and a 3-pound sledge hammer, you'll have to dig away mortar and bricks or stones or concrete blocks. Just

mason handle the work, unless you've got experience. Slipping that last brick or stone into place is a lot trickier than dropping the final brick or stone on the top of a wall.

In a frame house, closing up a window or door is as simple as removing the window or door and toenailing studs, 16 inches on center, in the void. Nail a piece of ⅝-inch or ¾-inch sheathing plywood on the outside of the studs and finish off the exterior with the appropriate siding. The inside is ready for whatever wall surface you intend to install eventually.

Rough-In

If you have taken your kitchen down to the stud frame, you will be in what builders call the "rough-in" stage. At this stage, the subfloor is intact, the studs and ceiling joists are in place, but no doors, windows or insulation have been installed. Before the insulation is added, heating ducts, electrical wiring and plumbing are installed.

In new construction, windows and doors are generally installed after sheathing and wall surfaces, and their installation is considered finish work. There is flexibility in the timing, though. Since windows and doors attach to the studs of the rough openings, they may be installed before interior walls. If you're remodeling the house you're living in, you will undoubtedly want to install windows and exterior doors, just as soon as the rough openings are ready for them. A door should be hung before the finish floor is installed so that the sill can be positioned correctly.

But you've done a lot of work to get as far as you have. Your new kitchen, which still looks far from the harvest kitchen you envisage, is roughed in. The next steps require a lot of coordination. There's wiring to be installed, and plumbing too. All the plaster you tore down must be replaced. There are cabinets to make, flooring to buy, a lot of work still to do.

add full-length studs

add a rough sill

Frame in an unwanted door opening by nailing a 2 x 4 to the floor between the trimmer studs and by toenailing 2 x 4 pieces to extend from the header to this new bottom plate.

Basic Wiring

It is easy to take kitchen wiring for granted. Yet those appliances that seem to multiply by themselves—the toaster, blender, food processor, mixer —all use electricity. Even something like a food dryer is often electrically powered. Many a kitchen stove is electric. And there are electric lights and the refrigerator, possibly a ventila-

tion fan and dishwasher: all electric.

A hundred years ago there was none of that. To keep food fresh, there was the springhouse or the icebox, a cabinet where food was cooled by a large block of ice delivered by the iceman. Food was also preserved by canning, salting, pickling and drying.

Since then, electrical use has increased steadily. Fifty years ago, 30-amp service was considered fully adequate. Now, 100-amp is the accepted minimum.

In spite of this trend, many homesteaders are getting more

selective in their use of electricity, feeling that with a little effort, and an eggbeater or a wire whisk, they can do as good a job as an electric beater. Some people feel they have more control using hand—or even pedal powered—devices, while others want to conserve energy. Still, there is little substitute for electric refrigeration and lighting. The best policy is to bring your kitchen up to current standards. These are not excessive, even if your energy needs are modest, and they will ensure that any electric equipment you use will function at maximum potential.

Fundamentals

A lot of people, including many experienced and capable handymen, are cowed by electricity. They'll tackle carpentry and plumbing, they'll run up the highest ladder and dance on the roof, but they won't touch the wiring. It's mysterious.

Oh, they know their house has a couple of 230-volt circuits to power the electric range and perhaps a clothes dryer or air conditioner. They know that all the other circuits in the house are 115 volts. They know there's a fuse or circuit breaker panel in the basement or a utility room, and that if they get too many appliances going at the same time, it'll "blow a fuse," prompting a walk to the panel to reset a breaker or replace a fuse.

But they don't really know what a volt is, or an amp, or even a circuit.

The truth of the matter is that

you can safely and successfully wire or rewire your harvest kitchen without taking a course in the fundamentals of electricity. But you do need a little background information.

Electricity comes to your house through wires extending from the electrical utility's pole through a meter, which measures how much power you use, to the main panel. The arrangement is called the service entrance. The typical residential system has three wires at the service entrance, delivering 230-volt, 60- to 200-amp service.

Volts are a measure of electromotive force; amps are a measure of flow. Think of them in terms of water: the water pressure (force) remains the same whether you have the faucet set for a trickle or for a gush (flow). Multiply the force by the flow to get the power,

which in electricity is measured in watts (or kilowatts). The voltage remains constant while the amperage, and thus the wattage, changes with the rise and fall in the demand for current.

If you examine the wiring at your fuse or breaker box, you will see one thick wire with black insulation, another with red insulation, and a third with white insulation. The red and the black wires, the "hot" wires, each carry 115 volts. These are referred to as the legs of the service. To run a 230-volt range, you must tap each leg of the service; to run a 115-volt grain mill, you need tap only one leg. The white wire is referred to as the neutral wire. It is interconnected to the ground by a wire attached either to the water line in a house supplied with community water, or a long rod driven into the ground.

Electricity doesn't simply run out of the wires, as water flows from a pipe. It must make a complete loop from generation point to a light or a piece of equipment in your home and back. On a lighting circuit it travels from the fuse box to the light bulb and back through a neutral wire to the fuse box. If the light bulb is removed from its fixture, the loop or circuit is broken and the electricity will not flow. Each circuit should have some load using the electricity flowing in a circuit—a light bulb, a motor, a heating element. The lower the resistance of the load, the more power it demands of the circuit. The wires carrying the electricity, called conductors, have almost no resistance. A circuit **81**

your house. That is why fuses or breakers are so important.

The main panel, which holds the fuses or breakers, is the electrical distribution center for the house. It has a switch that enables you to turn off *all* power beyond the panel. It has connections for all the circuits in the house; they all begin and end in the main panel. Each circuit has a "switch" in the main panel in the form of a fuse or circuit breaker. This switch enables you to turn off the power to a circuit so that you can safely work on it. More important, it is an automatic safety device that breaks the circuit if the electrical flow exceeds the capacity of the conductors carrying it; if, in other words, there is a short circuit or if the appliances on the circuit create an overload.

In principle, wiring a circuit involves running a cable from the main panel to the location of the electrical device you want to install. You strip insulation from the cable's individual conductors, attach the bare wires to the appropriate terminals of the device and to the main panel, and the circuit is wired.

As a practical matter, there is much more to it. You must choose materials and equipment capable of carrying the necessary electrical flow. You must install the equipment following tested and accepted procedures so your circuit will work safely and efficiently and so a handyman modifying your work 30 years from now will be able to decipher your installation. And you must follow safety routines so your project doesn't come to a shocking and premature end.

The Service Entrance

without load is a short circuit, which is potentially dangerous since the electrical flow will sim-

ply increase until the conductor itself overheats because it is overloaded, perhaps kindling

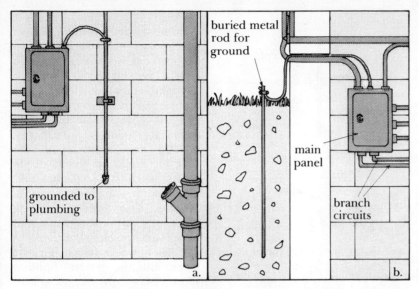

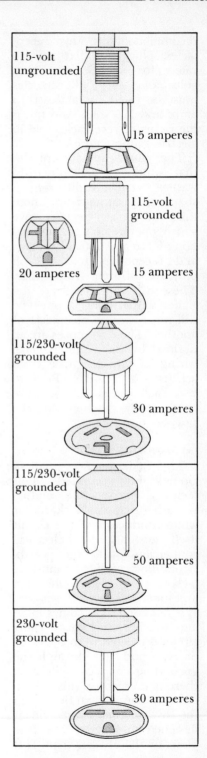

Your house's wiring may be grounded in either of two ways: a. to the plumbing, or b. to a metal rod driven into the ground. If the plumbing has a meter with rubber seals, a jumper must bypass the meter.

The National Electrical Code

Over the years, efforts to create safe and uniform wiring standards grew into a formal set of guidelines, called the National Electrical Code. These guidelines, referred to as the Code, do not have the force of law. The actual regulations are made by state and local governments, which adopt the Code and give it the force of law in their jurisdictions. Some agencies make slight changes when they write the regulations, such as defining who can do wiring and how to get new wiring inspected. Work on private dwellings by the persons living there is usually permitted, but often only after a permit has

been purchased. Always call the local city, county or township agency before you do any work. Some areas require step-by-step inspection and will make you tear out finished walls to uncover work that has not been approved.

General Requirements

The parts of the Code that are important to the home electrician concern such things as conductor size, overcurrent protection (fuses or breakers) for branch circuits and the main panel, prevention of overload and assurance that all receptacles, light fixtures and appliance cords are properly rated for the current they will carry.

Much of the protection that the Code offers can be had just by following manufacturers'

83

recommendations. Most receptacles, plugs and fixtures are rated for specific maximum volts and amps. Receptacles must be rated for at least 15 amps and 125 volts. And this is the rating of receptacles sold in electrical supply stores.

The plugs and receptacles that supply a 230-volt dishwasher circuit are different in shape and rating from those that supply an electric stove which operates on a combination of 115 and 230 volts. Plugs and receptacles for 115-volt only are different from either. These different types are designed so that a plug of one type will not fit into a receptacle of another. The differences are all defined by the Code to make wiring as safe and free from accidents as possible. Be sure that each component you use was actually designed for the purpose it will serve.

Grounding

The Code requires that all circuits be grounded. This means that a separate conductor, other than the black, red or white conductors of the circuit itself, must make good electrical connection with the earth. Grounding conductors must attach to every metal outlet box and junction box on the circuit. If a hot conductor comes loose and touches the box, a short circuit is created from the black or red conductor through the grounding conductor. Because there is no load on this circuit, more amperage then flows than the overcurrent protection is designed to handle. The fuse blows or the breaker trips. If it

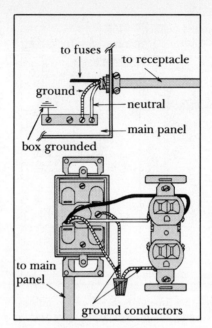

A receptacle safely grounded to the outlet box.

were not for the ground wire, the box would become live, but no current could flow, and so the fuse or breaker would be prevented from opening the circuit. A person touching the box would be shocked.

Kitchen Requirements

Because kitchens make use of so many small appliances, the Code requires that they be served by at least two 20-amp small-appliance circuits in addition to general lighting circuits. Lighting fixtures that are not part of an appliance may not be served by these two circuits. They are for receptacles only. These circuits can, however, serve receptacles in the pantry, breakfast room, dining room and family room in addition to

those in the kitchen. This is a minimum requirement. Most electricians nowadays use two 20-amp circuits for the kitchen only. The refrigerator may be plugged into one of these small-appliance circuits, but if you have room in the main panel for an extra circuit just for the refrigerator, you'd be wise to install it. Fixed appliances, such as a dishwasher, must be supplied on separate circuits. The general lighting circuit for the kitchen may not supply receptacles there, except one used solely for an electric clock. But the general lighting circuit may supply lighting outside the kitchen.

Receptacles are required in every 6 feet of wall space throughout the house, if the wall is more than 2 feet in length. In the kitchen and dining areas, the requirement is greater. Receptacles must be installed at each counter space longer than 12 inches. Counter tops separated by refrigerators, sinks or counter-top ranges are considered as separate counters and must have their own receptacles. Receptacles that cannot be reached because they are behind stationary appliances do not count as the required counter receptacles.

Appliances

The Code requires that appliances have a means of being disconnected from all hot conductors. Appliances using plugs and receptacles need no other disconnecting means. This includes portable appliances such as grain mills or blenders, and most stationary

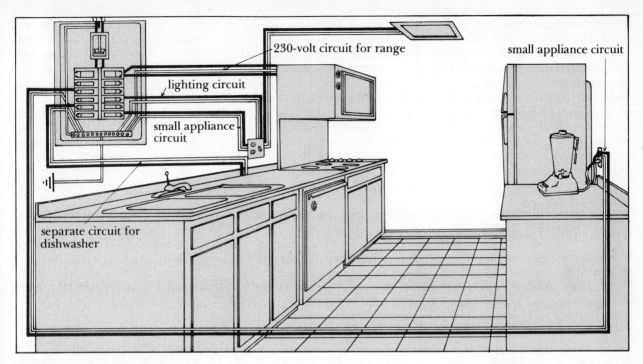

A simplified wiring schematic shows the light circuit, two small appliance circuits and separate circuits for the stove and dishwasher. Although not shown here, all circuits would be grounded.

appliances, such as the refrigerator. But for fixed appliances such as a built-in dishwasher or built-in range, that may not be enough. A fixed appliance with no plug and receptacle may be disconnected by means of a branch circuit switch or breaker if that is readily accessible to the user of the appliance.

Canadian Standards

In Canada, electrical standards are defined by the Cana-dian Electrical Code. Most of them are the same as in the United States, but the differences are worth noting.

Circuits supplying lighting fixtures are limited to 15 amps and no more than 12 fixtures and receptacles. The U.S. code allows general lighting to be supplied by either 15- or 20-amp circuits and has no set limit for the number of outlets.

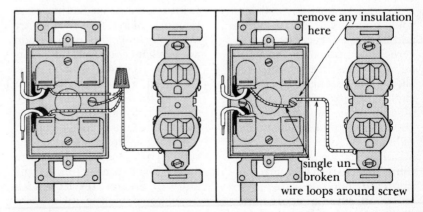

United States (left) versus Canadian (right) methods of attaching the ground to the box and receptacle.

The Canadian code does not favor wire nuts for the attachment of grounding conductor. The bare ground wire should be looped around a bonding screw and then continued without a break to the grounding terminal of the device. If another circuit enters the box, the ground wire for it should be attached to a different bonding screw.

Calculating Electrical Load

Before you get too far along planning the wiring for your kitchen, it's worthwhile to find out what the total load of your home service is. If the conductors that supply your main panel are large enough, and the present service load is small, you can run a couple of new circuits easily. But if your home is already drawing close to the maximum allowable for your service conductors, you may have to limit your plans or consider a larger service.

Total Home Load

To determine total load in your home, you don't merely add all the electrical devices together, because they are never on all at once. Instead, the Code allows an estimate of service load. There is one method for 60-amp service and another for 100-amp or greater service. No estimate is given for less than 60-amp service because anything less than that is now considered inadequate.

For an existing single-family dwelling with 60-amp, three-wire, 115/230-volt service, you may calculate the load according to this formula: the first 8,000 watts of load are figured at their actual value and the remainder at 40 percent. Load calculation includes allowance for lighting and portable appliances at 3 watts per square foot of living space. This includes all lighting fixtures and receptacles in the living area. It is not necessary to include an unfinished basement, attic or garage in this calculation. In addition, each 20-amp appliance circuit is listed at 1,500 watts. All other fixed appliances are figured at their nameplate rating. Don't separately calculate the appliances, such as the refrigerator, on a small-appliance circuit. These are covered by the 1,500-watt allowance for each circuit.

The sum of the first 8,000 watts and 40 percent of the remainder yields the total load. Since volts × amp = watts, 230 (the maximum volts available) × 60 (the maximum amps available) = 13,800 watts. Thus, a total load of up to 13,800 watts is possible with 60-amp service. If total load according to the Code's formula is less than that, you are okay. But if you are near the limit and plan to add an appliance circuit, you may need to upgrade your service. As noted, appliance circuits for the kitchen count for 1,500 watts in addition to the 3 watts per square foot of living space.

For a single-family dwelling served by a set of three-wire 115/230-volt conductors of 100 amps or greater, service load is determined a little differently. The following allowances must be made:

1. 1,500 watts for each 20-amp appliance circuit, including the laundry circuit and the kitchen circuits.

2. Three watts per square foot for general lighting and receptacles.

3. The nameplate rating of all fixed appliances, including four or more separately controlled space heaters.

4. The nameplate amp or kVA (kilovolt-amp) rating of all motors.

5. The larger of either the total heating or the total cooling load figured at: 100 percent of air-conditioning load, 65 percent of central electric space-heating load, 65 percent of the load of less than four separately controlled electric space-heating units, or 100 percent of the connected load of four or more separately controlled electric space-heating units.

Total load is the sum of the heating or air-conditioning (whichever is greater), 100 percent of the first 10,000 watts of all other load, and 40 percent of all remaining load.

If you do decide to install a larger service, you must replace the main panel (fuse or breaker box) with a larger-rated one, and the service conductors from the panel to the power pole. This requires arrangements with the power company and, doubtless, inspection and certification by local authorities. Find out the details before you do any work.

Single Circuit Load

While there is no particular limit on the number of receptacles that may be placed on a given circuit, it is important to consider what appliances and other load will be placed on it. The maximum possible load on a given circuit is found by multiplying the rating in amps (the size of the fuse or breaker on the circuit) by the voltage.

It is not a good idea to be near the maximum capacity of the circuit, especially when variable loads (receptacles) are present. A good margin for error is provided by having the load no greater than 80 percent of the capacity of the circuit.

Planning

The first step in planning your wiring is to draw two maps, one of your existing system, the other of your new one. Examine the existing wiring for the kitchen and map the circuits on paper. Shut off circuits one by one at the main panel and test receptacles and fixtures with a test light until you know exactly which circuits supply the kitchen and whether these circuits supply other parts of the house. Draw a floor plan of the kitchen, mark the location of each receptacle, switch and light, and label which circuit it is a part of. Find out how much power each of these circuits can supply. Make sure each cable is actually designed to supply the amount of power indicated by its fuse or breaker. Unfortunately, overfusing is a common and dangerous practice. Check conductor rating by shutting off the main fuses in the panel and measuring the diameter of each conductor. Insert the conductor into the smallest possible hole in a cable ripper. The number above the hole is the wire gauge. Finally, find out how much load the entire house uses and what the maximum capacity of your electrical service is. This will let you know if you can add new circuits.

Then draw up a new plan. You may be able to use some or all of the present circuits if the cable is in good condition. Go over your wiring plan until you are certain you understand every aspect. Even mild confusion is usually a sign that something is lacking in your knowledge. Don't make assumptions; don't guess. Partial knowledge can be dangerous in wiring if it leads you to make mistakes, and it probably will. Plan the route of each circuit or extension, exactly where the cable will go, how you will attach outlet boxes, what you will do to repair damage to walls or ceilings.

When you have a final plan, go over it mentally step by step. Actually walk along the routes you have chosen, visualizing where the cable will run and how you will connect every receptacle. It is likely you will realize something on the dry run that isn't right for one reason or another.

This is the point at which you should make your shopping list for materials and equipment. You can minimize extra trips for things you've forgotten or overlooked by putting all the details in the plan and by reviewing and re-reviewing carefully. Measure the approximate

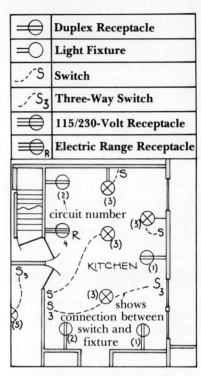

Mapping the existing wiring.

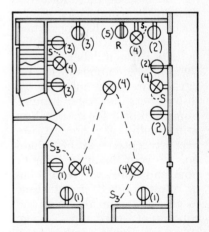

Mapping the new wiring.

distance of each cable run, following each bend and turn. You'll be surprised how much length goes into twists and turns. Allow a couple of feet extra at each device for attachment to the terminals. Make a list of the amount of cable you will need and in which sizes. Add to the list each box and device you will need, and all the connectors and miscellaneous hardware—wire nuts, brackets and so forth. Then go shopping.

As you do the actual wiring, double-check each step. Check each connection and box with a voltage tester. And take your time. Then you can be sure your wiring job will be right.

Probably the best attitude you can have when working with electricity is a very healthy respect. Not so much that you don't do your own wiring, because you *can* do it safely, but enough to make you careful.

Tools and Equipment

You can learn a lot about wiring just by going to an electrical supply store and examining the things on sale. In most places, only one or two different kinds of cable are sold. But each type comes in different sizes. The smaller the number printed on the outside of the cable, the thicker the conductors inside. Each size is rated for a certain number of amps and is used for definite jobs—number 14 cable for lighting, number 12 for kitchen circuits, number 10 for dishwashers and water heaters, number 6 or 8 for ranges. You won't really know how to connect a receptacle until you hold one in your hand, no matter how many times you read about it. Allow yourself enough time to get the feel of the tools and equipment used in wiring. When you finally start the project, at least you won't have to waste time getting acquainted with strange equipment.

Cable

For electrical purposes, a conductor is material capable of transmitting electricity. (Conductors are wires, but electricians don't usually call them that.) Cable is a combination of conductors insulated from each other and enclosed in a protective sheath.

Armored or BX Cable. This type of cable was in general use roughly 20 years ago and is still required in some areas. It consists of a flexible ridged metal sheath that contains the conductors. Although the metal sheath serves as a ground, a bare wire runs along with the insulated conductors to insure a good ground connection. BX cable should not be used in damp areas because the metal is subject to corrosion.

Nonmetallic Cable. Often called Romex cable, a brand name. This is the most familiar type of cable nowadays. The conductors are enclosed in a plastic or woven fabric sheath. The size and type of cable is printed on the plastic sheath. The ground conductor is not insulated. On some high-amperage cable, the ground consists of many small wires that must be twisted together in order to be screwed to a ground terminal in the main panel. The standard indoor cable suitable for a 15-amp circuit is 14/2 with ground type NM. The first number is the wire gauge, the second is the number of conductors. The same wire type with 14/3 would have a red insulated conductor added. Type NM is for dry indoor use only, while NMC may be used in either wet or dry locations.

Aluminum Wiring. While cop-

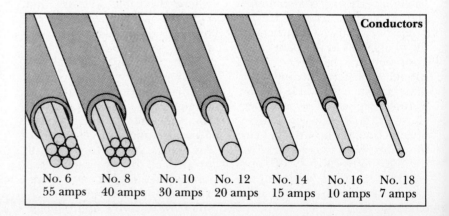

Conductors

| No. 6 | No. 8 | No. 10 | No. 12 | No. 14 | No. 16 | No. 18 |
| 55 amps | 40 amps | 30 amps | 20 amps | 15 amps | 10 amps | 7 amps |

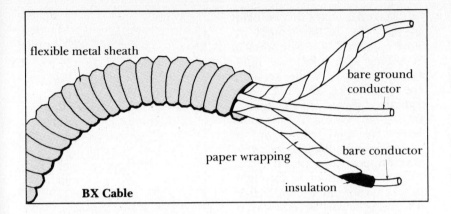

flexible metal sheath

bare ground conductor

paper wrapping

bare conductor

insulation

BX Cable

per conductors are by far the most widely used type in electrical installations, aluminum conductors are also used in many homes. Aluminum conductors are less costly, but they have drawbacks.

A thicker aluminum conductor than copper conductor is required for a given amperage. Number 12 copper conductor is rated for up to 20 amps. The same 20-amp rating with aluminum conductor would require number 10 wire.

Moreover, aluminum reacts with brass in a way that in-creases electrical resistance, so to avoid overheating, special fittings must be used with aluminum wiring. These special receptacles, switches and other devices are designated AL or CO/ALR or CU/AL. Aluminum also oxidizes rapidly when exposed to air, and this too increases the resistance in the conductor. Consequently, an anticorrosive paste must be smeared on the wire immediately after the insulation is stripped from it. The terminal screw should also be tightened enough to bite into the metal slightly. This assures good contact, even if corrosion is present.

Copper-clad aluminum is also used in residential wiring. The rating is the same as for aluminum—heavier-gauge wire is required for a given amperage than with copper. But copper-clad aluminum does not have the problems with corrosion or contact with brass that pure aluminum does. This makes it a safer bet than pure aluminum.

Color Coding. The conductors used in all residential wiring are color coded the same way in all areas of North America. Wire covered with black insulation is always hot. Wire with white insulation is always neutral. Ground wire is either bare

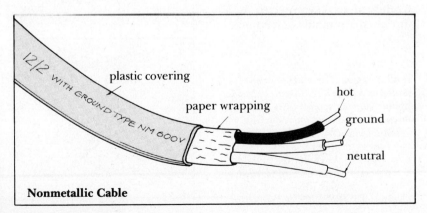

plastic covering

paper wrapping

hot

ground

neutral

12/2 WITH GROUND TYPE NM 600V

Nonmetallic Cable

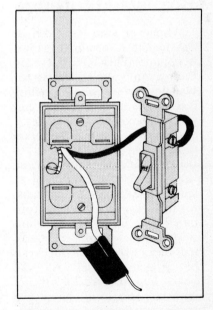

Whenever a white conductor will carry current, code it at each end with black tape so that it cannot be mistaken for a neutral conductor.

metal or covered with green insulation. But if two hot conductors are contained in a single cable, the second is coded red. This is three-wire cable. It is used in wiring 115/230-volt appliances and in some 115-volt circuits to distinguish between hot wires with different functions (one switched for a light and the other always hot for a receptacle, for example).

Sometimes, when wiring a switch loop, for example, it is necessary to code a white wire black. (See "Switch Loop" under "Wiring Additions.") Since both terminals of a switch are hot, the conductors must always be black in a two-wire system. If the wire must be coded, put black tape on each end where it meets a wire nut or a terminal.

Boxes and Fittings

Whenever wire is spliced or attached to a terminal, it must be contained in a box. There are three main types: wall boxes for switches and receptacles, ceiling boxes for light fixtures, and junction boxes for wire splices.

Wall Boxes. The most common type, they contain either switches or receptacles. Some have flanges for mounting to studs. Deep boxes are available for holding extra wires. To contain many wires or to mount several switches or receptacles together, two or more boxes can be ganged together. All wall boxes, however, are 3 × 2 inches on the face and have two mounting ears in a standard position for attachment to any switch or receptacle.

Ceiling Boxes. Ceiling-mount-

ed octagonal boxes can be held in place by an assortment of devices. (See "Box Supports.") A ceiling box holds the light fixture in place while keeping the spliced wire safely enclosed.

Junction Boxes. Since splices must be enclosed, junction boxes are used where wire is joined but no outlet is needed.

Box Supports. To fasten a box to wallboard rather than studs, a bracket of soft metal shaped like an upside-down "F" is inserted through the hole for the box and wrapped around one side of the box. Another bracket is similarly placed on the other side of the box. These two brackets prevent the box from slipping forward, toward the room. The screw mounts at the top and bottom of the box prevent it from falling the other way, into the wall.

A bar hanger, suspended between two joists to hold a ceiling box anywhere along the bar, allows great flexibility of location. The offset hanger is similar to the bar hanger except that it screws into the bottom of the joists and can be installed in a plaster and lath ceiling that cannot be reached from above.

Connectors. A connector is a device that establishes a connec-

Wall boxes: a. The bracket screwed or nailed directly to a stud secures this box. b. Side clamps expand when a screw is threaded into them and press the box against wallboard. c. "F" clamps hold the box to wallboard when they are folded around the front edge of the box. d. Two boxes can be ganged together by removing one side from each, fitting them together and tightening two screws.

90

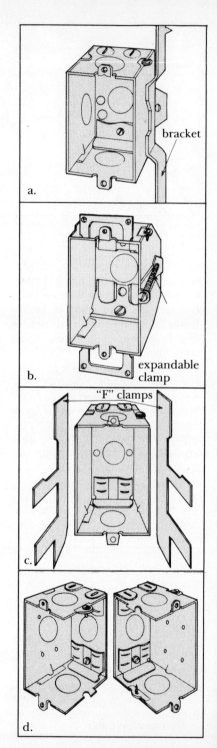

bracket

a.

expandable clamp

b.

"F" clamps

c.

d.

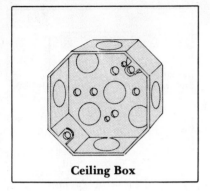

Ceiling Box

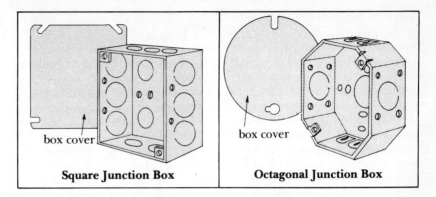

box cover

Square Junction Box

box cover

Octagonal Junction Box

tion between two or more conductors or between conductors and terminals. A wire nut is a connector. It is copper-threaded on the inside and is screwed onto the conductor wires like a cap onto a tube of toothpaste.

Another kind of connector secures cable to a box. The conductors run from the cable to the terminals inside the box. Box connectors consist of a threaded sleeve and a pressure clamp. The sleeve slips over the conductors. The pressure clamp fastens to the cable with screws. The threaded sleeve and the conductors are pushed into the box and a locknut is screwed onto the sleeve, anchoring the connector to the box. The final tightening of the locknut is done with a hammer and a screwdriver or nail set. Small teeth on the outside of the locknut allow it to be hammered tight.

A grounding clamp is another type of connector. A ground clamp clips to the side of a box. The ground wire is inserted and held in place by the clamp, forming a solid ground connection to the box.

Clamp. A clamp functions like a box connector, but instead of being purchased separately, it is built into the box.

Maximum Conductors per Box

The Code recommends a definite limit to the number of conductors in a box of a given size. A conductor running through the box counts as one, as does a conductor that ends in the box. Conductors that do not leave the box don't count (such as jumper wire from a wire run to the box, or connections between two devices in the same

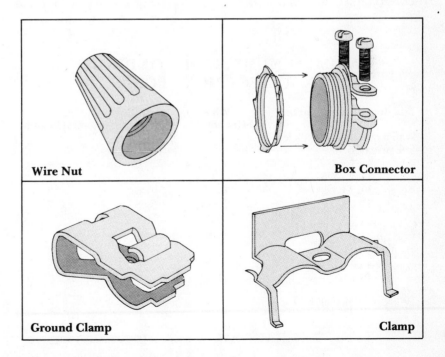

Wire Nut

Box Connector

Ground Clamp

Clamp

91

box). If the box contains one or more ground wires, the box is considered to have a capacity one less than is listed in the table. If the box contains any switches or receptacles, its capacity is also reduced by one. Finally, if the box contains any internal cable clamps or fixture studs, its capacity is reduced by one. (Fixture studs are threaded rods that support some kinds of light fixtures.) Some wiring additions such as the conversion of a switch to three-way use may involve enough extra wires to exceed the Code recommendations. If there is any question about capacity, replace the box, and the result will be safer. Too many conductors in a box can cause overheating. It is also difficult to stuff a lot of wires into a small box, and it is possible to damage them or loosen connections while trying.

Devices

According to the National Electrical Code, a device is a component of an electrical system that carries but does not use electricity, for example, a switch or a receptacle.

Receptacles. A receptacle is a contact device at an outlet for the connection of a plug. An outlet is the point on the wiring system where current is taken to supply equipment such as light bulbs, or, via the receptacles, drills, toasters and other plug-in equipment. Most receptacles are actually double receptacles, or duplexes, which will accept two plugs. A receptacle with a third hole is a grounding receptacle. If this kind is installed, the ground connection must be complete.

A receptacle has two brass

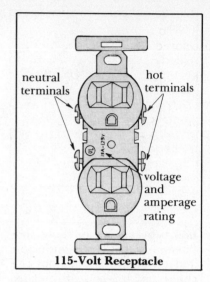

115-Volt Receptacle

terminals for hot wires and two silver-colored terminals for neutral. Between each of these pairs is a small conductor that can be broken off to separate the receptacles from each other. Because of this feature, it is possible to wire each receptacle on a different circuit, or to allow one to be controlled by a switch while the other is always hot. Most receptacles and switches have four pop-off ears that can be used as shims between the receptacle and the screw holes of the box to insure that the device will be flush with the wall. Most receptacles also have mounting slots to allow the receptacle to be vertical even if the box is not.

Switches. Most common is the single-pole, side-wired switch. Other types of single-pole switches have terminals in different locations to accommodate different installation problems. Switches usually have two brass terminals because techni-

MAXIMUM NUMBER OF CONDUCTORS
FOR ELECTRICAL BOXES

Box dimensions in inches	Wire gauge of conductors (copper)		
	#14(15 amp)	#12(20 amp)	#10(30 amp)
Wall boxes (for receptacles & switches)			
3 x 2 x 2¼	5	4	4
3 x 2 x 2½	6	5	5
3 x 2 x 2¾	7	6	5
3 x 2 x 3½	9	8	7
Ceiling boxes (round or octagonal)			
4 x 1¼	6	5	5
4 x 1½	7	6	6
4 x 2⅛	10	9	8
Junction boxes (square)			
4 x 1¼	9	8	7
4 x 1½	10	9	8
4 x 2⅛	15	13	12

cally both are hot, but some have one brass and one silver-colored. A switch is always installed on the hot conductor of a circuit. One reason for this is that if a hot conductor in an electric coffee maker or other appliance were to work loose, it would create a danger of electric shock. But to make it worse, if the appliance had its switch on the neutral conductor, the danger would remain even with the switch turned off. Except for this hidden danger, the appliance would function normally.

Some switches have wire holes in the back to allow easy attachment of the conductors. A clip inside the switch holds the conductors in place. Other switches have both terminal screws and wire holes, giving the user the option of which to use. A three-way switch has two brass or silver-colored terminals and a black or copper-colored one. There are no on-off markings on a three-way switch. A four-way switch has four brass-colored terminals and no on-off markings. Switches, like receptacles, usually have shims and mounting slots to aid installation. (See "Receptacles.")

Tools

Many of the tools needed for electrical work are familiar hand tools. Pliers, screwdrivers, hammers, a nail set and wire cutters all help get new wiring and fixtures in place. For cutting armored BX cable, a hacksaw is needed. There also are some specialized tools that are useful for electrical work. You can buy the essentials for

Single Pole Switch

Three-Way Switch

Four-Way Switch

what it would cost you to have an electrician fix a switch. If you install only one new circuit, you will have saved money. And with wiring, once you have done one job, you are likely to do another, because the actual in-

stallation is not hard. The trick is knowing what to do and having the confidence to do it. Once you have that, it's exciting to realize you can do a good job of something that seemed totally mysterious at one time.

Wire Stripper. A wire stripper looks a little like a pair of pliers, but it has holes sized for conductors to fit through. It will cut through the insulation on the conductor without damaging the wire when it is closed over the conductor. Most strippers will handle conductor sizes from about number 10 to number 18. The stripper is one tool that is a must. It makes the job of preparing conductor for attachment to terminals easy, and there is no other easy way.

There are actually two kinds of strippers. One costs only a few dollars, is the size of a small pair of pliers, and has no other function than stripping insulation. The other kind is larger. Besides removing insulation, it will cut small bolts, crimp certain kinds of connectors, and cut wire.

Wire Gauge. The holes on a wire stripper are a little larger than the wire and won't do for checking conductor size, at least, not until you have some practice at it. A combination wire gauge and cable stripper is designed to measure conductor size without guesswork. If the wire of the conductor will just fit through a hole, the number beside it is the correct size. Make sure the wire is cut clean. A small burr could prevent the wire from going through the right hole. The cable stripper that is part of the tool is almost useless unless you are psychic, **93**

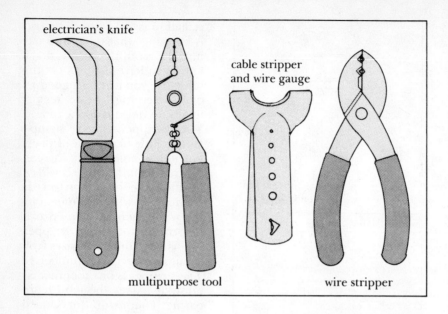

electrician's knife

cable stripper
and wire gauge

multipurpose tool

wire stripper

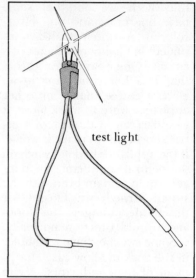

test light

because you can't see where the blade cuts through. Since the conductors can twist around each other in the cable, you have to see where the blade is to avoid slicing the conductors.

Electrician's Knife. This is the tool to use for cutting cable. With its hooked blade, it is easy to cut the cable insulation while keeping the blade tip between the conductors. Start at the end of the cable and work inward. This allows you to keep track of the conductors. When you have cut as far as you need, use the knife to cut completely around the cable insulation, taking care not to cut into the insulation of the conductors. Then you peel off the outer layer as you would a corn husk. It is very easy to nick the insulation of the conductors. If you do, discard the conductor as far as the nick. These small cuts can lead to short circuits later on because wires in a box or panel are usu-

ally crammed next to each other so they'll all fit in. A small nick can eventually become a break in the conductor, allowing the conductor to short against another conductor or the box. Always leave yourself plenty of leeway when working with cable.

Test Light. A test light consists of a small neon bulb encased in plastic and two short insulated conductors with metal tips. It is designed to test for voltage between roughly 90 and 600 volts. It is about the size of a pocket pen. *Buy one.* Always have it handy when you are working on any house wiring. When the metal probes are placed against uninsulated parts of one hot conductor and a neutral or ground, the bulb lights. If the probes are placed between two different live wires, corresponding to the two legs that come into the main panel, the tester will light. The voltage in this case will be 230, although the

tester will not indicate this, only current or lack of it. When you cut power to a circuit, the tester will verify that it is off. But it must be used alertly, because failure to light doesn't always mean there is no voltage present. If you place the probes at two different places on the hot conductor, it will not light. Likewise, if you place them between two *different* hot conductors that connect to the same leg of the main panel, it will not light. A similar tester, designed for automobile and small battery circuits, can handle only 12 volts. Make sure you get the right one.

Continuity Tester. This is used

Use of a test light: a. Receptacle is live. b. Receptacle and box are grounded. c. Ground is functioning. d. Current is present as far as the receptacle terminals.

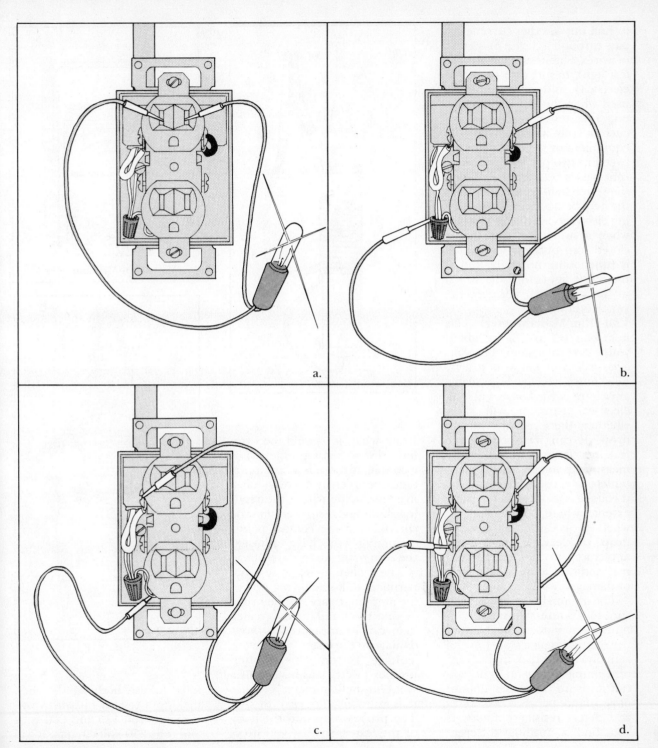

a.

b.

c.

d.

to find out whether current can pass through a device or section of wire. This tester, unlike the test light, has its own source of electricity and must never be used when the house current is on. The tester sends a small current from its battery into the equipment or the conductor between its two probes. If the current passes between the probes, the tester lights, indicating that the item being tested is conducting electricity. If the light shines when a switch is tested in the closed (on) position, the switch is functioning normally. But if the tester lights with the switch in the open (off) position, the switch is broken.

Volt-Ohm-Milliammeter. This item can tell you a lot about your electrical system. The voltage scale will tell you exactly how much voltage is available anywhere in the house. On long electrical runs, it will show whether there is any voltage drop. It can measure voltage leak in a circuit or appliance. By measuring voltage at different outlets on a circuit, you can tell if voltage is leaking, and to some extent where. Lost voltage, whether because of voltage drop or leakage, can cause appliances to run poorly and may indicate loose connections or damaged wire.

The ohmmeter scale will measure for continuity just as a continuity tester does. But because the reading is on a scale (several actually) rather than in the form of a simple yes or no light, you can measure the actual amount of resistance between two points and detect resistance faults. If you find a reading different

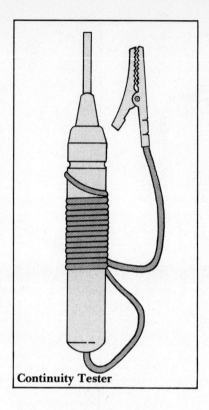

Continuity Tester

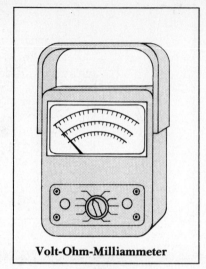

Volt-Ohm-Milliammeter

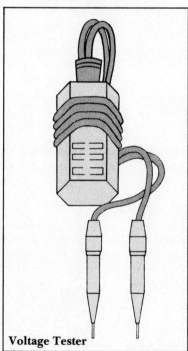

Voltage Tester

from what it should be, you have discovered a problem. For example, if there is a little resistance between two points on a live conductor where the reading should be zero, there may be corrosion at the contact points (assuming you have adjusted the zero point correctly).

The milliammeter scale is not pertinent to home wiring, where the amperages are on the order of one thousand times greater than can be measured without damage to the tester.

Voltage Tester. This is often used by electricians instead of a volt-ohm-milliammeter because it is durable and easy to use. The probes snap into the body of the tester, so that you don't

have to use both hands when making a test. It measures voltage between 115 and 600 volts and tests 230-volt circuits. It will

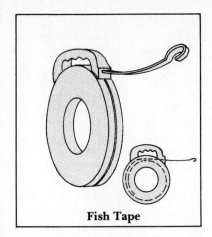

Fish Tape

not give you as much information as a volt-ohm-milliammeter. **Fish Tape or Fish Wire.** It is used to pull cable through walls or other inaccessible places. A flat steel ribbon, usually not more than ½ inch wide, fish tape comes in lengths of up to 30 feet and is usually tied in a coil. Sometimes you can find it in a container that makes it a little easier to handle. Two rolls are sometimes used together in difficult situations—one tape is fed into the wall or floor at one spot and the other is fed in somewhere else to catch the first and pull it out. Then cable can be fastened to the fish tape and pulled between the two spots. Fish tape is very useful in electrical work, but you might not need it to wire a kitchen. Most kitchens are over a basement. You may be able to drill through the floor plate of the 2 × 4 framing and feed the cable right on through.

Putting It Together

You should now be ready to do the wiring. No matter how carefully you plan, though, you may find yourself going back to the electrical supply store several times. Often, it's not until you have the equipment and tools in hand that you realize exactly how it all will go together.

The actual wiring is done in two different stages of the kitchen building project. The rough wiring is done in the rough-in stage. It consists simply of securing all the boxes to the frame of the house and running cable from box to box to main panel. Attach the cable to the boxes with standard electrical connectors. The wiring of devices in their boxes should be done while the finish work is being done. At that time, attach the devices to the conductors, secure them to their boxes, and put the coverplates in place.

The last step is at the main panel, where you shut off the main fuses or breakers and connect each circuit. Before turning the power back on, go over your work. There are safety rules to follow:

1. Before working on any circuit, shut off the power to it and to any circuit that could have live parts near where you will be working.

2. After you have turned off the power, check the circuit with a test light to be sure it is off. (Making the same test before you shut off the power to the circuit will let you know if the test light is functioning.) Test the hot conductor to both neutral and ground. Testing the ground lets you know that the ground is in working order. Then test neutral to ground to be sure there is no voltage present.

3. If you plan to cut, nail or screw into the wall, check to see what cables might be in the area. Shut off power to them before you do any work. If possible, make cuts where there are not likely to be any cables.

4. After completing work on a circuit, but before connecting it to the main panel or replacing the receptacle and switch covers, inspect all connections visually to be sure conductors are properly attached and the terminal screws are fully tightened.

5. Before connecting the cable to the main panel, test the circuit with a continuity tester to be sure there are no short circuits. Remove all light bulbs and plug-in appliances from their fixtures and receptacles. Turn on all the switches. Touch the probes of the tester to the black and white conductors that will attach to the main panel. If the light does not shine, no short is present. If there is a short, use the continuity tester to track it down.

6. When making connections to the main panel or any place where live power is nearby, stand on thick, dry wood, 2 × 4s or two pieces of ¾-inch plywood. Keep your free hand close to your side. Even though power to the main is shut off, voltage

is present at the service terminals where the conductors attach from the power pole.

7. Connect the circuit to the main panel, and replace any conductors that were moved to allow work on the circuit. Restore the power to the main panel. Then restore power to the branch circuit. If you are restoring power to several circuits, turn them on one by one,

so that several motors kicking in all at the same time do not overload the system.

8. Check the ground connections by putting one probe of the test light or the voltage scale of the volt-ohm-milliammeter on a hot terminal and the other on a ground terminal. If the tester lights or the scale reads 115 volts, the ground connection is good.

siderable. Consequently, the ceiling surface can't be expected to support the box, as the wall surface sometimes is; the box has got to be attached to the joists.

Whenever the joists are exposed, as in new construction, installing ceiling boxes is done without a hitch. When the box can be against a joist, a box with a flange for such mounting is used. But when the box must be located in the space between joists, a bar hanger must be used. This telescoping support is positioned between the joists, opened up so its ends are tight against the joists, then nailed fast. A threaded stud, which can

New Circuits

If your kitchen was not installed in the last ten years, it may not have the two 20-amp appliance circuits and separate lighting circuits required by the Code. The Code actually requires that remodeled kitchens be brought up to current standards. Even if that weren't true, it is a good idea to make sure there is plenty of power available. Heavily used circuits might not blow a fuse, but they will heat up when used at maximum power. Over a long period of time, insulation may become brittle and eventually fail. Once you have determined that extra power is available at your service entrance, you can plan the new circuits. If the cable of your kitchen circuits is old, rewire the kitchen. But you may need only to add a circuit if the cable is good.

Rough-In

In practice, the rough wiring work depends upon the extent of your kitchen project. If the framing is exposed, as in new

construction or an extensive remodeling job, the work is a snap. If the walls and ceiling are in good shape and you don't want to rip them down and replace them, you've got a lot of tedious work to do, cutting holes for boxes, fishing cable, then installing the boxes.

If you have torn out the walls and ceilings, it's easiest to install the box and then run and attach the cable. Before mounting the box, determine which knockouts must be removed and, using a nail set and hammer, punch them out. Then nail the boxes to studs and joists, just where you want them. Remember that you'll want the edges of each box to be flush with the finished wall surface; for now, the boxes will seem to jut into the room.

Ceiling boxes are a bit more difficult to install than wall boxes. In part this is because you are working overhead, usually perched on a stepladder. But ceiling boxes often have to support the weight of the fixture, which in some cases is con-

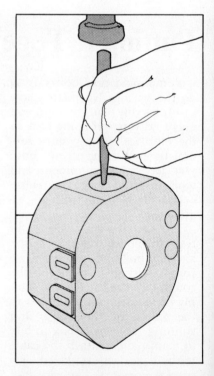

Removing a knockout from a box.

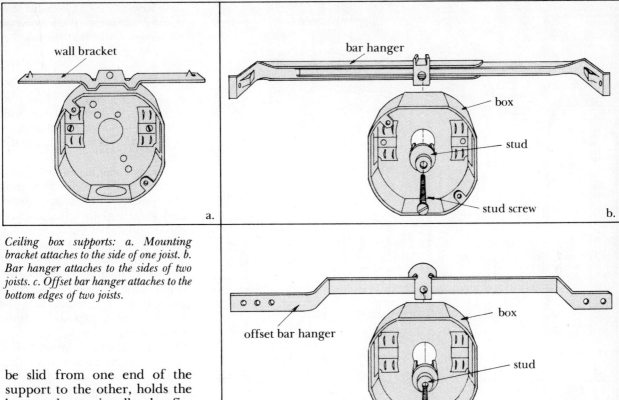

Ceiling box supports: a. Mounting
bracket attaches to the side of one joist. b.
Bar hanger attaches to the sides of two
joists. c. Offset bar hanger attaches to the
bottom edges of two joists.

be slid from one end of the
support to the other, holds the
box, and occasionally the fixture. A knockout in the back of
the box is removed, the box is
slipped over the stud and fastened with a nut.

Running Cable

The next step is to run the
cable. The basic procedure for
running cable is first to string it
from one outlet to another, leaving plenty of cable on each end
to allow attachment to terminals
in each box. The sequence of
each run should be worked out
in advance.

Code requirements for running cable and for securing
cable and boxes amount to little
more than common sense. If
cable runs through structural
members, it must not weaken

them. Cable and boxes must be
adequately supported. Cable
may not be exposed to unnecessary risk of damage during or
after installation and so on. The
National Electrical Code has
specifically defined these requirements, and the following is
a summary.

Structural Members. Cable may
run along or through joists, rafters or studs as long as it doesn't
weaken them structurally. It
should run through the approximate center of the structural
member. For studs, the hole

must either be no closer to the
edge than 1¼ inches or protected from nails or screws by a
metal plate ¹/₁₆ inch thick. The
metal plate should be fastened
to the stud between the cable
and the room and be large
enough to protect the cable
against someone's coming along
later and hammering a nail into
the cable because he didn't
know it was behind the wall.

Notches. Notches are permitted
in wood members where they
won't weaken the structure.
Wherever cable is run through a

99

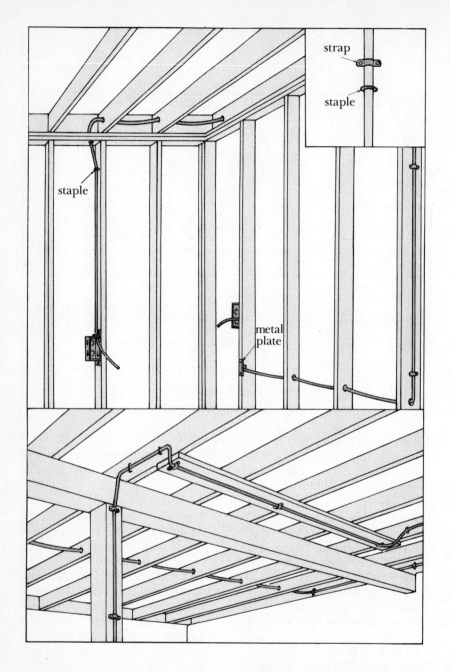

strap

staple

staple

metal
plate

Cable may run through joists and studs or along their length. When cable runs across them, it must be protected.

of cable sheathing to permit attachment to terminals or wire nuts. Each conductor must have at least 6 inches free of sheathing.

Securing Cable. Cable and boxes must be fastened securely along the run and at each outlet and switch point. In practice, this means that cable must be secured at intervals of at least 4½ feet and within 12 inches of any box. Fishing unsupported cable through dead air spaces is permitted. But wherever the cable becomes exposed, it must be supported.

Fire Protection. If there are fire prevention measures in a building, such as firestopping in the walls, the wiring must not interfere with them.

Dealing with Finished Walls

Installing circuits in situations where the walls haven't been stripped out is more difficult. Half the battle is cutting the openings for the boxes. And choosing the right box and mounting method is the other half. In between bouts you must fish the cables, no small battle in itself.

To start the rough-in work in this situation, you locate roughly where you want to place the box. Then you drill a small test hole to survey the wall cavity. Bend a piece of wire into an L shape with one leg at least 6 inches long. Insert that leg

notch, it must be protected by a metal plate 1/16 inch thick.

Cable. Sharp bends can damage cable. No bend in residential

cable may have a radius less than five times the diameter of the cable. Cable is also required to have enough conductor free

100

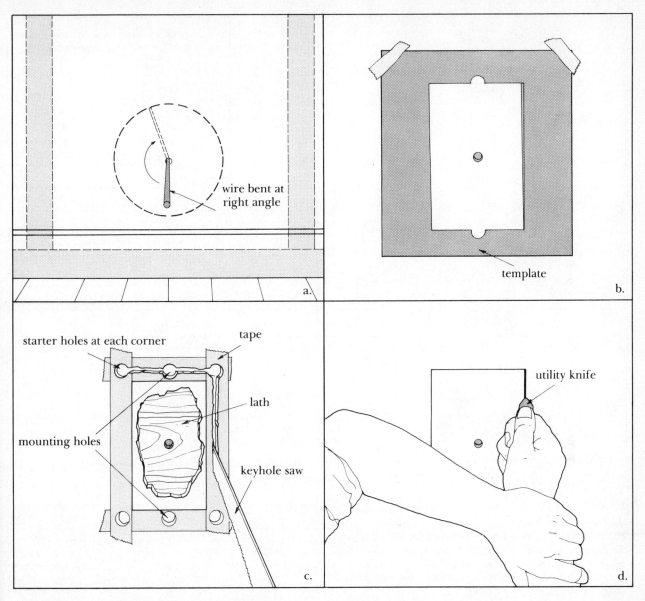

Cutting a hole for a wall-mounted box: a. Slip a piece of wire through a hole drilled in the wall to probe for studs. b. Using a cardboard template, mark the size and location of the box. c. To cut through a plaster-and-lath wall, use a keyhole saw. d. Wallboard can be cut using a utility knife.

into the hole and try to spin the wire. If there are cables or pipes in the cavity or if you're too close to a stud, the wire will hit the obstructions and you'll know you have to relocate the box.

Once you've got the location nailed down, you use a tem-plate—trace around the out-side of a box on a piece of cardboard, then cut out the template—to scribe exactly **101**

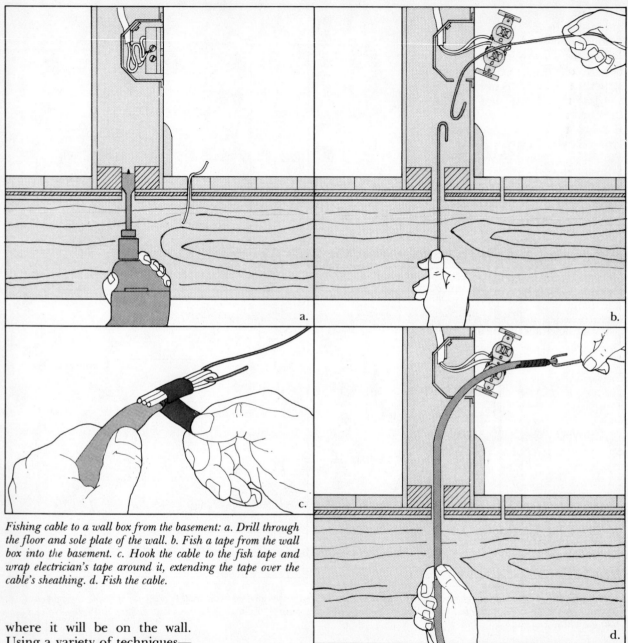

Fishing cable to a wall box from the basement: a. Drill through the floor and sole plate of the wall. b. Fish a tape from the wall box into the basement. c. Hook the cable to the fish tape and wrap electrician's tape around it, extending the tape over the cable's sheathing. d. Fish the cable.

where it will be on the wall. Using a variety of techniques— the construction of the wall has everything to do with the method you use—you cut a hole in the wall. With all the holes cut, you are ready to fish the cables.

Fishing Cable

Fishing is something of an art in itself. There are usually several ways to run cable from one place to another and often several possible sources of electricity for a new outlet. The idea is to choose a route that will cause the least damage, the least aggravation, and use the least amount of cable.

The trick in fishing cable is to be able to visualize the interior structure of the walls so that you can get around obstructions you can't actually see.

Basement to Finished Wall. One convenient place to string cable is an unfinished basement. Most kitchens are on the first floor. It is usually easier to drop cable down into the basement and run it along or through the joists and then up to where it is needed than it is to tear up finished walls. In most basements, the sole plate of the kitchen wall is accessible. The sole plate is the 2 × 4 that the wall studs rest on. If you haven't got enough room to drill up from the basement, you'll have to remove a section of wall in the kitchen and drill down into the bottom plate to make a hole for the cable. A ¾-inch spade bit will do the job nicely.

You can probably find the correct location in the basement by noting where pipes, other cables, or walls run. If you can't tell where the box is located, drill a ¹/₁₆-inch hole through the kitchen floor directly below the outlet. Stick a wire through the hole to help locate it in the basement.

After drilling the ¾-inch hole through the sole plate, go down to the basement and insert a length of fish tape into it. Feed this into the space between the studs. Have someone hook the fish tape and pull it out. If you are installing a new outlet, your helper may be able to reach into the outlet hole and get the fish tape. But if there is already a

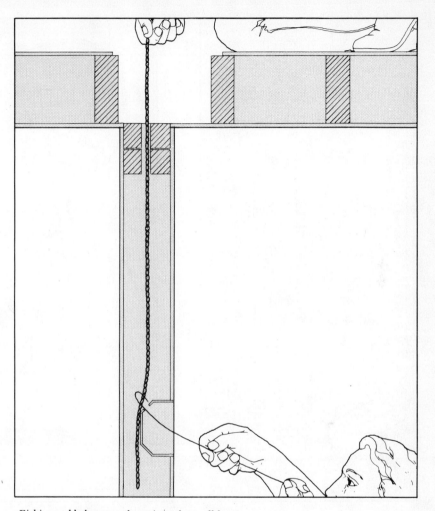

Fishing cable between the attic and a wall box.

box there, have the helper punch out a knockout hole and feed a short piece of fish tape or a piece of bent coat hanger wire into the hole, hook the section from the basement and pull it out.

Come upstairs and strip the sheathing from several inches of cable and the insulation from the exposed conductors. Bend the wire around the hook of the fish tape and wrap the whole

thing with electrical tape until there are no parts sticking out to snag. Have someone pull the cable down to the basement. If the box has a built-in clamp, you don't have to remove the box from the wall to attach the cable to it. But if it doesn't, and you can't find an extra, you'll have to remove the box to attach a standard two-part connector. In that case, you might as well pull the box out before you fish the

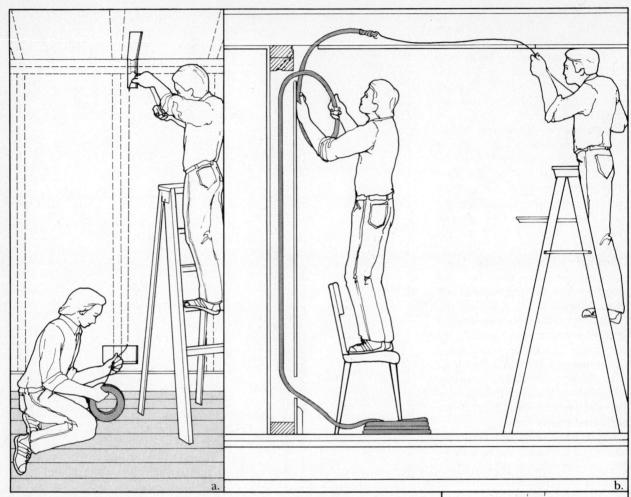

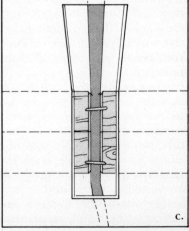

Fishing cable through a wall to a ceiling fixture: a. Cut access holes at the base and top of the wall and the edge of the ceiling through which to work with the fish tapes. b. Fish the cable through the wall, then through the space above the ceiling. c. The cable is then stapled in a notch chiseled in the doubled top plate covered with a metal strap and the access hole repaired.

cable. It will make hooking the fish tape a little easier.

Run the end of the cable that you fished to the basement along or through the joists either to the main panel or to the point where you will tap into an existing circuit.

104 **Attic to Ceiling Fixture.** If there

is an unfinished attic above the kitchen, it may be used for running cable, just as the basement can. An accessible space above the kitchen, even a crawl space, makes locating a ceiling fixture easier than when you have to fish cable in the ceiling. Instead of using fish tape from the attic,

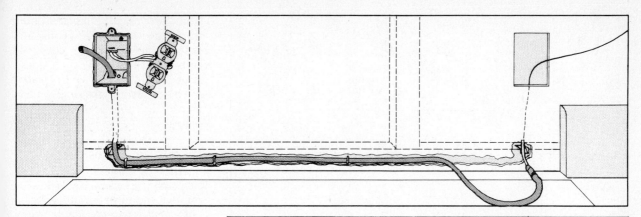

Cable can be run behind a baseboard in a channel chipped in the plaster. Be sure not to nail through the cable when reinstalling the baseboard.

drop a light chain down to an existing wall outlet. The kind of chain used for counterweights in windows is about right. Most hardware stores sell it.

To run cable from the wall box to a new fixture, drill a ¾-inch hole in the top plate and drop the chain through it. Have someone remove the receptacle from the box without disconnecting the conductors (but with power off, naturally). Have your helper punch out a knockout and poke fish tape through it to catch the chain. Make sure your chain is long enough to reach down as far as the box. Your helper pulls out the chain, tapes it to the fish tape, and you pull the tape into the attic. Tape the fish tape to the cable, and let your helper pull it down and out the box.

The cable may run to the fixture box over, through or along the joists. Be sure it is properly supported and protected.

Getting from the Wall to the Ceiling. You can get a cable

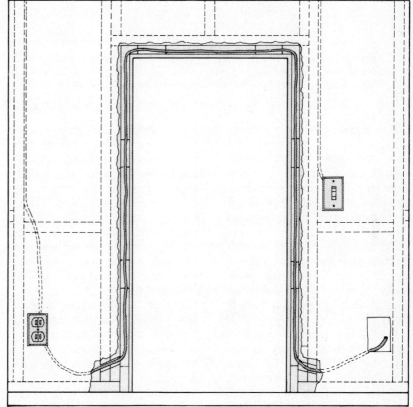

Cable can be run behind door or window casing, minimizing plaster damage.

from the wall to the ceiling space without tearing a big hole by running the cable against the top plate instead of through it. If the space above the ceiling is not accessible, you can fish the cable to the ceiling outlet as long as the joists run in the same direction as the cable.

105

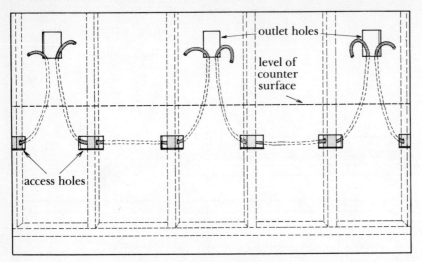

In a kitchen, outlets must be just above the counter top. Damage to walls can be minimized by locating access holes for fishing cables below the counter top. The cabinets will hide patching, or, if they have backs, will eliminate the need for patching.

Use a chisel to cut a narrow L-shaped channel where the wall and ceiling meet. The cut should extend below the top plate to allow access to the dead air space in the wall. A small cut in the ceiling will provide access there.

To make the cable flush with the top plate, use a wood chisel to cut a channel in the plate about ½ inch deep and wide enough for the cable (at least ¾ inch).

Run cable from an existing wall outlet to a new ceiling fixture, by pushing the fish tape through the access hole down into the wall space. Remove the receptacle but leave the conductors in place (power off). Have someone insert a short length of fish tape through a knockout hole in the box to hook the other fish tape, and pull it out. After your helper has taped the cable to the fish tape, pull it out at the ceiling-wall access hole. Have your helper insert fish tape into the opening for the ceiling fixture, and hook it with a short length of fish tape at the ceiling-wall access hole. Tape the cable to the fish tape, and let your helper pull it out the ceiling hole. Staple the cable to the channel in the top plate and cover the channel with a ¹/₁₆-inch steel plate.

Running Cable along a Finished Wall. You can run cable along a wall by cutting a channel behind the baseboard. Pry off the baseboard carefully with a chisel or pry bar. Cut a channel along the wall to a point below the opening for the new outlet. Fish the cable down to the channel from the existing box, run it along the channel and fish it up to the new opening.

The cable may run through ¾-inch holes drilled in the studs, or may lie against the studs. If the cable runs in notches, it should be covered with metal plates ¹/₁₆ inch thick at each stud. When you replace the baseboard, make sure to nail above the cable and any metal plates.

Installing Boxes

With the cables run, it's time to install the boxes. Be sure you remove the appropriate knockouts and have the cable with connector attached ready to slip into place as you install each box. You won't be able to remove knockouts or install connectors after the box is screwed to the wall. But after the box is secured to the wall, you can turn the lock nut on the connector and gingerly tighten it. Installing ceiling boxes can be a lot more trouble because you must cut a big hole in the ceiling surface to accommodate the supports. The patching can be extensive.

In some situations, you can gain access to the ceiling cavity from the floor above. In a single story house, you may have an attic or crawl space above the kitchen. Or you may be able to carefully remove a floorboard or two in the second-floor room above the kitchen. In such cases, the patching is minimal, since you cut a hole in the ceiling only as big as the box. Use a bar hanger or a box with a flange.

A special ceiling box support made for remodeling situations is called the offset bar hanger. It is like the bar hanger, except that it's designed to be fastened to the edges of the joists, rather than the faces, and the area that

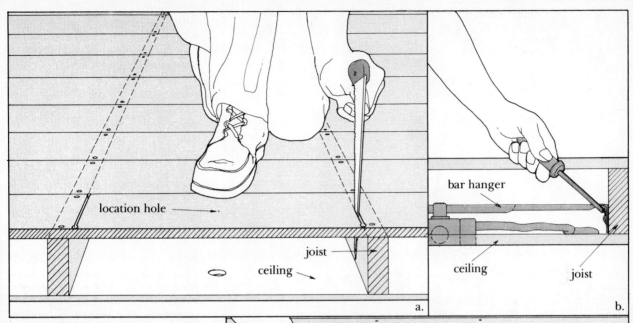

location hole

joist

ceiling

a.

bar hanger

ceiling

joist

b.

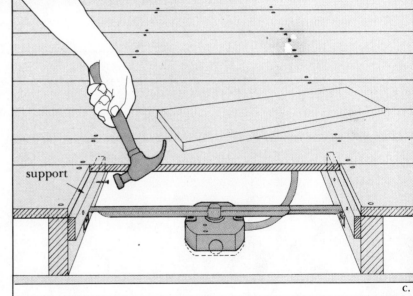

support

c.

Installing a ceiling box from the room above the kitchen: a. Using an auger bit, bore a hole through the ceiling and into the floorboard, just allowing the bit's spur to penetrate the floorboard, thus marking the board to be removed. Cut out a single board to gain access to the ceiling cavity. b. Cut a hole for the ceiling box and install the box. c. Nail cleats to the joists to support the floorboard, then reinstall it.

accommodates the mounting stud is offset. Instead of cutting a hole big enough to work through, you cut away only a box-size hole and a narrow strip from joist to joist for the hanger. The hanger is nailed to the joists, the stud positioned and the box installed. The offset is sufficient to allow the box edge to be flush with the ceiling surface.

In a limited number of cases where the ceiling surface is strong—like plaster on lath in good condition or a wooden

ceiling—and the fixture is lightweight, you can use a special bar support that uses the ceiling surface to support the box. This spreads the load over

most of the ceiling span between the two joists. Because it's unlikely that the ceiling is very thick or that you want the box jutting into the room, you

107

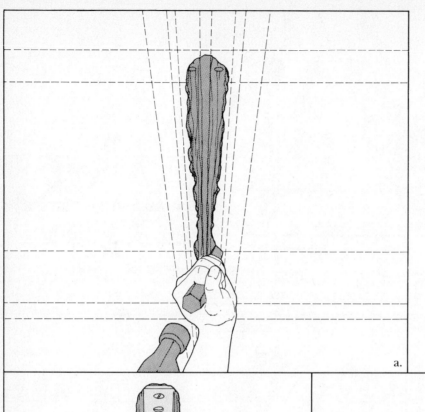

must use a special shallow box with this support. A hole for the box is cut in the ceiling and the support put into the cavity with the stud extending down through the hole. The box is installed and either tightened against lath that is deliberately not cut away for this purpose or tightened against the support. In the latter case, the box and hanger will be loose until the fixture is installed.

As with wall boxes, if you

Installing a ceiling box using an offset bar hanger: a. Chisel a channel in the plaster for the box and hanger bar, cutting away lath as necessary. b. Attach the offset bar hanger to the joists, then install the box. c. Repair the damage to the plaster.

a.

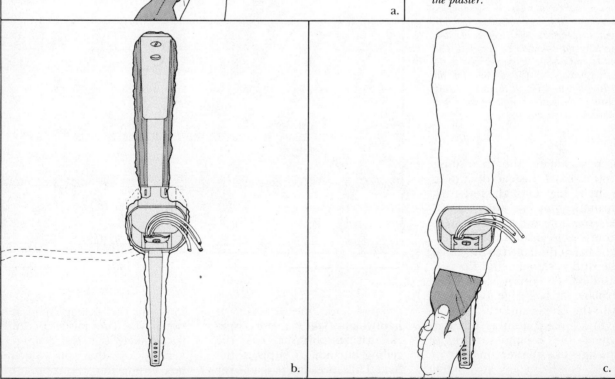

b.

c.

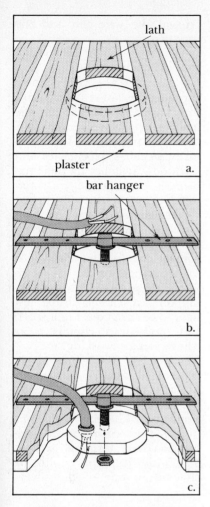

Installing a ceiling-supported box: a. Chip away the plaster for the box, and cut away the center lath, but not those at the periphery. b. Fish the cable to the hole, then insert a bar hanger with a mounting stud through the hole and lay it across the ceiling lath. c. Use a special shallow ceiling box. Fastening it on the stud will tighten it against the uncut lath, holding it in place. Only a lightweight fixture should be used, since the ceiling is supporting the weight of the fixture, rather than the joists.

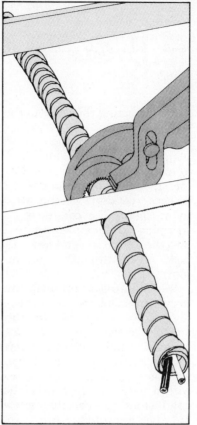

Cut BX cable with a hacksaw. Hold the cable with pliers and saw just enough to break through the armor but not enough to nick the conductors.

don't have free access to the stud space, you'll have to run the cable before installing the box. Clamp the cable in a connector, remove box knockouts and slip cable and connector into place as you slide the box into place. Turn the lockout onto the connector after the box is secured, and finish your wiring job.

Finish Wiring

With the rough wiring done, it's time to turn to other tasks. Eventually, however, you'll re-

turn to the wiring, to install receptacles, lights and switches.

Wiring—that is stripping insulation from conductors and connecting them to each other and to devices—is pretty straightforward work. But here are a few tips that can make the work easier and the result better.

If you are using nonmetallic cable, wait until the cable is secured to the box with a connector before you rip off the outer sheath and strip insulation. You'll be able to use a wire stripper efficiently. If you are using armored cable, however, you'll have to cut through the outer sheath with a hacksaw be-

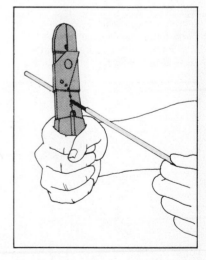

Removing insulation with a wire stripper.

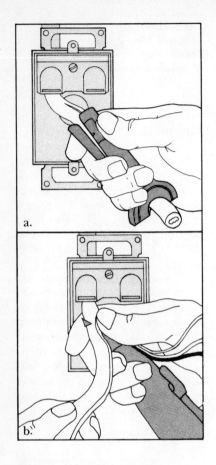

Joining the conductor to a terminal: a. Form a loop in end of conductor. b. Fit loop around screw so tightening screw (c.) will tighten loop.

Ripping nonmetallic cable. a. Rip the sheathing with the blade between the conductors to avoid damaging their insulation. b. Cut off the sheathing with a utility knife.

fore connecting the cable to the box.

In either case, use a wire stripper to remove about 1 inch of insulation from each conductor. (If you are using back-wired devices, you don't need to strip so much off the conductor; a stripping guide is incorporated into the device so you know just how much insulation to remove.)

When wiring a terminal, use needle-nose pliers to form a hook of the bare conductor and attach it to the terminal in such a way that tightening the screw also tightens the hook. If you are joining two or more wires with a wire nut, first twist the conductors together, then screw on the appropriate-size wire nut. If you have any fear that the nut may come loose, wrap a length of electrician's tape

around the wire nut and the conductors.

Wiring Additions

While there are many possible variations in home wiring once the branch circuit has left the main panel, there are only four basic situations to consider: fixtures, switches, receptacles and junctions. Switches by their nature always operate with fixtures or receptacles. Switched receptacles aren't too common, but they are sometimes used. Occasionally, several switches control one fixture, allowing it to be turned on or off from different places. Before working on any circuit, use a test light to be sure power to it is off. Cut power to circuits near where you are working.

Receptacles. The common receptacle is called a duplex receptacle because it is actually two receptacles joined into a single unit. The black (hot) conductor connects to one of the brass-colored terminal screws. The white (neutral) conductor attaches to one of the silver-

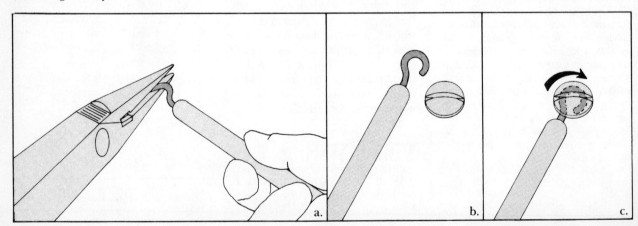

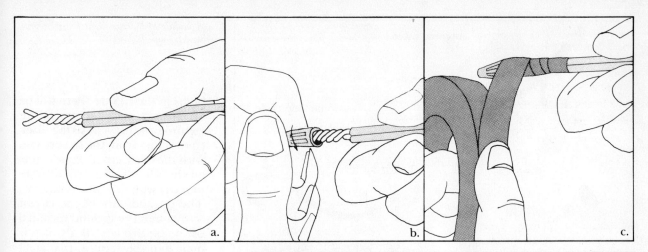

Joining conductors with a wire nut: a. Strip the conductors and twist the bare ends together. b. Turn the wire nut onto the conductors. c. If it seems necessary, wind electrician's tape around the conductors and wire nut.

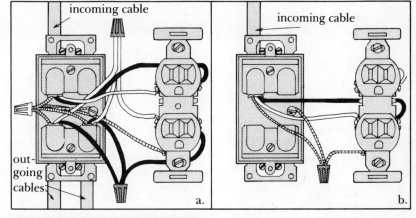

Wiring receptacles (right): a. Middle-of-the-run (incoming power cable also branches into two outgoing cables). b. End-of-the-run.

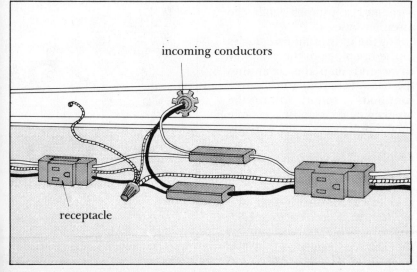

colored terminals. A small conductor between each set of terminals may be broken off, allowing each receptacle to be separated and placed on a different circuit.

Receptacle Strip. A surface-mounted receptacle strip is ideal for the harvest kitchen. Installed just above the counter tops, the strip provides an outlet

Wiring up surface-mounted receptacle strip.

111

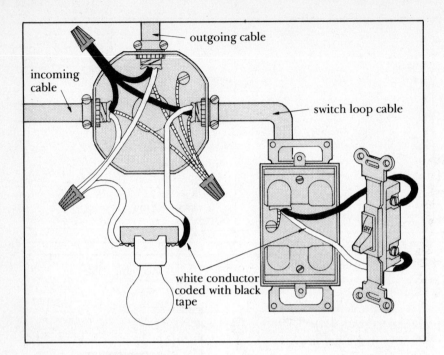

A middle-of-the-run light fixture with a switch loop.

bulbs in the fixture there will be several black and several white fixture conductors. All the black conductors from the fixture join with the black circuit conductor; all the white fixture conductors join the white circuit conductor. The ground wire of the circuit screws into the ground terminal of the fixture box. If a switch is built into the fixture, that is all there is to it. If not, the black conductor of the circuit is broken at some point by a separate switch. The details are explained under "Switches."

Middle-of-the-Run Switch. A switch is simply a place on the hot, black conductor where the circuit can be opened. The cir-

every foot or so of its run. The strips are available in a variety of lengths, ranging from 3 feet to 6 feet.

Installation is simple. Run a number 12 cable from the breaker panel to a point about 8 inches above the counter top. Remove a knockout from the receptacle strip assembly and secure the cable to the strip's base with a connector. Screw the base to the wall.

The assembly comes with the receptacles all wired. To tap into the system with the incoming power, simply cut the conductors near the power cable. Strip only a ½ inch of insulation from each conductor, then join the incoming black and white conductors to the assembly's black and white conductors using wire nuts or special pressure-type wire connectors

that are supplied with some assemblies. Since the Code does not allow the use of these connectors for ground wires, you must use a common wire nut to join the two green assembly wires, the power cable's bare wire and a jumper from the assembly base.

Put the individual receptacles in the openings in the assembly cover and snap the cover into the base. Test your work with a continuity tester, flip the breaker and a most versatile small-appliance circuit is ready to use.

Fixtures. These come in an astonishing variety, but the principle is always the same. One hot, black conductor and one neutral, white conductor of the circuit attach with wire nuts to the fixture conductors of the same color. If there are several

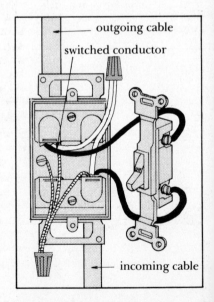

Middle-of-the-run switch.

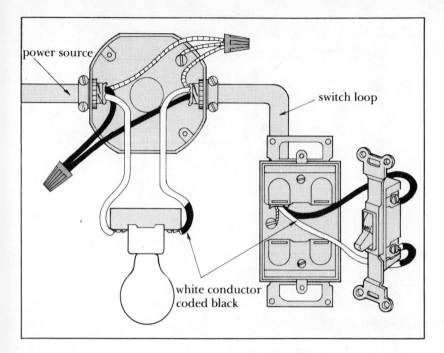

power source

switch loop

white conductor
coded black

A switch loop. Since the switch must be on the hot side of a fixture, both conductors leading to the switch are hot ones. One runs from the power source to the switch; the other returns to the fixture.

cuit is said to be open when the switch is off. A middle-of-the-run switch is located between the power source and the fixture controls. The power source is the preceding fixture or device on the run. To wire a middle-of-the-run switch, run a cable from the power source to the switch box. Attach the white conductor of this cable to the white conductor of the outgoing cable with a wire nut. The ground wire is attached with a wire nut to two wires, one screwed to the box and the other leading to the fixture with the outgoing conductors. The black conductor of the power cable is attached to one terminal of the switch. The black wire of the outgoing cable is attached to the other switch terminal. At the fixture, the ground wire is

screwed to the ceiling box, the white conductor is attached with a wire nut to the white fixture conductor, and the black conductor is attached with a wire nut to the black fixture conductor.

Switch Loop. The switch follows the fixture in this arrangement. A black (hot) conductor runs from the fixture to the switch and back. Since only the black conductor extends to the switch, a run cannot be extended from a switch loop. Install a regular two-wire cable with ground from the fixture to the switch, and code the white conductor with black tape at each end to indicate it is hot. This coded hot conductor is attached at the fixture to the black conductor from the source, with a wire nut. At the switch, it is attached to either terminal. The

black conductor of the switch-to-fixture cable is attached to the remaining switch terminal and, at the fixture, to the black conductor of the light fixture with a wire nut. The neutral white fixture conductor is attached with a wire nut to the white conductor from the power source. The ground wire of the incoming source cable is joined with a wire nut to the ground wire of the switch cable and to a short conductor or jumper attached to the fixture box. At the switch, the ground wire attaches to the box with a screw.

Three-Way Switch. This type of switch allows a fixture to be controlled from two locations. You can turn on a light in a barn or garage to light your way to the back door and then turn it off when inside. Of course, outdoor wiring must use cable suitable for that purpose. There are three possible configurations for three-way switches: fixture–switch–switch, switch–fixture–switch, and switch–switch–fixture. The three sequences follow one general pattern. The wires to the switches are all considered hot. Thus, the white neutral conductor continues along the run, never connecting with the switches. When it reaches the fixture box, it is attached to the white fixture conductor with a **113**

wire nut. A three-way switch has two brass or silver-colored terminals and one black or copper-colored one. The black conductor from the source attaches to the black or copper-colored terminal of one switch, and the black fixture conductor attaches to the black or copper-colored terminal of the other switch. The wires connecting the switches themselves attach only to the two brass or silver-colored carrier terminals on each switch. These connecting conductors always run between these carrier terminals in the same relative position on each switch, for example, bottom right to bottom right terminal and bottom left to bottom left. If the fixture is between the two switches, the connecting conductors from each switch are joined in the fixture box with wire nuts but have no contact with the fixture. Wiring a three-way switch requires three-wire cable and re-coding of some white conductors. See the illustrations for the three basic types. It is a good idea to use deep boxes or even two boxes ganged together to accommodate the extra wires needed for three-wire switches. Note the Code recommendations for the maximum number of conductors that can be run in boxes of various sizes.

Wiring the three sequences possible for three-way switches: a. Power source, switch, switch, fixture. b. Power source, fixture, switch, switch. c. Power source, switch, fixture, switch.

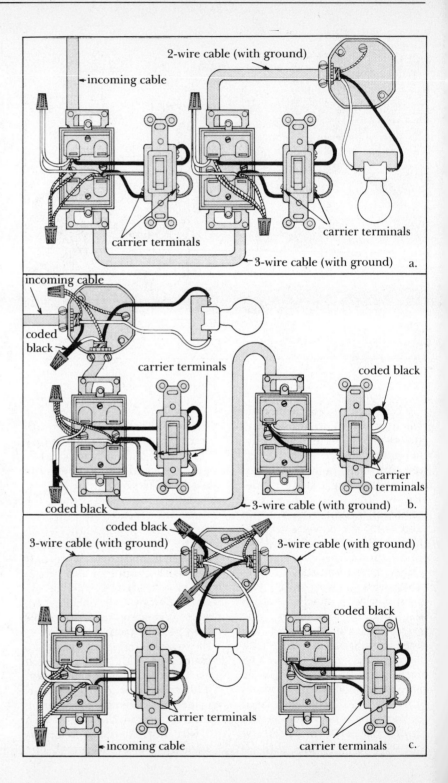

Working on the Main Panel

If you run a new circuit, instead of extending an existing circuit, you will have to attach the cable to the main panel or a subpanel. This is not difficult, but it requires shutting off current to the entire house. Also, after you shut off the main fuses in the panel, the service conductors that attach to the panel remain hot. That means you will be working on a panel that is live at two terminals, which can be sobering the first time. If for any reason the connections would be closer to the hot terminals than six inches, find another solution. Have the electric company shut off power to your home, or, if you know how, pull the meter. This will probably not be necessary. The service terminals are usually at the top of the panel, well away from the branch circuit terminals.

Attach the new circuit to an unused fuse or breaker location on the panel. Circuit breaker panels usually have extra spaces at the bottom of the panel. But, if yours doesn't, you can replace single breakers with two half-size breakers of the same amperage.

Circuit panels are wired so that there are two vertical rows of breakers in the panel. But these two rows do not correspond to the two legs of the

Common main panels: a. Circuit-breaker panel. b. Straight-bus panel.

115

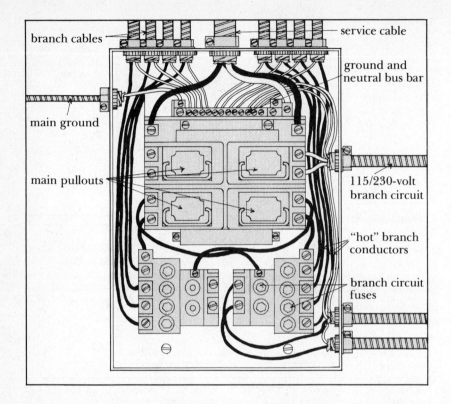

branch cables

service cable

ground and
neutral bus bar

main ground

115/230-volt
branch circuit

main pullouts

"hot" branch
conductors

branch circuit
fuses

service. Instead, the first two *horizontal* contacts are supplied by one leg of the service, the second two horizontal contacts are supplied by the other. Each contact can supply one 115-volt breaker. But 230-volt supply requires one contact from each leg of the service. That is why 230-volt breakers are twice as big; they actually cover two contacts. Snap new breakers in place, then attach the conductors to the terminal screws or insert holes.

The contacts and breaker terminals correspond to the hot conductors, either black for 115-volt circuits, or red and black for 230-volt circuits. The neutral conductors of each circuit attach with terminal screws to a single bar called the

grounding bus. The neutral service conductor attaches to it, as does the ground for the panel. This is normally the only place where the ground and neutral conductors meet, because the purpose of the ground is to provide an alternate route for current in case of a fault in the wiring.

If your main panel has fuses instead of breakers, there may not be any extra spots to run new circuits. You will have to add a subpanel as described below. If there are extras, the hot terminal is below the fuse socket. The neutral terminal, as in a breaker panel, is on the grounding bus. The cable enters the panel through a knockout hole, just as it does in a box or a breaker panel. It attaches to

the panel with connectors.

The most common type of fuse panel has a main pullout that controls current to the entire house. The pullout contains two cartridge fuses, one for each leg of the service. Next to it is another pullout for the range. It also contains two cartridge fuses, usually 40 amps each. In one variety of this type, the main pullout controls all other current, including the range. In this kind, the amperage of the main fuses is the same as the rating of the house service. The other variety also has two pullouts next to each other. But the range pullout is separate from the main. Pulling the main does not cut power to the range. In this case, the amperage of the main fuses is less than the service rating, to allow for the range. In both types, the pullouts are below the branch-circuit fuses.

Another type of fuse panel sometimes encountered is called the split bus panel. It has up to six pullouts with two cartridge fuses in each pullout. Each one must be pulled in order to shut off all power in the house. The second variety of panel mentioned above could be considered a split bus in the most elementary form, two pullouts. In the split bus with four to six pullouts, the branch fuses are generally supplied from one or two of the pullouts. The others supply appliances such as range, clothes dryer and hot water heater.

You can run a subpanel from the main panel if there are no extra sockets for new circuits. The cable to the subpanel attaches to take-off terminals located between the fuse sockets in a standard main panel. The cable must be three-wire and of the same rating as the subpanel. Each of the two hot conductors is attached to one of the take-off terminals and the neutral to the grounding bus.

Extending Existing Circuits

The kitchen you are wiring may be supplied with two or more 20-amp appliance circuits and with other general lighting circuits. If so, it is part of a rare, but growing breed, the modern kitchen. Take advantage of the situation by running new outlets from the exising circuits. There is no need to waste time and money running new circuits if the present ones are adequate for the job. Once you have checked to be sure that the new outlets you plan will not overload any circuits, use the following examples to find how to make the connections from whatever outlet you want to use to start the extension.

The examples given are referred to as end-of-the-run or middle-of-the-run. This refers to the position of the device with respect to others on the circuit. A branch circuit cable begins at the main panel. The entire circuit is called a run. The section of cable from the panel to the first device (switch, fixture or receptacle) is called the home run. A device that has other devices on both sides of it is called middle-of-the-run. The last device on a run is called end-of-the-run. Remember that while the run is a circuit, both conductors of the circuit are contained in one cable. When cable connects to an end-of-the-run device, no other conductors connect to the device. Any middle-of-the-run device, however, will connect to at least two cables.

Receptacles

End-of-the-Run Receptacle.
The easiest way to extend wiring is to start at the last receptacle on a circuit. The only conductors to it are a black one to the brass terminal and a white one to the silver-colored terminal. If the circuit is grounded, there will also be three bare wires attached with a wire nut. They connect the box, the ground terminal and the ground wire of the run. To extend the run, attach a black conductor to the unused brass terminal and a white one to the remaining silver-colored terminal. If the receptacle is grounded, the new section should also have a ground wire. Insert the bare ground wire of the new section into the wire nut connecting the the other three ground wires. You may need a larger wire nut for this. The jumpers between the wire nut, the box and the receptacle may be green insulated wire or bare wire.

Middle-of-the-Run Receptacle. Leave one set of black and white conductors attached to the receptacle terminals. Remove the other black and white pair. Attach the black conductor to the new run and to a short piece of black conductor with a wire nut.

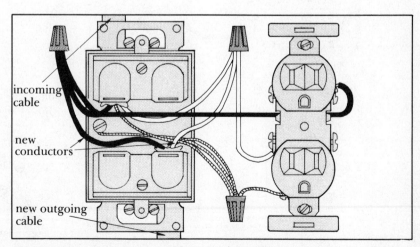

Extending the wiring from an end-of-the-run receptacle.

117

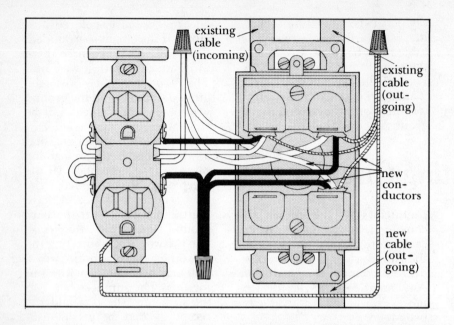

Extending the wiring from a middle-of-the-run receptacle.

jumper, using a wire nut. Attach the jumper to the remaining silver-colored terminal.

Switches

Extra wiring can be added to a switch in the middle of an electrical run. You must find which of the two black conductors carries the power from the service panel by shutting off the power, removing the switch from the box, restoring the power, then checking the two wires with a voltage tester. The

Attach the short piece as a jumper to the remaining brass terminal (the one where you re-moved the black conductor). Then connect the white conductor to the new run and to a

Extending the wiring from: a. a middle-of-the-run switch, or b. a middle-of-the-run light fixture.

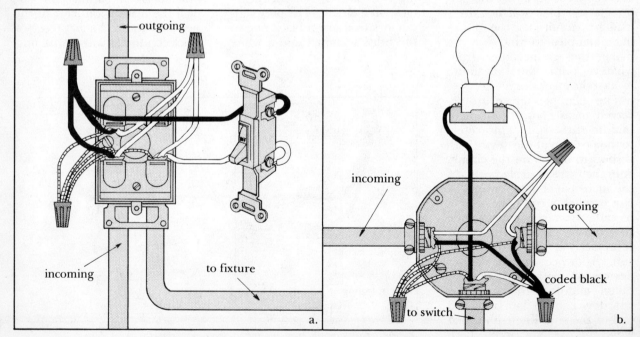

conductor to the panel will test hot whether the switch is on or off. Turn the power off again. Disconnect the black conductor that leads to the panel from its terminal and attach it with a wire nut to the black conductor of the new run and to a jumper to the terminal. The white conductor and the ground wire of the new run are attached to the two existing wire nuts, white to white and ground to ground.

A run cannot be extended from a switch loop because it is only served by one conductor, the black one carrying the current.

Fixtures

To extend a circuit from a fixture in the middle of a run, attach the new conductors to the existing wire nuts, making sure to avoid the line that goes to the switch which is attached at a wire nut to the black fixture conductor. The black conductor of the new run is added to the incoming black conductor. You will find this incoming black conductor attached with a wire nut to a black conductor leading out of the box, to the switch. One of the conductors to the switch will be white, coded black with tape. The white conductor and the bare ground wire are connected to the proper existing wire nuts. The new white conductor attaches to the white conductors, and the ground wire attaches to the other two ground wires. You must test to be certain the fixture is in the middle of the run. If it is not, your new line will go dead every time the light switch is turned

off. If the fixture is in the middle of the run, one black wire will always test hot, even if the light switch is turned off.

Remember when extending from fixtures or switches that the Code does not allow light fixtures to be supplied by the two small-appliance circuits required for the kitchen, or kitchen receptacles to be supplied by the general lighting circuit.

Junction Boxes

If more than one circuit passes through the junction box, determine which one is the circuit you want to tap. First, have someone turn off the house wiring; next, remove the wire nuts from the black conductors, making sure the exposed wires do not touch the box or any other conductor. Have someone turn on everything but the circuit you want to tap. Then, determine with a voltage tester which set of black conductors has no current;

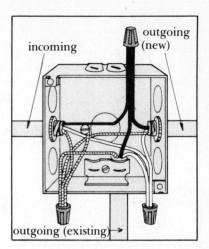

Extending the wiring from a junction box.

those are the ones you want to tap. Shut off the power; add the black conductor of the new run to them with a wire nut. Add the white conductor of the new run to the wire nut containing the white conductors of the circuit you are tapping. Attach the new ground wire to the wire nut that contains all the ground wires.

Appliance Circuits _____

Many appliances must be supplied by separate branch circuits. The two 20-amp circuits required by the Code for small kitchen appliances do not supply enough electricity for large fixed appliances. Any motorized appliance that draws over six amps must be supplied by a separate branch circuit. An electric range must be on a separate circuit.

All appliances must have a

means of being disconnected from the branch circuit, either with a plug and receptacle or, for a motorized appliance over ⅛ horsepower, with a switch located within sight of the appliance.

The conductors of any branch circuit must be rated for the load they will carry. The rating for a circuit serving a motorized appliance must be 125 percent of the nameplate **119**

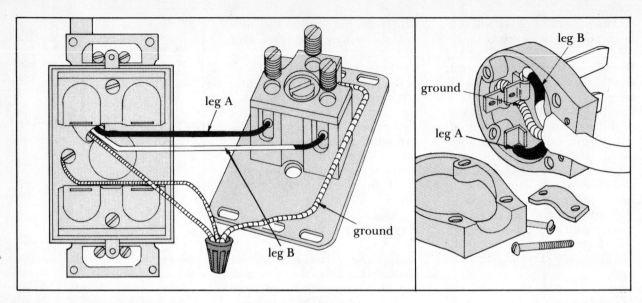

Wiring a 230-volt plug and receptacle.

rating of the appliance to allow for the extra current it draws at start-up.

Wiring a 115/230-volt plug and receptacle.

Three-Wire Circuits

230 Volts Only. An appliance such as an electric water heater uses only 230-volt power. When the load is between two hot conductors on different legs of the service (corresponding to the two separate hot service conductors that enter the main panel) the voltage is 230. Such an appliance has no need of

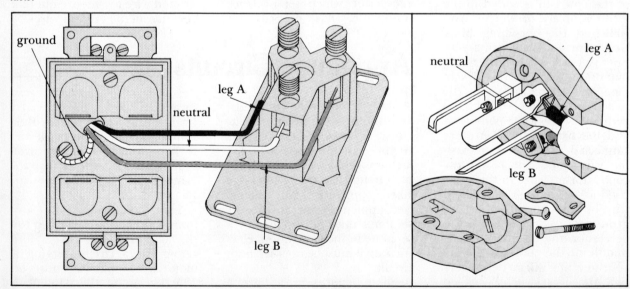

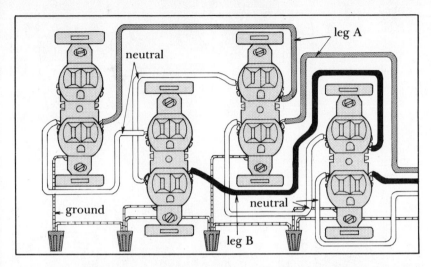

Wiring two separate 115-volt circuits using a single three-wire cable.

a neutral conductor. It is wired with two hot conductors and a ground wire, nothing else. Thus, a 230-volt circuit may be supplied by two-wire cable with ground. You must recode the white conductor with red tape at each terminal so that anyone working on the circuit will know that both conductors are hot.

Combined 115/230 Volts. Most large appliances use a combination of 115 and 230 volts. An electric range draws 115 volts to supply the clock, lights and the burners on low. It draws 230 volts for burners on high. Dishwashers also draw combined voltage. Cable to supply these appliances is three-wire with ground. The terminals on the appliance are generally marked to show how to attach the conductors.

Three-Wire, 115-Volt Circuit. If there was once an electric stove in your kitchen, you can use the 230-volt line that served

it to make two 115-volt circuits. Or you can run a new three-wire cable to supply two 115-volt circuits—this is easier than fishing two separate cables. The advantage of having two 115-volt circuits supplied by one cable is that adjacent receptacles can be on different circuits.

If load is placed between the two hot wires, as in an electric stove, the voltage is 230. But if the load is placed between one hot wire and the neutral, the voltage is 115. To get 115 volts at one receptacle, attach the neutral and the red conductors to the proper terminals of one receptacle for the first circuit. Attach the neutral and black conductors to the terminals of the next receptacle for the second circuit. The neutral is shared by the two circuits. By connecting the hot wires of the three-wire cable to the two take-off terminals of the service panel, you can get the required

power. Make sure you use the take-off terminals from the two different sides of the panel, corresponding to the two different hot wires entering the house. If you should take both hot wires from one side of the panel, both hot conductors would be on the same leg of the service and the neutral wire would carry a double load. Since the neutral is not protected by a fuse, this could result in overheating and fire.

Both hot wires in a three-wire circuit should carry approximately the same current. When this is true, the neutral carries nothing. But if there is an imbalance, 15 amps operating on one circuit and 10 on the other, the neutral carries the difference, 5 amps. For that reason, it is a good idea to arrange the load so that both circuits operate at roughly the same level. In cases of extreme imbalance, the circuit with the higher load may experience voltage drop (where current is most needed) and the other circuit may experience voltage increase.

This is true of any three-wire circuit connected to different legs of the service, whether on the main panel or on any subpanels. To avoid problems, design the system so that each leg carries approximately the same load. In other words, balance the load on the two legs.

Electric Range

An electric range is the largest single user of electricity in most homes. In older homes, a special pullout for the range fuses **121**

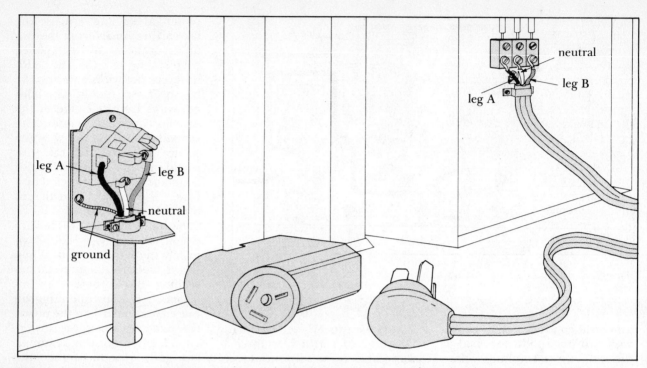

Wiring an electric range (combined 115/230 volts).

was often located right next to the main pullout, controlling at least 40 percent of the total power available (40 amps in a 100-amp service). If your home has this type of arrangement, even if you no longer have an electric range, there is probably sufficient power already running to the kitchen for electric cooking equipment. Or, with a circuit breaker panel, you can probably add 230-volt breakers of the proper amperage to spaces at the bottom of the panel reserved for new circuits.

The most likely wiring changes for cooking equipment are either relocation of the existing range or its replacement by

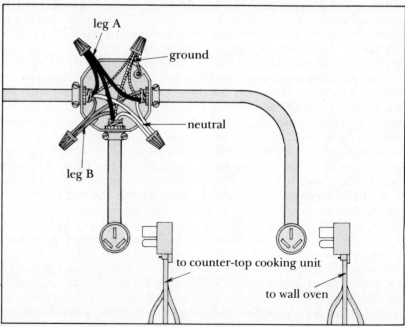

Wiring a counter-top cooking unit and separate wall oven on a single branch line (115/230 volts, 40 amps).

a wall-mounted oven and a counter-mounted cooking unit. Fortunately, the Code allows up to two wall ovens and one counter-top unit to be supplied by one branch circuit and to be considered together as far as demand load is concerned. Demand load is the amount of current a piece of equipment draws from the circuit. If your existing cable has the capacity to supply the sum of the nameplate rating of the new units, you can wire them up with no changes.

If the existing cable is not large enough for the load required by the new equipment, you may have to replace the cable with one of a larger size or run a new circuit to one of the units. If you have circuit breakers, running another circuit to the cooking equipment is no problem. But, with a fuse panel, take-off terminals may already be in use, and replacement of the range conductors would require you to work with range terminals located next to the terminals for the main pullout. These main terminals are hot even with the main fuses pulled, and this makes it unsafe to work near them unless the power coming into the house is shut off. You can shut it off by making arrangements with the power company or by pulling the glass-covered meter that measures the amount of electricity you use. This meter is a plug, and its removal in a properly wired system will shut off all power to the main panel and the entire house.

If the maximum rating on your new cooking units is only slightly over the capacity of the cable supplying them, it may still be safe to use the existing cable. A range with a nameplate rating of less than 12 kilowatts may be considered to be only 8 kilowatts (kW) for the purpose of judging load on the feeder and branch circuit serving it. Up to two wall-mounted ovens and one counter-mounted cooking unit in the same room may be served by a single circuit and considered together by adding the nameplate ratings of all the units. If the result for either a freestanding range or the combination (up to two wall ovens and one counter unit) is between 1¾ and 8¾ kW, you may calculate the demand at 80 percent of the nameplate values.

Appliances must have a means of being disconnected from all hot conductors. Whether the cooking equipment you install is freestanding or not, plug and receptacle connection to the circuit is preferable and will serve as the required means of disconnection provided you can reach it without moving the stove. A plug and receptacle make removal of the range easier, whether for cleaning, servicing or maintenance. Range receptacles may be fastened to the wall. They do not have to be mounted flush.

Dishwasher

A dishwasher is considered a fixed appliance and must be supplied by a separate circuit, unless it is a portable, plug-in model on rollers. This is so even if it only operates at 115 volts. Most dishwashers operate at a combined 115/230 volts.

The dishwasher may be connected to the circuit either at a junction box near the appliance or with a plug and receptacle. The use of a plug allows easier disconnection and removal for servicing and maintenance. Be sure to use a plug and receptacle that are designed for the proper voltage and amperage. This will probably be a combined 115/230 volts at 30 amps, but the actual rating will be listed on the rear of the appliance.

Ventilation Fan

Although a ventilation fan is a fixed appliance, it may be included on a small-appliance circuit (but not general lighting) since it will draw less than six amps. It may be connected to the circuit either at a junction box near the fan or with a plug and receptacle. The Code requires that the fuse or breaker on the circuit not exceed the full-load rating of the motor beyond a set amount. The idea is to ensure that the circuit will open if the motor suffers severe overload, such as could occur if an obstruction prevented it from starting. A time-delay fuse on a circuit may not be more than 225 percent of the full-load rating of the motor, a regular fuse 400 percent, an inverse-time circuit breaker 400 percent, and an instantaneous trip breaker 1,300 percent.

If the fan motor is over ⅛ horsepower, a means of disconnection other than the branch circuit fuse or breaker must be within sight of the fan. If the **123**

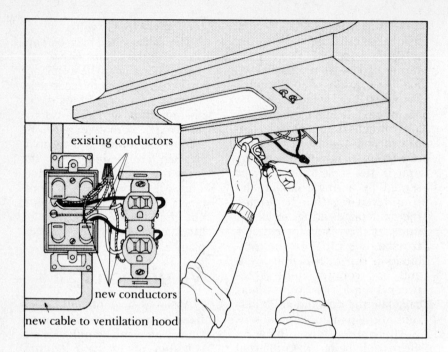

Wiring a ventilation hood from an end-of-the-run receptacle.

existing conductors

new conductors

new cable to ventilation hood

fan is connected by plug, no other switch is needed. If the unit has a built-in switch with the off position marked on it, that will do. Otherwise, a motor-rated switch must be installed.

Doing the Work

Wiring your harvest kitchen is not a once-and-done job. Like the plumbing work, it extends throughout the duration of your building project. You'll install boxes and run cable at the rough-in stage, install receptacles, fixtures and switches early in the finishing stage, and screw switch and receptacle plates in place as a final act.

Wiring a kitchen is *not* difficult. Many otherwise capable people avoid messing with their home's wiring because they are afraid of it. Follow the safety rules and never work with a live circuit. Buy and use a circuit tester. With the circuit you want to work on tested and proven dead, there's nothing to fear.

Plan carefully, work carefully, check your finished circuits. You'll find it's true: you *can* do it yourself.

Kitchen Plumbing

Plumbing, like wiring, is best done when the kitchen is in its most stripped-down state. It is easier then to reach what you are working on, and there's less chance of damaging finished surfaces. But if you do do plumbing work with some finished surfaces remaining, the trick is to minimize the damage.

The rough plumbing is run in

between or through the studs and framing plates. Some holes will probably be cut through framing. New plumbing must be tied into the existing system and old pipes removed while the water is kept running as much of the time as possible.

After the rough plumbing is in place as far as the stub-outs (short pipes that stick out of the floor or wall), you proceed with the finish work—lighting, cabinets, walls, windows. When all that is done, you go back and finish up the plumbing. Parts that will be visible in the room have a chrome finish. You mount the fixtures on the sink, set it in its cabinet, and hook into the stub-outs. So the plumbing isn't really finished until the kitchen is.

Getting Started

Don't spend a lot of time learning procedures you won't use. Once you've decided on copper pipe, the information on joining plastic won't do much for you. If you are going to replace but not move the sink, the details of venting and drainage are not necessary.

If you *are* thinking of a new sink location, understanding the drain-waste-vent system is necessary, along with the basics of how to make connections. Drainpipe must be pitched correctly and it must be vented. If a sink is relocated by more than a few feet, there is a very good chance that back venting or a new stack will be required. Back venting means running drainpipe up higher than the sink and then over to the drain stack. This can involve a lot of work and is something you should definitely examine in detail before you commit yourself to a new sink location.

There are many kinds of pipe and fittings—copper, galvanized steel, cast iron, plastic. In kitchen plumbing, often one kind of pipe is used for supply and another for waste, though the same kind can be used for both. Connections can be made between whatever type of pipe is already in place and the kind you choose. Transition fittings are available that connect all types of supply and drain pipe.

Getting the Materials

When the time comes to do the plumbing, map out the work that must be done, make a materials list and take it to a supplier. The clearer idea you have of what you need, the less trouble you'll have at the supply house and the fewer times you'll go back. No matter how careful the plan, you will have to go back. And if you have a big project, the salespeople may get to know you very well. Find a store you like.

Salespeople in home improvement centers or large department stores like Sears may not know much about plumbing. If you aren't looking for advice, the prices and quality are generally competitive. There is an advantage in that most of the merchandise is displayed openly where it can be picked up and handled. Doing so is a good way to learn.

Plumbing supply stores that sell to the professional are a possible source of information as well as parts. The people who work in them are usually very knowledgeable. There may be a communication problem, though. Sometimes they are so used to the jargon of the trade that they have trouble understanding what you want even when you ask for the right thing. But once they find out what you are planning, they will often anticipate parts you'll need that you might otherwise forget.

The goods in such stores are generally not on display. You must be able to specify what you want. Since you are acting as your own contractor, you may be able to get the professional discount. If not, compare prices. Retail prices at outlets selling to the trade are sometimes very high.

Before you buy your materials and tools, get familiar with all the pipes and fittings you plan to use. You will also need to know about the tools you'll need.

Roughing-In the Plumbing

Plumbing, like wiring, is done as much as possible during the rough-in stage. In new construction, this occurs after the framing is up but before the walls, ceiling or finish flooring are done.

When a kitchen is remodeled, something is usually left as it was, if only the ceiling or a wall. That means there are usually some finished parts to look out for and to work around. But think in terms of the rough-in stage. As much as possible, take out everything that is going out. The plumbing will be a lot easier.

Rough-in plumbing includes tapping into the existing supply

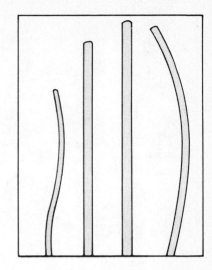

Rigid and flexible copper tubing. Flexible tubing is sold in rolls and retains a slight bend, even when installed.

and drain lines and running the pipe to the place where it will be used. Actually hooking up fixtures and appliances is finish work, to be done after the walls, cabinets and floors are completed. Rough-in plumbing ends where the pipes leave the walls or floors. The pipes left sticking out during finish work are called stub-outs.

Pipes and Fittings

Several different kinds of pipe can be used in home systems. As noted, it is not necessary to use the same kind of pipes that are already in the house because special transition fittings allow easy connection between all types of pipe. The decision of what types of pipe to use involves a balance of cost, convenience and durability. But local plumbing codes vary, and some codes specify certain kinds of pipe. Check with the local building inspector before you start.

Copper and plastic can be used either for supply or drainage. Unthreaded copper is generally referred to as tubing, while threaded copper or brass is simply called pipe. Threaded galvanized steel pipe is used mostly for supply, cast iron only for drainage. The drainage and supply systems are really two different systems and often are composed of different kinds of pipe. The drainage system is known as the drain-waste-vent (DWV) system. This system must be properly vented to keep waste gases from escaping into the house.

Copper Pipe

Copper tubing is still generally favored for water supply, while plastic pipe is used more and more for drainage. Copper is fairly light and easy to work with but strong enough to stand some abuse. It is smoother than galvanized pipe, allowing the use of one size smaller diameter pipe. If a run requires ¾-inch galvanized, then ½-inch copper would do the job.

Flexible or Rigid

Copper tubing is available either flexible or rigid. The flexible kind, called soft temper, comes in 30-, 60- or 100-foot rolls. It is very easy to work with, and the measurements between fittings do not have to be as exact as with rigid pipe. But since soft temper retains the shape of the original coil, installations with it never look quite as professional as those with rigid pipe. Rigid, hard-temper pipe comes in 10- and 20-foot lengths, and many supply houses will cut it to any length over 1 foot.

Copper Fittings

There are different copper fittings for each type of joint. Smooth fittings that are soldered to the pipe are called sweat fittings. Some fittings have both smooth and threaded ends, for joining copper to steel. Fittings that join different kinds of pipe are called adapters or transition fittings. In the case of a steel-to-copper adapter, its design must prevent corrosion caused by electrolytic action. This can occur when two types

127

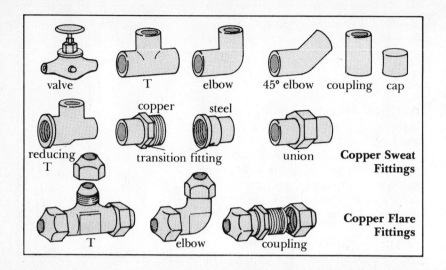

valve T elbow 45° elbow coupling cap

copper steel

reducing T transition fitting union **Copper Sweat Fittings**

T elbow coupling **Copper Flare Fittings**

of metal are next to each other in the presence of water. A miniature battery is created that causes one of the metals to corrode. Some fittings connect pipes of different sizes, others cap off a pipe, and some, a faucet, for example, allow water to be turned off and on.

Pipe Thickness

In addition to the two tempers, copper pipe is available in three different wall thicknesses, types K, L and M. The heaviest, type K, is used primarily for buried runs. It is available in either rigid or flexible pipe. Medium-walled type L is used for interior plumbing. It also is available in either flexible or rigid. The least expensive is thin-walled type M, available only in rigid hard-temper. It is perfectly suitable for interior plumbing.

Copper pipe is sized so that the outside diameter is always ⅛ inch more than the stated, or nominal, size. The nominal size

approximates the inside diameter of the pipe, although since the three types of pipe, K, L and M, have different wall thicknesses, their inside diameters vary accordingly. Because of this, type M will always permit more water to flow than type K or L of the same nominal size. Pipe size is always expressed in terms of the nominal inside dimension unless the letters O.D. (outside diameter) accompany the measurement.

Cutting Copper

The best way to cut copper is with a tubing cutter. Most cutters have a retractable triangular blade that is used to remove burrs from the inside of freshly cut pipe. The pipe is cut by rotating the cutter around the pipe. After every couple of turns, tighten the handle slightly to increase the pressure on the pipe. It is fairly easy to overtighten and flatten the pipe. If this happens, you will save time by discarding the pipe or cutting it down for use elsewhere. After the pipe is cut, use the reamer attachment to remove burrs.

A hacksaw can also be used to cut copper pipe or tubing. The saw should be used in a miter box to keep the cut straight and help hold the tubing. A vise tends to flatten pipe and should not be used. Tubing that will be used for a flare fitting must be perfectly square. If necessary, file it square. If the tubing will be used with a compression ring, there can be no ridge on the outside edge or the ring won't fit over it. File any ridge

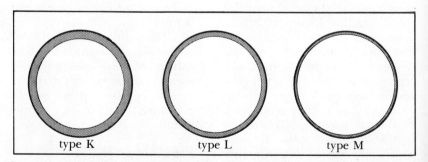

type K type L type M

Copper tubing is sold in three thicknesses: thick-walled type K for buried installations, medium-walled type L for most home use and inexpensive, thin-walled type M for installations where damage is not likely.

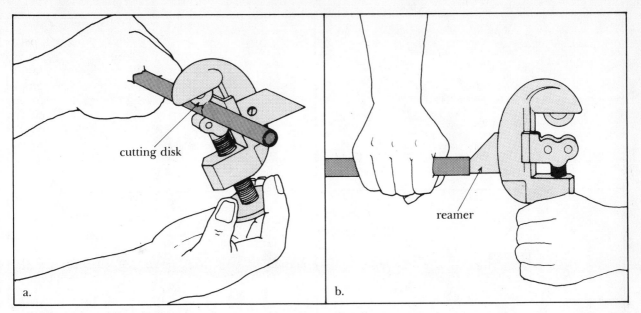

a.

cutting disk

b.

reamer

Using a tubing cutter: a. Rotate the cutter around the tubing, screwing down the handle occasionally to keep the blade snug against the tubing. Don't over-tighten. b. Use the retractable reamer to remove burrs from the inside of the tubing.

carefully. If the pipe has been flattened at all, the compression ring won't fit, either.

Sweating Joints

The usual means of joining copper tubing to fittings is by sweating the joints with solder. Sweating is the least expensive way to join copper.

To prepare a joint for solder, polish the outside of the tubing and the inside of the fitting with emery cloth, fine sandpaper or steel wool. This removes the oxidized copper, leaving bare metal for the solder to adhere to. Brush a thin coat of flux onto the polished parts of the pipe and fitting, then slip the

fitting onto the pipe. If the fitting is a valve, remove the stem and washer. Some people wrap a wet rag around the valve stem as a way to protect the washer from heat without removing it. While using a rag may prevent damage to the washer, it also makes it difficult to heat the joint properly, risking a weak joint.

Heat the fitting with a propane torch. The flame is hottest about 1 inch from the nozzle. When solder melts if held against the side of the fitting opposite the flame, move the flame to the pipe. The flame should not be closer than 1 inch to the joint. If it is, the flux may overheat. Flux removes any oxidized copper left after polishing, but charred flux does not perform this function properly. If you overheat the flux, you'll get a weak joint.

When solder will melt on the side of the pipe away from the

flame, move the flame back to the fitting and insert solid wire solder into the side of the joint opposite the flame. Keep feeding the solder into the joint until a rim of solder appears completely around the joint. When this happens, the molten solder has completely filled the joint by capillary attraction. The ring of hot solder is bright and shiny. When it becomes dull, the joint has cooled and, after about a minute, may be moved. Don't handle the pipe or fitting during or soon after the heating. Copper tubing conducts heat well enough to burn you at some distance from the flame. If you must move the joint soon after the solder has dulled, slosh a little water on it first to be sure it is cool enough to handle.

If you sweat a joint near wood framing, stick a piece of asbestos between the joint and the wood. Don't set down a lit torch. The **129**

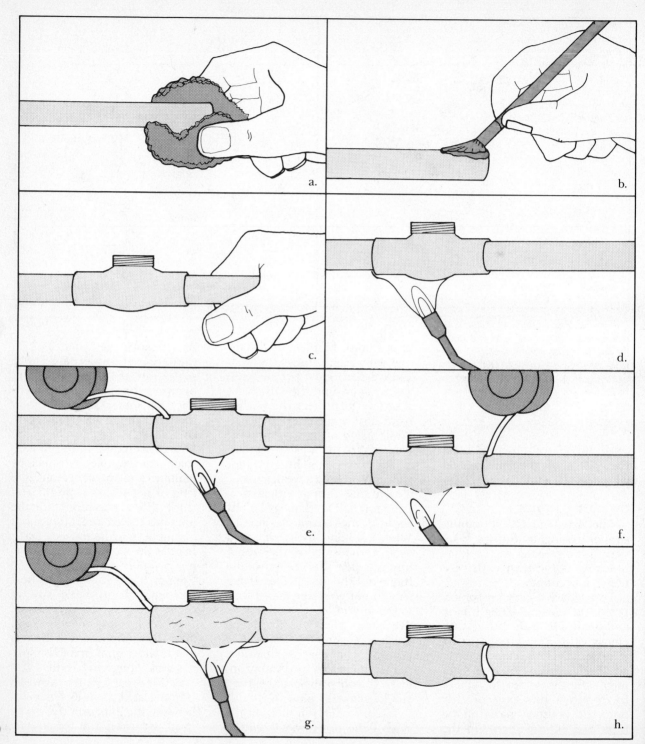

Sweating a joint: a. Remove oxidation from the mating surfaces of pipe and fitting with emery cloth or steel wool. b. Apply flux. c. Fit the pipe into the fitting. d. Heat the fitting, not the pipe. e. Test the temperature by touching the solder to the fitting; if the solder melts, the temperature is correct. f. Touch the solder to the seam between pipe and fitting; g. and h. It will melt and be drawn into the gap, bonding the pieces and sealing the joint.

flame is very quiet and can be almost invisible. You might reach into the flame while trying to get something else. A

device that makes restarting the torch easy is a spark starter. It is inexpensive and easier to use than matches.

Flare Joints

Flare joints are generally used only on soft-temper tubing. The fittings are fairly expensive but are easy to make and may be taken apart and put together easily. Some local codes do not permit flare joints.

A flare joint is made by slipping a flare nut over the end of copper tubing and inserting the tubing into the flaring tool. The flaring tool consists of a reamer

and a two-part die with holes of different sizes to accommodate different diameters of tubing. The reamer screws into the tubing, molding it permanently into the flare shape. The tubing must be free of burrs on the inside and ridges on the outside before it is inserted into the die. The end of the tubing is placed flush with the surface of the die

Fabricating a flare joint: a. A flare nut is first slid onto the tubing. b. The tubing is clamped in the flaring die. c. A reamer is used to flare the tube. d. Finally, the joint is completed by inserting the male fitting into the flared tubing and secured with the flare nut.

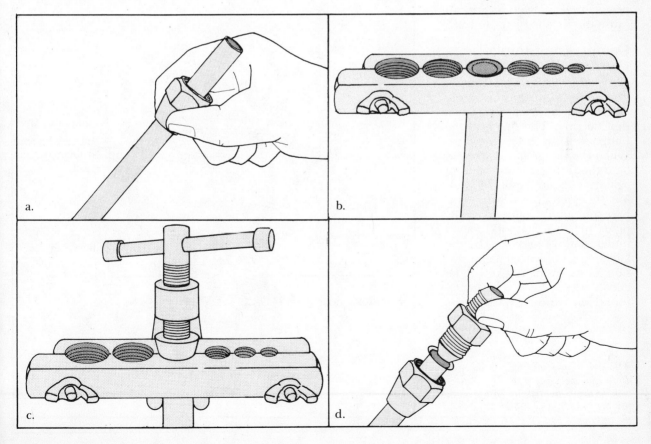

a.

b.

c.

d.

131

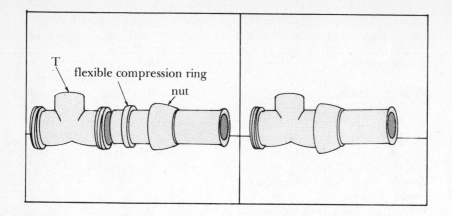

T flexible compression ring

nut

Compression joint. A nut presses the flexible compression ring against the pipe, forming a watertight joint.

and must be perfectly square. If it is not, file it carefully. The die and the end of the reamer, as well as the tubing itself, must be perfectly clean. Sand or grit can cause the finished joint to leak.

Compression Joints— Copper and Brass

A compression joint consists of a flange nut, a pipe, a fitting and either a metal ring or a flexible ring. The ring and the flange nut fit over the pipe. When the flange nut is screwed onto the fitting, it pulls the ring against a seat in the fitting, sealing the joint. Metal-ring compression joints connect supply pipe to the shut-off valves under bathroom sinks. In the kitchen, flexible-ring compression joints are more likely to be encountered. These are usually found on exposed waste pipes

A flexible-ring joint connects the sink drain and the waste pipe. The ends of both the drain and the pipe have a small lip; the flexible ring is pressed between the two lips to make the seal watertight.

under the kitchen sink where thin-walled brass pipe is used. These joints are generally used to connect waste pipes to cross or T fittings.

Another kind of flexible-ring joint that is common in kitchen plumbing connects the waste pipe to the basket drain of the kitchen sink. This joint is really a kind of union. The waste pipe has a small lip around the end, as does the basket drain. In this type of joint, the flexible ring is pressed between the basket drain and the waste pipe. To assemble the joint, slip the

bottom of sink

basket

bottom of sink

rubber washer

nut

strainer body

compression ring

locknut

tailpiece

flange nut over the other end of the pipe from the lip. Place the compression ring on the lip and press the pipe and ring against the lip of the basket drain. Screw the flange nut to the drain. If the ring is placed on the wrong side of the pipe lip, the metal of the pipe will be pressed against the metal drain lip, and the joint will leak. Use a wrench to tighten the flange nut, but don't overtighten. As with all compression fittings, light pressure will do. If you overtighten the nut, you may distort the fitting. This would make it difficult to reassemble properly, so that it doesn't leak.

Plastic Pipe

The main advantage of plastic pipe is that it's easy to install. Connections are made with solvent cement and a brush. The solvent actually melts a little of the pipe and fitting. The result, obtained in a couple of minutes, is a heatless weld that when left

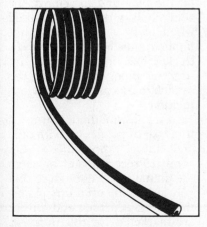

Flexible polyethylene tubing.

overnight is stronger than the pipe itself. Plastic pipe is resistant to corrosion and may be used underground.

There are several kinds of plastic pipe, some flexible, some rigid. The latest development in rigid pipe allows the use of hot water heated up to 180°F. The hot water pipe is a chemically hardened version of an old standby, PVC (polyvinyl chloride). It is called CPVC (chlorinated polyvinyl chloride). A less expensive rigid pipe is called ABS (acrylonitrile-butadiene styrene). It can only be used for cold water but costs only one-fifth as much as CPVC.

Flexible plastic pipe, called polyethylene or poly, is black in color and, like ABS, can only be used for cold water. Because poly is resistant to corrosion, it is excellent for buried runs. Its flexibility means it can be used in an uneven trench and also that it will not burst, even in a hard freeze.

A drawback in using these materials is that some of the resins used to make plastic pipe are carcinogens. During manufacture, they are changed chemically into a safe form. But tiny amounts of the original material remain. The concern is over how much of them remain in the finished pipe and at what rate they migrate into the water. While this question has not been answered conclusively, indications are that concentrations of harmful material are extremely low. On the other hand, the effects of exposure to low levels of toxins are not conclusively known either. In the meantime, consider using plastic only for

your drain-waste-vent system, where the benefit of lightweight, large-diameter pipe is greatest. One last word. Plastic pipe is more resistant to corrosion than copper or galvanized steel. If your water is acid and soft, there is some risk of contamination from dissolved copper or zinc. In that one case, you would probably be better off with plastic.

Joining Plastic with Couplings

Flexible plastic tubing is joined with ribbed couplings rather than by solvent welding. The pipe is pushed over the couplings and held in place with clamps. The clamps, the same kind as used on a car radiator hose, have slotted metal straps that are tightened by turning a screw. Transition couplings are also available for flexible tubing. The threaded plastic-to-steel transition couplings are generally made of steel because threaded plastic is weak. Poly is available in several grades. The better grades will hold pressure up to 100 pounds per square inch (psi), the same as with rigid plastic.

Joining Rigid Plastic Tubing

Working with plastic tubing is easy, but the cement used to join it dries quickly, in two to three minutes, and this makes it important to have everything worked out in advance. Cut and fit the pipes before gluing them, and test the fit between each pipe and fitting. Then apply solvent cement to the inside of the fitting and the outside of the **133**

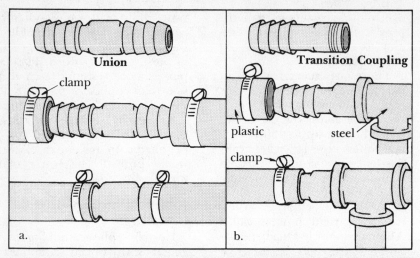

Joining polyethylene tubing with couplings: a. Plastic to plastic. b. Plastic to steel.

pipe with a small brush. Allow for the distance the tubing will go into the fittings. (This distance is called the make-up distance.) Plastic fittings vary slightly in size. If a pipe does not touch lightly all around the fit-

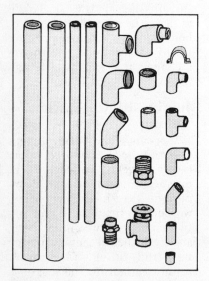

134 *Plastic tubing and fittings.*

ting, the joint may leak. If the fit is too tight, there won't be enough glue to seal the joint properly.

Make sure the solvent you use is in good condition. It gets thick with age, or if the temperature is too low. Drying time depends on temperature and humidity, with 40°F. as a rough minimum for successful joining. The joint may be moved after a few minutes, but not before. After an hour it will hold water, but it is better to wait overnight or about 16 hours before testing under pressure. Make sure the solvent is designed for the type of pipe you are using. Use solvent only in a well-ventilated area; the vapors are harmful.

First cut the pipe with a 24-tooth-per-inch hacksaw blade or with a tubing cutter. To make a square cut, place the pipe in a miter box. The burrs inside the tubing can be removed with a small penknife or with a reamer on a tubing cutter. Any burrs on

the outside should also be removed to ensure a tight joint.

Before you apply solvent, make sure that there is no water or grease on either the pipe or fitting. Grease prevents adhesion, and water slows drying. Place a scratch mark on both the pipe and the fitting when they are correctly aligned. This will allow you to align the joint quickly during final installation, before the solvent sets.

There are several ways of applying solvent to prepare tubing for joining. The first is to sand the shiny finish off the pipe end. Then brush a light coat of solvent on the inside of the fitting and a thicker but even coat on the outside of the pipe end. This method allows the most time before the joint sets.

Insert the pipe in the fitting and twist the pipe about a quarter of a turn, until the scratch marks line up. This spreads the solvent all around the joint, just as heat spreads the solder in a sweated copper joint.

In the second method, you use a very light coat of solvent on the pipe end to remove the shine. Follow this, as you would when using sandpaper, with a light coat inside the fitting and a thicker one on the tubing. Insert the pipe and line up the scratch marks as in the previous method.

In the last method, you use a thin coat of primer on both pipe and fitting. Apply the solvent about 15 seconds later or when the plastic is soft enough so that you can scrape off a tiny paper-thin piece. A primer and solvent are marketed for this purpose. Insert the pipe and line up the

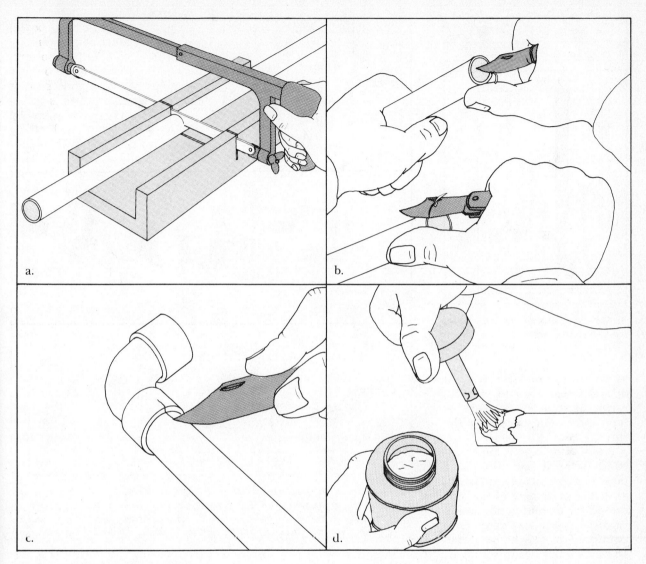

Joining rigid plastic tubing: a. Cut the tubing with a hacksaw or tubing cutter. b. Trim the burrs. c. Dry fit tubing and fitting and score both to indicate the desired alignment. d. Apply solvent, then joint tubing and fitting, lining up the scored marks immediately.

scratch marks after the second coat. If the solvent hardens before a joint is properly posi-

tioned, cut it off and discard it. If you are careless, it can become expensive.

Because plastic is not rated higher than 100 psi, you must protect your runs from water hammer caused by the opening and closing of valves. A rapidly closed valve can create a momentary pressure of up to

500 psi. The answer, and it is a good idea with copper, too, is to make air chambers near each valve. Make an air chamber by extending pipe from a T near the valve. Cap the pipe. The air trapped inside acts as a cushion. The solenoid-controlled valves of a dishwasher need an air chamber of 18 inches of pipe **135**

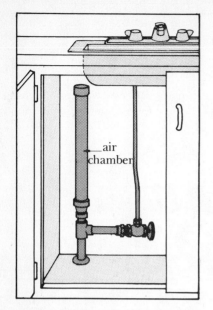

An air chamber near the valve keeps pipes from knocking.

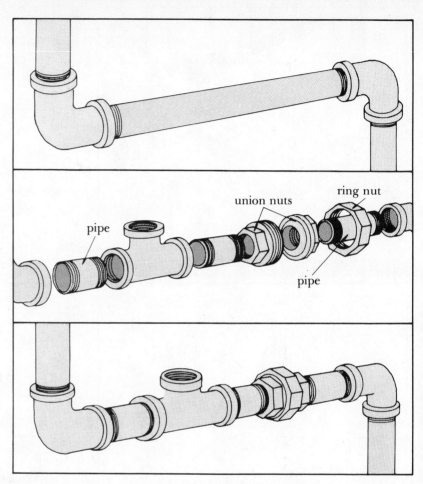

A union joint is the only way to replace a length of threaded galvanized steel pipe without removing the entire run. For example, tap into a line: a. Cut the pipe on an angle to ease removal of the two pieces. b. Screw the various pieces of pipe and the fittings into place in sequence, finishing with the union. c. The completed alteration.

which must be one size larger in diameter than the run. Regular valves need only 12 inches of pipe of the same diameter as the run.

Plastic hot water pipe expands when it gets hot. Plastic pipe hangers allow expansion, as well as movement of the pipe caused by opening and closing valves. Don't allow water temperature to get higher than 180°F. A water heater setting of 140-150°F. is a practical maximum, more than enough for home use; a lower setting is safer and more energy efficient.

Galvanized Pipe

Galvanized steel pipe has a coating of zinc inside and out. It is available unthreaded (solderable) and threaded. The **136** threaded kind is used most often. Galvanized steel is the most durable type of supply pipe. The trouble is that it is heavy, and existing runs are hard to take apart. As galvanized pipe is assembled, each fitting and piece of pipe is screwed onto the one before, and the run is built up step by step. But once the run is installed, unscrewing a piece in the middle is impossible—screwing the pipe out of one fitting would tighten it into the other. To work on the run without taking the whole thing apart, you must cut out a section. The section can be replaced by two smaller pieces that are joined by a union. The union is the key to working with threaded pipe, because it allows the joining of threaded pipe in

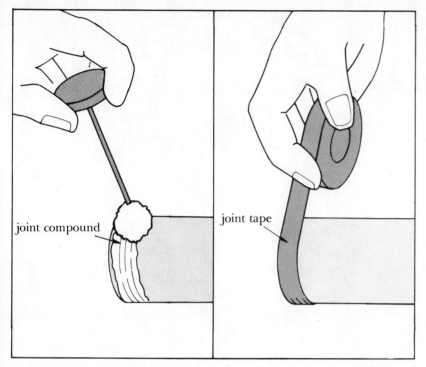

joint compound

joint tape

Applying the joint sealers to the threads of galvanized steel pipe. If the joint is an old one, you may have to wind in a few turns of lamp wick on top of the plastic tape or joint compound.

the middle of a run.

Galvanized pipe is available cut to order, or in 10- and 21-foot lengths. If you buy it cut to size, you can have it threaded at the same time. Naturally, if you do this you must measure what you need carefully beforehand. If you plan extensive plumbing changes, and if galvanized is your choice, you can rent the

Tightening a fitting to a pipe with the help of two pipe wrenches. The open end of the wrench should face in the direction that force is applied.

equipment needed to cut and thread your own pipe.

Joining threaded pipe is easy. The threads of the pipe should be brushed with pipe-joint compound or wrapped with plastic joint tape. The compound lubricates the joint, protects the threads from corrosion and seals the joint against leakage. If the joint is an old one, it may be necessary to wrap a few turns of lamp wick into the threads to seal it.

The threads on pipe are tapered. The farther you screw in the pipe, the tighter the joint. Each time the joint is taken apart and reassembled, the pipe must screw a little farther into the fitting. At first, about three threads should be visible. But,

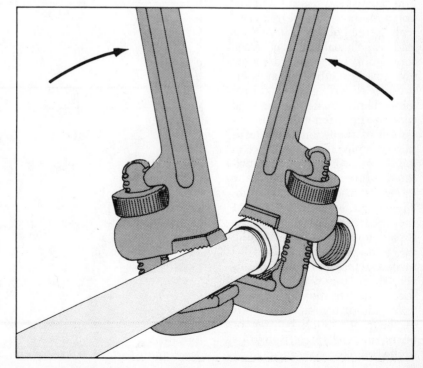

Joining hubless cast-iron pipe with a neoprene sleeve and a clamp—no lead solder is required. Although a screwdriver or wrench speeds initial fitting, the final tightening must be done with a torque wrench.

you should never tighten the joint after none of the threads are visible, or the fitting might break. The joint is assembled by holding the pipe with one pipe wrench and turning the fitting with another. Apply pressure on the wrench in the direction in which the jaws point.

Cast-Iron Pipe

Cast-iron pipe is used only for drain-waste-vent runs. It is the most durable and inexpensive kind to use. But, until recently, it has been hard to install. Cast-iron pipe is heavy, and the traditional method of joining it is by sealing the joints with molten lead and oakum, a time-consuming job. There are now two easier methods that both produce strong, leakproof joints. Unfortunately, some local codes do not permit their use.

One of them joins standard, hub-type pipe using compression joints. A neoprene gasket, lubricated inside and out with soapy water, is inserted in the hub. The spigot, which is the end of the pipe without the hub, is forced into the gasket, sealing the joint. When the spigot is properly inserted, the joint is very durable and will even absorb some vibration and deflection without leaking. The ends of the pipe should be free of burrs, and the spigot should be of the beadless type.

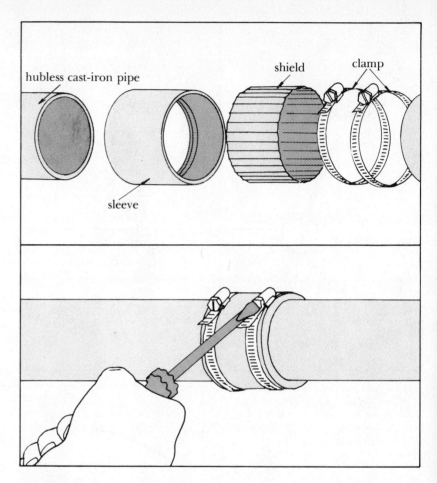

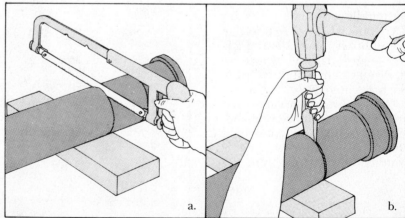

Cutting cast-iron pipe: a. Scoring the pipe. b. Breaking it along the scored line with a hammer and chisel.

No-hub joints connect pipe or fittings that are butted together in the second joining method. The pipe ends are inserted into a neoprene sleeve until they butt against an internal rim. The make-up distance for this type is only the width of the rim, about ¼ inch. A stainless steel sleeve is placed over the neoprene one and tightened with screw clamps like those on a car radiator hose. The stainless steel sleeve is slit to allow it to be tightened without kinking.

Because the joint is not much wider than the pipe, 3-inch no-hub soil pipe (toilet drain-pipe) can be used inside a wall supported by 2 × 4 studs without shimming out the wall. A special tool is designed to tighten the screw clamps to the proper tightness. Or you can use a torque wrench to tighten them to 60 inch-pounds.

Cast-iron pipe can be cut with a tool called a pipe cracker. A cutting chain is wrapped around the pipe and tightened. When the two long handles of the cracker are brought together, the pipe snaps neatly. If you use a hacksaw or chisel to cut pipe, the pipe must be supported on a 2 × 4. If the pipe to be cut has a hub, the 2 × 4 must lift it off the ground. Mark a line where the cut is to be made, and be sure it is square. The 2 × 4 should be right under the mark, allowing the short piece to fall clear when the cut is made.

With a coarse-toothed hacksaw, cut completely around the pipe about ¹/₁₆ inch deep. Then, tap the short piece close to the cut with a heavy hammer until

a crack forms and splits the pipe.

To cut with a hammer and chisel, a shallow groove is made along the mark completely around the pipe. Continue tapping the chisel in the groove until the pipe fractures.

Tools

There aren't a lot of basic plumbing tools, and many of them are used only with one or two kinds of pipe. A propane torch is basically just for copper, a tube bender for copper only. Some tools, a seat wrench, for example, are primarily for repair. Certain tools are necessary for almost any plumbing. These include at least one pipe wrench, locking-grip pliers, and a pair of large adjustable pliers. A tubing cutter is invaluable for cutting small-diameter pipe.

Pipe Wrench. The pipe wrench is designed to hold a pipe in a grip proportional to the pressure applied. The more you push on the wrench handle, the tighter the pipe is gripped. It is invaluable for holding or turning threaded pipe and fittings. Two wrenches are usually used together, one to hold and the other to turn. The drawback is that since the pipe wrench works by digging into the pipe, it will mar chrome-covered supply pipes if tape is not first wrapped around the pipe. The wrench should face in the direction in which pressure is applied.

Locking-Grip Pliers. These are similar in appearance to a pair of regular pliers, but the jaws of

these pliers lock into place. This proves invaluable in certain situations where quarters are cramped. If the locking pliers are wedged in place, they can sometimes hold the nut or faucet, freeing the hands to work on the other fitting.

Tube Cutter. Better than a hacksaw for cutting pipe, a tube cutter has a disk that rolls around the pipe under pressure. After it has cut into the pipe a little bit, you tighten a screw handle to increase the pressure. Eventually the cutter goes all the way through the pipe, making a clean cut. Most cutters have a retractable reamer that will remove the burrs on the inside of the pipe. Cutters are made in many sizes, but one that will cut pipe up to 1¼ inches handles most home plumbing jobs involving the supply lines. To cut drainpipe, use a hacksaw or pipe cracker.

Tube Bender. A tube bender looks like a large screen-door spring. You insert copper tubing inside the spring and carefully bend it with your hands, moving them from one end of the bender to the other. The bender evens out the pressure and prevents the pipe from kinking. Tube benders come in

Even with the new joints for cast iron, plastic is lighter and easier to work with. It is becoming the standard for new drain-waste-vent installations in many areas.

139

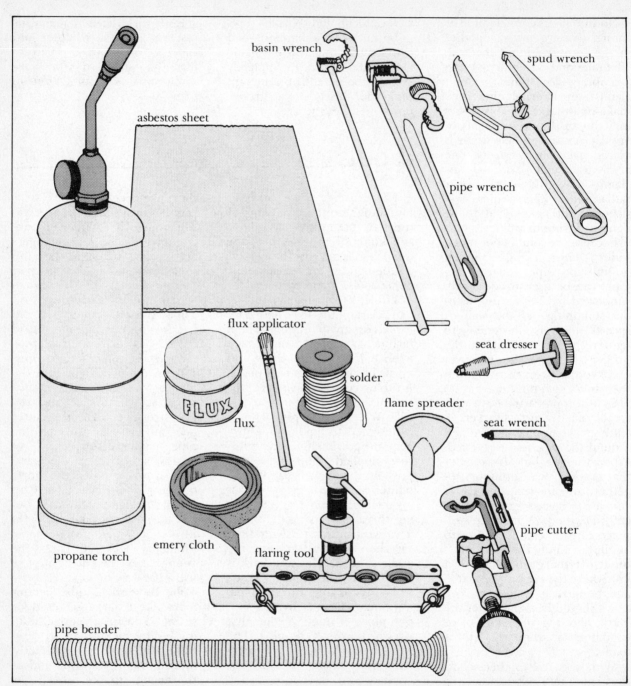

basin wrench

spud wrench

asbestos sheet

pipe wrench

flux applicator

seat dresser

solder

flame spreader

seat wrench

flux

emery cloth

flaring tool

pipe cutter

propane torch

pipe bender

several sizes, and it is important not to use one that is too big, or the pipe may still kink.

140 Propane Torch. The propane torch with its accessories—spark starter, solder and flux—is essential for working with copper pipe. With this equipment you can permanently solder all types of copper tubing to copper or brass sweat fittings. A brass nozzle with a disposable tank of propane doesn't cost much. Solder is fairly expensive, but a little goes a long way. Replacement tanks of propane are widely available.

Seat Wrench. The seat wrench allows you to remove the valve seat without removing the faucet. There are two types of seat wrench, one straight and the other bent at right angles. Both of them have one square end and one octagonal end to fit the two main types of valve seat. The straight seat remover must be turned with a wrench or a pair of pliers. If you replace a washer and the faucet still leaks, the seat has probably been chewed up. The only way to fix it is to replace either the seat or the whole faucet. Since valve seats and seat wrenches are much cheaper than faucets, it makes sense to try changing the valve seat first. It is hard to get exactly the right valve seat, but your chances are better if you take the old valve seat to a hardware store and buy one to match it.

Flaring Tool. The flaring tool, used to make flare joints, consists of a die to hold the tubing and a reamer to flare the tubing. The die has several holes to accommodate different sizes of tubing. The reamer screws down into the tube. A special fitting fits into the flared end. If the tube is square at the end, and no dirt or metal chips are present, the joint will not leak and may be taken apart and reassembled any number of times.

Basin Wrench. The basin wrench is dandy for gripping nuts under sinks and in other cramped places. You can usu-

ally get by with other tools. Locking pliers, in particular, are good at turning hard-to-reach nuts.

Spud Wrench. A spud wrench will remove large nuts. This tool

Plumbing Basics

Once you can make a leak-proof joint, plumbing is largely a matter of measuring carefully and working around and through what is already there. Plan the whole job before you figure the exact distance for each pipe. The less damage to walls and floors, the better. And, naturally, shorter runs are cheaper. If you are working with finished walls, running pipe through the joists of an unfinished basement below the kitchen may save time. Supply pipe, since it carries water under pressure, can run down and then up. Drainpipe, since it must always slope downward and must be properly vented, usually requires more thought and effort.

Measurement

To get an accurate measurement for running pipe, the amount that the pipe goes into the fitting and the space taken up by the fitting must be determined. The distance that the pipe goes into the fitting is called the make-up distance, and the space taken up by the fitting is the fitting gain. There are several ways to measure them.

The most obvious, but not always the easiest, is to put the

is useful for some sink fittings, but, as with the basin wrench, the work *can* be done with other tools, such as large channel-lock pliers, or a large pipe wrench.

pipes and fitting in place, without joining them permanently. Unless you are working with plastic pipe, this is tiresome but relatively foolproof. Don't screw galvanized steel together without pipe dope, though. It might not come apart. If you need to measure between two fixed fittings, you have to account for the make-up distance. Place a pipe directly above the fitting and overlap one fitting by how far the pipe would go in one fitting. You can estimate this distance by inserting pipe in a spare fitting. Make a mark where the other end would stop in the second fitting. When cut at the mark, the pipe will be the proper length. Of course, the fixed pipes must have enough play to allow the new piece to be inserted.

Instead of using pipe to find the length, you can use a tape measure. Insert the tape into one fitting as far as the pipe would go and measure to where the pipe would end inside the second fitting. If the second fitting is not in place, have someone hold it at the right spot and measure. An alternative method is to measure between the facing ends of each fitting and add on the make-up distance for each fitting.

Fitting gain is so standard that **141**

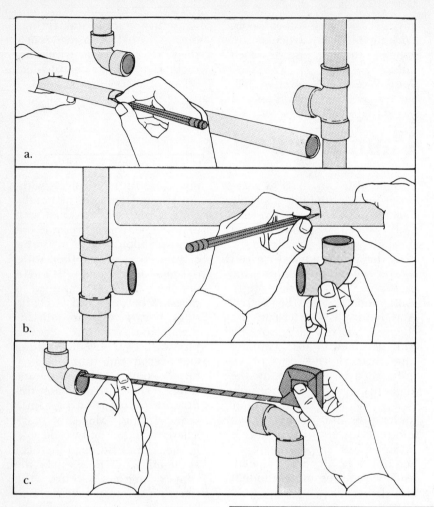

a.

b.

c.

Three ways to measure the make-up distance: a. By holding a length of pipe between the fittings. b. By holding the pipe in place while someone else holds one fitting (for making up a new run). c. By using a tape measure between the fittings.

Fitting gain—the space occupied by the fitting—is simply the distance between the faces (or ends). But where the fitting changes direction, the fitting gain is the distance from the middle of the run of pipe to the opposite face of the fitting. Note that if the angled fitting is a T, that only accounts for half the T. The fitting gain would be the same for the other angle. The straight-through fitting gain of the T—the distance face to face—would be double the two angle gains.

Support

Pipes in an unfinished basement usually run below the joists, attached with pipe hangers. Steel and rigid copper supply pipes should be supported every 7 to 10 feet. Plastic pipe should be supported at

Calculating the length of a new piece of pipe requires that you take into account the make-up distance and the fitting gain.

there are tables that give the amount for each type and size of fitting. The only trouble with these tables is that different brands of fittings sometimes vary slightly from the standard. It is best to key the measurements to your own actual run.

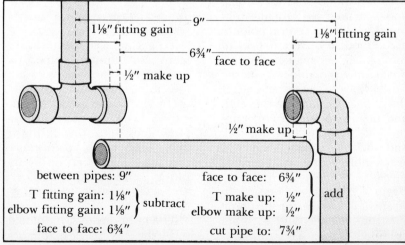

9″

1⅛″ fitting gain   1⅛″ fitting gain

6¾″ face to face

½″ make up

½″ make up

between pipes: 9″   face to face: 6¾″

T fitting gain: 1⅛″ }   T make up: ½″   } add
elbow fitting gain: 1⅛″ } subtract   elbow make up: ½″

face to face: 6¾″   cut pipe to: 7¾″

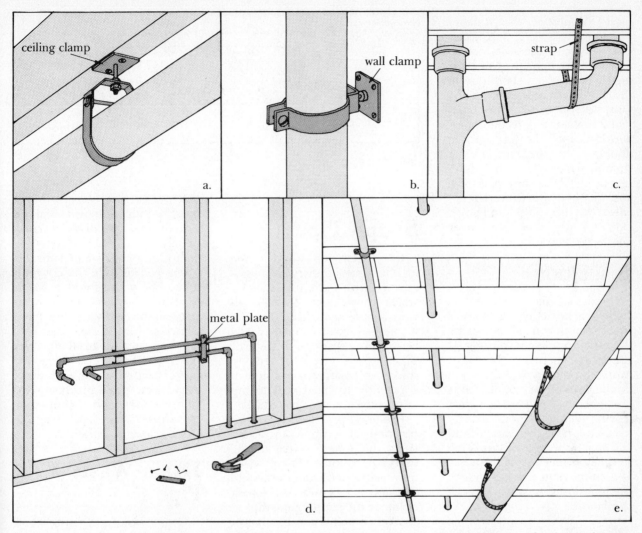

Supporting new pipes: a. and b. Hubless cast-iron pipe must be securely supported at every joint in both horizontal and vertical runs. c. Hubbed cast-iron pipe can be supported with perforated metal strap in horizontal runs. d. Studs may be notched for pipes, but metal straps at least 1/16 inch thick should cover the notches to protect the pipes. e. It's easiest to hang pipes from joists using perforated strap or special pipe straps, but you can drill holes for pipe through the center of joists.

least every 3 feet, and soft-temper copper every 16 inches. Drain-waste-vent pipe should be supported every 4 feet, or about every third joist. No-hub cast-iron pipe should be supported at each joist.

Notching Studs and Joists

Remodeling work sometimes requires that pipes run along a partition or cross floor joists. If there is no extra room, you may have to go through the studs or joists. You can notch the studs supporting a partition as long as the cut is no deeper than half the width (1½ inches for a 2 × 4). After the pipe is in **143** place, reinforce the notches with metal plates. If it is necessary to notch floor joists, cut no more than one quarter of their depth. The notch should be in the center half of the length of a joist. If you exceed this limit, nail 2 × 4s or 2 × 6s on one or both sides of the joist. These doublers, as they are called, should be 3 or 4 feet long. Holes can be drilled at any part of a joist if they are centered between the top and bottom edge. Don't locate one hole over another; stagger them.

Insulation

If part of the run is in an unheated area, such as a crawl space, you may need to insulate the pipes to prevent freezing. If the run is between the joists, insulation placed over them will do the job with no trouble. Joists are generally 8 to 12 inches high, leaving enough room to run plumbing near the flooring and still attach the batts of insulation to the bottom edge of the joists. If the pipes run across the joists, the pipes must be wrapped with insulation.

Pipe Size

Pipe size is fairly standard, although galvanized steel may require one size larger diameter than copper or plastic. The water service entrance is usually 1 inch in diameter. Hot and cold mains are usually ¾ inch. Branches to the sink are generally ½ inch. Soil stacks and house drains are 3 to 4 inches, roof vents are at least 3 inches, and branch drains from sinks and dishwashers are 1½ inches.

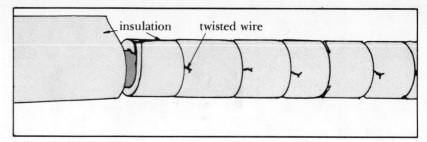

Insulating pipes.

Supply Pipe

Installation of supply pipe is fairly straightforward compared with drain-waste-vent work. In practice, there is always a little something to make it interesting, of course. It may be reaching through a tangle of pipes to the one you need to solder, or having to rip a hole in a recently finished wall to tap into a pipe you overlooked.

It is good practice to run supply pipe at a slight angle, up from the water source to the faucet or fixture. Then, water may be drained from the system through a faucet at the lowest point. If the supply pipe dips at any other point, another faucet must be located there so that the system can be drained completely.

Hot and cold water runs are often side by side for convenience, but you should leave at least 6 inches between them to prevent the cold water line from drawing heat from the hot, wasting energy. Insulating the hot water pipe (and the water heater) will save a lot of energy, too. Plastic pipes are better insulators than either copper or galvanized steel and may be placed closer together.

Drain-Waste-Vent Pipe

Drain-waste-vent installation

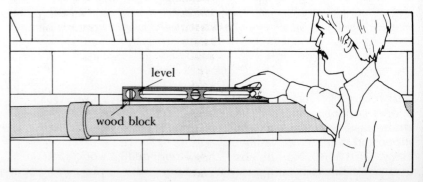

Checking the pitch of the pipe with a carpenter's level.

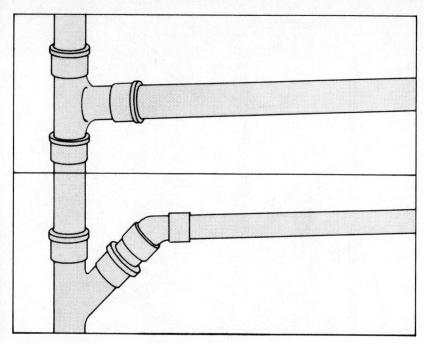

If it is impossible to run drainpipe at the correct pitch (top), run as much as you can at the normal ½-inch-per-foot drop and the rest at 45 degrees (bottom).

is more complicated than supply because the drain system must prevent poisonous sewer gas from escaping. This is accomplished by venting drainpipes to the outside air and by placing traps after each fixture. A trap is generally a U-, J- or S-shaped section of pipe. The bend in the pipe always remains filled with water. This seals the drain and prevents sewer gas from escaping into the house. Some fixtures, toilets for example, have built-in traps.

Pitch

The drainpipes must be pitched slightly to allow waste water to run out of the building. The angle of pitch and the size of the pipes are more important than with supply pipe. The re-

quired pitch is between ¼ inch and ½ inch per foot, with the optimum about ¼ inch per foot. If the pitch is over ½ inch per foot, the water may run off, leaving behind solid wastes that can eventually clog the pipe. Use a block of wood taped to a level to measure the pitch. For a two-foot level, use a ½-inch block taped at the end. If you cannot get less than ½ inch per foot in a horizontal drain run, do as much as you can at ½ inch or ¼ inch per foot and the rest at 45 degrees. There is seldom any problem with clogging in a drop tilted at 45 degreees or more.

Drainpipe Diameter

As drainpipe increases in diameter, the flow of a given

amount of water slows down. Because free-running drains depend on the scouring action of swiftly moving water, correct drain size is important. If the drain is too small, of course, clogging also becomes likely. The recommended pipe size for kitchen sink drains is 1½ inches. Two sinks on one trap require 2-inch drains. A dishwasher needs only 1¼-inch drain.

Traps

Every fixture is required to drain through a trap. Up to three sinks may drain through a single trap, but no fixture can drain through two traps—for example, if a sink on one floor has its own trap, its drain cannot connect to the drainpipe between a fixture on a lower floor and the trap for that fixture. Instead, the connection would have to be made beyond the trap on the lower floor. Some fixtures, like toilets, have built-in traps. They do not require, indeed are not permitted to have, any other trap. No trap is necessary if the waste connection is open to the air, as is the case with a washing machine that drains into a wash sink. Naturally, the sink will have a trap.

The diameter of the trap must be the same as that of the pipe that runs to it. If the drain is of 2-inch pipe, the trap and following pipe must also be 2 inches in diameter. This prevents buildup of solid wastes that could clog the trap.

Cleanouts

Cleanout plugs must be installed at every point on the drain where a turn of more than 45 degrees is made and at any **145**

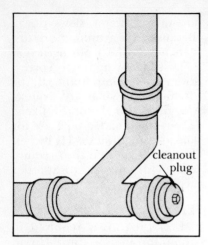

A cleanout plug allows you to remove clogged material without taking the pipe apart.

place where it would be difficult to insert a snake through the trap and into the following drain. A cleanout must also be installed if there is a run of more than 45 feet of horizontal pipe following the previous cleanout. A cleanout is required before the drain passes through the foundation. A final trap is often required there as well. Such a trap is the only exception to the rule that a drain may not pass through two traps.

Venting

After waste water leaves the fixtures, it travels a distance in the horizontal branch drain, then drops into the large vertical pipe, called the soil stack, or if no toilets drain into it, the waste stack. Often, all fixtures in a home drain into the soil stack, although if fixtures are on opposite sides of the house, there may be more than one stack. **146** The stack carries waste down to

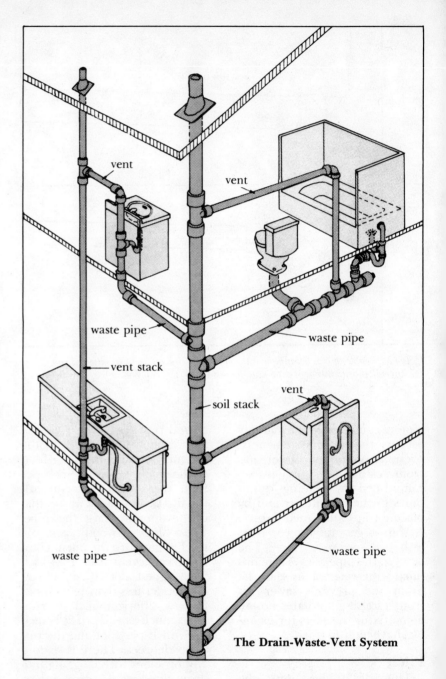

The Drain-Waste-Vent System

a horizontal drain in the basement or crawl space of a house that takes the waste through the foundation of the house, either

to a sewer pipe or a septic tank. The stack also goes straight up through the roof and is open, or vented to the outside air. Vent-

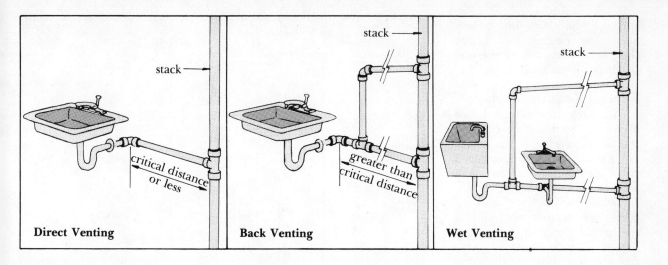

Direct Venting   **Back Venting**   **Wet Venting**

ing prevents air pressure from building up in front of draining waste and slowing the flow. Venting also allows air to enter behind the waste water, preventing water in a trap from being sucked out by siphoning. The vent also prevents sewer gas from concentrating in the stack. If a trap does fail, most of the gas will escape through the vent, rather than into the house.

Direct Venting

If a fixture is within a certain distance of the stack, it can simply be connected to the stack. This is called direct venting. The allowed distance is known as the critical distance and is equal to 48 diameters of the drainpipe, with a drop of no more than one pipe diameter. The trap cannot be any closer to the stack than two pipe diameters.

There is a reason for all this. If the vent is too far from the trap, the trap will not function properly. With standard sink drainpipe of 1½ inches, the critical distance is 48 times 1½

inches, or 72 inches. The measurement is from the part of the stack nearest the trap to the trap weir. This is the point where water in the trap overflows into the drain.

The drain cannot drop more than one pipe diameter below the overflow level in the trap because a greater drop would risk emptying the trap by siphoning. If the stack were located closer than two pipe diameters to the trap weir, water could be pulled out of the trap by suction.

Back Venting

Every fixture must be vented within the critical distance. If the stack is farther away than that, a separate vent must run to the stack from a point within the critical distance. This is called back venting. The vent must enter the stack at least 6 inches above the flood level of the highest fixture connected to the stack to prevent the vent from filling with water if a fixture overflows. The vent rises verti-

cally from the drain until it is above the fixture. Then, it runs at a normal drain pitch of ½ inch to ¼ inch per foot. An alternative to back venting is to run the vent straight up through the roof, creating a vent stack.

Wet Venting

If several fixtures other than a toilet are on a branch drain, some local codes do permit all the fixtures that require back venting to use a common vent. The usual practice, however, is to vent each fixture within its critical distance. The use of a single vent is called wet venting because some of the venting takes place in a drain that also carries water. Make sure your local code allows wet venting. It is easier than running individual vents, but not if an inspector makes you do the whole job over. If you are relocating your sink, venting can be a big factor. A new sink across the room from the stack can mean not only running a drain   **147** through the floor, but a vent above the ceiling, too. Either that, or a new stack all the way up through the roof.

Special Requirements

The stack must extend 1 foot above the roof and be open to the air. If you live in the northern part of the country, it is a good idea to have a vent of at least 3 inches diameter, even if the stack itself is less than that. This prevents ice from building up and closing off the vent. There is nothing wrong with making the top of the vent larger than the stack, but the stack itself must be at least as large as any branch that enters it. A branch cannot get smaller as it runs downward toward the stack. The obvious reason is that decreasing size could cause clogging. A branch drain can get larger, though. If a toilet that requires a 3-inch drain is near the stack, only the drain following it must be 3 inches. A sink farther from the stack on the same branch could be drained with 1½-inch pipe as far as the toilet. But if the toilet rather than the sink were farther away from the stack, the entire branch would need 3-inch-diameter pipe.

Only special fittings, called sanitary fittings, may be used in drain-waste-vent runs. They are specially designed not to impede the water flow or allow buildup of solid matter. Long sweeps are preferable on angle fittings for the same reason.

Remodeling

The reason it is harder to change existing plumbing than

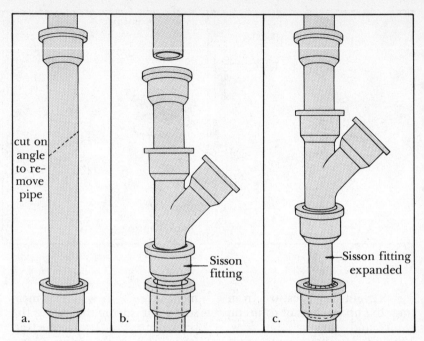

cut on angle to remove pipe

a.

b. Sisson fitting

c. Sisson fitting expanded

A Sisson fitting enables you to tap into cast-iron pipe without disrupting the entire run. The outside diameter of the fitting is the same as the inside diameter of cast-iron pipe, allowing it to drop inside the pipe of the run you are tapping into. After the new fittings are installed, the Sisson fitting is pulled up into place and sealed.

to install plumbing while a house is being constructed is that in the former case you don't know exactly where the pipes are located in the walls or floors, and you must support the existing pipes while making an addition.

A stack is required to be exposed at some point, even if only in a crawl space or basement. A stack usually runs straight up, although one will sometimes angle around some unseen obstruction inside the walls. Get someone to listen at the wall while you bang on the exposed pipe to try to locate the stack. Or you can measure the stack's distance from a wall in the basement and then measure from the same wall on the floor where you need to locate it. Supply pipe can often be traced from an existing fixture. But at some

point, you have to chop into the wall or whatever to see if the pipes are there.

If you need to tap into a cast-iron drain, a cleanout plug is an easy place to do it. Try to use no-hub joints if you have to tap into the stack itself. If your local code does not permit no-hub, you will have to use a Sisson joint, which is an expandable joint. In either case, make sure the stack is well supported above the section you cut out. Once the new T or Y joint and the Sisson joint are in place, the

148

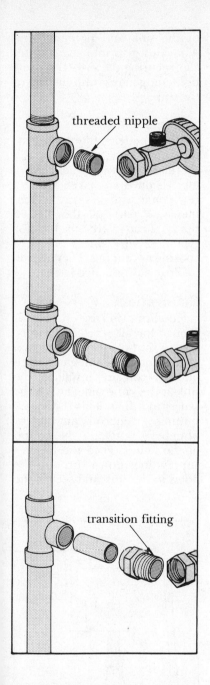

The supply stub-outs are the parts of the rough plumbing that project through the finished walls. Variations include: a. Short-nipple stub-out used with galvanized steel pipe. b. Projecting stub-out used with steel pipe. c. Projecting stub-out used with plastic or copper pipe. The cut-off valve is common, but ordinary elbows could be substituted.

the same as working with supply pipe, except for the size.

Stub-Outs

The stub-outs are the last part of the rough-in plumbing. The installation of fixtures and appliances is done after finish work on walls, floors and cabinets is complete. When the rough-in is complete, cap all the stub-outs or stick a rag into the openings to prevent anything from falling in. In the case of drainpipes, this will also keep sewer gas from escaping into the house. The caps are purchased along with the rest of the plumbing supplies in the dimension of the pipe you buy. The caps don't need to be soldered or solvent welded unless water will be in the new lines before final hookup.

Water Supply Stub-Outs

If the stub-out will be visible, it may be chrome plated like the rest of the finish plumbing. But with kitchen plumbing this is seldom important since sinks are usually installed in a counter top and the pipes leading to the sink are hidden in the cabinet below. If it is easier to bring the stub-out through the wall a couple of feet to one side or the other of the faucet, you can. The supply lines are run from the stub-out along the wall to the faucet. You can use the same kind of pipe as behind the wall.

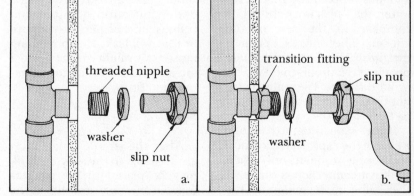

Transition fittings to connect the drainpipe to the stub-out: a. The close nipple allows the slip nut to be screwed tight to join the drainpipe to threaded galvanized pipes. b. The threaded adapter is welded or soldered to plastic or copper stub-outs to allow the drainpipe to be screwed to it with the slip nut.

Sisson is expanded to the proper length and then sealed with lead and oakum. Working with copper or plastic drains is

Whether the stub-out terminates in a threaded or smooth fitting depends upon what it is to join. The height of the stub-out is not important because it is easy to vary the length of the vertical pipe to the faucet. But a shut-off valve should be located on the supply line under the sink.

Drain Stub-Outs

Use only drain fittings with drain stub-outs, and make sure the stub-out angles up toward the fixture. The pipes from stub-out to sink are joined with compression fittings. The first piece of pipe is called the drain-pipe and usually joins the drain stub-out right at the wall.

Some type of transition fitting must join the stub-out to the drainpipe. If the drain is threaded galvanized steel, a piece called a close nipple is screwed into the drain fitting. This piece gives the threaded slip nut the necessary means of connecting the threads. After the close nipple is screwed into the drain fitting, the slip nut and then a flexible compression ring are slipped over the drain-pipe, which is then inserted in the nipple. When the slip nut is tightened over the nipple, a watertight joint results. If the drain uses sweated copper or welded plastic connections, a threaded adapter is welded or soldered to the drain fitting. The compression ring and slip nut are placed over the drain-pipe and tightened as with the galvanized pipe. The stub-out and drainpipes for the sink should be 1½ inches.

Finish Installation

Before you do the final installation of sinks, traps, faucets, and any appliances that draw water, the finish work should be complete in the rest of the kitchen. The only exception is the finish flooring, which some people save until the last, to avoid damage. The walls might not be painted, but they should be up.

If the water is on, turn it off. Remove the caps from the drain and supply stub-outs only when the final connection is made. If the stub-out is soldered, the water must not only be turned off, it must be drained from the line.

150   After the final connection is made, check for leaks. The rough plumbing in the walls should have already been tested under pressure. Compression fittings must be perfectly square or they will leak. Flexible tubing must be straight for at least 2 inches where it leads to a compression fitting.

Sinks

After the strainer and faucet are fastened to the sink, the sink may be placed in the counter top. Set the sink carefully in the hole in the counter on a ¼-inch bead of plumber's putty. Slide at least eight clips into the four channels that rim the underside of the sink and tighten them. The clips grip into the counter top, securing the sink. But over-tightening may crimp the rim of the sink.

Faucets

Most modern faucets are of the single-lever type, although there are plenty of dual control models on the market. Quite a few come with a spray attachment as part of the faucet. Spray heads are useful for cleaning vegetables prior to cooking or canning. They are valuable in a productive kitchen.

Connections

Hooking up the supply is similar for all types of faucets. First, a shut-off valve is attached to the hot and cold water stub-outs. If you are installing the sink at the same time, attach the faucet to it first. This is done by putting a generous amount of plumber's putty on the botton of the faucet. Feed the faucet's supply lines down through the holes in the sink and secure the

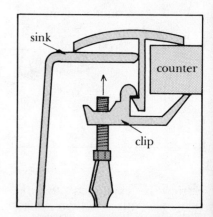

Interlocking clips hold the sink tightly against the edge of the counter top.

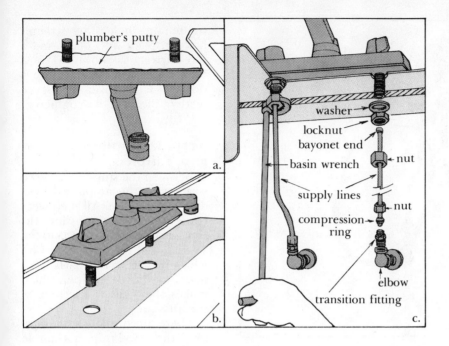

plumber's putty

a.

b.

washer

locknut

bayonet end

basin wrench

supply lines

compression ring

nut

nut

elbow

transition fitting

c.

Installing a faucet in the sink: a. Coat the bottom with a generous layer of plumber's putty. b. Put the fixture shanks through the holes in the sink. c. Tighten the locknuts with a basin wrench and complete connections.

goes through each hole. If there is a spray head, the supply to it attaches under the spout; the spray is controlled by a diverter valve in the faucet body. The spray head itself is not part of the faucet body, but rests in a fitting to one side of it.

Single Lever Faucet

There are several types of single levers, but the installation is standard. Instead of two holes, the single lever requires three. One, in the center under the lever, is for the supply lines and the spray hose. The spray head rests in one of the end holes. The fitting for the sprayer also serves to secure the faucet body to the sink. The other end hole is for a bolt, washer, and hex nut. The only problem comes if you want to

faucet underneath with a washer and hex nut. If the faucet has a spray head, it too is held in place with a hex nut. Connect the two faucet supply lines to lengths of copper or plastic tubing by using compression fittings. Attach the other end of the tubing to the shut-off valves, also with compression fittings.

The branch supply line for a kitchen sink is usually ½ inch, while the supply lines attached to the faucet are usually ⅜ inch. The shut-off valve accepts the ½-inch tubing at one end and the ⅜-inch tubing at the other. If you don't use a shut-off valve,

you'll need a reduction fitting to make the connection.

Dual Control Faucet

This type usually requires two holes in the sink, one under each handle. One supply line

A dual control faucet with a spray head requires three holes in the sink directly under the faucet and a fourth to one side for the spray head.

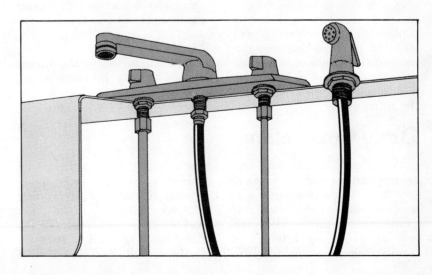

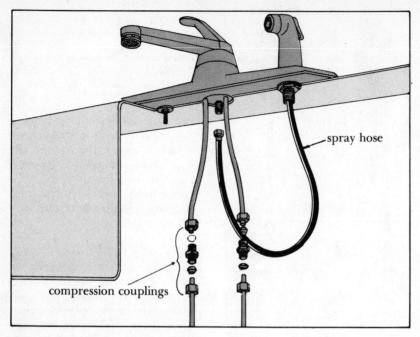

compression couplings

spray hose

Installing a single lever faucet with a spray head involves straightening the copper supply tubes to fit easily through the center hole of the sink, setting the faucet in place and inserting the sprayer hose through the hole next to the faucet lever. Then attach the supply tubes and the faucet hose.

replace a dual control faucet with a single lever but keep the old sink. If the sink only has two holes, you have to drill out the middle hole. It isn't easy, but it's the only way.

Drain Connections

The finish connections for kitchen drains are the bright spot in the drain-waste-vent system. All the connections are compression fittings. They are not as prone to leaking as compression-type fittings for the supply lines, and there is no venting to worry about in the finish stage. The sink is the main fixture. If there is a dishwasher, the waste water can pass through the sink drain, using the sink's trap. This is an example of wet venting.

Strainer

The strainer and the faucet should both be installed before the sink is attached to the counter top. The strainer is made of several parts that screw together. The strainer body is set in the sink on an ⅛-inch bead of putty. Under the sink, a rubber washer and large metal washer fit over the protruding strainer body. Thread the locknut onto the strainer body, hand turning until it rests on the bottom of the sink. For final

tightening, hold the strainer body in place with pliers and a screwdriver, as shown. Have a helper use a hammer to tap a dowel or screwdriver against the teeth of the locknut to tighten it.

Trap, Drainpipe and Tailpiece

Between the stub-out and the strainer are the last pieces of the drain installation. All the pieces connect with compression fittings. A tailpiece connects to the strainer and the trap. The trap, which may be in two parts, connects to the drainpipe, which makes the final connection to the stub-out.

There are two kinds of traps. One, the swivel trap, is a simple J and can be angled if the drainpipe and tailpiece are not perfectly in line. Another version of the same type consists of a U-shaped trap with an elbow that makes the connection to the drainpipe.

The other kind of trap is fixed. It has the same shape as the U and elbow combined. But since it is in one piece, the strainer and the drainpipe must be perfectly in line. There is no reason to use this type if you are doing your own installation. It just means aggravation. If you encounter one already in place, you can remove it by loosening the tailpiece and swiveling the trap and drainpipe 45 degrees. Then remove the trap from the drainpipe.

These drain pieces are chrome covered. The slip nuts may be tightened with large adjustable pliers or pipe wrenches. Whichever you use, protect the

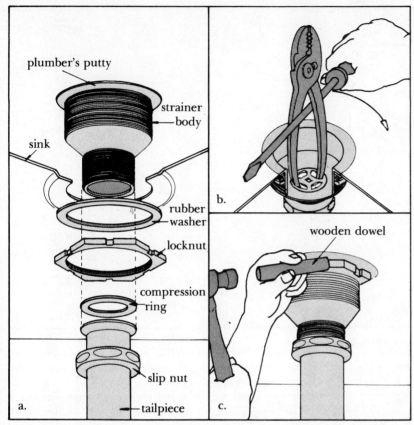

line to the dishwasher. The water supply line should be ½ inch, the recommended diameter for a kitchen sink branch.

The washer itself is equipped with a flexible drain hose, terminating in a threaded female screw coupling of the garden-hose type. The shut-off valve should have a comparable male thread. It can be attached to any convenient place.

Installing a sink strainer: a. Fitting the washers and locknut over the strainer body once it has been seated in the sink. b. Holding the strainer body in place with the handle of a pair of pliers. c. Tightening the locknut by hammering it with a wooden dowel.

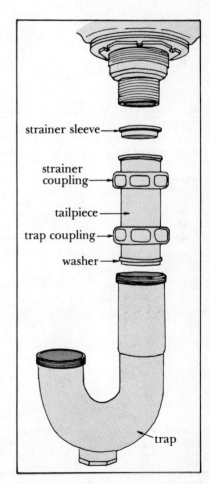

Fitting the tailpiece and trap to the strainer with compression couplings.

finish of the slip nuts by wrapping a couple of layers of tape around the pliers or wrench.

Dishwasher

A dishwasher is usually installed near the sink to make hookup of the water and waste lines easier, but this is not essential. The electrical and plumbing connections are made after the cabinet has been installed. The best course for electrical connections is to put in a receptacle and plug in the dishwasher. This makes removal for servicing easy.

The water supply taps into the hot water line leading to the sink, giving the maximum water temperature. The hot water line is cut and a T installed. The tap should be made ahead of the sink shut-off valve, so that the sink can be independent of the dishwasher. Another shut-off valve should be part of the

153

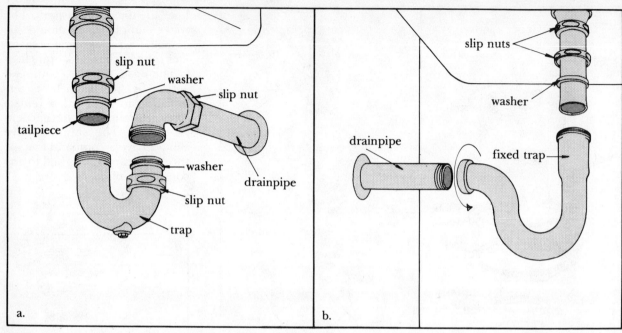

Replacing traps (above): a. Just loosen the coupling nuts to remove swivel trap. b. A fixed trap is removed by loosening the tailpiece from the drain and swiveling the entire trap.

Installing a dishwasher (below): a. Attach the hot water supply below the shut-off valve for the sink. b. Attach the washer drain hose to a special waste T.

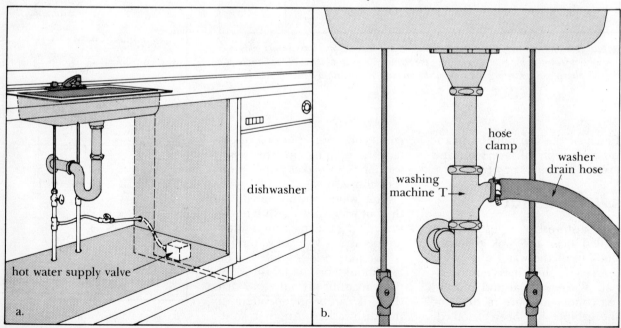

154

Drain Connection

The drain connection is made above the sink's trap. The connection is made with a washing-machine T. Most washer drain hoses terminate in female-thread garden-hose couplings. The T should have a male thread. But if the hose is smooth on the end, it can be attached with hose clamps to a T with a smooth side connection.

A washing-machine T can replace the tailpiece entirely. The top has a lip that is pulled against the strainer and strainer sleeve by the threaded slip nut as described under "Trap, Drainpipe and Tailpiece." The bottom of the T is smooth and fits into the trap. This is the end that can be cut to size. It is joined to the threaded trap with a slip nut and washer.

If you don't want to replace the entire tailpiece, you can use a waste T. The bottom of the waste T fits into the trap just as a tailpiece does. The top is threaded like the trap to accept the smooth tailpiece. Since the bottom of the tailpiece is smooth, it can be cut to allow the waste T to be inserted.

A Garbage Disposal?

A garbage disposal is a handy item, but it is designed primarily for organic wastes, the heart and soul of a good compost heap. Because recycling organic material is essential to gardening that is not dependent on pesticides and manufactured fertilizers, a disposal has no place in the harvest kitchen. Even in an urban setting, it is possible to reuse kitchen wastes without causing odors or attracting any critters. The trick is to fast-compost the food scraps in a well-sealed container with sawdust or straw.

That's all there is to kitchen plumbing. When it's finished down to the faucets and sink hookup, your kitchen is finished too.

Lighting

What's important about lighting? It affects the quality of work you do in the kitchen and, because of that, the way you feel about the work. Good lighting can help make your kitchen a comfortable, productive place. On the other hand, poor lighting can make an otherwise terrific design seen harsh, uninviting and awkward. It can cause

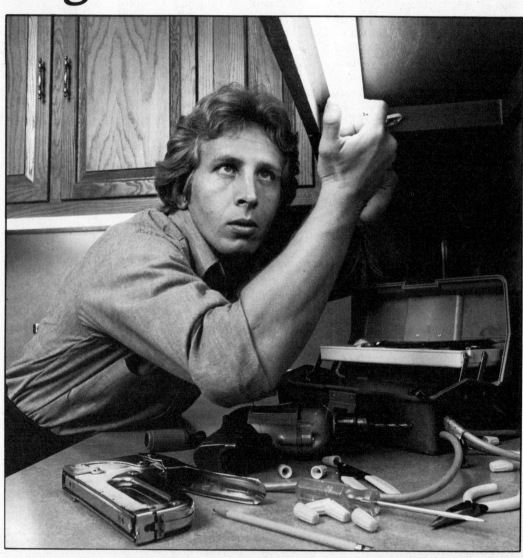

fatigue and eyestrain.

Good lighting doesn't have to be complex. The main idea is to provide the kitchen with a comfortable level of general illumination and additional light at work areas. The general or background light should be fairly even because it is tiring to look at things that differ drastically in brightness. You'll want some variation, though, to keep the kitchen from appearing flat and uninteresting.

The variation is provided by accent or mood lighting, which can be anything from spotlights highlighting a textured wall to a stained glass window. Accent lighting is used to create a mood in the kitchen, and while this aspect must be secondary to the need for a well-lit cutting board, for example, it is important. Especially if the kitchen will be used as a general gathering place, it should look warm and inviting.

Good lighting needn't mean track lights and illuminated ceilings, either. The sun provides excellent light. Give some thought to the placement of windows and doors as a source of light. A skylight may be able to brighten the otherwise dim recesses of a kitchen. Outside light is never dull because it is always changing, with the weather, the seasons and the time of day. But because outside light is bright, the side of a kitchen away from windows may seem dark. A light-colored wall facing the windows will help to brighten it up and will even brighten the whole kitchen when the sun goes down and the lights come on. If you find that you need extra lights for the dark interior part of the kitchen during the day, put them on a separate switch. Then they can be shut off at night to keep the lighting balanced.

The tendency in recent years has been toward more and more light in the kitchen, both for background light and for task lighting. It adds up to a lot of energy. Twenty-four percent of all electricity is used for light. In many cases, excessive lighting has contributed to the somewhat uninviting look of many modern kitchens. If your kitchen will be a place where people spend a lot of time, you certainly want it to look comfortable and appealing.

How Much Is Enough?

The reason for the ever-increasing levels of lighting in the kitchen avowedly has been to prevent eyestrain resulting from dim light and to avoid sharp contrasts in the level of light. Research confirms, however, that too much light causes fatigue and eyestrain more easily than too little. While you certainly want a comfortable level of background light, the important thing is to have good light at the working areas, glarefree and without sharp shadows. After all, you are trying to make a harvest kitchen, not a laboratory. Laboratories are notoriously overlit, anyway.

How much is enough?

A favorably located window can provide an excellent source of daytime light, as well as a refreshing view.

Whether you need two or three overhead fixtures to provide adequate general lighting depends on the size and the layout of your kitchen. You can find the comfortable level by varying the wattages of the lamps after the fixtures are in place. Dimmer switches allow you to vary the light at will. It is more energy efficient to use a single high-watt bulb than several low-watt ones. One 100-watt bulb produces 50 to 75 percent more light than four 25-watt bulbs. This favors single-bulb fixtures, but it is still better to use several fixtures for background lights—keeps the shadows from being too harsh.

The rest of the lighting is either task light for local work areas, or mood lighting. Despite the somewhat negative connotation of the latter, with its images of chrome fixtures and walls awash with light, lighting is critical to the character of a room. But the quantity depends entirely on your tastes.

The most important lighting, finally, is where you do the work. Where vegetables are chopped, dough is rolled or preserves are made, adequate lighting is essential. This light may be provided in several ways, but it should not be left to the background lighting. How much depends on the placement as much as on the wattage. Two 100-watt spotlights mounted on the ceiling would provide no more light to a work area than two 20-watt fluorescent tubes mounted over a counter.

Different Kinds of Light for Different Jobs

The trick in planning the light is to make all sources work together. The system must be flexible enough so that fixtures can be turned off easily when they are not needed. The mix of different kinds of light should be pleasing to the eye. Work areas must be well lit. Whether it is day or night, the balance of light should be good.

Natural Light

The view out the windows is so important that it's easy to forget the light coming in. But the shifting patterns of light from outside can be an asset as long as you plan well. If daylight provides an important part of the background or task lighting, you may have problems when clouds pass, or even when the seasons change. Other sources of light must be available.

It's free. You never have to turn off the skylight. But, again, planning is important. If you live in cold climes, bear in mind that you would lose a lot of heat through a north window in winter, so unless you want your kitchen to double as an artist's studio, try to avoid putting windows in the north wall. Remember that all windows let heat escape at night. To get the most out of the free daylight, make sure the windows are sealed tight, and use storm windows or Thermopane glass. Although heat goes out at night, light generates heat when it strikes a surface. If the windows can be arranged so that light falls on masonry, brick or stone, the heat will be stored until nighttime. This will result in a net saving of energy (and money) if you cover your windows with insulating shades at night.

That's good news. Now, some of the problems. Daylight is higher in blue light than either incandescent or fluorescent lamps. Be aware of this in balancing the light. If the kitchen gets a lot of daylight and the dining room is lit by artificial light, or vice versa, the food may look different in each room. As the amount of daylight changes, the quality of light will change.

Light drops off quickly as you move away from a window. It's not uncommon for the natural light to be ten times dimmer across the kitchen from a window than at the window. The answer to this is to position windows and doors on at least two walls. If possible, paint the wall across from the windows a light color. This reflects the light that does reach the wall, raising the general level of illumination. Another thing you can do to keep the level of natural light high, if you happen to have no second floor over the kitchen, is to put in a skylight.

Morning light in the kitchen or eating area is usually pleasant. If you can, position win-

Concrete, brick and stone store energy from sunlight and release it in the form of heat.

dows to let in some morning light. Afternoon light, on the other hand, can be hot and uncomfortable. If windows will face west, provide some means of shading them.

When positioning windows, remember their main function, providing a view of the outdoors. A view of the garden can make life in the kitchen more pleasant. If children have a favorite play area near the kitchen, put a window facing it. The person who has to keep an eye on them while cooking will have an easier time of it.

Fluorescent or Incandescent?

Fluorescent fixtures produce about twice as much light per watt as incandescent ones. They also last seven times longer and give off much less heat. Eighty

percent of the energy produced by an incandescent bulb is given

off as heat. That's important in a kitchen where the stove produces so much heat. Ready to switch?

Incandescent also has some advantages. The main one is its warm tone, which casts a cozy glow into the room. Fluorescent can't match this, even though there are several shades available. Warm white or deluxe warm white blend well with incandescent lighting. Incandescent light is also easier to control. Dimmer switches allow in-

A skylight can brighten the interior of a dark room.

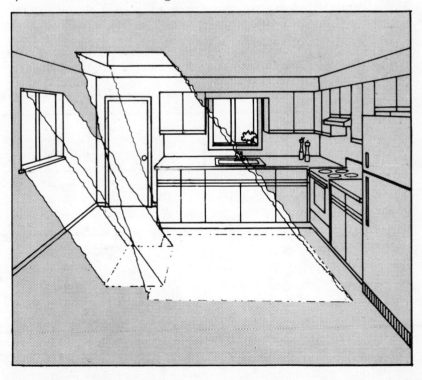

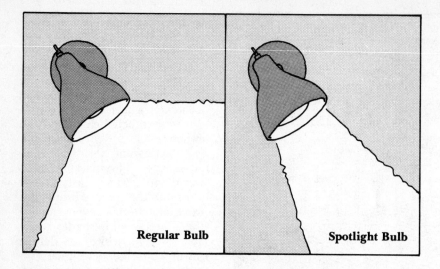

Regular Bulb

Spotlight Bulb

Straight fluorescents are available in lengths from 9 to 60 inches, ranging from 6 to 100 watts. Two-foot, 20-watt and 4-foot, 40-watt tubes are the most common. Circular tubes for special ceiling fixtures are available.

Incandescent bulbs for standard sockets range from 15 watts up to 300 watts. The usual range for a single incandescent ceiling fixture is between 100 and 200 total watts, produced by one to three bulbs. A fluorescent ceiling fixture will total between 40 and 80 watts.

Background Light

Most of the light in a kitchen used to be provided by one overhead fixture. The trouble was, it cast shadows where the work was being done, the worst place, and made the corners of

candescent bulbs to be dimmed at will, making it easier to balance the light and control mood. Dimmers for fluorescents are expensive and bulky. Fluorescent fixtures emit a slight hum. Fixtures with old tubes or defective starters sometimes flicker.

Spotlights and other fixtures that cast a narrow beam of light are always incandescent. A regular bulb in a spotlight fixture will cast a soft beam, while a special bulb with a reflector surface will cast a sharper, more focused beam. Fluorescent tubes are usually used for valances, cornices and counter-top or under-the-counter fixtures.

Some of the many types of ceiling fixtures available.

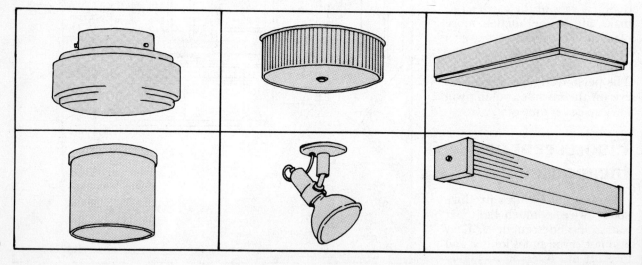

General background illumination is provided by the wall bracket on the left, which keeps the side of the room away from the window from being too dark, and by three spotlights throwing light onto the ceiling.

large kitchen, should be plenty. Background light may also be provided by other means. Spotlights aimed at the walls or ceiling, or used as overhead lights with regular bulbs, will add to the general light in a kitchen and add an unusual lighting touch if handled well. Recessed fixtures and light panels in the ceiling can add to the background light, as can lighting strips along the walls or ceiling. These strips should be mounted behind boards, called faceboards, to prevent the light from being directly visible.

the room dim. Nowadays, kitchens are often too bright.

All you want from the background lighting is a pleasant amount of light, enough to read the labels on cans, enough to get around, but not so much that you want to leave the room.

One overhead fixture is probably not enough. Two, or even three in an L-shaped or

Single-tube fluorescents located under wall cabinets make excellent task lighting. The overhang of the cabinet keeps them from being seen directly, and it can even provide a convenient mounting surface.

Lighting strips are usually single-tube fluorescent fixtures. The fluorescents can easily be hidden behind 6- to 10-inch faceboards, and being long, they require fewer fixtures and fewer electrical connections.

Single-bulb fixtures are often mounted every 3 or 4 feet to provide extra background light to a particular area. Such an arrangement is useful for lighting the dim interior away from the windows. When used in this manner, the fixtures should be on a separate switch from the other background lights. When the sun sets the extras can be switched off, maintaining balance.

Local or Task Lighting

Task lighting is the most important to the person who works and spends time chopping and canning vegetables, baking, and preparing meals. If the task lighting is planned skillfully, the general level of illumination may remain moderate while plenty of light is available where it counts.

Put the switches where the light falls. That way, you don't have to run around to turn on the light after you have walked to the work area and are ready to start.

Counter tops located under cabinets are most easily lit with single fluorescent tubes mounted under the cabinets. The overhang of the cabinets makes spotlights impractical. The fluorescents may be fastened to the front edge of the cabinet or to the wall, but they

Recessed fixtures are flush with the ceiling. They are unobtrusive sources of background light.

must be shielded so that they cannot be seen directly. A 20-watt, single-tube fixture is about 18 inches long, and one of these for every 3 feet of counter space will produce a brightly lit area.

Cooking surfaces require light. If you get a ventilation hood, lighting will be built in. A stove hood is worthwhile because it removes heat and moisture as well as cooking odors. If you have to do without one, put a recessed fixture or a light panel over the stove. Two spotlights of 75 watts each, one on each side, will also provide shadow-free illumination.

Recessed fixtures vary from single bulb sockets up to large units holding four 40-watt fluorescent tubes. A fixture with two 75-watt or three 60-watt incandescents or two 40-watt

fluorescents would provide adequate light for the cooking surface.

Soffit Fixture

If the sink is lit with ceiling fixtures, the requirements are

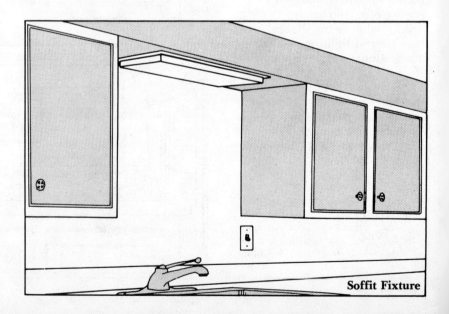

Soffit Fixture

Lighting adds a decorative touch: a. A spotlight emphasizes a large plant. b. An old-fashioned brass lamp casts a warm glow.

the same as for the stove. Sometimes, however, the sink is flanked by cabinets with an overhang above the sink, called a soffit. The soffit can accommodate fixtures. These will be closer to the work surface than a ceiling installation and provide more light. Two 60-watt incandescents or a 40-watt fluorescent will do the job.

Work areas that don't have cabinets above may be lit in a number of ways. Any of the above approaches could be adapted. But many other kinds of fixtures are available, from lighting strips that stick to the bottom of a cabinet and plug into a receptacle to single-bulb recessed fixtures that may be aimed where you want.

Accent Lighting

All the lights in your kitchen add to the overall character of the room in some way. But those lights whose main purpose is to highlight a feature of the room itself or to produce an effect with light are known as accent or mood lights.

While you may not want chrome spots throwing pools of light across the ceiling, there is nothing wrong with using light intentionally to emphasize aspects of the harvest kitchen. Beautiful hand-hewn beams might be nearly invisible without extra light on them. The idea is to keep the lighting in harmony with the kitchen, not the other way around.

The way shadows fall on objects helps us to see them in three dimensions. Accent light can take advantage of this ef-fect. Highly directional light picks out more surface features than even light. Lights directed along the surface of a wall will emphasize the texture of the surface.

One or two spotlights on a large floor plant or on the objects on a shelf can provide a decorative touch. Stained glass definitely sets a tone. A cabinet with a stained glass door or panel can be lit from the inside.

Even the type of fixtures affect mood. A brass fixture hanging low over a table casts a warm, intimate light that makes you feel at home in the room. At the other extreme, chrome fixtures and cool hues tend to produce detachment.

Test Your Lighting Plan

You're making your plan. You've figured out how much background light you need and pinpointed the areas that need task lighting. You're making educated guesses about where to use fluorescent and incandescent light and what types of fix-

163

tures to use. Guesses? There's a better way. Make up an experimental kit. This will give you an idea of what the light will really look like.

Buy two or three portable lamps with metal shades. These come with clamps that allow them to be placed practically anywhere. They are great to have anyway. Get a couple of lengths of heavy-duty extension cord and a variety of light bulbs. You'll need several different wattages, say 60s, 100s and 150s. Also get a couple of spot bulbs of the indoor type. They are cone shaped and have a mirrored backing to direct the beam. With this equipment you can test the effect of most of the incandescent fixtures your plan calls for, local or general. You can even get a good idea of what effect a spotlight would give, though the beam from the spot bulb in the portable lamp will be less concentrated than one thrown by a proper spot fixture.

If you really want to do it right, make a fluorescent test fixture too. Fasten three single-tube fluorescents to a 6-foot length of 1 × 6, 6 inches apart. Mount a junction box to the board and run cable to each of the fixtures. Join conductors of the same color to conductors from heavy-duty (number 14) extension cord using wire nuts. The cord needs to be only a couple of feet long, terminating in a standard plug. Wire it so that the hot (black) conductors from the fixtures correspond to the smaller of the two prongs of the plug. If the prongs are the same size, don't worry about it; use either. If you use a three-

wire plug, attach the ground conductor to the bare conductors from the fixtures, using a wire nut. Your test fixture will be fully grounded. The components are reusable. With this you can see how valance, wall-bracket, cornice, and under-the-counter lighting would look. If you remove the tube from the

middle fixture, the other two will still work, giving you a 2½-foot spacing. You'll also need a stepladder and a gullible helper.

Now, with the portable lamps clamped into position and you and your helper holding the fluorescent test fixture, you can test the effect of your plan before putting it into action.

Installation

Installing the fixtures is part of the finish stage in the kitchen. The cable should be in place and the electrical boxes secure. Usually, the walls and cabinets are up, though painting may wait until later. The procedures for making changes at an existing outlet are the

same whether you are replacing old fixtures or putting fixtures in new places. Some information on placement of electrical boxes is included here, but the work is done earlier, as part of the wiring.

Some lights serve as both general and task lighting, possi-

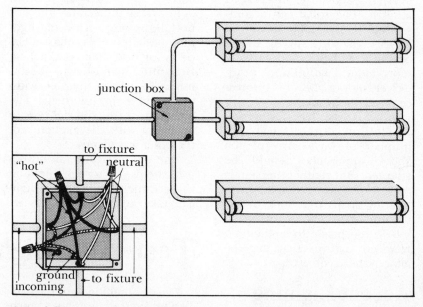

Several fixtures can be controlled by a single switch if they are wired together at a junction box.

bly even as accent lighting. The important point for installation is not what the light is for, but where it is located.

There are just two things to consider when you get to the point of actually mounting the various fixtures—support and wiring. The details of running cable and making connections are given in "Basic Wiring." That will get you as far as the outlet box. The support is often a matter of screwing the fixture onto the outlet box.

Naturally, there are some other things involved for the various kinds of fixtures. When several fluorescent fixtures are controlled by a single switch, it is often simpler to use one junction box to feed the fixtures, terminating the cable at the sheet-metal box that serves as a base for the lighting tube. Incandescent fixtures, though, are almost always attached to an outlet box.

Surface-Mounted Ceiling Fixtures

Ceiling installations are straightforward for either incandescent or fluorescent fixtures. In both cases, the fixture is supported by a metal outlet box mounted flush with the ceiling surface. The fixture is actually supported by the box, of which there are two main types. One contains a threaded stud, the other has two screw holes. In the first type, the fixture is placed over the stud and secured with a cap nut. Sometimes there is another fitting between the stud and the fixture. In the

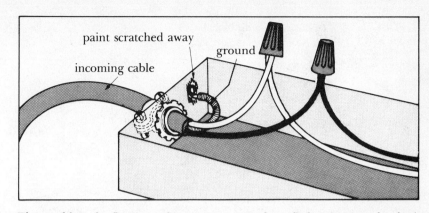

The metal box of a fluorescent fixture can serve as the outlet box. The branch cable is attached to it with a cable clamp. Attach the ground wire to the box at a nearby screw—but first scrape off the paint under the screw to assure a good connection.

second type, a strap is screwed into the holes in the outlet box. A nipple screws into a threaded hole in the strap. The fixture is placed over this nipple and fastened as before with a cap nut. Sometimes long mounting screws, instead of a nipple, fasten the fixture to the strap.

Both fluorescent and incandescent fixtures can be fastened to the outlet box, although fluorescents may also be screwed to structural members for additional support.

Whether the fixture itself is a standard ceiling light, a spotlight or a hanging fixture, the connection to the outlet box is the same. This means that you can make some changes in the lighting without doing any rewiring.

Track Lighting

Even track lighting can use an old outlet box that served a discarded fixture, if the box is in the right location. The strip itself must be fastened to clips

that screw into framing members. Track lighting works by having a metal track inside the frame that is electrically live. No matter where the lights are positioned, they draw electricity, sort of like a trolley car.

The outlet box is at one end of the track. Over it is screwed a box adapter and a connector that makes the electrical connection with the track. After these are positioned, draw a line beginning at the center of the connector, indicating where the track will be located. Use a rule as a guide. Find framing members and screw mounting clips into them. (Obviously, the location of ceiling joists may influence the location of your track.) Line the clips up on the line you drew. Push the track wires into the connector and force the track over the clips. There are usually side screws in the clips that you tighten when the track is in place. Snap the two-part cover over the connector.

Because the live track is par-

165

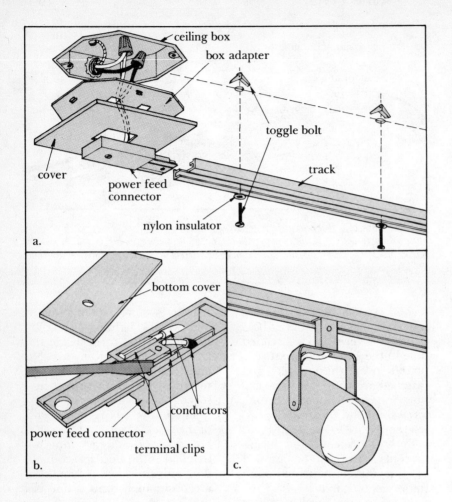

ceiling box

box adapter

toggle bolt

cover

track

power feed
connector

nylon insulator

a.

bottom cover

power feed connector

terminal clips

conductors

b.

c.

Installing track lighting: a. The track, which carries the power, is attached to the ceiling or wall, then connected to the wiring at an ordinary ceiling box using a power feed connector. b. In the most simple setups, a bit of insulation is stripped from the conductors, which are then thrust into a terminal clip in the power feed connector. Using a screwdriver to ease the clip's tension a bit makes insertion easier. c. Any of a wide variety of light units can be clipped into the track and positioned anywhere along its run.

sure that the light will not be visible directly.

The fixtures should be attached to the ceiling, either with screws into the joists or with a nipple attached to the outlet box. If you secure a fixture to the outlet box, put an additional screw or two into the joists.

The fixtures may be wired from an adjacent outlet box, or electrical cable may be run from a junction box to each fixture, provided that it is secured to the fixture with an approved electrical connector.

You only need one switch for the entire cornice, so the fixtures may be wired up together. Use one junction box to feed every three fixtures. The wiring sequence is the same as for the experimental fixture, above, except that instead of hooking up to a plug, the fixtures hook up to the source cable. Running more than three fixtures from one box would make it almost impossible to cram all the conductors and wire nuts into the box without damaging them. Even if you could, don't! The box would overheat.

If you need more than three

tially exposed, it should not be used where children might be able to poke something into it.

Cornice

A cornice installation runs along the ceiling near the wall. It consists of single-tube 20-watt fluorescents placed end to end and covered with a faceboard.

Secure the faceboard to the fixture with metal angle brackets. Since these fasten (with sheet-metal screws) to the bases of the fixtures, the brackets

must be attached before the fixtures are placed. The faceboard may be secured to the brackets before or after the fixture is up. If you decide to do it after, make sure that the lighting tube is not in the fixture when you're putting it up so that you'll have room to reach the wood screws for the faceboard. The center of the tube in a finished installation should be less than 3 inches from the wall or the faceboard bottom. The faceboard should be at least 6 inches wide to en-

angle bracket

at least 6″

3″

3″

faceboard

at least 6″

Keep the fluorescent tube away from the wall and the bottom of the faceboard to aid light diffusion and to keep the tube from being seen directly.

fluorescent fixture has a transformer, called the ballast, that boosts 115-volt current to the level required to light a fluorescent tube. The ballast is inside the fixture and looks like a black box. If you string the cable through the fixtures, connect each fixture with threaded conduit nipple fastened to each fixture with a locknut. The

fixtures, run the last cable through another outlet box, which then becomes the source for more cables. The wiring sequence in each box is straightforward. The black conductor of the source is fastened to all the other black conductors with a wire nut, the white source to all the whites, the neutral source to neutrals, ground to grounds and to the box.

Another possibility is to run the cable right through each fixture from the outlet box. This requires heat-resistant THHN or equivalent cable. Conductors may not pass the ballast unless they are heat resistant. Every

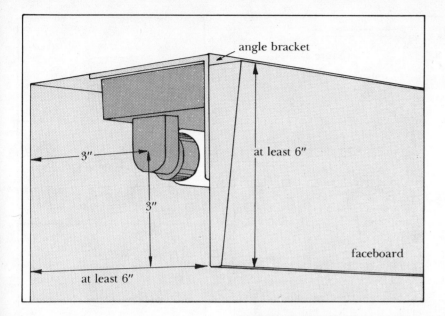

A cornice installation positions the light at the ceiling along a wall and conceals the bulbs or tubes from view with a faceboard.

167

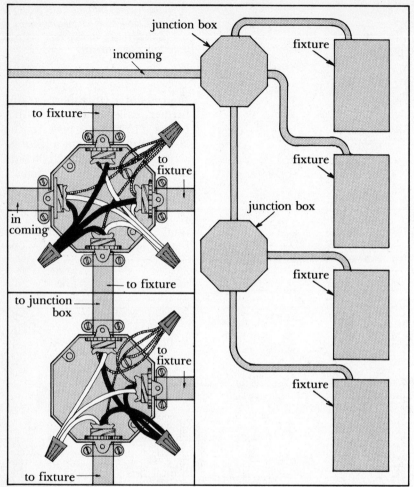

Overcrowded electrical boxes can be avoided by using extra junction boxes to supply power to a bank of fixtures.

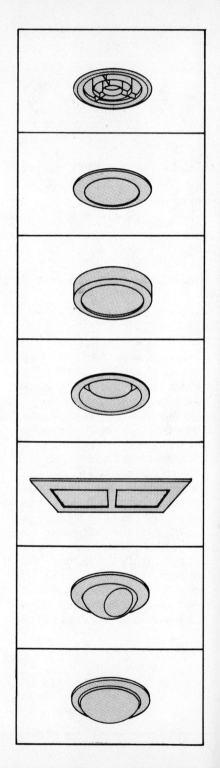

cable goes through the conduit.

How many fixtures do you need? Again, this is somewhat a matter of opinion. It depends on the other light in the room and on what you like. You should use 40-watt tubes since they are high up. They may be spaced anywhere from right next to each other to every 2 or even 3 feet. Rig up a test with fixtures attached to a long board. If you can mount it temporarily or have some helpers hold it up, you'll get an idea of what you need.

Some of the many types of recessed fixtures that are available.

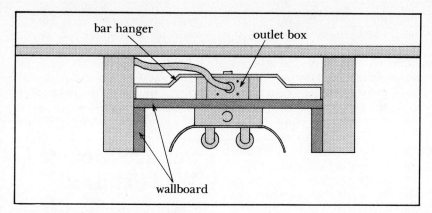

Outlet box for a fluorescent fixture positioned above it and attached to the joists with a bar hanger.

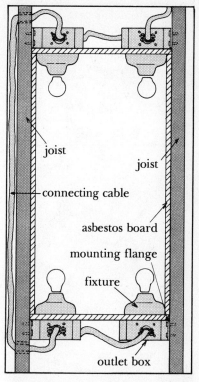

Four incandescent fixtures provide the light for a built-in recessed unit lined with asbestos board. The outlet boxes for each fixture are attached to the joists with mounting flanges.

Recessed Fixtures

There are two main types of recessed fixture, store-bought and built-in. The store-bought variety is designed to be mounted more or less flush with the surface of the ceiling. Electrical connections are outlined in the manufacturer's specifications.

Store-Bought Fixtures

Many, many kinds are available. The range of styles and types is a little bewildering. Shop around. And make sure the ones you buy really suit the kitchen you have in mind. It's easy to get sucked overboard by the impressive variety.

Built-In Fixtures

The built-in kind of recessed installation may consist of standard fixtures mounted in a finished space between the joists. The space may be square or rectangular, with either fluorescent or incandescent fix-

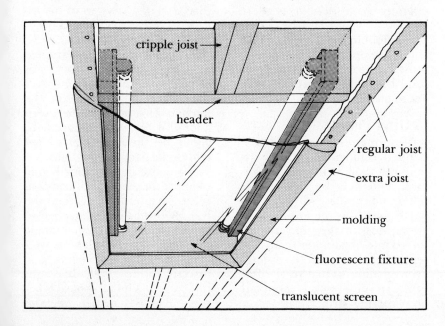

A large installation where part of a joist has been removed to accommodate two fluorescent fixtures.

169

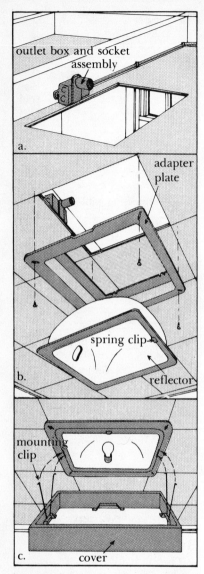

a.

adapter plate

spring clip

b.

reflector

mounting clip

c.   cover

Installing a recessed ceiling fixture. The adapter plate replaces a ceiling tile and, once attached to furring strips, supports a socket assembly, a reflector and a cover. The mounting clips for the cover allow it to be pulled down enough to replace bulbs.

tures. If you use incandescent, the entire cavity should be lined with adhesive asbestos board.

For fluorescent fixtures, it may be boxed in with wallboard. You'll need to run nailer strips between the joists so there's something to nail into.

If there is enough room, you can mount the outlet boxes above the cavity with a bar hanger. If there is not enough room above, position each outlet box against the joists with a flange. Mount the box against the wallboard that runs between joists, with the box facing the cavity. Or you can run cable from a junction box located nearby if an outlet box is not required.

The light is finished off by nailing molding around the edge to hold up a glass or plastic diffusing screen, or a louvered surface.

A really large installation consisting of single- or double-tube fluorescent fixtures requires structural changes. You cut out part of a joist and box in the opening with double headers the same width as the joists. Then double the two joists that frame the opening. The cut joist must be supported at each cut until the headers and doublers are in place.

Ceiling Panels

Most manufacturers of suspended ceilings offer light assemblies that fit into their ceilings. You may be able to get other units that will fit, but make sure the dimensions are right. Most of the units are inserted into an adapter plate that reduces the size of the ceiling grid opening to that of the fixture. An outlet box is mounted on a furring strip and a socket assembly attached to it. A metal reflector with a hole for the socket fits into the adapter plate. A translucent cover fits over the assembly. Fluorescent models are available. The outlet box should be installed according to the manufacturer's instructions.

Surface-Mounted Wall Fixtures

Incandescent fixtures can be mounted on walls the same way as in ceilings. They are fastened to the outlet box with a capnut. That is all the support you need for single- or double-bulb fixtures. Several single-tube fluorescent fixtures are sometimes attached to walls and shielded from direct view with a faceboard. Mounting procedures for these follow.

Valance

A valance is a short curtain placed across the top of a window. A light can be placed behind it, right above the window, usually to illuminate the drapes.

Valances are commonly associated with living rooms, but they can find a place in the kitchen. In a small kitchen with a lot of windows, a valance light could be the best way to get additional background light.

A valance light is usually one or more single-tube fluorescent fixtures mounted against the wall. A faceboard is attached to the fixtures with metal angle brackets. The faceboard prevents the lights from being seen directly and bounces some light downward. The faceboard is between 6 and 10 inches wide and

soffit

face-
board

Valance lighting mounted on the soffit. Usually, the fixture is mounted directly on the wall and shielded—as is the case here—with a faceboard mounted on metal angle brackets.

no closer than 2 inches to the middle of the fluorescent tube. The top of the faceboard is flush with the top of the fixtures to allow plenty of light to spread along the ceiling. There should be at least 10 inches between the ceiling and the top of the fixture.

The angle brackets fasten to the faceboard with wood screws and to the fixtures with sheet-metal screws. If the fixtures are mounted over curtains, the fluorescent tubes should be about 2 inches beyond the curtains. Mount the fixtures on a strip of wood to position them away from the wall, over the curtain. Either a single 2×2 nailed to the wall or a 2×2 with a 1×2 nailed over it should allow the proper distance. The strips are nailed to the wall surface. The fixtures screw into the strips.

When the fixtures are shimmed out with wood strips, they cannot attach directly to the outlet box. Instead, a short length of cable must run between the box and the fixture, attached at each end with standard electrical connectors. This means that you must drill a hole through the wood strips before attaching them to the wall. Make the hole large enough for a connector where it will rest against the fixture.

Wall Bracket

A wall bracket is a valance with no window under it. There are two varieties of wall brackets, a high bracket and a low bracket. Any installation where the distance from the floor to the bottom of the faceboard is 6½ feet or greater is of the high type. The top of the fixture should be flush with the top of

the faceboard and no closer to the ceiling than 10 inches.

If the bracket is lower than 6½ feet, it is of the low-bracket type. Low brackets are good for local or task lighting. Under-the-counter fixtures are of the low-bracket type. The fixture should not be lower than 2 inches above the bottom of the faceboard. The fixture may be mounted directly to the outlet box, or it may be attached to the wall or studs and serve as the outlet box itself. In that case, the cable is secured to the fixture with a standard electrical connector and attached to the fixture conductors with wire nuts.

Over-the-Counter Fixtures

Over-the-counter lights may be installed either on the wall or directly on the outer edge of the cabinet. When mounted against **171**

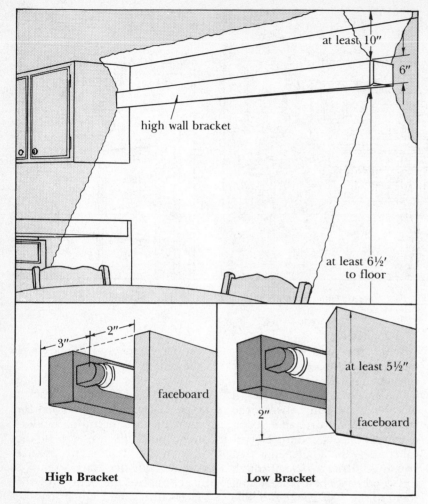

Installing wall brackets.

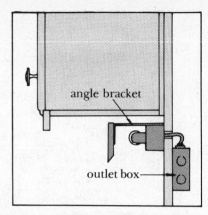

Installing a low-bracket over-the-counter fixture.

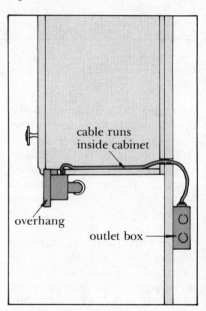

Mounting a fluorescent fixture on the cabinet overhang.

the wall, the lamp is shielded by a 1 × 3 faceboard attached to the fixture with angle brackets. The base of the fixture is placed against the wall, as with the wall-bracket type of mounting. The outlet box is in the wall behind the fixture.

When mounted on the cabinet, the fixture is shielded by the overhang of the cabinet. Screw the base of the fixture to the overhang so that the tubes face the wall. Rather than try to find room for the outlet box, locate a junction box in the wall and run cable from it along the bottom of the cabinet to the fixture. Secure the cable to the fixture with an electrical connector.

A series of such fixtures—as with valance or cornice lighting—can be wired by using one junction box to feed up to three fixtures. All the fixtures in a given run of counter may use a single switch.

Automatic Lights

When you start to think about it, you realize that the average kitchen is full of automatic

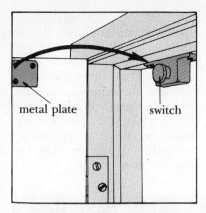

metal plate   switch

An automatic light will switch on whenever you open the pantry door.

lights. Refrigerators have them; ovens and dishwashers often do. In appliances, they are either built in or not. There's not much you can do once you have the appliance. But pantries, closets and cabinets can be rigged with a switch that turns on a light when the door is opened.

You can rig up an automatic light without any special wiring. Screw a small unit into the door frame and plug it into a nearby receptacle. On one side of the unit is a socket for the bulb and on the other a small button that remains pushed in as long as the door is closed. When the door opens, the button is released and the light goes on. Simple. Of course, if you don't happen to have a receptacle inside the pantry or cabinet, you'll have to wire that up.

Just don't leave the door standing open.

Rewards

All the planning and wiring you do mean that you will have a harvest kitchen that's a pleasant place to be in, to work in. There's no justification for ripping up walls and floors, then failing to make the effort to install proper lighting where the day-to-day cooking and seasonal food processing will be done. It's easy to do, and it doesn't cost much.

By all means, light your harvest kitchen properly.

Ventilation, Heat and Comfort

As you plan and build your kitchen, keep in mind that it must be properly heated and ventilated to be a really comfortable place to work. The humidity shouldn't be too high, fresh air should slowly replace the old air and the temperature should be moderate throughout the room no matter what the season or time of day.

You've got to make several things work together to create this comfort. You need good ventilation, not only from windows and doors, but, just as important, from an exhaust fan located over the stove. Good ventilation gets rid of the heat and odors that are a by-product of a working kitchen. It keeps the air fresh and the environment comfortable.

In cool weather, some kind of heating is essential, either as part of your home's central heating or as a separate kitchen unit. Take stock of your situation and develop a comfort system that will work in your kitchen. You may simply decide to use central heating throughout the house, including the kitchen, or you may decide to combine the central heating with a wood stove or a wood-burning range. If you do that, make sure you can easily close off the central heat to the kitchen. Another option is to have wood for your main heating system and use individual thermostatically controlled units to keep the house warm when the fire is out.

Options and Work Sequence

The floor plan of your kitchen should include such things as the location of new heating pipes. If the stove will be relocated, the final location should be influenced by such things as how hard it will be to run ventilation to the outside. By now the basic layout, including such considerations, should be complete.

Whatever new wiring and plumbing are going to be in your kitchen should also be installed as far as the stub-outs and outlet boxes. The final connections come later. Now is the time for putting in or relocating any ventilation ducts, heating ducts or pipes. If a wood stove or range is part of your plan, you'll have to install a flue or put an existing one into working condition.

In a major renovation, the walls will probably have been removed. You'll do the heating and ventilation right after wiring and plumbing. Before you replace the walls, put insulation in exterior walls and a vapor barrier between the insulation and the room. These keep your heating bills down and prevent moist kitchen air from damaging exterior paint or even sheathing or studs.

For a more modest effort, try to integrate any new heating or ventilation with new plumbing or wiring to minimize damage to walls. If you are using central heating, you may only have to route ducts or pipes to a few new locations to accommodate the floor plan.

If you want to insulate the exterior walls, you can have insulation blown into the wall cavity or you can remove the interior surface and install batts. For a masonry wall, the operation could require studding out a wall, installing batts or foam insulation between the framing members and then covering all with wallboard. Balance the total expense of installation against the long-range savings in heating costs. Good insulation will save you money. But even if you decide against insulation, go ahead with weather stripping. It doesn't cost much and is a good investment.

Weather stripping is applied to the edges of window sashes and doors in the finishing stage. Good weather stripping prevents infiltration of cold air into the room. This not only improves the insulating quality of the whole wall, it prevents drafts. Weather stripping is just as important as insulation in assuring a comfortable, energy-efficient kitchen.

Heating

There are three main kinds of central heating: steam or hot-water, electric, and hot air. Both steam and hot-water systems are made of pipes, usually steel, but sometimes copper. The actual connections and hardware are covered in "Kitchen Plumbing," while the specifics of the systems are covered here. Electric units, similarly, are installed in the same manner and with the same tools as other fixtures described in "Basic Wiring." That's where you'll find information on how many units to run on a circuit, what size cable to use and so on. The actual steps in wiring up an electric heater are included here.

Electric heaters are part of the central electrical system. If **175** your house has electric heat, it doubtless has at least 200-amp service. If your electrical system cannot handle full electric heat but has some extra capacity, you may still use electric units as local space heaters. This can be a welcome option if you build a new room for your harvest kitchen. You may find it easier to wire in electric baseboard units than to tie the room into the central heating. Or the central furnace may already be working at capacity.

Forced hot-air systems are the most common kind of central heating system. In both gas- and oil-fired versions, air is heated in the furnace and blown to various rooms through the heat-ing ducts. Running the ducts is described in this section.

In all central-heating systems, the placement of the registers, radiators, or baseboard units is done as finishing work with the walls in place, patched and painted and with the baseboard molding installed. For electric or hot-water baseboard units, you can install the molding af-terward, since the heating unit actually takes the place of some of the molding.

There are other ways to heat your kitchen: solar and wood. The sun can add appreciably to the heat in the room, especially where windows are placed to let the light fall on masonry. If you don't have an expanse of masonry to store the heat, though, the temperature may rise to uncomfortable levels. You'll also need insulating panels over the windows at night to hold in the heat radiated by the storage medium.

You can heat your kitchen with a wood range or a wood stove. A wood range is a cookstove while a wood stove is a heating stove (though the flat top of a wood heating stove can be used for certain cooking jobs). In the sections on installa-tion the term "wood stove" is used loosely to refer to either a wood stove or a wood range.

A wood range can make your kitchen into a cozy gathering place on cold winter days. Un-like a gas or electric range, a wood range stores heat and radiates it slowly long after the fire is out. In summer, the heat of a wood range may be un-wanted. If you have a big room, you may be able to have both a wood range and a more conven-tional type. Or put the wood range in a laundry room or on an underused porch. Add sim-ple counters and shelves, keep all your canning equipment there, and you'll have a summer kitchen.

A good-quality cast-iron wood stove is another good source of heat for a harvest kitchen.

A summer kitchen adjoining the main kitchen provides space for storage of canned fruits and vegetables. During the canning season, the room can be devoted to food preservation without dis-rupting the normal functioning of the kitchen.

Well-designed units burn for a long time with a minimum of tending, continue to radiate heat if the fire is low or out, and restart easily. If you want to take advantage of the heat of a wood stove or a wood range, but you don't want to be tied to keeping the stove or range burning day and night, an independently controlled heater will be better than central heating as a back-up. If you're committed to a wood heater or range, you really need no backup unless you'll be away from the house for days at a time during cold weather.

than oil, gas or electricity. If you have a woodlot, wood heat costs little more than your time and the amount you spend on gas and upkeep for a chainsaw. For some people, the ritual of attention that wood heat requires is part of the pleasure. And there is no denying it, wood heat is very pleasant.

If you decide on wood heat, get a good heating unit. It will give you more even heat, more heat per log and more safety. Get a solid cast-iron stove and expect to pay more than a few hundred dollars. You may have to settle for a secondhand wood range. There's not a lot that can go wrong, but try to make sure it works properly before you pay.

Wood Heat

When you're dreaming about your harvest kitchen and a big wood range, it's easy to imagine a scene like this: Hot muffins come out of the range, done perfectly (because the hot air from the firebox circulates all around the oven, providing the even heat that's best for bread); there is a faint, pleasant hint of wood smoke in the air, which mingles with the smell of sausage and griddle cakes cooking; someone comes stamping out of the snow and stands gratefully beside the range.

It can be like that, and a wood stove can provide a similar atmosphere with less tending. But wood stoves and ranges do require time and attention. Wood must be cut and split into pieces. These must be fairly small for a range. Ash must be shoveled out every few days and hauled out of the house. Pieces of wood and ash must be cleaned from the floor. At least once a year the chimney and stove must be

cleaned, for efficiency and safety.

Wood stoves and ranges must be located far enough from flammable materials so that there is no danger of fire. Smoke must be vented from the house safely. This can be done through a sound masonry chimney or through a double-walled, insulated metal flue.

On the plus side, logs are cheaper, calorie for calorie,

Installation

The first step in locating a stove in your kitchen is to estab-

You'll need an ash bucket and a box for split wood to keep the area around your wood stove clean and neat.

A sound masonry chimney is hard to make. You should have the assistance of a competent mason.

Concrete-Block or Brick Chimneys

Brick or concrete-block chimneys are considered the best. Properly constructed, a ma-

lish where the flue will run. If there is an old chimney in the kitchen, even if it's plastered up, there's a chance you can use it for the flue. The flue is the vertical part of the venting that runs through the house and out the roof or, sometimes, up the outside wall of the house. You may be able to vent the stove through a fireplace. Some heating stoves are designed for this.

You have three venting options. You can use an existing flue, you can run metal chimney pipe, or you can build (or have someone build) a masonry **178** chimney. Unless you are confi-

dent of your ability, the latter option should be left to a competent mason who has built chimneys before.

If you want to put in your own chimney, use insulated pipe. It's not difficult to install, and it's perfectly safe. It is quite expensive but not as expensive as having a brick chimney constructed.

Check for leaks in the chimney by blocking the flue opening. Mark where smoke escapes. This works best with a good airtight stove that won't smoke up the house too much while you're checking.

mark each leak

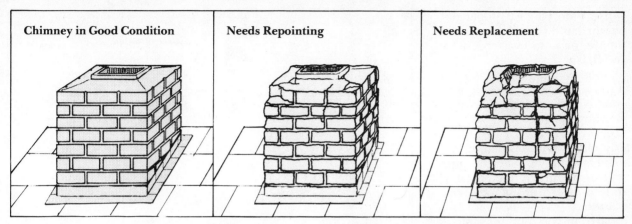

Chimney in Good Condition · **Needs Repointing** · **Needs Replacement**

Locate old flue openings by tapping the wall with a mallet and listening for a hollow sound at the opening. Make sure you have located all such openings before you fire up a new stove.

sonry chimney will last as long as the house. Nowadays, chimneys are installed with ceramic flue linings inside. The smooth surface offers less resistance to the smoke than brick and mortar and is not likely to leak smoke or, worse, fire.

One problem with *old* brick chimneys is that they were constructed without flue linings and the old mortar may be crumbling both inside and out. Chimneys without ceramic linings are frowned on by many building inspectors. But if the mortar in yours is in good condition, you can use it safely. To check, build a fire and have someone stuff rags or a straw-filled bag into the top of the chimney. Any smoke coming through the chimney means leaks. Look at the cap on top of the chimney. The mortar should be in good condition. Shine a powerful flashlight down the opening. If the flue is in good condition there won't be any gaps visible and the mortar will not be crumbling.

It is possible to repair minor

flaws, but again, if you are in doubt, get a mason to look at it. A misjudgment can cause your

house to burn down. Major reconstruction is an expensive proposition, but even a small job

179

you can do yourself might not be worth it if the chimney is still unsafe, or is so declared, after you finish.

Another thing to check, even if the inside of the chimney is in good condition, is that any previous openings to the flue have been properly sealed off. Properly means with nonflammable material. Many an old stovepipe hole in an unused flue has been stuffed with newspaper and plastered over—a real fire hazard if you put in a stove downstairs and start a blaze. Look carefully at that "free" flue you've discovered for your stove. It may be serviceable, but if you don't check well, it could cost you your house.

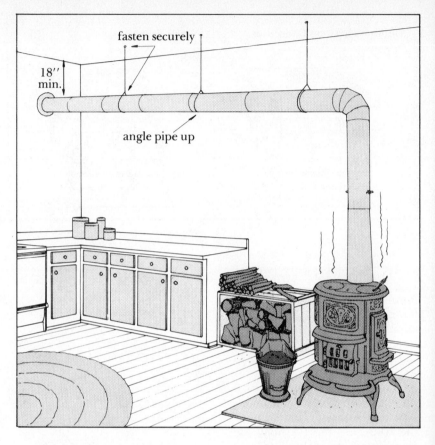

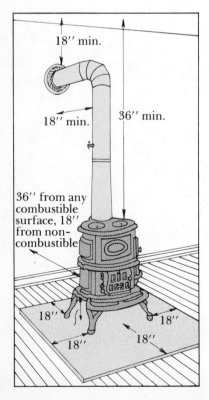

Locate the stove a safe distance from any combustibles.

Locating the Stove or Range

Locate your stove or range at least 36 inches from unprotected flammable material. If the flammable material is shielded, it may be as close to the stove as 18 inches. The shielding may be stone, bricks, asbestos board or sheet metal. Sheet metal or asbestos board must be 1 inch from the flammable material to leave an

A long run of stovepipe must be moored securely, yet be easily dismantled for routine cleaning. This vital maintenance must not be neglected.

air space, and air should be able to circulate through the space.

Place a layer of brick or stone on the floor and locate the stove on top of it. The brick or stone should extend beyond the stove at least 18 inches on all sides, to protect the floor from heat and sparks. The rule of thumb is that no flammable material should ever be so close to the stove that it becomes too hot to touch comfortably.

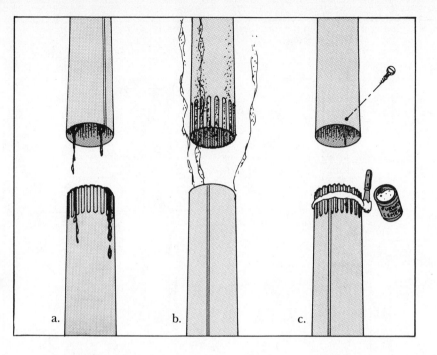

Several ways to assemble stovepipe: a. With the crimped end up, you may get creosote leaks. b. With the crimped end down, you may get smoke leaks. c. With the crimped end up and the joint sealed with furnace cement, you'll have no leaks.

can actually cause more creosote to form. It slows down the smoke, giving it a chance to cool before it leaves the flue, and smoke forms creosote as it cools. Slow-burning airtight stoves produce more creosote than fast burners, but there is always some creosote. If there is a problem with leakage, the solution is to cement the seams with furnace cement. This makes the removal of pipes more of a production, however.

Insulated Chimney Pipe

This is the kind of pipe to use if you are doing it yourself. Make sure you get pipe that is

The actual placement of your stove will depend largely on where it is practical to run the chimney. If the chimney is located on an outside wall, you *can* place the stove toward the middle of the room, running stovepipe across the room to the chimney flue. But the long run of stovepipe will quickly collect creosote deposits, becoming a safety hazard and a maintenance burden. Put in a long run if you are willing to trade extra installation costs and a regular cleaning chore for the extra heat. Better to keep the stove and flue in close proximity.

When installing stovepipe, point the crimped end away from the stove. This is the same as for ventilation or hot-air heating. Some people install their pipes the other way, crimped end toward the stove, on the theory that any creosote that drips down will not run to the outside of the pipe and drip on the floor. But pointing the crimped end toward the stove

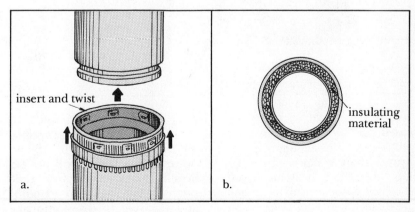

insert and twist

insulating material

Insulated chimney pipe: a. A twist-lock connection joins pipe securely. b. A cross-sectional drawing of insulated pipe.

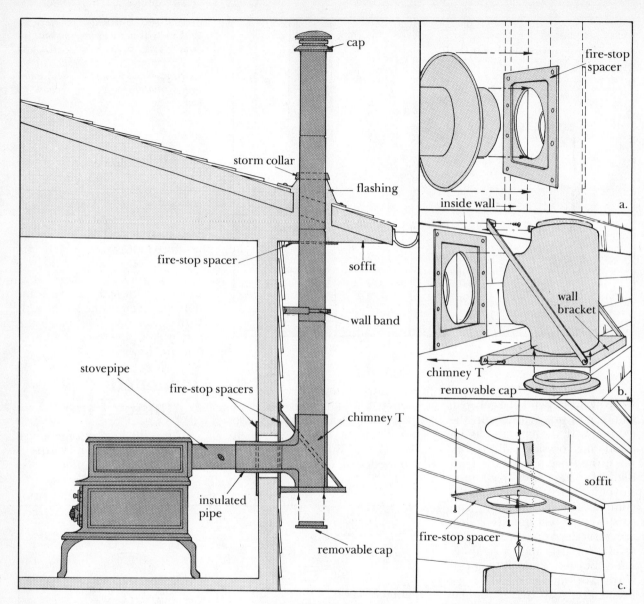

cap

fire-stop spacer

storm collar

flashing

fire-stop spacer

soffit

inside wall

a.

wall band

wall bracket

stovepipe

chimney T

fire-stop spacers

chimney T

removable cap

b.

insulated pipe

soffit

removable cap

fire-stop spacer

c.

Installing insulated chimney pipe to extend through the wall and up the outside of the house: a. A hole must be cut through the house wall and a fire-stop spacer installed. b. A wall bracket is installed outside to support the chimney T. c. A hole must also be cut through the soffit and roof and a fire-stop spacer installed there.

rated for "all fuels." This kind will stand much higher temperatures than exhaust pipes for gas hot water heaters, which look the same. Insulated metal pipe has a twist-lock connection at each end.

Locate the chimney if possible on the downwind side of the house and where it will not be near tall structures or trees that might cause the wind to eddy and the flue to draw improperly. Make the run as vertical as

182

possible for bends heat up and wear out faster than straight runs. Bends also slow down the smoke, allowing it to cool and form creosote.

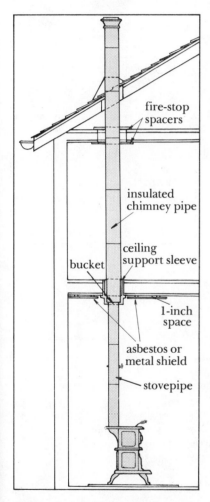

Chimney installed inside the house. The safest installation is one where the uninsulated stovepipe is no closer than 18 inches to flammable parts of the house. Here the ceiling is protected from the stovepipe by shield mounted 1 inch from the ceiling.

Fire-Stops

If you run insulated pipe through the wall and up the side of the house, it must pass through a metal fire-stop mounted between the studs. Stovepipe can run as far as the fire-stop. From there on, use the twist-locking insulated pipe. Run the insulated pipe into the room for at least 18 inches, or cover the wall surface within 18 inches of the pipe with fireproof material. The first section outside is a chimney T with a removable cap that allows cleaning. The T rests on a wall bracket that is attached to the wall with screws. The pipe sections are held with adjustable wall bands that are secured to the wall. If the chimney passes a roof overhang, either cut

through the overlap and mount the pipe in a fire-stop spacer or go around the overhang with a pair of insulated elbows.

Roof Fixture

Where the chimney goes through the ceiling or roof, there must be a support sleeve mounted on the framing to hold the pipe. Before you mount it, run the pipe up from the stove to within 18 inches of the ceiling or roof. Use a plumb line from the ceiling to the edge of the pipe to find out where the pipe will enter the ceiling or roof. Make several marks where the plumb line meets the ceiling or roof, with the plumb bob directly over the edge of the pipe. Connect the dots to outline the hole and cut it out with a saber saw or a keyhole saw.

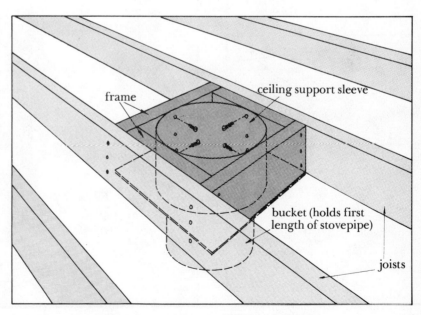

Screw the ceiling support sleeve to a frame nailed between the joists.   **183**

Don't run stovepipe up to the support sleeve in the ceiling, for this puts hot pipe too near the flammable parts of the wood frame. Either mount insulating material on the ceiling or use a sleeve that allows you to insert insulated pipe at least 18 inches into the room. The kind of fitting used on pitched roofs will do. It can be mounted in the ceiling just as easily as in the roof. The other means of protecting the ceiling is to mount asbestos or metal sheets on 1-inch spacers mounted on the ceiling. Leave a little gap at the sleeve to allow air to circulate. Of course, if you want to play it safe, you can run the insulated pipe right down to the stove.

The ceiling support sleeve is mounted between the joists. You'll have to place the stove so that the pipe will run between

Joining the stovepipe to the roof fitting from inside the house. The bottom of the roof fitting extends into the room, and stovepipe with a finishing collar attached fits into it. The finishing collar is then secured to the roof fitting.

the joists. Build a frame between the joists and, inside the frame, place blocking parallel to the joists to secure the sleeve. Nail through the sleeve into the frame and blocking. The sleeve holds the pipe steady and also serves as a spacer to keep the pipe away from wood framing.

By the time you're ready to put the roof fitting in place, you should have installed the pipe as far as the floor below. Make

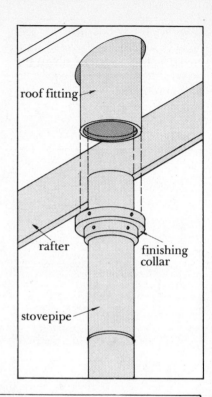

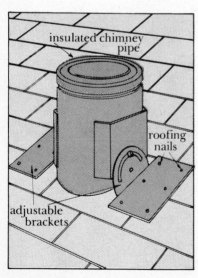

Securing pipe extending through the roof with adjustable brackets.

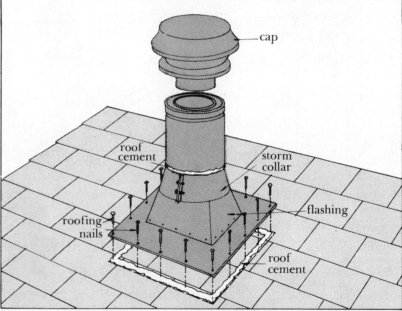

Installing the flashing, storm collar and chimney cap.

sure all fittings are compatible and distances carefully measured before you begin installation. The roof fitting is designed to accommodate the pitch of the roof. Get up on the roof and insert the pipe end of the fitting into the hole in the roof until the brackets lie flat against the roof. Nail the brackets in place and screw a section of pipe onto the end of the fitting. Then go back inside and install the rest of the pipe.

The roof fitting accepts stovepipe from below. A collar is screwed to the stovepipe and then to the roof fitting when the pipe is in place. The adjustable collar lets you insert the stovepipe into the roof fitting, fasten it to the stove below, and

then tighten the collar at the correct spot. But if you are also using a roof fitting in the floor, make sure that there is provision for adjusting the height of the pipe and that all the fittings are compatible.

Installing the Flashing

Attach enough insulated pipe to make the chimney 2 feet higher than any structure within 10 feet and 3 feet higher than the point at which the pipe

emerges. Place roofing cement where the edges of the flashing will lie and place the flashing over the roof fitting. Nail the flashing to the roof and cover the nails and the edges of the flashing with roofing cement. Lap the cement over the edges. Place a storm collar over the pipe and cement the seam between the collar and the pipe. Mount the chimney cap. The last step is to tack a trim collar to the ceiling inside.

Central Heating

If you do use a wood stove or range, you can shut off the central heat to the kitchen. But if you want backup capability or if your central system is the heat source for the kitchen, you'll need to consider one of the three main types: hot-water or steam, hot-air or electric.

Whether you are relocating a register or a radiator, the trick is in getting the heat where you want it with as little damage as possible to walls and without weakening the framing. If possible, run the heating supply lines between joists in basement space below, then up between

¾" nails (one every fifth rectangle)

grommets

trim collar

Installing the trim collar.

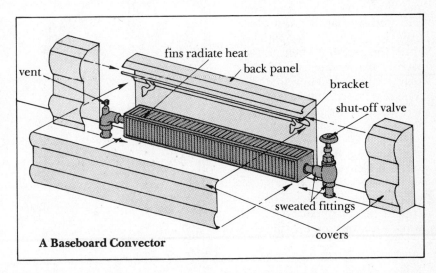

vent

fins radiate heat

back panel

bracket

shut-off valve

sweated fittings

covers

A Baseboard Convector

the studs. But bear in mind that each kitchen is unique and you must work out the particulars.

Hot-Water or Steam

Radiators take up a lot of room. In the kitchen, wall space is usually at a premium. The solution? Without moving any radiators, you can change the type of heating unit to gain space. Baseboard units are generally longer than radiators but are much less obtrusive.

Baseboard heaters are called convectors. As the name implies, they produce most of their heat by convection, heating air so that it will rise and warm other parts of the room. Convectors are made with aluminum or cast-iron fins that transfer the heat. There are two kinds, the baseboard variety and an upright convector that stands about 2 feet high. Baseboard convectors produce less heat per linear foot than radiators. This means that they must be a little longer than the radiator they replace, but their advantage is that cabinets or shelves may be placed closer to them. The less concentrated heat will not damage the paint or stored items.

Replacing a Radiator with a Convector

The risers to supply a convector may be of either steel or copper pipe. Copper is easier to work with, but some local codes

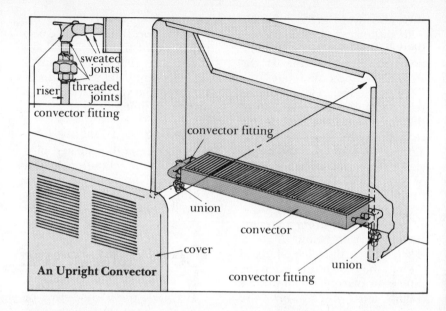

convector fitting
sweated joints
riser
threaded joints
convector fitting

An Upright Convector

convector fitting
union
convector
union
cover
convector fitting

do not allow it. It may happen that the risers are in the same location as the pipes for the new convector, but if they're not, you'll have to adjust the risers to meet the convector.

Empty the water from the entire heating system. This is done by first shutting off the furnace at the main switch and waiting until the water is lukewarm as indicated by the pressure-

union

temperature gauge. Then open all the bleeder valves on radiators or convectors throughout the house. Shut off the water supply to the furnace at the valve nearest the furnace. Attach a garden hose to the drain faucet attached to the furnace. As long as the end of the hose is lower than the drain faucet, the entire system will drain by siphoning—you may run the hose up to a basement window and down to a drain as long as the drain is lower than the drain faucet. Turn on the drain faucet.

After the water is removed from the system, use a pipe wrench to remove the unions on each side of the radiator. A small tray placed under each union will catch any excess water that drips out when it is disconnected. Stick some rags in the openings of the radiator to prevent dripping and haul it away.

If the new convector is wider than the radiator, you'll have to make new holes in the floor for the pipes. Center the heating element over the existing risers and mark on the floor where the new risers should run. Check in the basement or crawl space to be sure there are no joists or other obstructions in the way of the new risers. You may have to move the heater slightly to one side or the other.

Before running the new plumbing or drilling the holes for the risers, mount the baseboard heater on the wall. Upright convectors don't need this step because the cover is merely placed over the heating element. To mount the unit,

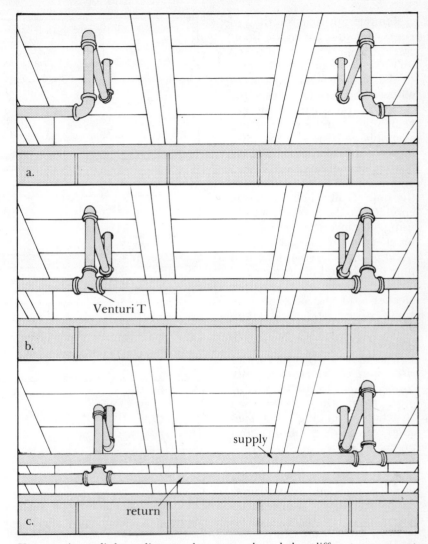

Hot water is supplied to radiators and convectors through three different arrangements of pipes. a. The series loop directs all the hot water through all the radiators. b. The single-pipe system diverts some water to each radiator using Venturi Ts to control the flow. c. The two-pipe system involves a lot of plumbing, having separate supply and return pipes.

first remove the baseboard from the wall. Find and mark the locations of the studs behind the wall. Place the back panel of the unit in position and slide on the brackets that hold the heating element. Position the brackets over the studs nearest each end of the unit. A long unit should have additional brackets for every second stud. Screw the brackets into the studs.

187

Remove any part of the old risers that stick above the floor. Sweat (copper) or thread (steel) an angle valve on the inlet pipe to the heating element and an elbow with a bleeder valve to the outlet. If you sweat the fittings, remember to remove the valve assembly and the bleeder valve to prevent heat damage. Set the heating element on the brackets and mark the exact location for the hole. Drill a hole just large enough for the size pipe you're using. Remove the heating element from the brackets and sweat or thread a short length of pipe to each end of the element. One length should run to the bleeder and the other to the angle valve. Replace the element with the pipe extending through the holes.

Take apart the rest of the old risers until you can conveniently connect them to the lengths of pipe from the heater. See "Kitchen Plumbing" for specifics on joining fittings and pipe.

Attach the front panel and place end caps over the exposed pipes at each end of the unit. Fill the system with water.

A New Convector or Radiator

You may want to add a new heating unit or move an existing one to a new location to make way for cabinets or appliances. The installation of the new units is the same as for replacing a radiator with a convector except that you tap into the supply mains instead of making connections with existing risers. There are three pos-

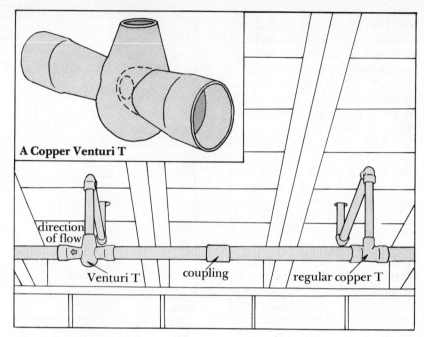

Connecting a single-line copper system.

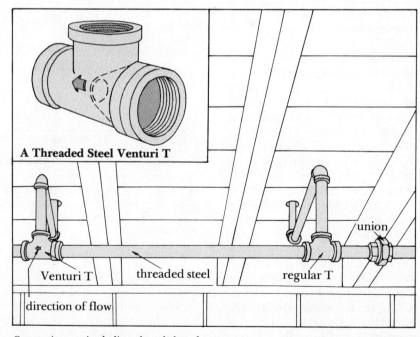

Connecting a single-line threaded-steel system.

sible arrangements of the supply lines: a two-pipe system with a supply and a return line, a single-pipe system in which all water flows through each heating unit in turn, and a single-line system in which each unit is served by a separate loop off the main supply line.

In the latter system, the supply riser feeds a heating unit and a little further along the pipe a return riser takes water back to the main. The return fitting in this case must be something call a Venturi T. This fitting creates internal suction that assures an even flow of water through both the risers and the supply line. The connection between the risers is a standard T at the supply and the Venturi T at the return.

The single-pipe system has no supply line between the risers. All the water passes through each unit. Check the plumbing of your other heating units to see which you have. To add a heater to the single-pipe system, cut out the pipe between the two new risers (after draining the water as described above). Use elbows and short lengths of pipe to divert the supply line up to the unit. Run the return to the supply line from the return end of the heating unit.

The last system for supplying hot water to the heaters is the two-pipe variety. To add a new unit, tap into the supply main with a T. Run the riser from it to the heater. Run a return riser from the heater return outlet to a T in the return main. A Venturi T is not required for this type, just a standard T.

After you have hooked up the units to the risers, fill the entire system with water.

Steam

In a steam system, there may be a supply line only. The pipe runs at a slight pitch so that as steam cools and condenses, it trickles back down the supply pipe to the furnace. You can add a steam radiator by tapping into the supply line with a T and running a riser to the radiator. Convectors are not used frequently with steam because they clog up more readily than radiators.

Forced Hot-Air

In a forced hot-air heating system, the furnace heats air that is blown to all parts of the house through ducts. One or two large return vents keep the air circulating. To prevent moisture from being circulated throughout the house the returns should not be in the kitchen. You may have to move a hot-air register to rearrange kitchen appliances or cabinets.

You may be able to move the register by disassembling the old branch duct and rerouting it to the new location. Or you can block off the old outlet and run new duct.

In a hot-air system, the branch ducts have dampers, usually near the beginning of the branch. These may be adjusted to control the flow of air so that if you run a new branch, you can rebalance the flow in the ducts to compensate for the extra air. You won't have this problem if you are merely routing an existing duct to a new register location. The procedure for balancing the flow is described in "Balancing the Heat" later in this section.

Working with forced-air heat is work that's out of the ordi-

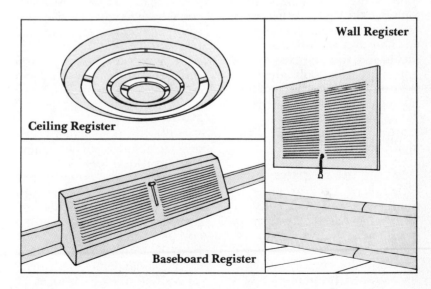

Ceiling Register

Wall Register

Baseboard Register

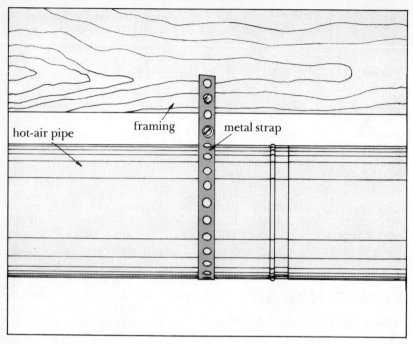

Installing a hanger to support hot-air ducting.

nary. Hot-water and steam systems are basically plumbing, while electric systems are basically wiring. Forced-air is unlike either, and unlike other work you've done thus far in your kitchen. But the work isn't difficult, and, with the exception of tin snips, the tools are commonplace: hammer, screwdriver, pliers. Always wear heavy gloves when working with duct. It's easy to get cut if you don't.

Moving the Register

If you're going to move the register, you can block off the old branch at the damper or disassemble the whole branch. If there's a chance you might ever use the branch, just close the damper. If the new register is supplied by the same branch as the old one, you'll be better off dismantling the ducts that go to the old register. Otherwise you'll have to add new dampers where the branch separates and take out the old one at the beginning of the run—just so you can close the damper to the old register.

Round Ducts

Hot-air ducts are either round or rectangular. The round kind, usually at least 6 inches in diameter, has a crimped end and a plain end. The crimped end of one section fits into the plain end of another, with the crimped end pointing away from the furnace so the air flow is not impeded. Sheet-metal screws hold the pieces together where the two sections meet. Disassembly is a matter of removing the screws and pulling the sections apart.

Pipe sections are suspended from joists and other framing members with metal straps. The sections are light, and there is a certain amount of play. Once the screws have been removed, two sections can usually be pulled apart easily.

Run the duct to the spot where the new register will be located, assembling the sections as you go, screwing them together with sheet-metal screws and hanging them from the framing with metal straps. The fitting to which the register is mounted is called a boot. It is round at one end and rectangular at the other. The register is inserted in the rectangular part and screwed in place. The register screws pass on both sides of the boot and and fasten to the wall or floor. The boot is mounted so that it will be flush with the wall or floor surface. Since the duct should be run during the rough-in stage, make sure to allow for the thickness of the wall or floor that has yet to be installed. If you are adding a register but not an entire wall or floor, you'll have the existing surface as a guide.

When the branch duct runs through the floor, it must be supported. If the boot ends in the floor itself, the metal straps holding the ducts on the joists below will provide sufficient support, especially if the boot fits snugly into the floor opening. But if the duct continues on up to a register near the ceiling or to the floor above, some sup-

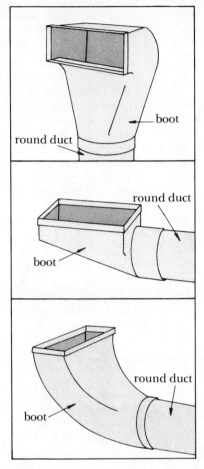

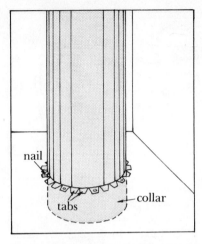

face of the floor. Tack every second or third tab to the floor.

Round ducts are sold disassembled in flat sheets. There are two kinds, snap lock and hammer lock. Both kinds are cut to size at the plain rather than the crimped end.

The snap-lock seam has a slot into which an angled tongue is inserted, starting at one end of the section and working to the other. When the two parts are joined, the duct will hold its round shape permanently. Do not hammer the seam of a snap-lock duct.

The hammer-lock seam is simpler. Each side of the sheet is folded back. These two folds are interlocked and form the seam. Place the duct over a 2×4 resting across two sawhorses or other supports. Hammer the seam, moving from one end to the other. Check each part before you hammer. If part of the seam separates, the hammer blow will squash the folds and

Boots of many varieties connect round heating ducts to the register opening.

Use a collar of the type used to tap into rectangular ducts as a support for round duct passing through a floor. Nail every third tab to the floor.

most cases) below the crimped end so that 4 to 6 inches of duct for making connections will protrude into the room below. Poke the whole works through the hole in the floor. The tabs should come to rest on the sur-

port is needed where the duct passes the floor. This can be provided with a collar of the type used to tap into a rectangular run of duct. (See "Running a New Branch" in this section.) One end of the collar has metal tabs and the other has a standard crimped end. Separate the collar at its seam and wrap it around the duct with the crimped end down. Leave enough duct (about a foot in

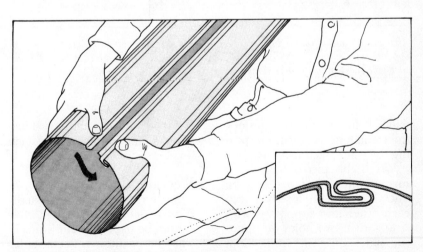

A snap-lock seam can be fitted together by hand. Bow the pipe into shape and, starting at one end and working toward the other, slip the tongue into the seam.

191

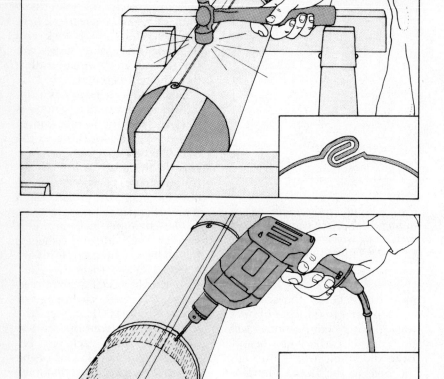

The hammer-lock seam must be hooked by hand, then hammered to lock it.

Some small rectangular ducts simply snap together, but most fit together with clips. On installed ducts, these clips form a metal band nearly an inch wide that goes completely around the duct. The band is made of four clips, S clips on the top and bottom of the duct and drive clips on the sides. The S clips are sheet metal folded in such a way that the cross section forms a squashed letter S. The sections of duct fit into the top and bottom of the S from opposite directions. The drive clips pull the two S clips tight and hold the sections together.

After two sections of round duct have been coupled, secure them by drilling two holes on opposite sides of each joint and tightening a sheet-metal screw into each hole. Be sure each hole goes through both sections of duct.

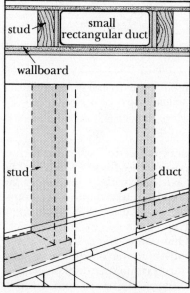

Rectangular ducts are available in sizes small enough to fit between the studs in a wall.

make it impossible to interlock the remaining part without prying the whole section apart.

When the pieces have been formed into round duct and the ducts have been inserted into each other and supported with straps, drill two holes on opposite sides of each connection. The holes should penetrate the plain end of one section and the crimped end of another. Turn sheet-metal screws into each hole.

Rectangular Ducts

Since round ducts are usually 6 or 7 inches in diameter, they cannot be used between studs in walls or partitions. Rectangular ducts, however, are available in widths that fit inside walls.

To separate sections, pry apart the tabs at the top and bottom of each drive clip with a screwdriver. Pull the drive clips down and off with pliers. Then pull the duct sections out of the S clips. To join sections together, reverse this procedure. Ducts are supported by metal straps nailed to joists and secured to the ducts with sheet-metal screws.

Duct Tape

Seams between both round and rectangular ducts may be wrapped with duct tape which provides a tight seal, reducing the air leaks that cause loss of both pressure and heat. The tape is a couple of inches wide and is designed to adhere for extended periods to the hot-air ducts. Duct tape, when used with fiberglass insulation wrapped around ducts in unheated areas, will keep heat loss to a minimum.

Tapping a Wall Duct

When rectangular ducts are placed between studs in a wall, one side is very close to the interior wall surface. Tapping the duct to mount a wall register is a matter of cutting through the wall and into the duct.

First mark on the wall the dimensions of the inside of the register, the part that will be inserted into the duct. Poke small holes through the wall at each corner of your outline to be certain you have the entire area over the duct. Cut out the wall at the marks.

Mark a rectangle on the duct 1⅝ inches in from each edge of the wall cut. Place the edge of an old screwdriver in the center of the rectangle and hit it with a hammer. When you've opened the hole enough to insert the tin snips, cut to the edge of the rectangle you've marked. Cut out the rectangle and remove it. Then make cuts from the corners of the opening on the duct to the corners of the wall opening. This creates four flanges at the duct opening. Fold them around the wall opening. The flanges provide support for the duct. Drill holes in the flanges corresponding to the holes in the register. Mount the register and fasten it to the flanges with sheet-metal screws.

Running a New Branch

When you are changing the location of a register, it is sometimes easier to run a completely new branch then to use the old one. The procedures for joining

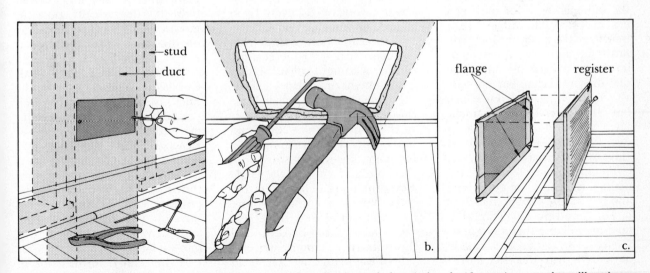

Tapping into an existing duct is easy. a. Poke wire through the wall to locate the hot-air duct. b. After cutting away the wallboard, start a hole in the duct by driving the tip of a screwdriver into the duct with a hammer blow. c. Make diagonal cuts at each corner of the duct opening to make flanges, and fold them at right angles to support the register.

193

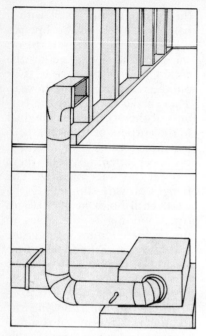

Running a new branch.

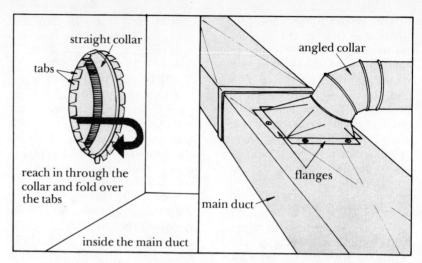

A straight collar (left) for round duct has tabs on one end that are folded against the inside of the duct to hold the collar against a metal bead. An angled collar (right) for round duct ends in a rectangular opening. It also has tabs on the inside that hold the main duct against four flanges.

duct sections and mounting the register in a new run are much the same as those for moving a branch duct. The difference is that to make a new branch you must tap into a main duct or into the furnace plenum. The plenum is a chamber directly above the furnace from which hot air is forced into the ducts. Each branch duct must have its own damper, preferably placed close to the furnace.

To tap into the plenum or to a main duct, you must cut a hole and mount the branch duct over it. For round duct, you'll need a take-off collar, either straight or angled. A straight collar is made of round duct that fits into a round hole in the plenum or the main duct, while an angled col-**194** lar is rectangular where it at-

taches to the plenum or the main duct but round at the other end. Angled collars are available in many varieties. You should be able to find one suitable for your needs, even if you require an unusual shape.

If the run extends away from the main duct at 90 degrees, you can use a straight collar. Mark a circle on the main duct exactly the same size as the collar. Place the edge of an old screwdriver in the center of the circle and strike the screwdriver with a hammer. Insert tin snips into the hole and cut out the circle along the mark. The end of the collar has a series of tabs around its perimeter. Insert these into the hole until the bead around the collar rests against the outside of the main duct. The bead stops the collar at the proper depth. Stick your hand through the collar into the duct and fold

over the tabs until they lie flat against the inside of the duct.

Use an angled collar if your run extends away from the main duct at any angle other than 90 degrees. If possible, mount the take-off collar on top of the duct. The rectangular end of the collar has tabs, similar to those on a straight collar. Cut a rectangular hole in the duct just large enough to admit the tabbed end. Push the collar in until the flanges stop it. Reach through the collar and bend over the tabs. The collar is held to the duct by the tabs on the inside and the flanges on the outside. Drill or punch holes through two opposite flanges and drive sheet-metal screws into each hole.

If the branch run is made of rectangular duct, you don't need a take-off collar. You can attach the branch directly to the main duct by making flanges at the end of the branch to secure it to the main duct. Make a 1-inch cut into the duct at each corner. Bend the 1-inch strip of each of the four sides out, forming flanges. Cut a rectangle the size of the branch in the main duct, using the method described above. Punch or drill holes in each of the flanges and fasten the flanges to the main duct with sheet-metal screws.

Installing a Damper

You can buy 2-foot sections of round duct with a damper already installed. Use them as part of the run.

Be prepared to make a damper for rectangular duct, though. The essential hardware is two spring-loaded clips that let the damper swivel. The damper itself is cut out of a piece of sheet metal.

Cut a sheet-metal rectangle 1 inch longer and wider than the dimensions of the duct. Mark a rectangle the size of the duct inside this piece. Cut off the corners of the piece by making 45-degree cuts that just touch the corners of the inner rectangle. Fold the edges marked along the inner rectangle with a pair of broad-billed pliers until each strip rests flat against the sheet metal. Place the clips over the edges of the two short sides of the sheet-metal rectangle, right in the middle of each side. The end of each clip has a point that will rest against the sheet, toward the center. Hammer each point through the metal. Drill a hole the size of the clip pivots in the sides of the duct. If the hole is midway between top

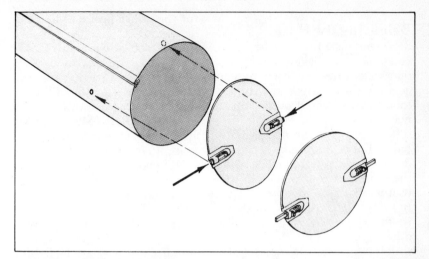

Installing a damper in a round duct.

and bottom, the damper will open or close fully. Often, however, the holes are made a couple of inches toward the bottom of the duct, to prevent the damper from being completely closed off. Insert the damper into the duct while holding in the spring-loaded pivots; then allow them to pop into the two holes. Attach a handle to one of the pivots.

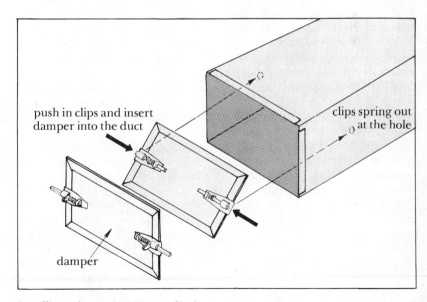

push in clips and insert damper into the duct

clips spring out at the hole

damper

Installing a damper in a rectangular duct.

Balancing the Heat

If you install a new branch you'll need to balance the system to ensure that each room gets the right proportion of the total heat delivered by the furnace. Balancing the system after installing a new branch is not hard, but it may take several days. The idea is to partly close the dampers on branches to rooms that are too hot. This reduces the airflow to the hot rooms while increasing air to all other rooms. The damper is wide open when the handle of the damper is parallel to the run of the duct. When the handle is perpendicular to the run, the damper is fully closed. Measure the temperature of the hottest room between waist and shoulder height on the opposite side of the room from the register. Reset the damper and wait six or eight hours. Measure the temperature of the room again and compare it with the earlier temperature. Keep shutting down the dampers on the hotter rooms and opening them on cooler rooms until the temperatures are all about the same.

When the room with the thermostat is too warm and the rest of the house too cool, shut down the damper to that room, even to the point of closing it completely. This prevents the room from heating up too quickly and fooling the thermostat into believing the whole house is warm.

Electric

Individual electric units may be used either as central heat for the entire house or as space heaters. They may be switched on and off indiviudally or have individual thermostatic controls.

A kitchen can benefit from the individual control offered by electric heat. Many kitchen appliances generate heat, and more than half of the energy used in cooking escapes as heat, so there are times when the kitchen does not need any extra heating. But with steam, hot-air or hot-water, you have little choice. Some degree of individual control is available with these, but the simplest way to get individual control is to use electric heating units.

Even with a wood range as a source of heat, a harvest kitchen can benefit from a thermostatically controlled backup device. Use the backup to even out the heat and provide comfortable working conditions until the range warms up. More important, use the backup to provide heat to prevent plumbing freeze-ups—during those cold-weather times when no one is around to tend a fire.

Wiring a built-in electric heater is like wiring any other fixed appliance in the kitchen. You'll find details on running cable, calculating load and connecting circuits to the main panel in "Basic Wiring."

There are three basic types of electric heater: wall, baseboard, and under-the-cabinet. Radiant heaters, which may be ceiling-mounted, are not suitable for kitchens because they are designed to provide occasional short-term heat in a restricted area in front of the unit. In contrast to radiant heaters, the other three kinds heat the air and thus provide warmth throughout the room.

Wall Units

Wall units usually have a built-in thermostat or off-on switch, either one of which is part of the internal wiring of the unit. A fan blows the heated air into the room. To install a unit, mount the heater housing in the wall by attaching it to a stud. The heater housing is basically just a large electrical box, part of the rough-in wiring. The electrical cable is secured to the housing with a connector, as with any other electrical box.

When you get to the finish stage of your wiring, after you have replaced any walls that needed it, connect the internal conductors of the circuit and mount the assembly in the housing. Whether the unit operates at 115 volts or at 230 volts, connect the ground conductor of the incoming cable to a ground screw on the housing.

If the unit uses 230 volts, code the white incoming conductor with black tape to indicate it is hot. Attach this coded conductor to one terminal of the assembly and the black conductor to the other. For 115-volt units, attach the incoming black conductor to one terminal and the incoming white conductor to the other.

For the purpose of deciding how to organize devices on your circuits, consider any heating unit as an appliance. Do not use heaters on general lighting circuits. Even with appliance circuits, it is best to be cautious

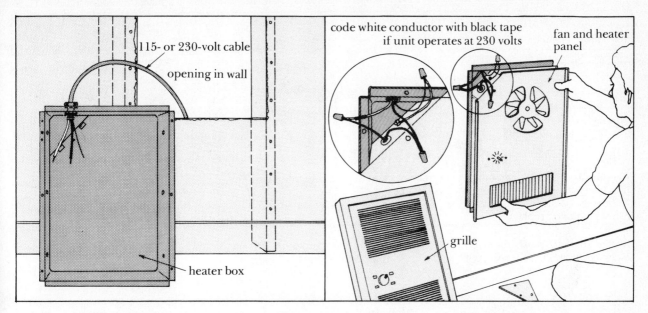

115- or 230-volt cable

opening in wall

code white conductor with black tape
if unit operates at 230 volts

fan and heater
panel

heater box

grille

*Installing a wall unit. If the unit oper-
ates on 230 volts, the white conductor
must be coded black. After the fan and
heater panel is mounted in the wall,
fasten the grille over the assembly.*

about adding heaters. Be sure that no combination of the heater and any appliances that could be on simultaneously draws close to the maximum for the circuit (20 amps on an appliance circuit). The best method, especially for more than one heating unit, is to put the heaters on a separate circuit, or more than one if their rating demands it.

Remember: The rating of the unit in watts divided by the voltage it draws (115 or 230) equals the amperage. To be on the safe side, the amperage of devices on the circuit should not be more than 80 percent of the maximum rating of the cable.

Baseboard Units

Baseboard heaters are sold in lengths from slightly over 2 feet to 10 feet. Several units can be ganged together. Units are only 7½ inches high and 3 inches deep. As the name implies, they are mounted on the wall and replace the baseboard.

Screw the units to the wall studs. Attach electrical cable to the back of the units with connectors; no outlet box is necessary. Use a wire nut to connect the line conductors (those from the incoming cable) to the internal heater conductors. For a 115-volt unit, attach white to white and black to black. For 230-volt, code the white line conductor with black tape and attach it to either heater conductor. Attach the black line conductor to the other heater conductor. For either 115- or 230-volt, fasten the line ground conductor to a ground screw in the unit.

Units may be set side by side and screwed together. Remove the knockout holes between the units. Insert a bushing (supplied with the heater) through the hole and fasten it with a locknut. Run jumpers from the first unit through the bushing to the conductors of the second unit. The ground conductor does not have to be run to the second unit, since the bushing itself will ground the two to each other. The two jumpers run from the wire nuts of the first unit to the wire nuts of the second. If the units are 115-volt, run white to white and black to black, but if they are 230-volt, the order does not matter. Connect either wire nut in the first unit with a jumper to one in the second and the remaining wire nut in the first unit to the remaining one in the second, using another jumper.

197

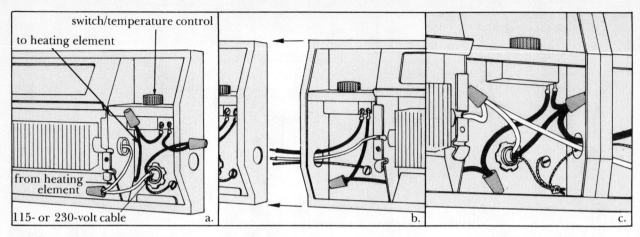

Wiring an electric baseboard unit. In every situation, if the unit operates on 230 volts, the wire conductors must be coded black. a. A single baseboard unit. b. Adding a second unit. c. Wiring the two together.

Under-the-Cabinet Units

Under-the-cabinet units are often mounted as a backup source of heat and provided with a wall-mounted timer switch. Such a unit will fit under many cabinets. It has a built-in fan to blow the hot air out into the room.

If possible, build this heater as an integral part of the cabinet. Cut a hole in the kick space of the cabinet. Run cable from the main panel to the wall location of the switch and then to the cabinet, either through the wall or under the floor. Pull out enough cable to make the connections before the unit is installed under the cabinet. Fasten the cable to the housing of the heater with a connector. Fasten conductors as with the other heaters: white to white and black to black for 115-volt; for 230-volt, one line conductor to a heater conductor and the other line conductor to the

other heater conductor. Fasten them with wire nuts. In this type of unit, there may also be an internal ground conductor. Use a wire nut to fasten the line ground to the heater ground and run a jumper from the ground wire nut to a ground terminal on the unit. Then in-

sert the unit into the hole and secure the grille to the cabinet.

Adding the Switch

Wall-mounted units have built-in switches or thermostats but a baseboard or under-the-cabinet unit may need a separate wall-mounted switch. See

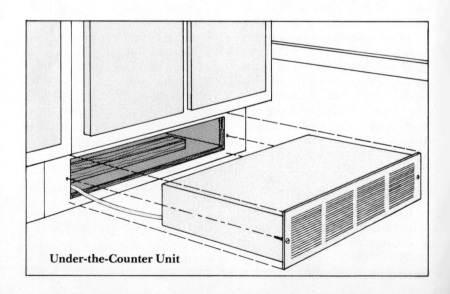

Under-the-Counter Unit

198

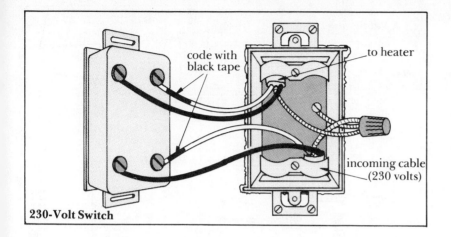

230-Volt Switch

code with black tape

to heater

incoming cable (230 volts)

It may be necessary—or simply desirable—to control an electric heater with a switch. In wiring the 230-volt variety, be sure to code white conductors black.

"Basic Wiring" for switch details. The wiring is the same as for a single-pole switch if the unit is 115-volt. If it is 230-volt, you must use a four-terminal 230-volt switch. The line conductors attach to the top terminals and the outgoing (load) conductors attach to the bottom terminals. Remember to recode all white conductors on a 230-volt circuit with black tape at each terminal.

Ventilation_____

Ever noticed that fragrance of dinner cooking that seems to fill the whole house? That's a sign of poor ventilation. It may smell nice, but it's not only the smell that wafts from room to room. It is also moisture, grease and heat.

Cooking releases a lot of steam; even frying vegetables produce steam. As the steam mixes with the air in the room, it produces a warm, moisture-laden blend. When this moist air comes in contact with cooler surfaces, water condenses. The same surfaces may receive this condensation over and over. Windows, doors, underinsulated walls and other cool surfaces will remain moist, until in the long run wallpaper peels, paint comes off or wood rots.

Besides that, poor ventilation from the kitchen can result in hot, humid working conditions. And the grease carried aloft by the steam presents an extra cleaning problem. The solution is to install a fan to carry excess heat and moisture to the outside. This fan may be simply mounted in a wall opening, or it may be part of a hood connected to a long duct running through the floors of the house and venting through the roof. The ventilation you get from windows and doors is important when the weather is mild, but won't take care of the heat and moisture from your stove.

For good ventilation from windows, try to locate them on opposite walls for a cross breeze. If you only have one set of windows in the kitchen, use the fan to get the air moving.

What Kind, How Much?

So you need ventilation. Is this going to mess up your plan? Will it cost a fortune? No and no. You can spend a fortune, just as you can on most anything else. But a sturdy top-of-the-line hood with fan, built-in lights, all the necessary ducts and a vent cap to protect against the weather will run you less than a good food processor if you install it yourself. A large hood suitable for mounting over a kitchen island is more, of course, but the basic equipment for moving out the heat and moisture is not exorbitant.

The fan you use, be it wall-mounted or part of a hood, should be able to change the air in the kitchen about every four minutes. Store-bought hoods are designed with the so-called average kitchen in mind. If you are not sure your kitchen is the usual size, check the rating of the fan. Fans are rated in cubic feet moved per minute **199**

(CFM). The fan you use should be rated at one-fourth the total volume of the room. A fan that is too powerful for the room will pull in too much cold air in the winter, while one that is too small may not do an adequate job of ventilation.

Another factor that influences the required capacity of the fan is the length of the ducts. Ducting produces significant resistance to airflow. Twists and turns also slow the air. A 90-degree turn produces the same resistance as 10 feet of duct. As a rule of thumb, add 50 CFM to the capacity of the fan for every 10 feet or each 90-degree turn. (Two 45-degree turns equal one of 90-degrees.)

A two-speed fan gives you more flexibility. Use the high speed when doing a lot of cooking or canning and the low speed when you want to pull as little air as possible during the winter months.

One other form of ventilation should be mentioned. This is the closed-cycle hood. It pulls the air from the stove through a charcoal filter and blows it back into the room. It is good for removing odors, but it cannot remove moisture or heat from the air. Because of that, it should be considered the choice of last resort. As far as doing a real job of ventilation goes, a simple wall-mounted fan on any outside wall of the kitchen will do more than one of these.

Hoods

Hoods are available in many sizes, shapes and prices. You can buy a vast one of beaten copper to hang over an elabo-

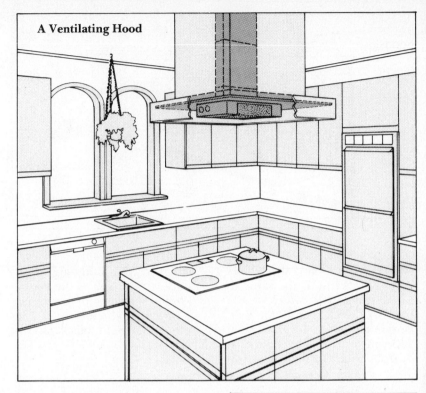

A Ventilating Hood

rate kitchen island, or you can build a serviceable one yourself of ¾-inch plywood. Stained and finished off with trim, this homemade kind can match your cabinets. Most hoods are sold prewired, with a fan and a light built in. A junction box is usually part of the hood, making the electrical tie-in fairly simple. The main work of installation is in mounting the hood and running the ducts.

Wall Fans

As an alternative to a hood, you can mount a fan in an exterior wall. This will provide adequate ventilation if the fan is located over the stove and the capacity of the fan is adequate,

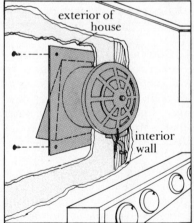

Installing a wall-mounted fan.

but more of the smoke and steam is bound to escape into the room than with a hood. This type of ventilation was widely used in the 1940s and 50s, but has been largely superseded by hoods.

Cook-Top Fans

Another type of ventilator pulls the air down instead of up. The fan is mounted between the burners as an integral part of the stove. The ducts in this type usually run between the floor joists to an outside wall. If running the ducts through the walls or ceiling really presents a problem, this type may be worth considering.

Installation

Unless you want your ventilation ducts to be part of the decor, you'll have to figure out how to run them from the hood to the ouside without their

being seen. Several ways of doing this are described below. Study each one before you decide where to put your stove—you don't want suddenly to run up against a brick wall.

Mounting the Hood

A hood, whether you buy or build one, will usually attach to overhead supports. These can be the bottoms of cabinets, ceiling joists, or the framing of a soffit. In the kitchen, a soffit is often built to fill in the space between ceiling and cabinets. Some hoods may also be attached to the framing of the wall, as well as to overhead supports.

Once you have decided where the duct will run, punch out the knockout at either the back or top of the hood and have some-

one hold up the hood while you mark around the opening for the duct. Shut off power to all circuits running through or to the kitchen. Use a keyhole saw to cut out the opening. If you are determined to use a saber saw, use heavy-duty extension cord and run it to a room with live circuits.

The top of the hood generally has holes for screws at each corner. Drive the mounting screws into something strong enough to support the hood. If the hood will attach to ceiling or soffit framing, use screws that are long enough to reach the wood framing.

Running the Ducts

Round ducts 7 inches in diameter are usually the easiest to install, but if you run the ducts between studs, you may need rectangular ones. Most hoods come with a duct connection that screws onto the hood. You can buy one if you are building your own hood. This connector has a rectangular opening. If you use a round duct get a transition fitting, which is round at one end and rectangular at the other, to make the hood connection.

The stove undoubtedly will be located either against a wall or in a kitchen island. Consider the location of the stove with respect to the outside walls, and what obstructions are in the way.

Mounting the hood to the bottom of cabinets. Though the duct runs through the cabinet, you can still use it for storage.

201

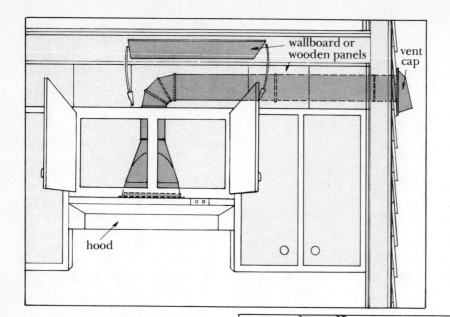

wallboard or wooden panels

vent cap

hood

The duct from the ventilating hood can run above the cabinets in a soffit, which may be finished to match either the walls or the cabinets.

floors is hard; there would be a lot of ducting to box in or hide, and the long run might not draw well.

Running duct through the roof may be necessary for a kitchen island stove. With the stove located in the middle of the room, it can be hard to hide the ducting. Running it straight up could solve that problem.

There are several ways to run ducting. The most common arrangement is to run the duct through a cabinet located above the stove. From there it may run inside a soffit above the cabinets. Or the duct may vent directly outside if the stove is against an exterior wall. If there is no space above the cabinets, you can even run the ducting inside the cabinets. You'll lose a bit of storage space, naturally.

You may run the ducting straight up through the roof. If yours is a one-story house, this is fairly straightforward. Once you get the duct into the attic, it can be routed to avoid rafters. If the house is more than one story, try to find an alternate route. Running duct through several

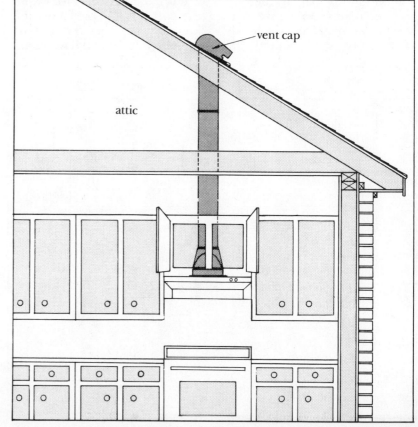

vent cap

attic

Ventilation ducts can be installed vertically from the hood to the roof.

Other options include hiding the ducts above a dropped ceiling, or running them along the joists inside the ceiling. Or you may frame a soffit for the sole purpose of hiding the ducts. Brass or copper ducts (expensive) may even be exposed, turning a problem into part of the decor.

The ducts are light enough that they are generally supported only at the hood and at the outside vent cap. But for long runs, additional support may be provided with coat-hanger wire, 1 × 2s, or pipe strap nailed to framing.

The Vent Cap

There are two kinds of vent caps, one for installation in the wall and the other in the roof. These keep wind, rain, insects and twigs out of the house. The vent cap opens downward and is protected by a screen or grate. Inside, there is a damper that opens when the fan is on. When the fan is off, it closes to keep outside air from blowing in.

To mount a wall cap, cut a hole in the wall slightly larger than the duct. Check the cap to see how it fits over the duct from inside. Usually the cap is designed to fit snugly over ducting cut flush with the wall. Place the cap over the duct from the outside, making sure that it fits tightly. Make sure the damper is free to move. Caulk around the edge of the wall cap to prevent moisture from seeping in.

Installation of a roof cap is more involved, but basically not difficult. Any time you poke a hole in the roof, though, you

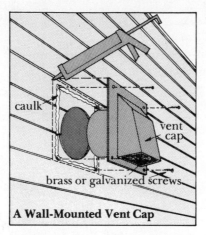

caulk
vent cap
brass or galvanized screws

A Wall-Mounted Vent Cap

Installing a wall-mounted vent cap.

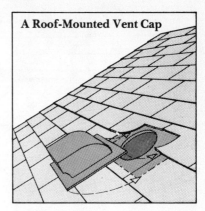

A Roof-Mounted Vent Cap

Installing a roof-mounted vent cap.

risk causing a leak. Water can seep its way past flashing that appears well sealed. Check for leakage during a heavy rain to make sure.

Cut a hole in the roof slightly larger than the duct. Cut the duct at the same angle as the pitch of the roof. The duct should stick up about ½ inch past the roof surface. Have a helper in the attic remove the duct from the hole. Apply roof cement to the underside of the roof cap flashing. Stick the upper part of the flashing under the shingles. Finally apply roof cement to the underside of the shingles that overlap the flashing. Then, hold the cap in place while the helper inserts the duct. You can finish up by placing a coat of roof cement on top of the flashing edges.

Soffit Installation

In some cases, the duct may end at the soffit formed by the eaves of the roof. In a one-story

home in which the ducts run along or above the ceiling joists, a soffit is the best place to vent the duct. In a one-story brick veneer home, the ducts may be run through the attic to avoid having to break a hole in the brick. The duct passes over the top course of the bricks, then down to the soffit. A simple grate in the soffit will keep out the bugs and moisture, since the grate faces downward. If you have been using round ducts, switch to rectangular with a transition fitting where the duct passes above the wall. Fit the grate securely into the last piece of duct and secure the grate to the soffit with screws.

Wiring

You have mounted the hood, run the ducts, and placed the vent cap. All that remains is to tie the electrical conductors into a branch circuit. The electrical code allows a small ventilating fan to be part of a general lighting circuit—the only Code-approved use of a motor on a

203

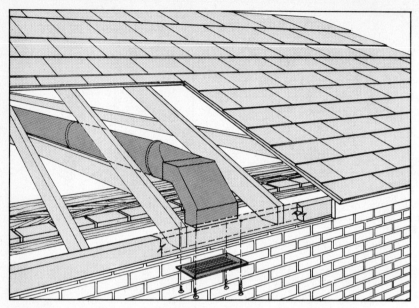

Exhausting a ventilation fan through the soffit.

lighting circuit in a kitchen. Since a store-bought hood will have built-in lighting, you cannot tie the hood into an appliance circuit.

Find the nearest lighting circuit. Make sure the additional load of the hood will not exceed the rating of the circuit. Shut off the power. Run cable from the most convenient receptacle, junction box, or fixture on the circuit to the built-in junction box in the hood. Models may vary in the final wiring details, so follow manufacturer's instructions. In general, though, the conductors from the built-in junction box will feed a receptacle for the fan. This allows the fan to be disconnected, as required by the Code, even if the switch on the hood should fail to operate. The conductors from the hood junction box also feed the light.

All this is typically accomplished as follows. The black conductor from the branch circuit (line) attaches with a wire nut to the black conductor of the internal wiring of the hood. The internal wiring feeds both the light and fan switch. The return from the fan switch is usually a red conductor, indicating a switched (not a 230-volt) conductor. Attach this red conductor to the black conductor from the fan receptacle using a wire nut. Attach the white conductor from the branch circuit to the white conductors from the fan receptacle and the internal hood wiring, all with a wire nut. Attach the branch ground conductor to the ground screw of the hood junction box. If there is no ground connection between the hood and the fan receptacle, attach ground conductor from the receptacle ground terminal to the branch circuit ground conductor using a wire nut (rather than attaching the branch ground directly to the junction box ground screw). Then, run a jumper from the wire nut to the ground screw of the junction box.

A Comfortable Kitchen

Your kitchen should be even in temperature from one side of the room to the other, day or night, winter or summer. And it will be if you have considered how the different elements work together. The heating should have enough reserve capacity to maintain a comfortable temperature in the coldest weather, of course, but it should be flexible and well balanced enough so that it doesn't overheat the room.

Good ventilation from an exhaust fan and well-placed windows will keep the air fresh and temperate. You should realize that the fan is pushing air out of the house. The air must be replaced from somewhere, and that somewhere is the outside. No matter how tight your house, some air infiltrates. With an exhaust fan, this infiltration is more pronounced. Even though there is some heat loss, this slow infiltration is

Stapling fiberglass insulation batts between the studs.

necessary to prevent air stagnation. But you must keep it to a minimum in order to have a comfortable energy-efficient kitchen.

This is done with weather stripping. Good weather stripping around windows and doors saves energy and keeps the room temperature even by reducing drafts of cold air. To round out your comfort system, you'll need storm windows and insulation in exterior walls. These act as a blanket to hold the heat in your kitchen.

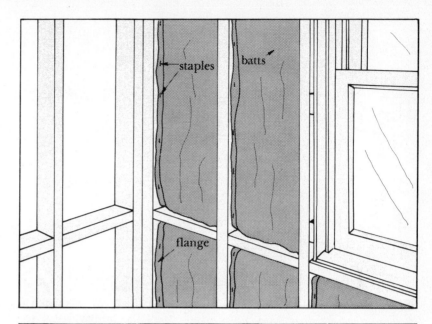

Vapor Barriers and Insulation

If you add insulation between the studs in your kitchen walls—and you'll save on heating costs if you do—make sure to include a vapor barrier. Warm air holds more moisture than cold. If there is nothing to stop the water vapor, it will move from the warm kitchen into the walls. As it cools near the outside of the house, water will condense in the insulation. This is harmful both to the insulation and to the wood and paint. The vapor barrier should be inside the insulation—always on the warm side.

Some fiberglass batts have a foil backing that acts as a vapor barrier. There are gaps at the studs, however, that allow moisture-laden air to get in. The best barrier is polyethylene sheets stapled over the studs. These can be used in addition to

Staple sheets of polyethylene over the insulation as a vapor barrier.

foil-backed insulation. If yours is a one-story house, or if your kitchen is an addition, put a vapor barrier in the ceiling too. It is hard to staple the sheeting to the underside of the ceiling

joists, but doing that is best. Otherwise, after the ceiling is up, cut sheets of polyethylene a **205**

A storm window reduces heat loss through a window by 50 percent.

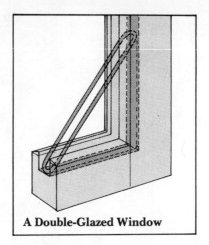

A Double-Glazed Window

few inches wider than the spaces between the joists. Working in the attic, lay them between the joists and place the batts or other insulation on top. Do not lay sheets over the joists. That might trap water against the joists.

Storm Windows, Caulking, Weather Stripping

Reduce heat loss through windows by installing good-quality storm windows or double or triple glazing.

Even if the room is held at a suitable even temperature, it may not seem temperate. Large unshaded windows facing the afternoon sun may make you

feel decidedly hot, even if the air temperature of the room is not high. A poorly insulated window lets in cool drafts of air that may make you feel cold even if room temperature is adequate. If you stand near a single-pane window in winter, you will feel cool, even if the window is well caulked. The reason is that heat radiates easily out the window. Since it is

cold outside, little heat is radiating in, and the result—a net loss of heat from your body—feels chilly. If there are two panes, more heat is reflected back by the surfaces of the glass, and still more is absorbed and radiated back from the air space. As a result, you aren't chilled near a double-glazed window.

Check windows and doors carefully for drafts. As a test, hang plastic food wrapping from a coat hanger and move it around the edges of windows or doors. If you hold it steady, any air leaks will show up as movement of the plastic. Caulk or weather-strip to reduce leakage.

Caulking is applied by loading a caulking gun with a disposable cylinder of caulk. Don't use it if the temperature where you are working is less than 40 degrees F. Clean dirt, loose paint and old caulk from the area to be filled. Go slowly at first. Have a rag handy to wipe up any excess.

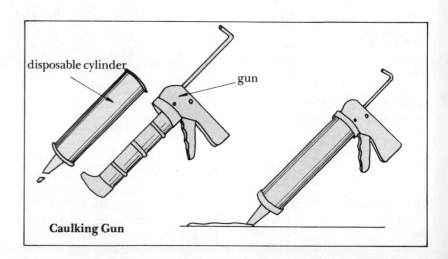

Caulking Gun

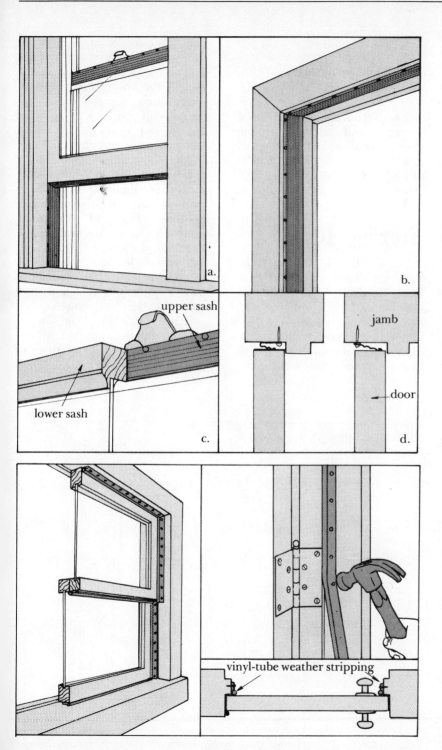

upper sash

lower sash

a.

b.

jamb

door

c.

d.

vinyl-tube weather stripping

Spring-metal weather stripping can be used for windows and doors. a. Tack it into the window channels and along the lower sash's bottom. b. To weather-strip a door, tack it to the jambs. c. The space between the upper and lower window sashes is weather-stripped by tacking the metal to the upper sash. d. The two types of this weather stripping that are available.

Removable storm windows can be weather-stripped by placing a thin felt or adhesive foam strip around the perimeter of the frame. Place the storm window on top of the strip. Adhesive foam is more durable and insulates better. Costs more, too. Triple-action, permanently installed storms have their own weather stripping built in.

The main windows should also be weather-stripped. The best weather stripping is folded spring-metal placed between the window sash and the frame. If there is not enough play between the sash and the frame, mount vinyl-tube weather stripping to the frame outside the sash. A metal strip nailed to the frame holds the vinyl tube in position to seal gaps between sashes and between sash and frame.

Another type of weather stripping, the combination type,

Vinyl-tube weather stripping is useful where there is not enough room in the window or door channels for spring-metal weather stripping. Tack the vinyl tube on the outside of the house, along the window or door channel.

207

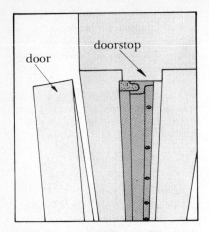

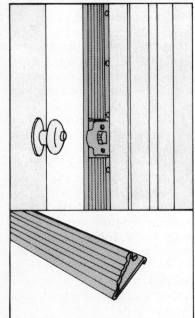

Folded spring metal is the best weather stripping for doors. It is nailed to the jamb between the doorstop and the door.

consists of a metal strip attached to a foam strip. This type is often attached to doorstops so that the closed door butts against the foam. The metal is

Combination weather stripping is mounted to the doorstop so that the door butts against it when closed.

screwed into the stop. Folded spring metal all around the door, including the hinge side, is better. One side of the metal is tacked to the door frame. The crease faces toward the door as it closes.

Storing Heat

You can take advantage of the fact that some materials store heat. Masonry, brick and stone may be poor insulators, but they absorb heat. If parts of the kitchen that receive direct sunlight during the day are made of these materials, they will radiate heat far into the night. If window surfaces are covered during the night with insulating panels, the energy lost through the window for the entire 24 hours will be less than the energy that comes in. Thus you will have a net heat gain.

The increasing use of solar energy has given some new ideas to the building trade. Heat gain is one; heat storage is another. The old textbooks used to describe insulation only in terms of the rate of heat loss to the outside. Now it is recognized that a window can gain heat if it is properly oriented toward the sun, has good weather stripping, a heat-storage medium in the room and is covered with insulating panels at night.

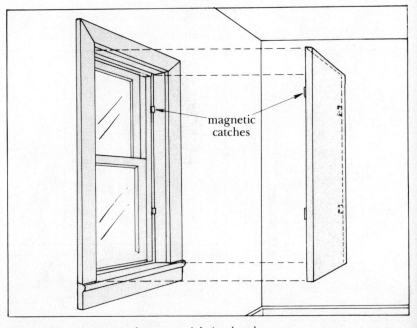

Removable insulating panels prevent nighttime heat loss.

Using Color

Even color and light influence comfort. Warm colors make you feel warmer than cool tones—that's why they're referred to as warm and cool. Warm colors also stimulate greater physical movement, which generates warmth. Fast-food restaurants often use warm tones to stimulate you right out of the building, making room for other customers. Don't overdo the warm colors—in the summer, you'll want some relief. Nor do you want the colors to be tiring. A balance is needed. The browns of wood cabinets and tables suggest warmth without over-stimulating. Some large green plants provide relaxing places for the eye to wander.

Ceiling Fans

One novel method of maintaining a comfortable temperature in the harvest kitchen is to install an old style ceiling fan. The fan adds to the decor and is a real energy saver. You'll need a high ceiling, though. The fan circulates air that otherwise tends to separate in layers with the warmer air near the ceiling where it does no good. Don't locate your fan above a wood stove or it may interfere with the draft.

In the summer, a ceiling fan will lower the temperature significantly. Several companies are selling ceiling fans in a number of styles, and demand is growing fast as people discover their energy-saving features. Best of all, ceiling fans don't use a lot of energy, usually only about 60 watts, a light bulb's worth.

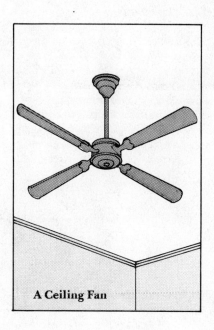

A Ceiling Fan

The finishing stage can both satisfy and horrify, gratify and grieve. You see all your careful work begin to assume final shape; the gutted carcass assumes new flesh. Yet, you know many tasks remain to be done. And it's sometimes hard to maintain your momentum. The basic plumbing, wiring and framing stand ready for sink

Finishing

and faucets, switches and receptacles, cabinets and windows and doors. Scheduling the finishing jobs will enable you to move methodically from one job to the next until every tile is neatly laid, every molding strip firmly tacked, every door swinging freely.

Work Sequence

The work sequence should be arranged to minimize damage to new work. Ideally, the first step is to complete the windows and doors. Then do the ceilings, finally the walls. There is a bit of leeway here, however. If doors or windows are new, the rough openings should be framed in and ready. But if you're replacing an old sash with new, you can wait for a convenient time, even after the interior walls are up.

You will have to resign yourself to a certain amount of backtracking to tie up loose ends that could have been tied up earlier—patching the hole you accidentally jabbed with the screwdriver, for example. Even professionals do some of it, just a little less often. What you want to avoid is making extra work for yourself by cutting corners unnecessarily. Take the time to get the right tool and material for the job. When you have finished a project, protect it from dust and splatters of work going on nearby. And if you meet a problem, take time to cool off. It is easy to damage something when frustration wells up or when you are concentrating too closely on another task.

After the ceiling and walls are installed—or patched if that's all they need—painting, papering or wainscoting is usually the next step. If you follow this sequence, you will spare yourself the trouble of protecting floors and cabinets from paint drips and the like. But if you are installing a new wood floor or sanding an old one, do that first, including the finishing. Cover the floor with drop cloths when you do the wall finishing and then install the cabinets.

Cabinets, counters and molding are installed after the ceilings and walls have been finished. Even if the woodwork will match the walls, it is often easier to paint it separately. This allows you to countersink molding nails and fill the holes with wood filler without damaging your paint job. If wood trim and molding will match the cabinets, finish it along with them.

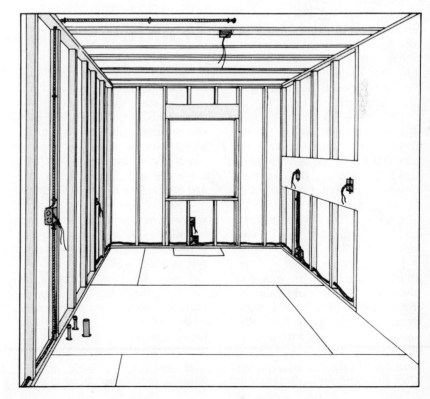

In a complete kitchen renovation, cabinets, walls and fixtures may be stripped away, allowing construction to proceed as in new construction.

Install wall cabinets first, followed by the floor cabinets. There is no need to paint the wall behind cabinets unless it will be visible when the cabinets are open. The wall is visible with built-in-place cabinets, since the wall forms the interior surface. Built-in-place cabinets will have to be finished in place, and should be finished just as soon after construction as possible. Prefabbed cabinets should be finished before installation.

Resilient floors are generally installed after all the other work is done, again, to minimize damage. They butt against the walls and floor cabinets. Baseboard molding covers any gaps. No molding is required under the toe space of counters.

An extra strip of shoe molding is often used with wood floors. Install the baseboard before laying the floor, which then butts against the baseboard. The shoe molding is nailed over the gap between the floor and the baseboard.

The final work on the kitchen involves the plumbing, wiring and heating. Once you've completed the faucets, light fixtures and heating units, your kitchen should be ready for cooking and canning. After you finish work on each type of service, go back and check all parts of the system.

This sequence is, of course, an ideal one. If you are going to make do with your old cabinets for a while, you'll have to tape them when you paint the walls, keep them covered with a drop cloth and remove any dripped paint. You might even discover after finishing the walls that you must put in another electrical circuit. Well, it happens. Then you'll have to go back and tear out part of your new wall. Your particular situation will never be quite the same as the ideal. Just keep the general sequence in mind as a guide and make changes from it as necessary.

Tools

The tools you'll be using at this stage of the kitchen work are those tools you've been using all along. Any carpentry work will require the hammer and saw, the framing square and level that you used in framing your kitchen. Completing the wiring and plumbing will involve the screwdrivers and wrenches and pliers you used at the outset of those aspects of the project.

There are some additions you'll have to make, though. Finish work introduces new tasks, such as laying flooring and putting up wallboard. Some of the basic tools are needed to do these new tasks, but there are some specialized tools you'll need too. Some can be rented, like a wallpaper steamer. Others, like paintbrushes, you are just going to have to buy. Make a list of those special tools you'll need for those special jobs you have to do. If you can't borrow or rent what you need, see if inexpensive or makeshift tools will get your job done. As a last resort, buy the tool.

Windows and Doors

Mounting windows and doors in their frames is not exactly rough construction and not quite finishing. There is a certain amount of flexibility as to when you do it. If you are replacing old windows, you can leave the old ones in until you are ready. But if you are cutting a hole in the wall for a new window, you'll probably want to install it as soon as the framing is finished, rather than leave an unprotected hole.

Install new windows or doors after all rough framing is complete but before you put up new walls. Plumbing, wiring and heating may be installed before or after the windows.

If you are replacing an old window or door without changing the size of the opening, remove everything inside the rough stud frame. If the interior wall is in place and extends past the studs into the rough opening, you'll have to cut it back even with the studs to do the leveling. Usually, the interior wall ends flush with the stud frame.

The frame of a window or door is made of stock that is nominally 1 inch or 1¼ inches thick. The bottom of a window frame is called a sill. The bottom of an exterior door frame is called a threshold; interior doors have no threshold. The sides and top of both window and door frames are called jambs. The frame is secured inside the rough stud opening so that the door or window is plumb and level.

After the windows or doors have been set in their openings, put up the walls or do any patching needed on the existing walls. Before you paint or paper, nail the window and door casing in place. Casing is a type of molding that extends around the perimeter of the opening, giving a finished appearance. It must fit with the other kitchen molding and can often be installed at the same time.

Windows

Windows are available complete and ready to install. There are double-hung windows, casement windows, horizontal-sliding windows, awning windows and stationary windows. They differ in the ways they open. If a window opens outward, make sure it won't interfere with movement outside on a porch or walkway next to the house.

Ready-Made Windows

Most new windows come assembled and ready to install. The exterior casing is already attached to the jamb, and the sashes are in place. You put the entire unit into the rough opening, level it and nail the casing to the studs. These windows are usually packed with stops to keep the movable parts stationary until installation is complete.

Double-Hung Window. The double-hung window is what most people consider the standard window. It consists of two sashes mounted in vertical channels. The top sash moves up and down in a channel a little to the outside of the bottom sash. When the window is closed, the two sashes overlap to prevent air leaks. Counterweights attached to the sashes hold them in any position along the channel.

Sliding Window

Double-Hung Window

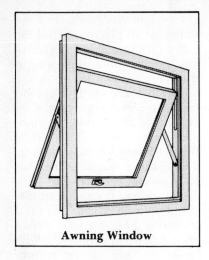

Awning Window

Casement Windows. Casement windows are hinged along one side and usually crank open. They are a good type to locate over a sink or counter, where reaching the sash can be difficult.

Horizontal-Sliding Window. A window useful above counters is the horizontal-slide type. Because it's easier to pull sideways when you're reaching than it is to push up, you'll find it easier to open a sliding window than a double-hung window in such a situation.

Awning Window. Another possible over-the-counter type is the awning window. This pushes out from the bottom. Often it is mounted on sliding friction hinges that allow the top rail of the sash to move down as the bottom of the sash is pushed out. The older variety was simply hinged at the top. If you do use an awning type above a counter, make sure you don't have to reach too far to open it. This is important only if it does not open with a crank.

Stationary Window. You can buy a stationary window ready to set in the rough opening and install. The ready-made version is installed just like the other manufactured types by using pairs of wedges to level and plumb. It must look level and be weathertight. Since there are no moving parts, leveling and plumbing are not quite as exacting as with other types.

Each of these windows is available in a range of sizes. After you decide exactly what you want, shop around to find out if you can get it.

Installation

Ready-made windows usually fit into the rough frame opening from the outside. The exterior window casing covers the rough frame. After it is plumbed and leveled, secure the window by nailing through the casing into the stud frame.

Insert ready-made windows through the rough opening from the outside, and level the sill with wooden wedges manipulated from the inside.

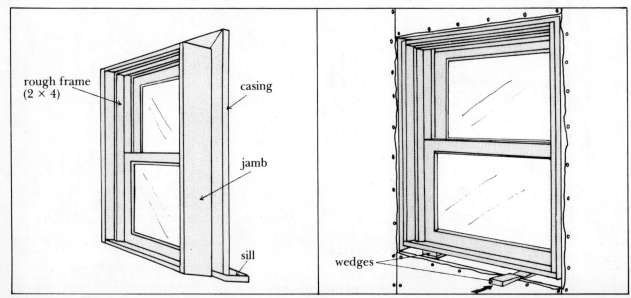

rough frame
(2 × 4)

casing

jamb

sill

wedges

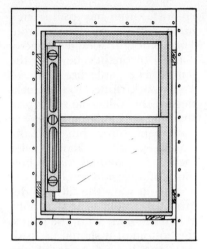

Use wedges at the side jambs to make the window plumb. Check both sides with a carpenter's level.

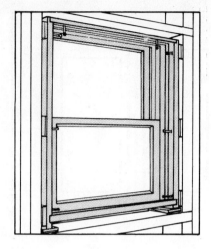

Secure the window by face-nailing through the casing into the studs of the rough frame. You may also anchor the shims, or wedges, by nailing through the jambs and wedges into the rough frame.

Putting in a window is a job for two people. After you remove the window from its packing—without removing stops or temporary braces—check to be sure the window is the right size, 1 inch narrower and ¾ inch shorter than the rough opening. Tack strips of building paper along the studs, header and sill, overlapping the exterior sheathing. This will help prevent drafts when the installation is completed.

Insert the window into the rough opening and place wedges under the sill to raise it into place and level it. For practical purposes, once the rough frame is built, the window's correct height is simply that height at which enough of the casing laps over the top of the opening that the window can be nailed in place.

Wedges are used in pairs. Wooden shingles work well. By pushing them toward each other, you raise the window. Use two or three pairs, depending on whether the window is long enough to sag in the middle. Place the wedges at right angles to the sill and tap the end that sticks out with a hammer.

When the window is at the correct height, place a carpenter's level on the sill and "fine tune" the wedges until the sill is level. Nail through the lower part of both side casings. Plumb the side jambs. Then put nails partway through the upper part of the side casing, one nail on each side. Check that the window is plumb and level all around. Open the window to ensure the frame isn't distorted. Secure the window by driving 8d or 10d galvanized or aluminum casing nails through the casing, spacing them 16 inches apart. The casing dents easily. Finish driving the nails with a nail set, countersinking them. Fill the holes with wood filler. Saw off any protruding portion of the shims.

Often several windows are installed next to each other. They are separated by a vertical wooden member called a mullion. In the case of a two-part window, perhaps with one stationary pane and one opening pane, the mullion is part of the complete unit. Installation of such a unit is the same as for a single window. But if two separate windows are mounted side by side, they are separated by a vertical stud. The casing is nailed to the stud, and molding completely covers it. This is called a support mullion because the stud helps hold the windows in place. The side casing from each window meets over the support mullion. There should be no gap between the casings.

Jambs are part of ready-made windows. Since different types of wall are sometimes different thicknesses, manufacturers include jamb extensions that may be used to make the jamb flush with the surface of the wall.

Found Windows

You may be able to salvage interesting windows from old houses or buy them in antique stores. Many people like old glass, with its ripples caused by manufacturing imperfections. You may even find a stained-glass or translucent window. If you plan to install salvaged win-

215

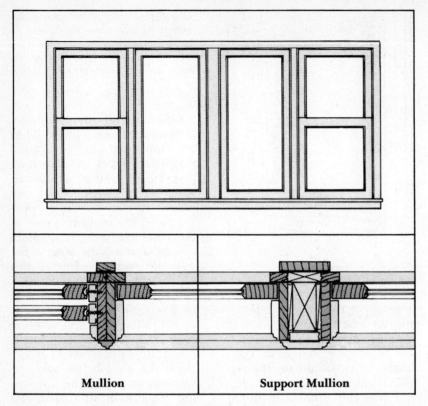

| Mullion | Support Mullion |

A mullion is the vertical wooden member between two adjacent windows. It is essentially the two jambs butted together. A support mullion houses a load-bearing stud and is formed by butting the jambs of adjacent windows against the stud.

run off. Either buy a sill from a lumberyard or rip it to size from 1 × 8 stock. It should project a couple of inches beyond the jambs. The jambs are made of 1 × 6 stock ripped to the thickness of the wall—the studs plus the interior wall and the exterior sheathing but not the siding—usually about 4½ inches. Cut dadoes in the bottoms of the side jambs at the angle you want the sill—15 degrees is enough for runoff. When the sill is set in the jambs, the bottom of it should be flush with the bottom ends of the jambs.

If you'd rather not try a dado, cut the bottom of the side jambs at the proper angle, set them over the ends of the sill, and nail through the side jambs into the sill. Or you can use a sill from a lumberyard with a sloped edge and a channel on the bottom for the siding. In this situation, cut a rabbet across the jamb for the sill. The sill may be cut even

dows, keep the project simple. Make a fixed installation or mount the side of the sash on the jamb with hinges.

Jamb and Sill

The first step is to make the jambs and sill. It is easier to build them as a unit before you install them in the rough frame. The sill must pitch toward the outside to allow rainwater to

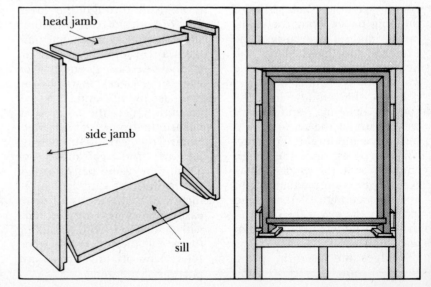

Building and installing a homemade window frame.

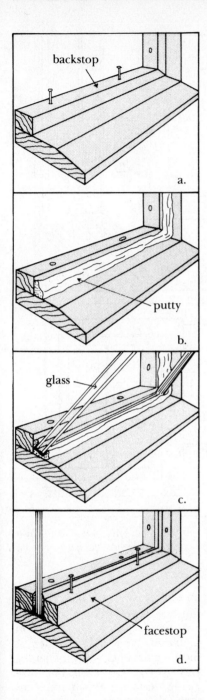

backstop

a.

putty

b.

glass

c.

facestop

d.

with the jambs, or it may extend beyond the rough opening onto the sheathing.

Installing a double-paned window in a homemade frame. a. Nail backstop to sill and jambs. b. Lay a bead of putty around the outside corner of the stop. c. Set the glass into the putty. d. Nail a facestop around the glass (but don't toenail it).

Nail through the face of the jambs into the ends of the sill. Set the top jamb inside the side jambs, and nail through the side jambs into the top jamb. Set the unit into the rough frame and use wedges at the bottom and sides to plumb and level. Secure by nailing through the side jambs and wedges into the rough frame. Make sure the corners of the frame are square.

Stationary Window

If you are installing a salvaged window as a permanent, stationary unit, nail a backstop to each jamb and sill, flush with the interior edges. Mitered corners for the stops are best. Apply a bed of glazing compound to the exterior corner of the stop and sill. Apply enough at the top and side jambs to provide a weathertight seal. With a double-glazed window, the jambs and sill should be ½ inch larger than the window to allow room for the snap-on spacer strips. Set the window into the compound, bottom edge first, and press it against the stops. Nail stops to the sill and jambs to hold the window in place. Don't toenail the stops or you may crack the glass. Nail straight down into the sill or jambs.

Hinged Window

Putting in a hinged window is the same as putting in a stationary one up to the point where you put down glazing compound. Instead, attach two hinges to the side of the sash. A gain (or mortise) for the hinge must be chiseled into the sash so the hinge will be flush with it. Set the window against the stops, then open it enough to be able to mark where the screws will go to hold the other leaf of the hinge to the jamb. Chisel a gain in the jamb for the hinge and screw the hinge into place. Attach a latch to the sash opposite the hinges on the inside of the window. If the entire sill is mounted at an angle, the bottom of the sash must match the angle.

Exterior Trim

Whether you use a stationary or a hinged window, the casing will be the same. The jamb is flush with the sheathing. The casing rests on the part of the sill that laps over the sheathing and must be cut at the same angle on the bottom as the sill. Place the side casing over the jambs and the sheathing with ¼ inch of the jamb edge showing. The portion of the jamb edge that's exposed is called the reveal. Cut the casing so that the head casing will also reveal ¼ inch of the top jamb by making the side casing ¼ inch higher than the lower face of the head jamb. The siding butts against the casing in the completed unit.

If the sill ends at the jamb, the casing won't look right, so make **217**

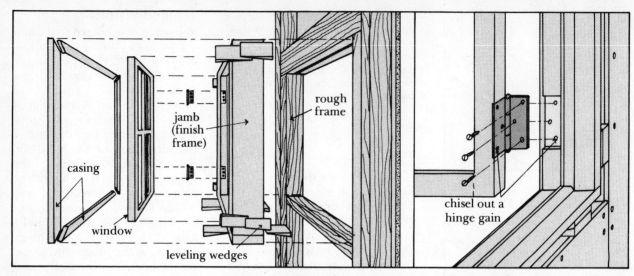

Installing a hinged window.

the jamb flush with the siding (instead of the sheathing) and leave the casing off. If you must use casing, use 1 × 2 cut off at the bottom even with the bottom of the sill.

The top piece of casing rests on the side pieces. Nail them into the stud frame with aluminum or galvanized casing nails, as with ready-made windows.

Interior Trim

Install the interior window trim after the wall is up. The wall ends flush with the rough opening to make leveling with the wedges easier. The interior casing will cover the gap between the wall frame and the window frame. Staple a vapor barrier to the backs of the jambs. Stuff the gaps between the jambs and studs with insulation, then fold the vapor barrier

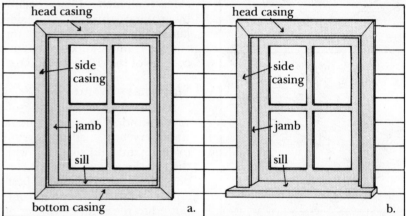

Casing the window. a. If the sill is to end flush with the jambs, you can nail casing over it to finish the bottom of the window. b. If the sill projects beyond the jambs, rest the casing on it.

over the insulation and staple it to the exposed studs.

The stool, which is the interior sill, is the first piece of trim. Like the sill, it may be bought in the lumberyard or ripped from dimension stock (1 × 4 or 1 × 6). If you buy a sill, buy a stool to match. The store-bought kind often fits over the

sill and serves as a stop for the window. If you are making your own stool, notch a corner on each end. When it is installed, it should extend beyond the jambs and overlap the wall. The side casing rests on this part. Nail through the edge of the stool with 8d or 10d casing nails. You'll be nailing through the

218

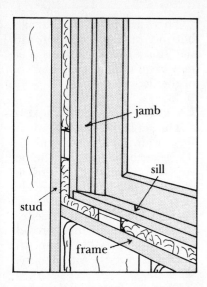

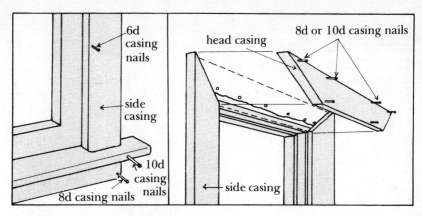

Installing the interior window trim.

Stuff insulation between the windowsill and the stud frame and between the jambs and the frame. When you install the plastic vapor barrier, be sure you cover this area.

wall to the stud.

The side casing, installed next, is nailed to the studs with 8d or 10d casing nails and into the edge of the jamb with 6d nails. The casing may be flush with the jamb or may have a ¼-inch reveal as with the exterior casing. Place the head casing on the side casing and nail with 8d or 10d casing nails. For a better corner, miter the ends at 45-degree angles where the head casing meets the side casing. Place an apron under the stool, and your window is finished. The apron may be a piece of molding or simply a piece of dimension stock cut to length.

Any good grade of lumber may be used for the casing and trim. Pine is commonly used. You can use hardwood, but it is expensive and, because it is sold rough-sawn, it presents extra work to ready it for use. Another possibility, especially with found windows, is to salvage lumber for the trim. And depending upon your design, you may make use of rough-sawn lumber here and elsewhere in your harvest kitchen.

Refurbishing Windows

If your windows are peeling and wind seeps through, you may not have to throw them away. Some minor repairs may be all that are needed.

Weather stripping will take care of most air leaks.

If the counterweight is missing or broken, you can install friction weather stripping between the sash and the jamb to hold the window in any position. But often the problem is merely a broken sash cord. Replacing a sash cord isn't always easy, but it *can* be done.

New caulk in place of crumbling caulk will seal the window. Reputty the panes to stop rattling and drafts. If the window is very loose in its channel, you may have to reposition the stops. Lightly plane them and the sash to get a smooth fit. Rub the moving surfaces lightly with soap before replacing the stops.

Scrape the old paint, sand, prime and repaint for windows that look new.

Doors

Installation of doors is similar to that of windows. The frame for both consists of jambs and a

sill leveled with wedges and attached to a rough frame. Door units may be bought with the **219**

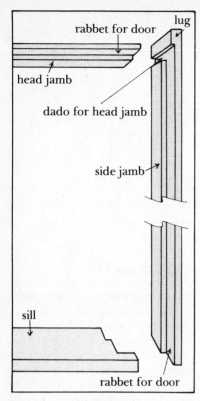

The frame of a ready-made door is rabbeted to receive the door.

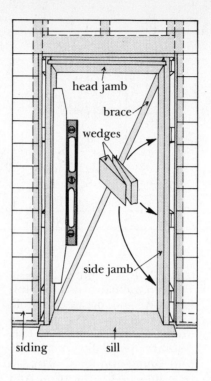

Installing the jambs for an exterior door.

casing and jambs already assembled and ready to nail to the rough frame. Or doors can be salvaged and hung onto hand-cut jambs and casings.

Exterior Doors

Exterior doors are surprisingly heavy. To support them, the frame is made of what is called $^5/_4$ stock, nominally 1¼ inches thick, but actually 1 inch thick. This frame goes into a rough opening 2½ inches larger than the door. Side entrances of the kind you'd need for a kitchen entrance are 30 or 32 inches wide; that's the actual width of the door. The standard height for any kind of door is 80 inches.

Ready-made door units are cut at a mill and may be delivered assembled or "knocked down." Details vary and it's important to follow the manufacturer's instructions carefully. Generally, these units have ½–inch-deep rabbets in the head and jamb to receive the door. Stock door frames are designed for standard stud frame with siding construction, but can be adapted for brick veneer. The frame can also be fitted with extensions to accommodate different wall thicknesses.

There are many kinds of sills, but the top is always even with the finish floor. Making it so may require trimming the top of the floor joist.

Exterior Door Installation

The jamb and head should be flush with the interior wall and the exterior sheathing. Before you start, check the dimensions of the frame—length, width and depth—to be sure it will fit. If jamb extensions are needed, check to be sure they provide the proper width. Trim the floor joist for the sill, if necessary.

Place the frame in the opening, center it in horizontally, and nail a temporary brace from the top of one jamb to the lower part of the other. Nail through the face of the brace into the edges of the jambs. Level the sill with shims and pairs of wedges. Make sure the sill will be even with the finish flooring. Drive an aluminum or galvanized casing nail (8d or 10d) into the lower part of the casing on each side.

Place pairs of wedges between the tops of the jambs and the studs. Adjust the wedges until a 4-foot level held vertically against each jamb shows they are plumb. Drive a nail through each jamb and its wedges and into the studs. You'll need a helper to hold the level, and you may have to hold the wedges in place by nailing under them through the jambs and partway into the studs. Don't drive the nails home. Place wedges where the hinges and doorknob will be. There are three hinges on an exterior door. Use at least

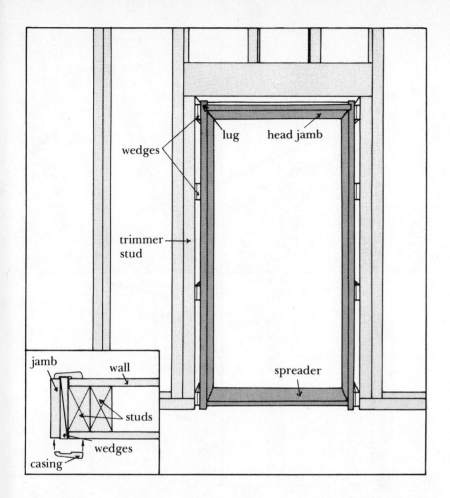

threshold sit on top of it. Before the frame is set in place, lay a strip of sealing compound across the floor joist to insure a weathertight seal. The sill must be perfectly level and straight for the doors to slide smoothly. Plumb and brace the frame with wedges, as with regular door frames. Use about four pairs of wedges per side. Space casing nails 16 inches on center.

Interior Doors

Interior doors do not have a sill. The head jamb fits into dado channels cut just below the top of the side jamb. A small gap is left between the top of the side jamb and the header. To keep the frame square during installation, you must use a board; called a spreader, to hold jamb bottoms in position.

You'll probably buy milled jambs and casing, then cut and nail them to length on location. Installing a salvaged exterior door is like interior installation, because you install all these pieces separately. The jamb is not rabbeted to receive an interior door. Instead, a stop is nailed to the head and jambs after the door is hung. Drive all nails through the jamb where they will be covered by the stop.

The width and height of an interior door is the same as for an outside kitchen door, 80 inches high and 30 or 32 inches wide. Closet doors may be 24 inches. Since interior doors are lighter than exterior doors, an

four pairs of wedges per side. Complete the installation by nailing the exterior casing in place with 8d or 10d casing nails spaced 16 inches on center. Cut off parts of wedges that extend beyond the jambs. After the door is hung, install a threshold over the sill (see "Thresholds").

Sliding Glass Doors

In a large kitchen, you may choose to install sliding glass doors. They can fill the room with natural light and provide an impressive view of the outside. Most varieties have double-glazed insulating glass to reduce heat loss in cool weather. You can reduce this loss even further by placing insulating panels over the doors at night.

The general installation is similar to other outside doors, but follow manufacturer's directions carefully. The sill is mounted flush with the finish floor, as with other exterior doors. The metal runners and a

221

interior door jamb is 1-inch dimension lumber, which measures an actual ¾ inch thick. This means the rough opening is 2¼ inches wider than the door, instead of 2½ inches for an exterior door.

Interior Door Installation

Check the length of the head and side jambs. The distance from the bottom of the head jamb to the surface of the finish floor should be 6 feet 8¹¹/₁₆ inches providing ⅝-inch clearance below the door and ¹/₁₆ inch above it. A 25-cent piece provides a handy approximation of ¹/₁₆ of an inch.

Place the frame in the opening and center it. If the finish flooring is not down, you'll need permanent blocks the height of the finish floor under the side jambs. Or you can cut the jambs that much longer if you're doing your own cutting. If there isn't enough clearance between the top of the jamb and the header, cut a bit off the top. The edges of the jambs should be beveled at about 2 degrees away from the door opening to insure that the casing will lie against it without any gaps. (A

Installing a split-jamb door: a. Separate the two sections. b. Mount the section with the door (but leave in the spacers between the door and the jambs). c. Use a level set against the casing to plumb the frame, then drive 10d casing nails through the face of the casing and into the stud frame. d. Move to the other side of the door and slip shims between the side casing and the rough frame. e. Install the second frame section. f. Nail the stops into the jambs and stud frame with 10d casing nails.

222

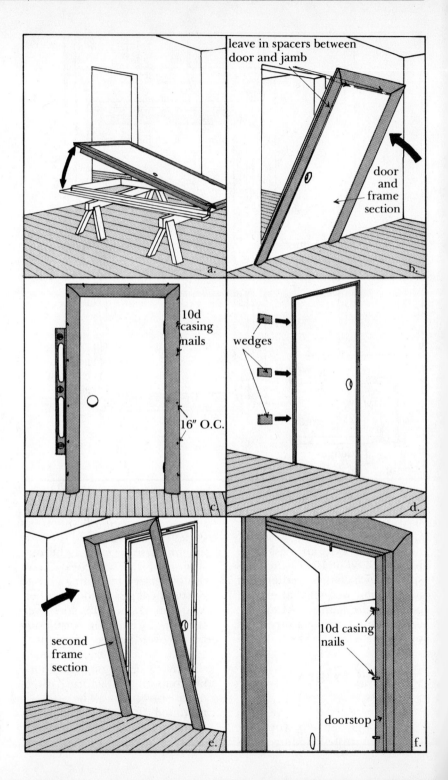

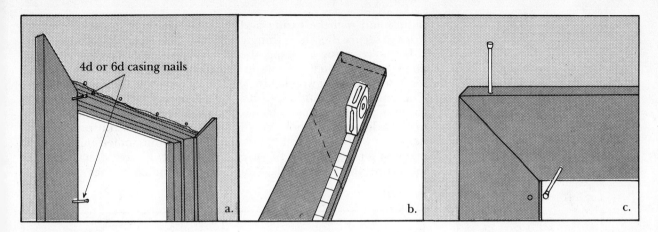

Installing door casing. a. Measure two pieces of side casing, cut them at 45 degrees, then nail them to the edges of the jambs and to the stud frame. b. Cut the head casing to fit between the side casing pieces, with each end mitered at 45 degrees. c. Nail the head casing in place, then lock-nail the head casing to the side casing.

2-degree bevel is about ¹/₃₂ inch in 1 inch.)

The jambs should be flush with the surface of the walls. For wallboard over studs, that's ⁵/₈ inch plus 3½ inches plus ⁵/₈ inch, or a total of 4³/₄ inches—the usual width of jambs. For plastered walls, the jambs will need to be 5¼ inches wide to accommodate the extra thickness of the plaster. You may use jamb extensions, split-jamb units or jambs cut to that dimension.

To accommodate varying wall thicknesses, split-jamb units with the door attached may be installed. The unit is plumbed with a level and the casing nailed to one side. Then a second frame is installed from the other side. It fits in a groove in the first part and is nailed to the studs and jamb.

Place the spreader at floor level between the side jambs. It is the length of the head jamb minus the depth of the dadoes, usually ½ inch each. Mark nailing lines on the jambs where the stops will be. Plumb the side jambs with a 4-foot level and pairs of wedges at the top and bottom of each jamb. Drive two nails, 8d or 10d, into each pair of wedges, staggered ½ inch on either side of the nailing line.

Nail casing over the edge of the jambs and the wall surface to cover the gap between the jambs and the wall. You can install a door before the wall is up if you take the wall's ultimate thickness into account, but the casing can't go up until after the wall is finished. The wall ends flush with the stud frame.

The corners of the casing should be mitered. You can usually buy premitered casing. But you can cut it yourself if you have a good quality miter box or wood trimmer. Set the casing in place, ¼ inch from the edge of the side jambs. Mark where the miter should be, take the casing down and make the cut. Drive the casing or finishing nails partway into the side casing and mark where the cuts will be made on the head casing. Cut the miters, and complete the installation. Use 4d or 6d nails along the jamb edge and 8d nails over the studs. Space each 16 inches on center.

Hanging a Door

Before you hang the door, double-check to see which way it will open. Be sure that no permanent object will be in the way of the swing and, if possible, that no other door could open into it. Make a mark on the door jamb that will receive the hinges and on the edges of the jamb where they will be mounted.

Before a door is hung, it must be trimmed to size, the lock edge of the door must be beveled, gains must be cut for the hinges, and holes must be bored for the lock and handle. Mills **223**

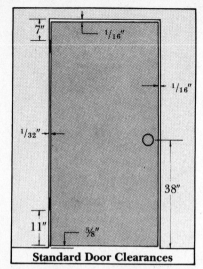

Standard Door Clearances

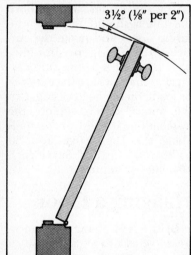

Bevel the lock side of the door to allow it to close freely.

plumb and nail the casing and stops to secure the whole thing.

If you're going to hang the door yourself, you'll need a router or a good set of wood chisels. The router will do its best with a routing template that attaches to the edge of the door. You'll need a well-sharpened block plane or a power plane. Be sure to secure the door well. You may clamp it to sawhorses or use a special clamp that holds the door on edge and protects the surface.

To mount the lock and handle you'll need some kind of drill and an adjustable bit. To do it perfectly you need a boring jig and something to cut a mortise. If you don't want to spend much money, however,

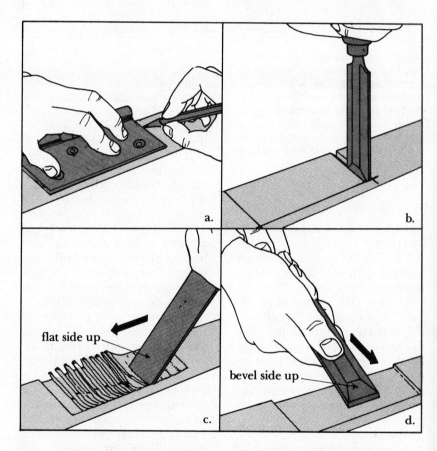

Cutting a mortise, or gain, for the hinge: a. Position the hinge on the door edge and mark its outline with a pencil. b. Make vertical cuts along the outline, tapping the chisel with a hammer. c. Make a series of shallow cuts inside the lines with the bevel side of the chisel down, then gouge out the pieces from the opposite direction with the bevel almost horizontal. d. Clean out the mortise by holding the chisel in both hands—perpendicular to the other cuts—and scraping off the rough spots with the flat side down.

sell doors with all this done except minor planing and sanding. They even sell frames with the door already hung. A split jamb unit is of this prehung **224** type. You place the unit, then

get the premilled door, or possibly settle for somewhat less than professional—but not bad—results. You can do a quality job with well-sharpened chisels, plane and drill. It just takes more time and patience.

Here's how to do it. Plane the door to allow clearance of between $1/16$ and $3/32$ inch on the lock side. Allow $1/32$ inch between the hinge side and the jamb, $1/16$ inch at the top and $5/8$ inch between the bottom of the door and the surface of the finish floor. For exterior doors with weather stripping, allow an additional $1/8$ inch at the top and on each side.

You need a bevel on the lock side of the door to allow it to close freely. Plane the edge $1/8$ inch over 2 inches. That's roughly $3½$ degrees. The usual width of the door is between $1⅜$ inches (interior) and $1¾$ inches (exterior). Plane the edges of the door slightly and sand them smooth.

Hinges, Locks and Stops

Use chisels or a router and template to cut the gain for the hinges. If you use the router, buy hinges with rounded corners. Then you won't need to chisel out the corners. Locate the top hinge 7 inches from the top of the door and the bottom one 11 inches from the bottom of the door. The jamb must also be mortised for the hinges. Screw each leaf of the hinges into place, mount the door, and drop each pin into place. Cor-

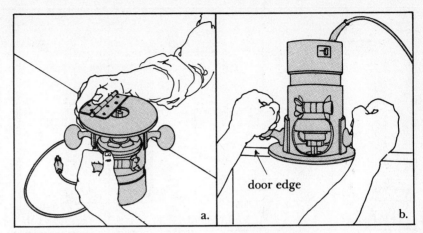

Cutting hinge mortises with a router: a. Set the depth of the cut to the thickness of the hinge. b. Then make the cut with the door set on edge and secured firmly.

rections are made by planing edges or altering the depth of the gains.

Minor adjustment can be made by placing small cardboard shims under one edge or the other of the hinges. Use the box the hinge came in to make the shims, cutting them the length of the hinge and about $¼$ inch wide. If the latch side scrapes, there is too much clearance at the hinge side; place the shims on the other side of the screws from the pin. That will force the door toward the hinge. If there isn't enough clearance on the hinge side, the hinges will bind before the door is closed. Place shims right at the edge of the jamb, between the screws and the pins. That will force the door away from the hinges. If the door scrapes part of the head jamb, one hinge

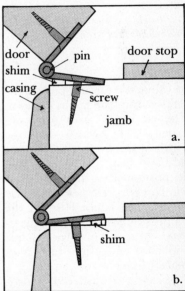

Use shims between the hinge and the door jamb to make minor adjustments: a. Shim between pin and screw if the door binds on the hinge sides. b. Shim on the side of the hinge away from the pin if the door binds on the latch side.

gain may be too deep. Shim it out and the door will even up.

Interior doors must have stops to prevent the door from

225

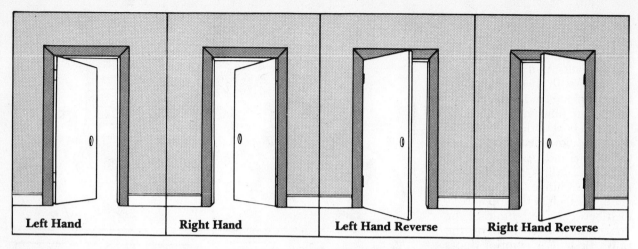

| Left Hand | Right Hand | Left Hand Reverse | Right Hand Reverse |

You'll need to know the "hand of the door" to buy the correct lock set.

traveling too far and pulling the screws from the jambs or door. The stop is a strip of wood, usually a bit wider than the width of the door, nailed to the side and head jambs. It should be positioned so that the door will come to rest perpendicular to the side jamb. Position the hinge stop with 1/16-inch clearance. Miter the corner joints and use 4d finishing nails spaced 16 inches on center.

Locksets are ordered according to the way the door opens. This is called the "hand of the door." Face the side where the key will be inserted into the lock. There are four possibilities: hinges on the left, door opens away from you (inward)—"left hand," LH; hinges on the right, door opens away (inward)—"right hand," RH; hinges on the left, door opens toward you (outward)— "left hand reverse," LHR; **226** hinges on the right, door opens

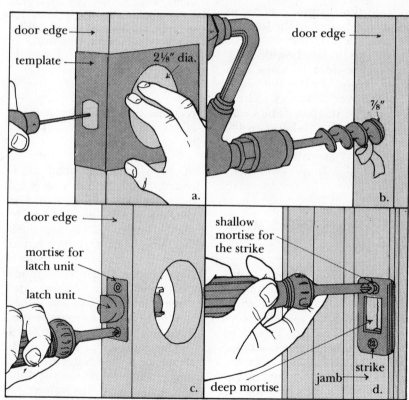

Installing a cylindrical lock set: a. Use a template to position holes in the door for the cylinder and the bolt. b. After boring the cylinder hole through the face of the door, bore the bolt hole through the edge and into the cylinder hole. Then cut a shallow mortise for the latch bolt unit's face plate. c. Install the latch bolt unit, then the cylinder, escutcheons and knobs. d. The final step is to install the strike plate on the jamb.

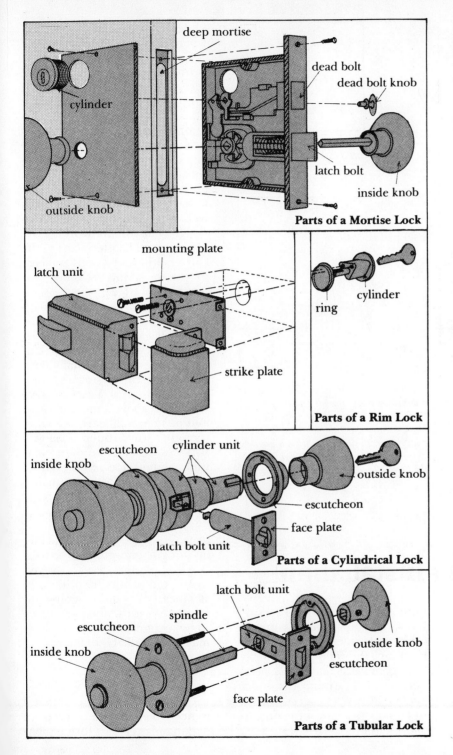

deep mortise

cylinder

outside knob

dead bolt

dead bolt knob

latch bolt

inside knob

Parts of a Mortise Lock

latch unit

mounting plate

strike plate

ring

cylinder

Parts of a Rim Lock

inside knob

escutcheon

cylinder unit

outside knob

escutcheon

face plate

latch bolt unit

Parts of a Cylindrical Lock

latch bolt unit

spindle

escutcheon

inside knob

outside knob

escutcheon

face plate

Parts of a Tubular Lock

toward you (outward)—"right hand reverse," RHR.

Locks come with detailed instructions and templates for locating the holes. Locks are usually placed 38 inches, sometimes 36 inches, above the finish floor. That distance is to the center of the doorknob hole. Cut a hole, usually 2⅛ inches in diameter, through the face of the door. Cut a smaller hole, usually ⅞ inch, through the edge of the door to the larger hole. Cut a mortise around the smaller hole to accommodate the latch unit. The strike is mounted in the jamb opposite the latch unit. It is usually in two parts, a box and a strike plate that fits over the box. Space for the box and the plate must be mortised. Two screws hold the pieces to the jamb.

A popular lockset for exterior doors is the mortise lock. Installation is similar, except that you'll need to cut a substantial mortise in the door edge for the lock. Rim locks are often used with mortise locks. The lock mechanism is mounted to the inside face of the door.

Thresholds

Exterior doors have a trim piece called a threshold mounted on the sill to make the door weathertight. The old ones were made of oak and other hardwoods. Nowadays, they are metal frames with vinyl inserts.

If you bevel the bottom of the door slightly, the door will close more easily. The shorter side of the door should reach the threshold first.

227

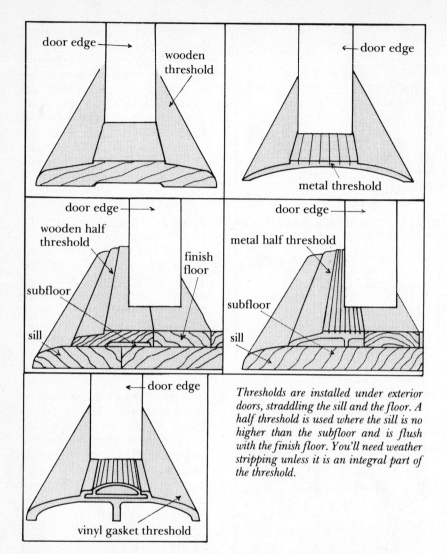

Thresholds are installed under exterior doors, straddling the sill and the floor. A half threshold is used where the sill is no higher than the subfloor and is flush with the finish floor. You'll need weather stripping unless it is an integral part of the threshold.

Wall and Ceiling Installation

When you're ready to put up the walls and ceiling, you have come pretty far. The basic service lines for electricity, water supply and drainage are in. Ventilation and heating should be installed and awaiting the final registers or heating units. Windows are up and doors hung. Now for the interior surfaces. If you've been running cable and pipes to lots of new locations, the walls are probably long gone. But maybe *you* need only to patch around the outlet boxes and cover up a few cracks. In either case, now is the time to make a final check to be sure the cables, vents and pipes are where they should be.

Ceilings are generally done before walls, simply because they are harder to reach. A dropped ceiling, though, is done after the walls. To minimize any possible aggravation with ceilings, take the time and effort to arrange good platforms and scaffolding. The secret of working on the ceiling is to have your tools and materials well organized and to be able to reach what you are working on. Molding will often cover the corners where the walls and ceiling meet—along with any gaps and ragged edges.

Walls may be finished with paint, wallpaper, fabric, ceramic tile, plastic laminates, even boards or sheet paneling. Unlike ceilings, which usually have only one type of surface, walls may have several. You may have wallpaper above a molding strip and painted wallboard below, or the other way around. The wall surfaces between counters and wall cabinets are often tiled or covered with plastic laminates, both materials that will resist spills and gouges.

The wall surface itself is usually wallboard, paneling or tongue-and-groove boards. Brick, plaster or salvaged weathered planks are other possibilities. If you're going to finish up with wallpaper, tile or some exotic surface, the base material should be wallboard.

Wallboard

Gypsum is a white mineral mined like coal and used in making plaster. It is formed into sheets that have heavy paper bonded to each side. These sheets, variously called wallboard, sheetrock and drywall can be nailed to studs or joists and painted or papered. Wallboard can be used to patch large holes in plaster walls. Wallboard is fire resistant and provides a good barrier to sound.

Standard sheets are 4 feet wide by 8, 10, 12, or 14 feet long. The usual dimension is 4 by 8 feet. Thicknesses are ¼ inch, ⅜ inch, ½ inch, and ⅝ inch. The ¼-inch stuff is used to cover old walls or ceilings. The ⅜-inch sheets are used in two-ply construction, in which one sheet is nailed up, then another is nailed on top of it. The ½-inch and ⅝-inch thicknesses are used for single-layer construction. The ⅝-inch sheets—the standard width for residential construction—provide greater durability, resistance to fire and sound control.

Installation

Apply the sheets to the ceiling first. You'll need braces to hold the sheets in place while you nail, and stepladders with heavy planks laid between them or scaffolding to stand on. Whatever you use, make sure it won't tip over easily.

Sometimes furring strips are applied to a plaster wall and the wallboard attached to them, for example, in a house where the plaster is right against a brick wall. But usually wallboard is applied to joists and studs.

Cutting and Measuring

Measure where wallboard

sheets will be installed. Take a measurement on each side of the sheet in case the framing is not square. Doing that also serves to catch simple measuring error.

Sheets are cut along the length or width by scoring a line along the face and breaking the sheet in two. Make the scoring line straight by pulling a utility knife along a straightedge. The sheet should be supported close to the scored line. Press on the back of the sheet beneath the line, and it will snap neatly. The paper on the back will still be attached, however. Cut it with the utility knife. The edge should be smoothed with coarse sandpaper if it won't be covered by molding.

Mark the location of electrical boxes and other holes before you put the wallboard in place. Then cut out the spaces with a saber saw or a keyhole saw. You may have to patch in small pieces around windows and doors, although with careful measurement and cutting, you can fit large sheets closely around openings.

After the ceiling is covered, place sheets horizontally, starting at the top of the wall. This leaves any ragged cuts at the bottom, where they will be covered by molding. If you plan to use molding between wall and

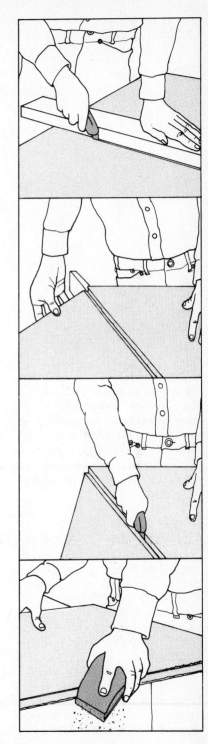

Cutting wallboard: a. Score the wallboard along a straightedge. b. Break the wallboard at the cut. c. Slice through the remaining backing paper. d. Smooth the edges with sandpaper.

229

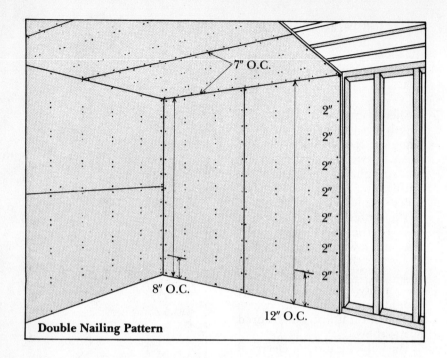

Double Nailing Pattern

7″ O.C.

2″
2″
2″
2″
2″
2″
2″

8″ O.C.

12″ O.C.

After all the nails are in, go back and drive another nail 2 inches from each of the first ones. This is for the middle only. Around the perimeter, space nails 7 inches on center for the ceiling and 8 inches on center for the walls.

Another method of reducing nail pops and cracking around corners is called floating angle construction. It applies only to inside corners. For ceilings, position the sheet with the long dimension parallel to the joists and set the row of nails along the short dimension 7 inches back from the walls. Nail the long dimension normally. For walls, set the top row of nails 8 inches below the ceiling. At inside corners of the wall, nail into the end stud on one side of the corner, but leave the other side free of nails, or "floating." This will mean that the vertical row

ceiling, however, it doesn't matter if you start the wallboard at the bottom. Although sheets may be installed vertically, they are just a bit harder to work with that way. Stagger joints to avoid having the end of one sheet directly under the end of another.

Single-Layer Construction

Joists and studs should be level. The framing must be well dried. This won't be a problem if you are remodeling, but in new construction, moisture can be a problem. As the framing shrinks, it pulls away from the wallboard and nails start to pop loose. Nail pops can be a problem even if the framing is dry because of normal stresses on a building. To minimize this possibility, use a double-nailing pat-

tern in the middle of each sheet. Space nails 12 inches on center.

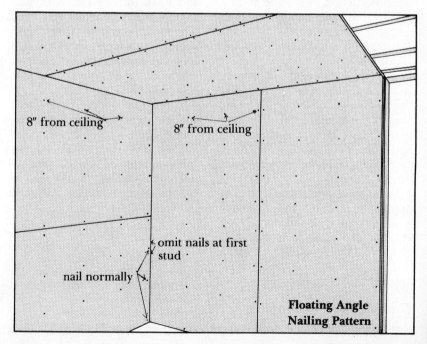

8″ from ceiling

8″ from ceiling

omit nails at first stud

nail normally

Floating Angle Nailing Pattern

on the floating side will be 16 inches back from the corner.

Nails used for wallboard are called annular ring nails. They have flat heads and rings around the shank. For single-layer construction, use 1¼-inch nails. The nailhead should be driven slightly below the surface of the wallboard, but without causing the paper surface to break. Do this by making the last hammer strokes very carefully. The head of the hammer must strike the nailhead evenly or the corner will dig into the wallboard. A properly driven nail rests in the center of a shallow dent made by the hammer head.

Special wallboard screws are sometimes used instead of nails. Screws are more resistant to popping than nails and may be spaced farther apart—12 inches for ceilings and 16 inches for walls. You need a power tool to make the use of screws tolerable. Use an electric drill equipped with a screwdriver that has a clutch attachment that disengages when the screw head reaches the surface. As with nails, screws should rest in a slight dimple in the unbroken surface. Don't use nails or screws closer than ⅜ inch from the edges.

Double Layer Construction

Double layer construction, sometimes called two-ply, offers greater sound resistance and fire protection than single-ply installations. One layer is laid down as a base. It may be ⅜-inch wallboard, backer board or sound-deadening board. It

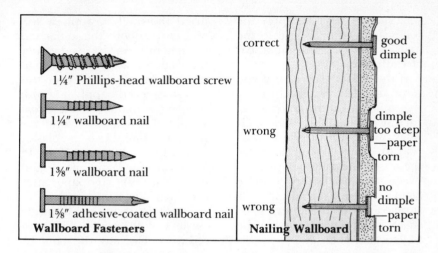

Wallboard Fasteners

1¼″ Phillips-head wallboard screw

1¼″ wallboard nail

1⅜″ wallboard nail

1⅝″ adhesive-coated wallboard nail

Nailing Wallboard

correct — good dimple

wrong — dimple too deep —paper torn

wrong — no dimple —paper torn

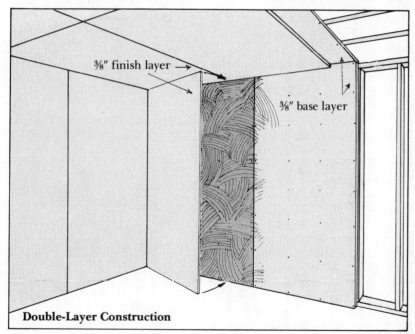

⅜″ finish layer

⅜″ base layer

Double-Layer Construction

isn't necessary to double-nail because double layer is resistant to nail pops. The second layer is ⅜-inch wallboard. It is fastened to the base layer with adhesive, usually applied to the entire base surface with a notched trowel. The joints of the finish layer should be offset at least 10 inches from those of the base layer. Nails or temporary bracing are often used to hold the finish layer in place until the adhesive sets.

Masonry Walls

You can install wallboard over brick or masonry walls. If the **231** wall surface is level, apply the wallboard directly to the masonry surface by using a special adhesive.

If the wall is uneven or if you want to add insulation, apply the wallboard to metal or wood furring strips. Use cut nails (they are rectangular instead of round), and if possible drive them into the mortar layers between the bricks or concrete blocks. Foam insulation may be sprayed between the strips, or sheets of rigid insulation may be fit between them.

Joints and Corners

In both single- and double-layer construction, joints between wallboard sheets must be taped and finished to a smooth surface. This is done with special paper tape and joint compound. Use a joint finishing knife to spread the joint compound into the indentation formed by the tapered edges of the wallboard. Lay the tape in the joint compound with the finishing knife held at an angle of 45 degrees and with sufficient pressure to remove excess compound. Apply a thin layer over the tape to prevent the edges from curling. Fill the nail or screw cavities. The dents around the screw or nailhead allow them to be covered easily.

After the compound has dried thoroughly, apply a second coat to both the joints and the nail or screw heads. Feather the second coat 2 inches beyond the first on all sides. After this coat has dried, apply a finish coat to the joints. This last coat should also extend beyond the previous one. Use a plaster trowel to apply a coat 12 to 14 inches wide. You may sand lightly with fine sandpaper after each coat.

Joint tape is applied to inside corners of the room. The procedure is basically the same as for flush joints. First apply joint compound to each side of the corner. Crease the tape down the middle and press it into the corner. Let the joint compound dry, then lay down two more layers, as with flush joints.

For outside corners, nail down metal corner beads. These are metal strips formed into a 90-degree angle. Each side is about an inch wide. The bead fits over the corner, extending from the top of the wall to the bottom. The corner beads are held in place by nails that extend through the wallboard and into the framing. Since the corner of the bead is raised, no joint tape is needed. The joint

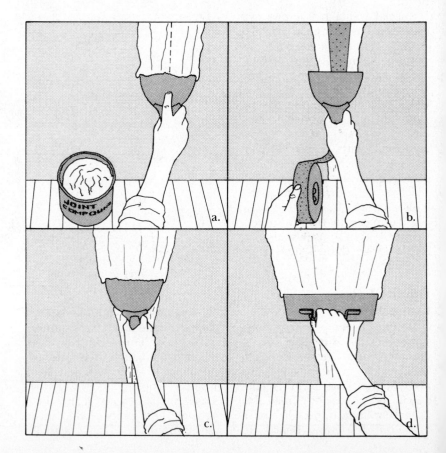

Finishing joints between sheets of wallboard: a. Spread joint compound along the seam. b. Lay the joint tape in the compound. c. Cover the tape with more joint compound. d. Apply a finish coat with a plaster trowel.

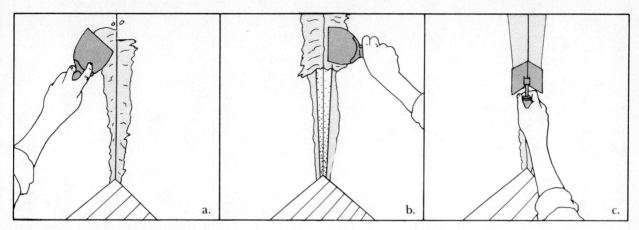

Finishing an inside corner joint: a. Apply joint compound. b. Lay joint tape in the compound, then use a taping knife to press it well into the compound. c. Apply a second and then a finish coat of compound with a corner tool.

compound is spread into each side of the bead. The raised part serves to keep the compound level. As with other joints, three coats feathered out successively will result in a smooth, finished joint. Seal the joint compound with primer-sealer before you apply paint or wallpaper.

Patching

Wallboard, joint compound and patching plaster can be used to patch damaged plaster or wallboard. Patching plaster has a consistency similar to joint compound, but it is designed especially for patching work. It is commonly used to fill in cracks and small holes. Before a crack is filled, it should be undercut with a sharp tool so that the opening at the surface is narrower than underneath.

This holds the patching plaster in place. The plaster is also used to fill around electrical boxes or anywhere that remodeling has left gaps in the wall surface.

Wallboard and joint com-

Finishing an outside corner: a. Spread joint compound over the corner. b. Apply the paper-flanged bead to the corner, pressing it into the compound. c. Apply a second, then a finish coat of compound. If all-metal corner bead is used, nail it in place before applying any compound, but finish it with two or three coats of compound.

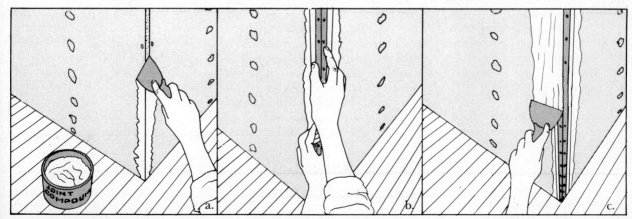

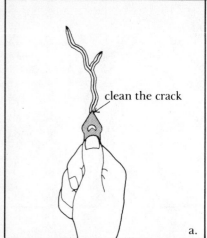

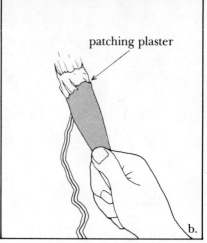

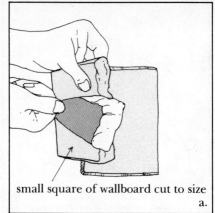

small square of wallboard cut to size

a.

Repairing a hairline crack in the plaster (above): a. Use a sharp tool to open up the crack for the patching compound and to remove loose plaster. A wider crack should be similarly cleaned, but should also be undercut. b. Use a putty knife to spread the patching compound.

Using wallboard to patch a hole (right): a. Cut a piece of wallboard to the exact size of the hole, turn a screw into its center to serve as a handle, then apply patching compound to the edges. b. Holding the patch by the screw, fit it into the hole. c. After the compound dries, sand away lumps, then apply a finish coat of compound with a trowel.

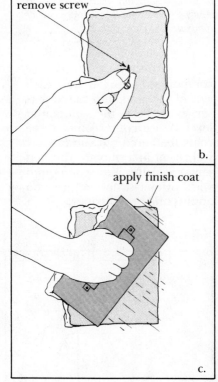

remove screw

b.

apply finish coat

c.

pound will fill in larger holes. Cut out the hole to a square or rectangular shape. Measure this hole and cut a piece of wallboard to fit. It is easier to cut a larger hole that exposes enough framing to support the wallboard than to worry about a small one that doesn't. Nail the piece of wallboard in place and apply joint tape and three layers of joint compound as with a standard joint.

Plaster

Some people prefer plaster walls to those finished with wallboard. Plaster walls make a more solid sound if you tap on them, and they don't give as much if you bump into them. Other than that, there's not a great deal of difference.

Plastering a large area is a job for a professional. The trick of finishing off to a level, smooth surface can't be learned on the first try. If you decide to hire a plasterer, remember to schedule his work with yours and allow for delays that may result if he doesn't start on time.

Plaster must season for three months before oil-base paint is applied. And oil-base paint is a good idea in the kitchen. You can put down a layer of latex while the plaster is curing to protect it from dirt and grease.

Tongue-and-Groove Paneling

Board paneling is applied di-

rectly over joists or furring. Tongue and groove is the most common form of board paneling, but board and batten or

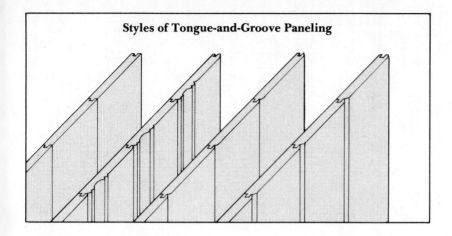

Styles of Tongue-and-Groove Paneling

don't want gaps to open between boards.

The boards range in width from 4 inches to 12 inches nominal. The actual thickness is ¾ inch. If you place the boards horizontally, you can nail them directly to the studs. For vertical placement, nail 1 × 3 furring to the studs and nail the boards into that. Countersink 6d finishing nails and fill the holes with wood filler that matches the wood. Narrow, 4- to 6-inch boards may be nailed at an angle through the base of the tongue (called blind-nailing). Insert the groove of the next board onto the already-nailed tongue of the first; then nail the second board's tongue. This secures the entire surface better than straight nailing would, and there are no nail holes to fill. Finish nailing with a

shiplap joints are used occasionally. You may choose from quite a variety of woods, both hardwoods and softwoods. You can salvage weathered planks or use rough-sawn lumber for a less finished look.

Use well-seasoned wood. The boards should be unpacked and left in the room where they will be used for several days or weeks before you install them. This allows the moisture content of the wood to adjust to the humidity level of the room. Wood shrinks as it dries; you

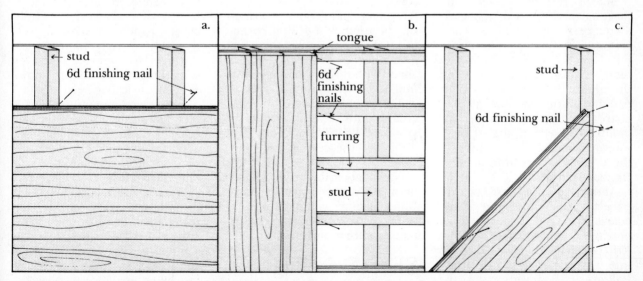

Installing tongue-and-groove paneling: a. When installing the boards horizontally, the first and last pieces must be face-nailed to the studs, and all pieces except the last blind-nailed through the tongue. b. To install the paneling vertically necessitates the installation first of horizontal furring strips. The tongue-and-groove stock is then nailed to the furring. c. A diagonal installation is blind-nailed through the tongues and the exposed ends into the studs.

235

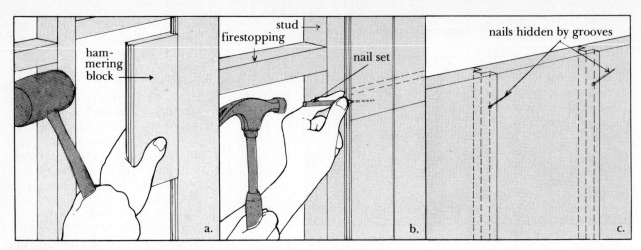

Installing the paneling: a. Tap boards tight, using a scrap piece as a hammering block to protect the tongue. b. Countersink the nails with a nail set to avoid damaging the tongue. c. The nails are hidden in the finished wall.

nail set to avoid smashing the tongue.

Boards can be installed in diagonal patterns. Cut them at 45-degree angles and nail to framing or furring. The ends must meet over a framing member. Install the boards with the tongue side up and blind-nail them. You can install all the boards at the same angle or mount one section angled one way and the next section angled the other way, creating a herringbone pattern.

Another way to use board panels is as wainscoting. The boards are nailed vertically to a height of about 4 feet and a strip of cap molding is placed on top. The upper portion of the wall is finished with paint or wallpaper. Wainscoting can be nailed over wallboard or directly to furring. If it is installed over wallboard, it will stick out from the wall slightly. You can also use sheet paneling for wainscoting. Using wainscot is a good way to get some wood into the room, perhaps to match cabinets or trim, without suffering the darkening effect of solid-wood walls.

Tongue-and-groove boards can be used as a ceiling covering. Like wainscoting, they can give a feel of real wood to the room without darkening it too much. A tongue-and-groove ceiling with painted walls creates an effective contrast. If you use boards for both the walls and the ceiling, use light wood.

Nail the boards at right angles or at 45 degrees to the joists. Blind-nailing will give you a ceiling with no visible nails and a more secure ceiling, too.

Sheet Paneling

Prefinished panels are widely used in the building trade. They are made from plywood or composition board (hardboard) that is finished on one side. There are hundreds of different finishes. Some resemble tongue-and-groove boards; others suggest inlaid wood. You can even get flashy colors with glitter added. Although substitutes cannot replace the warm beauty of real wood, carefully chosen panels can make a positive addition to the room. Paneling an entire room always leaves something to be desired, however, so use it sparingly.

Panels are generally 4 by 8 feet and ¼ inch thick, although other lengths and thicknesses are available. Panels are commonly nailed to a backer board, but you can fasten them to studs or furring with staples, screws, or adhesives. The reason for using a backer board is that the panels are thin and will give slightly if they are not well-supported. The backer board can be either ⁵/₁₆-inch plywood or ⅜-inch wallboard. To attach panels to a masonry wall, use horizontal furring spaced 16

236

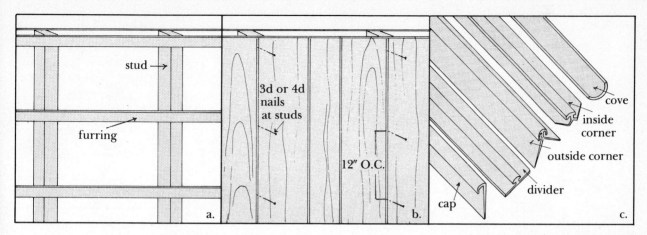

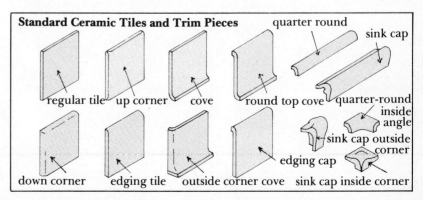

Attaching sheet panels to furring strips: a. First nail furring strips across the studding. b. Nail the panels to the furring and studding. c. Various types of molding are made especially for use with sheet paneling.

inches on center. Place strips of vertical furring between the horizontal strips, and space it every 48 inches.

The panels may be butted directly together. If the seam is visible, it can be concealed under strips of molding. There are many types of molding designed for paneling. With some types, the panels slip into channels, leaving only a strip of molding visible at the seam on the surface of the panel.

Leave panels in the room where they will be installed for at least two days to allow moisture in them to adjust to the room's humidity level. Use a plumb line or level to ensure that the first panel is installed plumb. Leave ¼ inch between the edge of the panel and the facing wall to allow for expansion. Nail panels with 3d or 4d nails, 6 inches apart at the edges and 12 inches apart elsewhere. For some types of hardboard, you'll have to predrill the holes. Cut the panels face up with a handsaw and face down with a circular saw or a saber saw. The

edges of all panels must fall on supporting framing.

If you use adhesive, cut and place the panels carefully. Once the panel makes contact with the adhesive, it is very difficult to move it. Adhesive is usually laid down in strips with a caulking gun. Where edges of paneling meet, use a zigzag pattern in laying down the adhesive.

Ceramic Wall Tile

Tile can be a great addition to a kitchen. The space between a counter and wall-hung cabinets

is a good one for tile, but there is no reason you can't use it anywhere as a decorative touch or as a border. Some of the best-looking tiles have hand-painted designs on them and are therefore fairly expensive —good enough reason to use them as decoration rather than as a complete wall covering. Hand-painted trim pieces may

237

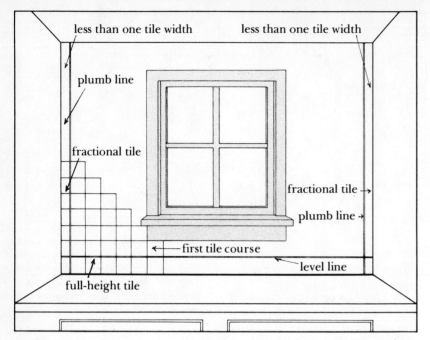

Where only a fraction of a tile will fit, hold a full-size tile in place and mark where to make the cut.

Marking off the wall section for ceramic tile.

not be available. Instead, you may have to make a border of wood molding to give the tile a finished edge.

The wall surface must be clean and level. Patch any cracks or holes. You can apply tile over a painted surface if the paint is not flaking. Wallboard must be firmly attached to framing. Any patches must be sealed with shellac. A plaster surface must cure for at least a month before

you tile it. You can apply tile to exterior-grade plywood but not to interior-grade.

Carefully measure the area you plan to cover. Measure the tiles. Standard ones are 4½ inches square, but you may run into other sizes. Divide the area height in inches by the height

Cutting ceramic tile: a. Using a commercial tile cutter. b. Using a glass cutter to score the glazed surface, then breaking the tile.

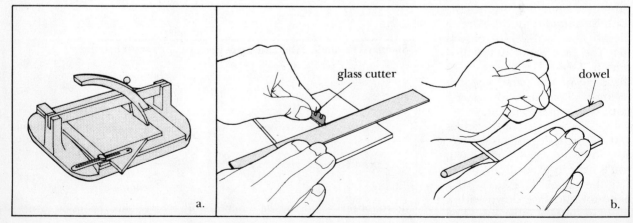

of the tile. Divide the area width by the width of the tile. Round off to the next higher number for each and multiply them together. The product is the number of tiles you will need. Add a few to cover possible breakage.

You'll need plumb lines and a horizontal line as a guide. Wall corners and even cabinets and counters are often out of plumb. Naturally, over short distances leveling is not as important, but it's worth the trouble to line up the tile. Find the lowest point of the area you're going to cover and make a mark the height of a tile above that point. Use a level to mark a horizontal line completely across the area.

Mark a 3- or 4-foot length of 1 × 2 with a series of lines equal to the width of a tile. Use this stick to position the tiles so that any fractions of a tile are equally divided between the two edges. Mark two vertical lines at each side of the area at the point where the full-length tiles end. First fill in the marked area with full-sized tiles, then cut and mount the fractional pieces. Tiles can be cut by scoring the glazed surface with a glass cutter, then snapping the tile in two along the line. Or you can rent a more elaborate tile cutter from a tile dealer.

Ceramic tile is fastened with wall-tile mastic adhesive, one gallon of which will cover about 50 square feet. Apply this adhesive with a notched trowel to an area no larger than 3 feet by 3 feet. Press hard enough that the beads of adhesive are no larger than the notches. Press the tiles straight into the adhesive. Don't

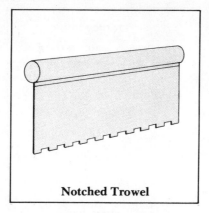

Notched Trowel

move them around once they have been placed because the mastic may get on the surface of the tile. Check each horizontal course with a level to make sure you are laying them straight.

Let the mastic set for 24 hours, then apply the grout with a rubber-surfaced trowel. Hold the trowel at a slight angle, and move it in an arc, forcing the grout down into the cracks. When the grout starts to set, wipe off the excess with a damp rag. After it has dried, rinse off the surface of the tiles and wipe it with a clean rag.

Ceiling Tile

Ceiling tile can be attached to furring strips, metal channels, or directly to an existing ceiling. Most tiles are 12 inches by 12 inches and have a ½-inch flange and channel on two sides and an overlapping flange on the other two sides. The flange is stapled to the support; then a second tile is fitted into the channel. The interlocking flanges secure the tiles without exposing staples.

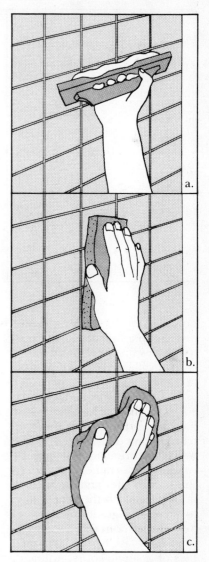

Grouting tile: a. Apply the grout with a rubber-surfaced trowel. b. Wipe up the excess with a damp sponge. c. Finish up with a dry cloth.

Before you put up the tile, snap chalk lines to serve as guides. Locate the middle of the two short walls. Snap a chalk line between these middle **239**

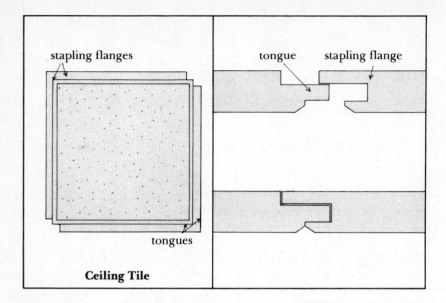

Ceiling Tile

place the tile face up with the cut over the edge of a table. Press down and the tile should break cleanly.

If the condition of your ceiling precludes attaching the tiles directly to it, you will have to fur it out. You do this by nailing 1 × 3 furring at right angles to the joists using 8d nails. The first strip should be at the edge of the ceiling and the second placed right along the chalk line that marks the border of the trimmed tiles. Set the rest of the furring as far apart as the tiles are wide, usually 12 inches on center. Double-check to be certain the edges of the tiles will center on the furring in actual installation. The furring must be level. As you nail it up, check with a four-foot level and shim with wedges to make sure it is. Use pairs of wedges between the joists and the furring. This is a

points to mark the long center line. Snap a line across the center of this line at right angles to it. You will lay your tiles parallel to these lines.

The courses of tile along the edges of the ceiling will usually have to be trimmed. It is best to trim courses equally on opposite walls. Before you put up the first tile, determine the width of the border tiles and snap chalk lines parallel to the center line, to serve as a guide for the border. If the room is not square—it usually isn't—the trimmed tiles of a single course will vary in width.

Trim the border tiles with a sharp utility knife and a straightedge. You'll have to change the blades often. Score the face of the tile deeply and

Installation of ceiling tile begins in a corner, but layout begins in the center. Snap chalk lines across the exact center of each dimension of ceiling. Then snap lines around perimeter of ceiling, parallel to main guidelines, to help size border tiles.

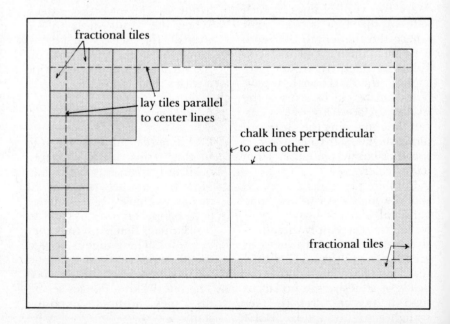

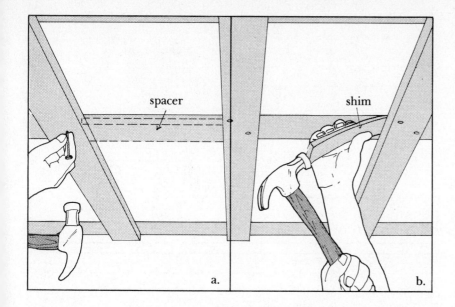

Furring out the ceiling for tile: a. Use a spacer to locate the furring strip, and nail the strip partway. b. Level the furring with shims, then drive the nail home.

tedious process, but a vital one: the finished ceiling will look terrible if it isn't square and level.

Fasten the tile with $^{9}/_{16}$-inch staples, three per side for 12-inch tiles and four per side for 16-inch tiles. The corner tiles will usually be cut on two sides. Since there is no flange on the trimmed side, you'll nail directly to the furring. Cover the nails with molding.

If the ceiling is reasonably level, you can apply tile directly to it with adhesive. Put a blob of adhesive at each corner and one in the middle of each tile. You may need to staple through the flange to the ceiling underneath to hold the tiles while the adhesive sets. Place the adhesive no closer to the edges than 1½ inches.

You can buy metal furring that is self-leveling. This makes it possible to install tiles on a ceiling that is not perfectly level. Metal furring is less likely to warp than wood. You do not have to remove the ceiling surface, although metal furring must be attached to joists. First nail metal molding to the walls 2 inches below the existing ceiling. Then nail the metal furring channels at right angles to the

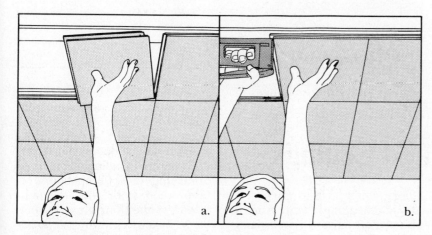

Installing ceiling tile: a. Position the tile. b. Staple the flanges.

Ceiling tiles are easily cut using a sharp utility knife.

241

You can use adhesive to install tile that attaches directly to the ceiling.

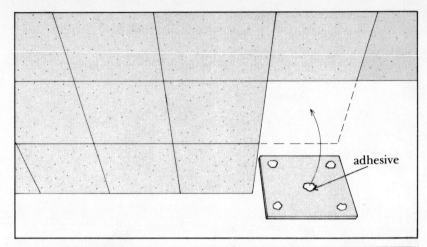

adhesive

joists. Locate the joists exactly before you start to nail. Finally, install the tiles. They are mounted in metal cross-Ts that give the tiles additional support.

Dropped Ceiling

A dropped ceiling is similar to the kind with metal furring except that the panels are suspended by a metal frame that hangs from the ceiling joists. This allows pipes or electrical cable to be concealed between the ceiling and the joists. The panels are typically 2 feet by 4 feet. After they have been installed, they can be lifted out of the frame to allow access to the space above the ceiling.

Nail a perimeter molding to the walls at the desired height for the ceiling. Attach hanger wire to the joists with screw eyes at 4-foot intervals. Fasten the main runners to these; then snap cross-Ts between the main runners and at right angles to them. The edges rest in the perimeter molding. Insert the panels through the openings in the frame and drop them into

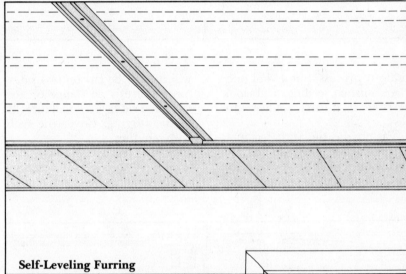

Self-Leveling Furring

place on the support flanges of the frame.

Finishing Walls and Ceilings

Do your painting and wallpapering right after the walls and ceilings have been installed or patched. If you do the painting before the cabinets and floors, you'll have to worry less about damaging them. And if you should harm the walls later while doing the floors or cabinets, repair is fairly easy—

no more than patching plaster and paint. Removing paint from unfinished cabinets, on the other hand, can be difficult. As noted, wood floors should be laid before installing cabinets or finishing walls. Cabinets rest on the wood floor, not the subfloor, so the floor must be done first. Likewise, if you are sanding down a wood floor, you obviously don't want all the saw-

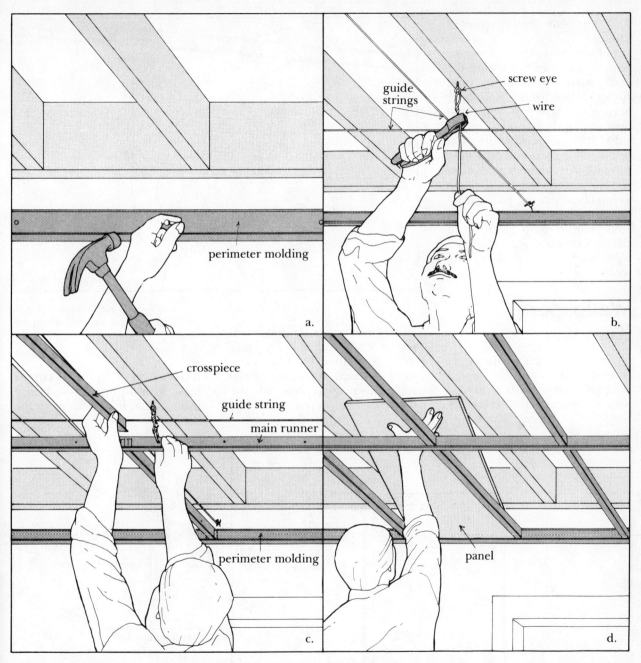

Installing a dropped ceiling: a. Nail perimeter molding to walls. b. Stretch guide strings across ceiling above molding and hang support wires to joists. c. Install support gridwork, leveling it to the guide strings with the wires. d. Drop ceiling panels into place.

243

dust on your freshly painted walls.

Before you can paint or paper, you must make sure the wall surface is clean and smooth. Remove any wallpaper before you paint. If you paint over unbuckled paper, the results may be satisfactory, but removing the paper will be very difficult. And there is always the chance that the paper will begin to buckle under the paint, forcing you to remove the paper. If you plan to strip paint from cabinets or woodwork, do it before you paint or paper the walls.

Wallpaper Removal

You can loosen wallpaper in several ways—with a rented steamer, a large plant mister, or with various chemical solutions.

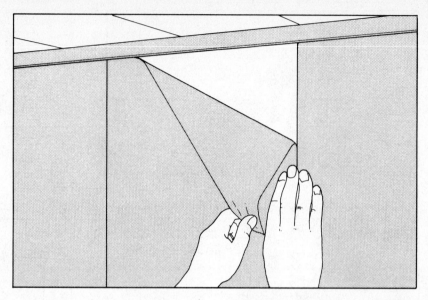

You may be able simply to pull fabric-backed paper from the wall if you are careful.

After the paper is loosened, scrape it off with a putty knife or a wallpaper scraper. Consider yourself fortunate if the wall covering is one of the fabric-backed types. All you have to do is pry one corner loose with a putty knife, fold it over so that it stays close to the

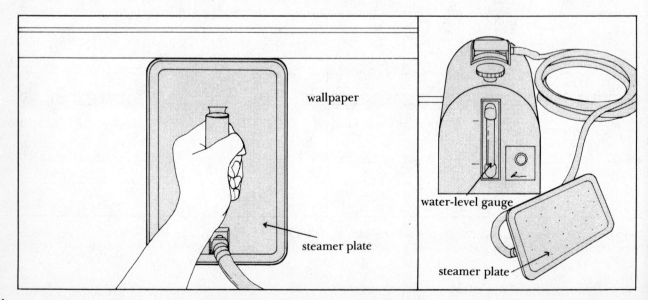

wallpaper

steamer plate

water-level gauge

steamer plate

A rented steamer will remove the most stubborn wallpaper, but don't use it on wallboard.

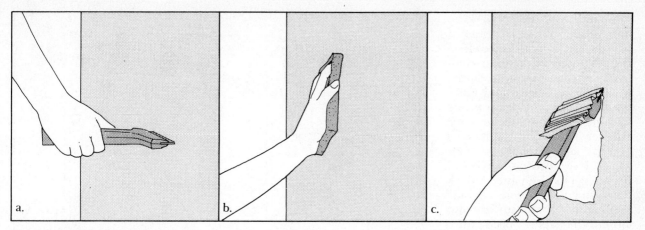

Removing wallpaper: a. Cut waterproof papers with sharp-edged tool. b. Dampen paper with water or a plant mister. c. Scrape off the paper.

wall, and pull slowly with an even force. Be careful to keep it angled close to the wall so that it won't tear. Should any parts tear and stick to the wall, moisten them with some water, and scrape them off with a putty knife or scraper. When removing wallpaper from wallboard, use special care. Don't get the surface so wet that the paper backing on the wallboard comes off.

Renting a steamer may be a good idea if you have a large wall area to strip. There are several different types, but they all operate on the same basic principle. Fill the storage tank with water and plug the unit into an outlet on a 20-amp circuit. The water heats to the boiling point, and the resulting steam travels through a hose to an applicator pan that has small holes on the face that allow the steam to escape—much like a steam iron. Hold the applicator face against the wallpaper until

the steam works through the paper and dissolves the paste. Scrape off the paper with a putty knife or a wallpaper scraper.

If your walls are composed of drywall, *do not* use a steamer. The high levels of moisture can be disastrous—the paper face of the drywall will probably come off with the wallpaper and ruin your wall surface. Steaming the walls may cause water spotting on the ceiling (keep that in mind if you are planning to leave the paper on your ceiling). The steam can also dissolve the paint on your woodwork if it is water soluble.

If your wallpaper is one of the newer, plastic-coated types, or if it has been painted over, run over it with a coarse grade of sandpaper to make holes for the steam to penetrate. Some of the older steamers take quite a while to heat the water, so pouring boiling water into the storage tank will significantly reduce your waiting time. Open all the windows before you begin, because the room will otherwise rapidly fill with steam. Close any doors leading into the room to prevent water

damage to adjoining areas.

Renting a steamer isn't the only way to get the job done. An electric steam iron, applied directly to the wall, works almost as well, if not as quickly.

A popular method is to spray the wall with a large plant mister and then scrape off the wallpaper with a sharp scraper. Spray in small areas, 3 or 4 feet square. The best way is to spray two adjacent areas. Go back and spray the first again after about ten minutes. Scrape the first area; then spray a third area. Spray the second area again, and scrape it. Continue in that pattern so that the water in each area has time to soak down to the paste.

A number of paste-dissolving solutions are also available. Generally sold in dry form, they are diluted with water and applied directly to the wall with a paintbrush, roller, or pump-type garden or paint sprayer. The solution contains chemicals that penetrate the paper and react with the paste. The loosened paper is then pulled or scraped off before the paper has time to dry.

245

Should you prefer to keep unfamiliar chemicals out of your house, you can make effective solutions with some common kitchen staples. Sudsy water or a vinegar-and-water solution (four parts water to one part vinegar), used in the same manner as the commercial brands, are old-time methods which have proven successful for many kinds of paste. A thick flour and water paste liberally applied to the wall surface also loosens the paper. This mixture dries slowly, so you have plenty of time to scrape. The kids will love to help you with this project!

Whichever method you decide upon, work on only one section of wallpaper at a time to keep things simple. Be sure to have ample cartons or bags for discarding the old wallpaper. Otherwise, you'll have bits and pieces of it stuck to everything in the room. Rubber gloves are a good idea if you are working with any strong solutions. And if you have several layers of paper to get through, you may have to repeat the process a few times to thoroughly clean the wall.

Paint and Varnish Removal

Stripping cabinets or wood trim requires patience and a gentle touch. Varnish is easier to remove than paint. Brush a liberal amount of varnish remover onto a small area, 1 or 2 square feet at a time. Wipe off the varnish with a rag. You'll need plenty of rags. If there is still some stubborn varnish,

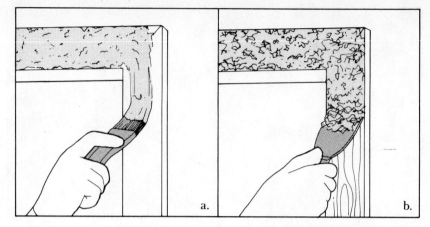

Brush on paint remover, let it stand until the paint blisters, and use a scraper to take it off.

apply more remover and wipe off the excess. You may need to finish up the job with steel wool and fine sandpaper, especially around corners and molding.

If you have only a single layer of paint to remove and if your woodwork doesn't have a lot of ornate molding and trim, you can use a power sander. Belt sanders work faster than orbital sanders. Remove all cabinet hardware before you begin. Start with a coarse grade of sandpaper. When the rough stripping is complete, switch to medium and finally to fine sandpaper. If you have access to an orbital sander, use it for the final sanding with fine paper. Orbital sanders are better for finish work. You'll have to finish up the corners and molding by hand. Fold the paper in half to reach down into cracks.

For several layers of paint and for ornate woodwork, use paint remover. It is available in liquid and paste form. The paste is better on vertical woodwork because dripping is minimized. Paint the remover on with a brush, stroking in one direction only, and wait until the paint starts to blister and wrinkle. Then scrape off the paint with a putty knife and steel wool. A waxy residue may remain after you have scraped off the paint, so wash off the woodwork with a cloth dipped in gum turpentine or denatured alcohol before refinishing it.

Remember that the active chemicals in paint and varnish remover are very powerful. Proper ventilation is a must; open as many doors and windows as possible. Always wear rubber gloves. Protect other surfaces with heavy layers of newspaper. It's a good idea to wear goggles if you're applying stripper to wall cabinets.

If you don't like the idea of using such potent chemicals in your home, mix up your own paint stripper. A solution that's mild on your hands but not on paint consists of three parts of lacquer thinner and one part of denatured alcohol. It works on all kinds of paint.

Wallpaper Application

Wallpaper can bring bright colors and designs as well as a durable surface into your kitchen. A heavy waterproof covering will not only stand up to the spills and moisture of a kitchen, but effectively hide cracks and minor roughness in the wall surface. For the same reason, such a covering is very effective as a ceiling finish.

Consider using boldly patterned wallpaper as a decorating element. Strong vertical patterns make a room seem higher than it is. Horizontal patterns will make it seem broader. Light colors make a room seem larger, while darker ones make it seem smaller.

Types and Sizes

Wallpaper rolls are a standard size. A roll contains 36 square feet, a double roll 72 square feet, and a triple roll, 108 square feet. Most rolls are 27 inches wide, although 54-inch widths are available. The width, however, does not change the standard area of a roll.

Some types come with a vinyl face instead of paper and in different weights. The lightweight kind can be hung with wallpaper paste, but the heavier kind needs special adhesive. The backing is either paper or fabric. Vinyl-faced rolls are referred to as wall covering rather

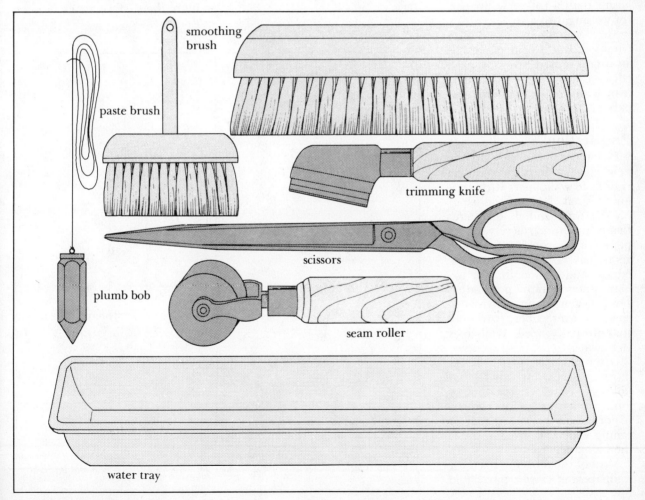

smoothing brush

paste brush

trimming knife

scissors

plumb bob

seam roller

water tray

than wallpaper. The vinyl surface makes the covering waterproof and thus particularly suited to kitchens. It is easy to clean, and it resists moisture and spills. Vinyl-faced covering with a fabric backing will do an amazing job on a problem ceiling.

Some wallpaper comes with paste already applied to the back. All you have to do is wet the back with water. This is not as messy as working with paste and a pasting table. You can buy a water tray, which is a little larger than a roll of wallpaper, for wetting the paper.

Most wallpaper is sold pretrimmed. But if your paper has an undecorated strip at each edge—called selvage—you must trim it off before hanging the paper.

Preparation

Before you can put up the new paper, you may have to get rid of old wallpaper. If there is only a single layer of wallpaper on the wall, and if it adheres firmly to the surface, you can paper right over it. A few loose spots may be removed and the edges sanded smooth, but too many spots indicate poor adhesion. Do not put vinyl-faced covering over paper. It will not stick properly. (See "Wallpaper Removal.")

After the old paper is removed, patch any cracks and holes and coat fresh patching or joint compound with primer-sealer. Coat the entire wall or ceiling with wall size and apply the wallpaper.

Most of the tools you need for wallpapering can be purchased

as a kit from the place you buy your wallpaper. The kit contains a brush to smooth out the wrinkles, a trimming knife with interchangeable blades, a seam roller, chalk and a plumb line. In addition, you'll find shears useful for cutting and trimming, a straightedge helpful in making even cuts, and rags and a sponge vital to wipe up excess paste. You'll need more only if you apply your own paste. Then you'll need a large paste brush, and some sawhorses and a sheet of plywood for a working surface.

Measurement

Before you can start, you have to figure out how much wallpaper you need. Measure the length and width of the room, ignoring windows and doors for the present. Add the lengths of the walls together to find the perimeter. Take the height of the room and multiply it by the perimeter. This product is the surface area of the walls. An 8-foot by 12-foot room would have a perimeter of 40 feet. If the walls were 8 feet high, the surface area would be

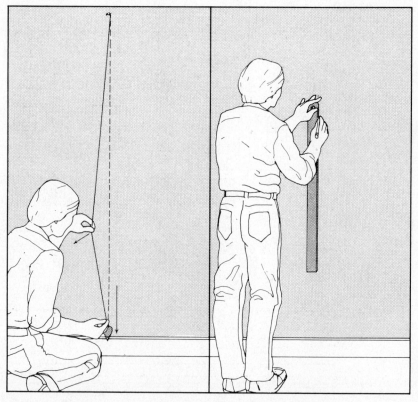

Snap a vertical chalk line and line up the first strip of wallpaper with it. You can substitute a metal straightedge for a plumb line: suspend it from a nail and it will hang plumb.

248

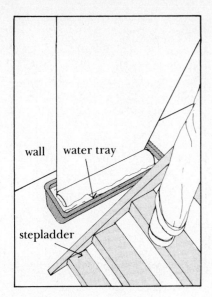

Using a water box.

320 feet. Each single roll, remember, has 36 square feet. To allow for waste, figure each single roll at 30 square feet, each double at 60 square feet and so on. Dividing 30 into the sample area of 320, we find that we need 10⅔ rolls, or 11 even rolls, to cover the total area. For each two windows, doors, or run of cabinets, deduct one roll. If the room has three windows, two doors, and one average-size run of cabinets, deduct three rolls for a total of eight. For ceilings, divide the area by 30 to find the number of single rolls needed.

Applying paste to the wallpaper: a. Lay the paper on a large table and spread paste. b. Fold a 2-foot section of the paper back on itself, without creasing it, so the paste is inside. c. Repeat the process at the other end.

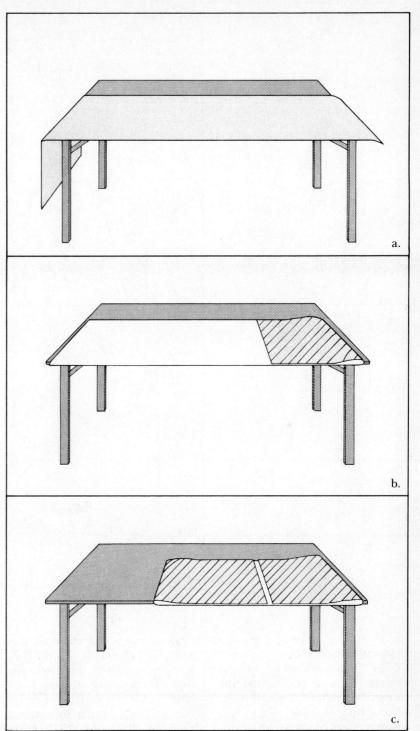

a.

b.

c.

249

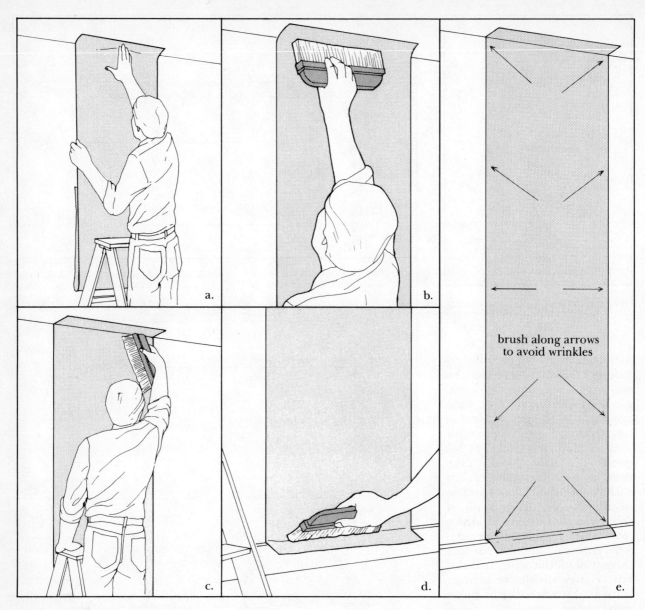

brush along arrows
to avoid wrinkles

Application

The first strip of wallpaper should be hung at a corner or along the edge of a window or door. But because walls are often not truly square, you must first mark true vertical so you can align the strip. To do this, suspend a plumb line from the top of the wall. It can be a length of string with a weight on the end. Chalk up the string, then let it hang until it stops

Hanging wallpaper: a. Unfold the top section and align the paper with the plumb line and allow a bit of ceiling overlap, which is trimmed off later. b. Press the paper to the wall with the brush. c. Stroke from the center to the edges. d. Open the bottom section and brush it on the wall. e. Brush out all the wrinkles and bubbles.

250

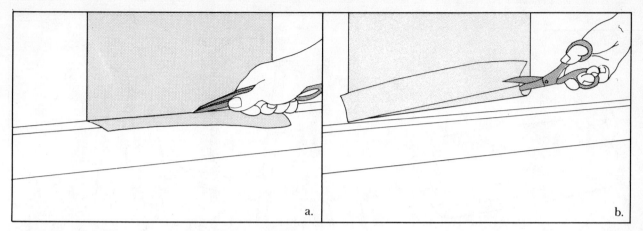

Trimming wallpaper: a. Use shears to crease paper. b. Pull the paper from the wall and cut, then brush paper back in place.

moving. Carefully pull the line taut without moving it from side to side, then snap it, transferring the chalk from the string to the wall, right on true vertical. Line up the strip of wallpaper with this chalk mark.

Work around the room until you end up where you started. Any variation from plumb will show up at the corner where the work begins and ends. Start the rolls in a corner that isn't a center of attention.

Cut each strip about 4 inches longer than the height of the wall. If you are applying paste, start at the middle top of the sheet. Leave an inch or 2 unpasted at the top. Make sure the paste covers each spot, especially at the edges. Fold the strips every 2 feet so that the pasted back of each half of the fold rests on the other back. This will keep paste off the decorated face. Don't crease at the

folds or you'll end up with a crease on the wall.

Line up the edge of the strip with the plumb line, the top of the paper overlapping the ceiling by about 2 inches. Brush the paper smooth, working from the center toward the edges. The paper can be moved a bit while it is wet, but if the entire length is out of plumb, it is easier to pull the paper away from the wall and try again. A helper is useful for hanging the strips.

All outlet and switch covers should be removed before you hang the paper. Hang it right over the wall boxes, then cut away the paper around them. Make the cut smaller than the cover, and there won't be any gaps. Work the paper into any edges that protrude, overlapping slightly. You may have to slit the edge of the paper to fit it around corners of cabinets or molding. Score the edges that overhang the ceiling and floor molding with a straightedge, then cut along this line with shears. After about 15 minutes,

press the seams lightly with the seam roller.

Ceilings

When covering a ceiling, apply the wallpaper strips along the shorter dimension—you'll have fewer problems. Cut the strips about 2 inches longer than the width of the ceiling. Fold the entire strip into 18- to 24-inch sections with the paste side of one fold pressed against the paste side of the other. Do not crease at the folds. A sturdy platform to work on can be made of a heavy plank set between two stepladders. When you are on the platform, your head should be about 6 inches from the ceiling. Have an assistant hold the folded strip while you work. You can also set up a platform to hold the strip, but you'll have to keep moving it. Start at either edge and work across the ceiling. Overlap each edge an inch. Slit the paper into wedge-shaped sections around light fixture holes. Trim off the excess and brush the paper flush with the holes.

251

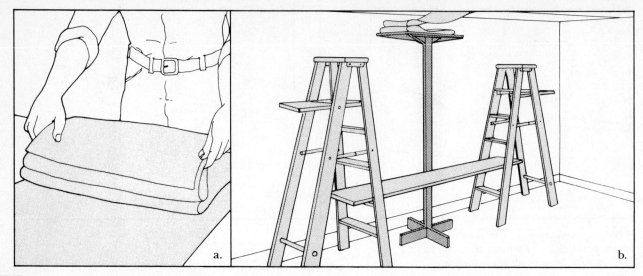

a.

b.

Papering a ceiling: a. Gather the pasted wallpaper accordion fashion. b. Have a helper or use a stand to hold the bulk of the paper while you apply it to the ceiling.

Fabric Wall Covering

You can achieve an interesting textural effect by using fabric instead of wallpaper. A lightweight cloth will adhere to the wall more firmly than will a heavy one. The application is basically the same as with wallpaper, except that you put the paste on the wall instead of the fabric. The fabric should overlap the ceiling and baseboard an inch. If parts of the fabric don't adhere after the paste is dry, paint the entire surface with watered-down paste—on top of the fabric. This will also help protect the surface, although the visual impact of actual cloth on the wall will be lessened a little.

Painting

You'll need durable paint if you choose to paint your harvest kitchen. There's extra moisture in a kitchen, even a well-ventilated one, and there are grease and spills you'll need to clean regularly. Flat-finish paint is often used for interior walls, but in a kitchen it isn't too practical. Kitchen walls should be painted with semigloss paint; it's easier to clean and holds up better to cleaning than does flat paint. Use semigloss or high gloss for woodwork.

The two main kinds of paint in use today for interior surfaces are latex and alkyd base. Oil-base paint isn't used much for interior painting. Latex paint is thinned with water. It is easier to put on and easier to clean up. Alkyd paint is thinned and cleaned with paint thinner or turpentine. It is a little harder to work with, but its covering

power is greater, and it is more durable than latex. Kitchen walls accumulate a lot of grease over the years. Even if you clean the walls with detergent, you're not going to get it all. Alkyd may be applied right over the grease. You can use an alkyd primer and finish up with latex semigloss. Even if the walls already have a coat of paint, use the alkyd primer before the finish coat.

Before you paint, all cracks, gouges, dents and nail holes must be filled with patching plaster. This plaster must be covered with a sealer before you paint unless the paint you get for a primer is a primer-sealer. Fresh plaster must cure for at least a month before it is painted.

Scrape away loose paint. If you are removing old paint from woodwork with paint remover, be sure you clean the newly revealed wood with turpentine. In any case, smooth the surface with fine grit sandpaper.

Before you apply the primer, wash the entire wall surface with detergent and water. Let it dry completely before you apply the paint. Use good-quality brushes or rollers and cover any finished floors or woodwork with drop cloths or masking tape. Remove the tape as soon as the paint starts to set. Using short strokes, paint in different directions, not all one direction. Level the paint by using a soft back-and-forth motion with the brush. Always remove excess paint from one side of the brush after you dip it into the paint can so that it won't drip. With a roller use an upward stroke when the roller is full of paint, then down, then up, until the paint is laid down. Smooth out this zigzag pattern with back-and-forth horizontal strokes.

Repointing

In repointing you remove old mortar from a brick wall and replace it with new material. It is usually done where the mortar has crumbled, and it will dress up a brick wall that has been exposed as a decorative touch in your kitchen.

You will be working with mortar. A good mortar mix is 1 part masonry cement to 3 parts of sand. Or one part portland cement to one part hydrated lime to four parts sand. Or you can buy easy-to-use mortar mix—you just add water. It is expensive, but if you have only a small job, mortar mix can be ideal. It certainly beats laying in 80 pounds of masonry cement

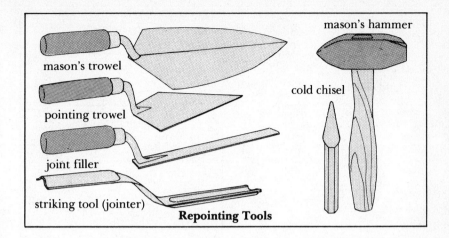

mason's trowel

pointing trowel

joint filler

striking tool (jointer)

mason's hammer

cold chisel

Repointing Tools

when you only need a bucketful.

To match your mortar to that of the old work, you also need some mortar coloring in either powder or paste form. There is some guesswork involved here, so you should mix a small trial batch. Make it a bit darker than the color you want to achieve since mortar lightens as it dries. Of course, if you are repointing all of your exposed wall, the match is not a problem.

Your tool collection should include a ¾-inch cold chisel and a hammer, preferably a 2½-pound mason's hammer, for cleaning out the old mortar. The basic tool used in the repointing is the mason's trowel, a tool with a flat, diamond-shaped blade attached to a handle. You'll also require a jointing tool, which has a long thin blade attached to a handle. A jointing tool fits between the bricks and smooths out the mortar. You can finish mortar with a corner of the trowel, but depending upon the type of joints you want, you may need a striking

tool. You will need something in which to mix the mortar, and when removing old work, you'll want some eye protection. A soft brush is good to clean up your finished wall. Use it before the mortar is completely set.

Work about 1 square yard of wall at a time. Remove the old mortar to a depth of ½ inch with the chisel, doing the vertical joints first, then the horizontal. Hold the chisel on a sharp angle, but be careful not to chew up the bricks themselves. Clean up with the brush, and mix your mortar.

Spray the bricks with water so that the water in your new mortar will not be absorbed too quickly. Scoop mortar onto the trowel, hold the trowel next to the joint and force mortar into the joints with the jointing tool. Do the verticals first. Leave the mortar flush with the brick and go back with your striking tool to finish the job.

After the mortar has set for a few days, you should consider applying a coat of clear brick **253**

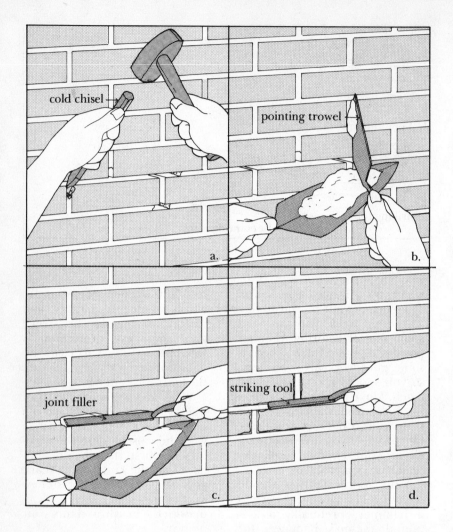

Repointing a brick wall: a. Chisel away old mortar. b. Use a pointing trowel to press mortar into vertical joints. c. Use a joint filler to press mortar into horizontal joints. d. Strike the joints.

cold chisel

pointing trowel

a.

b.

joint filler

striking tool

c.

d.

the time for a new floor. You can pull up the old surface and put down another, perhaps a new type.

Slate floors are durable and not beyond the ability of a home craftsperson. Ceramic tile, though more costly than resilient flooring, is both durable and quite beautiful.

If you want wood floors, they should be installed *before* the floor cabinets. Hardwood is beautiful, and if it is protected with several layers of tough finish, it will hold up well even in the kitchen. You may already have a hardwood floor under that old linoleum. If you can get the adhesive off, sand down the hardwood with a rented sander.

Resilient Flooring

There are two kinds of resilient floors, sheets and tiles. The sheets come in linoleum and vinyl and the tiles in asphalt, vinyl, vinyl-asbestos, and cork. Vinyl affords the brightest colors, while the vinyl-asbestos provides the most durability. For kitchens, vinyl-asbestos is the best bet with tile, vinyl with sheets. Cork tile coated with vinyl is durable and soft to walk on. It also deadens sounds.

Tile Flooring

The floor should be clean and well patched, free of peeling

sealer. It will waterproof the surface, make it easier to clean, and prevent any brick dust from dirtying your room.

Flooring

If you're using resilient, slate, or ceramic tile floor covering, the finish floor is the last thing to be done. That way you don't have to protect it every time you are working on some other part of the kitchen. Resilient floor-

ing, tiles or sheets, is most often used in kitchens. It is easy to clean and is available in many colors and patterns. After years of use, the surface of old resilient flooring will be so worn that it never looks fresh. That's

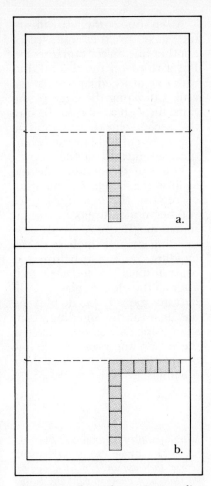

Positioning floor tile: a. Snap a line across the short dimension of the room and lay out tiles perpendicular to the line, repositioning the line if necessary. b. Lay out another row of tiles perpendicular to the first and reposition if necessary. Use the lines as guides.

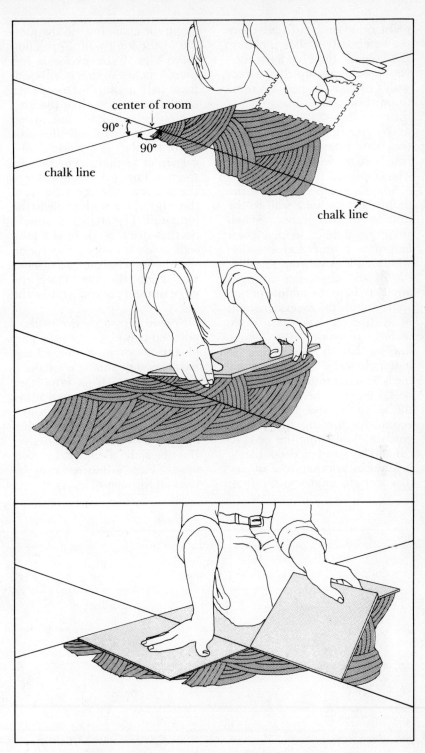

Laying down adhesive with a notched trowel and setting the tiles along a chalked guide mark.

255

paint or loose boards. Remove the baseboard or shoe molding. If an old tile floor has loose tiles, you should pry up the surface with a prybar and perhaps some wood chisels. Get up as much of the old adhesive as possible, and make sure that it doesn't make the floor uneven. Smooth out rough edges with sandpaper or a block plane.

Snap a chalk line from the middle of one long wall to the middle of the other. When snapping a line, snap a short length at a time. Lay out tiles without adhesive from the middle of the chalk line at right angles to it, to the middle of one short wall. If the excess (fraction of a tile) is less than three inches, reposition the center line so that the excess will be half a tile wide. Since most floor tile is 9 inches square, this would be 4½ inches. The excess will be the same at both sides of the room. By moving the layout, you are eliminating the need to cut and lay small pieces of tile.

Lay out another row of dry tiles at right angles to the first, along the chalk line, to the middle of the long wall. Reposition these tiles if the excess is less than 3 inches so that it will be at least half a tile. Snap another chalk line the length of the long dimension of the room, using the edge of the middle tile (after repositioning) as a guide. Use a carpenter's square to make sure the new line is perpendicular to the old one. Also measure from the edge of the middle tile to the long wall. The chalk line should be that distance from the long wall at each end of the room. Use the two chalk lines as guides for laying the tile. Place the edge of the first row against the lines.

Spread the adhesive with a notched trowel. Cover only part of the room at a time. Press hard enough that the excess is pushed away. It is important that there is not too much adhesive, or it may seep up through the cracks. Press the tiles straight down into the adhesive. Do not slide them. Take your time. The adhesive can be worked for several hours.

After you set the last full-size tile next to the wall, place another one directly on top of it. Put a third on the second, but with one of its edges against the wall. Cut along the edge of the third tile with a utility knife, into the second tile below it. The piece you cut will fit exactly into the space next to the wall.

You can either butt the tile against the baseboard molding or remove the molding before you begin measurement and installation. If there is a shoe molding strip at the base of the molding, remove it before you begin installation and replace it after all the tile is in place. It will hide any gaps. If you do butt the tile against the molding, consider using shoe molding even if there isn't one presently. Screw down metal thresholds at door openings.

Marking a tile for cutting: a. Place the tile to be cut atop one in the last full course, then use another, fitted against the wall, as a guide in marking. b. and c. At a corner, the process is much the same, but it must be done twice.

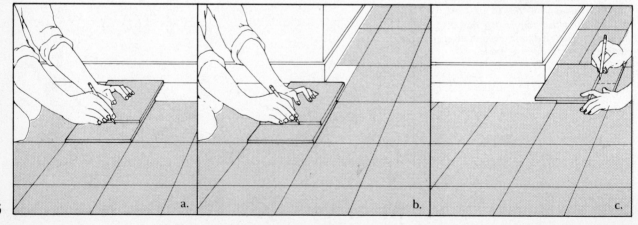

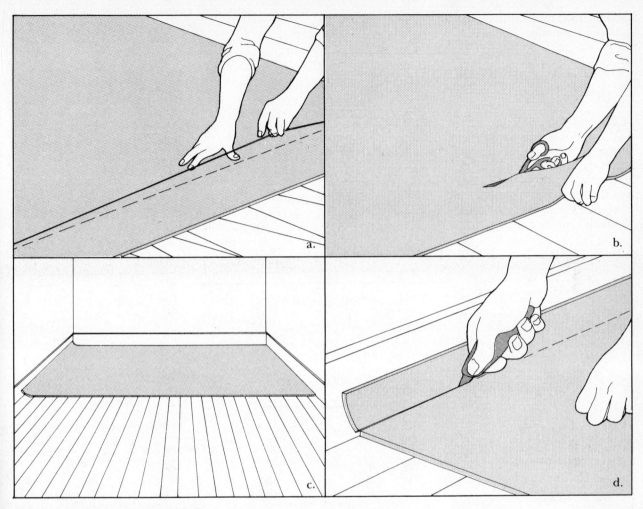

Fitting sheet flooring: a. Use a chalk line to mark longest dimension. b. Cut along the line with heavy shears. c. Fit the flooring in place with excess lapping against one wall. d. Carefully trim away the excess with a utility knife.

Sheet Flooring

The floor must be prepared as with resilient tile. Remove the baseboard or the shoe molding. Measure the room, including counters and irregularities. Roll out the sheet in another room and transfer the measurements to it. The sheets come in 6-, 9-, and 12-foot widths. Snap a chalk line at the longest dimension and cut along it with heavy shears.

Roll up the sheet and carry it into the kitchen. Butt the cut edge against the wall. Unroll the sheet and let it lap up where there is excess. Make slits to allow the sheet to fit over pipes or other protrusions.

Press the sheet into place against corners and trim it even with the edges of the room, leaving ⅛ inch to ¼ inch clearance between the wall and the sheet. It is simpler to trim in two steps, first most of the excess, then the last ½ inch or so. This makes errors less likely.

Roll back half of the sheet after it is perfectly cut to fit and apply adhesive with a notched trowel. Carefully lay the sheet back down and repeat with the other side. Replace all molding. **257**

Screw down metal thresholds at all door openings.

Slate and Ceramic Tile

Slate and ceramic tile can be laid over any sound subfloor. Loose, uneven, or peeling surfaces should be repaired. Slate is available in random shapes or in different-size squares and rectangles. Ceramic tile, usually 4 inches or 6 inches square,

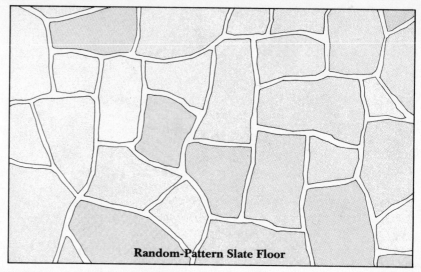

Random-Pattern Slate Floor

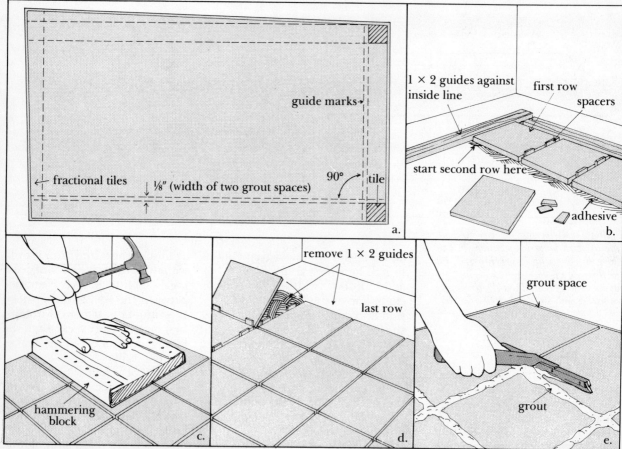

comes in many designs and patterns.

To achieve a random pattern, lay slates without adhesive and number the bottoms. The slates should be placed ⅜ inch apart, smooth side down. Remove 2- or 3-foot sections one at a time and spread adhesive on them. Replace the slates according to number.

Square slate and different-size rectangular pieces can be installed along chalk lines. Lay down the lines between the middle of each pair of opposite walls. Use this as a guide in laying out the slate. You'll need to rent a slate cutter to fit the pieces in at the edges of the room. Lay down the adhesive with a notched trowel in 2- or 3-foot sections. Place a board on top of each slate and tap the slate into place with a rubber mallet. Use a ⅜-inch spacer strip to keep the slates the proper distance apart.

For both random and rectangular slates, let the adhesive dry overnight. Use a rubber-surfaced trowel to apply grout

Laying out a ceramic tile floor (opposite): a. Make perpendicular chalk lines from the most square corner to each of the opposite walls. These guide marks should be away from each wall by one tile width plus ⅛" (two grout spaces). b. Lay out the rows of tile along 1 × 2 guides whose inside edge is on the guide marks. c. Use a hammering block to make sure the tiles are well seated and level. d. Remove the 1 × 2 guides and lay the final rows along the two perpendicular walls (there will be enough room for a grout space on each side of the tile). e. Apply grout.

into the cracks. As it begins to set, wipe off the excess with wet rags or a damp sponge. Polish with a dry cloth.

Ceramic tile is applied in the same manner that it is attached to walls, except that you should use $^1/_{16}$-inch spacers to keep the tile separated slightly. The floor must be perfectly sound and level. Apply mastic in 3-foot sections. Press hard with the notched trowel to avoid excessive mastic. Allow the mastic to dry and apply grout.

Wood Flooring

Use either tongue-and-groove boards or random-width planks. If you don't have any real planks, you can buy random-width tongue-and-groove from the mill. A finished floor is somewhat risky in a kitchen. Use only hardwood and finish with at least three coats of polyurethane varnish. Then apply a compatible floor wax on top of that and keep it replenished. This will protect the floor from anything short of a major disaster.

Hardwood flooring is available in widths ranging from 1½ inches up to 3¼ inches. Standard thicknesses are ⅜, ½, and $^{25}/_{32}$ inch. You'll find the boards have tongues and grooves at the ends as well as the edges to ensure tight joints all around.

It is important to allow the flooring to acclimate to the humidity levels in your kitchen before you nail it down. Stack the flooring in the room, putting slender strips of wood, called stickers, between layers of flooring to accommodate air

circulation. Give it several days—several weeks is better—to adjust. If you don't, it's not unlikely the boards will dry and shrink slightly, opening tiny gaps between boards.

The subfloor must be clean, in good condition, and with all nails driven completely into place. Remove all molding. Lay 15-pound building paper over the subfloor, lapping the edges by 3 inches. Snap a chalk line on the paper to show the location of each joist. Lay the flooring at right angles to the joists.

Set the first board ½ inch from the wall and nail straight through it into the subfloor. Countersink and fill the nails on the first strip. The ½-inch space will be covered with baseboard and shoe molding. Face-nail pieces for the first strip along the edge of the wall. Leave ½ inch at both ends.

Blind-nail succeeding strips into the tongue at an angle of 45 to 50 degrees. Use a nail set for the last strokes to avoid damage to the tongue, or better yet, rent a portable nailer made specifically for nailing down flooring. The nail size depends on the floor thickness. Cut the pieces so that no joints on succeeding strips are within 6 inches of each other. Pull the last strip into place with a crowbar. The finished floor should have a ½-inch gap all around.

Finishing

Wood flooring may be bought prefinished, or you can do the job. If you are finishing an old floor, rent a drum sander, a disk sander, goggles, and earprotectors. Buy three grades of **259**

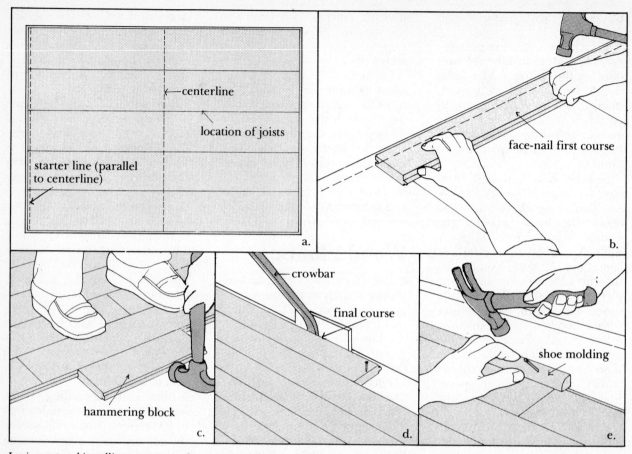

Laying out and installing a tongue-and-groove wood floor: a. Mark the locations of the joists, then locate and mark the centerline of the dimension perpendicular to the joists and a starting line ¼ to ½ inch from the wall, parallel to the centerline. b. Position the first board along the starting line, face-nail through the board as close to the grooved edge as possible, using pilot holes, then blind-nail through the tongue edge. c. Position subsequent boards, using a hammering block—a scrap of the flooring—and a hammer, then blind-nail them. d. The final course is fitted using a crowbar and secured by face-nailing. e. Installation of baseboards and shoe molding will hide the gaps between flooring and wall and cover the nails.

sandpaper to fit both sanders. Start with coarse paper on the drum sander. Start at one end and walk it across the floor. Keep the machine moving or you'll get a rippled, uneven floor. Go around the edges with the disk sander loaded with coarse paper. The molding should be off, naturally.

Work down to fine paper. You'll have to get tight spots with paint scrapers and block sanders. Sweep and vacuum all the dust, but wait a few hours for it to settle.

If you want a stain, paint it on, and after a few minutes, wipe off the excess with rags. You'll need plenty of them. A stain is not necessary, but applied lightly, especially on hardwood, it will do little more than emphasize the wood grain. Test the stain in an inconspicuous place or on a scrap of the flooring. If it goes on unevenly, paint the floor with a prestain before you apply the stain.

Finally, put down several

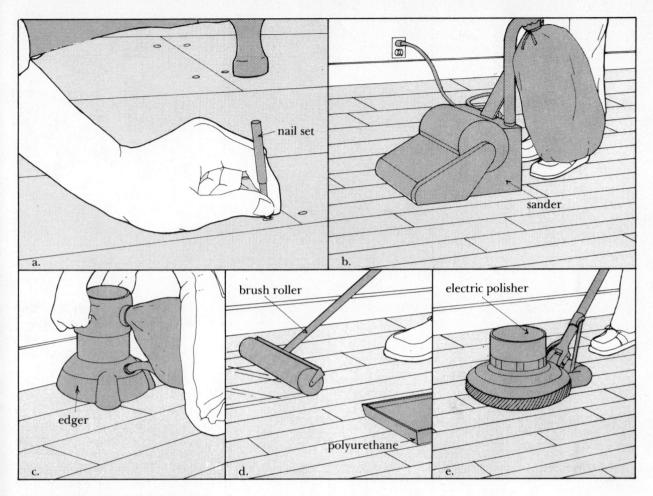

Finishing a wood floor: a. Set all nails. b. Sand with three grades of paper. c. Sand the edges with three grades of paper. d. After vacuuming thoroughly, apply finish. e. Wax if desired.

coats of varnish. Polyurethane is the best all-round finish. Do not shake the can or stir. The least mixing will cause bubbles that can remain when the finish dries. Brush it on very carefully. Let each coat dry completely.

Molding

Molding adds the finishing touch to a kitchen. Under it are the cracks, the gaps, the mistakes. But who's to know? Be careful when you attach it, though, because hammer dents, cracks, and bent nails stand out.

The window stool and interior window and door casing are part of the molding. Seams be-tween the paneling are often separated with a molding strip that hides the seam. The angles between the walls and the floors are always covered with a strip of broad baseboard; against it a small strip called a shoe is often added. Inside corners often have cove molding and outside ones have a cap of outside corner molding. The top of wainscoting is finished with cap molding.

261

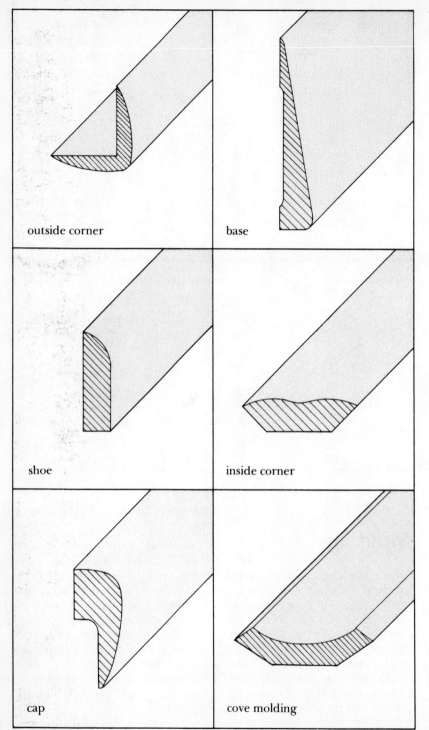

outside corner

base

shoe

inside corner

cap

cove molding

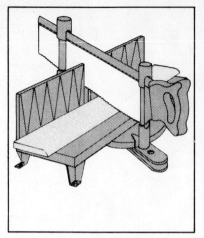

Use a miter box to cut molding.

Nail molding with finishing nails. Countersink them with a nail set and cover the holes with a wood filler—preferably one that matches the wood finish.

Outside corners must be mitered using a miter box or a wood trimmer.

For an inside corner, butt one piece of molding against the wall. Miter the other piece at 45 degrees. Then cut it with a coping saw, holding the blade at 90 degrees to the face of the molding and cutting along the end, following the line of the molding. Undercut slightly and the piece will butt perfectly against the first. This is called a coped joint.

You can do this finish carpentry using the same woodworking tools you used to cut and nail the framing, but that's not really being a finish carpenter.

Molding is made in a variety of shapes for a variety of purposes.

Coping a joint for an inside angle: a. After cutting a 45-degree miter on the molding, darken the edge of the miter with a pencil. b. Holding the coping saw perpendicular, cut along the line. The finished piece should fit tightly against another piece of the same molding.

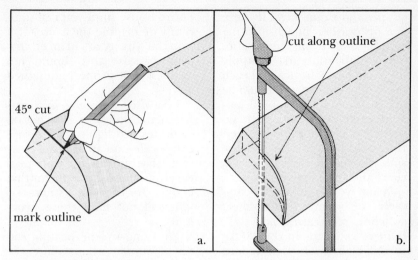

The better your tools, the better a job you'll be able to do.

A miter box or wood trimmer will cut molding at perfect angles. The wood trimmer, a guillotine-like device, does a better job with molding, but a miter box is more versatile. The best, and most expensive, models will cut anything up to framing studs at any angle you desire.

The saw used to cut molding and window casing in a miter box is called a backsaw. It has a broad rectangular blade with a heavy reinforcement along the top edge and 14 to 18 teeth per inch, for fine cuts. You'll also need a coping saw, for cutting those coped joints.

To nail the molding in place, use a 10- to 12-ounce claw hammer. This is more delicate work than spiking studs together, so use a more delicate hammer. And use a nail set to countersink the nails so you don't dent your expensive molding.

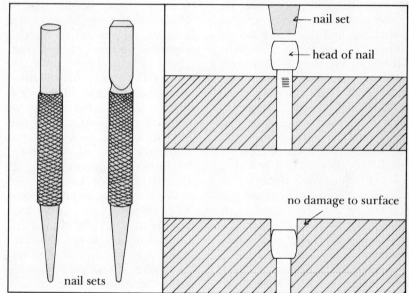

Complete the nailing of molding with a nail set to avoid damage to the surface.

Wrapping Up the Job

Your harvest kitchen is almost done. Soon you will be canning tomatoes by the bushel, baking bread in fragrant loaves, and cooking, hopefully with more ease than you thought possible. All that remains is the final set of connections for your plumbing, wiring, and heating systems.

The finish work of plumbing involves connecting the stubouts to faucets and drains. Mount the sink in the counter, install the faucets and the drain, and make the connections to **263** supply and drain lines. If there is a dishwasher, attach it to the supply and drain lines also. Turn on the water to the supply lines and check for leaks at each new joint. The faucets should be off at first. They should not drip under pressure and no water should appear between the base of the faucet and the sink. Turn on the water and check the drain lines for leaks.

When you're ready to complete the wiring, first connect switches, receptacles, and light fixtures to the conductors. Make sure that all ground connections are made, that there are no loose connections or bare wires touching, and that there are no other obvious faults. Carefully insert all the devices into their outlet boxes and fasten cover plates or light fixtures into place. Finally, turn off power to the main fuse or breaker box, and attach each circuit to it. Remove all the fuses or turn off each breaker. Turn on the power to the house, then restore the power to the old circuits one by one by replacing the fuse or switching on the breaker. Finally, restore power to the new circuits, one by one.

Check the operation of every single device and fixture on the new circuits. Be alert for such things as flickering lights, which indicate a possible loose connection, dimming of lights when appliances switch on, or even the smell of smoke. In the latter case, shut down power to the entire house until you can definitely determine the cause. If it is in the wiring, call in an electrician, because this should not happen in a properly designed system.

Likewise, dimming of lights when an applicance switches on indicates that lights are improperly located on an appliance circuit. If you draw up your plan carefully and use conductor that is rated for the load it will carry, you will not have these problems.

Finishing up the heating can be as simple as installing the registers in a hot-air system. Make connections for electric heaters as you do with other electrical fixtures. Install radiators or convectors after the rest of the finish work is done. When your heating units are in place, check that they are operating properly. You may have to wait for cool weather to make the final adjustments to balance the kitchen heat with that in the rest of the house.

Now the last switch plate is screwed tight, the faucets actually spout water, the drains drip not a drop, the floors shine, the walls are smooth and cheery with color, the windows sparkle, and the doors close snugly. Even your tools are tucked away, cleaned and oiled, ready for a rest. It's time for you too to rest and bask in the pleasure of your family's comfort and your friends' compliments.

Part III

Appliances, Large and Small

Tools are essential to any workplace; in many cases, tools are pivotal to the design, layout and use of the workplace. In a working harvest kitchen, the appliances and other kitchen equipment are the tools. As you design your harvest kitchen, it is vital to know the size and working characteristics of each appliance you want to install. It's vital to know what other tools—pots and pans, small appliances, knives and gizmos—you'll have, to work with and to store. Moreover, it's likely the harvest kitchen will have some out-of-the-ordinary equipment: it won't have a Baconer, it will have a grain mill. In choosing these tools for your harvest kitchen, look beyond color and style, characteristics so dear to American kitchen consultants. Look instead for the characteristics that will make them useful, efficient tools to help you in your kitchen work.

The Heart of the Kitchen

If you are a gardener who puts food by for the winter, the kitchen is the most important room in your house. Not for you the compulsive consumer's kitchen, equipped with a can opener, microwave or toaster oven, hot plate and midget fridge or freezer. You spend a lot of time in the kitchen pre-

serving the harvest bounty so that you can eat well all year round, and your kitchen must be designed and equipped so that you can do this efficiently.

The cornerstone of the harvest kitchen is the basic equipment—the appliances, large and small, that you work with daily and depend on completely at harvesttime. Your "large" appliances should really be large if they are to handle the big quantities of food processed in a harvest kitchen. Each piece must be sturdy, in proper working condition, and must work well, both at its own job and as a member of the team you have assembled. No maneuvers in kitchen design can compensate for the failure or lack of an appliance.

Good organization is the other main requirement for an efficient harvest kitchen. Sometimes, for example, when all the tomatoes ripen at once and you want to get them all canned, you need several cooks working in an assembly line to expedite the different stages of processing. At times like this, your kitchen must function like the kitchen of a small, well-run restaurant, with nothing hidden, no attempt to conceal rational clutter. On the other hand, when there is only one cook, operations must move just as smoothly and swiftly. Foods can spoil in the time it takes to carry them from a distant preparation center to the stove.

The secret of success in running a harvest kitchen lies in careful organization and sound basic equipment, including large-scale major appliances.

Establish Your Criteria

When you choose your basic appliances, criteria of size, durability and simplicity come into play. So does a thorough knowledge of what you hope to accomplish in your harvest kitchen.

Size

How large a scale? Well that, along with much else in a kitchen, depends on the cook, or cooks. A good many people are learning that when it comes to the complexities of harvest cooking, a four-burner universe is too confining. On the other hand, some cooks say it's not the number of burners that matters, but their size and placement. There must be free space to set hot pans and kettles on, and burners or elements should be large enough to heat the bottom of huge pots evenly. Other harvest cooks, who bake a lot or dry foods in the oven, are more often interested in oven size. Some want separate cooktops and built-in ovens organized into work areas. The important thing to remember with stoves is that for harvest quantities they must be big.

There's more disagreement about the size for refrigerators. Americans often wonder how Europeans get along with such small refrigerators. The answer is that in addition to shopping more frequently, Europeans don't use refrigerators for cold pantries the way we do.

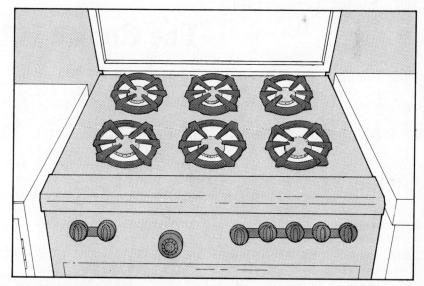

Many find conventional stoves just won't do when harvest season arrives. Restaurant stoves are ideal for large-scale harvesting operations—the burners are larger, more widely spaced, and there are usually more of them.

The household that eats food fresh from the garden in summer and direct from the pantry shelves and freezer in winter doesn't have much use for a large refrigerator. But stocking purchased or home-produced meat, fruit or dairy products in bulk may make a large refrigerator attractive to you.

Durability

A harvest kitchen, one that may have to provide for six or seven separate processing activities at once, takes a terrible beating. A big part of that beating is delivered to appliances, so they should be selected for their strong materials, their sound design and their ability to last. Avoid the flimsy, the unsteady, the complicated device with many moving parts. Like a restaurant kitchen, a harvest kitchen should stick to business and to basics. You'll find no easily broken built-in timers, no refrigerator-door drink dispensers in a restaurant.

Avoid easily chipped enamel, easily bent chrome and all that is fussy, purely decorative or unsubstantial. A kettle of applesauce comes down pretty hard on a cooking surface when it weighs 20 pounds or so.

Simplicity

When you're keeping four separate timing schedules in mind on an August day, the last thing you need is a ten-minute hunt through cabinets and drawers for a misplaced processor blade. A good knife kept at eye level may actually get the job done faster. At times of pressure, organization is all, and simplifying is the key to organization. In choosing minor appliances, steer clear of those that perform only one operation. They take up as much room in your cabinets and in your mental "thing index" as ones that really earn their keep. If you have a stove that will cook a hamburger do you really *need* a gadget to do it? In eliminating unnecessary appliances from your shelves or your "wish list," examine your own ways and habits. How often would you really need square eggs? Do you really need that special appliance that cooks eggs in little cubes?

In general, the rule modern

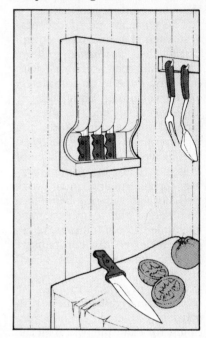

Storing equipment you use every day, such as a favorite knife, within sight and easy reach, eliminates frustrating searches.

interior designers apply to living room furniture works all the better for kitchen appliances: keep them big and few.

The Choice Is Yours

There are at least four thoroughly interrelated factors you will need to consider in establishing criteria for selecting appliances. Ask yourself how much you can or should pay for them. Then ask yourself how much you can or should (in ecological as well as direct cost) pay to run them. Then think about what you plan to use them for—what they should be able to do for you. Finally, consider how these appliances will fit into your general living patterns, both present and future. You will find that as you mull these things, categories will mesh and melt together and even more factors will emerge.

Economy

The economy of the rich is to buy for the future; the economy of the poor is often to make do with relics from the past. If you're just starting out your homestead or harvest home career and your negotiable assets are few, the best place to put what you *do* have is probably *not* into kitchen appliances. The price of a sturdy new restaurant-style range is high, and you can do cooking and baking and canning—on a less-grand appliance. As you can or dry in small batches instead of freezing in large ones, however, keep one eye on the future (however remote it seems) so you don't box yourself into your present restrictions. If you save space for future "dream" appliances, their installation will cost you less. You will find you have to be clever and adaptable when you live in the present and future simulta-

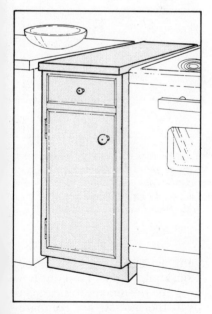

Planning for future appliances may leave you with some gaps in your present layout. A filler cabinet offers continuity as well as extra storage space.

neously so that your kitchen can grow along with your assets while functioning at top capacity now. If you measure your dream range and find it a foot longer than the second-hand stove you now own, build a temporary cabinet to make up the difference. You can use the cabinet elsewhere when you eventually get your dream range.

Keeping one eye on the future will often mean you skip intermediate steps and make do with *less* than you could afford at a given time. If it would really take a twelve-cubic-foot chest freezer to hold all your excess garden produce, but you can afford only a six-foot one now, it may be wisest to keep on canning until you can have exactly what you want.

Buying Secondhand

With time, effort and intelligent judgment you can save money by buying used appliances. There are stores that sell only secondhand, reconditioned or demonstrator appliances, and others that combine used and new sales. There are also auctions, yard and garage sales, and classified ads through which individuals sell used appliances. One important fact to remember in looking for appliance bargains is that even if the time limit has not expired, a manufacturer's warranty will no longer apply once an appliance has changed hands. Some secondhand dealers offer their own, generally short-term, warranties, but it

is important to check, through Better Business Bureau or through experienced friends, on the reliability of any dealer you may have to trust.

Buying from individuals or at auctions means even greater risk for the bargain-hunter unless you know the people you are dealing with personally or know how to examine an appliance for potential problems.

In buying reconditioned appliances from a store, find out which parts have been replaced or repaired and, if possible, why the repair was made. The "reconditioning" of ranges is often just a thorough cleaning or repainting. Check repainted enamel to make sure that it has been baked on and will not chip easily. When enamel has been sprayed on to cover up scratches or rust, it usually has an uneven or milky look. Sometimes you can detect small lumps or bubbles on the sprayed area. If you suspect that a used appliance has been spray painted all over as a touch-up measure, find a hidden surface like a flange on the back or the interior of a drawer, and see if the new paint scratches or peels when you apply a thumbnail or the side of a coin.

A privately sold range or dishwasher may not have been cleaned. Try to determine if it works, preferably by demonstration, then estimate to what extent you can improve appearance and performance by giving it your own thorough cleaning.

On an electric range, test each element to see if it becomes completely red when turned on. **271**

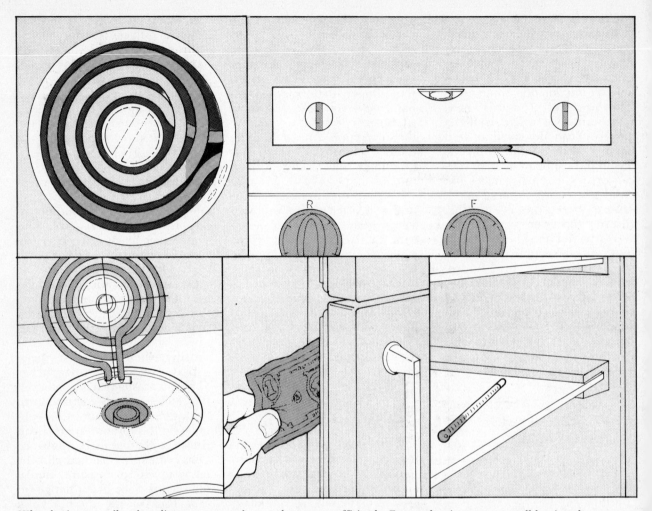

When buying secondhand appliances, test to make sure they operate efficiently. For an electric range, turn all heating elements on to high to see that they turn completely red, and use a straightedge to determine whether burners are perfectly flat. On any range, check that the oven vent is free of obstruction, since the vent assures even heat distribution and removes excess moisture. Test refrigerator and freezer gaskets by closing the door over a dollar bill; if there is no resistance when you pull the bill out, the gasket is defective. And use a thermometer to check that the temperatures inside the refrigerator fall between 32 and 45°F. in the fresh-food compartment and 0 and 10°F. in the freezer section.

Check to see that elements are level and flat. If they are warped or dead, determine if they can be replaced and add replacement cost to the price you are considering. Use a dependable thermometer to check oven thermostat settings, and go over ovens for poor hinges, rusty racks or rack holders and warped liners. Check insulation.

On gas ranges, in addition, check for rust on oven floors, on baffles under the floor and on pipes and burners For your own safety, see that the oven vent is clear of obstruction. Check pilot lights. Find out how long the oven takes to heat. Gas oven thermostats are comparatively easy to adjust. Try to estimate whether or not you can unclog holes in the burners to increase efficiency.

In buying a used refrigerator the most important matter is to find out if it will cool satisfactorily. Look at an advertised refrigerator only when it is plugged in and has been running for a day. It should register 32 to 45°F. in the food compartment and 0 to 10°F. in the freezer, preferably the lower temperature. If no thermometer is available, see if ice crystals form within an hour on water put into the freezer compartment. Check refrigerator cabinets for foul odors and test gaskets by putting a piece of paper between the door and the side wall and seeing if it is hard to remove with the door closed. Gaskets are easy to replace, but this adds to the total cost.

When buying used or new appliances, it is always good to check with manufacturers to ascertain the ease with which replacement parts can be gotten. There are horror stories about people who've had to buy a whole door when a handle was sprung. A general observation is that the simpler, more comprehensible, less automatic a machine is, the easier it will be to keep in repair and the less chance there will be of getting stung if you buy it used.

Buying It New

In buying new appliances, the key to economy is knowing what you need and learning what is available and where to find it least expensively. This means planning and intelligent shopping. You will have to learn both the names of reliable dealers and the range of prod-ucts they carry or can order. In addition to time and effort, intelligent shopping takes a certain amount of patient sales resistance—singlemindedness in the face of glamour and trendiness. That's where knowledge of your own harvest needs comes in. Don't buy under pressure—your own or the dealer's. It's better to choose what you want before you can afford it than to see it later when you've settled for a permanently installed second best.

Energy Savings

When you buy a bed or chair you've paid for its use; with appliances the cost continues—even doubles over time—in your utility bills. Always measure economy of use along with economy of purchase.

The principal factors in energy saving with appliances are (1) choice of fuel, (2) choice of model, (3) placement and (4) use patterns and maintenance. Cooking, lighting, refrigeration, water heating and the use of small appliances account for about 9 percent of total energy consumed today in the United States. It is important to know which appliances are heavy users and which make little difference to our utility bills. See chart.

Choice of Fuel

Only a few years ago it cost less to run natural gas ranges than electric ones. Since federal deregulation of natural gas prices, this is no longer universally true. In deciding between an electric and a gas stove, make a careful comparison of costs in your area. Agricultural extension economists may be willing to help you with this.

If you have your own woodlot, using a wood range will save you money. There is, however, a trade-off in labor and comfort for savings when you burn wood.

Model Choices

In some models of gas ranges the principal energy cost goes into maintaining constant automatic pilot lights for burners and ovens. Pilot lights on newer models use "microflames" that consume less energy or have electrical igniters. The old-fashioned match is the cheapest igniter, but make sure gas flowing to the pilot light on your range can be turned off before you decide to use matches.

Ranges with self-cleaning ovens and smooth cooktops are generally high energy consumers, while microwave ovens, for all their other problems, are low in energy use. Chest freezers are substantially less costly to operate than upright ones or side-by-side refrigerator-freezers. A few frost-free refrigerators have energy-saving switches. Manual defrosting, if done often, may actually cost **273**

APPLIANCE OPERATING COSTS
By the Minute, Hour, Day or Job

Electric Product	Typical Wattage	Cost	Time
Air Conditioner			
Bedroom	1,000	4¢*	1 hr.
Family or Living Area	1,500	5.9¢*	1 hr.
Multiple Rooms	3,000	11.9¢*	1 hr.
Baby Food Warmer	165	1/10 of 1¢	10 min.
Blender	385	1/25 of 1¢	1 min.
Broiler (Portable)	1,500	3.9¢	30 min.
Can Opener	100	9/1000 of 1¢	1 min.
Carving Knife	92	1/25 of 1¢	5 min.
Clock	2	7.6¢	1 mo.
Coffee Maker	850	7/10 of 1¢	10 min.
Cooker (Egg)	516	1/5 of 1¢	5 min.
Deep Fat Fryer	1,500	4.8¢	1 hr.
Dehumidifier	240	1.2¢	1 hr.
Dishwasher	1,200	3.7¢	normal cycle
Disposer	420	1/25 of 1¢	1 min.
Fans			
Attic	375	2¢	1 hr.
Circulating	88	1/2¢	1 hr.
Exhaust-small	200	1¢	1 hr.
Furnace	660	3.4¢	1 hr.
Rollabout	171	9/10 of 1¢	1 hr.
Window	200	1¢	1 hr.
Floor Waxer/Cleaner	350	1.8¢	1 hr.
Fondue/Chafing Dish	800	2.1¢	1 hr.
Freezer (15 cu. ft.)	341	$5.50*	1 mo.
Frostless (15 cu. ft.)	440	$7.77*	1 mo.
Fry Pan	1,150	3.7¢	1 hr.
Griddle	1,200	2.3¢	30 min.
Hot Plate	1,250	3.3¢	30 min.
Humidifier	175	2.2¢	1 day
Ice Crusher	100	1/25 of 1¢	5 min.
Knife Sharpener	100	1/25¢	5 min.
Lights† (100-watt bulb)	100	5.3¢	10 hr.
Microwave Oven	1,500	2¢	15 min.
Mixer			
Hand	80	1/5 of 1¢	30 min.
Standing	150	2/5 of 1¢	30 min.
Radio	75	2/5 of 1¢	1 hr.
Range			
Small Surface Unit	1,300	6/10 of 1¢	5 min. (high heat)
Large Surface Unit	2,400	1.1¢	5 min. (high heat)
Oven (non-self-cleaning)	3,200	5.5¢*	1 hr.
(self-cleaning)	3,200	4.2¢*	1 hr.
Broiler Unit	3,600	4.8¢	15 min.
Self-Cleaning Feature	4,000	18¢–30.8¢*	2 hr.

APPLIANCE OPERATING COSTS
By the Minute, Hour, Day or Job

Electric Product	Typical Wattage	Cost	Time
Refrigerator/Freezer (14 cu. ft.)	330	$5.29*	1 mo.
Frostless (17 cu. ft.)	350	$7.93*	1 mo.
Roaster	1,350	4.3¢*	1 hr.
Slow Cooker-Low	75	2/5 of 1¢	1 hr.
-High	150	7/10 of 1¢	1 hr.
Space Heater	1,300	6.9¢	1 hr.
Toaster	1,200	1/5 of 1¢	2 min.
Trash Compactor	400	1/5¢	5 min.
Waffle Iron	1,200	2.5¢*	30 min.
Warming Tray	140	7/10 of 1¢	1 hr.
Water Heater (Quick Recovery)	4,500	12.3¢–30.8¢	per person/day
Water Pump	1,080	5.7¢	1 hr.

*Thermostatically controlled. Cost based on appliance estimated "On" time.

†Many factors affect lighting costs: size of the home, type of lighting, etc. But keep in mind—fluorescent lights are more efficient and more economical to operate.

Source: Edison Electric Institute, New York, N.Y.
Association of Home Appliance Manufacturers (AHAM), Chicago, Ill.
Various Appliance Manufacturers

Adapted from William H. Morrell, *Energy Miser's Manual* (Eliot, Me.: The Grist Mill, 1976).

more than using some frost-free refrigerators because food must be recooled after being removed from the cabinet. Even a dishwasher can save energy costs over some alternatives to its use.

Placement

Stoves should be separated from refrigerators, and freezers usually don't belong in a kitchen at all. Some freezers use half as much energy in a basement as they do in a kitchen kept at

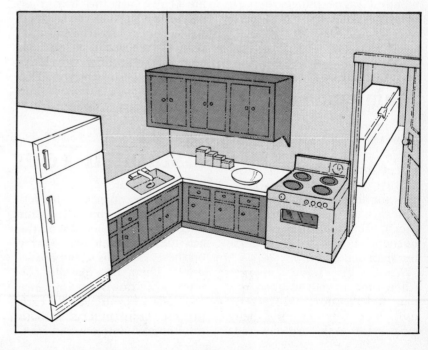

Proper placement of major appliances will save energy. A refrigerator next to the stove will run more than one located across the room from the stove.

Refrigerator and oven-door gaskets affect airflow and help maintain proper temperatures. For an oven, remove the old gasket by pulling it off, and simply clip on the new one. For refrigerators, loosen the retaining screws (do not remove them) and pull the gasket out from behind the retainer. Install the new gasket by pushing the bead under the retainer.

75°F. By using a cellar, cool pantry, utility room or porch for a freezer chest, you'll save kitchen floor space and, we hope, learn to manage trips to the chest with efficiency that will cut costs still further. Don't, however, exile the chest to the Siberia of an unheated, detached garage or shed. Its thermostat may not work at subzero temperatures.

If the freezer is out of sight you won't have to scold household members for holding its door or lid open while they manifest vague hunger or curiosity and enjoy a bit of coolness in summer.

Use Patterns and Maintenance

Gazing into freezers isn't the only bad habit we slip into. Some others are failing to replace stove and refrigerator gaskets, using unnecessary gadgets for simple tasks, using hot water and dishwashers too much, using small pans on large burners and running freezers less than half full.

Appliances waste energy when they are not in good repair. Refrigerators and freezers use more power if their evaporator coils are covered

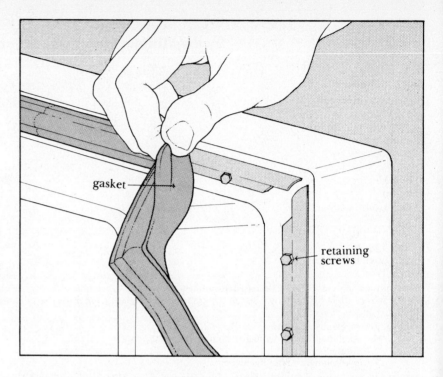

gasket

retaining screws

with frost. Their condensers must give off the heat they extract from the refrigerated space, so it is important to provide an air space of at least two inches around them. Check the temperatures of freezers and refrigerators from time to time, adjusting them upward (one dial number per ten degrees F.) if they're cooler than they need to be.

Keep refrigerator condensers clean of dust. The bearings of older refrigerators and freezers need occasional inspection and oiling. Test the fan motor shaft to see if it turns smoothly.

Establish Your Needs

At some quiet, off-harvest period before you plan your ideal harvest kitchen, list all the activities you would like to carry on there. Be realistic, but not *too* timid. Then, in a parallel column, write down the appliance or appliances you need for each process. Think in terms of both minimum investment and maximum ease. Also consider your tastes and established patterns. Does your family prefer canned foods to frozen? How many times has your present stove seemed too small? Would you find time to grind flour if you had a mill?

If you're considering enlarging your stocking-up repertoire, ask yourself how much a new technique would save, how much effort the task would take and what the benefits to quality and nutrition would be. Can the process be done by hand or with an appliance you already own? Try it first. Many an American kitchen cabinet holds a bread-kneading machine used once and forgotten while its owner, still buying the family bread, remains denied the tactile delight of hand kneading. Many a dishwasher owner on vacation in a cabin wonders how he or she ever got the idea that washing dishes by hand was a dreary chore.

Who Are You?

Then there are the social and psychological factors. How large is your household? Is it growing or shrinking? Is yours the home where the larger family gathers for Thanksgiving? Imagine the ideal dinner party with harvest food. Would it be large or cozy? What is the maximum number of cooks that has ever hovered over your stove at one time? Can you always depend on help in harvest cooking? Call for a household planning symposium, but remember that too many cooks can ruin the choice of freezer as quickly as the broth, so you'd better let the top chef have two votes.

Are you a weekend wonder who can work away from home five days a week and pack harvesting activities into summer Saturdays? Try to remember the longest and the shortest day you've ever spent in your kitchen. You may be surprised at the seasonal variation.

Do you have a tendency to overestimate your own energy? How stubborn are you? How adaptable? Are you easy to work with, or have you a strong sense of kitchen territoriality? Are you formal, easy-going, neat, messy or. all of the above depending on occasion?

Census statistics and psychological profiles may seem a bit excessive if you're only trying to decide whether to buy a bean sprouter, but some appliances have major impact on our lives and personalities.

Learn What's Available

The next step in choosing appliances is to find out what's available. This is the point at which you get out and around, visiting stores, talking to salespeople, consultants and friends.

Kitchen Designers

One way to begin your search for appliances is in the Yellow Pages, under "kitchens." As a do-it-yourselfer, you certainly don't need a kitchen "expert" to relieve you of the choices you're on your way to making. Skip this step if you wish. What a kitchen designer will do for you

Always allow at least 2 inches of air space behind and above any refrigerator. This permits proper cooling of the condenser coils, which is necessary to keep the appliance running efficiently.

wall

condenser coils

at least 2"

277

is provide a little free entertainment, let you practice sales resistance and teach you a little about what appliances are available.

Kitchen experts are generally interested in selling cabinets, floors and lighting. You often find them working for lumberyards or department or furniture stores. In talking with you, they will emphasize appearance, labor savings and high technology. They'll try to convince you to buy your kitchen all in one step by paying in installments for a package that includes design, equipment, materials, labor and supervision. Some designers allow you to do part of the labor yourself, but then charge you for drawings and plans.

Appliance Stores

Visit the biggest and best appliance showroom in your area, even if that means a day's trip to a nearby city. Come home with measurements, capacity and energy-use statistics, price lists, brochures and the addresses of manufacturers, but, most importantly, with keen visual and tactile memories of actual appliances. Go around the showroom with a salesperson, asking questions, but at some point shake the clerk and spend quiet time alone, testing gaskets and thinking.

In the days and weeks after your visit, read up on the appliance models that make most sense to you. Write to their manufacturers for information, price lists and the name of their dealer closest to your home.

Measure the appliance at the store to make sure it will fit into your space. Every inch counts.

Study the brochures well, learning to resist the glamour of full-color photographs of "cooks" in evening dress. Learn to spot and be wary of phrases like "ultimate technological advance," "revolution in the art of cooking," "feature-packed units" and "custom-designed food preparation systems." Keep in mind the criteria you have established for your harvest needs: economy of purchase, economy of use, quality of product and compatibility with personal style. These firm criteria, in the priority you have assigned them, will be the wax in your ear to mute the siren songs.

Restaurant Supply Houses

If you've already determined that you need a large major appliance, try taking a totally different tack. Find out the name of the nearest restaurant supply house. It's a good idea not to go there until your sales resistance is well built up, for you may be overwhelmed by the size and quantity of what you see. Instead of aisles of small oven fronts in this season's favorite pastel color, you'll see a bastion of stainless steel and cast iron.

At first you may feel out of place there because the other customers will be businessmen, but you will find the restaurant supply salespeople will understand your harvest-quantity needs more than anyone you've talked with so far. And you do belong there. The new high-tech fad is daily bringing more retail customers to these suppliers. Don't be surprised if no one rushes to wait on you. Turn neglect to advantage by wandering, testing, picking up brochures.

The chances are that your local restaurant supplier will display only a few of the models he can order for you. His catalogs will contain dimensioned drawings, specifications and price lists—and no glamour shots. Find out how you can get copies of them. Don't be either flattered or frightened if the clerk inquires about your "establishment." It's his way of determining if you should receive a discount. You shouldn't, but when you see the price lists you'll wish you could.

Make sure you understand electrical current demands and cycles when you consider restaurant stoves and cooling units. If the equipment you see displayed looks too massive to fit in your kitchen, inquire about smaller major appliances designed for use in small restaurants, schools, nursing homes and churches. Avoid built-in deep fryers and steam tables; they are not for your kind of cooking. Ask about replacement parts and service.

Some restaurant appliances are stripped-down in comparison with domestic ones. Ovens, for example, may contain no broiling units since in a restaurant broiling would normally be done on a separate appliance. Restaurant stove ovens may also lack adjustable shelves.

The best you may accomplish in the enchanted land of iron and steel may be only to renew appreciation of durability and simplicity. Carry this with you when you go back to the appliance showroom, and it may help you narrow your choices. If money is the problem—and it usually will be—look for used restaurant appliances. Small restaurants often go out of business with down-to-the-bare-walls sales or auctions. You'll meet interesting people at those, but remember what you've learned about testing and inspecting all used appliances.

Read Your Way to Selection

Not all the people who write about appliances write sales brochures. There are experts who have very little or nothing at stake in your choice. At public libraries you can find consumers' guides and magazines, books on kitchen design, home processing and specialized harvest cooking, and household magazines.

Consumers' guides give ratings on individual models. The consumers' magazines also discuss the ways in which appliances were tested, and you can learn from them what features to look for. Remember that they are geared to the *average* consumer, so you must keep your special needs in mind as you compare your ratings with theirs.

Agricultural extension services and the home economics departments of state universities are a source of pamphlets and advice on home appliances. Though they never mention models or brands, they give excellent safety information.

Sometimes you can find magazine articles by or about famous cooks or experienced gardener-cooks who have chosen their appliances carefully.

Word of Mouth

Last but not least, trust your friends, especially those who cook and think the way you do. Ask them all the questions you've been asking yourself. Invite yourself over to cook a meal for them on the stove you've admired. Borrow small appliances, perhaps in exchange for a share of the product made with them.

If you're tempted to the restaurant supply route, interview a restaurant chef while he works. See how his patterns of motion differ from yours and how work is shared in a restaurant kitchen. If you want to sell homestead produce or products eventually, seek out someone who sells it now, perhaps someone at the local farmers' market stand. Ask to tour his preparation and storage area.

However you go about your research, do go about it diligently. You aren't Madison Avenue's typical consumer, so don't act like one. You're a special person with special needs. The care and thoroughness with which you shop for the appliances that are the heart of your kitchen are the measure of how well your harvest kitchen will meet your special needs.

The Major Appliances

When it comes down to paying for a kitchen appliance these days, nearly every one takes on a significant characteristic of "major." Nearly every kitchen appliance is expensive.

But for our purposes here, a major appliance is a critical appliance, one that makes your kitchen work. It's not difficult to imagine doing without Bacon-

ers, corn poppers, hot dog cookers and their ilk. Most folks can imagine doing without a dishwasher, even, or a garbage disposal or an instant-hot-water spout. But try doing without a stove or a refrigerator; these are The Major Appliances.

The Range

Some homes in cool climates can get by without refrigerators, but every home, and especially every harvesting home, needs a place to cook. The stove, therefore, is the most significant of all appliances.

Wood Cookstoves

Using a wood-burning range will change your life. You get a real sense of working with a tool—controlling, making choices, employing your senses and your sense.

Using a wood stove is demanding. You must learn what woods to use for different cooking temperatures, and you must fell trees, split logs, and stack, season and carry wood. But wood cooking is the only means that allows you complete independence from commercial, nonrenewable energy sources.

Getting a Wood Range

Almost any new wood range will cook adequately. Both American and European models are expensive, you have to wait for them to be delivered, and some of the American-alloyed cast-iron ones are not as durable or warp-proof as older wood stoves.

Some of the choices to be made in selecting a new wood range concern size (from about 21 to 52 inches wide and various heights and depths), materials (enamel, cast iron or steel), color (some enamels come in color), extra features (second ovens, water reservoirs, griddles), number of cooking lids (two to eight), size of cooking lids (7 or 8 inches), alternate fuel capacities (some burn coal, charcoal, trash or cobs), size of oven (about 9 inches by 11 inches by 12 inches to 14 inches by 18 inches by 20 inches) and single or dual top-cooking fuel (a few are wood-electric or wood-gas).

The heat from a fire has to be distributed throughout a wood range for the range to cook. Internal baffles channel hot smoke and gases directly into the flue when you want to heat only the cooktop, or divert them around the oven when you want to heat it too.

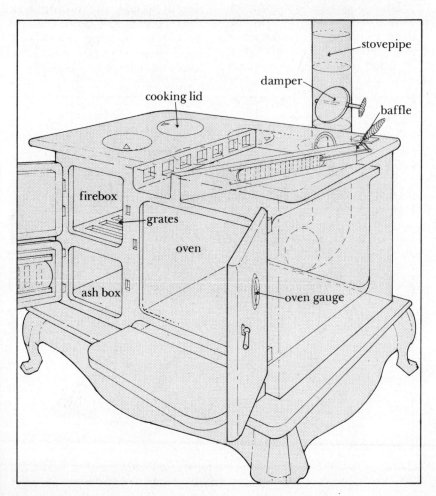

281

Cooking with Wood

Wood cooking is not for everyone. Bringing a wood stove into a kitchen involves about as much adjustment and adaptation as bringing home a new member of the family. A wood stove changes your sense of timing, forces you to adjust to its rhythm and teaches you patience—much as a baby does. Like babies, wood stoves also take much feeding and cleaning up after.

The essence of wood stove top cooking is: Build a hot fire and move pots around on the stovetop till you find the temperature you want. When there is a hot fire going, the entire steel or cast-iron top is hot enough to boil water if lids are in place, though the very hottest part is over the back of the fuel box. This general heat would seem to be ideal for the food processor whose work requires large quantities of boiling water for blanching, steaming or open-kettle canning. But the general heat—welcome in winter—may be too hot for comfortable work during canning time. Moreover, wood stoves can burn you (even without a flame in them), melt plastic handles, blacken your pans with soot and give your pressure canners nervous breakdowns. It is unreasonable to think you can maintain a steady high or medium temperature on a wood stove unless you devote constant attention to shifting pans and stoking flames. Temperature fluctuations may cause loss of liquids from canning jars and cause pressure to build up in pressure canners too fast. Can-

ning is possible with wood fires, but difficult.

Water reservoirs on wood stoves may be used for boiling-water-bath canning since the entire bottom of the compartment maintains a boil as long as the fire is stoked.

On the other hand, cast-iron surfaces and beds of coals hold warmth for long periods and allow slow and gentle cooking. Using wood when cooking times are long is a genuine economy move. Incomparable tomato sauce is made on wood stoves.

Drying can be done on or over wood ranges. Dry in the oven using an old banked fire and adding only one small stick of wood at a time, or suspend

produce on racks or strings over the rangetop.

The upper shelves of stoves that burn wood stay warm day and night, furnishing ideal spots for proofing yeast, raising bread, souring milk or sprouting seeds.

Wood range baking involves even more labor than rangetop cooking, but most wood cooks say it is worth it. Each oven, and every fire, has its own personality; no wood oven heats evenly. The baking heat is controlled by using dampers, by burning different woods, by shifting and turning pans and (to cool ovens down) by opening doors and adding cool objects. No hot air is run through wood range ovens

The upper shelves of a wood cookstove stay warm continuously, providing an ideal spot for sprouting, bread raising and yogurt making—even on the coldest of days.

as it is through gas and electric ones; rather, heat radiates from almost every direction. Wood oven baking requires the use of all your senses, but it also rewards them bountifully.

If You Can't Stand the Heat

In southern European countries today, as in pioneer days in America, summertime cooking is done either outdoors or in a summer kitchen. Some folks keep wood stoves in sheds near their gardens for maximum freshness in canning, as well as comfort. Others adapt barbecue pits or incinerators for slow cooking of apple butter in the old way, screening it from insects and falling leaves.

Winter canning and freezing can take advantage of wood stoves when they are welcome. Stored root crops, frozen produce and dried legumes or meat can be combined in soups, stews and casserole dishes, and cooked slowly in quantity. The food can then be frozen or canned for future use.

Cooking on a Heater

Many people for whom wood ranges are impractical provide all or part of their household heat with wood. In selecting a wood heating stove, especially if it is to go in or near the kitchen, make sure it has a flat top (preferably a soapstone one or one with cooking lids) so it can serve as a second range for supplementary, occasional or seasonal use.

Though wood heating stoves have no ovens, they can be used with small stove-top ovens or volcano cookers.* Small amounts

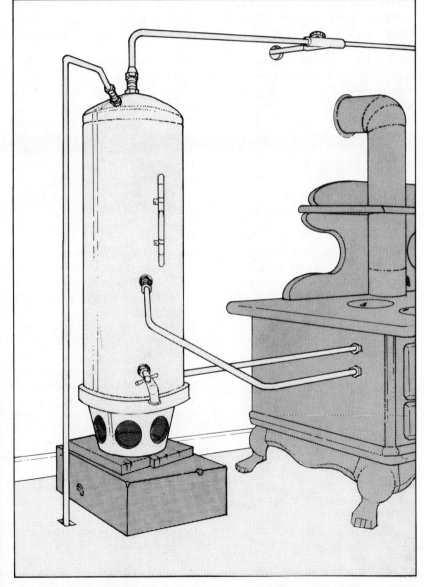

Some wood stoves are designed to heat water as well as living space, giving you an extra return on your investment.

*Volcano cookers, sold by camping equipment manufacturers, are set on a wire rack over a small stove-top opening. Heat circulates upward through the middle of the heavy Dutch-oven-type container and then downward over the top surface of the dough or batter, baking and browning evenly.

of baking may also be done in stovepipe ovens that attach to the stovepipes of the less efficient heating stoves and use exhaust heat.

Getting into Hot Water

If you choose wood to cook with because of its economy, consider buying a stove or range model with water-heating capacity. The electric water heater requires far more electricity to operate than any other piece of equipment in your house, unless your house is heated electrically. Several companies are bringing out devices for producing hot water by using wood heating or cooking stoves, either directly or through recapturing stovepipe exhaust heat. Installing these devices demands basic decisions in plumbing design that must be made before you install the stove or range. You may also want to consider installing (or keeping) a gas or electric water heater as a backup for seasonal use.

It should also be noted that though the location of an oil or gas water heater is determined by the need to vent it to a chimney, you can save money by placing an electric water heater close to the point of maximum hot water use. This often means putting it in the kitchen, within five or six feet of the faucet.

Safety First

A wood or coal range is always more dangerous to install and operate than a new gas or electric one. No wood or coal stove or its stovepipe should be placed near enough to combustible materials of any kind to make them too warm to put your hand on when a fire is burning in the stove. This means at least 18 inches of space should be left between radiating stove surfaces and all walls, floors and ceilings. Small children should be taught to respect range surfaces and should not play near them, and stoves and their chimneys should be inspected, cleaned and maintained regularly. Stove tops are self-cleaning on wood ranges, but fireboxes, flues, stovepipes and chimneys are not.

Coal Ranges

Coal contains more energy per unit of weight than wood and can be cheaper to use than gas or electricity, but the use of coal for cooking is a controversial subject for both ecological and health reasons. Read up on the controversy, studying the conclusions of experts before you come to your own. Coal-burning and wood-and-coal-burning ranges and stoves are available.

Gas and Electric Range Forms, Finishes and Features

Gas and electric ranges may cook differently, but they come in the same shapes and sizes and have the same general appearance.

Freestanding Ranges are the familiar ones that sit on the floor (or in some older and restaurant models, on legs), are self-contained, and stand independent of adjacent walls and cabinets. These ranges offer the widest assortment of prices, sizes and features.

High Oven Ranges are freestanding units with a square-cornered, built-in look. They have eye-level ovens, and sometimes another oven or a dishwasher beneath the cooktop. Eye-level ovens over burners save bending, but they can be awkward, or even dangerous.

Slide-in Ranges are designed to fit snugly between base cabinets. Their sides are left unfinished.

Drop-in or Built-in Ranges rest on special floor platforms or base cabinets, or sit on a flange under a counter.

Separate Cooktops and Built-in Ovens allow you to divide cooking from baking functions and to incorporate each into a separate working center. Single or double ovens can fit into a wall, either side by side at eye level or stacked, or they can fit under a counter. Cooktops with two to four burners or elements can be fashioned into counters, or into work islands or peninsulas. You'll have to use more kitchen space if you separate cooking and baking activities, but with separate surface and oven units you can choose one electric and one gas.

When you are choosing among these forms of ranges, consider the total layout of your harvest kitchen, and, most of all, think about what you need to be able to do there. If you bake a lot, for example, you may want an extra-large wall oven or two ovens that can be used at the

same time. You can locate working space for milling, kneading, rising, cooling, mixing, pastry rolling and cookie cutting, and storage space for pans and sheets, racks, pastry marble, rolling pins, grains, flours and other baking supplies near the oven. If you added a small built-in surface unit (or a hot plate) for heating butter and scalding milk or doing the other small cooking tasks associated with baking, you would create a "mini-bakery" corner where you could work without disturbing other cooks who are blanching or boiling on the main stove or counter unit.

If your kitchen is always full of cooks, an island surface unit will allow them to work from different sides at the same time, but it may add to the cost of wiring or gas connections. Some safety experts recommend allowing 18 inches of fireproof counter space on either side of ranges and surface units and 24 inches on at least one side of a separate wall unit. This will give busy cooks a place to deposit hot pans quickly, and it allows pan handles to project sideways so they won't be accidentally struck and tipped. Some harvest cooks who use big kettles on back burners or elements like their rangetops set lower than normal so they can see into their pots.

When choosing a gas or electric range, consider your personal needs as well as your kitchen design and layout. Six major stove types are (clockwise from top left): built-in oven, separate cooktop, drop-in, high oven, freestanding and slide-in.

A mini-bakery designed right into the kitchen provides ample space for preparation and baking, and keeps ingredients and equipment centrally located.

Most cooking ranges or units are finished in stainless steel, brushed chrome, porcelain enamel or a combination of these materials. Porcelain enamel comes in various colors, and there are also different finishes for stainless steel. A cook whose range gets heavy use will want the most durable finish he or she can afford. Stainless steel, usually the most expensive, won't chip the way porcelain will, but it may dent with heavy use.

If you bake in quantity or like to bake several foods at once to save fuel, or if you use your oven for drying, make sure the oven racks adjust to various levels. Oven doors with glass panels offer you the convenience of being able to watch a cake rise without causing it to fall, but the panels have been known to shatter at high temperatures or when heavy objects are dropped on them.

Both gas and electric ovens come with optional cleaning systems: manual, pyrolitic (self-cleaning) and catalytic (continu-ous cleaning). If you bake little, if you think the best means to a clean oven is the conscientious prevention of spills, if you don't think any surface is clean until you've scrubbed it yourself or if you need to economize, dare to be old-fashioned and stick with an ordinary enamel or steel surface for your oven liner. With that kind of surface you need not be afraid to use cleansers and ammonia when spills occur or when you think your oven's efficiency will be improved by a cleaning.

Whatever the cleaning system you use, you will need to scrub your oven racks from time to time. Consider this fact when you choose a sink for your kitchen and get one large enough to soak oven racks in. A large sink can always be divided by setting an old-fashioned dish-pan in it, but a modern divided one will often confine you when you're doing jobs like vegetable scrubbing or rack cleaning.

Continuous or catalytic ovens have linings coated with a por-ous, baked-on finish containing a catalyst that helps in oxidizing, and thus removing, spills and splashes. The finish works every time the oven is heated hot enough for baking. The cataly-tic method does only a mediocre job of cleaning. Heavy or gooey spills still have to be wiped up, and after a while, spots remain. If you try to clean them more thoroughly, you may chip away the unique finish and lose its advantages or even mar the sur-face. Once chipped, the surface deteriorates quickly. Probably the best thing to be said about catalytic ovens is that they relieve the consciences of busy cooks by at least *looking* reasonably clean.

In a pyrolytic or self-cleaning oven, the temperature is gradually raised to about 900°F. to burn up and convert to dust all spills and spatters. The process takes about three hours, and the cleaning of all six sides is generally thorough. Not only does the self-cleaning feature add to the cost of a stove, but each cleaning costs something too. Because of their high heating capacity, self-cleaning ovens tend to be smaller than others, but they are so well insulated with inorganic materials that can take high heat that they bake economically under normal temperatures.

Self-cleaning ovens, and those with built-in rotisseries, automatic timers and thermostats, griddles and probe thermometers are bought at a high price. You should remember that a plain model may cook and bake just as well as a fancy one.

Check stoves for their cleanability. Harvest cooking is often a messy business. Large and snug-fitting drip pans under surface units, up-tilting electric elements, removable rings, removable gas burners and pipes and drip trays make cleaning easier. Some stoves have removable oven doors to make it possible for you to reach and clean the back panel of the oven.

If you have extra money to invest and want the advantage of uniform, very low heat over a wide area (the quality you may have most admired in wood ranges), it makes sense to look for this in a restaurant stove which has the burners under a cast-iron top, rather than to put money into the fancy modular convertible rangetops or the plug-in elements of high-priced home ranges.

Gas Ranges

Gas burners are designed to give a circular flame pattern. The intensity of the flame and its height is controlled by a throttling valve. In choosing a gas range look for models with electric or manual ignition or with energy-saving small pilots. These will save you fuel.

To cook with gas you must either arrange for gas to be piped into your home, or you must purchase, provide room for and install gas in bottles,

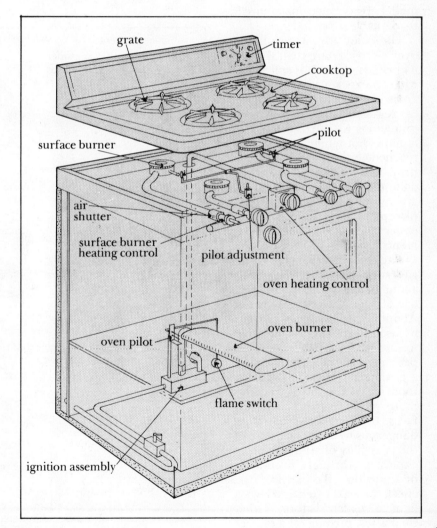

The parts of a gas range.

canisters or tanks. The latter two are usually placed outside but near the kitchen. If gas is not piped into your locality, or if there is a long waiting list for new customers, make sure that there is a dependable bottled gas supplier in your area, and discuss with him installation of tank or bottle, costs, and the frequency and dependability of his delivery. In choosing a model of gas range, make sure it is adaptable to bottled gas.

The chief advantages of gas over electricity are that, though its price is rising, it is still somewhat cheaper to use in some areas of the country, it is easier to regulate and offers more gradations for surface cooking, it allows hot temperatures to be reached quickly and heat to drop rapidly when it is turned on and off, and the units it uses are more durable, need replacement less often and are easier to clean than electric elements.

The chief disadvantage is that gas surface burners are only about half as efficient in their use of fuel as electric elements. About 80 percent of the electricity used in cooking is converted to useful heat, while only 40 percent of the heat produced by a gas burner goes into cooking food. Gas is also dirtier; it leaves more oil film on kitchen surfaces. It is also somewhat more dangerous to use gas because of the possibility of asphyxiation or explosion through misuse or malfunction. To avoid risk, check for leaks often and always light a match before, rather than after, turning on a surface unit or oven.

Gas and electric ranges of similar design are usually comparable in price, though gas restaurant-size ranges tend to cost less (and be more common) than electric ones.

A recent study conducted in London, England, sought to isolate the cause for a higher frequency of respiratory disease among schoolchildren from homes where gas, rather than electricity, was used for cooking. Concentrations of atmospheric nitrogen dioxide (NO_2) were measured and compared in otherwise environmentally matched gas and electric kitchens. The average hourly concentration of NO_2 in gas kitchens was found to be more than seven times greater than in electric kitchens. Though further research is needed to determine

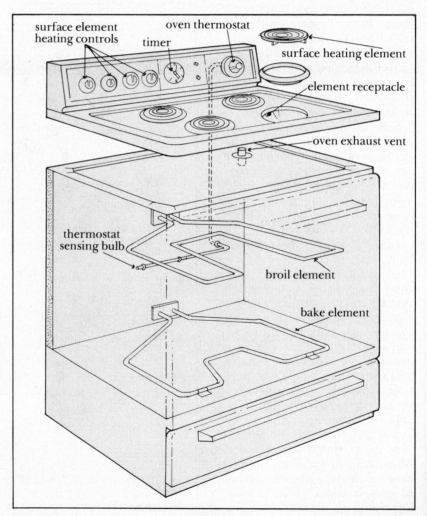

The parts of an electric range.

how the pollutant NO_2 influences respiratory disease in humans, this gas has been shown to increase susceptibility to respiratory infection in animals.

Electric Ranges

Electric surface units are usually equipped with heating elements of metallic-sheathed, resistant wire in spiral shape. Some burners have inner and outer coils to accommodate smaller or larger pans. Since coils glow only at higher settings, many models have indicator lights to show when the elements are in use.

Since all but the most isolated homes in this country are wired for electricity, electric stoves are easier to install than gas ones. However, it is important to make sure the wiring of your house is adequate in voltage and amperage for the requirements of the stove you select. This is especially important when you choose pyrolytic ovens or large restaurant-style ranges.

Electric ranges require a 230-volt hookup. If you must add to your household electric capacity, it will substantially increase the total cost of acquiring an electric stove. Most homes built since World War II provide space for a 230-volt circuit.

Restaurant ranges require a lot of power to operate. Typically, they require three-phase wiring, although single-phase models are available. Residential wiring is single phase; three phase is commercial wiring. Be sure the range you buy is compatible with your house's wiring.

Ceramic Cook-Tops

A relatively new development in electric ranges is the one-piece ceramic cooktop which can be part of a freestanding or a drop-in, counter-mounted unit. A cook-top's glass-ceramic slab is usually ¼ inch thick and masks a set of electric elements hidden under decorative patterns. The typical ceramic cook-top has four elements: a small, low-wattage pair under patterns about 6½ inches in diameter and a larger, medium- or high-wattage pair under patterns 7½ or 8½ inches across. Some models have a separate ceramic plate for each unit.

The chief selling point of ceramic tops is that they give a furniturelike appearance to a kitchen, concealing its function; this is something no harvest cook needs. A second claim is that they are easier to keep clean since drips or spills are prevented from going below the flat surface. It is true that the chore of cleaning drip pans and rings is eliminated with these units, but this is more than cancelled out by the fact that the tops themselves require tedious care both in cleaning and in use. Certain cleansing pads and cleansers cannot be used on them, bottoms of pots and pans

must be scrubbed free of grit or they will scar the tops, and permanent stains will result from sliding aluminum or copper-bottomed utensils on the surface, or from wiping drips of water from it with a soiled cloth or sponge. Spills must be removed only after the material has cooled, and baked-on spills are extremely difficult to clean up, though they are a little easier to get off glassy-finished ceramic than mat-finished. Some models are recommended for use only with flat-bottomed ceramic Pyrex-type pans.

Claims for the efficiency of operation of ceramic tops have also been made. The truth is that ceramic tops heat up more slowly and require 25 percent more energy to heat than ordinary electric elements. They do hold foods at steady low temperatures, and they deliver even heat if used with perfectly flat-bottomed utensils, but they take much longer to cool down—45 minutes to an hour. Some manufacturers recommend turning off the element before cooking is finished.

There is no need to belabor the point—smooth-top units are *not* for you. And think of the poor naughty family cat. From the floor it can't tell whether it's leaping to a counter surface or a hot ceramic stove!

The Refrigerator

A refrigerator is in operation around-the-clock, lasts 15 to 20 years, seldom needs service and consumes more energy than any other appliance except water and space heaters.

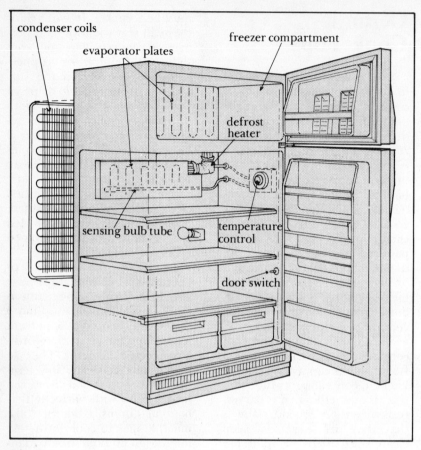

condenser coils

evaporator plates

freezer compartment

defrost heater

sensing bulb tube

temperature control

door switch

The storage compartments of a refrigerator-freezer.

After determining the size refrigerator you need to fit your habits and your needs (chief factors in this choice are how swiftly you process perishables and how many you feed), decide whether you need a freezer section and if so, how large it should be.

The refrigerator consists of a compressor that pumps the refrigerant, a cabinet, an evaporator or plate that gets cool and chills the cabinet, and a condenser to transfer heat away from the cabinet. In a refrigerator of the old type, frost collects on the coils surrounding the freezer storage space. There is only one temperature control.

Basic features in refrigerators include shelving, crispers, ice cube trays, a freezing compartment and a light. Special features for refrigerators include rollers to enable you to clean under them easily, special meat and butter compartments, ice makers, egg holders and convertible doors.

Manually defrosted refrigerators with small freezing compartments are the least expensive of all units both to buy and to operate. Their drawbacks are: They require defrosting about once a month; they are common only in the small or kitchen-cabinet size and difficult to find in the 17- to 20-foot range; their freezing or ice cube compartments go down to only 10 to 20°F. so cannot be used for freezing but only for short-term storage of frozen foods. If you own, or plan to buy, a chest freezer, a small manually defrosted refrigerator may be all you need. They come in both freestanding and built-in models. Most have enamel finish.

Refrigerator-Freezers

In combination refrigerator-freezers, there are two separately insulated units with separate exterior doors and controls. In most models, one method of defrosting is used for both sections, but there are a few models available with manual defrost for the freezer and automatic defrost for the refrigerator. These are the most economical to use, but they are hard to find.

In a frostless refrigerator-freezer, the coils are not visible from the exterior of the cabinet, and defrost water is carried in pipes to a motor compressor compartment where it is evaporated. All refrigerator-freezers require more energy to operate than refrigerators. Their advantage is that they will freeze food. A refrigerator-freezer will make it possible for you to freeze some garden produce. Some gardeners who freeze produce in economical-to-operate, but difficult-to-reach-into chest-style freezers buy refrigerator-freezers that will hold a week's worth of frozen food. These enable them to plan menus by the week and stock a week's worth of food close at hand, saving trips to a distant freezer.

Horizontal, freezer-on-top models are the most common style of refrigerator-freezers, though occasionally you may find one with the freezer on the bottom. Side-by-side, vertical freezer models provide more orderly space, and their freezers are proportionately larger, but they are also inefficient to operate and cost more initially.

There are top-freezer models that do a good job on 25 to 30 percent less electricity than is used by the average model, or at around 100 kilowatt-hours per month as compared to 120 to 170. These can be identified by the Association of Home Appliance Manufacturers' (AHAM) energy certification labels they bear. The AHAM (20 N. Wacker Drive, Chicago, IL 60606) also publishes a handbook that supplies energy ratings on standard models and costs 50 cents. The low-energy-using models generally feature manually switched heaters to keep condensation from forming on the doorsills, rather than more energy-consuming automatic heat tubes.

The temperature inside a refrigerator should be around 37°F., and a freezer should be around 0°F. Both sections should be able to maintain their temperatures, even when the weather, or the kitchen, is hot.

Check the insides of a refrigerator or refrigerator-freezer for durable materials and ease of cleaning, and for removable and adjustable shelves rather than for abundant or elaborate compartments like deli-trays and wine racks. You will learn that when you *do* need a refrigerator for harvesttime storage, you need it free of clutter.

Make sure the doors of the refrigerator are hinged so that they swing wide, and then place it so that there are no walls, shelves or other doors to interfere with its opening. Models are available with both right- and left-hand opening doors.

The Refrigerator of the Future

An engineer at the Quantum Institute of the University of California at Santa Barbara has constructed a horizontal refrigerator that resembles a kitchen base cabinet on the outside, but is lined and insulated with foam coated with fiberglass and resin like a surfboard. Top openings give access to two refrigerator compartments flanking a central freezer compartment. Heat loss is minimized by the freezer's placement, by the horizontal design that concentrates cold air inside and keeps air moisture outside and by the placement of the pump motor assembly at a distance from the cabinet. Coils are located above and to the rear of the cabinet. The machine can save on electric bills, but it is still experimental and not yet available.

Restaurant Refrigerators

The quality and efficiency of refrigerator-insulating materials has improved in recent years, so that now almost all standard refrigerators and refrigerator-freezers are reasonably well built and airtight with magnetically sealed doors. If you want truly durable materials like stainless steel, or if you require extra cold-storage space, you should look into restaurant or commercial refrigerators.

Few harvest kitchens prepare large enough quantities of perishables regularly enough to justify the enormous cost of commercial refrigeration or the proportionately high use cost in electricity. If you buy a commercial refrigerator, check to see if additional house wiring is needed. Walk-in and reach-in models are available, usually also built-in, but sometimes freestanding. Doors are usually divided like oversized side-by-side units so they won't block large areas.

Freezers

If you raise a lot of fruits and vegetables and freeze them or if you have an inexpensive source of meat, fish or game that you **291** freeze, a freezer will save you money in spite of its high operating costs. Forget all the statistics kitchen designers will give you based on family size and entertaining patterns and just go out and buy the largest freezer you can afford and can make room for. Put it in a cool area like a basement or unheated utility room. Sizes of domestic freezers run up to 30 cubic feet, but if you are thinking that large you might consider two 12- to 16-cubic-foot chests, if wiring and space will allow. With these you can clean one freezer at a time when frozen harvest provisions run low around May, and then shut one down for the hot summer or until the other is full.

Keeping freezers full saves on operating cost. During the slack season, put semiperishable items like flour, cheese, nuts and seeds in the freezer, You can also freeze enough bread ahead for the summer or prepare convenience foods for busy harvest days.

A chest freezer is more economical than an upright one, because it holds more food per cubic foot and because its temperature is less affected by door openings. People buy uprights for their convenience in organizing, but there are means to make chests organizationally efficient. Interior dividers will section a chest into areas for meat, vegetables and fruit. Some harvesters use large shallow plastic trays, large plastic bags or wire baskets (even bicycle baskets) to contain categories. This makes it easier to keep track of use, which in turn helps in planning future plantings to meet household need.

No-frost upright units are an unwarranted extravagance in energy costs. It is true that a freezer works better when kept free of frost, but defrosting a well-insulated machine with tight gaskets seldom needs to be done more than once or twice a year.

Check the energy rating of any freezer you are considering. Some freezers have exterior lights to indicate they are running, and some models have interior lights like refrigerators.

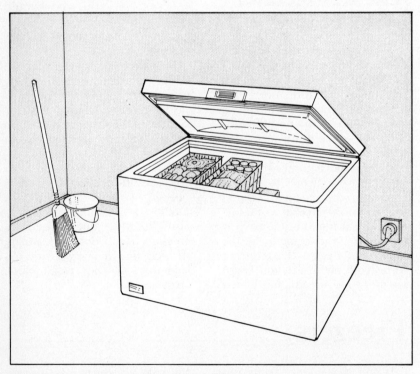

Chest freezers operate most efficiently when filled to capacity, so don't buy one that's too large.

The Optional Appliances

When you move beyond stoves and refrigerators, you've progressed from need to want; from necessity to luxury. A new set of criteria now comes into play as you ask yourself such questions as: What would this machine allow me to do that I can't do now? Would it improve efficiency? Are there better places to put the money? How

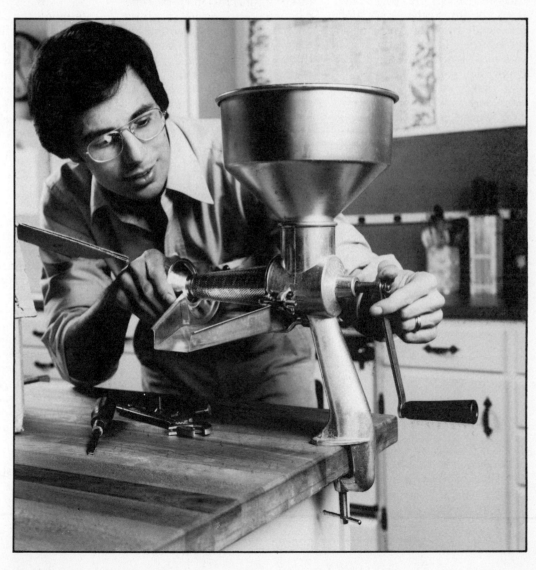

much energy does it use? Is it ecologically responsible to use it? How will it change household life?

Dishwashers

No home that has a sink really *needs* a dishwasher. (Speaking of sinks, a utility sink outside the kitchen where the worst muck can be rinsed off vegetables frees not only kitchen sinks, but also needed working space near appliances.) There are two factors most apt to determine if a dishwasher is desirable for you. The first is whether it can save time and save energy money. The second is how it fits into your life pattern.

To some harvest cooks the chief advantage of a dishwasher is psychological. It's a place to put dirty dishes so you don't have to deal with them immediately and can get on with more important matters. The perpetual washing-up in a busy kitchen can be a human energy drain. There's also the need for the social life after a large dinner party. Everyone really knows that a dishwasher alone won't clean up the dinner mess by magic, but when guests really want to sit back and chat, it's good to be able to pretend it will. Some sneaky-clever cooks

achieve the same result without a dishwasher, by hiding dirty dishes in a cabinet and washing them later.

If used properly, dishwashers save both time and energy. A cardinal rule is: Never run a dishwasher partly full. A corollary is: Use it for dishes, glassware and silver only, not for space-consuming items like pots and pans. By this method, a household of five will use a standard-size dishwasher once a day. If the dishwasher does an adequate job without extensive prerinsing, and if the alternative would be spending an average of half an hour *three* times a day to wash the dishes by hand, over an hour will be saved, even if 15 minutes goes into loading. A small family may only have to use a dishwasher twice a week when using the dish-only method.

Now for energy. More energy is used to heat the water that goes into a dishwasher than to run the dishwasher itself (unless the model has a device to raise the heat of incoming water). If your method of washing by hand involves rinsing under running hot water and you wash after each meal, washing by hand may actually be more energy-consuming and expensive than using a dishwasher. Of course this doesn't take into consideration the cost of the dishwasher.

Dishwashers don't sterilize dishes, but dishes washed in a dishwasher are generally freer of bacteria than those washed by hand, a factor to consider. You may even want a machine with a sani-cycle for times of illness. A

A dishwasher certainly is not a must *for the harvest kitchen. But if it is used efficiently, it can actually be an energy saver.*

sani-cycle raises water temperature to the point at which it kills most bacteria.

If energy saving is your primary concern, however, it's not the sani-cycle you'll be interested in, but the machines with a *light* cycle. This cycle does one wash as opposed to two in regular cycles, and two-to-six rinses as compared to three-to-six, using an average of around 8 gallons of water, as opposed to 13 for the regular. In most models the light cycle will do the job, as long as sticky things like eggs are previously removed by hand, or with a rinse-and-hold cycle. Study dishwasher manuals for loading instructions to get maximum cleaning from your machine. Another important way to save energy is to open the machine and let the dishes air-dry instead of using the energy-consuming hot-air drying cycle.

If the arguments (other than energy-saving ones) *for* dishwashers are psychological, the arguments *against* (other than purchase cost ones) are social and personal. Many cooks feel much the same about the activity of washing dishes by hand as they do about kneading. It's a peaceful, relaxing, undemanding chore that leaves the mind free for problem solving, contemplative thought, planning and useful fantasy.

There is something about water play or hydrotherapy that brings people together. On some days in a busy family, dinner and dishwashing time are the only family times, and it is here that children learn that work has its social dimension

and its obligations. On the other hand, particularly as children grow older, they may have too many other things to do after dinner and may not want to help. If dishwashing time starts being the occasion for hassles rather than harmony, that may be the signal to bring in a machine. A dishwasher won't give you much company, but neither will it give you "lip." Harvesting households have no dearth of other useful chores at better times for kids.

Dishwasher Models

There are three basic types of dishwashers: the built-in or undercounter permanently installed and plumbed one, usually front loading, with no side panels or top; the portable, which is freestanding and rolls on coasters to the sink to be connected to the hot water; and the convertible, which is similar to the portable but has removable side panels for later permanent mounting. The convertible makes sense for temporarily located householders who plan to build or buy permanent homes later.

Portables cost more than lighter built-ins, but the cost may be worth it to the person who seldom uses the dishwasher and

doesn't want to give up precious bottom cabinet space near the sink, or pay for permanent plumbing and wiring. Portables can be wheeled to a table for immediate loading and, after washing, to cabinets and drawers, even in a different room, for unloading. If you are buying a portable, make sure your kitchen plan includes parking space for it—both near the sink and out-of-the-way.

One advantage of a built-in is that your sink is not out of commission while the machine is being used. Short cycles take around 45 minutes; long ones, over an hour. Built-in machines with one cycle only are cheapest to buy and easiest to repair.

The wash chamber of a dishwasher may be of porcelain enamel, plastic-coated steel or stainless steel. Stainless is most durable and most expensive. Porcelainized surfaces are resistant to detergent and food staining, but they chip. Plastic coating stains, and can be punctured, but is easy to repair and less apt than enamel to break dishes accidentally dropped into the machine.

Commercial dishwashers, except for one or two fast-operating and energy-costly ones, have such large capacities and cost so much to buy and use that very few harvesting households would find them necessary.

Supplementary Ovens_____

Two new kinds of ovens are being sold as separate built-in or portable units, or as part of a

few ranges. They embody newly discovered or newly home-adapted principles of baking, **295** and they are still sufficiently experimental to be somewhat controversial—especially one of them—and to be expensive. Definitely in the luxury category are the convection oven and the microwave oven. Other small electric broiler- or toaster-ovens, while high in energy use, may relieve a large range oven of small jobs and save you money.

The Convection Oven works by continuously circulating air heated from the top and bottom of the oven with a fan, to achieve even temperature throughout. Air brushing against food has a sort of reverse windchill factor, a "heat-boost factor," that makes baking time as much as one-third shorter and allows settings of up to 50°F. lower, as well as eliminating the need to baste or turn. Convection ovens are simpler to clean than regular ovens, though this is partly because the models out now are smaller than most range ovens.

Convection ovens have been used for commercial baking for many years because even when food is crowded into them, they bake evenly. Home models would especially appeal to harvest cooks who bake frequently. Convection ovens are used with metal or glass utensils. They warm or bake frozen foods quickly.

The Microwave Oven uses very short waves of radio frequency that penetrate materials, setting up movement between molecules that acts to cook food. Microwaves enter food from all sides, passing into it from the bottom through special glass shelves and through special utensils of glass, ceramic, pottery or paper. Utensils do not warm up. Food cooks simultaneously in all its parts, not from the surface inward. The Federal Communications Commission has assigned a special frequency for microwave ovens. Most microwave units are portable and about 12 inches by 7 inches by 14 inches, but units can be combined with conventional ranges and ovens. Some models come with an option to allow browning the food after it is cooked, because microwaves alone will not brown. Foods like vegetables and eggs, normally cooked on a stove top, can be cooked in a microwave oven.

Microwave units cook much more rapidly than either conventional or convection ovens. Waves are generated by a magnetron and travel, following channels, in straight lines like light. At the end of the channel the waves strike a stirrer, a slowly rotating fan. Fan blades reflect the microwaves, causing them to bounce off metal oven liners. Some units have revolving shelves to accomplish the same end as stirring.

Experts agree that microwave ovens save both time and energy when you are preparing a small quantity of food, that food is nutritionally superior when cooked by this method and that the microwave oven is most handy when used as a supplement to, rather than as a substitute for, the conventional range

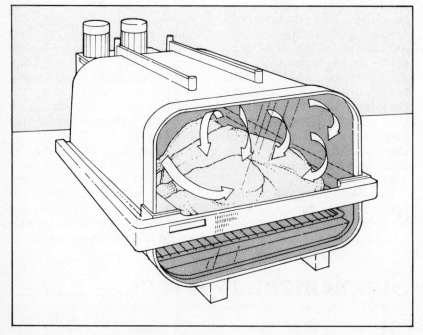

Convection ovens are good auxiliary cookers. They bake faster, more evenly and at lower temperature settings than conventional ovens.

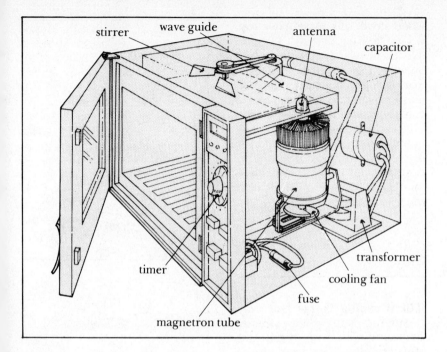

stirrer wave guide antenna

capacitor

timer

magnetron tube

transformer

cooling fan

fuse

In a microwave oven, electromagnetic waves agitate the food molecules, heating them up. Baking times are dramatically reduced.

partment of health or a trained repairman. If you have qualms about using something so new, you may wish to wait until there is more information available on the effects of microwave exposure.

Waiting makes sense for other reasons too. The price may go down, and the major drawback to microwave cooking may be overcome. That drawback is chronic unevenness of cooking. If you bake a lot, you can ill-afford to risk having soggy, underdone pockets in the bread.

Microwave ovens also cause radio and television interference and should not be used near heart pacemakers. Some nutritionists say that cooking in

and oven. What experts don't agree on is the safety issue. Concern has been expressed, for example, over the fact that microwaves and human brainwaves have certain similarities. You will have to do your own reading and soul-searching on this subject. There is no record of injury or health impairment from properly used microwave ovens *so far,* but like any source of radiation, including the sun, there may be more to be learned about their effect.

Microwave ovens have interlocks as a safety measure and come under the United States Department of Health, Educa-

tion and Welfare standards for leakage limits. Leakage should be checked once a year by an inspector from the state de-

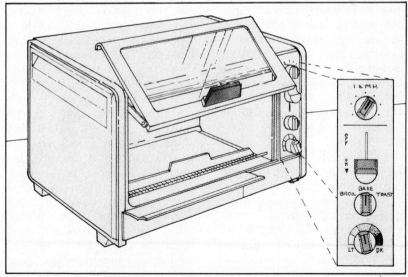

Toaster- and broiler-ovens are more versatile than conventional toasters and are great for jobs that are too small for a regular oven.

a microwave oven changes the form of the fatty acids in the food. These changed forms, or trans-fatty acids, have been implicated in arteriosclerosis.

Toaster- and Broiler-Ovens are small, portable and usually poorly insulated ovens that are useful for relieving a large oven of small jobs. There's nothing better than toasted homemade bread, but homemade bread won't always fit the standard pop-up toaster. If you have a wood stove, of course, your top is your toaster, but if a pop-up toaster brings you nothing but burned toast, crumbs in the workings and constant repair, a toaster-oven may be the answer. It is also useful for grilled cheese sandwiches, for heating small quantities of frozen food and for use as a warming oven when the regular oven is tied up. Broiler models do even more, but cost more to operate.

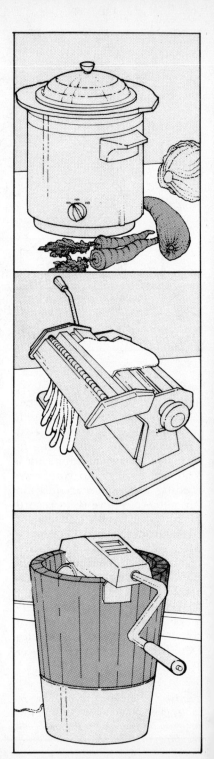

Other Luxuries

Each cook has his or her own "not-essential-but-oh-so-nice" list. Some candidates for this would be:

The Crock-Pot, which cooks slowly and nutritionally by electricity, but whose products can be duplicated by long, slow, range or oven cooking in heavy casseroles.

The Mixer, which saves arm-muscle-straining labor on doughs and batters and is handy for beating eggs, cream, sauces, and so forth. Large mixers are hard to find counter space for, and a harvester's good right (or left) arm, extended by a rotary beater, whisk, spoon or spatula, will do as good a job or better.

The Blender, which is useful when harvesting chores include pureeing, liquefying or making soups. Nearly everything else a blender can do a processor or mixer can do better, or you (given enough time) can do as well with sieves, mortar and pestles, food mills, hand choppers, knives or whisks to help you.

The Warming Top or Hot Tray (assuming you don't already have one with your restaurant stove or wood-burning range) which can help you with many processes that require low, constant warmth. These include dinner plate warming, yeast proofing, bread raising, sprouting and yogurt and cheese making. For some of these tasks you can use ovens, oven racks, radiators, clothes dryers, thermos bottles, electric heating pads or containers wrapped in down-filled clothing or bedding.

The Ice Cream Maker, which comes in hand- and electric-powered models, including some that work in a freezer, provides a treat in quantity. Unless you have dairy animals, cream is a luxury and homemade ice cream a rare dish.

The Pasta Maker, which is useful if you favor pasta dishes. Hand ones are easy to use for medium-size quantities, but there are electric models which come

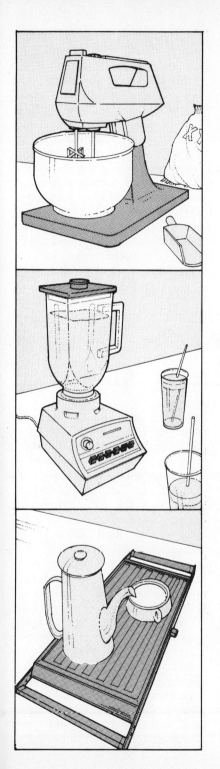

Your kitchen is probably stocked with all the equipment you really need to do what these specialty appliances do (clockwise from top left): Crock-Pot, mixer, blender, hot tray, ice cream maker and pasta maker.

separately or as attachments to food processors. The pasta-making job can be done by hand with a rolling pin.

Miscellaneous electrical appliances are either frivolous dupliations of easy-to-use tools (can openers, knives, knife sharpeners) or utensils (skillets, tea kettles), or one-operation luxuries (waffle irons, rotisseries, milkshake machines, deep fryers, coffee makers) that have little or nothing to do with processing the harvest.

Some items that are very useful like pressure canners and cookers, kettles, cherry pitters or tofu makers, are really utensils or tools, not appliances.

Unnecessary Appliances

There are two widely used and increasingly popular appliances that no harvest kitchen needs or should have—the garbage disposal unit and the trash compactor.

Disposals

Any gardener worthy of the name knows that the proper place for garbage is not in the already over-taxed sewage system or the septic tank, where it may cause pollution of streams, but back in the soil in the form of compost. The only ecologically responsible disposal is a model that grinds and centrifuges garbage put down a sink, but retains it in a slurry form suitable for use in compost piles and worm pits. These models exist, but are hard to find. The amount of water required to cool the motor of a garbage grinder while it is in operation and to coagulate grease and carry ground waste away is about two to four gal-

lons, though most owners of disposal units use more than this. Water, therefore, is wasted along with potential compost.

Though some cities, in order to protect sewage facilities, ban the use of disposals, a few cities with poor or nonexistent collection services require their installation in new homes. There's an outside chance you may have to pay for a garbage grinder you won't use.

If you have a home composting toilet, your garbage-flow system will be an integral part of your kitchen and house. A composting toilet ends dependence on wasteful municipal sewers and can save the average family 40,000 to 50,000 gallons of water a year, while slowly providing a small quantity of usable compost for the garden. These toilets resemble ordinary plumbing fixtures, but use no water. Human wastes from the toilet gradually mix with vegetable wastes from the kitchen in a special container. The unit, set

299

at a distance beneath both kitchen and bathroom, is primed with organic material to provide optimum conditions for humus-building organisms. In the kitchen of a house with a compost toilet, as you pare, stone or trim fruits and vegetables, you just shove the rejected portion over to a slot in the cabinet top, and it goes down a chute to the composting container where it joins toilet wastes (in some less-complex models, kitchen refuse must be put into the toilet) and starts turning to compost.

Gardeners with conventional toilets and outdoor compost bins, on the other hand, will need an indoor (though perhaps not an outdoor) garbage pail. This should be allowed for in kitchen design. Some harvesters like flip-top cans kept under the sink, while others combine garbage receptacles into a consealed or exposed recycling center. In either case, trips to the outdoor compost will be frequent, especially in summer, but they will not be unpleasant, for they will remind you of the cycle of transformation that lies at the heart of harvesting.

Trash Compactors

Trash compactors use electric motors to press and reduce the volume of household refuse (sometimes including garbage) so that it is easier to manage and prepare for collection. Harvesting households, in maintaining a relatively waste-free and packaging-free existence, produce less refuse than others. Their members reuse canning jars, freezer containers, better-quality paper and plastic bags and some of the other paper, containers and foil they buy or acquire. What they don't reuse, they should, to be ecologically responsible, recycle. Recycling takes only slightly more time than ordinary disposing, and it cuts down on pollution, land destruction and waste. It does demand organization, which is probably why people are attracted to compactors.

Locate, or begin, a recycling center near your home, or talk with a junk dealer who is interested in the materials you accumulate. Then set up a corner of the kitchen, or a nearby porch or utility room, with containers for each category of waste the center or dealer handles. These are usually glass, paper and metal. Chutes or bins can be built into cabinets and sometimes even constructed so they can be emptied from an outdoor porch or entryway. Few harvesting households need to carry their collections to a recycling center more than once a month. Some trash collectors (should you still need one) charge reduced rates for infrequent or plastics-and-miscellaneous-only service.

Special Harvest Kitchen Appliances

You are probably already doing kinds of cooking and food processing in your kitchen that are foreign to the average American kitchen. And in your new harvest kitchen, you'll want some of those specialized appliances that will do many of those jobs better with less work and in less time. But don't let your guard down because they're your kind of kitchen tools. You've still got to look carefully into what's available, what you can afford, what you have room for and what you *really* need.

Grain Mills

Very few folks who have developed the habit of home baking would willingly go back to using bread from the grocery store or bakery. The economy of home baking is considerable, but the satisfaction and nutritional advantage is even greater. People who have ground their own flour for baking feel the same sort of reluctance to settle for ready-milled flour. The wheat berries needed to produce flour cost less per pound than flour. Most prepackaged whole wheat flour contains an extra dose of preservatives to compensate for the highly perishable wheat germ it contains. Wheat berries can be stored in quantity. Having a home mill allows you to grind just enough flour for baking, so you know your flour is fresh and full of nutrients, not preservatives. If you have land and

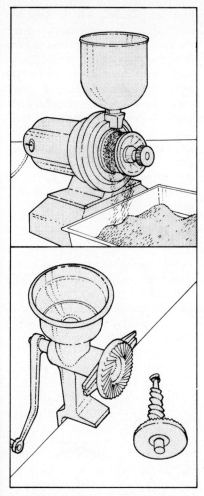

The many domestic grain mills all have either stones or metal burrs to do the grinding. Both electric and hand-operated mills are available.

time, you can push self-sufficiency a step further and raise, harvest, thresh and winnow your own wheat.

Bread flour is just one of the many products you can make with mills. Other wheat products include bran, cracked wheat, grits and fine pastry flour. You can also grind whole flours and meals from other grains, like corn, rye, millet and rice, and, if you have a burr mill, make nut butters, tahini (sesame seed butter) and soy pastes.

To pick the best mill for your needs you must make several choices. Decide what you want the mill to do and select the type that will do it best. The two main types are stone mills, which, like miniature grist mills, press and crush grains between revolving stones, and burr mills, which use two metal plates to do the same thing. (The plates have a rough texture or pattern so that flour can filter through the spaces.) To make matters more complex, there are a few combination models.

Stone Mills

If it's only whole-grain flour you're after, a stone mill, either hand or electric, is the best choice. Stones are generally limited to grinding dry materials. In addition to wheat, they will grind some other dry grains and well-dried non-oily seeds, but oily seeds or soybeans will glaze most stones and interfere with grinding. Should a stone become glazed, it can be cleaned by running popcorn through the mill on a wide setting. *No stone, either man-made or natural, should ever be washed.* Most companies now sell man-made stones of vitrified bauxite clay.

The space between the stones determines the fineness of the flour, and this space is controlled by an adjustment mechanism, which is present on every mill. (On some mills it is conveniently located on the front where you can see the setting you want, while on others it is on the back and not as easy to return to a familiar setting.) It's possible in every mill to adjust the stones so close that they touch, but a mill should never be run that way. For the finest grind possible, adjust the stones until you hear the clicking noise of them beginning to touch and then back off slightly until the noise goes away. Study the coarseness adjustment to make sure you can grind coarsely too. If the setting can be made wide enough, a mill can be used to hull sunflower seeds. If that's one of your goals, find a mill with stones or burrs that open up to ¼ inch.

Alignment of the stones also affects the grind. If one stone is tilted slightly, there will be a gap between the stones on one side and the stones will be touching on the other. The result is a coarser grade of flour because the grain will follow the path of least resistance and escape through the gap.

Burr Mills

The big advantage of burr mills is their versatility. They can grind oily beans and seeds and some models can pulverize dry vegetables or roots, or spices. If you intend to work with oily substances, make sure the insides of the mill you choose are stainless steel; iron and copper may spread a rancid taste if not used with care. The plates are usually removable and washable. Some burr mills can be used to grind peanut butter—but you'd better see how difficult cleanup is going to be before attempting that one.

Burr mills will also grind grains. With an inexpensive hand model, however, you may have to run the grain through two or three times to get a fine flour. Expensive hand mills, whether stone or burr, can produce fine flour in one pass.

There are two kinds of combination mills. One, the older model, has a stationary, permanent burr plate and interchangeable stone and burr. The burr/burr combination offers versatility for oily beans and seeds while the burr/stone combination makes grinding to a bread flour easier. There can also be two options on the burrs for coarse or fine grinding.

Today, combinations are available with interchangeable stationary grinding surfaces so that you can have three options: burr/burr, burr/stone and stone/stone.

Electric or Hand

The key factor in deciding between power and hand mills is cost. To go electric you must be willing and able to pay for the time and labor saved—you must do enough baking to justify it. The cheapest electric mill is probably a bare-bones model you build from a kit. Some companies sell milling units alone, and you supply a one- or two-horsepower motor, a V-belt and mountings.

Find out how much cranking a hand mill takes to produce the amount of flour you use in one baking. The minimum will probably be 10 to 15 minutes on a better mill and 30 to 40 minutes on a cheaper model. Long handles, counterweights, verti-

cal-motion mountings and grain-feeding flow devices will speed the rate and save labor. Permanently mount any hand mill on a solid table. If the table wobbles while you're cranking, it's being moved by your energy—energy that could be better spent grinding grain.

In shopping for electric mills, you will find you may have to order by mail, so having enough information is crucial. Ask about the speed of running—fast ones can create heat and vapor that may heat up or pack flour. The speed of electric mills for grinding ten pounds of flour ranges from 14 minutes to an hour. Check the ease of disassembling for cleaning, and learn the size of the hopper and cabinet to determine how frequent refilling and emptying will be. See if there is apt to be a problem with dust flying during grinding.

Combination Machines

If you are in the market for a food processor or a top-quality mixer or blender, you may want to exercise the principle of few-and-large by buying an electric mill attachment along with it. One model of mixer, which also comes with a meat grinder and a slicer-shredder, has a burr plate mill that grinds ten cups of flour in 21 minutes. Another model comes with a slicer-shredder, a blender, a berry press, a pasta maker and a citrus squeezer, and has a stone mill that produces one cup of fine flour every 2 minutes. A

blender model, which has attachments for juicing, yogurt making and mixing, has a system for producing bread, one loaf at a time, from grain to oven, in an advertised 5 minutes. Some juicers are sold with grain-grinding attachments. Still another combination machine, used with a mixer, grinds beans and seeds as well as flour, and the mixer with it can power a juicer, coffee mill, pea huller, meat grinder and slicer-shredder.

Processors

An appliance that will cost about as much as a low-cost electric mill is the food processor. Next to the microwave oven, it is the most-advertised and most-discussed kitchen appliance today. Already such machines fill the cabinets of many people

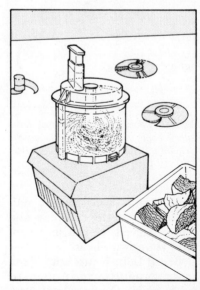

Food processors vary in the number of tasks they perform, so before investing in one, make sure it suits your harvesting needs.

who neither harvest nor cook very much. Advertisements usually emphasize both the versatility of these machines and their use in expert cooking.

The heart of the processor is a very powerful motor over which a fairly small receptacle with a top and a feeder-chute fits. The motor powers and drives interchangeable blades for different chopping and mixing operations and additional rotating disks for shredding and slicing at fantastic speeds. The processor does everything a blender can and does it better, with certain exceptions. It will not grind hard or porous materials like coffee, corn or some spices. Nor will it puree neatly or in large quantity, nor liquefy the way a blender will. It could entirely replace the mixer, except for beating egg whites, if only its receptacle and blades were larger. (Models large enough to knead a full recipe of bread are even more expensive than the standard ones.)

The big question to ask is: What will the processor do for me? More efficiently than any of the machines it competes with, a processor will shred, slice, grate and chop fresh vegetables. This makes the preparation of raw vegetables so easy that gardeners will eat more of them and so get the greatest nutritional benefit from their fresh garden produce in season. The second advantage of the processor is that it will save you labor if you make and preserve sliced vegetables or fruits or combination dishes using them. The processor is also a big help in preparing food for drying. It

will "grind" meat, fruit, nuts, seeds and soaked beans as well, actually by high-powered chopping, and some models have juicer attachments.

Make sure any processor you are considering can perform all operations smoothly and that the motor that powers it can handle every job.

Commercial Food Dryers

Drying is a low-energy-consuming natural method of preserving foods. When 80 to 90 percent of their natural water is removed foods become inhospitable to destructive microorganisms. Home-dried foods shrink by one-sixth to one-third,

so storage space is conserved by this method. Storage should, however, be in a cool, dry, dark area. The most important consideration in deciding how much drying you should do is your own taste. Other considerations are the cost and availability of energy sources in your area, the need for time both in processing dried foods and in reconstituting them for use, the need to check dried foods frequently for mold and the fading of the nutritional value of some dried foods after a period of five to six months.

Small commercial units dry food by maintaining a constant low heat. Some circulate warm air around food racks. The appliances are low in energy use. Some have thermostats and

Although commercial dehydrators can process only a small quantity of food at a time, they cost only pennies to operate.

A juicer separates the juice from the fiber and pulp of most fresh fruits and vegetables to provide a healthy beverage.

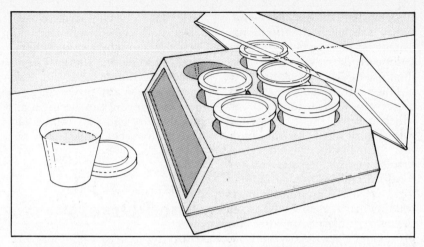

Individual-serving-size containers that come with most electric yogurt makers allow you to concoct a variety of flavors with each batch.

The wire mesh jar-covers of a commercial seed sprouter make a convenient filter when you're rinsing the sprouting seeds.

tubular heating elements and can be used to make yogurt or raise bread. Most of them, however, are small in capacity, and this means that drying during harvest period will have to be done every day.

Home-dried vegetables and fruits are drier than commercially dried ones, and therefore require no sulfur for a preservative. A dryer can be as simple as a screen tray suspended over a warm place like the top of a wood stove or over a gas pilot light or a bank of electric light-bulbs. A thermometer can be used to help you monitor for a steady temperature of 140°F. during the first half of the drying process and a temperature of from 95 to 100°F. during the remaining half. In consistently sunny, dry climates, drying may be done by sun outdoors.

304 Drying can be done in larger quantity in gas or electric ovens by presteaming sliced or chopped foods and spreading them on sheets to fill oven racks. Set the oven temperature between 130 and 160°F. and use only the bottom element of an electric oven. Prop the door open 3 inches so the steam can escape. The disadvantage of oven-drying is that it ties up the oven and heats up the kitchen. If you dry a large portion of your produce, investment in one of the larger commercial dryers may be worthwhile.

Juicers

Several of the multipurpose machines discussed earlier come with juicer attachments and some juicers have blender attachments. Juicers are different from liquefiers in that they separate fiber and pulp from juice, ejecting the pulp and al-

lowing the juice to be used clear. This is an important consideration if your harvesting includes much jelly making, but it is also of benefit in letting you convert almost any garden-fresh fruit or vegetable into a healthy beverage form. Some juicers are called extractors. Almost all are electrical, but there are a few hand-operated ones. If a juicer uses steam for extraction, it will require a power source for heat. Make sure a steam juicer is not aluminum, for this material may be harmful if used with acid foods. An added advantage of steam juicers is that they can be used for blanching, steam cooking of meats and vegetables, presteaming of dried foods and for steaming grains. Vegetables and fruits used in steam juicers need not be peeled, and the juice is hot enough to put in jars or to use for jelly directly. On the other hand, juice produced by steam is less nutritious than raw juice.

In purchasing a juicer, check for juicing efficiency (test especially with difficult items like carrots), for ease of cleaning, for a tendency to clog with pulp and for the amount of juice delivered with each operation (there can be a 20 percent variation). Some electric juicer models have two or more speeds.

Substitutes for juicers are blenders and liquefiers (these pulverize pulp and mix it in), hand mills, hand presses and cider presses, table-top wine presses and jelly bags or filters, especially when the latter are combined with food grinders, choppers and mills. Juice made with juicers, or by hand methods, can be stored in jars and bottles before use or processing to filter out all impurities. For harvest home use, however, absolutely clear jelly is silly to try for.

Yogurt Makers

Electric yogurt makers make some sense for anyone who uses a pint of yogurt or more a day, especially if he or she takes it to work in small containers. All they really do is provide a constantly warm place of exactly the right temperature so that a biological process can operate without guesswork. Most commercial units make good creamy yogurt.

Seed Sprouters

Commercial seed sprouters save you the trouble of improvising cheesecloth-covered jars to sprout seeds and beans in. Some are little more than wire mesh jar covers to replace the cheesecloth, but others provide tiers for different seeds and allow water to filter through to all levels while you rinse. You'll still have to provide a warm place and find time for rinsing. No organic gardener needs to be told about the nutritional advantages of fresh sprouts.

Tempeh Incubators

Tempeh, an easily digested fermented soybean product, is made much as yogurt is, maturing in a warm place. A food drier or a light bulb in an insulated picnic chest may be used in making tempeh, but you can sometimes find special tempeh incubators in oriental specialty shops.

The Choice Is Yours

Appliances large and appliances small—from the indispensable stove to the easily improvised sprouter—they are yours to choose among. They can help you lead a happy, productive, self-sufficient and self-reliant life, or they can clutter and complicate your existence, rule your patterns and make an ordinary August processing day a nightmare of waste and despair. It's up to you to choose them intelligently, following criteria of quality, durability, economy, ecological responsibility and personal style.

The next step will be to design, build and install them in your harvest kitchen so that you can get the most out of them, and so that they can work their best for you.

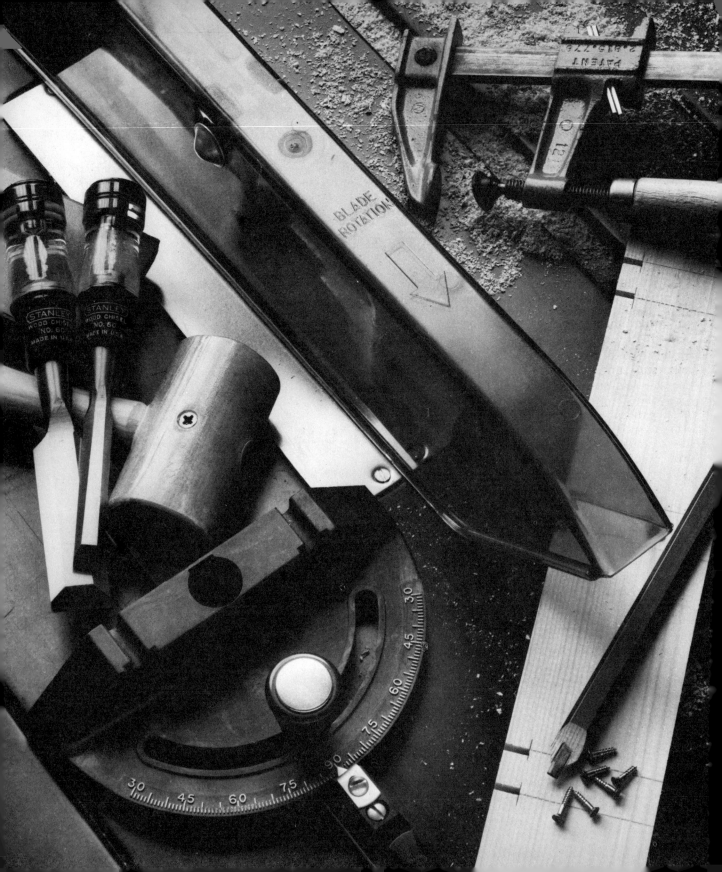

Part IV

Cabinets and Storage

Saw teeth bite into wood. Shavings curl from the plane. Glue oozes from a joint as clamps press it tight. Cabinetmaking. Because no kitchen that's short of storage and work space can be a satisfactory place to work, the cabinets can be regarded as the heart of a kitchen building or remodeling project. Sadly, the cabinets are the element most often left to professional cabinetmakers or industry's assembly lines. With careful planning, the kind of planning that relates your skills to your needs, you *can* build your own kitchen cabinets. It takes an understanding of various woodworking materials, techniques and tools. It takes time, money, space, equipment and diligent care. But most determined people can produce cabinets. Even you.

307

The Cabinetmaker's Craft

Kitchen cabinets can be the most expensive part of your harvest kitchen. They are certainly pivotal to the appearance of the room. What you do about kitchen cabinets is without question a major decision in building your harvest kitchen.

You can have cabinets. Or you can not have cabinets. You can buy the services of a custom

cabinetmaker and have cabinets crafted especially for your kitchen. Or you can buy cabinet modules and fit them to your space. Or you can build your own.

And if you've got the skills and gumption to take on a kitchen-building project in the first place, you've surely got the skills and gumption to build your own kitchen cabinets.

Don't be afraid, first of all, of being different. Just because all your friends and neighbors have tiers of cabinets of a certain style or character doesn't mean you have to have them. As part of your overall kitchen planning you've got to think seriously about this matter. You've got to meld your desires with your skills, your tools, your budget and your time. If shelves, rather than traditional cabinets, are best for you, don't be reluctant to have them. If you *can* build cabinets, but not the sort that the kitchen cabinet industry grinds out, be proud of yourself.

After all, you are doing it yourself. Your neighbors probably can't say that.

To Build or to Buy

The first step is to analyze your storage needs. How much cupboard space do you need? How about bin storage? Do you *really* need all those cupboards, or will shelves serve as well in place of some—or all—of them? Can you use furniture instead of cabinets? Do all have to be in the kitchen? How much counter space does the family cook really need? Could benches be used

instead of counters? Do you *need* doors? And drawers?

Once you have sorted it all out, you'll have some information to help you decide whether you have the time and money to build what you want, indeed, whether you *can* build what you want. There is no easy way to determine how long building your cabinets will take. It's a question of how skilled you are to begin with, as well as one of how fast you learn and how fast you work. It is also a question of the tools you own, that are available to you or that you intend to buy.

If you decide to buy cabinets, there are two options. You can have cabinets custom-built to fit your kitchen. Or you can buy standard units, assembling the modules that will provide you with the capacity you need and that will fit into your kitchen.

You may decide to build some components and buy some. Plastic laminated counter tops, for instance, are available ready-made. Butcher block is also available; the special tools and techniques required to make butcher block recommend that you purchase it. You can also buy drawers and doors and apply your own finish and

hardware. You can even buy kits.

Like everything else in the world, there is a vast difference in quality, even when the prices are similar. The quality of materials and workmanship in commercial cabinets can vary enormously. Some manufactured cabinets approximate the quality of fine furniture. And they look it. Others use materials that are too light, joinery that doesn't provide the necessary strength at critical points, finishes that will fade, chip, peel and crack long before they should. They don't look like much either.

If you are fussy about the appearance and durability of your harvest kitchen cabinetry, you should expect to spend substantially, if not lavishly, to obtain the effect you want. If you hire a custom cabinetmaker, the expense will be wholly monetary. If you do it yourself, you'll have to know, or learn, how to make the various joints that cabinetmakers use, their relative merits, and where they are most appropriate for their strength, appearance or both. If you decide, after learning about cabinetmaking, not to build your own, your knowledge of joinery will help you judge the quality of what you can buy.

Understanding the Principles

Kitchen cabinets are essentially elaborations of shelves and boxes. A cupboard is a box with shelves inside and a hinged door. Or it may have drawers. But the idea is still appropriate as you contemplate its construc-

tion. The need is, therefore, to construct a box that will withstand years of hard use, that will fulfill your aesthetic requirements, and that you can build with the tools available and within the time available.

309

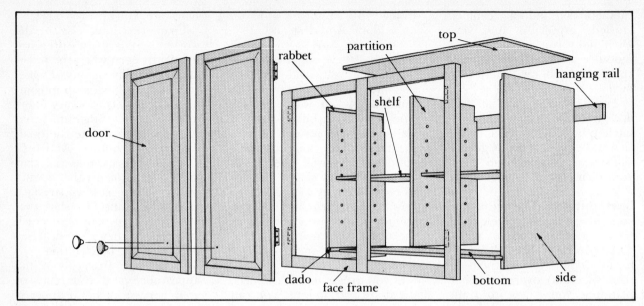

door

rabbet

partition

shelf

top

hanging rail

dado

face frame

bottom

side

Wall cabinets generally have but three elements: case, face frame and doors.

If you have decided to build, there are two basic ways of proceeding. You can prefabricate or you can build-in. Both methods have advantages and disadvantages. Prefabrication means that you build the cabinet in the shop and then install it at a future time. Its principal advantage is that the kitchen is not dismantled until the cabinets are all ready to be installed. Therefore, your present kitchen is usable as a kitchen while you build cabinets in your shop. When you build in, you monopolize the kitchen for a longer time, since dismantling starts even before you start to build. Of course, that may be just the pressure you need to get the job done once you start.

The disadvantage of prefabrication is that you use more materials. You probably will not be able to use the wall of the kitchen as the back of the cabinets, for example. Therefore prefabrication is more costly. This disadvantage may be more than offset by the fact that if you have a fairly complete shop that includes nonportable shop tools, you will make far better use of them if you don't have to run back and forth from kitchen to shop.

The typical kitchen base cabinet consists of five elements: the case, the face frame, the drawers, the doors and the counter top. The case is commonly constructed of plywood and board lumber. It's an ugly shell. The addition of the face frame, composed of vertical members called stiles and horizontal members called rails, starts to spruce up the cabinet. Drawers break the storage space into accessible compartments (as do shelves, which are part of the

case), and the doors shield the cabinet's contents from view.

The appearance of the cabinet—its style—is set by the doors and drawer fronts almost exclusively. The material chosen for the visible portions of the cabinet plays a role, but the doors and drawer fronts are what make the cabinet ornate, refined or simply stark.

If you visit a kitchen dealer's showroom, you may be impressed initially by the array of cabinets and styles available. But you'll discover that one cabinet is intrinsically like another. Only changes in trim and finish are required to change the style. The array is not what it seems.

After the cabinets are in place, either because they were

310

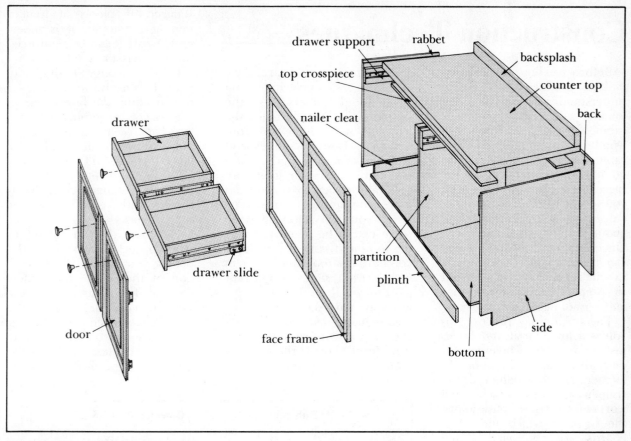

The typical base cabinet is composed of five elements: case, face frame, doors, drawers and counter top. Not every cabinet will have all the elements, but most will.

built there or because they've been installed there, a counter top is constructed, tying them all together. The foundation stock for the counter top is commonly particle board, a ¾- or 1½-inch slab of it. A finish surface, plastic laminate, tile or the like, is applied to the particle board.

The final step is to cover the raw plywood of any exposed side with a face panel to complement the style established and the materials used in the face frame, doors and drawers. This facing can be a ¼-inch plywood panel or something more elaborate.

Building kitchen cabinets is not necessarily fine cabinetmaking. It *can* be, but it doesn't have to be. Create a design that's compatible with your skills. Select materials that you can afford, that you can work with,

that fit the design. Don't expect to build a battery of solid cherry, raised-panel cabinets if you've no experience as a woodworker. On the other hand, don't feel you have to buy cabinets or assemble kit-cabinets if you've got little woodworking experience. You don't necessarily need a shop full of expensive tools to make attractive and serviceable shelves and cabinets.

All it takes is some thoughtful planning, a little sweat and a lot of care. Don't be intimidated. You *can* do it.

311

Construction Techniques

Before tackling any cabinet-making project, you've got to understand the rudiments of joinery. You can't design your cabinets if you don't know how wood is cut and joined, how cabinets are constructed. You've got to know about laying out the pieces you need on the stock you've got to work with, about cutting them out accurately and about joining them securely. Once you know the options, you can begin to plan the specific cabinets or shelves you want and to prepare working drawings and a list of necessary materials.

The planning process involves a lot of trial and error, just as does the whole task of designing and building a kitchen. But basic joinery is the framework within which you'll work. First learn the basic joints, the ways in which individual boards are connected. Then learn the techniques used to fabricate and bond the joints.

Joints

The joints that you make in your harvest kitchen's cabinets will have a lot to do with their final appearance and their durability. There are more than a hundred kinds of joints that can be made, but they all fall into a few basic categories that are modified to suit special needs. Modern technology, specifically in the area of adhesives, has reduced the need for some of the more complicated joints —provided you make the simple

joints accurately and carefully.

Some basic principles still apply to all joinery. Use the simplest joint that will assure the strength needed in the construction. Dowels, splines and glue blocks add strength to simple joints and such joints are generally easier to make than more complicated joints. The joints you will select must to some extent be determined by the tools and skills you have. If you have few tools but use them with care and skill, a simple butt joint may be best. If you have a table saw and a dado head, by all means make dado joints wherever they are appropriate.

Butt Joint. This is the simplest joint, formed by butting two

squared-off pieces of lumber together. Though it is inherently weak, it can be reinforced with dowels or a spline to become a strong, high-quality joint. It is useful in framing or for attaching the face frame to the case or for joining the sides and back of a drawer, though more discriminating and capable craftsmen will want to use other drawer joints. In framing, butt joints sometimes are reinforced with glue blocks or corner blocks.

Edge Joint. If you intend to glue up stock to make large flat panels, you will use some variation of the edge joint. Unless you cut the pieces on a power saw with a carbide-tipped blade, the edges will require surfacing to remove the roughness left by the saw blade. Traditionally, this surfacing, called jointing, is

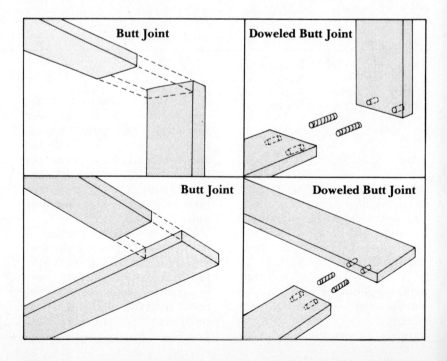

Butt Joint

Doweled Butt Joint

Butt Joint

Doweled Butt Joint

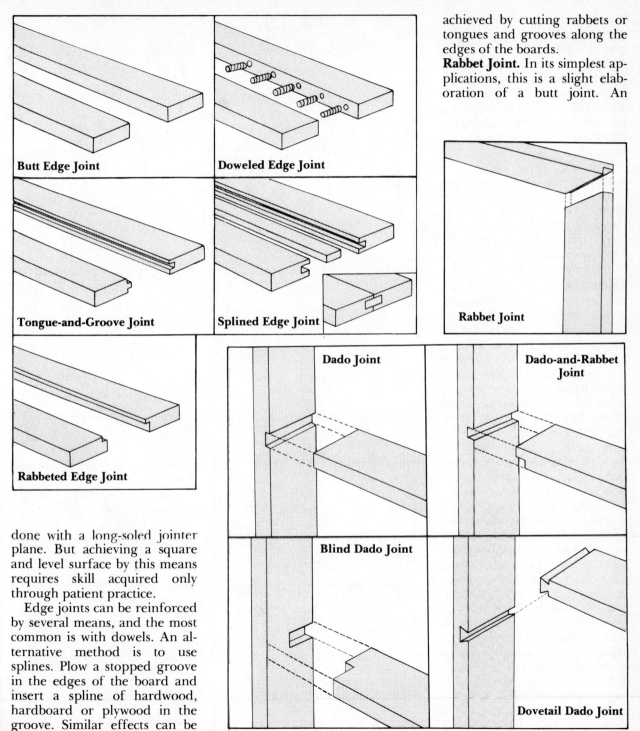

Butt Edge Joint

Doweled Edge Joint

Tongue-and-Groove Joint

Splined Edge Joint

Rabbeted Edge Joint

Rabbet Joint

Dado Joint

Dado-and-Rabbet Joint

Blind Dado Joint

Dovetail Dado Joint

achieved by cutting rabbets or tongues and grooves along the edges of the boards.

Rabbet Joint. In its simplest applications, this is a slight elaboration of a butt joint. An

done with a long-soled jointer plane. But achieving a square and level surface by this means requires skill acquired only through patient practice.

Edge joints can be reinforced by several means, and the most common is with dowels. An alternative method is to use splines. Plow a stopped groove in the edges of the board and insert a spline of hardwood, hardboard or plywood in the groove. Similar effects can be

313

L-shaped groove is cut into the end or edge of one of the pieces and the other fits into it. The width of the rabbet should match the thickness of the piece to fit into it, and the depth should be one-half to two-thirds the thickness of the board being rabbeted. A variation is to rabbet both pieces.

The virtue of the rabbet joint is that it conceals the end grain of one of the pieces being joined, and it reduces the tendency of the joint to twist. It is frequently used to join the sides and fronts of drawers and to install cabinet backs.

Dado Joint. A dado is a groove cut across the grain. It is commonly used where the joint is to provide support for a horizontal member, as in a bookshelf or a cabinet bottom. If you object to the appearance of the notch, you can make a blind or stopped dado, terminating the dado about ½ inch from the front edge of the supporting piece. The piece to be inserted will have to be notched accordingly, but the result will have the appearance of a butt joint and the strength of a dado joint.

There are elegant variations to the dado joint that make it one of the most versatile joints you can use. As a corner dado, it provides support for a lower shelf in a table, with dadoes cut into the legs and the corners of the shelf trimmed to fit into the dadoes. For added strength and rigidity, a combination dado-and-rabbet joint has one member rabbeted and the supporting member dadoed. A fancy, and strong, variation is the dovetail dado, which can be cut

314

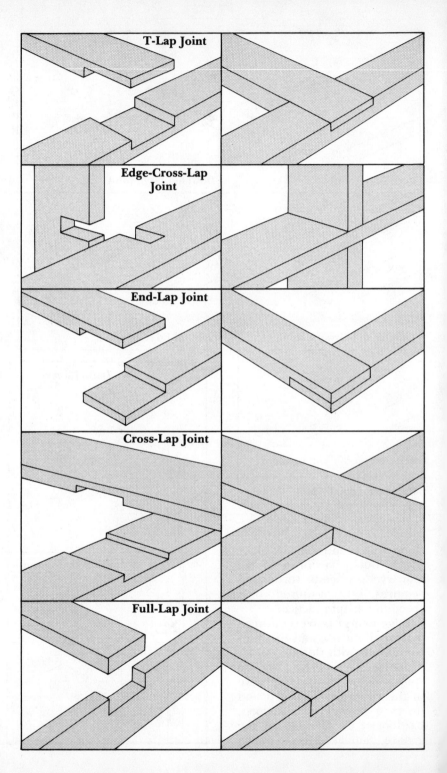

T-Lap Joint

Edge-Cross-Lap Joint

End-Lap Joint

Cross-Lap Joint

Full-Lap Joint

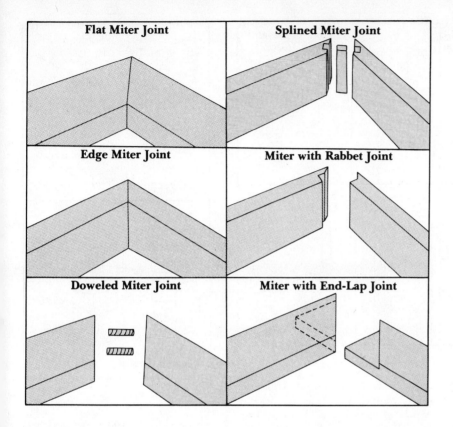

Flat Miter Joint	Splined Miter Joint
Edge Miter Joint	Miter with Rabbet Joint
Doweled Miter Joint	Miter with End-Lap Joint

with a dovetail bit in a router. The supporting member is dadoed with a dovetail slot, while the other member has a matching dovetail pin cut in its end.

Lap Joint. A joint in which one member is notched to accept the other member is a lap joint. Essentially, the joint consists of dadoes or rabbets cut in one or both pieces. The pieces are thus interlocked with their faces flush. In a full-lap joint, only one piece is notched; the other's full dimension is set into the notch. In any of the half-lap joints, both members are notched, usually with half the total material to be removed coming from each piece.

Within these broad categories, there are many variations. In the end-lap joint, both members are lapped at their ends. In a cross-lap joint, the laps are somewhere other than the ends; the members can cross at any angle. In a T-lap joint, one member is lapped in the middle, the other at an end. In an edge-cross-lap joint, the members are notched rather than dadoed so that the lapping is edge to edge, rather than face to face.

Miter Joint. This angled joint hides the end grain of both pieces being joined. While the pieces usually form right angles, they can also form acute or obtuse angles. The miter joint is

most familiar in picture frames, but it is also commonly used in constructing furniture casework. If you use it at all in your kitchen cabinetry, it would be in constructing door frames and face frames or in finishing the exposed edges of all-wood counter tops.

Pure miter joints are not particularly strong joints, and consequently must be reinforced with dowels, a spline or a key. There are a number of hybrid miter joints used in casework that combine miters with rabbets and dadoes and these are stronger than simple miters.

Miter joints run in several main groups: the flat miters, in which the angled cuts run across the face of the pieces, the edge miters, in which the pieces to be joined are actually beveled rather than mitered, and the compound miters, in which the pieces are cut with combination miter and bevel cuts.

Mortise-and-Tenon Joint. This classic joint is not one you are very likely to use unless you are building a table to go into your harvest kitchen. The most common application of the mortise-and-tenon joint is in leg and rail construction—the framing and legs of a table. But mortise-and-tenon joints are used in constructing frames for panel doors.

Mortise-and-tenon joints take many different forms. The basic elements are the mortise, which is a hole—round, square or rectangular—and the tenon, which is a tongue cut on the end of the joining member to fit the mortise. There are joints known as blind mortise-and-

315

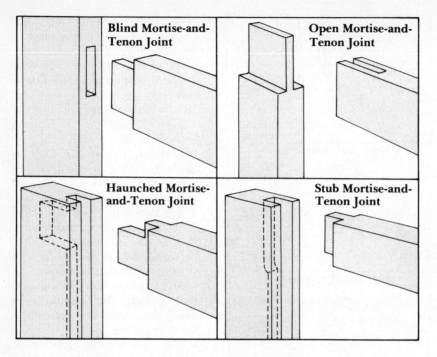

Blind Mortise-and-Tenon Joint

Open Mortise-and-Tenon Joint

Haunched Mortise-and-Tenon Joint

Stub Mortise-and-Tenon Joint

Finger Joint

Dovetail Joint

tenon, haunched mortise-and-tenon, open mortise-and-tenon.

In general, the mortise ought to be at least $5/16$ inch from the outside face of the work, and at least $1/8$ inch deeper than the tenon is long. The tenon should be about half the thickness of the stock. A slight taper on the tenon is advisable so that it will fit easily yet snugly into the mortise.

Dovetail Joint. This is the classic joint found in quality drawer construction. In handmade furniture, dovetails are often used to join casework. When properly executed, the dovetail joint is extremely strong, and it is attractive to boot.

Dovetailing is an enterprise that used to separate the cabinetmaker from the woodbutcher. The pins and slots had to be carefully designed and laid out, everything had to be cut and chiseled by hand. The finished product had to fit perfectly. Now it's possible for most anyone to make first-class dovetail joints using a router and dovetailing template.

The mechanized approach will produce a single kind of dovetail, however, while the skilled craftsman can make lap dovetails and stopped-lap dovetails, as well as the traditional through dovetails. And he can vary the size and shape of the dovetails too.

A simpler yet strong as well as decorative joint that resembles the dovetail is the finger joint. The interlocking pins, instead of being tapered, are parallel. They are therefore easily cut on a table saw.

These joints are what joinery is all about. The joiner is the person who fabricates them. While a cabinetmaker is more than a joiner, he's got to have the joiner's skills mastered for his cabinets to be successful.

Joinery is the process of fabricating parts and assembling them. In a simple project, fabrication may be merely cutting boards into pieces, assembly may be merely nailing them together. But even a simple project can be done well or done poorly. If the pieces aren't laid out accurately, if they aren't cut out carefully, if the nails aren't driven true, the simple project can be a disappointment. If all is done skillfully and carefully, the

316

project can be an object of pride.

No matter how skilled the craftsman, how complex the project, how sophisticated the tools and materials, the success or failure of the finished product will be determined by the basics. As you approach the cabinetmaking phase of your kitchen project, ground yourself in the basics.

Safety

Before you begin, there's a very important subject to consider. That's safety.

Safety is the subject to which everyone gives at least lip service. Too, it is a subject about which many people get sanctimonious. Unfortunately, neither lip service nor sanctimoniousness will prevent you from rapping your thumb with the hammer, ripping your flesh with a chisel or rattling your bones stumbling over clutter on the shop floor. You've got to practice safety every moment you are working.

Most cabinetmakers can tell some pretty grisly tales of fingers consumed by the tools of their trade. Anybody with any sense at all knows that a power

tool will cut whatever you feed into it, including fingers. But a lot of folks who exercise all due caution around a table saw get blasé with a chisel and shed blood anyhow.

Safety isn't simply a matter of using the blade guard and wearing goggles. It's working thoughtfully, alertly. It's keeping tools in good repair. It's using the correct tool for each job. It's routinely cleaning up after yourself. It's having a helper around when you need extra hands, and not having distractions around when you need to concentrate. It's walking away

from the job when you are tired or when the damn tools and boards won't cooperate. A blade guard won't protect the inattentive or reckless woodworker, any more than a lathe will be careful not to grab you by your necktie.

Here are some general safety guidelines:

- Be ready mentally for the work. Don't drag yourself out to the shop if you are tired, irritable, distracted or preoccupied. Don't try to work yourself out of a snit by ripping boards; spade the

Accessories for the well-dressed cabinet-maker: a. Ear protectors of the earmuff variety are better than ear plugs or cotton balls for cutting the shriek of power tools. b. Face mask filters the dust from the air. c., d., e. Eye protection is afforded by a variety of goggles and face shields.

garden or take a long walk instead. Don't force yourself to get those cabinets done if you're exhausted. You are doing this because it's fun, because you enjoy it. And if you are enjoying yourself, you are more inclined to be alert, thoughtful, *careful*.

- Dress the part. Leave the jewelry, including your wedding ring and watch, on the dresser. Wear fairly close-fitting clothes, and roll up your sleeves. If you are working with a power tool that generates a lot of sawdust, wear goggles, even a respirator if it seems appropriate. You are in your own shop, so don't worry about what the neighbors will think.

- Maintain a well-ordered workplace. Get yourself a big waste barrel, use it, and empty it regularly. Sweep up when you finish work, picking up scraps of wood. Keep materials stored neatly, accessibly, *and* out of the way. Have a place for every tool, and keep it there when you aren't actively using it. Give yourself enough room to work around each shop tool you have, and don't use the tool's table as a workbench.

- Know your tools. If you've got the money to buy a tool, you should have the sense to learn how to use it properly. And properly is safely. Read a book about it, or take a course, or at the least talk to a cabinetmaker who has all his fingers. Think. Take the time to maintain your tools.

Take the time to set up for a task, using firm work supports and whatever clamps, jigs, guides or guards are necessary and appropriate. Every shortcut can endanger your well-being.

Finally, be prepared for accidents. Get a first aid kit and keep it handy. Know how to use it. It is almost inevitable that you will at least get a splinter or two in the course of building a kitchenful of shelves and cabinets. Be prepared for it, though not necessarily resigned to it.

Woodworking is a lot of fun, especially if you do it safely.

Layout

The first construction stage in any project is laying out the pieces of the cabinet on the material from which each piece will be fabricated. Ofttimes this is as simple as scribing a line across the face of a board. But other times it involves marking the locations of holes to be drilled, rabbets and dadoes and grooves to be cut, partitions to be attached.

This is a critical process. It's going to be tough to get the cabinet right if you lay it out wrong. Shop teachers tell their

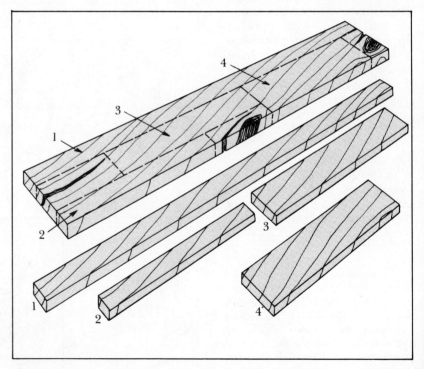

Judicious layout enables you to cut usable pieces from a board that has knots or other defects.

pupils to "measure twice and cut once," and that's good advice. A hole drilled in the wrong place can be plugged with a piece of dowel, perhaps, and a mispositioned groove can sometimes be patched with a strip of wood. But a board can't be stretched to the proper size if you cut it too short.

So measure twice and cut once.

As you lay out a project, examine your materials. Look for defects in the wood that will affect the use of the board in your cabinet. Of course, you *should* check your lumber at the lumberyard, and you *should* refuse to accept defective lumber. But sometimes you discover blemishes after the board is yours, and you have to work with it.

Defects are relative. Warped or twisted or cupped boards may be totally unusable. The defective ends of a board afflicted with checking can be cut off. A board with a loose knot may be okay as a framing piece, but not where it would be visible. You may decide that defects and blemishes are unacceptable in any exposed part of your cabinets, while your neighbor may find that knots and the like add something to the character of his or her cabinets.

In any case, examine your

To make the most economical use of your materials, use a pencil and tape measure to roughly lay out all the pieces you need before you cut any of them.

material and decide how to deal with it.

The next step is to start laying out and cutting individual pieces. When dealing with the rough-sawn lumber, the cabinetmaker cuts the pieces to a rough size, one that's larger than needed. The faces and edges are planed and jointed, the board is ripped to the desired width and finally, the board is crosscut to the desired length. When dealing with board lumber and plywood, you can in most cases skip the preliminaries and cut to specific lengths. One exception would be when you are cutting boards to be glued edge to edge to form a panel. In such a case, the individual pieces should be cut over-

length, glued up, then the panel cut to the specific length.

Laying out a whole project at one time may not be the best approach. Sometimes you'll want to cut pieces as you go, cutting them to fit rather than to a size specified on paper. You'll have to judge individual situations.

In doing the layouts, remember that your saw will consume some of the wood, turning it into sawdust on the shop floor. Saw kerfs vary. Generally, a power saw will create a wider kerf than a handsaw. You should have given yourself some leeway when you drew up your materials list, so you should have enough wood. Perhaps you'll

319

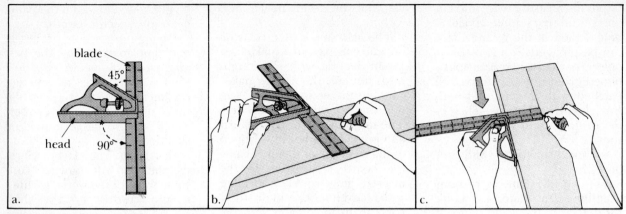

Using a combination square: a. The tool. b. Laying out a crosscut. c. Laying out a rip cut.

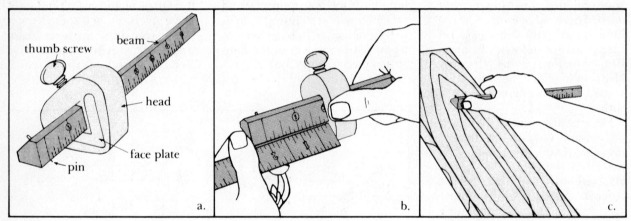

Using a marking gauge: a. The tool. b. Setting the gauge. c. Marking the cut.

find it advisable to "sketch" out each piece to be sure you know where each piece is coming from, then measure and cut as you go.

The key tools for layout work are a rule, a square and a scriber. The rule can be a tape measure, folding rule or yardstick, the square a try square or framing square, the scriber a pencil, knife or awl. For some jobs, you may need a compass or dividers, for others a marking gauge. For laying out long cuts on plywood, you may find a chalk line useful.

The routine for laying out crosscuts on lumber is to measure from the end of the board, after having first checked to be sure the end is square, and make a small mark at the desired point. Using a square set at the point, scribe a line across the board. Precision here is a sign of craftsmanship. For rough work a pencil line is okay, but for fine work, use a knife to score the line, making the line more precise and cutting the surface fibers of the wood that could splinter when you saw.

To lay out a rip cut, measure from the edge you know is true (because you jointed it or at least checked it with a straightedge). Use a chalk line or a marking gauge to mark the line. The marking gauge, because it will score the wood, is a better tool to use for fine work.

If you have shop tools, such as a radial arm saw or a table saw, some of your layout work will be

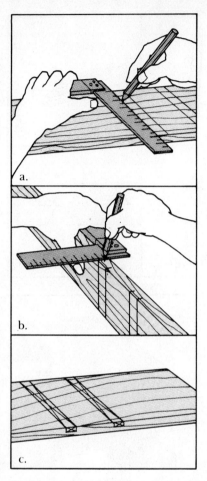

Laying out a dado that's to be cut by hand.

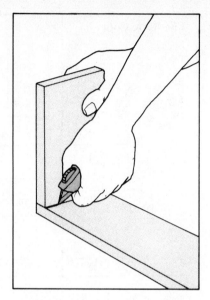

Using the pieces to be joined to lay out a joint.

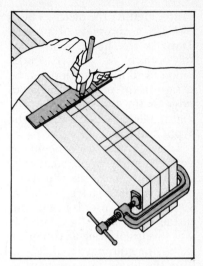

Marking several pieces at one time.

cutting work. That's because you can set up a variety of cutting guides on these power saws that help you to cut the size of pieces you want. It takes some time and care to set up the guides, but once they're set, they'll allow you to produce as many uniform pieces as you need. The most skilled craftsman can't produce uniform pieces with hand tools the

way a woodbutcher can with a table saw.

Marking pieces to be cut from larger boards or panels isn't the only layout work you'll have to do in making cabinets. There may be dadoes and grooves to be laid out, or holes to be drilled. When you do this kind of layout work, make your measurements from a common point. And remember where that point is so that it remains your single point of reference. You'll thus avoid errors that would otherwise be inevitable.

Keep the process in mind as you do your layout, so you make marks that are pertinent. No need to mark more than the center point of a hole to be drilled, for example. If you are plowing a groove with a router, a single position line will suffice; the router's setting and bit will determine the width and depth.

But if doing the work with hand-powered tools, you'll have to mark the edges of the groove as well as its depth.

A trick used by skilled woodworkers is to use the parts being joined as measuring devices. In other words, if you are joining two pieces of 1-inch stock at right angles using a rabbet joint, mark off your rabbet using a piece of the wood instead of measuring the desired width with a rule.

If you have duplicate pieces to fabricate, lay them out at the same time. If possible, clamp the pieces together and use a single measurement and marking to indicate locations of grooves or notches in all the pieces. The goal of duplication can be approached, if not achieved, if these pieces can be cut as they were marked, together. It's not always possible, but if it is, do it.

Finally, but of primary impor-   **321**

tance, identify the pieces. This is vital in a complicated project. Don't be shy, lightly write "top" or "bottom" or "part A" on the wood. And if orientation may be a significant problem, mark an edge as the top, another as the right, perhaps one side as the front and the other as the back.

Identification can begin as you examine your materials. Mark one face as the best; cabinetmakers have a little squiggle they use, but you can just as easily write "best face." It will surely continue as you mark parts for joining, so that you glue the tenon into the mortise you spent so much time fitting it to, rather than one of the others in the project.

Just write lightly, so your notes can be sanded away as you prepare the cabinet for finishing.

Cutting

The next major step in cabinet construction is the fabrication of the pieces. In a simple project, fabrication isn't fabrication at all, it's cutting out pieces. But, depending upon how you've chosen to join the pieces, you may have to do much more.

In sophisticated cabinetry, you may have to surface hardwood to prepare it for use, plow grooves and cut dadoes, drill holes and chisel mortises.

However you have chosen to construct your cabinets, you will have to cut out the pieces—if only as the first step in fabrication. Cutting is a fundamental part of woodworking. There are dozens of tools for cutting, ranging from saws through

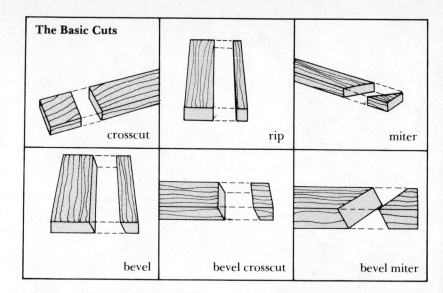

The Basic Cuts

crosscut   rip   miter

bevel   bevel crosscut   bevel miter

chisels to drills. How well you understand and master the various woodcutting processes will determine how well you'll do as a cabinetmaker. You *will* have to cut wood to make your kitchen cabinets.

The cutting picks up where the layout leaves off. If you don't cut accurately, all the precision in layout is wasted. The piece will come out too long or too short, the dado will be a hair off, the cabinet will be just a mite crooked or wobbly. So apply yourself to the cutting as you did to the layout.

The bulk of the cutting you will do in building kitchen cabinets is either crosscutting or ripping. Crosscutting is cutting across the grain of the wood. Ripping is cutting with the grain. Cutting plywood or particle board can be considered crosscutting, although for the best results it should be approached as a special kind of work all its own.

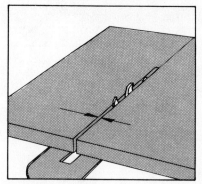

The kerf is created by the removal of material by the saw teeth during the cutting process.

Whichever cutting you are doing, one of the keys to success is to always cut on the waste side of your cutting line. This is important because of the saw kerf, the gap created by the saw's removal of material. With a table saw, the kerf may be ⅛ inch or more wide. Cutting on the wrong side of the line will produce a piece ⅛ inch short.

Ripping and crosscutting are

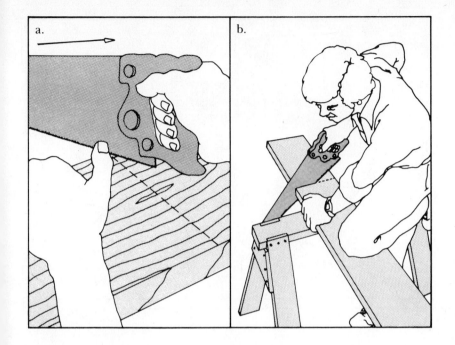

Using a handsaw to make a crosscut: a. The thumb guides the saw on the initial strokes. b. Saw with steady, even strokes, the line of teeth at a 45° angle to the board.

(this is what sawhorses are made for), lean over the board, placing one hand (your left, if you are right handed) on the board. Hold the saw in your other hand. Place the saw against the far edge of the board. Using the thumb of your left hand to guide the blade, start the kerf just on the waste side of the line by drawing the saw toward you. Once you have the kerf started, get your thumb out of the way and begin sawing in earnest. The saw will do about 75 percent of its cutting on the downstroke, and you will be wise to develop a steady, even rhythm. Keep the toothed edge of the saw blade at about a 45-degree angle to the surface of the wood. Keep your eye on

done with different saws (or saw blades). There are combination rip and crosscut circular saw blades, and for most work such a blade is okay. But finer cuts are achieved using rip blades for ripping, crosscut blades for crosscutting, and plywood blades for cutting plywood, hardboard or particle board.

Crosscutting

Crosscutting is what most people think of when you talk about cutting wood, and it's surely the most common cutting procedure in a woodworking project. Almost invariably, the materials must be crosscut to length as a first step. Often, this

is the only cutting required.

With a handsaw, crosscutting is easy enough. After marking the cutting line and laying the board across knee-high support

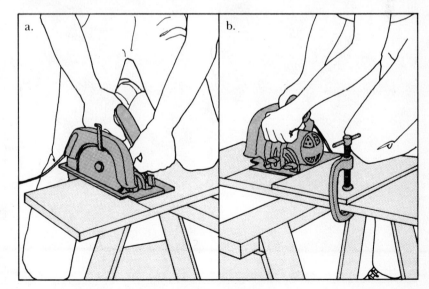

Using a portable circular saw to make a crosscut: a. Cutting freehand along a line. b. Using a guide.

Using a miter box will enable you to get precision crosscuts and miters.

where you are going and the blade cutting along a straight line. As you approach the end of the cut, reach across the saw with your left hand to grasp the

Using a radial arm to make a crosscut: a. With the board held against the fence, start the saw and pull it toward you, cutting the board. b. Extension tables on each side of the saw support long boards. c. A stop tacked to the extension table allows many pieces to be easily cut to exactly the same length. d. A clamp attached to the fence serves the same purpose.

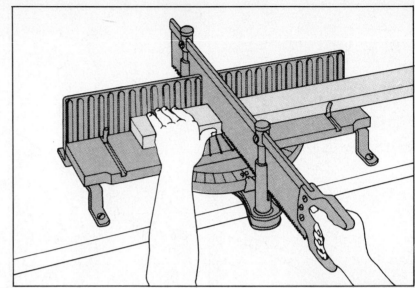

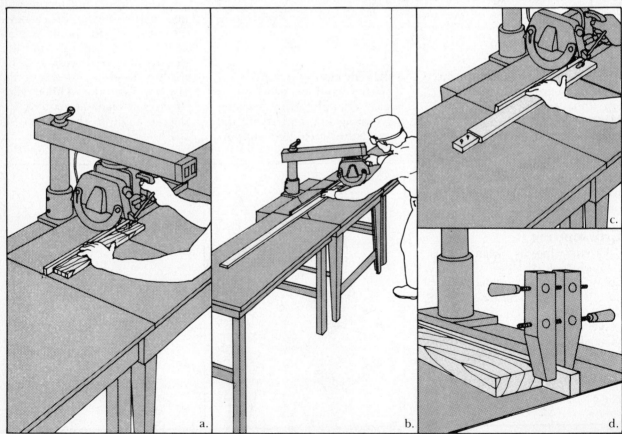

a.

b.

c.

d.

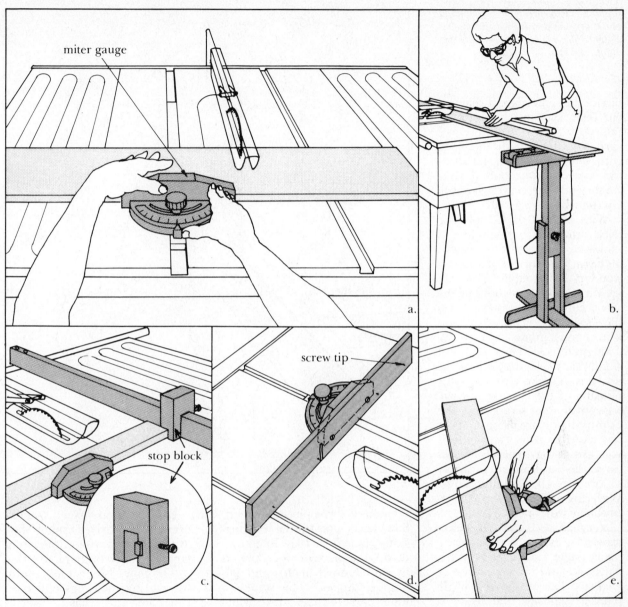

Crosscutting on a table saw: a. The miter gauge is always used to guide the board in crosscutting. b. Boards that extend well beyond the saw table should be supported by a stand or helper. c. A stop attached to the rip fence allows the cutting of many pieces of exactly the same size. d. A wooden facing attached to the miter gauge eases the cutting of long pieces; screws with their points just breaking the surface help secure the work, especially when cutting miters. e. Cutting a miter.

waste piece, so its weight doesn't tear a huge splinter out of the good piece before you can cut it all the way off.

The procedure when using a portable circular saw is very

325

Ripping a long board with a handsaw could be considered good exercise. A wedge in the kerf keeps it open, preventing it from binding the blade.

nearly the same, except that you cut from the near edge to the far edge. And you use a lot of care. You don't guide the blade with your thumb. A handsaw can take a chunk out of your finger, but the power saw will zip the whole finger off.

With both of these tools, the trick is to cut in a straight line. A handsaw moves pretty slowly, and you can correct if the saw wanders off course. You can with a circular saw too, but the saw is cutting a lot faster, so you have to react quickly. A solution is to clamp a guide to the board. The guide can be a scrap of wood that's at least as long as the board is wide. Be sure the motor housing of the circular saw will pass over the scrap and the clamps, if you are using a power saw. And be sure it's a scrap if you are using a handsaw, because the handsaw will probably scrape up the guiding edge. With care and with practice, you probably won't need a guide.

Very fine and accurate crosscuts, including those made on an angle, can be made with a backsaw and miter box. A backsaw has a shorter blade than a handsaw, the blade is stiffened with a heavy metal backbone, and it has very fine teeth. It cuts slowly, but the cut is fine, and because the blade is stiff, the cut is straight and true.

The miter box is a saw guide. In its simplest, most inexpensive form, the miter box is a channel

wedge

formed of three pieces of wood. Saw kerfs cut in the channel sides guide a backsaw in cutting through a piece of wood placed in the channel at 45- and 90-degree angles. This type of miter box you can make yourself. In its most sophisticated and expensive form, the miter box has a backsaw, or a variation of it, mounted in a pivoting guide over a saw table. The guide has settings that allow you to cut angles ranging from 45 degrees to 135 degrees.

For the weak-armed, there's even a motorized miter box available, with a portable circular saw in a pivoting mount.

The miter box is most useful for cutting moldings and interior trim, but it has its uses in cabinetmaking. And one of its uses is in crosscutting relatively narrow boards with considerable accuracy.

Crosscutting can be done on either a table saw or a radial arm saw. It is most easily done on a radial arm saw, because that's

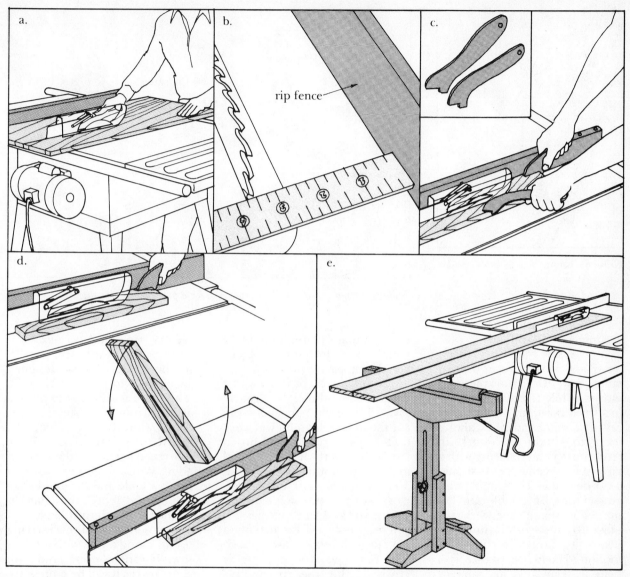

a.

b.

rip fence

c.

d.

e.

Ripping with a table saw: a. The rip fence is always used to guide a rip cut. b. Setting the fence so a board of the proper width will be cut. c. Use push sticks when ripping narrow pieces; use the blade guard-antikickback finger-splitter always. d. Ripping long or narrow stock is eased by cutting only half the length, shutting off the saw, withdrawing the work and flipping it end for end, then completing the cut. e. A stand or a helper can also be used to support long stock during a ripping operation.

what the saw does best. The board is laid on the table and the saw is pulled along an overhead track toward the operator, cutting through the board. Miters, which are cuts made at an angle across the board's face, and bevels, which are cuts made at an angle through the board's

thickness, are easily made. And in all cases, the work remains stationary while the blade is

moved. If auxiliary tables are set up on either side of the saw itself, extremely long work- **327**

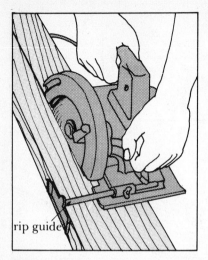

Using a rip guide on a portable circular saw.

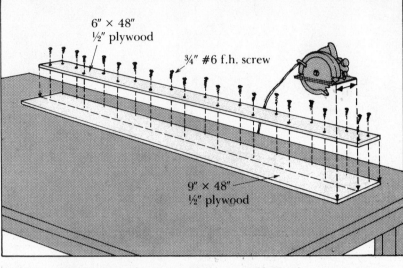

6" × 48"
½" plywood

¾" #6 f.h. screw

9" × 48"
½" plywood

Making a ripping and panel-cutting guide for a portable circular saw.

pieces can be laid in place for cutting without difficulty.

A table saw will also crosscut, miter and bevel. But in using a table saw, the workpiece is moved, while the blade remains in a fixed position. An accessory called a miter gauge is always used to guide the work in crosscutting and mitering with a table saw. Freehand cuts should *never* be made. The trouble with crosscutting on a table saw lies in the fact that it's the work that moves. If the work is an 8-foot board, it is tough to control its motion. Having assistance is a help, as is an auxiliary table or stand positioned to support the work.

Ripping

Ripping is done to establish or change the width or thickness of a board. It has a lot in common with cutting panels. It is best to avoid this cut if you can't make **328** it with machinelike precision,

but if you are planning to build your own kitchen cabinets, you'd best learn how to rip.

A short rip can be done with a crosscut handsaw. A coarse saw—5½ teeth per inch—will cut the quickest, and it will work quite well for ripping. But a ripsaw has teeth that are shaped and sharpened differently than a crosscut saw. For the fastest, cleanest rip cuts, use a true rip-saw or ripsaw blade.

The procedure for making a rip cut with a handsaw is much the same as for making a crosscut. But the ripsaw cuts best when held at a 60-degree angle to the work, rather than a 45-degree angle.

As with the crosscut, the trick in ripping is getting a clean, straight, square cut. But because most rip cuts are a lot longer than most crosscuts, this trick is more of a challenge. The table saw will give you the most satis-

factory rip cuts, because it is equipped with a fence, parallel to the blade, that is designed specifically to produce rip cuts. The fence is adjusted to place it as far from the blade as the board width that's desired. The board to be ripped must have one trued surface and one trued edge. With the good surface on the saw table and the good edge against the fence, the board is pushed through the blade.

The antithesis of this is trying to saw along a line with a hand-saw. It can be done, and with short pieces it will be quite satisfactory. But freehanding a 4-foot cut isn't going to yield the same result time after time as will using a table saw. A wooden guide can be used, but after several uses, the scrap guide will really be scrap, unusable even as a guide.

A portable circular saw lies somewhere between the table

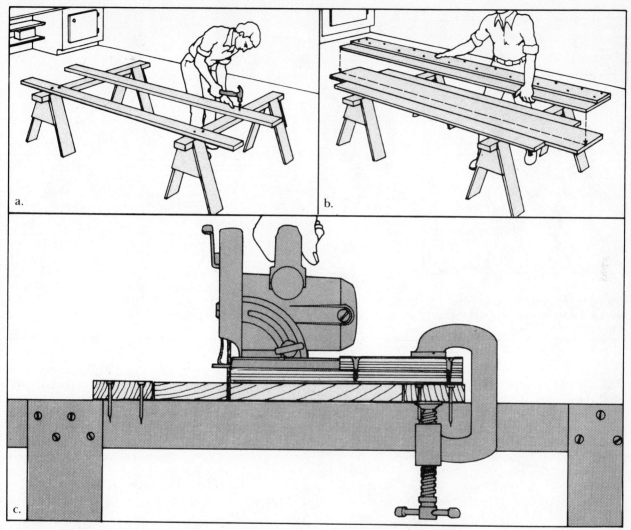

a.

b.

c.

saw and the handsaw. It doesn't require the physical stamina to operate that the handsaw does, and it cuts a lot faster. But it isn't terribly accurate over a long cut unless you use a guide of some sort. Most circular saws are delivered with a "rip guide," which is only good if it can slide along a trued edge. At best, it is a makeshift solution to the problem.

A better solution is to build a guide. You can use it for ripping and for cutting panels. A 4-foot one can be made by cutting a 4-inch-wide strip and a foot-wide strip from the 4-foot dimension of a plywood or particle-board panel. Be sure the narrow strip has the factory edge, which will be true. Glue and screw the narrow strip atop the wide strip, with the true

edge facing in. The face of the saw's shoe will ride on the broad strip, while the edge of the shoe glides against the edge of the narrow strip. The first cut you make will trim the broad strip to the proper width for your particular saw.

329

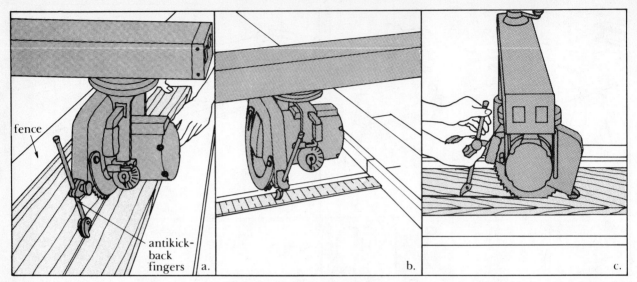

fence

antikick-
back
fingers | a.

b.

c.

Cutting a plywood or particle-board panel with a portable circular saw and a homemade guide.

Ripping with a radial arm saw: a. The motor and blade are pivoted and locked in position, and the board is pushed through the saw. b. Setting the saw the proper distance from the fence. c. Adjusting the antikickback fingers so they grip the board.

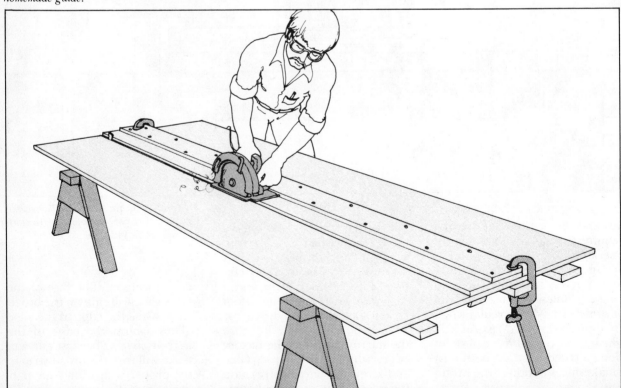

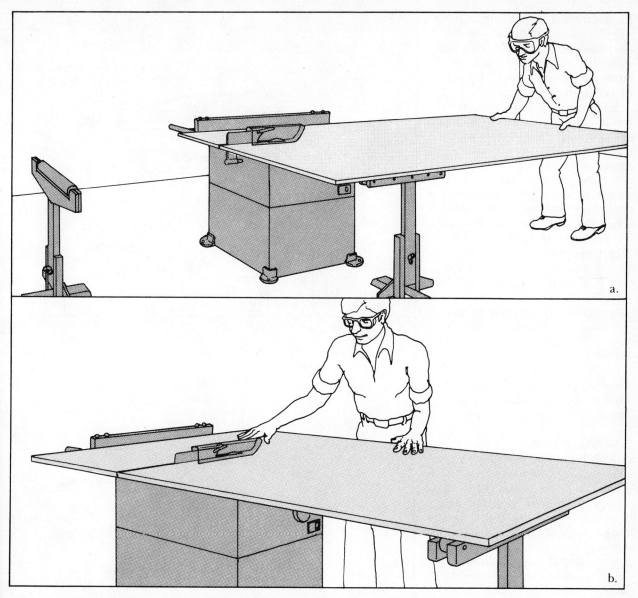

Cutting a panel with a table saw: a. Cutting along the long dimension. b. Cutting along the short dimension. In either situation the use of a support stand or a helper is vital.

To use the guide, clamp or tack it to the board to be ripped, lining up the sawn edge of the guide with the cutting line. Then slide the circular saw along the guide and cut the board. It may be necessary, with narrow stock, to lay a second board beside the one to be cut so that the guide has sound bearing.

Further, it's a good idea to **331**

measure your saw before making the guide, so you can make the narrow strip sufficiently wide that clamps you use to secure the guide will be cleared by the motor housing.

You can also rip boards on a radial arm saw. But just as crosscutting is sometimes awkward on a table saw, ripping is sometimes awkward on a radial arm saw. To rip, the saw and motor must be pivoted on the arm and locked in position. Then the unit is adjusted to rip the board to the proper width. Then, as with the table saw, the board is held against the fence and pushed through the blade. This works without a hitch if your access to the ends of the saw table is unhindered. But if you've set up your saw properly for crosscutting with sizable extension tables on either side of the saw, you can't really get behind the board to push it. It isn't impossible, it's just awkward.

Cutting Panels

The best material to use in making kitchen cabinets is plywood. Its drawback is that it comes in unwieldy 4-foot by 8-foot sheets; these sheets are tough to cut accurately. And because of the glues used in creating these and other man-made building materials like particle board and hardboard, saws quickly become dulled.

Here's how to deal with this special cutting problem.

First, use the tools you'd use to crosscut, unless you feel the extent of your project merits further investment. Remember that man-made panels will dull the blades quickly, so sharpen

your blades, or have them sharpened, more frequently than you normally would. Or invest in a carbide-tipped blade for your power saw. Such a blade will easily cost twice as much as a

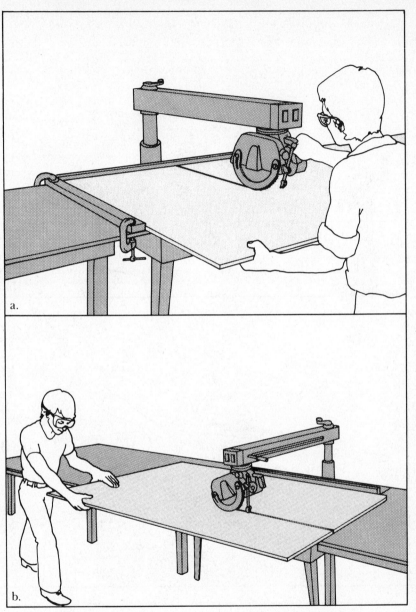

Cutting a panel with a radial arm saw: a. Cutting along the short dimension involves setting a temporary fence parallel to the saw's arm, cutting part way through the panel, stopping the saw, flipping the panel, then completing the cut. b. Cutting along the long dimension is essentially rip cutting.

regular blade, but it will last ten times longer. The more tips the blade has, the more the blade will cost. Thus, a special plywood blade, which has more teeth than a crosscut blade, will cost a startling amount of money.

Next, don't plan to construct tiers of plywood cabinets using only a handsaw to do the cutting unless you've got lots of time and energy, and unless you are remarkably skilled. Cutting 2-foot by 3-foot cabinet ends from 4-foot by 8-foot sheets means you've got a lot of cutting to do. And the cuts have got to be straight and true or you will end up with only a mediocre product. Better you should use a portable circular saw and a guide board or two.

Finally, build several sturdy sawhorses and use them, together with several expendable 8-foot 2 × 4s, to support the plywood as you cut. Lay the 2 × 4s across the sawhorses, then lay the plywood atop the 2 × 4s, good side down. After scribing the cutting lines, you are ready to cut. Clamp your guide board, made as previously described, along the first cutting line. Set the depth of cut of the saw just ¹⁄₁₆ to ¹⁄₈ inch greater than the thickness of the plywood, plug in the saw and cut. You'll cut shallow kerfs through the 2 × 4s, but as long as you set the depth of cut carefully, you won't seriously erode their strength.

Plywood panels can be cut using a table saw or a radial arm saw, but their large size makes them difficult to deal with on these shop tools. A good compromise is to halve or quarter the sheet with a circular saw,

Checking a board for flatness and squareness: a. A cupped board and a board with wind. b. Using a try square to check for cupping. c. Using a framing square to check for wind. d. Using a try square to check an edge for squareness.

then make any further cuts using one of the shop saws. In the interests of safety, and to avoid botching an expensive piece of plywood, you should have someone help you maneuver a piece 4 × 4 or larger.

When cutting plywood, you will want to minimize splintering damage to the best face. You can do this by cutting with the good face up with a handsaw, table saw or radial arm saw, and with the good face down with a circular saw. The splintering occurs when the teeth leave the cut. The differences in approach reflect the different directions in which the various power saws turn.

Dressing Hardwoods

Hardwoods present a special problem for the home woodworker, because they are stocked at the lumberyard in a very different state than softwood board lumber. They are stocked rough-sawn; the wood's been dried, but it is otherwise just as it left the blade at the sawmill.

Before you can work with this kind of wood, you've got to dress the surface. It is possible to have much of the work done for you by the lumberyard, a

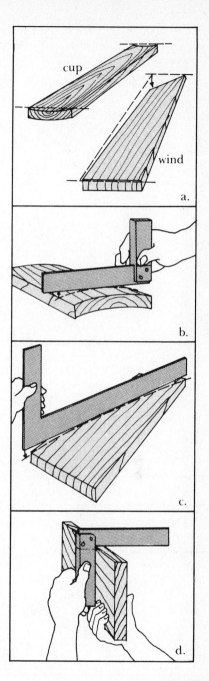

millwork company or a custom cabinet shop. But you should understand what has to be done **333**

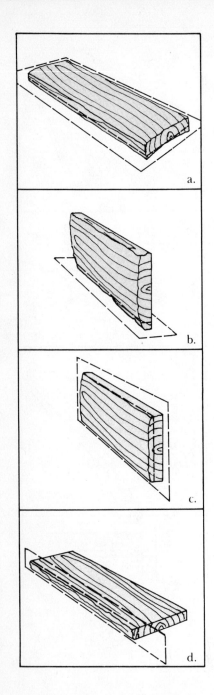

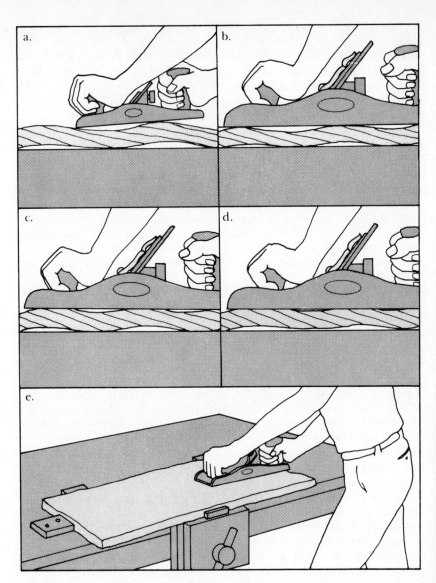

Dressing a rough-sawn board: a. A face is planed or jointed flat. b. An edge is jointed flat and square to the dressed face. c. The second face is planed or resawn flat and parallel to the first. d. The board is ripped to width, dressing the second edge parallel to the first and square with the faces in the process.

Dressing a board with hand planes: a. A short-soled smoothing plane won't flatten a board's wavy contours. b. A long-soled jointer plane bridges the crests. c. It shaves them lower with each pass. d. The ultimate result is a flat board. e. Clamp the board between a bench dog and woodworker's vise to plane it, always planing with the grain.

and decide whether or not you can handle it yourself—a lot
334 depends upon the tools you

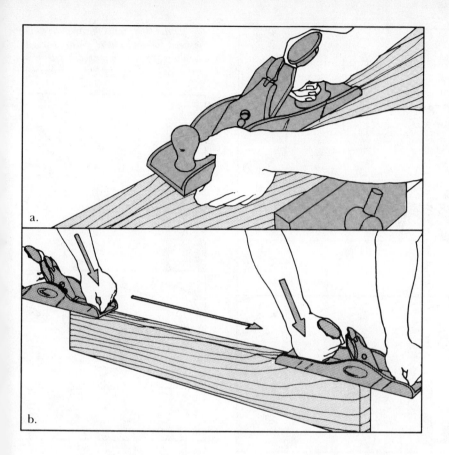

a.

b.

have—before farming out the work. Or giving up on hardwoods entirely.

The goal is to have the opposing surfaces flat, true and parallel and the adjacent surfaces square. The professional shop has impressive machines designed to help achieve the goal. A very skilled woodworker can achieve the goal using a variety of hand tools. You can do the same in your home shop if you've got a jointer and a table saw.

Briefly, the routine is this: Plane a face and an edge of the board on the jointer. Turn to the table saw, and rip the board

to width, trueing the second edge. Then resaw the board to true up the second broad face. Return to the jointer to clean up the second face and edge with a very shallow cut or two. And the board is ready for the next phase of joinery.

Traditional Methods

In traditional woodworking, rough boards are dressed using hand planes. A 2-foot-long jointer plane is used to do the initial planing, trimming down the high spots and producing a flat surface. The long sole rides on the high spots on the board, bridging the hollows. With each

pass, the high spots are trimmed a little lower, until eventually the surface is perfectly flat. Then a smoothing plane is used to plane out all traces of roughness.

The routine here is to plane one face, always working with the grain. Then the board is flipped end for end, and the second face is planed. The best edge is the third surface to be planed, again working with the grain. The second edge can be planed in the same fashion immediately if the board is the correct width, or just after it has been ripped to width. The trick is to do all this hand work and achieve the goal: opposing surfaces flat, true and parallel, adjacent surfaces square.

Don't endeavor to pick up this skill whilst cobbling up a battery of cherry kitchen cabinets.

Using the Jointer

The jointer is a power plane. It has three knives mounted in a horizontal cylinder, which is in turn mounted between two machined, cast-iron tables, one called the infeed table, the other called the outfeed table. The outfeed table is adjusted so it is tangent to the cutting circle of the knives, while the infeed table is set a tad below that cir- **335**

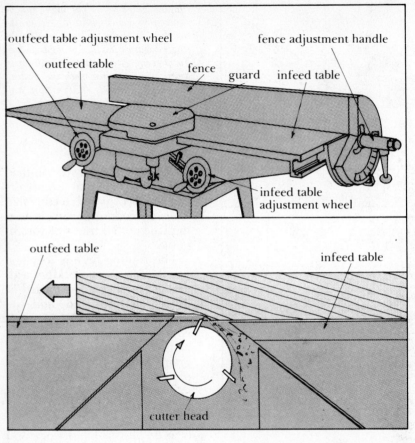

outfeed table adjustment wheel
fence adjustment handle
outfeed table
fence
guard
infeed table
infeed table adjustment wheel

outfeed table
infeed table
cutter head

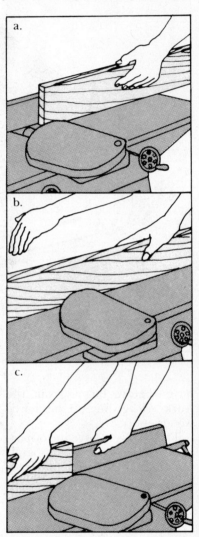

The jointer (left) takes the drudgery and the need for skill out of planing wood. Revolving knives do the work, cast-iron feed tables and fence ensure accuracy.

a.

b.

c.

Jointing the edge of a board (above): a. Starting the cut. b. Moving the left hand over and beyond the knives. c. Completing the cut, with the right hand clear of the knives.

Planing the face of a board on the jointer (left). Use a pusher so that your hands are not holding down the board as it passes over the knives.

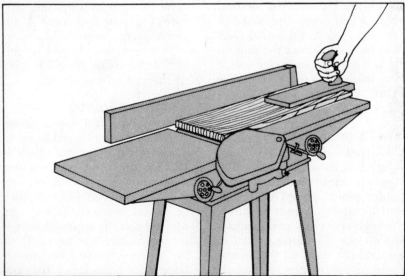

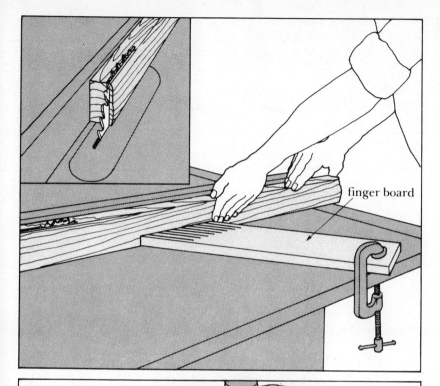

Resawing a narrow board on a table saw. The finger board, positioned ahead of the blade, keeps the board pressed against the fence, allowing the operator to concentrate on feeding the board to the saw.

finger board

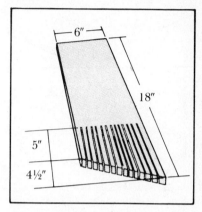

A finger board should be one of the first objects made with a new table saw. There's nothing to do but saw.

cle. The board to be planed or jointed is slid across the infeed table, over the revolving knives and onto the outfeed table. The tad of wood that finds itself between the surface of the infeed table and the cutting circle is sliced away.

Begin dressing a rough board by examining the board itself to determine the direction the grain runs in and to determine which face bears most firmly on the infeed table. Plane that face. Feed it into the knives in the direction the grain is running. If you plane against the grain, you will tear up the surface fi-

Resawing a board on a band saw (left). Note the homemade fence clamped to the saw table.

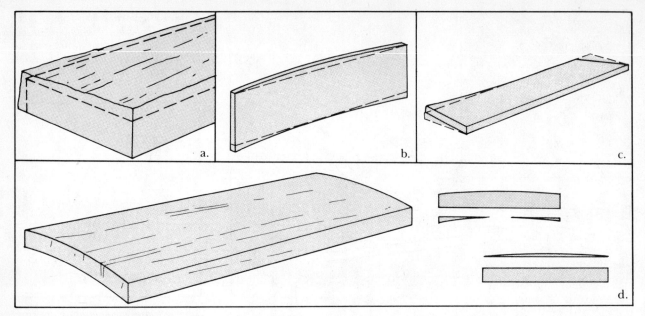

Squaring up warped stock: a. The basic technique is to plane a face and an adjoining edge, then to thickness plane or resaw the other face and rip the board to width. b. The concave edge of a crooked board should be jointed, the convex edge ripped. c. A board in wind can be almost impossible to square unless the distortion can be minimized by cutting the board into smaller pieces. d. If the board is cupped, plane the concave side, then plane or resaw the convex side.

bers of the wood, roughening it and sometimes taking splinters and chunks out of it. Don't try to remove too much material with one cut. Better to make several shallow cuts.

Plane the face completely.

Next, set the jointer's fence, checking to be sure it is perpendicular to the tables. Holding the planed face against the fence, joint the best edge, again endeavoring to cut with the grain. Of course, it isn't always possible to do this at this point. By making shallow cuts and easing up on the rate of feed, you can minimize the ill effects. You may choose to joint the edge that has the grain running in the right direction.

These two steps—planing a face and jointing an edge—are sometimes the first taken when working with hardwood. After this is done, layout work is started and the parts are crosscut to rough sizes.

But just as frequently, the dressing process continues. In a professional shop, the next step is to thickness-plane the board using a planer. The planer has knives similar to a jointer, but they are mounted above the feed table, so that they remove material from the top of the board. The board bears on the surface planed on the jointer, and the process ensures the faces will be level and parallel.

The process is called thickness-planing, because the woodworker keeps planing until a predetermined thickness is achieved. If a number of boards are necessary for a single project, all are planed at the same time to ensure that they will be of a uniform thickness.

A planer is too specialized and expensive a tool for most home shops, so most home woodworkers turn to other techniques. Some try planing the second face on the jointer. But it's difficult if not impossible to achieve the goal of parallel opposing faces this way. A better approach is resawing.

Resawing

Resawing is making a special rip cut to reduce the thickness of a board. In a sense, it is a

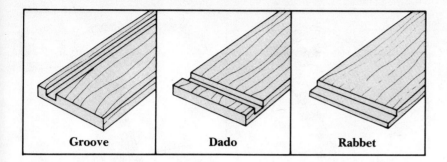

Groove	Dado	Rabbet

repeat of the cutting done to produce a board from a log, hence the term resawing. If you are working with a board of sufficient thickness, you *can* get two or more boards from one. But quite often, resawing is simply a substitute for thickness-planing, turning a given board into a thinner board and a pile of sawdust. As such, it is an important part of surfacing a rough-sawn board in the home shop.

Resawing can be done on a table saw or a band saw.

Using a band saw, resawing is a matter of setting up a fence and slowly feeding the stock into the blade. Naturally, the width of board that can be cut is limited by the depth of cut on your particular band saw. The best blade to use is the widest blade your saw will take. It should, of course, be good and sharp.

Using a table saw, the procedure is much the same, except that you should set up a finger board to hold the board against the fence, and you should figure on cutting only half the width of the board in a single pass unless it's very narrow. The best you'll be able to do on a table saw is resaw a board that's

got a width of less than twice the depth of cut of your saw, unless you complete the work with a handsaw. Make one pass, flip the board over, end for end, and make the second pass. Then, if necessary, finish up with a handsaw.

A finger board, which is useful for more than resawing, can be made from an 18-inch length of 1 × 6. Cut off one end at a 60-degree angle. Make a series of stopped rip cuts into the mitered end, leaving a ¼-inch finger of wood between each kerf. The longest finger should be about 8 inches.

To use the finger board, clamp it with a C clamp to the left side of the saw table. With the saw turned off, hold the board to be resawed against the fence, which has been set for the appropriate width of cut. Position the finger board so that its fingers will hold the board in position, and allow you to push it into the blade, but will prevent

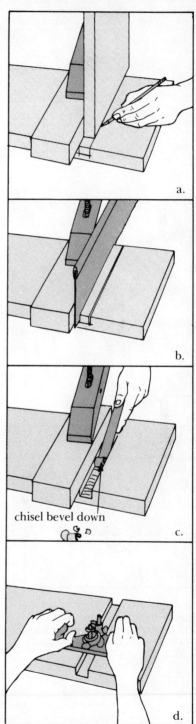

chisel bevel down

Cutting a dado by hand: a. Lay out the dado and clamp a saw guide to the work. b. Carefully cut the sides of the channel with a backsaw. c. Chisel out the waste. d. Use a router plane to clean the bottom of the dado.

339

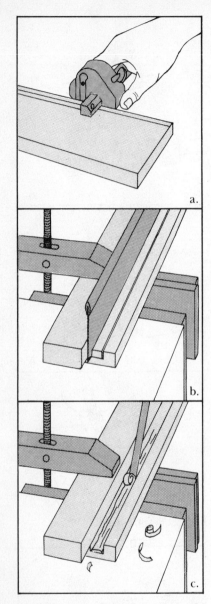

Cutting a groove by hand: a. Lay out the groove using a marking gauge. b. Saw the sides of the channel with a backsaw. c. Chisel out the waste, then clear up the bottom with a router plane.

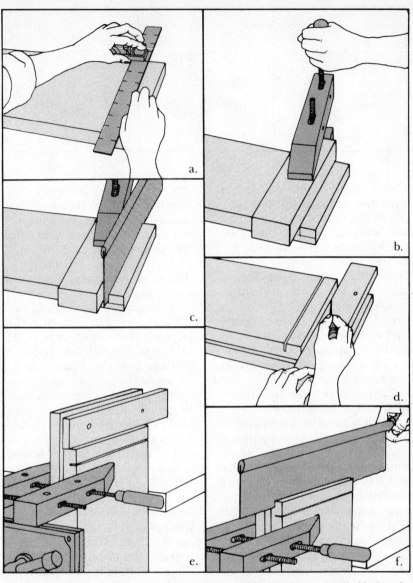

Cutting a rabbet with a backsaw: a. Lay out the rabbet. b. Clamp a guide block to the work. c. Make the cheek cut. d. Lay the work in a jig and mark the bottom cut. e. Clamp the work to the jig and place them both in a vise. f. Make the bottom cut.

it from being kicked back at you. Tighten the clamp and set to work.

After the board is resawed, you will probably find it advisable to plane the sawn face on the jointer to remove the marks left by the blade.

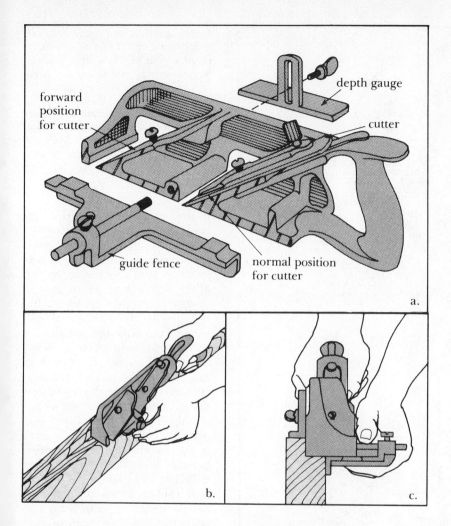

forward
position
for cutter

depth gauge

cutter

guide fence

normal position
for cutter

a.

b.

c.

Cutting a rabbet with a rabbet plane: a. The rabbet plane and its major components. b. Using the plane c. The rabbet is easily cut if the depth gauge and guide fence are set correctly.

Grooving, Dadoing and Rabbeting

Depending upon how sophisticated you get with your cabinetry, you may get into cutting grooves, dadoes and rabbets. In woodworking parlance, a groove is a channel cut into a board running with the grain. When a groove cuts across the grain, it is a dado. When it is cut at the edge of a board, so that it has only one side, it is a rabbet, whether it runs with or across the grain. When cut in conjunction with the making of a lap joint, rabbets and dadoes are usually called laps. If any of these channels is referred to as being blind or stopped, it means that the channel does not extend completely from edge to edge, it ends shy of either or both edges.

These channels need not be a part of your woodworking repertory for you to make excellent kitchen cabinets. But by being able to cut them, you'll vastly expand the number of different joints you are able to make, and you'll be able to make stronger joints. Remember, though, that poorly cut grooves, dadoes and rabbets may be worse than none at all; they must be carefully done.

All of these channels can be cut with hand tools, but it is a demanding task. It takes time and patience, skill and care, and a number of specialized planes

Dressing the board is completed when you rip the board to width.

Dressing hardwoods can be done before or after cutting. As a practical matter, you'll find it easier to maneuver boards that have been cut to rough length. They'll be ripped to their finished width in the course of dressing them. And the final cut to finished length must be made before any additional fabrication is possible.

Fabrication

The fabrication of the pieces doesn't begin in earnest until the parts have been cut to size. In a simple project, that cutting is all the fabrication there is. But in a complex cabinet, there are grooves, dadoes and rabbets to be cut for the various joints. Holes have to be drilled for dowels to reinforce joints. Occasionally, mortises have to be chiseled out. This is fabrication.

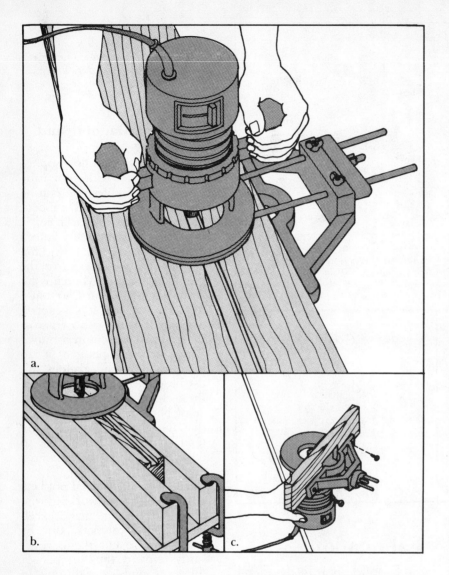

a.

b.

c.

Cutting a dado with a router and commercial guide: a. The guide rides along the edge of the board, holding the router in position to cut a dado parallel to the edge. b. To dado an edge, clamp the work between two thick boards to broaden the bearing surface for the router. c. The guide's bearing can be improved by attaching to the guide a scrap board with a cutout for the bit.

groove is too big and thus no good; if they are too close together, the groove is too small, and it will be frustratingly difficult to resaw one side or the other just a mite to make the groove the right size. (Actually, if a groove that's to accept another board is too small, it's usually easier to plane or sand that board to fit). Be sure you monitor the depth of the saw cuts, so that you don't cut too deep. Clean out the waste with a chisel. Again, monitor your progress so that you don't gouge too deeply. Finally, clean up the bottom of the groove with a router plane.

A rabbet across the grain is cut in much the same way, but both the side and bottom cuts can be made with the backsaw. The plane to use in this situation is a rabbet plane. To avoid splitting out the end grain in planing the rabbet, plane from the ends of the rabbet toward the middle.

A rabbet cut with the grain can be cut using the rabbet plane alone. It has an adjustable fence to control the width of the rabbet, but the operator has to ensure that the bottom is true and cut to the correct depth.

in addition to some more common tools.

The hand-cutting of a groove or dado starts with a rather elaborate layout. The groove must be traced across the face and the edges of the board, so that you know how wide and deep it will be, as well as exactly **342** where it is to be. If another board is to fit into the groove or dado, that board should be used in doing the layout. A backsaw is then used to cut the sides of the groove; it's a good idea to use a scrap of wood as a guide to ensure that the cuts will be perpendicular to the face of the wood. The cuts must be perfect. If they are too far apart, the

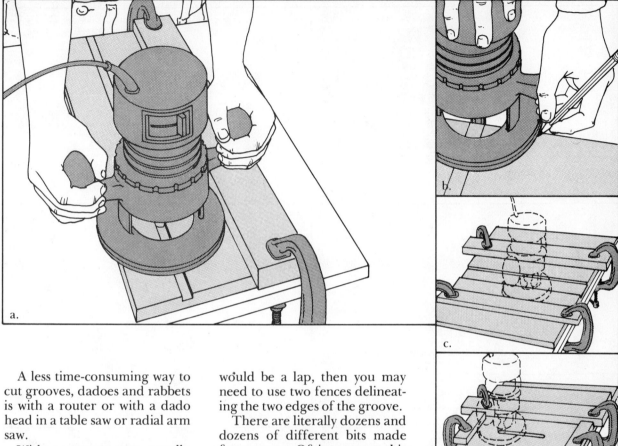

Cutting a dado with a router and homemade fence: a. Clamp a scrap with one true edge to the work; the router base edge rides along this guide. b. The fence is set by placing the router at the edge of the board with the bit in position, then marking the work at the edge of the router base. c. A groove or dado wider than the bit can be cut using two fences. d. A stop clamped to the work helps position the end of a stopped groove or dado.

A less time-consuming way to cut grooves, dadoes and rabbets is with a router or with a dado head in a table saw or radial arm saw.

With a router, you usually need lay out only the position of one edge of the groove. The diameter of the bit and the depth setting of the router will determine its width and depth. Edge guides are available for all routers; these fences slide along an edge of the board, holding the router in a fixed relationship to that edge, thus ensuring that a rabbet or groove is a constant distance from the edge. When such a procedure won't work, a makeshift fence can be clamped or tacked to the work to guide the router. If the groove is unusually wide, as

would be a lap, then you may need to use two fences delineating the two edges of the groove.

There are literally dozens and dozens of different bits made for routers. Of interest at this point are veining, straight and rabbeting bits. All veining bits will make grooves, but some create a concave bottom to the groove, and all produce very narrow cuts. Straight bits are most commonly used for grooving and dadoing. The straight bit cuts a clean groove with a flat bottom and perpendicular sides. The diameter of the bit determines the width of the groove, and unless the channel to be cut is unusually wide, it's far wiser to cut a groove with a single pass of the proper-size bit than to make repeated passes

343

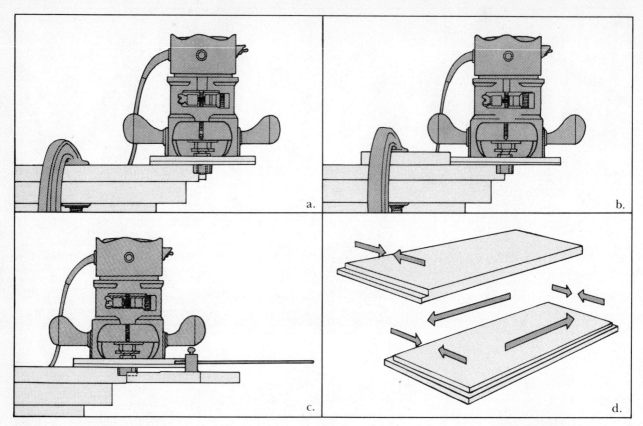

a.

b.

c.

d.

Cutting a rabbet with a router: a. A rabbeting bit has a pilot that rides on the edge of the work and governs the rabbet's width. b. A guide clamped to the work allows the use of a straight bit to cut a rabbet. c. A commercial edge guide can be used to guide a rabbet cut. d. To avoid splitting out the grain, cut first across the grain, then with the grain; end grain should be cut from the outer corners toward the middle.

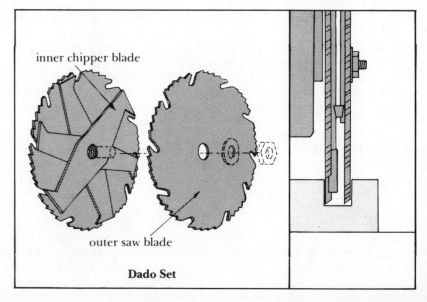

inner chipper blade

outer saw blade

Dado Set

with a too-small bit. Special rabbeting bits have a shank that extends below the cutters, forming a pilot that rides along the edge of the board, controlling the width of the cut. With such bits, the bit itself is the guide,

344

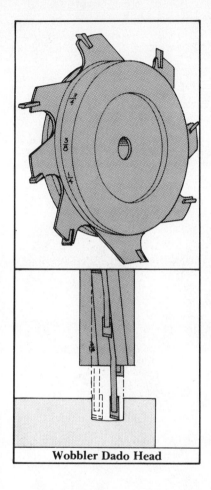

Wobbler Dado Head

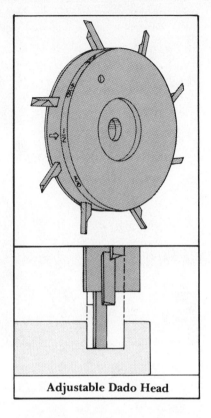

Adjustable Dado Head

a kerf wider than the thickness of the blade. The angle of skew is infinitely adjustable within a given range, usually the same range as a traditional dado head. Wobblers are less costly than other dado sets, but they don't cut as clean a groove either. The bottom of the cut is invariably slightly concave.

The third kind of dado assembly is a compromise between the previous two designs. It has a hub with teeth that individually skew as the unit is adjusted. It doesn't wobble, so it doesn't produce a rounded bottom cut, and it has infinitely adjustable settings within the common range of ¼ to ¾ inch.

In all cases, the depth of cut is adjusted by the saw mechanism.

Mounted in a power saw, the dado head cuts grooves and some rabbets as it would rip, dadoes and other rabbets as it would crosscut. The layout required is simply to delineate the position of the channel; its width and depth are established by the tool.

For most such work, the process is as simple as that. For some specialized joinery, the use of special jigs, fences, guides and stops is advisable, partly so that the work is done properly and partly so that it is done safely. This situation occurs more frequently with the table saw than with the radial arm saw, because the blade settings are less flexible on the table saw. The radial arm saw's blade can be adjusted in degrees from a plumb vertical to a level horizontal, while the table saw's blade will only adjust from a

and nothing else is needed. For cutting a groove in the edge of a board, a special slotting cutter is used.

If you have a table or radial arm saw, you can cut grooves, dadoes and rabbets with repeated cuts, or you can buy and use a dado assembly, often called a dado head, which will cut various-size grooves with a single pass.

Dado heads come in several varieties. Probably the best design is the traditional multi-bladed assembly, which consists of two circular blades and several chippers of different thicknesses. The chippers are sandwiched between the circular blades. The number and thicknesses of chippers used determine the width of the groove. Most dado assemblies will cut grooves ranging from ¼ inch to ¾ inch in width, but the variety of groove widths possible within that range is limited.

The wobbler is the second type of dado head. It has a saw blade set in a hub so that the plane of the blade is skewed from perpendicular. When the blade spins, it wobbles, creating

345

Cutting a rabbet on a table saw: a. and b. A regular rip blade and two passes can yield a rabbet. c. A dado across a board can be cut with a dado head, using the miter gauge to guide the work. d. A finger board clamped to the rip fence can help control the feed in a long rabbet cut.

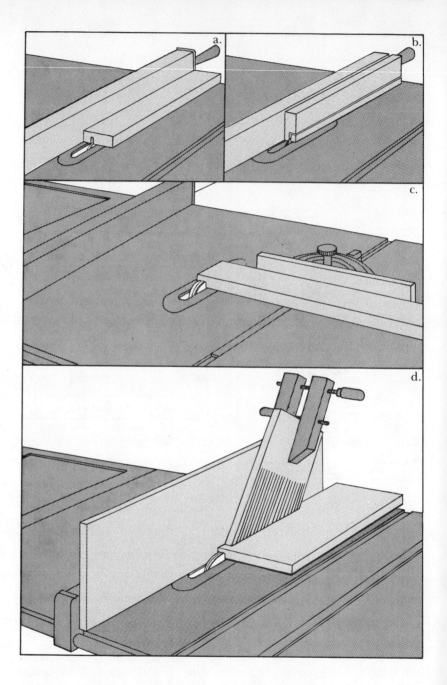

plumb vertical to a 45-degree angle. Thus most cuts can be made with the radial arm saw while the work lies flat and secure on the table, while to make some of the same cuts with the table saw will require the work to be stood on end or on edge. In all cases, the work is moved on the table saw while it usually is stationary on the radial arm saw. Moreover, the blade on the radial arm saw is always above the work, right where you can see it, while the work ofttimes obstructs your view of the blade on a table saw.

Drilling Holes

Holes are made by drilling.

Well, there is a little more to it than that. There are a number of different bits available and a number of different ways of powering the bits. And there are tricks for drilling holes exactly where and how you want them. And in drilling holes as in crosscutting and grooving, precision is important.

A pertinent question to ask when preparing to drill holes is: What is the hole for? The answer can help determine what tool and bit should be used to do the job.

A pilot hole for a nail can be

drilled with a hand drill and an ordinary twist drill bit.

A pilot hole for a screw can be drilled the same way, but a bet-

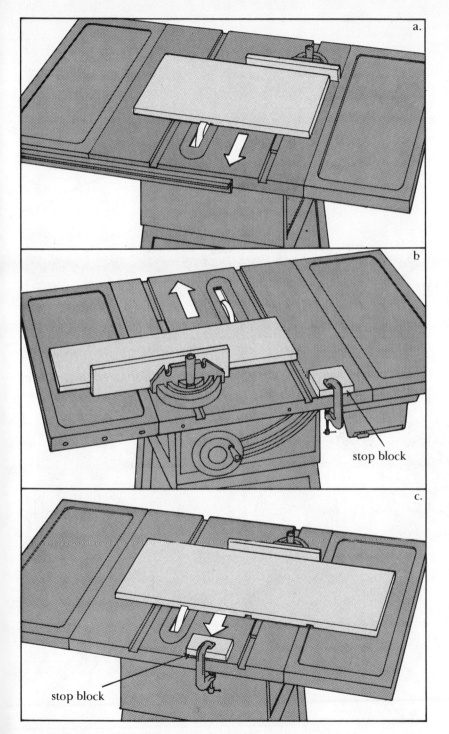

Cutting a dado on a table saw: a. Using the miter gauge to guide the cut. b. A stop block clamped to the saw table or the rip fence helps position dado cuts. c. The length of a stopped dado can be controlled with a stop block clamped to the back edge of the saw table.

stop block

stop block

ter approach, especially since most screws will be countersunk in cabinetmaking, is to use a special combination countersink-twist drill bit. These bits are available for number 6 through 12 screws. The countersink sleeve adjusts with a setscrew to the different screw lengths. You select the appropriate bit, adjust it for the length of screw you are using, fit it into a drill and drill your hole. It will be the proper depth and size, done in one step.

For screws smaller than number 6 and larger than number 12, you'll have to use the traditional approach of drilling the pilot hole with a twist drill bit and countersinking with a separate countersink bit.

If you need a fairly large hole, you may have to abandon the twist drills, although twist drills are available in diameters up to 1½ inches. Auger bits, which are driven with a cranklike tool called a brace, stop at the 1-inch size. Spade bits, which need to be driven at high speeds—2,000–3,000 rpm—to work well, are available in sizes up to 1½ inches. Expansive bits, driven with a brace, are adjustable and are available in sizes that will cut holes up to 3 inches in diameter.

347

Tenons are cut on a table saw by clamping the work vertically in a tenoning jig and sliding it past the saw blade. A jig can be made to fit over and slide on the rip fence. A C clamp holds the work in place.

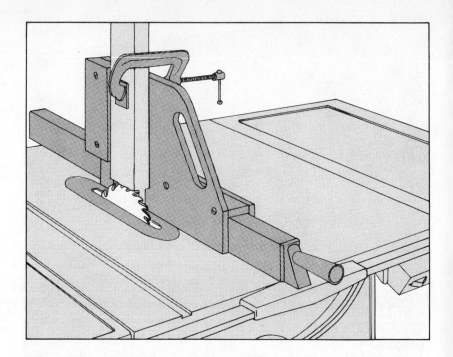

The most demanding drilling job in cabinetmaking is drilling dowel holes for dowel joints. The holes must be drilled precisely on the mark and precisely in alignment. If only one hole is a bit cocked or a bit off-center, the joint won't join. It's gotta be precise.

The best bit to use for this work is one that has a center spur to get the hole started in

Using a radial arm saw for dadoing and grooving: a. Cutting a dado. b. Plowing a groove.

precisely the correct spot. An auger bit has such a spur, as

does a spur-wood bit, which, other than its spur, is much like

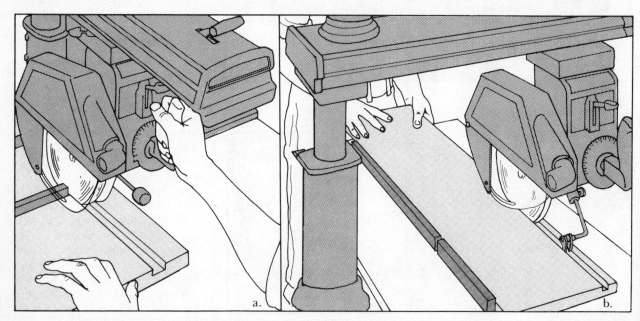

a.

b.

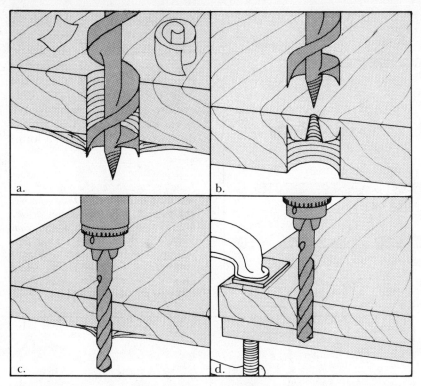

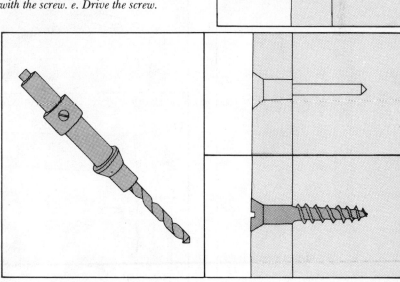

Boring clean holes: a. Drilling straight through the work will split away wood on the bottom. b. With an auger bit, bore until the spur breaks through, then turn the work over and complete the hole. c. A twist drill bit will split away wood too. d. Clamp a scrap of wood to the bottom of the work to prevent splintering.

Installing a flathead screw: a. Drill the shank hole. b. Drill the pilot hole. c. Countersink. d. Check countersinking with the screw. e. Drive the screw.

a twist drill bit. The twist drill bit, lacking a centering spur, tends to wander on the surface of the wood before it bites and begins cutting its hole.

The best drive tool is the drill press. You can clamp the work

A combination countersink-twist drill bit bores shank and pilot holes and countersinks in a single operation.

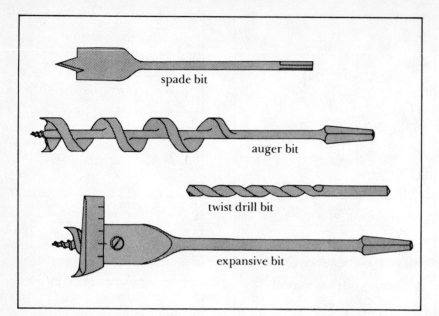

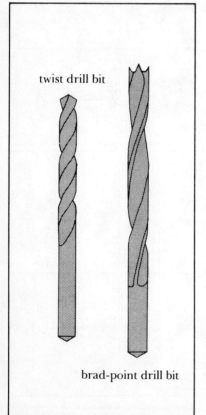

to the drill press table and be confident that the finished hole will be in the proper alignment. With a hand drill of any kind, it is very easy to waver and get the hole cocked, even if it's only ever so slightly. A compromise is to use a hand drill with a doweling jig. There are a lot of

Installing dowels: a. Use a doweling jig and a tightly spiraled bit to bore holes in one piece. b. Put dowel points in each hole. c. Line up one edge of the second piece with the first and swing them together; the dowel points will mark center points for holes on the second piece. d. Drill the holes, install dowels and joint the pieces.

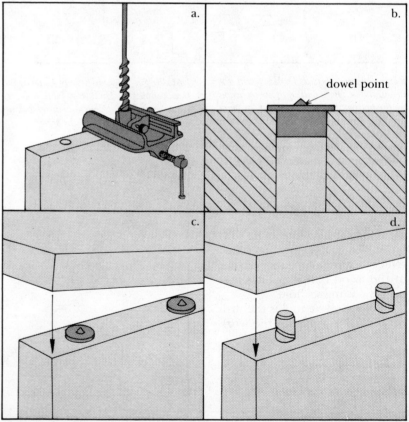

different versions of the doweling jig, but all in some way or other provide a tubular guide for the bit, so that it will be held perpendicular to the board as the hole is drilled. Twist drill bits work best with these jigs, but they don't have the spur that's so vital. Auger bits don't work well with the jigs. Hence, the best combination of tools for someone without a drill press is a spur bit in a hand drill with a doweling jig.

Doweling jigs, whatever variety you have, and there are quite a few different designs, are clamped to the edge of the board that's to be drilled. An index or alignment mark on the jig is used to position the device along the board; you line up the mark on the jig with a mark you make on the board, then tighten the jig's clamp. Then the position of the tubular guide is adjusted to position the hole.

The key to the use of the doweling jig is the marking of the pieces. You always use the same face of each board as the reference face, using that face

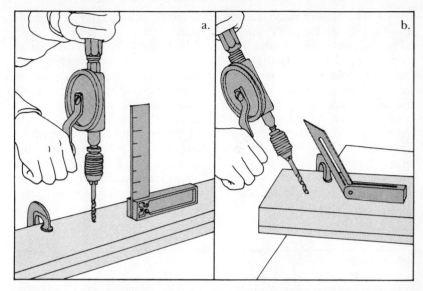

to position the jig on the board. And you set the position of the tubular guide once and keep it the same for every hole in a joint.

The routine, then, is to lay out the pieces to be joined just as they will be in the completed joint. Using a try square as a guide, mark the faces of both pieces with a single pencil or awl

Lining up a hole: a. To bore a vertical hole with a hand drill, try lining up the drill with a try square set beside the work. b. Use a sliding T bevel instead of a square when boring holes on an angle.

Making a drilling jig: a. Mark off the desired angle on a scrap of wood, then drill vertically through it. b. Cut along the line delineating the desired angle. c. Clamp the jig to the wood; the hole will hold the bit at the proper angle.

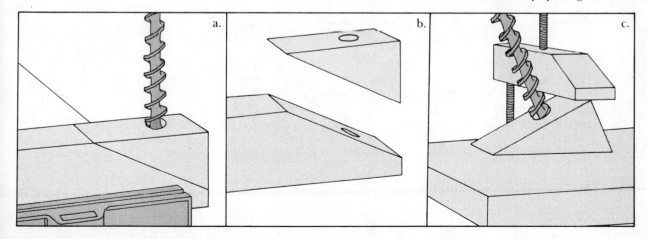

stroke. The holes will be drilled into the edge of the piece, parallel to the pencil line. Set the jig, then clamp it to the first piece. Drill the hole. Then move the jig to the second piece, aligning the jig's index mark with your position line. As long as you maintain a common reference face, the hole will always be properly aligned from piece to piece. So mark carefully and drill carefully, and you are practically done with the joint.

Occasionally, you purposely want to drill a hole at an angle. The bugbear here is the same as the bugbear in doweling. It's tough to maintain a steady position when using a hand drill. You *can* set the angle on a sliding T bevel, position it next to the drill and try to eyeball the alignment. A more accurate method is to fabricate a drilling jig just for your particular job. Get a scrap block of wood, such as a piece of 2 × 4, and drill a

hole of the size you want perpendicularly through the block. Then lay out the angle you want

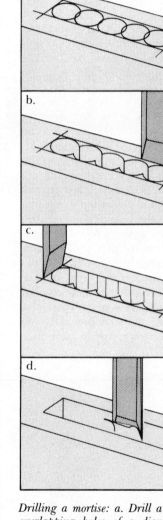

Drilling a mortise: a. Drill a series of overlapping holes of a diameter just smaller than the width of the mortise. b. Using a chisel, clean the remaining waste from the sides. c. Clean the ends of the mortise. d. Pare the mortise to fit the tenon.

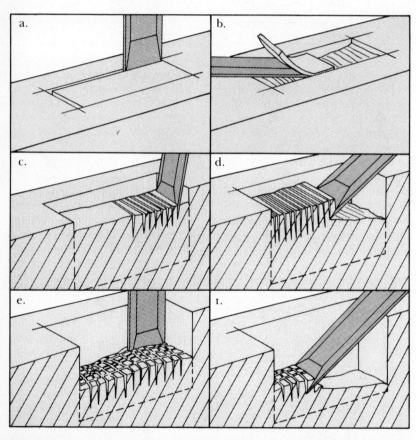

Chiseling out a mortise: a. Cut along the layout lines with the bevel in. b. Start to excavate with shallow cuts. c. and d. As the mortise gets deeper, chisel into the bottom and cut off the slivers of material. e. and f. Cutting in a crosshatch fashion can ease the work in deep mortises.

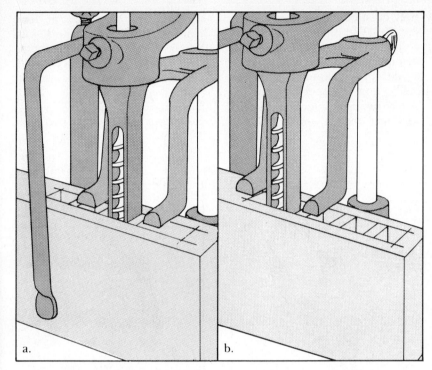

a.

b.

Using a mortising attachment on a drill press: a. Set up the attachment and secure the work in position. b. The usual procedure is to cut a series of nonoverlapping holes, then to cut away intervening material; with hardwoods, it is sometimes necessary to cut overlapping holes because of the difficulty of penetrating the material.

on the side of the block, cut the block in two along the line, and you have your jig. Tack or clamp it to the work and use it, as you would a doweling jig, to guide the bit as you drill the angled hole.

Cutting Mortises

You aren't likely to have to cut mortises in building kitchen cabinets. You *can* use them in constructing panel doors, and

depending upon the hardware you select, you may have to cut shallow mortises for hinges. The mortises called for in these situations seem to be quite different, but in fact they are cut in almost the same way. The principal difference is their depths.

Cutting hinge mortises is explained in "Finishing" in Part II.

Cutting a deeper mortise for a mortise-and-tenon joint is traditionally done with a mallet and chisel. The work goes faster if you excavate the bulk of the waste for the mortise by drilling a series of holes, then clean up the sides with a chisel.

The most remarkable way to cut mortises is with a mortising attachment on a drill press. This combination drill and chisel actually "drills" a square hole. By

drilling a series of these square holes, you can create almost any size of mortise you want. The attachment is not inexpensive, however, and setting it up takes a lot of time. For cutting only a few mortises, use the traditional approach.

Assembly

Here is the moment of truth. You are going to find out if, indeed, you have planned thoroughly and worked meticulously. You are ready to assemble your cabinet. If you've done well, this phase of the work will go without a hitch. If you've not done well, you may be in for disappointment.

In practice, assembly is seldom one protracted operation. Rather, it is something you do periodically as you construct your cabinets. You work in subassemblies. Often, you must assemble one part of a cabinet so that you know exactly how big to make the next element to be constructed. So you lay out and fabricate the case pieces, then assemble it. Then, after measuring the case, you construct the face frame and assemble it. Then you do the drawers and doors.

Assembly is a change-of-pace operation. After the deliberation of layout and fabrication, assembly is working pell-mell. The pieces must be set out, glue applied, the pieces joined together and nails or screws driven or clamps applied all before the glue dries. It is a process that should be preplanned and well rehearsed.

Thus, when the work pro-   **353**

gresses to the assembly stage, the first thing to do is dry-fit each subassembly or assembly. A dry-fitting is simply a dress rehearsal, an assembly without glue. You'll determine whether or not all the joints fit properly—snug but not so tight that they must be hammered together. You'll pinpoint the task's confusing aspects—keeping the orientation of a particular piece straight, for example—or physically taxing aspects—keeping three separate pieces balanced in place until a fourth is lined up and set. You'll learn what clamps you'll need and just where and how to set them. You'll learn just what has to be done after the glue is spread.

Clamping

Clamps are used for two pur-

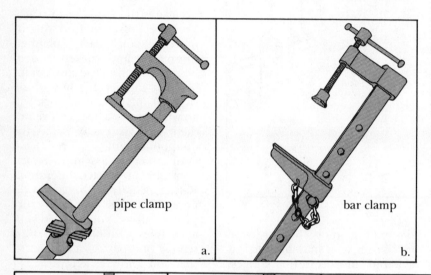

pipe clamp

a.

bar clamp

b.

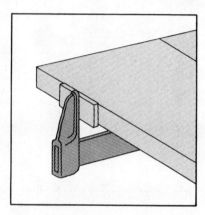

Use a caul—a scrap of wood—between the jaw of a metal clamp and the work to avoid denting the work.

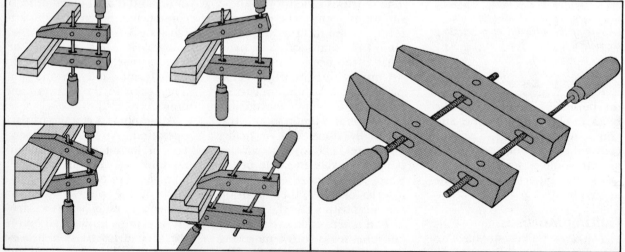

The hand screw's design allows it to be used for a variety of awkward clamping jobs. Its construction obviates the need for cauls, since its wooden jaws won't damage other wood. The jaws distribute the clamp's pressure over a broader area than most other clamps.

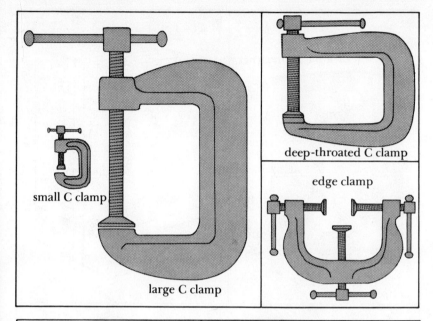

small C clamp

large C clamp

deep-throated C clamp

edge clamp

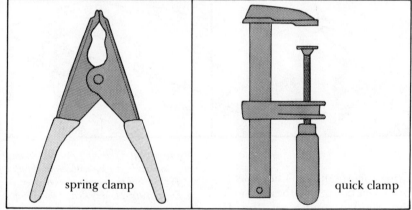

spring clamp

quick clamp

poses during assembly. At first, some clamps can be used to help position the various pieces to be assembled. After the glue is spread and the parts joined, clamps are used to compress the joint as tightly as possible and maintain the pressure until the glue dries.

There are many different clamping jobs, and there are many different clamps to do them. Most clamps, however, are versatile and can serve you in a variety of ways.

Bar or Pipe Clamps. These clamps are invaluable in cabinetmaking, because their jaws can span such great distances. They are used in edge-to-edge gluing, in assembling casework, face frames, drawers, door frames and in similar situations.

Half a dozen sets of these clamps is not too many to have for a major cabinetmaking project. Bar clamps are probably the best because their bar is stronger, more rigid than a pipe, but they are expensive. Less costly, and for all practical purposes just as good, are pipe clamps, which are created by mounting the jaws on a length—any length—of ordinary black or galvanized steel pipe.

In use, the movable jaw is adjusted to the appropriate position along the bar or pipe. The clamp is placed around the work (or the work is laid out across the bar or pipe between the jaws) and the clamp is tightened by turning the screw on the fixed jaw. Scraps of wood, called cauls, should always be slipped between the jaws and the work to prevent it from being dented or otherwise marred. Allow the work to set for five or ten minutes, then retighten the clamps.

Hand Screws. These wooden-jawed clamps are dandy for routine clamping jobs, because the jaws won't mar surfaces. They come in sizes ranging from those with 4-inch-long jaws that open 2 inches to those with 24-inch-long jaws that open a maximum of 17 inches. All are expensive.

The jaws are moved by turning the spindles. To roughly adjust the hand screw, you use a cranking motion, flopping the jaws over and over. Once the clamp is positioned and you want to tighten it, you twist the spindles. The final tightening

355

should be done by twisting only the rear spindle; this way the front spindle acts as a fulcrum to multiply the pressure being applied.

While there aren't too many gluing jobs you use these clamps on in making kitchen cabinets, you will find them useful in assembly.

C Clamps. These clamps have a C-shaped metal frame. One end has an integral pad, the other mounts a threaded rod that closes in on the work and clamps it against the pad. Cauls should always be used, for C clamps can severely dent wood.

All sizes and styles of C clamps are available, ranging from little ones with a maximum opening of only an inch or 2 through giants that open to a foot or more. Deep-throated clamps allow you to get a deeper bite on the work. A variety known as edge clamps have a pressure screw mounted in the center of the throat, perpendicular to the standard pressure screw. This clamp can be attached to a counter top and the second pressure screw used to clamp an edging strip in place.

Spring Clamps. These clamps are a lot like pliers with a big spring in them to keep the jaws tightly closed. They are available in many sizes, but none can exert the pressure of other types of clamps.

Spring clamps may be of occasional use in assembly.

Quick Clamps. A hybrid of the C clamp and the bar clamp, quick clamps are adjustable to a

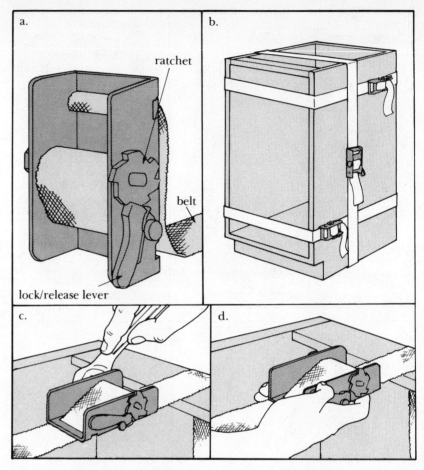

Using a band clamp: a. The clamp mechanism. b. A case with band clamps. c. Tightening the clamp with a wrench. d. Depressing a lever releases the clamp.

range of openings. Their flexibility is a boon, but they haven't the rigid strength of the C clamp.

Band Clamps. Imagine putting a ratcheting device on your belt to replace the buckle. That's what a band clamp has: a long canvas or nylon belt with a ratchet/lock device to cinch it tight. This clamp can secure round, square, rectangular or irregularly shaped objects with equal ease. It could be useful in assembling frames and drawers,

if not in casework assembly.

The effect of the band clamp can be duplicated by wrapping a cord around the assembly and tightening it as you would a tourniquet.

Corner Clamps. These little clamps hold two pieces at right angles to each other. The most common use for them is in mak-

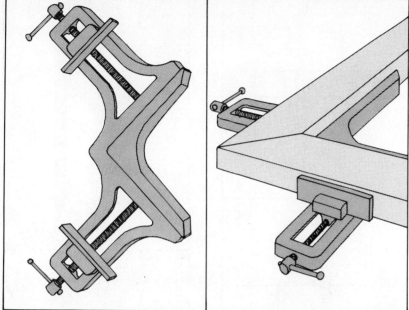

Corner clamps secure two pieces at right angles to each other. They can be used as an extra pair of hands in assembly work.

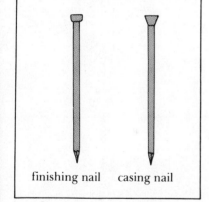

finishing nail   casing nail

ing picture frames. But you will find them particularly useful in assembling casework by yourself. Use them to position the sides, top and bottom of a cabinet until you get it fastened together. Don't expect to use them to exert much pressure for gluing, however.

Your dry-fitting will help you determine which of these many clamps you'll need just to help you get the pieces together and which you'll need to clamp the works together until the glue dries. It will also help you position fasteners you'll use, and any hardware that figures in the assembly.

Fasteners

Nails and screws are the only fasteners you are likely to use in constructing kitchen cabinets. And in much of the assembly, you won't use any fasteners at all. The glue you use will hold the parts together.

Nails. Of all the dozens of kinds of nails available, only two or three are of any use in cabinetry. Here and there, you'll be able to use common nails.

But wherever the nail would show and detract from the appearance of the cabinet, you must use either finishing nails or casing nails. Each has an almost nonexistent head that can, with a countersink, be driven below the surface of the wood, so that it can be concealed with a wood filler.

Nail sizes are designated by pennyweights. The higher the pennyweight, from 2 penny up to 60 penny, the longer the nail, and correspondingly, the heavier its shank. The abbreviation for penny is d. Among the common sizes you'll use are 1½-inch 4d, 2-inch 6d and 2½-inch 8d.

Some nails are available with a cement or resin coating. This coating increases the holding power of the nails. It's especially useful where you must nail into the end grain of plywood, which, because of all its layers, doesn't hold nails all that well.

A general guide to selecting nail sizes is to use a nail that is long enough that two-thirds of its shank will penetrate the second of the two members being joined. Thus, to nail a ¾-inch board to another, you should use a 3d nail.

In assembling cabinets, you can increase the holding power of any nails you use by driving them at a slight angle. Try to avoid positioning two nails along a line in the grain, for this **357**

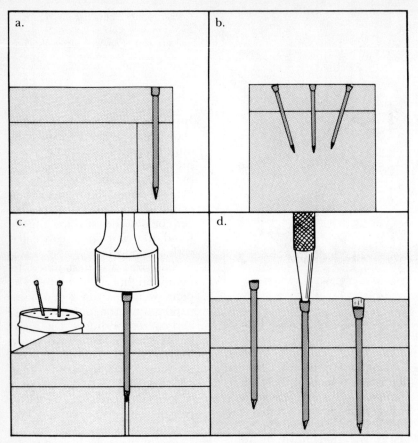

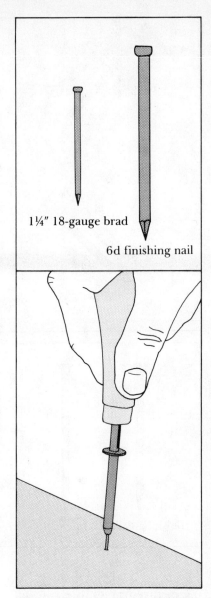

1¼″ 18-gauge brad

6d finishing nail

Driving nails: a. A nail of the proper length has two-thirds of its shank in the second of the two pieces being joined. b. Position the nails at a slight angle to increase their holding power. c. When nailing hardwoods, drill pilot holes and lubricate the nails with beeswax or soap. d. Drive each nail nearly flush with the wood's surface, then set it with a nail set and cover it with wood filler.

Brads, much more slender than nails, are pushed, rather than hammered, into wood. A brad driver is a tool specially made for the purpose.

will likely split the wood. Keep your eye on the nail as you hammer, hit the nail squarely. If you control your swing so that the hammer handle is parallel to the work at the moment of impact, you'll be hitting the nail squarely. If you don't do this, you'll bend the nail. You'll find that nails will penetrate softwood easily enough, but not so with hardwoods. Drill a pilot **358** hole, using a bit somewhat smaller than the shank of the nail. And push the point of the nail into a block of beeswax before driving it. The same techniques will prevent nails from splitting softwoods.

Brads. In certain situations, you need a nail that's smaller than 2d, often because the shank of a 2d nail is too big. Clearly, this is fine work, but you may be doing it. Use brads. Brads are slender nails made of mild steel wire.

They come in lengths ranging from ½ inch to 1½ inches and in gauge sizes from 20 to 14.

The heavier brads can be driv-

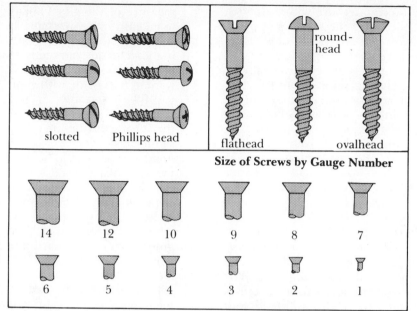

slotted   Phillips head   flathead   round-head   ovalhead

Size of Screws by Gauge Number

14   12   10   9   8   7

6   5   4   3   2   1

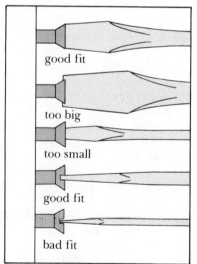

The screwdriver must be properly fitted to the screw so that the slot isn't damaged. A damaged slot can prevent the screw from being completely driven into place or extracted.

good fit

too big

too small

good fit

bad fit

Screws are available in astonishing variety. Most common are slotted and Phillips head screws with flat, round or oval heads. The sizes, regardless of style, are given in shank length (in inches) and girth (in gauge).

en with a light hammer, but the most slender should be driv-

en with an awllike tool called a brad driver. The tool grips the brad so that it extends from the driver's shank, and you merely push it into the wood.

You can drill pilot holes for brads too. Use a brad as a bit.

Screws. Like nails, screws come in a welter of shapes, styles and sizes. In the main, it's the shape and pattern of the head that's different from screw to screw. The shank sizing follows the same system for all.

You will undoubtedly use slotted flathead wood screws, if you use screws at all. These have a flat head with a slot in it for a standard screwdriver. There's an unthreaded section, called

the shank, then a section of threaded shaft tapering to a point. When you drill pilot holes, and you should, you must use a combination bit made specifically for the purpose, or you must drill a hole for the shank and a smaller pilot hole for the threaded section, then use a countersink bit to create the depression for the head to rest in. It's faster and easier to use a combination bit.

Other than slotted flathead wood screws, you'll find the hardware store has ovalhead and roundhead screws, Phillips head screws and sheet-metal screws, screws made of mild steel, aluminum, brass, and screws with various coatings.

Screws come in sizes ranging from number 0 (the smallest) to number 24 (the largest) with lengths ranging from 3/16 inch to 6 inches. You use screws in the 6-8-10-12 range, in lengths determined, as with the nails, by the situation. You should try to use a length great enough to get two-thirds of the screw—all of the threads—into the second piece. Where the screw will be anchored in end grain, use a longer screw. And don't use too fat a screw; always opt for more length and less diameter.

Screws, of course, are driven with screwdrivers. But there are screwdrivers and there are screwdrivers. Keystone tip screwdrivers are most familiar, but the taper of the tip will tear up the wood if you countersink too deeply. If you use a cabinet tip screwdriver for this work, then damage will never occur. Always match the screw size to the screwdriver size. Using a **359**

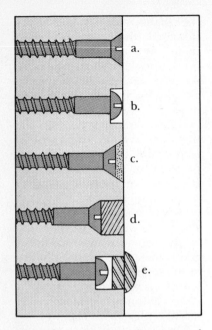

Concealing screws: a. A countersunk screw. b. A counterbored screw. c. A screw countersunk and puttied over. d. A screw in a counterbored hole, concealed beneath a flush plug. e. A round-head screw in a counterbored hole, concealed beneath a button plug.

mismatched tool will tear up the slot. Use a bit of beeswax on the screws to ease the work.

Other than standard screwdrivers, you can use a screwdriver bit in a brace. Or you can use a pump action screwdriver, which has a mechanism that twists the interchangeable tips when you push on the handle.

It's most likely that you'll want to conceal any screws you use. The most obvious ploy is to locate the screws where they can't be seen. Failing that, you can countersink them deeply and putty over them. Better to counterbore for the screws and fill

360

the counterbore with a wooden plug after the screw is in place. You can buy plugs, or you can make them with a plug cutter, a tool that is driven by a drill.

Having selected your fasteners and figured out how you are going to carry out your assembly operation and how you are going to clamp your work, you have one last decision to make before you actually assemble your cabinet. You've got to pick a glue.

Gluing

Glue is the adhesive that will bond your carefully crafted pieces of wood together. You may drive a few nails or screws. But glue is what will hold your cabinets together.

There are quite a number of different glues, all with different combinations of characteristics that are important to cabinetmakers. Among those characteristics are:

- *Assembly time.* This is the length of time you have to play around before the glue dries. A quick-setting glue is said to have a short assembly time: you have to work swiftly to get pieces assembled and clamped with such a glue.
- *Clamping time.* This is the length of time you must keep a joint clamped. Clamping times range from 30 minutes to more than 10 hours. If you have only a few clamps, you may want to use a glue with a short clamping time so that you can speed assembly work.
- *Gap-filling quality.* This is the

measure of the glue's ability to take up space in a joint. If you aren't too good at crafting joints, and yours tend to be a bit loose-fitting, you'll want to use a glue with good gap-filling qualities. If you craft snug joints, however, this characteristic isn't that significant to you.

- *Moisture resistance.* This is a measure of just what it says. For the bulk of your kitchen cabinetmaking, the moisture resistance of the glue won't be significant. But if you glue up a cutting board, use a moisture-resistant glue.
- *Heat resistance.* Some glues will soften when heated, meaning that you'd be able to unglue a joint by heating it. In practice, such a glue could surrender if the cabinet it bonds is too close to a woodburning range for too long. Its squeeze-out would gum up a sanding belt too.
- *Special preparation or use needs.* The best glue for you may be the one that comes ready-to-use in a plastic squeeze bottle, the worst the one that has separate ingredients. There are glues of both types.

Consider your project and your needs and select a glue from one of the following kinds of glue.

White Glue. The most popular woodworking glue has to be white glue, which is, more properly, polyvinyl resin emulsion glue. It has short assembly (5 to 10 minutes) and clamping (30 to 60 minutes) times, so-so gap-filling qualities, no moisture resistance and little heat resistance. Its lack of moisture resistance lies in the fact that it's a water-soluble glue; you can rinse it off your fingers and wash it out of your clothes. It dries as its moisture soaks into the wood or evaporates. But even after it has dried, it remains somewhat plastic, making it somewhat less sensitive than some other glues to the stresses of wood's response to humidity changes. It will soften when heated.

Comes in a plastic squeeze bottle. And available everywhere.

Yellow Glue. Properly called aliphatic resin glue, yellow glue (the most common brand is Titebond) is becoming increasingly popular. It has all the advantages of white glue, fewer of its disadvantages, and it is stronger. The assembly and clamping times are about the same, as are its gap-filling and moisture resistance qualities. But yellow glue is more heat resistant, which means that it's easier to sand and that it stands up better in the heat of a kitchen.

Yellow glue, too, comes in a squeeze bottle, ready to apply.

Hide Glue. This is the stuff old horses are made into. At one time, before the chemical blitz, hide glue was The Glue in cabinetmaking. It is still available and is still used, and is still good stuff. It has fairly long assembly and clamping times, about 30 minutes and 2 to 3 hours respectively, and good heat resistance. It is probably the best gap-filling glue. It's not

particularly moisture resistant, however.

Hide glue comes in two forms: as a liquid, ready to apply, and in flakes, which must be dissolved in water and heated for a time. It should be applied and allowed to become tacky before the wood is actually joined.

Casein Glue. Another natural glue, casein glue is made from milk curd. It shares a lot of the characteristics of hide glue—fairly long assembly and clamping times, good gap-filling quality and heat resistance—and it is considered moisture resistant besides (not waterproof, but water resistant).

Its drawbacks are that the glue powder must be carefully mixed with water to just the right, creamy consistency before each use and that it stains some commonly used hardwoods like oak and maple. It has an abrasive effect on cutting tools.

Plastic Resin Glue. Another moisture-resistant glue, this one is made strictly from chemicals. It has very long assembly and clamping (10 to 12 hours isn't too long) times. It is very strong, but it is also somewhat brittle in poorly fitted joints; it's not a good gap-filler, in other words. Its heat resistance is good, and its moisture resistance is very high—the glue is nearly waterproof, making it good to use to glue up cutting boards.

Plastic resin glue is another powdered glue that must be mixed with water just before use. It must be used in 70°F. or warmer temperatures, which can be a disadvantage in cold weather.

Resorcinol Resin Glue. Usually called simply resorcinol glue, this adhesive is very strong and totally waterproof. Use it to glue up a wooden sink for your kitchen. Resorcinol glue has a lengthy assembly time, but a long clamping time, too. It has good gap-filling qualities, good heat resistance and, of course, terrific moisture resistance.

Two ingredients, a powder and a liquid resin, must be mixed just before use, something of a drawback. A bigger negative is that the glue dries to a dark film. Like plastic resin glue, it must be used at temperatures at or above 70°F. The higher the heat, the faster the glue will set.

Contact Cement. You are most likely to use contact cement if you construct plastic laminated counter tops. But it comes in handy in any situation in which clamping is difficult or impossible, for it bonds upon contact. It doesn't deserve comparison to other adhesives because of its specialized nature.

To use contact cement, you brush a liberal coat on each of the mating surfaces. After the glue has dried—in about 30 minutes—sufficiently that a piece of paper won't stick to it, you press the surfaces firmly together, and they will stick to each other. Since the bonding is immediate, the alignment better be correct the first time.

The rubber-based variety of contact cement is noxious and highly flammable. It should be used in a very well ventilated shop, well away from the wood stove or any other potential source of ignition. In spite of **361**

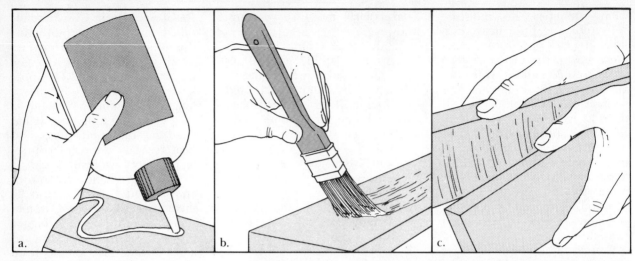

Spreading glue: a. Using a squeeze bottle. b. Using a brush. c. Evening the spread by rubbing the mating surfaces together.

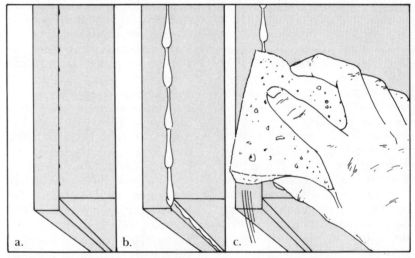

Squeeze-out is the excess glue expelled from a joint as it is clamped: a. A modest squeeze-out indicates a good spread. b. Excessive squeeze-out indicates that too much glue was spread. c. Water soluble glues can be cleaned up with a damp rag before the glue sets.

this drawback, the rubber-based contact cement is the best variety to use, for it bonds most strongly.

The most commonly available contact cement in home improvement centers and hardware stores is a water-based adhesive. It won't burn, but it doesn't bond as well as the flammable variety.

Epoxy Resin Glue. This is another specialized glue, one that's useful for bonding non-wooden parts to wooden parts. Like resorcinol glue, you mix two ingredients to get the bonding substance. It is strong, fills gaps well and is completely waterproof.

Having chosen just the right glue for your job, you are ready to actually assemble the cabinet.

First, make sure your mating surfaces are clean and smooth.

362

Then spread glue on both. This is called a double spread. If spreading from a squeeze bottle, trail a zigzag bead of glue. If you are using a mixed glue, use a glue brush or a stick to slather the stuff on the wood. When possible, rub the two pieces to

be joined together to even the spread. End grain sucks up a lot of glue, so spread a second coat there after the first has had a chance to soak in.

Press the pieces together and clamp or fasten with nails or screws. Beads of glue should

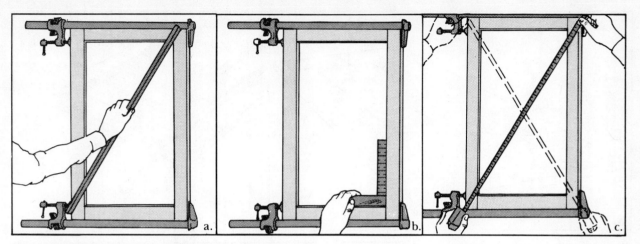

Checking the alignment of an assembly: a. Use a long straightedge to check the levelness. b. Use a try or framing square to check squareness. c. The squareness of a case or frame can be checked by measuring diagonally from corner to corner; the diagonals will be equal in a unit that's square.

well up from the joint in most cases. In the ideal, you'll have just tiny beads; rivulets mean you've used too much. This squeeze-out should be cleaned from surfaces already prepared for finishing as quickly and completely as possible. Stains and other finishes won't adhere to glue, and while you may not be able to see it before you finish the cabinet, you'll certainly see it, and weep, afterwards. Scrape up the glue with a sharp knife or chisel or scraper, then use a damp sponge to wipe up. If you've still got to sand the work to prepare it for finishing, you needn't worry about the squeeze-out.

The modest squeeze-out is a good sign, a sign that you won't have a starved joint. That's one

that didn't get enough glue; it'll come apart sooner or later.

Don't be afraid to tighten the clamps. While it's theoretically possible to get a starved joint from applying too much pressure and squeezing too much glue out, it is unlikely to happen. The more common error here is to apply too little pressure.

As you put the screws to the clamps, be sure to use a framing square to check the cabinet to be sure it's level and square. You can measure diagonals to be sure any boxlike assembly is square. It is easy to distort a cabinet at this point, so check and recheck as you work.

The clamps are unnecessary at this point if you've used nails or screws to fasten the joint.

How fast you must do all this depends upon the assembly time for the glue you use. Clamps should stay on, where appropriate, as long as the glue manufacturer specifies. It's not a bad idea to leave them on at least overnight, even with fast-

setting glues. If you must press the clamps into service elsewhere, do so. But most glues will gain strength after a period of drying or curing that's longer than the clamping time. So set the glued object aside, protected from jars and jolts, for a day or more.

Gluing Up Stock

Gluing up stock is a special assembly procedure required to produce broad boards or panels of solid wood. It is simply the process of gluing boards together-edge-to-edge. In making cabinets of solid wood rather than of plywood, for example, you must glue up stock for the cases. You may also need to glue up stock in making raised-panel doors. You should learn how to do it.

Preparation of the stock is the first step. The individual boards should not be too broad, certainly not more than 6 inches wide. If you have broader boards, rip them into narrower widths, as strange as that may

363

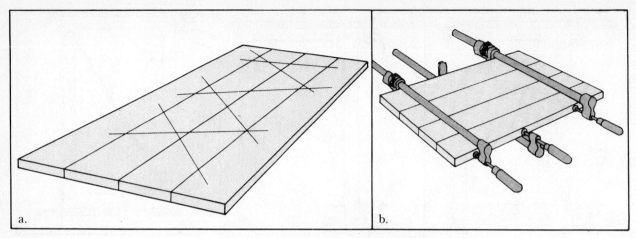

Gluing up: a. Before actually gluing up boards, lay them out to assess fit and appearance, then mark each board to speed gluing and clamping. b. In applying clamps, they should be alternated from face to face to counteract any tendency of the boards collectively to bow.

seem, before gluing them up. The goal here is to minimize cupping in the individual boards; the broader they are, the more likely they are to cup. The cupping could lead to distortion or splitting of the finished panel.

The edges to be mated should be planed on a jointer or with a jointer plane to ensure that they are flat and square.

Next, the boards should be laid out and switched around until a suitable arrangement is found. A suitable arrangement will have the grain of all boards running in the same direction and will, again to temper cupping, either have the pattern of growth rings on the butt ends of the boards alternated or matched. The arrangement of

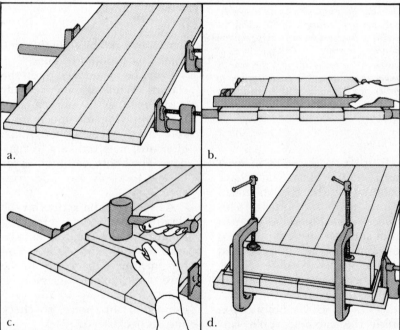

Aligning the surfaces of boards being glued up: a. Boards are loosely clamped. b. They are not properly lined up with each other. c. The boards, still clamped loosely, are brought into alignment by striking their surfaces with a hammer or mallet and a scrap of wood; with the boards in alignment, the clamps are tightened. d. An alternative method is to clamp a board or two across the stock being glued up; sheets of wax paper between the alignment boards and the work will prevent them from being glued together by the squeeze-out.

364

the boards shouldn't be haphazard. Mark the boards so that you can quickly duplicate the arrangement as you spread the glue and apply the clamps.

If you choose to reinforce the edge joints with splines or dowels, now is the time to do that work.

In clamping the boards after applying the glue, you want to place clamps across each broad surface to counteract any tendency to cup that would be generated by having the clamps all across one face. You want to have a clamp near each end and one every 15 inches or so in between.

The best assembly sequence to follow is to lay out however many clamps you plan to have beneath the boards. Set the jaws. Lay out the boards according to your markings. Working from one side to the other, apply glue to each mating surface, briefly rubbing the mating surfaces together to spread the glue evenly over the surfaces. Then press the boards together, insert the cauls, and start tightening the clamps. Use a framing square or other straightedge to check the surface, sighting along the surface of the wood to see any gap between the straightedge and the wood. Check across the grain and diagonally from corner to corner. Whack the boards into alignment with a mallet, using a scrap of wood to protect the surface from denting. If need be, you can clamp a straight board across each end with C clamps to keep the boards in alignment. If you do this, slip a sheet of waxed paper between

the stock being glued and the gluing cleat so that the cleat doesn't get glued to the work. Finally, add the clamps across the top surface and tighten them. Check the alignment once again (as best you can) and tighten the clamps as tight as you can. After a few minutes rest, retighten the clamps one last time.

Finishing

There's only one step left to complete your woodworking project, and that is to apply a finish. You can do the easy thing and paint it. You can stain it, varnish it, oil it. But whatever you do, you've got to prepare the wood surface first.

Preparing the surface means sanding. The sanding, depending upon the project, is something that is often done at the tail end of the fabrication process. Sometimes it's easier to sand the pieces than it is to sand the assembled object. If you haven't thought this out beforehand, certainly give it some consideration during the dry-fitting that begins the assembly process.

When you do finish-sand the pieces before assembly, you must take some special precautions during gluing to avoid having the finish spoiled by glue that's been slopped on the exposed surfaces of the wood.

Unless you've been extremely careful (and perhaps lucky) in your woodworking and thoughtful in your designing and planning, you'll have a few imperfections to deal with. There may be holes left where

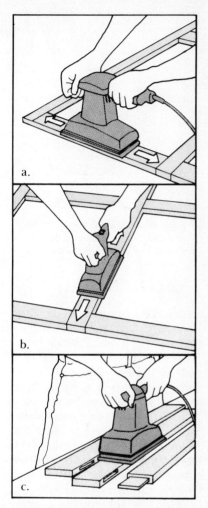

When sanding a completed assembly, such as a face frame, care must be taken to avoid cutting across the grain: a. Sand the rails. b. Then sand the stiles. c. The best approach often is to sand the pieces of an assembly before they are glued together.

nails were countersunk, perhaps a slight dent where you lost control of your hammer. The little holes and hollows can be filled with a wood filler like plastic wood, wood dough or wood **365**

Shallow dents in wood can sometimes be steamed out. Place a damp cloth over the dent and iron it with an electric iron.

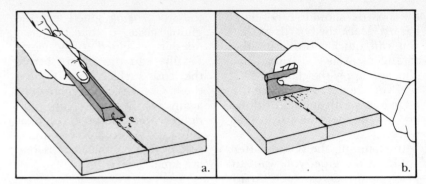

Removing dried glue squeeze-out: a. Pare with a chisel. b. Scrape with a cabinet scraper.

putty. You can even make your own filler by mixing sawdust with glue. Think ahead here. You want to use a material that will be compatible with wood *after* the finish is applied. Paint covers all. Stains will accentuate wood fillers, making them stand out from the wood because the filler will react differently to the stain than will the wood. In this situation, try to use a filler that will match the finished wood.

The best solution, of course, is to minimize or eliminate completely the need for nail holes where they'll be visible. It can be done.

Shallow dents can be raised, usually, by laying a damp cloth over the dent, then placing a hot iron on top of it. This should raise the grain and allow you to sand the surface even. Use some discretion and don't get the wood too wet.

Finally, before actually sanding, be sure to scrape off all the glue squeeze-out for reasons al-

ready mentioned. Trying to sand the glue away will only force it into the pores of the wood, creating an imperfection. Rather, you should use a sharp chisel or a cabinet scraper to remove it.

Sanding

Sanding is work that can drive you nuts. It takes a lot of elbow grease and patience to do correctly, and usually you have to do it when the project is *almost* done and you are getting anxious to see what it's really going to look like. And if you don't sand it well, it's going to look like, well, a disappointment.

Sanding can be done with machines or by hand. In any case, the final sanding should be done by hand.

There are several sandpapers you can use, and you probably should plan to use several different grits of whatever paper you do use, beginning with a fairly coarse grit and winding up with a very fine grit. The least expensive, and ultimately the least satisfactory sandpaper is flint paper. It uses a natural

abrasive (quartz) and is merely graded extra coarse through very fine, with no grit numbers. Flint paper is okay for hand-sanding.

Garnet paper is a good all-around paper for machine and hand-sanding. It too uses a natural material, almandite, but this abrasive is harder than quartz. It is graded numerically according to grit sizes.

Aluminum oxide, a man-made material that's harder than either flint or garnet, may be the best sandpaper for you to use, although it is the most expensive of the three. It is graded similarly to garnet paper.

In grit and grading terms, very coarse paper is graded 4 through 2½ with grits ranging from 16 to 30. Coarse paper is graded 2 through 1 with grits of 36 to 50. Medium is ½ through 2/0 with 60 to 100 grit, fine 3/0 through 5/0 with 120 to 180 grit, and very fine is 6/0 through 10/0 with 220 to 400 grit.

The grade of paper you use to start your sanding depends upon the state of the project. If

Using a belt sander: a. Keep the sander flat and move it back and forth to avoid gouging the work; sand with the grain for typical jobs. b. To remove material quickly, sand across the grain.

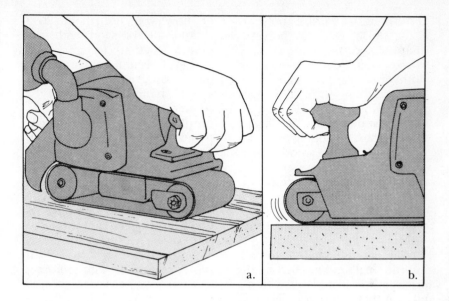

the wood is pretty rough, with lots of tool marks, you should start with a fairly coarse paper, say a 50 grit (1). Otherwise, a medium or fine paper is suitable for the initial sanding. A carefully planed surface could be sanded initially with a 150 grit (4/0) paper.

When jumping from one sanding stage to another, don't jump more than two grades of paper. Move from an 80 grit paper to a 120 grit paper to a 180 grit paper. It will take far more effort than anyone would want to expend to use 180 grit paper to remove the scratches left by 80 grit paper. And 180 grit is sufficiently fine paper to

use for the final sanding.

For the very best finish, you should raise the grain by dampening the wood before the final sanding. Whenever you apply moisture to the wood surface,

the wood fibers soak up the moisture, standing up as they do so. If you do this to a surface you think is finish-sanded, you'll discover that the surface isn't as smooth as you thought.

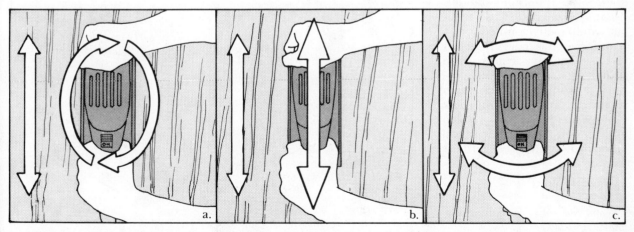

All finishing sanders work with one or more actions: a. Orbital. b. Straight line. c. Multimotion. Only a straight-line action sander allows you to avoid cross-grain abrasion. Work the sander back and forth in a straight line, moving parallel to the grain, overlapping successive strokes slightly.

367

If the moisture you are applying is the finish, you may be very disappointed. So, dampen the wood, using a damp sponge or cloth, and give the cabinet a finish-sanding with 220 grit paper. No need to flood the wood, just dampen it. You'll get those fibers standing up so you can sand the wood really smooth. Once the grain is raised, it's raised, and additional moisture won't roughen the surface. You won't be disappointed when you apply the finish.

You can use sanders for all but the final sanding. Belt sanders remove material the fastest, but they are a bit indelicate. Use a belt sander for rough-sanding large surfaces or individual pieces before assembly. The sander should be kept moving and should be kept flat on the surface. It is very easy to gouge the surface or precipitously break edges with a belt sander.

Second-stage sanding is best done with a finishing sander. All finishing sanders use regular sandpaper mounted on a pad. Different sanders have different sanding actions. The straight-line action is best, because it won't leave cross-grain scratches, so long as you don't sand across the grain. Orbital and multimotion sanders will leave such scratches, regardless

of how you use them. You should always sand with the grain, whether using a belt sander, finishing sander or your own elbow grease.

For hand-sanding, use a commercial sanding block, or simply wrap a piece of sandpaper around a scrap of wood. For odd shapes, use odd-shaped scraps, like a piece of dowel. Again, the final sanding should be done by hand.

After all your sanding is done, use a vacuum cleaner to remove the dust from the wood. Then wipe over it with a clean rag dampened with mineral spirits.

Choosing a Finish

You can spend as much time finishing a cabinet as you spent building it. There are all sorts of finishes and many of them take a long time to apply well. As a practical matter, however, you'll undoubtedly decide to steer clear of fancy furniture finishes in your harvest kitchen, not simply because they are laborious and tricky to apply, but because after all the work is done, they won't last.

Several considerations will affect your choice of a finish. Durability may well be the prime one. Others will include the appearance, the materials you've used and how patient you are.

How patient *are* you? The finest furniture finishing is a multiple-step procedure extending over many days. You start with a stain, which must be very carefully applied, then allowed to dry 12 hours or more.

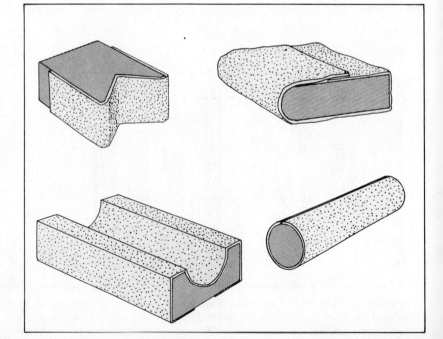

To sand odd shapes, wrap sandpaper around wood blocks crafted to match the surface to be sanded. Use a length of dowel or rubber hose or a block with a notch, hollow or nose.

Next, a shellac wash coat is brushed on, allowed to dry for a half-hour, sanded and cleaned. A paste filler is applied next; it takes a good 24 hours to dry. Varnish goes on next. It must be allowed to dry overnight, then be sanded and followed by a second coat, which also must dry overnight, then be sanded. The final step is to use pumice stone and oil and elbow grease to rub the finish to its final polished appearance.

It's a lot of work. And in the harvest kitchen its final polished appearance won't last too long.

But if you've used a good hardwood to build your cabinets, you probably should follow through and apply a good finish. Some version of that multiple-step procedure may be a good route. But there are shorter ones.

Paint. The shortest route of all is to simply paint the cabinets. It is an economical approach. Not only is a can of paint less of an investment than cans of stain, filler, shellac and varnish, but the materials used in the cabinets can be of a lower quality. You can use pine board lumber rather than hardwood, birch veneer-core plywood for doors rather than hardwood lumber-core plywood.

Use a good-quality oil-base, alkyd, epoxy or urethane paint or enamel. Avoid latex, though it is easy to work with. It won't produce the kind of finish you want for kitchen cabinets. The others will.

Follow the manufacturer's instructions regarding specifics of surface preparation, thinning of paint (seldom necessary), appli-

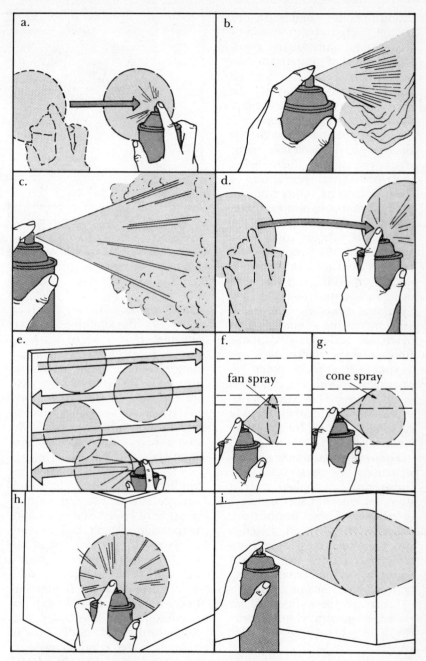

Special care must be used in applying finishes from spray cans: a. Always maintain a consistent and proper distance from the work. b. Too close and the finish will run. c. Too far away and it will be gritty with dust. d. Inconsistent and it will be both. e., f. and g. Maintain a consistent measure of overlap from pass to pass. h. Spray corners so the spray strikes both faces equally, rather than, i., unequally.

369

cation of an undercoat or primer coat, and application of second and subsequent coats. One point that's important is to be sure to shellac any and all knots. If you don't, you'll be surprised—and doubtless disappointed—to discover them mystically appearing through the paint, regardless of how many coats you apply. The shellac seals the knot, preventing it from oozing its resins into the paint. The resins will be there, regardless of the age of the knot, so if you are using recycled wood or reusing old cabinets, shellacking the knots is just as important as if you were using new materials.

Synthetic Finishes. There are an increasing number of urethane and other synthetic finishes on the market. Most are as simple to apply as paint, yet provide a smooth, clear, natural wood finish. They resist moisture, and that makes them a reasonable choice for finishing kitchen cabinets.

Follow the manufacturer's instructions. In most cases, the finish can be applied over a stain, but not over shellac, fillers or sealers. These finishes are supposed to do it all. Usually, two or three coats are recommended. If they are applied within a specified time, sanding between coats isn't necessary.

Some of these finishes are packaged in spray cans. A spray finish is generally regarded as superior to a brush-applied finish. Too, there's no brush to clean when you use a spray can. But your environment may preclude the use of spray applications.

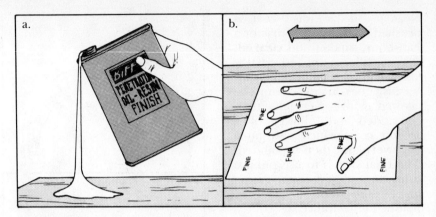

Applying a penetrating oil-resin finish: a. Pour a liberal amount of the finish on the wood. b. Keep the surface uniformly wet for 30 minutes or longer (until the finish no longer soaks into the wood), then sand lightly for a very short time and wipe the excess finish from the wood.

Oil Finishes. The oil finish is one of the all-time classy finishes. It is a *lot* of work to apply properly, and maintenance takes a lot of attention. But scratches and mars are easily repaired by applying more oil. It's a nice finish for a handcrafted end table, but probably not a wise choice for kitchen cabinets.

The traditional oil finish is applied by saturating the wood surface with a hot one to one mixture of boiled linseed oil and turpentine. (Don't boil linseed oil yourself; go to a paint or hardware store and buy a product called boiled linseed oil.) The mixture—a flammable one—is heated as indirectly as possible in a double boiler to a temperature of 80°F. It is spread on the wood, allowed to soak for a time, then wiped off. The process is repeated and repeated and repeated, with lots of rubbing between applications. Over the years, the oil

finish should be periodically renewed.

Paste wax can be applied to the oil finish to protect it.

Penetrating Oil-Resin Finishes. These are somewhat akin to oil finishes, but the oils and resins in them actually combine with the wood chemically, sealing, finishing and preserving the wood. The finish is fast and simple to apply. You'll have to decide if it is durable enough for your kitchen.

The wood should be sanded especially smooth, using 220 grit (6/0) paper, and, of course, thoroughly cleaned of dust. The surface can then be stained, and if necessary, filled with a mixture of the finishing material and an oil filler. The finishing material is applied liberally, really saturating the surface. Keep the wood wet for about a half-hour. Then, with the surface still wet, lightly sand the surface with 220 grit wet-dry sandpaper, lubricating the operation with oil. Only a minute or two of sanding is necessary. Finally, wipe off the excess oil and allow the cabinet to dry overnight. The finish can then be protected with a liquid carnauba wax.

As with oil finishes, the penetrating oil-resin finish is easily repaired of scratches or other marks by rubbing in more finishing material.

Stain-Filler-Sealer-Varnish. If you've determined that a multiple-ingredient finishing process is what your cabinets must have, be prepared to do a lot of research into the profusion of available ingredients, what they do and how they are used. And be prepared to do some testing on wood samples before putting your cabinets under the brush. Here's an introduction, but only an introduction.

The first ingredient of the finish is the stain. Stain puts color into wood, emphasizing the beauty of the grain, or "disguising" the wood as something it is not. You can make pine look kind of like walnut by using a walnut stain. Seems somehow deceitful, but it can be done.

Stain can be very tricky to apply well. The wood surface must be clean and smooth. Application must be done with synthetic bristle brushes with brass or rubber ferrules to prevent rust staining. The trickiest part is spreading the stain evenly and blending all the brushstrokes. It's all too easy to get variations in color and dark bands when brushstrokes overlap.

Water stain is the easiest to deal with. It is dye dissolved in water. It is very permanent, rather transparent but quite beautiful. The negative is that

because it is water-based, it raises the grain. Takes a long time to dry, too.

Alcohol stain, on the other hand, dries quite quickly, because it is dye dissolved in alcohol, a volatile spirit that evaporates rapidly. The quick-drying quality makes alcohol stain difficult to apply evenly. It is not as permanent as water stain.

Two types of oil stain are available: penetrating and pigmented. The penetrating type is dye mixed with oil. This stain is easily applied with a rag. It isn't very permanent, however, and tends to fade; it can be bleached out of the wood if the job is botched. Pigmented wiping stain is very heavily colored. This is the stain that colors one kind of wood to look like another.

After staining an open-grained wood like walnut, oak

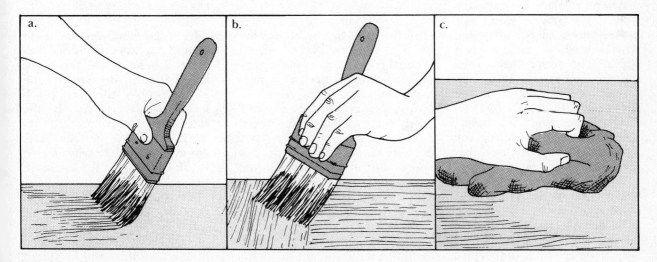

Applying wood filler: a. Use a stiff-bristle brush to apply the filler, stroking with the grain until the wood pores are partially filled. b. Using the same brush, apply another coat of filler, stroking across the grain. c. Gently scrape the excess filler from the surface, gliding a plastic or cardboard across the grain or wiping with a coarse rag.

or ash, you must apply a filler to fill up the wood's pores. You don't use wood dough, you use a completely different product that comes in paste and liquid forms. Some fillers are sold with oil stains mixed in, allowing you to do two procedures at one time.

Apply filler to a small area at a time, no larger than 2 square feet. Brush or wipe the filler first with the grain, then across the grain. After a short time, the filler will lose its wet appearance. That is the time to remove the excess by wiping across the grain with a coarse rag; a piece of burlap is excellent. If you wipe too soon, you'll pull the filler out of the pores, but if you wait too long, the filler will have dried and be very difficult to remove at all. This is where testing beforehand will demonstrate its worth. Get all the excess off. Don't let any accumulate in corners.

After the filler is dried, or, with a close-grained wood that doesn't need filling, after the stain is dried, you must apply a sealer. The sealer closes over the stain and filler and prevents them from bleeding into the finish coats.

The best sealer is shellac. Shellac is a lousy finish for kitchen cabinets by itself because it is too sensitive to water spotting and to alcohol, which will remove it. But as a sealer, covered by varnish, it is great.

Be sure you use a fresh shellac. After it is about six months old, it deteriorates and won't dry. Since the manufacturers don't date their product, you'll have to take the supplier's word

that it is fresh. Test it on a scrap. If it doesn't dry, take the can back and get another. And test *it*.

The usual store product is a 4 pound cut (4 pounds of shellac dissolved in a gallon of alcohol). This should be further cut one to one with alcohol for the sealer coat. Brush this sealer on, let it dry, then lightly sand it. Don't oversand or you'll cut through it and negate its seal. Shellac does have color—yellow to orange— to it, so be prepared for some alteration in the appearance of your stain. Again, a test will show you what you'll get before you do the whole job.

There are other sealers available. If the shellac doesn't suit, try one of them.

With the sealer applied, dried, sanded and cleaned thoroughly, it is finally time to apply the finish coats. You can use either a varnish or a lacquer, but in a kitchen, you are wise to use a varnish.

Lacquer will give you a better finish than a varnish. It doesn't darken the established finish color because it goes on in very thin, clear coats. Because it dries very quickly, it is both better to work with and harder to work with than varnish. The quick drying allows you to apply two or three coats in a day, which is good. But if you dawdle in the least, the lacquer can dry before you are done. It will dry up in the brush. All of which is bad.

Lacquer is fairly resistant to water, beverages and food. But, and this is the big but, lacquer is sensitive to excessive moisture, which can cause it to peel off the wood at worst and can cause

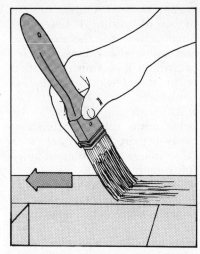

Lacquer must be applied using a heavily loaded brush and long, rapid, single-direction strokes. No sweeping back and forth as with paint. The lacquer will even out over the surface.

white water spots to develop at best. You have to decide whether or not you want to chance using lacquer.

If you must, then be sure you select a lacquer formulated for brush application. Spray lacquers dry much too fast to be brush applied. Be sure you use a compatible thinner, which means a thinner made by the same manufacturer as the lacquer. Stir the lacquer well. Apply it with a heavily loaded brush (don't wipe the brush on the rim of the can), using long, rapid strokes. Don't try to stroke back and forth as you would with paint or varnish. Just get it on quickly; it will even out to a tough, smooth finish. Each coat should dry at least 2 hours. Scuff the surface with 220 grit (6/0) sandpaper between coats.

Apply varnish to a small area at a time. Always apply it liberally, always stroking in a single direction, moving from dry to wet. a. Stroke first across the grain. b. Then cross the same area stroking with the grain. c. Begin a new section.

After the third coat, rub and polish the surface.

The strength of varnish is that it gives a sound, water-resistant finish, a finish good enough for exterior use. Its weakness is its long drying time. Each coat should dry 6 to 8 hours.

The first coat of varnish on your new cabinets should be thinned slightly, about 1 part mineral spirits or turpentine to 8 parts varnish. Subsequent coats should not be thinned.

Stir the varnish well. Using a clean, new brush, apply the varnish liberally to the wood. Stroke across the grain first, then lightly stroke with the grain, always in the same direction, always moving from the dry area to the wet area. Do a small area at a time.

Between coats, scuff the surface with 220 grit (6/0) sandpaper.

The final step in this laborious finishing process is the rubbing, polishing and cleaning. With kitchen cabinets, it's open to question as to whether or not you really need, or even want, a furniture finish, that glossy shine.

If you do, there are many ways to get it, but one of the best is to sand the finished surface with water and 400 grit (10/0) wet-dry sandpaper. Use a medium pressure. Wipe the surface clean, then rub it with a commercial polishing compound. Finally, apply wax.

Just when you finish your cabinets is another variable. If your cabinets have been built in place, obviously you'll finish them in place. But if you've prefabbed them in a shop, you can either finish them there or install them, then finish them.

Consider the environment. For finishing, you want to work in the cleanest, most dustfree conditions possible. It just may be that the kitchen is the place to do it. All the cabinets, doors and drawers can be done at one time. If woodwork or trim in the kitchen is to be finished to match, all can be done at one time. It will all match, surely.

But dust is the bugbear of finishing, especially with slow-drying materials. Vacuum the room, keep traffic entirely out of the area. Reclean after each sanding. A lot of trouble, but when the cabinets are installed, you'll see it was worth it. A well-applied finish will really finish off your labors.

Building a Kitchen Cabinet___

Such an apprenticeship you have served. You now know—on paper at least—all the basic woodworking techniques you need to master to make a cabinet. In fact, you probably know more than is necessary.

The challenge is to pull all the information together, identify those techniques you'll need to make *your* harvest kitchen shelves or cabinets, and put the rest aside. How do you pull the techniques you need out of the preceding welter of how-to?

The first step is to get a good picture in your mind of just what a cabinet is. Picture three shelves hanging on a wall. Nothing more, just the three shelves. Now put on sides, tying the three horizontal boards together and making a box with a single shelf in it. You are almost to cabinethood. Put doors on your bookcase and you're there. You've got a wall cabinet. Simple, unsophisticated, but a cabinet.

A base cabinet is deeper, and it has a toe space, but basically it's the same.

A drawer is a refinement of an open-topped box, sitting on the shelf.

A counter is a refinement of the top. It has an overhang at the front and perhaps on the sides. It has a durable surface of some kind. But it's just the top of the box.

With that picture in mind, begin constructing a cabinet in your mind. Start with the case, then progress to the face frame, then to the doors and drawers, finally to the counter top. Not every cabinet will have each of these elements. Cabinets can be made without face frames. And certainly not all cabinets have both drawers and doors. In fact, you may choose to eschew "cabinets" altogether and just have shelves in your kitchen.

Break your cabinet down into its several components, and plan the best way to cut, fabri-

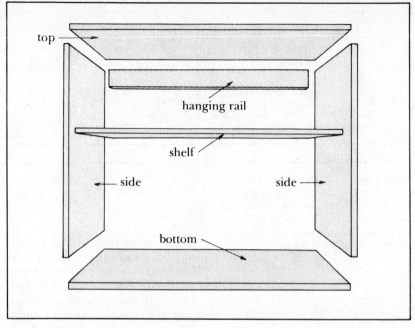

Assembling the case of a wall cabinet.

cate and joint the pieces needed to make each component. Just as there are a multitude of ways to lift the hide from a cat, there are usually a multitude of ways to join a cabinet's components. Just remember the caveat: The simplest joint that does the job is the best.

Constructing the Case

The case is the basic box. It's the three shelves with the sides. In constructing a wall cabinet, constructing the case is as simple as cutting ordinary board lumber into a top and bottom and two sides and nailing them together, forming a box. The case can have a back, although it doesn't need it. It does need a hanging rail, however, which is

a board across the back through which it is attached to the wall.

For a base cabinet, the case is a bottom and two sides, sometimes a back, other times merely a back cross-member, and certainly at least one, but usually two, top crosspieces. The back cross-member is important because it gives you some means to moor the cabinet to the wall: You drive nails, screws or lag bolts through it into the wall. The top cross-members serve a somewhat similar purpose: You drive screws through them, eventually, into the counter top to install it.

In almost every kitchen cabinet these days, the sides, bottom and any shelves or partitions are plywood. The material is strong and dimensionally sta-

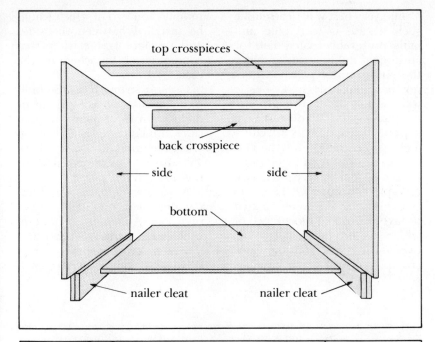

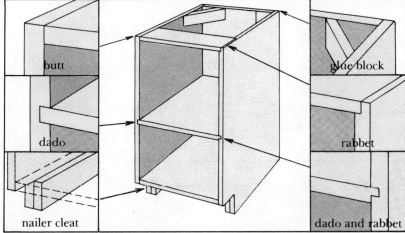

A variety of joints can be used in case construction, ranging from simple butt joints to more complicated—but stronger—dado-and-rabbet joints.

Assembling the case of a base cabinet.

In situations where the cabinet side will be against a wall or another cabinet, you can use a lower grade of plywood. It need have only one good side, the side you'll see when you open the cabinet. (Actually, even *that* side can be lower grade if you aren't picky but are on a tight budget.) If it's a cabinet of drawers only, you don't need a good side for the interior.

Where the cabinet side will be visible, you can buy a plywood with an attractive face veneer—walnut, maple, oak, cherry, whatever hardwood you want. Or you can build the case of ordinary plywood, then apply a facing of ¼-inch hardwood plywood or a piece of sheet paneling.

Of course, you can glue up stock to make the sides. It's a lot of work. The result won't have the stability of plywood, but it may look better, assuming you use an attractive wood. Presumably, you wouldn't use glued-up panels for sides that won't be visible. There you would use a frame. Or a piece of plywood.

Wall cabinets usually are also made from plywood. However, the architectural standard for wall cabinets is to make them 12 inches deep. If you subtract ¾ inch for the face frame, the sides need to be 11¼ inches deep, which means you can use 1 × 12 for the case. The drawback is that it's not unlikely that a 1 × 12 will want to cup or twist with changes in humidity. If the cabinet is well joined, it won't be

ble. It won't swell and shrink with changes in humidity as will panels glued up from lumber.

The movement, though imperceptible to you, is hell on joints. In addition, plywood is readily available, relatively inexpensive and doesn't have to be glued up. You simply lay out the pieces on a sheet of plywood and cut them out.

375

able to. At least not right away. But the stresses will torture your joinery and ultimately could loosen the joints.

You can sidestep the whole issue by using plywood to build the wall cabinets as well as the base cabinets.

The architectural standard for a base cabinet for the kitchen calls for it to be 36 inches high and 24 inches deep. Subtract for the face frame and for the counter top and cut your plywood sides to size. If you want to build your cabinets to your standard, and not the architectural standard, make whatever adjustments in size you find necessary. Cut a notch for the toe space, removing one corner from each side piece. The toe space is about 4 inches high and 3 inches deep.

Installing drawer supports: a. The drawer support is a spacer board attached to the side; it is only thick enough to be flush with the inner edge of the face frame stile. b. An internal partition, if offset so that one face is flush with the stile, will need only one drawer support.

The very best way to assemble such a case is with glue and nails, preferably coated nails for additional holding power, since the end grain of plywood does not hold nails or screws overly well. Butt joints, though elementary, will do. You can help support the bottom by attaching a cleat to each side for the bottom to rest on. Again, you don't need a back. You do need a back crosspiece, though. The top crosspieces could be eliminated in favor of corner blocks, two of which would be installed between the sides and the back crosspiece during the case as-sembly, and two of which would be installed between the sides and the face frame when that component is attached to the case.

Greater strength can be built into the case by using dado or dado-and-rabbet joints to join sides and bottom. Using full top cross members and a full back will also add to the strength of the unit.

A case may have a vertical partition. Use another piece of plywood. Attach it to bottom, back or back cross-member and the top cross-members. Use dado joints for greater strength.

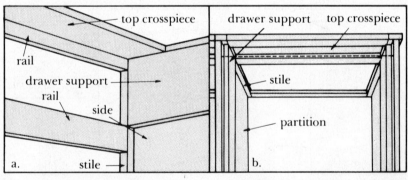

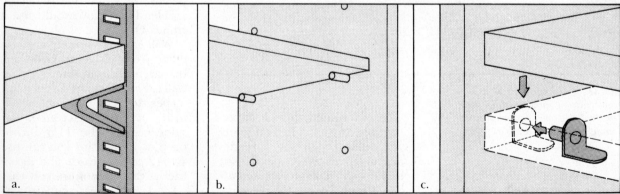

Supporting adjustable shelves: a. Metal tracks and clips. b. Short pieces of dowel inserted in holes in the case sides. c. Commercial shelf support pins.

If the cabinet is ultimately to have drawers, you may need to install frame pieces that will support runners or drawer hardware. Such pieces should be attached to the sides so that their faces will be flush with the inner edge of the face frame when it is attached. One (or more) could be attached to the top cross-members and the back or back cross-member.

If the partition figures into the need for drawer supports, be sure to plan how it will relate to the face frame. You should offset the partition in a double-bay cabinet so that it will be flush with one side of the center piece of the face frame. A drawer runner will fasten directly to the partition on that

side. A spacer will be needed on the other side.

In this sort of case, shelves can be glued and nailed in a fixed position. This, of course, will contribute to the strength and rigidity of the cabinet, but it will limit the flexibility of it for storage. As with the bottom, joining a fixed shelf to the case with a dado joint or a dado-and-rabbet joint will add to the strength of the unit.

More flexibility can be had by making any shelf a movable one. You can use metal tracks and clips, a pair on each side. Or you can create your own adjustment tracks by drilling two rows of shallow holes in each side and using shelf clips or bits of dowel stuck into the holes to

support the shelves. These holes should be laid out and drilled before assembly.

Actual assembly can be expedited with a little forethought. If you are using butt joints, a line in the right place can help you align the various parts. With dado joints you won't have to worry about this. A nailing line can help you get the nails driven dead center without a lot of guesswork.

A helper or a few corner clamps can expedite assembly too. The panels can be a bit unwieldy if you are working by yourself. You have to spread glue, fit the parts together, then drive nails. Corner clamps can act as an extra pair of hands by securely holding the bottom

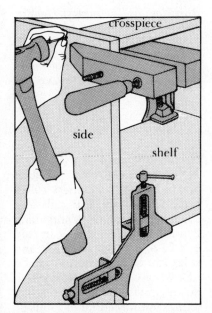

Clamps, expecially corner clamps, can be used to hold pieces of the case in position while nails or screws are being driven.

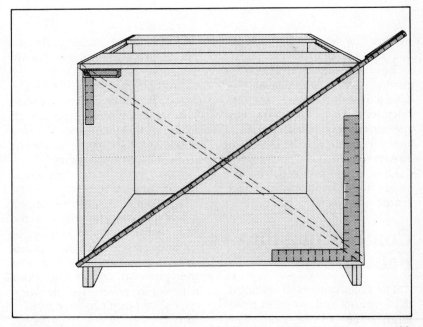

Check the case for squareness as it is assembled by using a try or framing square and by comparing diagonal measurements, which should be equal.

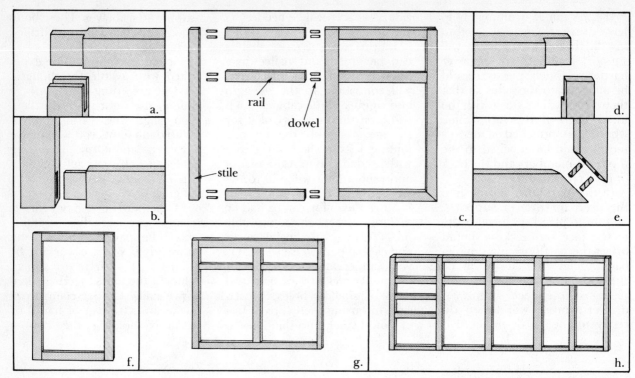

rail

dowel

stile

a.

b.

c.

d.

e.

f.

g.

h.

Assembling the face frame: a. Using an open mortise and tenon. b. Using a blind mortise and tenon. c. Using dowels. d. Using lap joints. e. Using dowel-reinforced miter joints. f. A wall cabinet face frame. g. A face frame with the intermediate stile extending from top rail to bottom rail. h. A complex face frame.

against the side, or by positioning a partition.

Be very sure you keep the case square as you assemble it. Use a framing square to check corners. And take diagonal measurements; if both diagonal measurements are the same, the case is square.

Once it is assembled, you are ready to think about the face frame.

Constructing the Face Frame

The face frame is an assembly that encases and dresses up the front edges of the case. The cabinet will begin to look like a cabinet when this component is nailed in place. Because the face frame helps to establish the appearance of the cabinet, it should be made of an attractive wood. It can be ordinary board lumber, but it ought to be a high grade of it. Most often, the face frame is a hardwood, as are the drawer fronts and doors.

In a very basic, economy-model cabinet, there may not be a face frame. Part of the frame's job is to cover the edges of the case, which, if it's made of plywood, aren't all that attractive. If you band the edges of the plywood, or if the door completely covers the plywood edges, you don't have to build a face frame. But you probably will.

The face frame is composed of vertical members called stiles and horizontal members called rails. Ordinarily, the rails and stiles are ¾ inch thick and about 2 inches wide. You can use 1 × 2s or 1 × 3s. The rails and stiles can be laid out and joined in a variety of ways. Most often, dowel joints are used, but lap joints, reinforced miter joints or even mortise-and-tenon joints can be used.

The usual layout is to have all

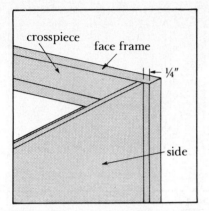

The face frame should extend at least ¼ inch beyond an unexposed case side.

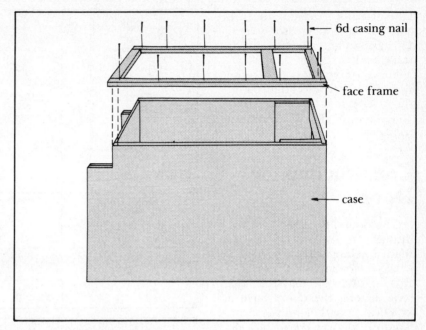

Gluing and nailing the face frame to the case.

the rails fit between the stiles. Certainly you want to avoid exposing the end grain of the rails, so you'd always have the side stiles extend the full height of the cabinet front. But you could have the top and bottom rails extend completely from side stile to side stile, with the center or any intermediate stiles fitting between them. Any intermediate rails would fit between the stiles regardless.

Several important considerations figure into the size of the face frame. The top edge is always flush with the top of the case. The upper edge of the bottom rail is always flush with the top surface of the case bottom. How the edges of the side stiles fit with the case sides depends upon the cabinet. The side stile should overhang any unexposed side by at least ¼ inch. Where the cabinet abuts a wall or another cabinet, this overhang allows some room for finagling to level the cabinets. The side stile should be flush with any exposed side, unless

you choose to dress up the side of the cabinet with a facing of ¼-inch hardwood plywood, in which case you need the ¼-inch overhang.

You have to think about the drawers and their runners in earnest at this point. If you are building a double-bay cabinet, with drawers side by side, you should have the center partition offset slightly, so that one side of it will be flush with the edge of the center stile. A spacer attached to the partition will be flush with the other side of the stile. If you mount the partition dead center, you need spacers on both sides; either that or a very narrow center stile.

Measure the case and do your figuring carefully. You should really have this all planned out ahead of time, but it's a good

idea to create the face frame to fit the case. That way you can accommodate any variations that may have developed as you built the case.

Cut all the pieces precisely. A good fit is important to the appearance of the cabinet.

The finished frame is usually attached to the case with glue and nails. Lay the case on its back, spread glue on its front edges and on the frame. Set the frame in place. Using 6d casing or finishing nails, nail it fast. Be sure the frame is flush with the case at the appropriate places and that the sides of the case aren't bowed.

If you are working with a built-in-place cabinet, temporarily securing the frame in the proper alignment whilst you nail will be tricky. Try using **379** hand screws to clamp the top stile to the top cross-member. Or have an extra pair of hands standing by.

However you do it, get the face frame firmly attached to the case. When it is, the cabinet is ready for the drawers and doors.

Constructing the Doors

The doors, together with the drawer fronts, will do more than anything else to establish what your cabinets will look like. But in addition to being the style setters, the doors have a practical function to perform. To do it, they've got to fit well, be flat and square and be easy to open, yet easy to keep closed.

There are three basic types of doors. The first is the *flush door*. The flush door fits within the face frame or the cabinet edges, so the face of the door is flush with the cabinet front. This is probably the most difficult door to hang properly. The face frame has to be square, as does the door. It must fit just right or it will be either too loose, with an unsightly gap, or too tight,

Making plywood doors: a. The overlapping door is most easily made; edge-banding hides the plywood's core layers. b. Cutting a bevel along each edge slightly changes the overlapping door's appearance; it too can be edge-banded. c. Rounding over the exterior edge can be done with a router; core plies are difficult to conceal. d. The lipped door has a rabbet along each interior edge; the exterior edges can be left square, rounded or beveled.

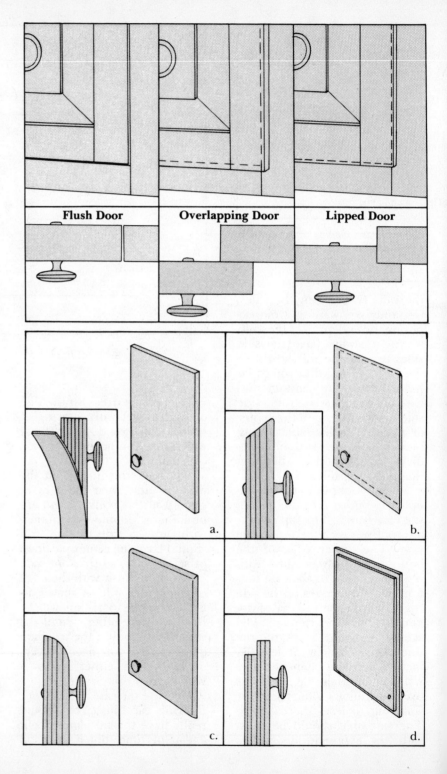

Flush Door   Overlapping Door   Lipped Door

a.

b.

c.

d.

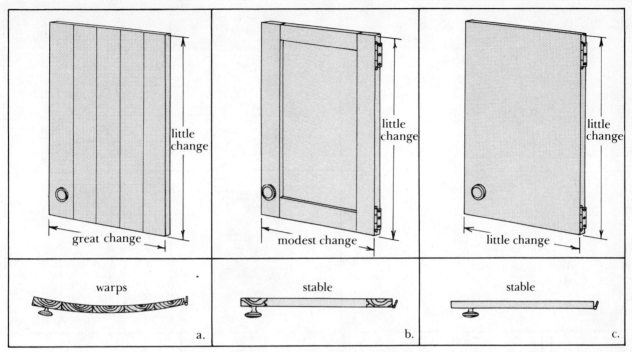

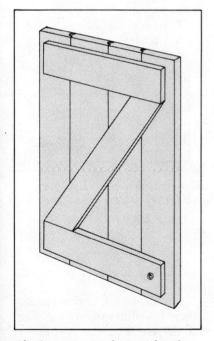

The dimensional stability of a cabinet door depends upon the materials and construction: a. A door glued up from solid stock is least stable. b. A frame-and-panel door, again of solid stock, is much more stable. c. A plywood door is most stable, resisting expansion and shrinkage and warpage.

Cleating tongue-and-groove boards together to make a cabinet door.

with irksome sticking. Make this door about ⅛ inch shorter and narrower than the opening.

The *overlapping door* is the antithesis of the flush door. It just lies on the face frame or the case edges, the way a refrigerator door fits the refrigerator. This door is much easier to fit and install, and it hides a lot of flaws that you just might want to hide. Make it about ½ to ¾ inch taller and wider than the opening.

The *lipped door* is a compromise. It has a rabbet cut around its perimeter so that the inner face fits into the opening, while the outer surface overlaps the frame. The advantage to this

type is that it is as easy to install as an overlapping door, while giving a better appearance. It is a bit more difficult to fabricate, only because of the need to rabbet it. It is usually made ½ inch taller and wider than the opening, and the rabbet is ⅜ inch wide and deep.

Each of these doors can be made in a number of different ways. The easiest in each case is to cut the door from a sheet of plywood.

Using plywood offers a lot of advantages. Foremost is that it is quick and easy to use. Lay out the door and cut it out. Voilà, the door is finished but for the **381**

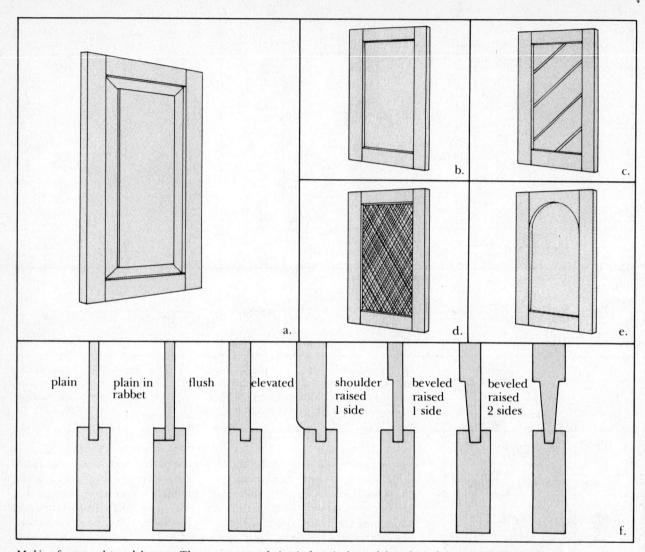

Making frame-and-panel doors: a. The most common design is the raised-panel door. b. A plain panel door is easier to make. c. Grooves can dress up a plain panel. d. Expanded metal, glass or caning can be substituted for the panel. e. The frame can be modified into an arch. f. The shape of the panel and its position in the frame affects the door's appearance.

installation. Oh, you can fancy up the edges by cutting them on a bevel or by shaping them with a router or by edge-banding. But that's true of any door you make. But with any other door, you've got some fabricating and assembling to do, sometimes very intricate fabricating and assembling.

A less obvious advantage to plywood is that it is dimensionally stable. It won't swell and shrink. It can warp, but it is much less likely to than solid lumber.

The drawback is the appearance. It's pretty plain Jane. Certainly you'd use a variety to match the face frame, but you still have only a plain slab of

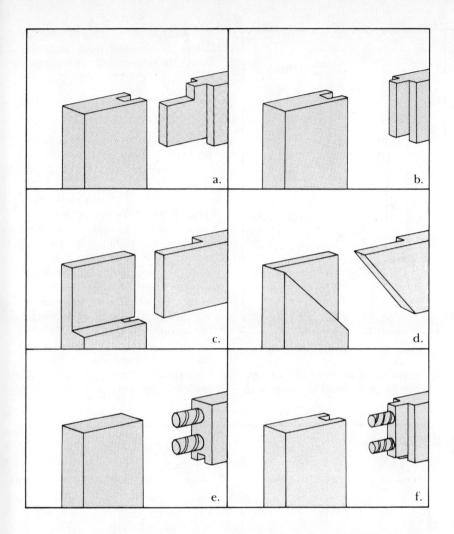

door, a frame of stiles and rails is constructed to surround a panel of some sort or to accept glass. The frame contributes dimensional stability, the panel contributes good looks.

The framework can be any wood, but commonly it's a wood to match the face frame. The material should be a minimum of ¾ inch thick, and while it's common for the stiles and rails to be of a uniform width of 1½ inches to 2½ inches, the rails could be thicker or thinner, or even shaped, for example, so as to present a door with an archlike appearance.

The panel too is ordinarily a matching wood, but it could be contrasting. The most simple panel would be hardwood plywood matching the frame and the cabinets. This panel can be set flush with either the front or the back edge of the frame, or it can be elevated so that it projects beyond the frame. Usually, it is centered in the frame. The most familiar variation may be the so-called raised panel, with a beveled or shouldered band around the perimeter of the panel.

Even a material other than wood could be used for the panel. Glass can be set in the frame. In such a case, perhaps the framed area would be broken up further with muntins; difficult to make, but a unique touch. Leaded glass could be

wood to look at.

You can glue up lumber to make door panels. But it's a lot of work, the door will be unstable and likely will warp. The door may not look any better than a hardwood plywood door unless you carefully select the boards for special patterns of the grain. If you do do this, you will, of course, have very special and beautiful doors, and consequently cabinets.

In certain instances, you may build doors by cleating several pieces of tongue-and-groove stock together, then ripping the tongue and the groove from the exposed edges. Such doors certainly won't be the best, unless the cabinets are of such a design that they demand those doors and no others for the design to work.

Frame-and-panel doors are the most difficult to build but have the most flexible design and the best appearance. In this

383

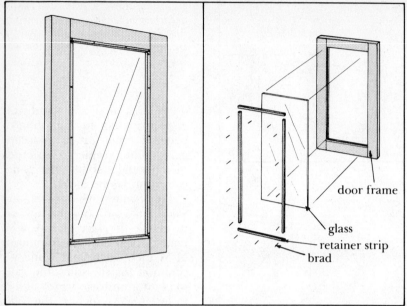

door frame

glass

retainer strip

brad

thin strips of wood or very light molding. This is the frame you'd use if you want glass doors.

A more sophisticated approach is to plow a groove in the inner edges of the rails and stiles for the panel. The groove ordinarily is ⅜ inch deep and is wide enough to accommodate the thickness of whatever panel is being used. However, where the panel will be solid lumber, the groove in the stiles should be deep enough to accommodate cross-grain expansion of the panel during periods of high humidity.

used. Expanded metal sheets or punched tin sheets. Caning. Use your imagination.

Name a joint, and it can probably be used to join a frame-and-panel door. A doweled or splined butt joint, one of the many variations on the mortise-and-tenon joint or one of several lap joints could be used to join the door frame. The panel could be set in a rabbet or groove cut in the frame. And the panel could be edge-glued from several narrow boards.

The simplest approach is to build the frame using dowel joints, then to cut a rabbet around the inner edge and set the panel or glass in the rabbet. Either can be held in place with

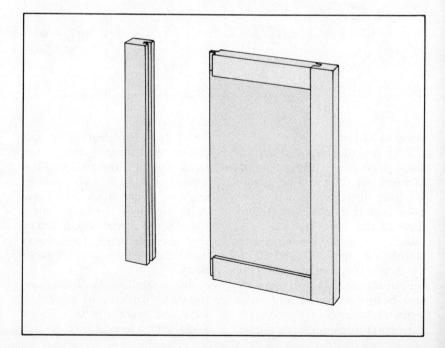

The most common and attractive method of installing wooden panels is to set them in a groove cut in the rails and stiles.

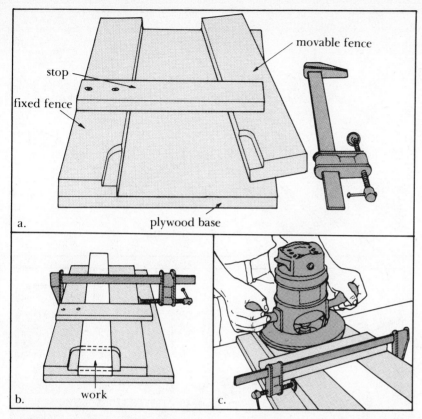

a.

stop

fixed fence

movable fence

plywood base

b.

work

c.

Cutting tenons with a router and jig: a. The jig is made by attaching a fence to a plywood base, then attaching a stop to the fence. b. The work is fitted under the stop, lined up flush with the jig's end and clamped between the fixed fence and a second, movable one. c. The router, adjusted for depth of cut, rides the stop, cutting the appropriate length of tenon; the fences prevent the router from tearing out splinters from the edges of the work.

tack the works together with cleats across the ends. Use a router-mounted guide to position the groove, making it as wide as the panel is thick and about ⅜ inch deep, except at the ends of the stiles. Here, cut the groove as deep as you can, forming mortises. Adjust the length of the tenons to match the depth of the mortises. Plow the appropriate groove in the rails, then plow the grooves and mortises in the stiles. There really isn't a need to square off the inner edges of the mortises, since the tenons and the panel will conceal the grooves. Finally, reset the router and cut rabbets across both faces of both ends of the rail, forming the tenons.

The frame isn't assembled, of course, until the panel is ready. When it is, glue is spread only where it will secure the frame. The panel should not be glued in place; you must allow it to move ever so slightly. Assemble the frame around the panel and clamp it with bar clamps or quick clamps or even thick rubber bands cut from an old inner tube. Be sure it is flat and square before the glue sets, of course.

A variation on this approach would be to cut the tenons only as long as the panel groove is deep, then set dowels into them. You would naturally change the fabrication of the stiles to accommodate the difference. This approach would involve a bit more work.

A second variation, more difficult than either of the first two, would be to cut a haunch into the tenons, then cut a blind groove in the stiles with a mor-

The time of the year in which you are working is also significant here. If it's winter, the boards are probably as shrunken as they will ever be; you must allow room for expansion, perhaps ⅛ to ¼ inch over a 2-foot-wide door. However, if it's summer, the boards are probably as swollen as they will ever get; no need to allow for expansion.

A good frame can be made using a router. Cut the rails long enough to allow you to cut approximately 1-inch tenons on each end. The tenons, which can be cut with a router, should be as thick as the panel.

To groove the rails and the stiles, set up a jig to hold the pieces on edge and provide bearing for the router. Sandwich the rail or stile between two pieces of 2 × 3 or 2 × 4 (or four pieces for more bearing) and

385

*Making a raised panel with hand tools:
a. Cutting the edge of the raised portion
of the panel. b. Planing the bevels.*

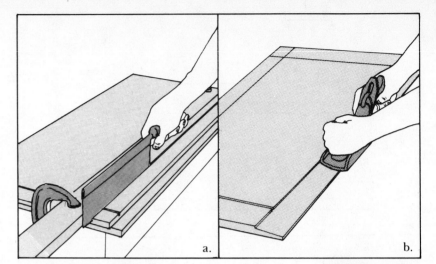

a.

b.

tise at each end. The mortises thus would have to be cut with hammer and chisel or with a mortiser on a drill press.

A plain panel can be cut from a piece of plywood. But a raised panel should be cut from solid lumber. Whether or not you'll have to glue up stock for the panel will depend upon its size.

A raised panel can be made with a shop saw (table or radial arm) or with skilled planing with a hand plane. A raised panel with a relatively narrow beveled area, say ¾ inch wide, can be created with a router. This sort of panel has a distinctive appearance all its own. A shouldered panel, in which the area of reduced thickness has a flat, rather than a beveled, face can also be made with a router. A shop tool called a shaper, the router's big brother, can also be used to make raised panels, and it is so used in production-line situations.

With a hand plane, the task involves marking the width of the band to be beveled with a marking gauge, then scoring the panel along the marks with a backsaw to a depth of about $1/16$ inch. Then the panel must be beveled with a plane, tapering the band from the score to the edge. Not easy to do well.

With a table saw, the panel must also be scored about $1/16$ inch deep to mark the inner perimeter of the beveled band and to create the band's shoul-

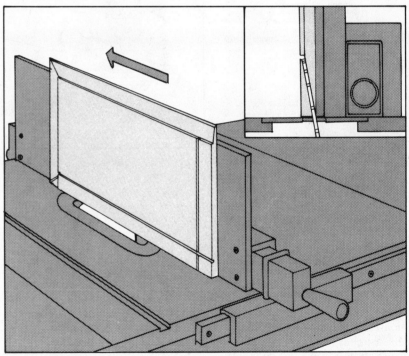

A raised panel is easily made with a table saw. First, cut the edge of the raised portion of the panel, then cut the bevels, standing the panel against a high facing attached to the rip fence.

der. You have to remove the saw guard and splitter to do this, so be careful. After these

cuts have been made, move the fence to the left side of the blade and attach a tall wooden facing

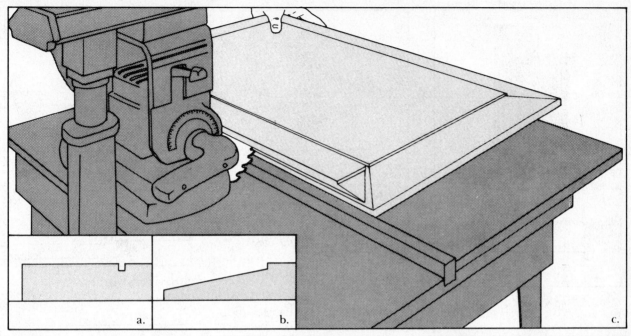

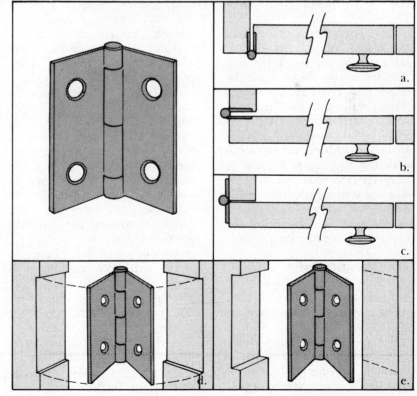

Making a raised panel with a radial arm saw: a. Cut the edge of panel's raised area. b. Cut the bevels. c. This is handled as a ripping process, with the blade and motor locked in a nearly horizontal position.

to it. Then set it to within $^3/_{16}$ inch of the blade. Tilt the blade to about 15 degrees from vertical (about 75 degrees on the saw's indicator). Raise the blade the width of the band. When you are sure it is correctly set (you might want to make a test cut or two on expendable boards), cut the bevel.

Butt hinge: a. Mounted on a flush door. b. Mounted on an overlapping door. c. Alternate mounting on an overlapped door. d. A hinge gain can be cut for one leaf in the door and one in the frame for a flush mounting. e. An alternative is to cut a gain for both leaves in the door and none in the frame.

387

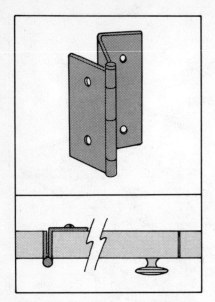

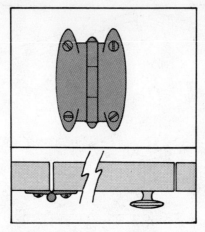

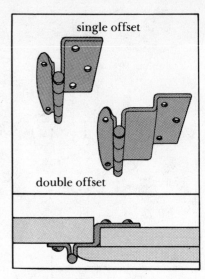

single offset

double offset

Semiconcealed offset hinges and their installation.

Concealed offset hinge and its installation.

Surface hinge and its installation.

The setup for a radial arm saw is a bit more involved. First set the saw for bevel ripping, with the saw in the outward position and tilted to the 80- to 85-degree mark on the bevel scale. Set the depth of cut by moving the saw toward or away from the column and locking it with the rip clamp. It may be necessary to use an 8-inch blade to avoid striking the column. To make the cuts, the work is moved past the blade, doing the end grain, then the long grain.

Hinges and Pulls

Before the finished doors can be installed, you have to have hinges. And once they are installed, you usually have to install some sort of knob, handle or pull so that the doors can be opened. And a catch has to be installed to keep them closed.

The type of hinge you use depends to some degree upon what sort of door it is. There are butt hinges, surface hinges, offset hinges and semiconcealed hinges.

Butt hinges are used on flush and overlapping doors. They are commonplace, easy to find, cheap to buy. Installed, only the barrel of the hinge is visible. The hinge can be installed so that one leaf is mortised into the door, while the other is mortised into the face frame, or space for both leaves can be made in the door by cutting an extra deep mortise there and surface-mounting the hinge at the face frame.

This is not a good hinge to use when mounting plywood doors, since the end grain of the plywood won't hold the screws well. For flush doors, it is better to use offset hinges, which have one regular leaf and one oversized, L-shaped leaf that is screwed fast to both the edge and face of the door.

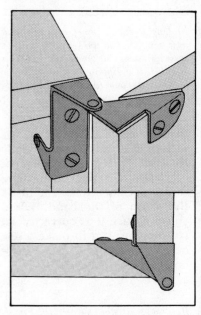

Pivot hinge and its installation.

You could also use surface hinges in this situation. Surface hinges are designed to be seen.

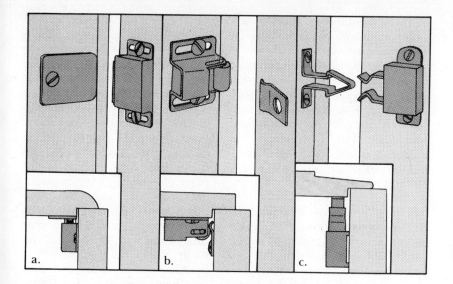

Door catches: a. Magnetic. b. Single-roller. c. Friction.

There are varieties made for flush doors, as well as special ones for lipped doors. These are much easier to install than butt hinges, since there's no mortising to do and because alignment of the hinge pins—important for the door to be free-swinging—is easier.

Perhaps the most commonly used hinge with lipped doors is the semiconcealed hinge. Installed, one leaf and the barrel of this hinge are visible, while the second leaf is hidden by the door. There are double-offset varieties available for use with lipped doors, and simple offset varieties for use with overlapping doors. If you use the double-offset variety, be sure the rabbet is matched to the hinge.

Pivot hinges, still another type, are practically invisible when installed at the top and bottom of overlapping doors. The door leaf fits into a shallow, angled rabbet cut into the door's edge, while the other leaf mounts on the face frame.

Unless your doors are unusually large—more than 3 feet high or 2 feet wide—you will need only two hinges for each. Usually the door with two hinges has them located a quarter of the way from the top and bottom edges. But in a run of cabinets with different-size doors that are all aligned top or bottom, you may want to align the hinges too.

Door pulls come in endless variety. Clearly, you'll want to match the pulls on the doors and the drawers, and, depending upon the type you use, you may want to match the hinges too. There are wooden, plastic, metal, glass and ceramic knobs of varying shapes and sizes. There are handles and latches. You can even make your own pulls. Use your imagination.

There are three basic types of catches. Magnetic catches have a magnet in a plastic or metal mounting that is attached to the cabinet, and a striking plate that is attached to the door. The magnet catches the striker plate and holds the door closed. Friction catches have a ball-headed screw or similar device for mounting on the door and a pincer device to catch and hold it for mounting on the cabinet. These have to be carefully aligned, but they work well. The roller catch, which can be regarded as a variation on the friction catch but is its own distinct type, has a door-mounted roller that rides over a humped plate on the cabinet when the door is closed, keeping it closed.

Constructing the Drawers

The drawer is a storage compartment. It's an excellent one, because it allows you to segregate items to be stored, and it stores them in clean, out-of-sight places. Yet when you want them, a tug brings them out where you can easily see them. No peering into dark, just-out-of-reach corners.

For the cabinetmaker, the drawer is the acid test. Because of all the pushing and pulling that a drawer is subjected to, it has to be well constructed to survive. And knowing that a good drawer is not easy to make, that's where judges of cabinetmaking look. If the drawer is well made, they fig- **389** ure, then the cabinetmaker should have been able to craft a sound cabinet as well. Keep in mind, then, that the drawers you make will be a measure of the cabinets you have made.

There are three basic types of drawers, and, not so surprisingly, they correspond to the types of doors there are: flush, overlapping and lipped. The flush drawer, of course, fits flush with the face frame. The overlapping drawer seats against the face frame, while the lipped drawer is rabbeted to fit into and against it. Your choice of drawers, clearly, will be influenced by your choice of doors.

But there's more to consider than that. Don't confine the drawers in your cabinets to the expected locations and uses. Because of their capacity to bring what's stored out of the cabinet, drawers are delightful substitutes for the shelves you'd store your heavy mixer or electric grain mill on. You can make

drawers shallow or deep, or build in partitions, even tiered racks for pots and pans.

A drawer shelf hidden behind closed doors need be only a tray with pronounced sides. It doesn't have to have a front or back, so long as the bottom is sturdy enough. Just how you design and construct the drawers in your cabinets is up to you, so long as you master the basics of drawer construction.

There are two elements to drawer construction. First, the pieces must be fabricated and assembled. Then the drawer has to be installed in the cabinet in such a way that it opens and closes without binding.

The drawer has a front and a back, two sides and a bottom. Almost invariably, the front is a piece of ¾-inch stock, usually solid lumber, while the sides and back range from ½ inch to ¾ inch in thickness, either plywood or lumber. The bottom is usually ¼-inch plywood or

hardboard. The drawers can be as shallow or as deep as you want to make them.

There are literally a dozen or more ways to craft and assemble these pieces. The most simplistic is to use butt joints throughout, gluing and nailing the sides, front and back together, then tacking the bottom onto the frame they form. If you aren't particular, such a drawer might do, though it won't look like much (because it isn't much). A far stronger drawer has the bottom riding in a groove and the front and sides joined with a double-dado joint and the sides and back joined with a dado-and-rabbet joint.

In between these extremes are rabbet, dado and dovetail joints of one sort or another.

Decide first how you are going to join your drawers. Don't necessarily select the most complex joint. Dovetails aren't any stronger than dado or rabbet joints unless they are very

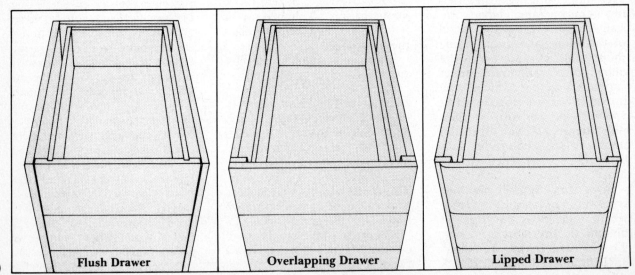

| **Flush Drawer** | **Overlapping Drawer** | **Lipped Drawer** |

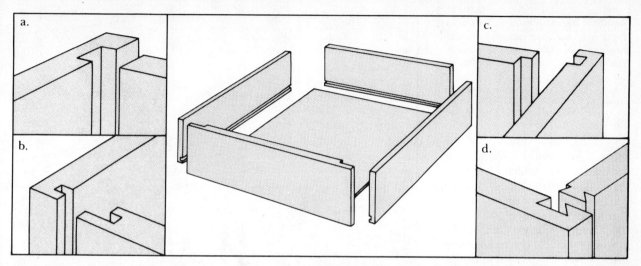

Constructing a drawer using simple butt and rabbet joints. Optional joints to use in constructing a drawer are: a. Dado. b. Double dado (often called a drawer corner joint). c. Dado and rabbet. d. Dovetail dado.

skillfully made. Stick with a tightly fitted butt joint, well glued and securely nailed.

Just how to fit the drawers to the case, that is, how big to make them, depends upon the type of drawer you are making and what sort of guides you'll be using.

An excellent albeit expensive solution is to use commercial drawer slides. These metal tracks attach to drawer and case with screws, as detailed on the packaging. Drawers suspended on these tracks glide open and closed without a hitch in all kinds of weather. The slides have built-in stops to keep the drawer from gliding all the way out of the case onto the floor. But the drawer is easily removed for cleaning.

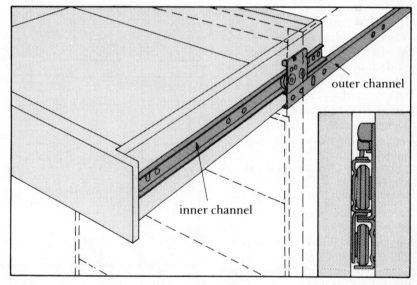

outer channel

inner channel

Commercial drawer slides are the most durable and troublefree system for supporting and guiding the opening and closing of drawers.

Perhaps the nicest thing about commercial slides is that they take no extra fabrication and they are easy to install. But there are other, considerably less expensive options open to you: side runners and center runners.

A center runner is installed beneath the drawer. Installing it is a bit cumbersome, and it isn't entirely satisfactory in use. But if you have a very wide drawer, it should be supported in the center, and the center runner does that. The center runner is **391**

Installing a center runner: Groove a length of 2 x 2 long enough to extend from the face frame to the case back. Nail it in place, with the groove bottom flush with the edge of the rail. Attach a strip of wood just smaller than the groove to the bottom of the drawer.

most frequently found in cabinetry assembled with a series of horizontal frames with dust panels in them; these frames are an integral part of the casework, and they serve, among other things, to separate one drawer space from another. In this situation, a center runner is a natural part of the frame. The drawer is supported by the frame and is merely guided by the runner. But in the type of cabinet you'll be making, the center runner would have to extend from face frame to case back. It would support the drawer as well as guide it.

A simple ¾-inch square strip of hardwood will do, but barely. The back of the drawer that is to ride this runner should extend below the bottom and should be notched to accept the runner. This is the simplest way to do it, though it is also the least durable. The life of the drawer can be extended by plowing a groove a tad wider than the runner in a strip of hardwood

Installing side runners: a. Mark the position of the runner on the inside of the drawer support block. b. Mark the centerline of the runner on the outside of the case. c. Attach the runner with screws. d. Groove the drawer sides for the runner.

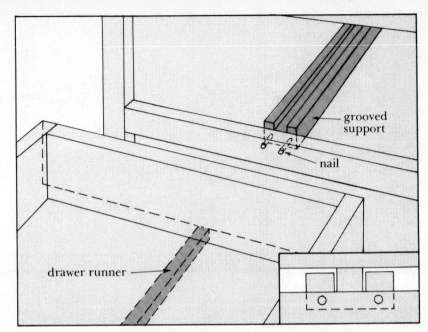

grooved support

nail

drawer runner

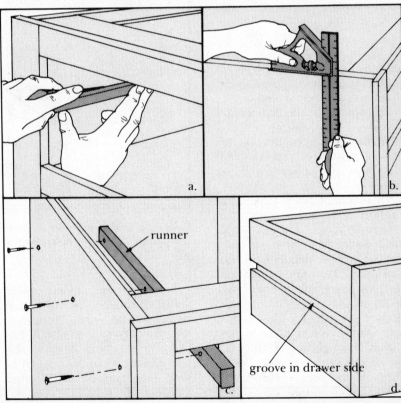

a.

b.

runner

groove in drawer side

c.

d.

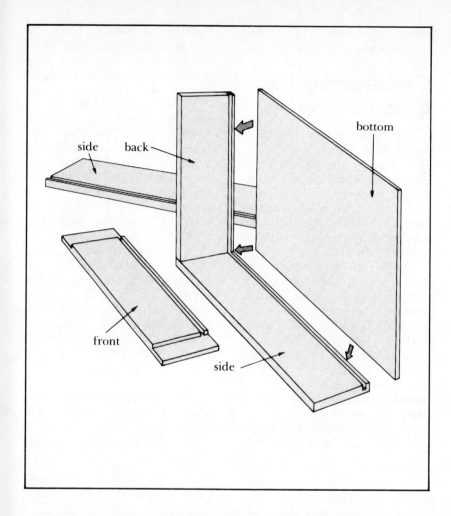

side   back

bottom

front

side

Assembling a drawer: Fasten a side and the back together, then slip the bottom into place. Then attach the second slide and the front.

At this point, you should have determined how you are going to join your drawers and how you are going to install them. Still to decide is whether they'll be flush, overlapping or lipped. And that's probably been decided too, by the style of doors you've built.

Now to make them.

Where you use the overlapping drawer front, the front that overlaps is a false front, unless you either fabricate it from a board that's 1½ inches thick or use a stopped-dado or dovetail joint to join front to sides. You've got to have ¾ inch of stock overlapping or the drawers won't match the doors. With the thick board, you can cut a ¾-inch-deep perimeter rabbet and join front and sides with a rabbet joint. If you choose the false front approach, you construct the drawer as a box, then glue and screw the false front to the structural front.

Where you use commercial drawer slides, you have to make the drawer narrower than the opening to accommodate the glides. Generally, you need a ½ inch space between drawer and case on each side for the slides. The front has to be designed to hide the slides when the drawer is closed. A wide rabbet will do it, and provide a joint as well.

It's a good idea to extend the sides of the drawer beyond the drawer back. The sides can then

that you then attach to the bottom of the drawer. The runner fits into the groove.

When using the center runner approach, be sure to install kickers, against which the top edges of the drawer sides will ride at each side of the cabinet. The kickers prevent the drawer from diving floorward when you pull it open.

A far better approach for the cabinets you'll be making is to use side runners. You'll have the drawer firmly supported on

both sides. You won't need kickers.

Use strips of ½-inch by ¾-inch wood for the runners. In the drawer sides, plow a ¾-inch-wide by ½-inch-deep groove for the runner to fit into. To allow the drawers to slide without binding, run a plane along the runners, skimming about ¹/₃₂ inch from them. Then wax them well. The runners are glued and nailed either to the sides of the case or to spacers attached to the sides.

act as a stop when the drawer is closed, and they can act as kickers when the drawer is open.

If side runners are being used, the drawer sides should be ¾ inch thick. Otherwise, ½-inch stock will do.

With all these factors in mind, lay out and cut out your drawer pieces. Plow a groove in each piece for the bottom, cut rabbets in the front and dadoes in the sides. The front can be gussied up to match the doors at this point. The edges can be beveled, rounded over or otherwise shaped. You can cut a beveled band around the front to match a raised-panel door.

Dry-fit the drawer, and if all is well, glue it together. Glue and nail only the sides to the front and back. Do not glue the bottom in its groove. Be sure, of course, that the drawer is square when you clamp it.

All that remains is to fit the drawers in the cabinet and attach pulls. The drawer pulls,

naturally, will match those used on the doors.

Constructing the Counter Top

Putting a top on your cabinet is the final step in its construction. Usually, the counter top is constructed and installed after all the cabinets are installed in the kitchen. A single counter ties them all together. But you can build a single freestanding cabinet with its own top.

In brief, the routine is to construct a base for the counter, called a core, using particle board or plywood. The core is then covered with a finish material, be it plastic laminate, ceramic tile or some other stuff. A backsplash is usually a part of the finished counter, but a number of variables govern when it is installed.

A very popular alternative, and one that's difficult to make

yourself, is butcher block. In this situation, there is no core; the counter is one thick slab, glued up from narrow strips of hard maple.

If you choose this alternative, the most rational approach would be to purchase the counter ready-made and install it yourself. To fabricate your own butcher block requires a great deal of millwork, surfacing hard maple for gluing up. And the gluing is a major endeavor of its own, requiring dozens of bar clamps. After gluing, the counter must be carefully surfaced and finished. Try gluing up a small butcher-block-style cutting board, then decide for yourself whether you really want to make your own butcher-block counter tops.

It can be done. But it's a lot of work.

The quicker, less expensive, more manageable project is to construct a core and cover it with plastic laminate or tile.

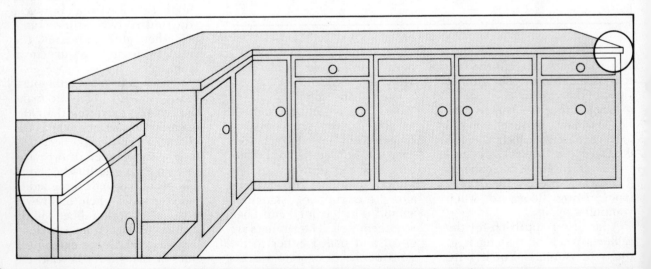

394 *The usual counter top has a 1½-inch-thick core. It overhangs the cabinet front and sides by 1 inch.*

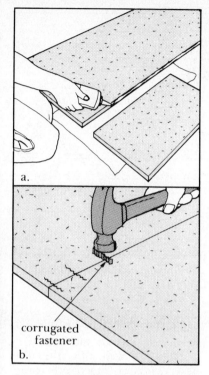

Constructing the core for an L-shaped counter top: a. Spread glue on the edges of the two pieces forming the L. b. Press the two pieces together and drive corrugated fasteners into the core across the seam.

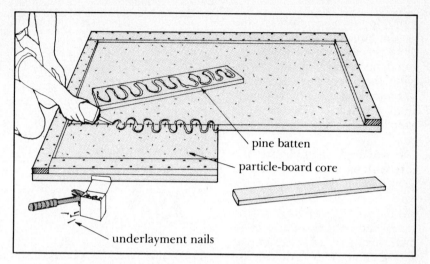

The finished thickness of the core can be achieved by gluing and nailing battens to the bottom of the core. Install battens around the perimeter of the core and across any seams.

The counter must cover all the cabinets and project an inch beyond the last counter on each end of the run and in front. That is, in a straight run of cabinets, the counter will be 2 inches longer than the run and 1 inch wider than the cabinets are deep. The core will ultimately be 1½ inches thick. It can be made by gluing two pieces of particle board together or by gluing and nailing battens to one side of a piece of particle board. Using the battens is probably a bit more economical, but laminating two pieces of particle board will probably be done faster and be a bit stronger.

In any case, take your measurements and lay them out on your particle board. If the counter is longer than 8 feet or if it makes a turn, you can join two pieces of particle board with

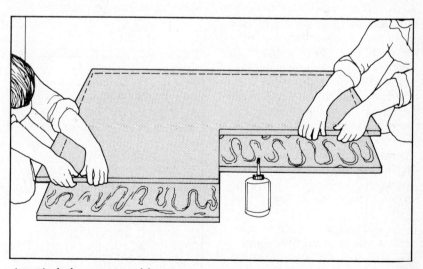

A particularly strong—and heavy—core can be made by bonding two particle-board layers together. Lay one core element on the floor, against a wall, and set the second element on edge atop it, leaning against the wall. Spread glue, then "close" the core, as you would lower the lid on a trunk.

395

a simple butt joint. Spread glue on the edges to be joined, butt them together and drive corrugated fasteners into the pieces, tying them together. Space the fasteners about 1½ inches apart along the seam. Turn the core over and drive in more fasteners.

If you are going to bolster the core with battens, apply them to what will be the bottom of the core. Begin by cutting strips to outline the perimeter of the core. The battens should be ¾ inch thick, of course, and at least 2 inches wide. You can use particle board, but lumber is better. Glue and nail them in place. Cover each joint in the counter top with a batten 4 to 6 inches wide to reinforce it.

Laminating two complete units to make a solid core simply requires you to build a second counter unit of particle board, being sure that you don't have joints in the same place in both. Spread the glue on both core elements. Remember that they have to be precisely aligned. It's best to have a helper when laying one element atop the other. Particle board is relatively heavy; don't be too sure you can handle the job alone. When the two elements are aligned, clamp them, at one or two spots, then drive underlayment nails through one piece into the other. Don't drive nails into both faces.

Now lay out any holes that have to be cut into the counter, for the sink or a counter-top range, for example. Use a saber saw to actually cut such openings.

This is the time to add the

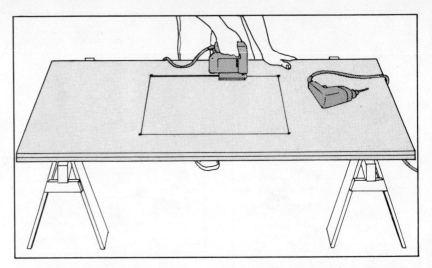

After marking the sink opening on the core, cut it out with a saber saw. Drill a hole at each corner to ease starting the cut for each side of the opening.

backsplash. The backsplash is used to protect the wall adjoining the counter from spills and splashes. If the wall doesn't need to be protected because of how it is finished, the backsplash can be omitted. For example, a tiled counter can have a course or more of tiles put on the wall, obviating the need to be protected because of how it is finished, the lumber or particle board, ¾ inch thick and 3½ to 4 inches

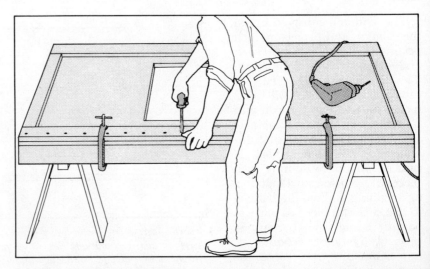

Glue and clamp the backsplash to the core, then drive screws through the core into it.

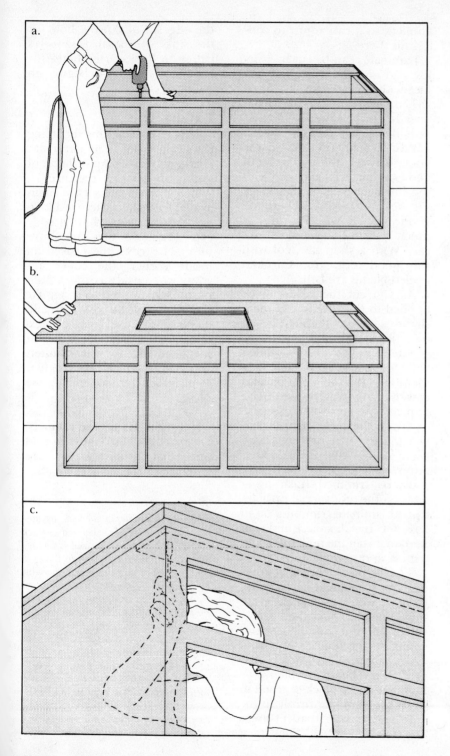

wide. Then glue and nail it to the back edge of the core. At this point the core is completed.

If the core is to be covered with plastic laminate, it is much easier to apply the laminate, then install the top. But tiling is better done after the counter is installed.

Installing the counter is simply a matter of positioning it on the cabinets and driving screws through the top crosspieces into the core. Obviously, you have to match the length of the screws to the combined thickness of the core and the crosspieces so you don't drive the screws all the way through the finished surface.

Because particle board has no grain structure, it doesn't hold screws very well. Be sure you don't make the pilot holes for the screws too large, for this will only compound the problem. You *do* need pilot holes, but rather than using the work-saving combination bit to drill and countersink the holes in one operation, bore the proper-size shank hole in the crosspieces, then bore very fine pilot holes in the core.

Don't glue the counter in place. You may live to regret it.

Applying a Plastic Laminate

Plastic laminates are popular for covering counters because

Installing the counter top: a. Drill holes through the upper crosspieces. b. Position the counter top. c. Drive screws through the crosspieces into the core.

397

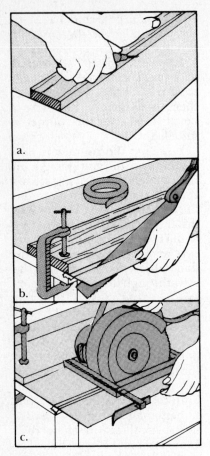

Cutting plastic laminate: a. Score the good surface deeply with an awl, then carefully break it. b. With the laminate firmly supported and the good side up, cut with a crosscut saw held at a very shallow angle. c. Turn the good side down to cut laminate with circular or saber saw.

they are durable, colorful, relatively inexpensive and certainly easy to apply. There are many different brands, but all are handled in the same way. The material is sensitive to humidity in the same way wood is; it should be stored for several **398** days in the kitchen before it's

applied, so it can adjust to conditions there.

Laminates can be cut by scoring a groove into the good surface with repeated strokes of an awl, then breaking it along the line. It can be sawed with most saws if you use caution. With a handsaw, maintain a very acute angle between the line of teeth and the surface, and cut with the finish side up. With a saber saw or circular saw, cut with the good side down. Provide as much backing support as you can. With a shop saw, cut with the good side up. Carbide-tipped blades are best.

As you cut the pieces to be applied to the core, make them slightly—about ¼ inch in all directions—oversize.

The laminates are applied with contact cement. Remember, this is volatile and evil-smelling stuff, so exercise appropriate care when using it.

Apply the edge bands first, starting with the narrow edges, then doing the front edges. After each piece is attached, it must be trimmed flush using either a file or a special carbide-tipped laminate trimming bit in a router. Install a piece and trim it, then install the next piece and trim it, and so on.

The big pieces for the counter top can be aligned by covering the core with paper, then laying the laminate atop that. Carefully pull out the paper and complete the bond a little at a time. When the surface is covered, use a laminate roller or a hammer and a block of wood to press the laminate firmly to the core and ensure that all areas are firmly bonded. Then trim

the edges. Cut out the hole for the sink with a saber saw. It's better to drill starter holes for the saw than to try to begin with a plunge cut.

Laying Tile

If you've come this far, tiling the counter will be no particular challenge. It's a simple matter of gluing tile blocks to the core.

Investigate what sort of tile is available. Usually there is a variety of trim tiles including edge caps, bullnose tiles and cove tiles. The cove tiles cover an inside corner, the edge caps cover an outside corner. Bullnose tiles are used to terminate the tiled area, but they can also be used to cover outside corners. Unless you use wood or metal edging for the counter, you will need at least regular square tiles and some bullnose tiles.

Begin by laying out all the tile. It's like dry-fitting the cabinets. It certainly doesn't hurt to find out what problems you are

Applying laminate to the counter top core: a. Do edges first; spread contact cement on both core edge and laminate, then apply laminate to core. b. Using a router or a file, trim the excess laminate before applying another piece. c. After the edges are covered, apply laminate to the backsplash face. d. Doing the counter top itself can be tricky; lay sheets of paper on the core and put the laminate atop it, then remove a little of the paper at a time, completing the bond. e. and f. Use a hammer and block or a laminate roller to guarantee a firm bond over every square inch of counter. g. The completed and properly trimmed counter top has uniform bevels along each edge.

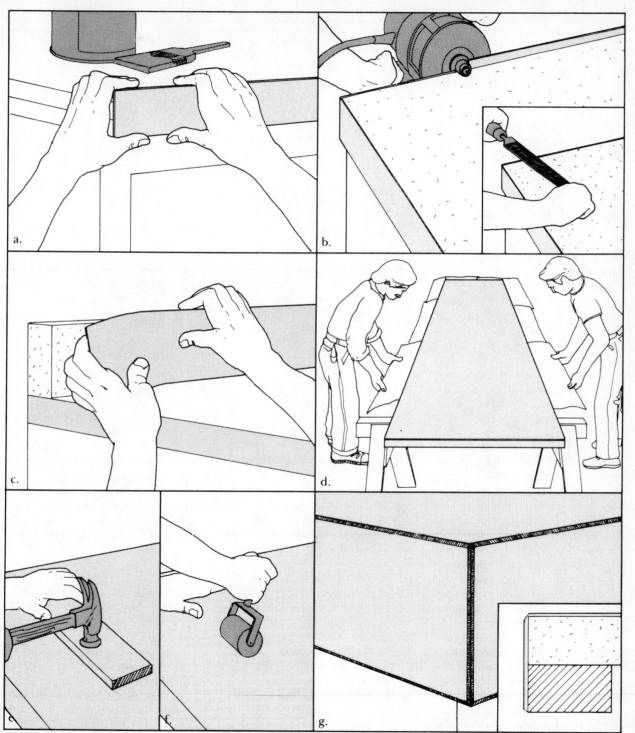

a.

b.

c.

d.

e.

f.

g.

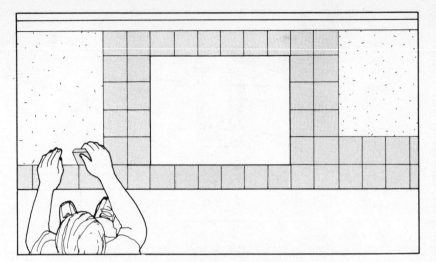

going to run into and see if you can work out easy solutions. Lay out the edge tiles first, then start at the sink opening, if there is one, and spread out the regular tiles. Try to work out an arrangement that relegates the tiles that have to be cut to the most obscure possible location. Certainly don't have them at the sink.

Decide whether or not you will tile the wall, and if so, how much of it. At the least, you should have a single course forming a tile backsplash on the wall. But quite often, the entire area between the counter and the wall cabinets will be tiled. If you are going onto the wall with tile, you can either use cove tiles to make the corner, or you can butt the wall tiles atop the counter tiles. If your backsplash is to be only a single course, make it a course of bullnose tiles.

If there are any special layout details you are afraid you might forget 'til you actually begin tiling, sketch them on the core. You certainly won't need to scribe the entire layout on the core, but in intricate spots, some notes can help.

Bond the tiles to the counter with mastic. There are other adhesives you could use, including epoxy adhesives, but the mastic sold at the tile dealer's store is more than adequate. When you buy the mastic, you'll

400

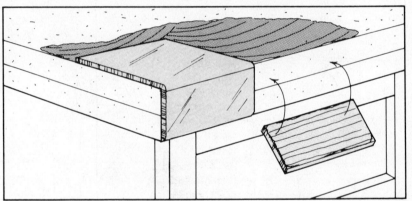

Apply tiles to the edges first. Spread mastic on the back of an edge tile, and position it on the core with a slight twisting motion. Spread mastic on the core, and lay tiles along its perimeter.

get a notched spreader that should help you to apply just about the right amount of mastic. If you don't get one, ask for it.

Start with the edge tiles. Instead of spreading mastic on the core edges, put it on the back of the individual tiles as you lay them. Set them in place with a slight twisting motion, which helps to spread the mastic. Line up these tiles carefully.

With the edges defined by the tiles, begin laying the regular tiles. Most such tiles have lugs on the edges that facilitate establishing the proper spacing. If your tiles don't have them, try to find tile spacers. These are small plastic crosses that can be pried up—carefully—before the mastic sets, or left in place and grouted over. An alternative is to use lengths of damp cord of the appropriate size.

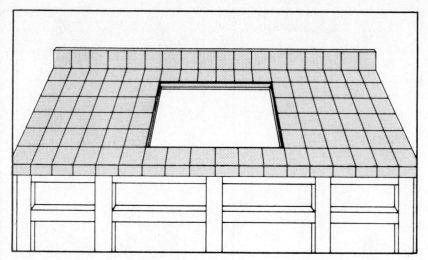

The completed counter top has any fractional tiles located in obscure positions whenever possible.

An old windshield-wiper blade is an excellent tool for spreading grout. Work the compound into the joints with a toothbrush handle. Sponge off the excess, and when dry, polish with a piece of towel.

Stretch them between the courses of tile to establish the spacing, removing them as the mastic sets.

Spread mastic over only a small area. Don't cover the entire counter core, because the mastic will probably set before you get all the tiles laid.

Tiles that must be cut can be cut with a tile cutter rented from the tile dealer. A somewhat less satisfactory technique is to score the glazed surface with a glass cutter, then place the tile over a nail, glazed side up, and snap the tile along the scored line. To notch corners or edges, nibble at the tile with tile nippers. Tiles that have to be cut should be placed along the wall or at the ends of the counter.

The mastic should be allowed to set at least 24 hours before grouting. There are a variety of grouts available. Mix the one you select according to the manufacturer's instructions. Spread it over the surface with a rubber float or a squeegee (an old windshield wiper blade will work swell). Work the grout into all gaps, using an old toothbrush handle, for example, to force it into voids. Sponge off the excess. When a haze forms on the tiles, buff them with a dry, soft cloth to remove the grout film.

There are, of course, many other options you have in constructing a counter top for your cabinets, just as there are in every phase of building the cabinets. But now that you understand just how the cabinets are assembled, you can work out those options for yourself.

What you must do now is select the materials you'll use and work out the specific plan you'll follow.

Tools and Materials

Cherry cabinets, made with plywood cases. Need some kind of cherry plywood to make the doors, though. Let's see, probably lumber-core. And some of that regular wood for cross-pieces. Hinges and pulls. Need some of those, and nails and screws and all that. Hmmm.

You are getting serious about building your own harvest kitchen cabinets when you start to think about the materials you'd use, about the tools you'd need. These are subjects that pervade cabinetmaking. You can't think about process without interrelating the materials and the tools involved. And you can't think about materials **401** without thinking about what you'd do with them and how you'd do it. And thinking about tools is foolish unless at the same time you think about what you'd use them for and whether you really need them to do what you want to do and with what materials you want to do it.

By now you should have a pretty good idea of the techniques involved. Along the way, you've picked up fundamental information on materials and tools. You've got to nail down a few more details about materials and tools, then you can begin to plan your cabinets in earnest.

Materials

Wood is the material you'll need the most of. In the complex project, you'll use dimension lumber, some hardwood, softwood and hardwood plywood in both veneer-core and lumber-core varieties, surely some particle board for counters, perhaps even some hardboard. By simplifying the plan, you can eliminate the hardwood and hardwood plywood and nix the hardboard. Here's how to select what you need.

Lumber

Lumber is the wood that comes from the sawmill. Solid wood. No glue, no fillers, no additives. There are two basic kinds of lumber, hardwood and softwood. The category in which a wood is placed has nothing to do with the actual hardness or softness of the wood itself, it has to do with the tree. If the tree is deciduous, dropping its leaves annually, then

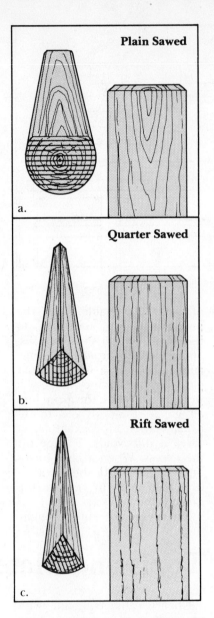

the wood is a hardwood. If the tree is evergreen, bearing needles and cones, then the wood is

Wood will shrink and distort as it dries, and the general characteristics of the distortion can be predicted, based on where in the log it is cut from.

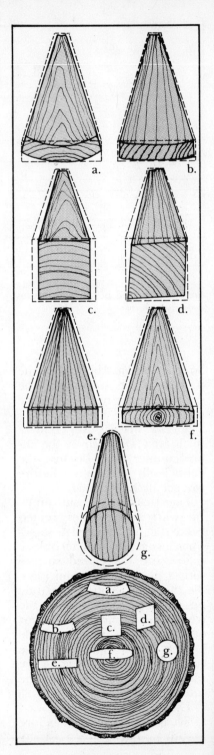

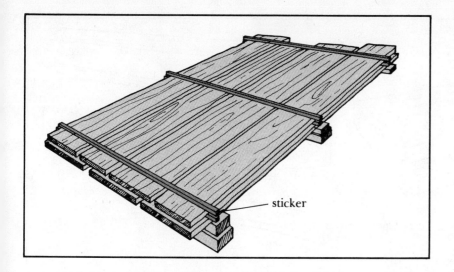

sticker

Stacking newly sawed boards for drying. Stickers placed between layers allow air to circulate completely around each board.

a softwood. In fact, some hardwoods, like poplar, are softer than some softwoods, like fir.

What's important at this point, perhaps, is the difference that these two categories make to you. Softwood is widely available, and is sold in a predictable, standard way throughout the country. Hardwood is difficult to find and is sold in a less predictable, though ostensibly a standard, way.

There are differences of appearance too. You are probably accustomed to seeing hardwood furniture and cabinets. You have a good idea of what cherry, maple, oak and walnut look like. You probably fancy having cabinets fashioned of those woods in your harvest kitchen. You probably also have a good picture of pine, the most common softwood lumber, and you may have some reservations about pine cabinets. Don't commit yourself too quickly.

There are similarities between hardwood lumber and softwood lumber. They all come from trees. They are sawed in much the same way, dried in much the same way.

Sawing. Boards are sawed from logs. There are several ways to do it. The easiest, and thus the most common, method is to saw tangent to the growth rings, squaring off the log. The first cuts remove the bark and create flat surfaces. Then boards are ripped from the log. Hardwoods sawed this way are called plain sawed, while softwoods cut this way are referred to as being flat grained. Wood sawed this way will shrink less in thickness than in width.

Another way to do it is to cut perpendicular to the growth rings. This is slower and generates more waste. Hardwoods sawed this way are called quarter sawed, while softwoods so cut are referred to as being edge grained. These boards will shrink more in width than in thickness.

A seldom seen compromise method is called rift sawing. Here the cuts are made at an angle to the growth rings, usually about 45 degrees. It is very unlikely you'll find any but plain sawed boards at the lumberyard.

Seasoning. When a tree is still a tree, it is full of sap. As soon as it is cut, turning it into a log, the sap begins to evaporate. As the wood dries, it shrinks. The shrinkage occurs largely across the grain, rather than with the grain, so boards will shrink in width and thickness, but little in length.

The wood will continue to dry, or season, until it reaches a certain moisture level, usually between 12 and 18 percent. There it will remain. The level can be further reduced, and the seasoning process much hastened, by drying the wood in kilns. The moisture level in kiln-dried lumber is routinely reduced to 10 to 15 percent, and for some cabinetmaking uses, even to 7 or 8 percent. Air-drying can take a year or more, kiln-drying a matter of weeks.

Regardless of how the wood is to be dried, and frequently a combination of methods is involved, the green wood is carefully stacked. The first layer of boards is elevated on blocks. A bit of a gap is left between boards. Then thin strips of wood called stickers are laid across the boards, and a second **403**

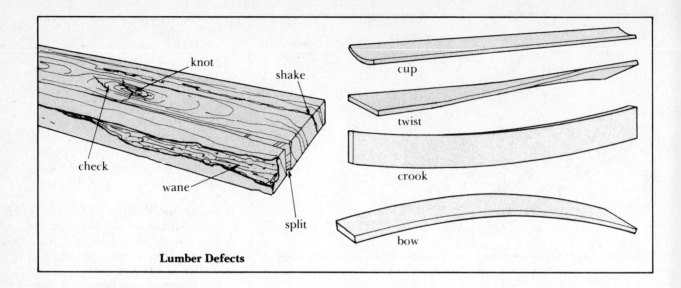

Lumber Defects

layer is put in place. Then more stickers, directly atop the first ones, and more boards. More stickers and more boards. Each board thus has air virtually all around it.

Wood destined to be air-dried is left stacked like this for a year or more, depending upon the thickness of the boards. The general rule is to allow a board to air-dry a year per inch of thickness. Some cabinetmakers who buy green lumber and season it themselves will have boards seasoning for years, even decades.

Lumber headed for the kiln is often left outdoors for a preliminary seasoning, then moved, still stacked with stickers, into the kiln. There steam is introduced. Gradually, the amount of steam is reduced and the heat is increased. This technique not only dries the wood, it does it in a way that reduces the stresses ordinarily found in air-dried wood.

Of course, all wood "breathes." This is an inaccurate way of saying that it will give off and take on moisture, depending upon the humidity. When it does this, it swells and shrinks, usually imperceptibly, but enough that a wise cabinetmaker compensates for it in his designs.

When you acquire lumber, regardless of whether it's a hardwood or a softwood, whether it's green or seasoned, whether it's been air-dried or kiln-dried, you should stack it with stickers, just as was done at the sawmill. If at all possible, stack it in the kitchen or a warm shop. Give it time to acclimate itself to the temperatures and humidity levels in its new home. Avoid building your cabinets in one climate, natural or artificial, then installing them in a significantly different climate. The first thing the wood will do is adjust, changing size—and sometimes shape—and creating unwarranted stresses.

Defects. Lumber, hardwood and softwood, has defects. Would that all of it was clear and unblemished, straight and true. But it isn't. Some of the defects affect the grading, but others don't. Thus, you can avoid getting boards with knots and pitch pockets by purchasing high grades of lumber. But warping and some other defects don't enter into the grading, and you can get stuck with boards afflicted with these defects.

The most obvious defects you'll run into are those lumped together under the term warp. A warped board simply isn't straight and flat. It may be bowed or crooked, which means it is curved from end to end, either in the plane of the width (bow) or of the thickness (crook). It may be cupped, which means that it is curved from edge to edge across the width. Or it may be twisted, which is worst of all.

There are various ways in

Spiked Knot	Intergrown Knot	Encased Knot	Knot Hole	Pitch Pocket

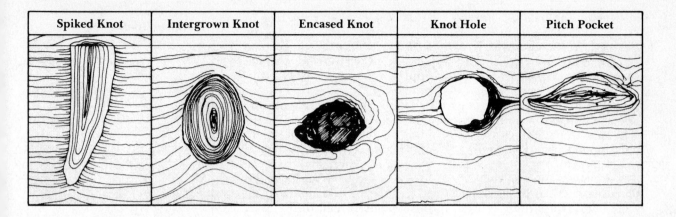

which you can attempt to remedy these defects, but you are better off trying to work around them. For example, a bowed, crooked or twisted board will usually yield many small, usable pieces, even though it would be totally unsuitable for use in one piece. A cupped board, if it isn't too severely cupped, can be planed and resawed flat. If the cupping is severe, it is sometimes possible to rip the board and plane and resaw the resulting two pieces into a usable form.

Splits, checks, and shakes are in another family of defects. All are separations in the wood. A shake is a separation between growth rings. A check is a separation across the rings, while a split is a major check that extends through the thickness of the board. All usually occur at the end of a board, and crop up during drying. The end grain gives off moisture better than the edge grain. Occasionally, a check will develop after you crosscut a board that wasn't as dry as you thought. This is one reason boards are cut to rough

sizes, then finish-cut to exact sizes by trimming a half to a full inch from each end.

The most common defects are knots and pitch pockets. All woods have knots. Pitch pockets are specialties of the softwoods, particularly pine, fir and spruce.

Pitch pockets are crevices filled with pitch, a sticky resin. No matter what you do, the pitch will continue to ooze from the pocket longer than you think it ever possibly could, and it will spoil many finishes, including paint. The best solution is to clean the pocket as thoroughly as possible with turpentine, then shellac it before finishing the board. This will seal any remaining pitch inside the pocket.

Knots are so commonplace that a whole lexicon has grown up around them. There are dimensional definitions for small, medium and large knots. There are encased, intergrown, not-firm and loose knots. There are red knots and black knots. There are spikes and branch knots.

Knots are the black holes of

woodworking. The grain eddies and swirls around a dense dark spot. Any saw strains to cut it. It resists cleaving. Nails bend in it. Resins and pitch ooze from it.

And all it is is a branch.

It's a good idea to try to steer clear of knots in your cabinet-making venture, particularly if you are a relatively inexperienced woodworker. It is true that knots in many woods are sources of great beauty, used as focal points in cabinets. But they are dealt with by craftsmen who know what they are doing—even when what they are doing is experimenting, taking a chance that their efforts will be rewarded. The exception would be if you've decided upon a knotty pine decor.

Knots—and pitch pockets—are relatively easy to avoid because they figure in lumber grading systems. The absence of knots makes a board more valued, thus winning it a higher grade than one with knots. Consequently, use a high-grade material anywhere that the wood will be exposed. No trouble with knots that way.

405

Softwood. The building industry is the biggest user of softwood. Your house surely is framed with softwood. The windows and doors are cased in it. The place is trimmed with it.

The softwoods are species like pine, fir, spruce, larch, hemlock. Most of these trees are cut into framing materials, lumber with a 2-inch or greater thickness, which is commonly called dimension lumber. But the pine is cut into 1-inch-thick boards and is commonly called board lumber. You will be primarily interested in the board lumber, at this point.

Individual sizes of board lumber are identified by their nominal sizes. There are 1 × 2s, 1 × 3s, 1 × 4s, 1 × 6s, 1 × 8s, 1 × 10s and 1 × 12s. All are actually ¾ inch thick. All are at least ½ inch narrower than their nominal sizes, with 1 × 8s, 10s and 12s being actually ¾ inch narrower. The explanation given for the discrepancy is that the nominal size is the actual size when the wood leaves the saw, but that shrinkage due to moisture loss and dressing reduces the board's cross-sectional size. Its length changes little.

It is true that lumber shrinks as it dries. And planing a board removes material. But the fact is that actual sizes of dimension and board lumber have been diminishing. Not too many years ago, the standard sizes were fractionally larger than they are now.

Regardless of the cross-sectional dimension, board lumber is delivered to the lumber-yard in lengths ranging from 8 feet up to 20 feet in 2-foot increments. It may be sold by the board foot in some places, but the most widespread approach is to sell it by the running foot.

There is no single, nationwide grading system for board lumber. The U. S. Department of Commerce has established some guidelines, and regional lumber industry associations have adopted and follow grading systems of their own.

In general terms, the material you are interested in here is classified as yard lumber. Yard lumber is graded as either Select, which is useful for finish work, or Common, which is useful for general utility or construction work. But there are numerous levels within each grade. The Select grade is subdivided into A, B, C and D levels. Grade A Select is the best of the lot, practically clear wood. Sometimes this quality of wood is graded Clear. Grade B Select lumber will have some few imperfections, such as checks or minor stains. Grades C and D have increasing numbers of imperfections, but they are still considered totally acceptable for finish work.

The Common grade is subdivided into numbered levels from 1 to 5. The differences lie in the number of knots and pitch pockets the individual boards have. Numbers 1 and 2 Common have some knots and pitch pockets but are considered to be usable without waste. Numbers 3 through 5 are usable, but with an increasing—though limited—amount of

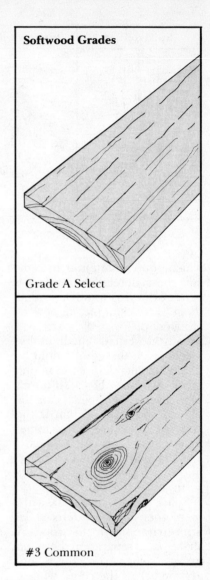

Softwood Grades

Grade A Select

#3 Common

waste. Sometimes the Number 1 grade is referred to as construction grade, Number 2 as standard grade, Number 3 as utility grade and Number 4 as economy grade.

Not every lumberyard will use

the same grading terminology, but if you ask for Select pine or Number 2 Common, you'll be understood. You may not find exactly what you want, however, if you are too picky about specific subdivisions of grades. No matter how large the yard, it's difficult for a lumberyard to stock a totally complete selection of lumber. Ordinarily, there will be a Select grade and one or two Common grades in the full complement of sizes and lengths.

The nice thing about board lumber, from the standpoint of a fledgling, underequipped woodworker, is that it is in as predictable and uniform a state as wood is ever likely to be. The sizes are the same from board to board. The surfaces are flat, square and parallel, as are the edges. It is entirely possible to build a set of cabinets using board lumber and never have to rip a board or plane an edge. You don't need a shop saw, or a jointer, or a thickness planer. And you don't have to pay for a lot of millwork.

Hardwood. Hardwood is on the other hand of lumber uniformity. It isn't uniform. The usual way to purchase it is by ordering a number of board feet of lumber, delivered in "random widths and lengths." Moreover, the local lumberyard isn't likely to have a wide selection in stock. And once you've got it, you need something better than the usual array of home handyman tools to work it.

So why bother?

Why? Because hardwoods look great. Pine is a poor match

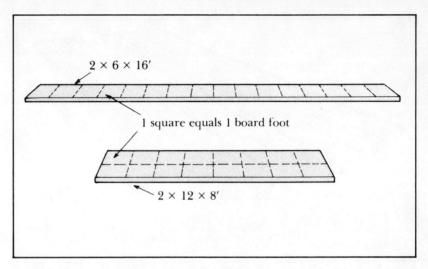

Two boards, though of different length and width, have the same board-foot measure. The board foot, a volume measure, equaling 144 cubic inches (or a piece 1 foot square by 1 inch thick), is widely used in the lumber industry, though few lumberyards use it in making retail sales.

for walnut. Or cherry. Or bird's-eye maple. Mahogany or red oak. Birch, pecan or ash. There is an astonishing array of hardwoods, many of them imported from foreign lands that are as exotic as the names of the woods. Macassar ebony. Red lauan. Zebrawood. Limba. Paldao. Primavera.

In building kitchen cabinets, it's unlikely you'll be working primavera or zebrawood. But by all means do consider working cherry or maple or oak. They are excellent woods, attractive, reasonably easy to work, and quite commonly available, if you look in the right places.

Hardwoods are cut into uniform thicknesses at the sawmill. The size of the log determines the width and length of individual boards. The goal at the

sawmill is to make maximum use of each log, so nothing is trimmed away to make boards of nice, neat widths and lengths. The ultimate user of the board, be it a furniture industry worker or an independent cabinetmaker, will decide just how to use it.

Thicknesses of hardwoods are often stated in terms of quarters of an inch. A 1-inch board is a 4/4 board. One that's 2 inches thick is an 8/4 board. Hardwood boards can be found in 4/4, 5/4, 6/4, 8/4 and greater thicknesses. As with softwoods, these are the actual thicknesses of the boards as they leave the saw. But seasoning shrinks hardwoods too, so the stated size quickly becomes a nominal size.

Hardwoods are sold by the board foot, a volume measure **407**

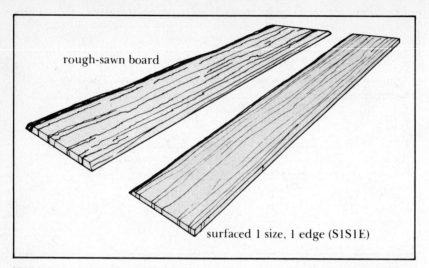

rough-sawn board

surfaced 1 size, 1 edge (S1S1E)

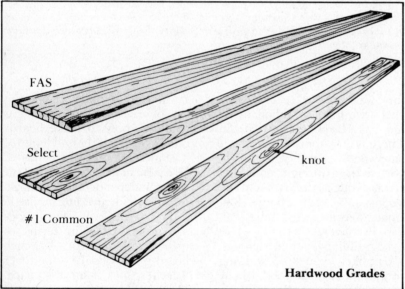

FAS

Select

knot

#1 Common

Hardwood Grades

wood surfaced on one (S1S) or both sides (S2S), and on one (S1E) or both edges (S2E), and in combinations thereof (S1S1E, S2S1E, S2S2E, S1S2E). When both sides and both edges are done, it's usually designated S4S, for surfaced four sides. If the lumberyard stocks the wood in a rough state, then the particular boards you select will be custom dressed to your specifications. There are standard dimensions for hardwoods, but you can have your wood planed to any thickness you want. The standard for a 4/4 board surfaced on one side is ⅞ inch, and surfaced on two sides ¹³/₁₆ inch. Surfacing a 5/4 board on two sides will reduce it to a thickness of 1¹/₁₆ inches.

The hardwood grading system is entirely different from the softwood system. The system was established to respond to the needs of the furniture industry, so it is based on getting as much clear wood out of each board as possible. Not only does the absence of knots and defects enter into the grade, but the width and length of the board does too.

The highest grade is Firsts, closely followed by Seconds. Invariably these grades are lumped together into Firsts and Seconds (FAS). FAS lumber must have a minimum width of 6 inches, a minimum length of 8 feet and must yield 85 to 90 percent clear cuttings. The grading is done from the poorer side of the board, curiously.

The next grade is Selects. A Select board must be 4 inches wide and 6 feet long and yield the same percentage of clear

determined by multiplying the thickness in inches times the width in inches times the length in feet and dividing by 12. A 1-foot length of 1 × 12 would be a board foot. So would a 2-foot length of 1 × 6. Board feet are always computed using the nominal sizes.

Hardwoods are stocked at the lumberyard in a rough condition. Of course, the wood must be planed before it can be used. If you haven't the equipment to do it, you should have the lumber surfaced.

Whereas with softwoods, you had no choice as to how it was surfaced, with hardwoods you usually do. You can buy the

408

cuttings as FAS boards. This grade is based on the better side; the poorer side must meet the standards for Number 1 Common grade.

Other grades include Number 1 Common, Number 2 Common, Sound Wormy, Number 3A Common and Number 3B Common. None of these grades reflects the nature of the defects so much as the amount of lumber left after the defect is eliminated.

As a practical matter, these grades may turn out to mean little or nothing to you. The grading is the servant of the hardwood furniture industry. A board's grade tells the industry woodworker just what uses he can put the board to. It tells him how much work is going to be required to extract the usable pieces from the raw board. But for the local lumberyard, the graded hardwoods are just another inventory headache.

There will be occasional exceptions, but in most instances, you'll be told to pick the boards you want from the stock on hand. This will make your job easier, but even so, there's more to buying hardwood than there is to buying softwood. The use of the board-foot measure makes it difficult to figure just how much running footage you are getting on the one hand, and on the other, just how much

the running footage you are selecting is going to cost at bill time. The grading system, if you run into it, is complicated. You've got to remember to specify the amount of surfacing you want, and what specific thickness you want.

But it's worth the trouble.

Wood Products

A lot of the materials you'll use in building your cabinets can be lumped together as wood products. They are largely wood in composition, but a lot has been done to the logs before they are sold to you. Plywood, particle board and moldings all fall into this category.

Plywood. The material you are most likely to use to construct

the cases of your cabinets is a man-made wood product called plywood. It is a wood sandwich, created by gluing thin sheets of wood together in layers. The sandwich comes in 4-foot by 8-foot panels.

Plywood is put to an enormous variety of uses, in the building industry, in the furniture industry, by almost anyone who has occasion to make things of wood. It isn't unreasonable to

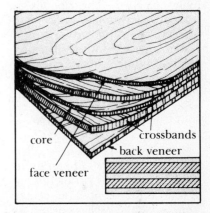

Plywood is created by gluing crisscrossing layers of wood veneers together, forming a rigid, strong and dimensionally stable panel.

core
crossbands
back veneer
face veneer

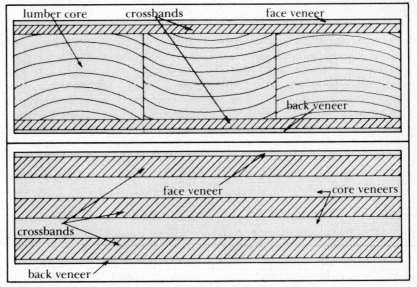

lumber core
crossbands
face veneer
back veneer

face veneer
core veneers
crossbands
back veneer

Lumber core plywood (top) has a core of solid lumber bonded between thin crossbands and surface veneers. It presents a more attractive edge and holds fasteners better than veneer core plywood (bottom).

409

think that the only mass-produced kitchen cabinets made in this country out of anything but plywood are those made of particle board or metal.

The principal virtues of plywood are its size and its stability. Both are consequences of its manufacture.

Plywood is created by unraveling colossal logs into thin sheets called veneers. A giant lathe is used. The thickness of the veneer can be controlled, knots can be cut out and the holes patched. The ribbons of veneer are chopped into 4 by 8 sheets, then crisscrossed and glued together with resin glues. An odd number of layers, either three, five or seven, is almost always used. A piece of plywood with four plies simply isn't as good as a piece with three or five plies.

The outer layers are called the face and back. The grain in them always runs parallel to the 8-foot dimension. The center veneer is called the core, and its grain usually runs in the same direction as the face and back veneers. Crossbands lie between the face and core and the back and core. The grain in them runs parallel to the short dimension of the plywood sheet. In a three-ply or a seven-ply panel, the core is in essence a crossband.

The core isn't always a veneer. Hardwood plywood is available with a lumber core, in which narrow strips of approximately ½-inch lumber are glued between crossbands and face and back veneers. The advantage of this construction is that the lumber will present a better appearance at the edges and it will hold nails, screws and dowels driven into the edge considerably better than will veneers.

Hardwood plywood is also made with a particle-board core.

The crisscrossing of grain patterns makes plywood a very strong and stable material. Regardless of humidity, it maintains its 4×8 dimensions. It doesn't check or split and rarely warps. It has strength both along and across the panel, something board lumber or glued-up stock can't offer.

There are a number of different kinds of plywood, but the two that are of interest here are the hardwood plywoods and the softwood or construction and industrial plywoods. The softwood plywoods may be the most familiar, since those having the distinct—and not particularly attractive—grain pattern that says, "Plywood!" are in this category. But since some of the woods used to manufacture these plywoods are actually hardwoods, it isn't totally accurate to call the product softwood plywood, hence the term construction and industrial plywood.

There are two basic types of plywood: interior and exterior. The difference is in the glue used to bond the veneers. In interior plywood, a water-resistant glue is used, but in exterior plywood, the glue used is waterproof. Naturally, the exterior variety is a bit more costly.

The construction and industrial plywoods are graded according to the quality of the veneers used to make them.

The highest grade veneer is designated N. It is intended to have a natural finish. Other grades are designated A through D, in order of descending quality. In applying these grades to a sheet of plywood, the first letter refers to the face veneer, the second to the back. The inner plies will be either C or D quality, depending upon the grading of the outer plies, but their grade is never specified. It is logical and proper to order plywood by the grade, face-veneer wood and type. Often, you will order a sheet of interior plywood having one or two good sides, rather than specifying an A-C or A-A grade. Unless you specify otherwise, you are likely to get fir plywood.

Construction and industrial plywood is the only such material you need to use to construct your kitchen cabinets. You'll paint the interiors of the cabinets, no doubt, and most of the exteriors will be hidden by other cabinets. Any exposed plywood can be covered with a decorative facing of sheet paneling or ¼-inch hardwood plywood. You can, as an alternative, use birch plywood, the most common of the hardwood plywoods, wherever the material will be exposed. Doors and drawer fronts can also be made of birch plywood.

Hardwood Plywood. You do have one other major plywood option, and that is the hardwood plywoods. These plywoods are faced with hardwood veneers. Think of a hardwood and it is probably available in a hardwood plywood. Your option, then, is to use hardwood plywood wherever the plywood will be exposed.

This calls for careful planning. Not all hardwood plywoods are immediately available everywhere. You may have to order the material. Such being the case, you can't just run back to the lumberyard if you run short, either because you misjudged or you made a mistake. You have to plan ahead,

order what you need, and be careful not to make mistakes.

The material is expensive. There's no reason to use it where the outer plies won't show. Use construction and industrial plywood there.

But hardwood plywood does expand your freedom to use a good hardwood for the face frames and even door frames. You won't have to feel compelled to glue up stock for exposed casework or for doors. You *can* use a matching plywood.

Perhaps the most widely used of the hardwood plywoods is birch plywood. It is just as strong, structurally, as fir plywood, and it has an attractive grain pattern. Birch plywood is frequently used to make plywood items that are going to have a natural finish or be painted. That plywood grain pattern tends to exhibit itself, even through several layers of paint.

Mahogany plywood, including plywood made from lauan mahogany, which is often simply called lauan plywood, is

another common variety. You may well use it for drawer bottoms. In fact, many lumberyards no longer stock softwood plywood in the ¼-inch thickness. Instead they stock lauan or mahogany plywood.

There are several types of hardwood plywood. You are most likely to use Type II, which is an interior type bonded with a water-resistant glue. But the material is also made with a moisture-resistant glue (Type III) and a waterproof glue (Type I).

The grading system is somewhat different from that of the other plywoods, and the terminology is different. The highest grade is Premium A or Number 1, which uses only selected, matched veneers with no defects or color contrasts. Good or Number 1 (also) grade is much the same as Premium, but the veneers are not as carefully matched. Sound or Number 2 grade will have grain and color contrasts, may have stains or streaks, but won't have obvious defects. Utility or Number 3 grade and Backing or Number 4 grade will have defects.

Like softwood plywood, hardwood plywood comes in 4-foot by 8-foot sheets. Thicknesses range from ⅛ inch through ¾ inch. Plywoods with particleboard and lumber cores are

Typical Plywood Grading Stamps

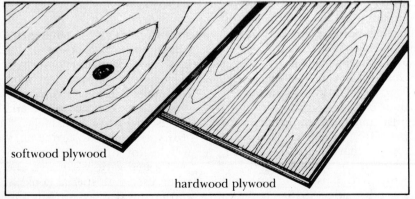

softwood plywood

hardwood plywood

Hardwood plywood has it all over softwood plywood in terms of appearance, though both are equal in terms of strength. Softwood plywood costs considerably less, however, and it is, unlike hardwood plywood, stocked by every lumberyard.

411

The best particle board—especially for covering with plastic laminates—has a layered composition with coarse particles inside, but fine particles at the surface. Coarser, less costly, single-layer particle board has the same composition throughout.

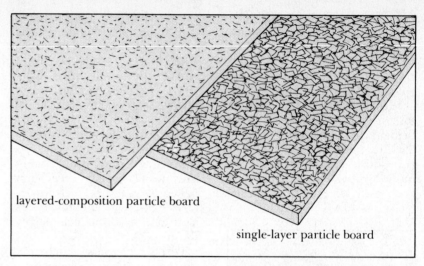

layered-composition particle board

single-layer particle board

made only in ¾-inch thicknesses.

It is probably worth pointing out that a great deal of hardwood plywood, including the commonly used birch and mahogany varieties, is imported. Since the United States is one of only four countries not using the metric system, don't be surprised to discover the plywood doesn't *quite* measure what you think it should. It may be a silly millimeter off. What this really means is that you should put a ruler to your hardwood plywood before plowing grooves. Your 6-millimeter plywood drawer bottom may rattle in its ¼-inch groove.

Particle Board. A truly man-made material is particle board. It is formed by combining glue with sawdust, wood chips or wood shavings in industrial presses. The result is a "wooden" panel. There are more than a dozen different kinds of particle board, engineered for specific uses. The most likely use you'll have for it is to make a core for your counter top, although it can be used to build the cases for cabinets.

Particle board is a heavy material, ranging from 30 to 50 pounds per cubic foot. It can be sanded very smooth, smoother, even, than plywood, which makes it a good core material. It

does not hold nails and screws particularly well, however, because it has no grain structure at all. If you are going to build cases with particle board, glue them, and perhaps use cement-coated nails, drywall screws or sheet-metal screws, which hold slightly better than wood screws. Only very small pilot holes are necessary.

Particle board is available in thicknesses ranging from ¼ inch to 2 inches, in widths ranging from 2 feet to 5 feet and in lengths ranging from 4 feet to 16 feet. Like plywood, it is most common in the 4 by 8 sheet, and in thicknesses from ⅜ inch to 1 inch.

Hardboard. Hardboard is a close relative of particle board. It too is a product of a process that combines processed sawdust and glue under heat and pressure. There are two main types of hardboard: Tempered, which is the stronger, and Untempered. It is made with one smooth side (S1S) or two

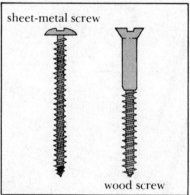

sheet-metal screw

wood screw

Sheet-metal screws (left) have their entire shanks threaded, giving them better holding power than regular wood screws (right).

smooth sides (S2S). While manufactured in thicknesses of ¹/₁₆ inch to ¾ inch, the ⅛-inch to ¼-inch thicknesses are most common. The standard panel is 4-feet by 8-feet, but wider and longer sheets are available.

If you use hardboard at all, it will be for drawer bottoms. A perforated variety is made, and when used with special hooks, it can create display storage. For

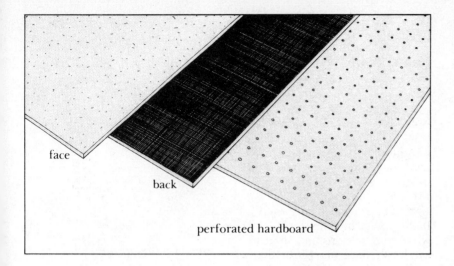

face

back

perforated hardboard

instance, you could use it to make a sliding partition on which you hang utensils.

Molding. You will probably use molding as a part of the room trim. But you may have need of it for counter edging or frame doors. There are dozens and dozens of different moldings made. Every lumberyard has a display of the moldings it stocks. Find out what is available to you before you get too firmly committed to using any particular size or style.

Hardware and Miscellaneous

Wood isn't the only thing you'll need to build your cabinets. You need hardware: nails and screws, hinges and pulls, catches, maybe drawer glides. You need glue. You need finishing materials. There are many choices you have to make, but you've already been given some guidelines to help you.

At this point, you have to meld your desires with the realities of what's available to you at the local hardware store or building supplies dealer. Think about where you'll get an unusual hinge before you commit yourself to using it.

Buying Materials

Buying your materials can be as big a project as using them. There are usually two kinds of places you can go for your materials: home improvement centers and lumberyards.

The home improvement center will probably have a big self-service showroom, stocked with the latest kitsch. While the place may seem to have everything, you will probably find it actually has a very limited selection. Anything that doesn't move in volume won't be stocked. Usually, what *is* in stock is available at a pretty good price, however.

A better place to go is the lumberyard. This is where the cabinetmaker and the building contractor go for their materials. Usually, this is a locally owned and operated concern, not a part of a chain. The showroom may be nonexistent. But invariably the salespeople know building materials. They are knowledgeable about what they have, what they can order, ofttimes about places to go for what they cannot supply.

As you get into this phase of your project, continue your research. Take some time to call around and find out what materials are available and what they cost. After you find out what things cost, you may want to alter your plans.

Tools

To tackle a large-scale cabinetmaking project, you're going to want more than the motley assortment of hand and power tools that most home handymen have. But you don't need a table saw and an expensive collection of chisels and planes. What you need is a thoughtfully amassed set of tools to do what it is you've chosen to do.

Look back at the cutting, fabrication and assembly operations. What joints do you propose to use? What materials will you use? What skills do you have? The answers to these questions will help you select the tools you will need.

As you think about these things, bear in mind that for **413** cutting and fabrication, hand tools require the most effort and the most skill to use, shop tools require the least effort and the least skill. Portable power tools lie somewhere in between. Now this does *not* mean that the acquisition of a radial arm saw will turn a novice into a master craftsman. It does mean the novice will have an easier time of plowing a groove with a radial arm saw than with a backsaw, chisel and router plane. But the job can be botched either way.

Another thing to keep in mind is expense. You can spend a fortune on hand tools, just as you can on power tools. You can get good tools and lousy tools. You usually—but not always—get what you pay for. To reiterate something that's been stated elsewhere, don't cheat yourself by buying cheap. A good tool is an investment, one that will help you build many more kitchens. A poor tool is a source of frustration, and you'll end up buying a good tool to replace it, nine times out of ten. Buy the good one in the first place.

Of course, you don't necessarily have to buy every tool you use. You can rent some, perhaps borrow others. It all depends on your situation. Again, think about the cabinets you want to make and about how they can best be made.

A fair number of the tools you collected to do the basic work will serve you in building cabinets. If you have done, or will be doing, framing work and finish carpentry, you'll have for those jobs the core tools for cabinetmaking: saws, hammer,

layout tools, screwdrivers, drills, perhaps even chisels and planes.

Hand Tools

All of the must-have tools are hand tools. You can build all your cabinets using hand tools only, but even if you do use power tools, you will need *some* hand tools. Again, most of these vital tools will be ones you'll use in other aspects of the kitchen project.

If you are really interested in hand tools and want to know what your options are, send for catalogs from some of the many mail-order tool dealers. There seems to be at least one in every corner of the country. Most sell the same tools, the majority of them imported from England and Germany. But the better dealers have a selection of each kind of tool. Visit the local hardware store and see what you can buy there. Then make some purchases.

Layout Tools. For layout work, you must have a tape or folding rule, a framing square and a pencil or knife of some sort. The work is eased if you also have a try square or combination square, a level, a yard-long straightedge, perhaps a sliding T bevel, a marking gauge and a pencil compass.

Cutting Tools. No matter what other tools you buy, like a circular saw or a shop saw, you should have a handsaw. This is another tool you should have

Basic layout tools: a. Carpenter's folding rule. b. Tape measure. c. Taking an inside measurement with each tool.

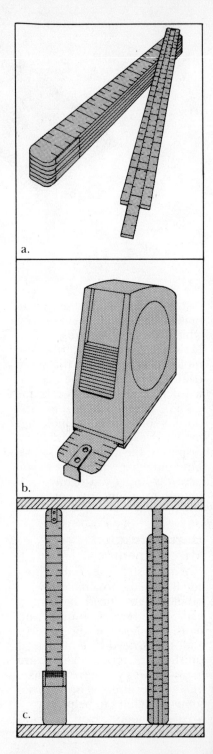

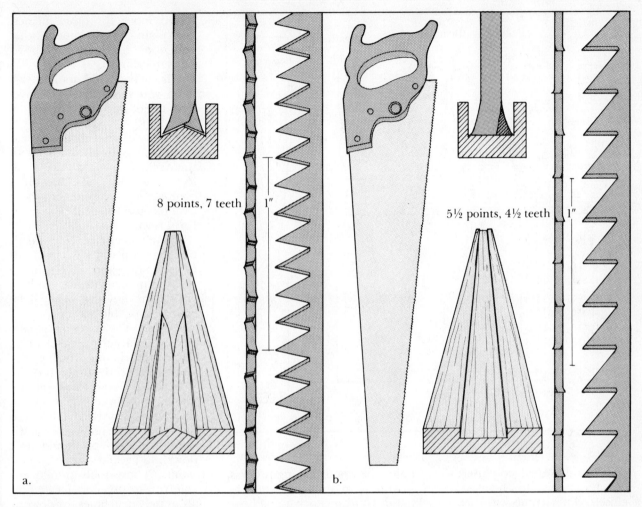

8 points, 7 teeth   1"

5½ points, 4½ teeth   1"

a.

b.

Handsaws come in two basic types, which, though superficially alike, are actually significantly different. a. Crosscut saws have teeth shaped, sharpened and set especially to slice across wood fibers; this skew-back saw has 8 points (7 teeth) per inch. b. Rip saws have teeth shaped, sharpened and set to chisel along the wood fibers; this rip saw has 4½ points per inch.

for other aspects of the total job.

A ripsaw you may get by without unless you are doing all handwork. Then you need one.

Be guided by the same general rules you followed in buying a handsaw for crosscutting, but buy a ripsaw with 4½ to 5½ teeth per inch. And be sure it is a ripsaw and not just a coarse crosscut saw.

The backsaw and miter box used in doing finish carpentry can be used in doing cabinetry. This is another tool in the category of vital if you are doing handwork, not important if you are using power saws.

For cutting dovetails, you may want a dovetail saw, for scrollwork a coping saw, for holes a keyhole saw.

There are other cutting tools besides saws, of course. Chisels are useful. They cut away big chunks or pare off wisps. They clean up dried glue squeeze-out, plow grooves and excavate mortises. You can easily drop a bundle on chisels, which are available in astonishing variety, from firmer chisels to mortising

415

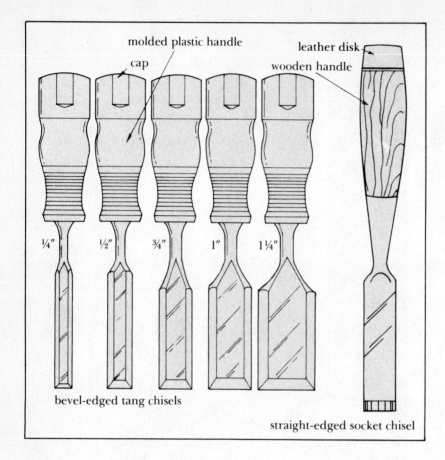

molded plastic handle

cap

leather disk

wooden handle

¼"   ½"   ¾"   1"   1¼"

bevel-edged tang chisels

straight-edged socket chisel

chisels to bevel-edged chisels to bench chisels to heavy-duty chisels. They come with plastic handles and wooden handles. They come in sets and individually, with cutting edges as narrow as ⅛ inch and as wide as 2 inches.

Decide what you are really going to need chisels for. A set of four—¼-, ½-, ¾- and 1-inch widths—with plastic handles will suffice for anyone other than a hand tool devotee.

Planes are like chisels, only worse. You really need only a metal block plane and a metal smoothing plane. But if you

enjoy the woodworking process, if you want to work wood by hand, you can stock a good-size shelf with planes, all different, each designed for a special job. Jointer planes, jack planes, rabbeting planes, router planes, even multiplanes that do the same work as a router, cutting fancy edge shapes. There are cast-iron planes and wooden planes. Each has its devotees.

Perhaps the best advice for the novice is to invest in a good block plane and a good smoothing plane and use them. Try squaring a small board. If the process leads you on, then

spend more for other planes. The plain truth is, though, that you don't need them to build kitchen cabinets.

Drills. The basic tools you'll need you should already have. You might go for a power tool here, but a good-quality egg-beater-style hand drill is an excellent, easy-to-use tool. With the drill, you should have a collection of drill bits, including combination countersink-twist drill bits used to drill pilot holes for screws.

It's not likely, but it is possible, that you will have occasion to use a brace and bit. The brace is a cranklike device with a chuck for holding auger bits, countersink bits, even screwdriver bits. The auger bits generally make larger-diameter holes than twist drill bits, which is why you might need a brace and bit.

If you propose to dowel any joints, you should buy several drilling accessories. First, the bits you use should be brad-point drill bits. You should get a doweling jig and a set of dowel points. These tools should enable you to precisely locate and accurately drill holes for dowels.

Hammers. That 22-ounce ripping hammer you bought to frame your kitchen won't be much good in cabinetry. But a 16-ouncer will serve in nailing casework together. If you feel clumsy using this size hammer to drive 6d and 4d nails, get a lighter one, about 10 or 12 ounces.

A wooden mallet may be a worthwhile investment. Such a tool is good for pounding on chisels, when pounding is called for, and for tapping the pieces

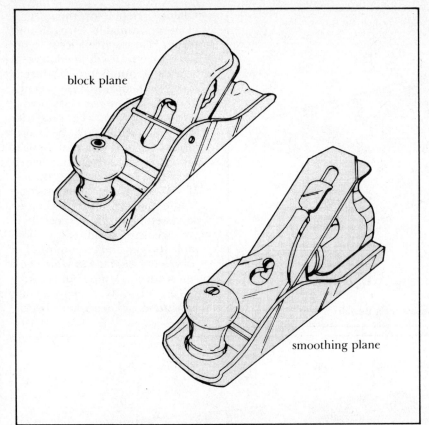

block plane

smoothing plane

Two planes—a block plane and a smoothing plane—will suffice for conventional kitchen cabinetmaking. If you get more involved in working with hand tools, many other planes, each with a special purpose, are available.

of an assembly into alignment.
Screwdrivers. The screwdrivers you used for preparing the shell and for wiring your kitchen will serve in cabinetmaking. These are most likely to be keystone tip screwdrivers. If you need to deeply countersink any screws, you may want to use a cabinet tip screwdriver, which has a straight or tapered rather than a flared tip, so you don't tear the wood surrounding the screw hole. If you have a lot of screws to drive, consider getting a pump action screwdriver, which has interchangeable tips, or a screwdriver bit for a brace, if you have one.

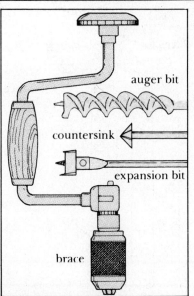

auger bit

countersink

expansion bit

brace

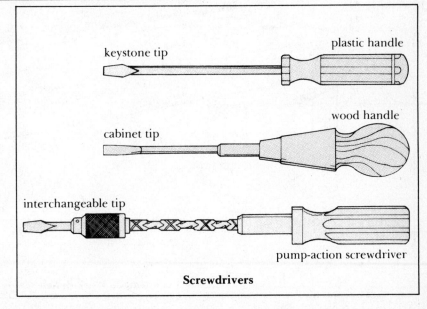

keystone tip

plastic handle

cabinet tip

wood handle

interchangeable tip

pump-action screwdriver

Screwdrivers

417

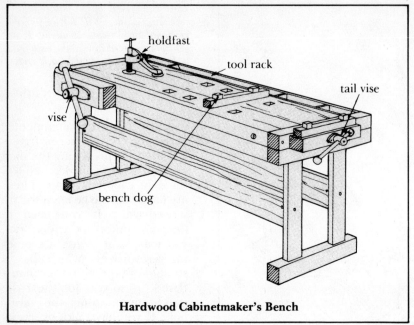

holdfast

tool rack

tail vise

vise

bench dog

Hardwood Cabinetmaker's Bench

Clamps. Details on the various clamps available are found under "Gluing." Suffice it to say here that you will need several sets of a number of different clamps, including pipe clamps and hand screws or C clamps.

An important clamping device that shouldn't be overlooked is a substantial bench-mounted vise. Even the bench itself can be a clamping device. If you are going to be crafting frame doors, drawers and other subassemblies, and especially if you are using hand tools or portable power tools, you need a solid work surface to which you can securely clamp your work.

The ideal is a high-quality hardwood cabinetmaker's bench,

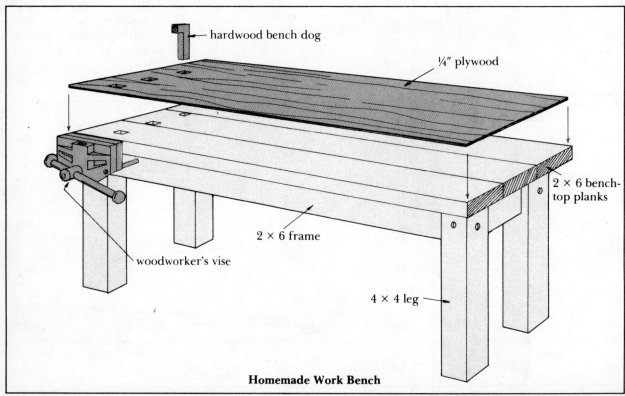

hardwood bench dog

¼" plywood

2 × 6 bench-top planks

2 × 6 frame

woodworker's vise

4 × 4 leg

Homemade Work Bench

with a vise at the left-hand front corner, another vise along the right-hand side, mortises for bench dogs along the front edge and a tray for tools at the rear. You can buy one for only a modest inheritance.

But you can also make a very durable workbench with 4 × 4 legs, 2 × 4 framing and a 2 × 6 plank top covered with a sheet of ¼-inch plywood. Hang a woodworker's vise on it, even two if you can afford them, cut some mortises for those bench dogs and you are in business. The legs and framing must be solid so the bench doesn't wince and wobble. The plywood can be replaced if it gets too torn up. The vises definitely should be woodworker's rather than machinist's vises. You can make bench dogs from hardwood, or you can buy metal ones. You can, in fact, forgo the dogs altogether if you nail temporary stops to the bench top itself.

Another alternative is to buy a metal leg-and-frame assembly and attach a plywood or particle-board top.

And still a fourth alternative is to use a freestanding vise stand, like the Workmate.

Whatever approach you choose, you do need something to which you can clamp wood for routing, chiseling, planing and sanding. It should be durable, and of course it should be wood.

Portable Power Tools

The first experience the average handyman has with power tools is with the portable power tools that are so common. Every one of these tools has a coun-

Workmate

terpart in the shop tool realm. The router compares to the shaper, the circular saw to the radial arm or table saw, the drill to the drill press. The shop tool is invariably more precision, but the work must be taken to the shop to be worked by a shop tool. The portable tool is carried to the work.

If you have a shop, the shop tool may be the best investment, especially if you are driven by a deeper desire than to merely build a few cabinets for your harvest kitchen. But for the handyman with no good shop area and no desire to make a heavy commitment to woodworking, portable tools are just the ticket.

The big problem with portable power tools is in making a wise choice. There are dozens and dozens of models to choose

from, ranging from discount store specials to commercial and industrial models. The home handyman models are inexpensive, but only because they are cheap. They aren't worth looking at, much less buying. The real commercial and industrial models probably aren't all that much better an investment considering the occasional use you'll give them. They are designed to work an 8-hour day, week in and week out.

Look for the most highly powered model you can reasonably afford. The amp rating of the tool can be a good indicator of the tool's power, as well as of the tool's energy consumption. Look too for roller-, needle- or ball-bearing construction. Look for tools you can grip comfortably and surely, tools that are easy to adjust.

419

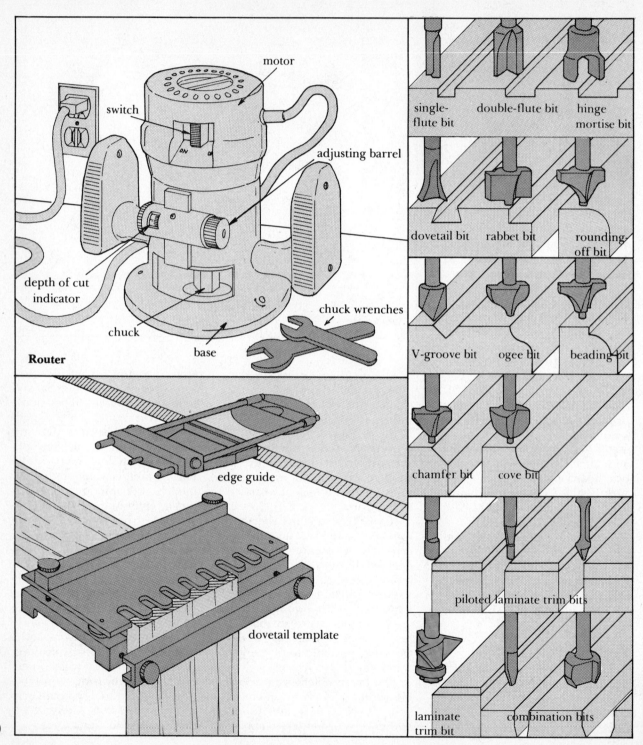

motor

switch

adjusting barrel

depth of cut
indicator

chuck

base

chuck wrenches

Router

edge guide

dovetail template

single-
flute bit

double-flute bit

hinge
mortise bit

dovetail bit

rabbet bit

rounding-
off bit

V-groove bit

ogee bit

beading bit

chamfer bit

cove bit

piloted laminate trim bits

laminate
trim bit

combination bits

420

There are four portable power tools you should consider. Two you may already own, having acquired them for other parts of your kitchen project.

Circular Saw. Using a circular saw will take a load off your arm. In making cabinets, there is a lot of plywood to be cut. With a guide, either commercial or homemade, you can use a circular saw to cut the plywood and do a better job of it than with any other tool. In addition, the circular saw will do reasonably good crosscutting and ripping.

It's likely that you already have a circular saw, having used it for doing framing work. A combination blade, which comes with most saws, is okay for that work, but not for cabinetmaking. Get a good set of blades, one for ripping, one for crosscutting, one for plywood cutting. The ripping and crosscutting blades should be carbide-tipped if you can afford them; you probably won't be able to find a plywood blade with carbide tips.

Power Drill. The electric drill is the other tool you may already have. It is the power tool that home handymen tend to buy before they buy any other. If you've prepared the framing and run new wiring and plumbing, a good power drill has been a help. It will continue to be in making your cabinets. But it's not absolutely necessary for cabinetmaking alone, unless you plan to screw or dowel nearly every joint.

Whatever can be said about buying a power saw or power drill has been said under "Preparing the Shell."

Router. A router will ease you into crafting more difficult joints. You can easily cut dadoes, grooves and rabbets with a router, the proper bit and a homemade jig or two. These basic cuts will allow you to build strong, more attractive cabinets. A router purchased for that reason alone is a good investment.

But once you have it, you'll find yourself using more elaborate joints routinely. You'll put fancy edges on things, perhaps even craft your own moldings.

A router is essentially a very high-speed motor—20,000 to 30,000 rpm—mounted vertically in an adjusting bracket. The bracket has a flat bearing surface that's exactly perpendicular to the plane of the motor shaft. The shaft has a collet-type chuck that holds cutting bits. The bit dictates the shape and size of the cut, the router adjustment dictates the depth of cut. The high speed ensures a smooth cut.

In looking at routers, be sure you get one with easy-to-grip handles, a sure adjustment system and a ¾-or more horsepower motor. Buy an edge guide. But get only those bits you are sure to use. Sets of bits can be enticing, but they always include a couple or three bits you'll never use. If you want dovetailed drawers, consider getting a dovetailing template setup.

In use, routers always cut best along the grain. Use extra care when cutting across or against the grain. Always work with left

to right action, since the router motor turns counterclockwise (when viewed from the top). Turn the router on, *then* place it against the work. Don't feed too fast—you can tell by the motor's sound whether or not you are overloading it. Turn the router off immediately upon removing it from the work; it's spinning at extremely high speed, and the bit is sharp.

Sanders. There are two types of sanders, either or both of which you may find useful in cabinetmaking. The belt sander is a relatively coarse tool, designed primarily to remove a lot of material quickly. It will, with the appropriate belt, put a medium-smooth finish on wood, but it won't match a finish sander in that regard. The finish sander will put a very smooth finish on wood, but isn't too good for rough-sanding.

The belt sander has a motor that drives an abrasive belt. The size of the sander is usually stated in terms of the width and circumference of the belt. The horsepower rating of the motor means something, too.

The belt sander should be started, then placed carefully against the work. If the sander isn't level, it will quickly create hollows, gouges or dents, all of them difficult to correct. Cutting across the grain will remove material the quickest, but it will leave cross-grain scratches that are the dickens to remove. Best to sand with the grain. Always keep the sander moving, overlapping strokes, with the sander aligned parallel with the grain.

The finish sander has a motor that wiggles a pad. Ordinary **421**

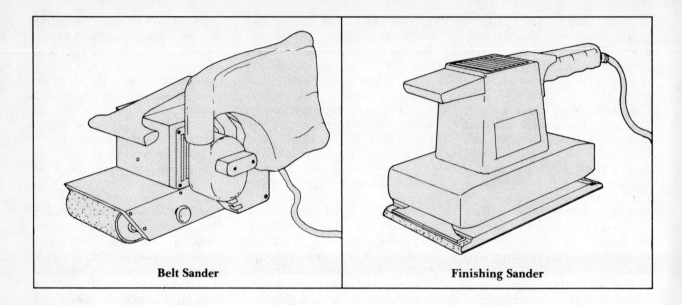

Belt Sander **Finishing Sander**

sandpaper—usually a quarter of a standard sheet—is mounted on the pad. Orbital sanders move the pad in a circular path, thus always cutting with and across the grain. Straight-line sanders only move the pad back and forth, putting you in control over sanding with or across the grain. Some sanders can operate both ways.

Sanders can skin you, but they aren't really dangerous in the sense a power saw is dangerous. They do generate a lot of dust, which can harm you, so a dust collection accessory is worth having.

Definitely do not get a disk sander. It will sand wood, but it will leave almost-impossible-to-remove swirls of scratches. Use it on your car, but not on your cabinets.

There are, of course, other portable power tools. You may, for example, have a saber saw. You can use it in your cabinet-

making, but it isn't sufficiently useful to warrant buying one just for making the cabinets. A circular saw is a better investment. If you are determined to motorize, but you haven't got a shop, the circular saw, drill, router and sanders are the tools to buy.

Shop Tools

Shop tools are motor-driven saws, shapers, jointers and planers, drills and sanders. They are generally large, heavy and costly. They take up space and using them requires even more space. You bring the work to them. With them, you can do precision, uniform work without having a great deal of skill. They all have to be used with caution, since they all tend to be dangerous.

It's been stated before, but it's worth stating again: You do not have to have shop tools to build sound, attractive kitchen cabi-

nets. Shop tools merely make the work easier. If you have a place for a permanent shop, and you have the money to invest, and you are going to do cabinetmaking beyond the kitchen project, by all means get shop tools. But don't be cowed into thinking you *have* to have them. You do not.

It is unlikely that merely because of the kitchen cabinet project you are going to set up a shop. The project may serve as the impetus to buy one or two shop tools, but you certainly wouldn't be right in the head if you spent the thousands of dollars necessary to get four or five good-quality shop tools just to make a few cabinets. It's common to start a shop by getting a shop saw of some kind. A table saw or radial arm saw is usually the heart of a shop. Other tools are added as money permits and as needs dictate. A jointer might be next, followed by a

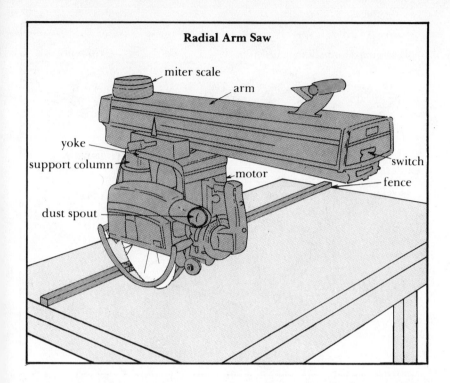

Radial Arm Saw

miter scale

arm

yoke

support column

motor

dust spout

switch

fence

drill press or a stationary sander. A router mounted in a table, either purchased or homemade, doubles as a shaper. The band saw, jigsaw and lathe have their uses in woodworking, but not in making cabinets.

Radial Arm Saw. The most versatile tool for the home shop is undoubtedly the radial arm saw. It is essentially a circular saw mounted in a yoke in which it can swivel and swing. The yoke is in turn mounted on an overhead arm that can be raised and lowered and swung from side to side.

The work is placed on a wooden saw table beneath the saw, and—for all but rip cuts—the saw is pulled along the arm, cutting through the work. Rip cuts are made by swiveling the

saw in its yoke 90 degrees, locking it there, then pushing the work through the saw. Miters are made by swinging the arm, bevels by swinging the saw, compound cuts by swinging the arm and the saw. Perfectly horizontal cuts can easily be made. Accessories allow the saw to make dado cuts, molding cuts, drill, sand and plane. It definitely doesn't do the latter three operations as well as tools made specifically for them, but it does do them serviceably well.

Originally, the radial arm saw was a contractor's tool, used to cut everything from framing members to finish trim. The portable circular saw has just about replaced it for such uses, but it has found a place in the home shop. Many cabinetmak-

ers look down their noses at the radial arm saw, perhaps because of its origins. The contention is that the radial arm saw is not as precise as the table saw, the *preferred* saw, because of all the joints in the mechanism. Each joint is an opportunity for looseness and imprecision to gain a foothold. But as a practical matter, the saw would have to be used hard for a long, long time before that would happen.

In fact, the radial arm saw is an ideal tool for someone who isn't planning to equip a quasi-commercial shop, primarily because it *is* versatile. In addition to versatility, the strong points of the radial arm saw are that it is reasonably safe and that it can be placed against a wall. The saw is "safe" because the blade is always above the work, always visible. In most situations, the work is stationary, the saw is moved. All saws are equipped with blade guards and, for ripping, antikickback fingers. Use them.

Positioning the saw against the wall is an advantage in the small shop, so long as the wall isn't too short. Working room is needed on only three sides. A table saw, in contrast, must be spotted in the center of an open area, so there is working room on all four sides of the unit.

The size of the saw is usually given in terms of the diameter of the blade it uses. A 10-inch saw is typical for the home shop, a 12-inch is within reason, but anything larger is for someone who's going into business. Look for ball-, roller-, needle-bearing construction, a 1- to 2-horse-power motor, and easy-to-use **423** controls. Get a saw with a blade brake, which prevents the blade from spinning seemingly interminably after the motor is switched off; a very worthwhile safety feature.

Information about the use of this tool can fill a small book. If you can afford to buy the tool, you can afford to buy a book detailing how to use it. Suffice it to say here that a radial arm saw would be a real boon on your kitchen cabinet project.

Table Saw. This is the saw *de rigueur* of cabinetmakers. It is a cast-iron table, machined to absolute flatness, with a circular saw blade projecting through its center. The blade can be raised or lowered to adjust the depth of cut, and it can be tilted to the right to make bevel cuts. An adjustable rip fence, extending across the saw table parallel to the blade, guides rip cuts. A miter gauge, which rides in slots machined into the table to the right and left of the blade, guides crosscuts and miter cuts. Dado blades and molding cutters can be used with the tool.

The work is always moved to be cut on a table saw, but it must always be guided, either by the rip fence or the miter gauge. Trying a freehand cut is the ideal way to find out why kickback is so dangerous. The table saw's blade, like that of the radial arm saw, spins clockwise, but whereas the effect of this movement with the radial arm saw is to push the work against the table and its backstop, with the table saw the effect is to push the work back at you. And if you get the work ever so cocked partway through the cut,

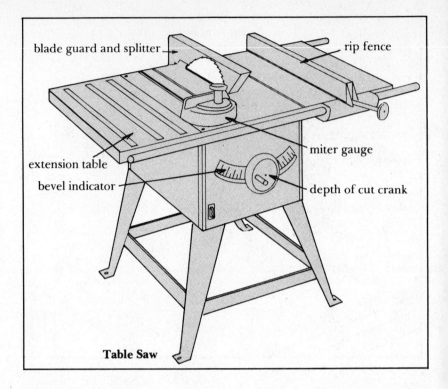

blade guard and splitter

rip fence

extension table

bevel indicator

miter gauge

depth of cut crank

Table Saw

it definitely *will* throw the work back at you. Hard. That's kickback.

You can do a number of things to avoid kickback. The first is to always use the guides, of course, and to use them properly. Never use the rip fence as a crosscutting guide. The piece being cut off surely will cock between blade and fence as it is severed, perhaps binding the blade and stalling it, perhaps being kicked back at you. Always use the splitter and any antikickback devices with which the saw is equipped. Never release the work until it is completely free of the blade. Never saw work that doesn't have a flat, sure bearing face (two such if you are ripping).

While kickback is a danger of

the table saw, so is the hidden blade. In some working situations, the blade is completely obscured by the work; you lose track of where it is and where your fingers are and they get together, to your everlasting regret. Using the blade guard is not a faultless defense, but it helps.

As previously noted, the table saw must be positioned so you have free access around the entire unit. If you intend to rip plywood from end to end, you'll need at least 10 or 12 feet of unrestricted space both in front and back of the saw. Your crosscutting capacity will be restricted by the space you have to the left of the blade, while your rip capacity will be restricted by the limits of the saw. If you are going to crowd the saw, crowd it on the right.

As with other power saws, the size of the table saw is given in terms of the blade diameter. Perhaps more important is the horsepower rating of the motor. Get at least a 1-horse model, and opt for more power if you can. Get extension tables, which increase the breadth of the saw table, providing increased bearing surface for cutting panels. Be sure the saw has at least 12 inches between the table's front edge and the blade so you can properly crosscut a 1 × 12. Again, consider the ease and sureness with which the controls work.

Mere acquisition of a table saw won't make you a cabinetmaker but it will ease your cabinetmaking. To find out all the marvelous things you can do with the tool, be sure to get and read a book detailing how to use the saw.

Jointer. If you plan to use hardwood stock or do a lot of edge-gluing, a jointer may be a worthwhile investment. Certainly it isn't the first shop tool you'd buy, and it is limited in its uses, but what it does it does better than any other tool, hand or powered.

The size of the machine is given in terms of the length of the cutters. Their length determines the width of board that can be planed. The typical home-shop-size tool is a 4-inch or 6-inch jointer. While it's nice to have good-size tables, the small-size tables of a 4-inch jointer don't limit it as much as the cutter length. If need be, you can set up an auxiliary sup-

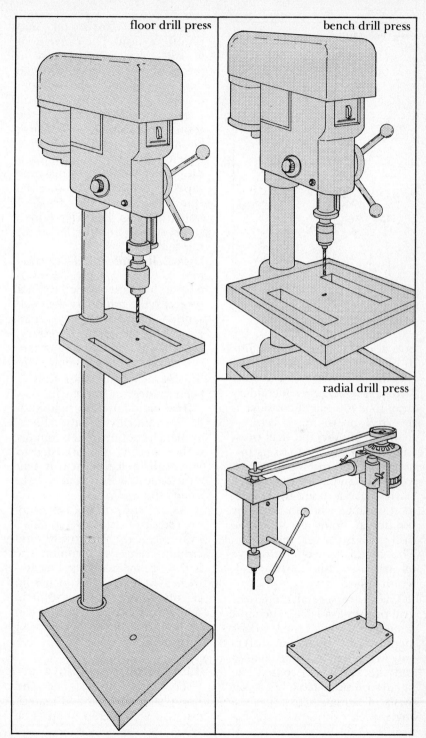

floor drill press

bench drill press

radial drill press

425

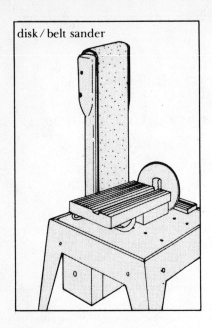

disk / belt sander

port at each end of the machine to help you when working long boards.

Drill Press. Another secondary shop tool you might consider is the drill press. More versatile than the jointer, the drill press will do tasks other than its primary one of drilling holes. It will rout, sand and cut mortises. If you have a desire to do a lot of doweling, wherein precisely positioned holes are vital, the drill press is the best tool to use. The same is true of cutting lots of mortises for mortise-and-tenon joints.

There are several models of drill presses available. The most familiar is probably the big floor model. A bench model differs only in the length of the column and the size of the base. The radial drill press has a head that twists, allowing you to adjust the angle of the bit anywhere be-tween level horizontal and plumb vertical. The capacity of a drill press is expressed in terms of the distance between the spindle and the column doubled. Thus, a 15-inch drill press can drill a hole in the center of a 15-inch-wide board, because there are 7½ inches between the column and the spindle. Other variables in machine capacity include the distance the spindle can travel (the depth of hole that can be drilled in a single stroke) and the length of the column.

Disk/Belt Sander. The last shop tool to warrant serious consideration for your kitchen cabinet project is the stationary disk/belt sander. It's useful for certain jobs, but far from necessary, especially if you have a portable belt sander. You will still have to finish-sand pieces after they've been sanded on this machine.

The stationary disk/belt sander is essentially a large, floor- or bench-mounted belt sander with a sanding disk attached to one of the belt rollers. It has an adjustable cast-iron table to help steady the work.

As with the portable belt sander, the size of this tool is stated in terms of the belt's width and circumference. A common size is 6 × 48, meaning the belt is 6 inches wide and 48 inches in circumference, with a 9-inch-diameter disk. Such a tool can be powered by a ¾-horsepower motor.

The Home Workplace

To build your cabinets and house all your tools and materials, you will need a shop. The shop may be the kitchen, especially if you are going to build your cabinets in place. But it's more satisfactory, in fact imperative if you've got shop tools, to have a separate room devoted solely to your woodworking.

The point here is not to explain how to organize a shop, but to establish the value of having a special place to work. Making cabinets will generate a lot of dust and considerable noise. Assembly requires some elbow room. Gluing requires warmth, since most glues must be used in 70°F. or better temperatures. You can't do a good job if you are relegated to a corner of a cluttered basement, or to an unheated garage or if you must use living space. You can make do with any space you can get, of course, but a shop is undeniably desirable.

Here are a few guidelines to help in picking your spot.

- It should have as much space as you can get. You need room to set up a workbench that you can work all around, room for shop tools (if you have them), room to assemble and perhaps store cabinets, room to store materials and tools properly.
- It should be sufficiently isolated from the living area that noise and dirt won't be troublesome. Of course, you should clean up after each session, so the dirt shouldn't be a cumulative thing.
- It should be warm, so you can glue in all kinds of weather. And apply finishes too.

- It should have good access. Don't build your cabinets, then discover you can't get them out of the shop and into the kitchen.
- It should be adequately wired, so you can have good lighting, both background and task, and enough power to start and run your power tools (a big shop saw can easily overload a 30-amp, 115-volt circuit starting up; better to run it on 230).

You have to survey your resources and do the best you can with what you have.

Planning Your Kitchen Cabinets

You are now ready—probably more than ready—to tackle the design and planning of your own harvest kitchen cabinets. It is a process not unlike that you used to design your harvest kitchen. You have to collect information, give it some time to meld with your desires in your head, then put it down on paper. In detail, great detail. And after all the wrinkles are worked out, you have to develop a list of pieces you must cut, turn it into a materials list for purchasing and work out a construction sequence.

It's a lot to do. And to do it well you have to have in mind not only the style of cabinets you want, but a good idea of just how you'll fit them together, what you'll make them out of,

Whatever setup you do establish, make sure you have a good, solid workbench, a couple of sturdy sawhorses and storage for tools and materials. It does no good to buy expensive kiln-dried lumber, then store it in a damp, unheated place for weeks or months on end. Likewise, it does no good to invest in expensive tools, then toss them in a box or leave them on the workbench or the floor. Even if you only arrange them on shelves you've taken a substantial step toward establishing a well-organized, safe and pleasant workplace.

and what tools you'll need to do the job.

How you go about the project as a whole depends entirely upon your ultimate goal. If you are looking for cabinets to be installed in your kitchen, pure and simple, you'll cut through what you might regard as folderol and get quickly to business. But if you have more personal or more artistic ambitions, you may spend much more time weighing options, thinking about materials and joints. Liking the process as much as the product, perhaps liking the process even *more* than the product, you may dwell on selection of stocks, on crafting pieces solely with hand tools. The project is a labor of love, a process of artistic creation.

Regardless, the way stations are the same. The difference is in the seriousness and the state of mind with which you approach them.

Scrutinizing and Scheming

Your first step, perhaps obviously, is to get on paper all the facts you can about the space you have to work with, the stuff you want to store and the standards you want to meet.

The space you have to work with presumably is set. You've plotted the room size, positioned the doors and windows, arranged the appliances and the sink. Get it on paper. To the fraction of an inch. The sizes of the appliances, the size of the sink, the locations of doors, windows, outlets and lights, the height of the ceiling, the length of walls. Lay it all out on graph paper.

Now collect information on what's to be stored. Talk to the cook, or the cooks. If you are he or she, so much the better. Jot down what you want to store and where you want to store it. Will there be a pantry? Must all the pots and pans and lids and utensils be in cabinets? Or will a rack be okay? All the dishes behind doors? And in one place? Or one place for everyday, another for good? How big are the canning jars? What about the mixer? The grain mill? Under the counter? How about a drawer rather than a shelf for these heavy items? Maybe movable hardware that will swing

A cabinetmaking project starts in the space to be filled with cabinets. On graph paper, plot the size of your kitchen, the locations and sizes of windows, doors and every other element that helps define the specific areas in which you can put cabinets.

Designing the layout is generally a trial and error process. Roughly sketch combinations of features that appeal to you, mixing and matching until you have a design that suits you and also fits the space you have to work with. You may hit the plan quickly. But it may as likely take dozens and dozens of sketches until you find your solution.

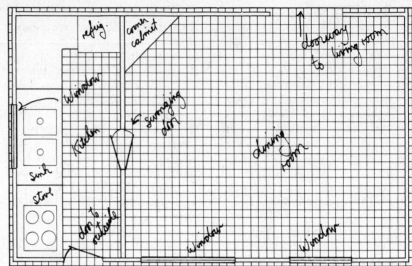

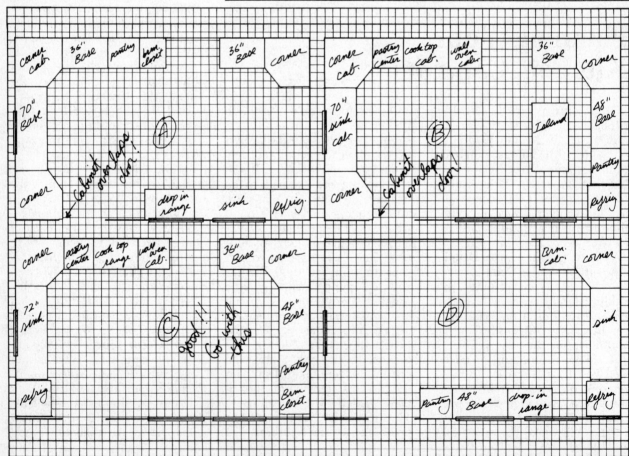

the shelf out of the cabinet and up to working height? What has to be stored in drawers? How many are needed?

Finally, compose a list of your standards. Do you want to build cabinets to conform to architectural standards? Or do you want to craft them to a size that's comfortable for the cook? Do you want cabinets at all? Will shelves be satisfactory? Do you want to reserve the right to change your mind periodically, and be able to move some things around, adjusting shelves, for instance? What do you want the cabinets to look like? Must the installation be a showpiece? Or is economy and function more important?

The scheming begins after all this scrutinizing is completed. Fiddle around with sketches. Turn things over in your mind. Weigh each given, each fact. Discard ideas that won't work, compromise your desires, alter the facts. Shuffle and scheme until it does work.

If you plan to prefab the cabinets, perhaps it would be useful to work with round-figure-size modules. Work with a 6-foot sink unit, a 3-foot double-door unit, a 4 foot double-door unit, a corner cabinet or two. If you have 42 inches in which to fit a cabinet, not 36 or 48, you know you have to adjust the dimensions of the cabinet. Perhaps you can split spaces into thirds or quarters, making drawers and doors of equal widths. For contrast, you could flank two wide doors with two narrow ones. Or vice versa.

Study existing cabinets that you like. Measure them and

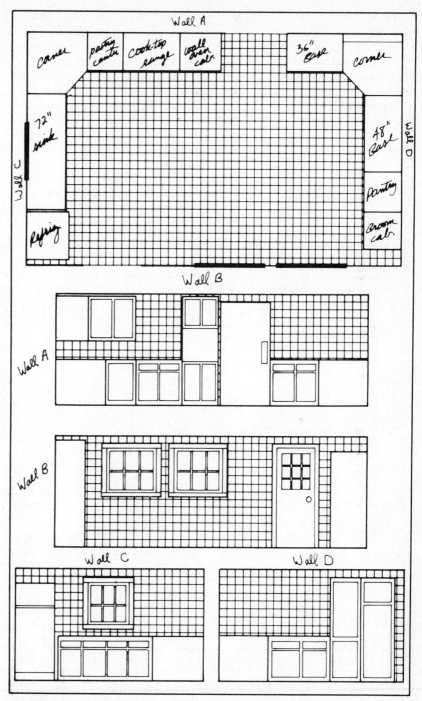

The final drawing of your solution to the cabinet problem should be as neat and realistic as you can make it. Work to scale, and use a straightedge. No sketching here.

make sketches. Try to analyze why they work for you, what makes them attractive to you. Think about their proportions, the balance of doors with drawers with other elements in the arrangement.

Use graph paper to prepare working drawings of each cabinet. Draw scale plans of top, front, side, back and bottom. Include any and all details you suspect may be troublesome to build. Solve every problem on paper before cutting a single board.

Blend your material wants into the stew. Walnut? Oak? Something inexpensive? Any particular hardware you like? Something homemade and individual? Again, take notes on design elements you've seen and like. Try to balance them with the cabinet design taking shape in your head and in rough sketches.

At some point you may simply have to be ruthless. You may have to reject ideas that simply

don't cut it, perhaps your husband's or wife's, perhaps your own. You can get lost and wander around in rough sketches if you aren't methodical and decisive.

All the while, of course, you as the cabinetmaker have to be looking at the realities of what you can build. Don't plan to dazzle the folks with the brilliance of your craftsmanship if you've never built a cabinet before. If your craftsmanship is

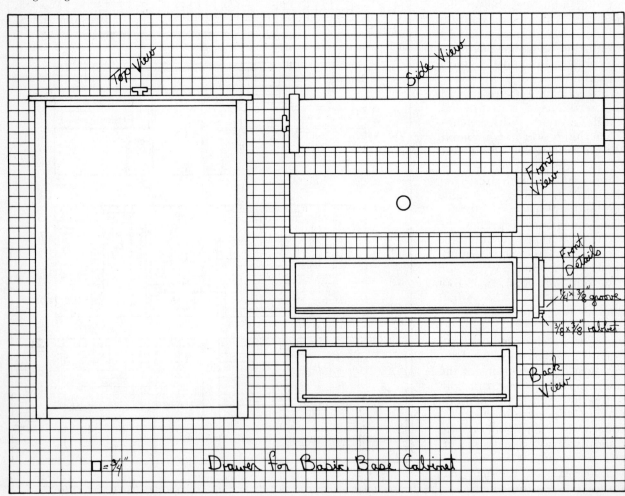

brilliant, they won't notice. If it comes through only dimly, they are sure to. Be honest with yourself. Remember that the best joint is the simplest one that does the job.

Commit your final scheme to paper. Sketch an overhead view, a frontal view. Do it as best you can and try to visualize exactly what you are planning to do. If you like it, if it seems realistic, if you think you can really build it, try to roughly estimate what it will cost. That may put the kibosh on the plan. No sense mapping it all out, only to find you can't afford it. If you can afford it, map it out.

Drawing the Cabinets

Your plan for the cabinets must now be committed in detail to paper. Use graph paper, a scale such as one block per inch, and prepare top, front, side, even back and bottom views. If necessary, draw details in actual size. You must know exactly what you are going to do. You must know exactly how big each piece must be, where the dadoes and holes must be, what the clearances must be. There can be no guesswork. Don't build in fudge factors, build in specific details.

The dimensions of everything must, of course, be known. You've got information on the kitchen. You should also know about lumber dimensions. You have to calculate joint dimensions. Making drawings helps you to visualize what it is you are going to do.

You want no surprises. Wood is too expensive to waste.

It is possible you know someone who jots a few sketches on a paper bag and cobbles up simply marvelous furniture and cabinets. It is possible. There are remarkably gifted woodworkers around. But it is also possible that the person has a remarkable pile of scrap wood. For every woodworker who can think and plan a project entirely in his head, there are a dozen intelligent and capable woodworkers who wouldn't dream of building something without first planning it on paper. In the end, it saves time, money and sanity.

Get your plans drawn up.

Organizing the Work

Two tasks remain before the chips can start to fly. You have to develop a specific materials list, and you have to plan your work sequence. Both grow out of your drawings.

The materials list starts with a list of pieces. First, give every piece a name or label. The label can be a number or a letter. Do what is easiest for you. Jot the label on the drawings. Then list the piece by label, dimensions and material. If the piece is lapped or has tenons, be sure you get the full dimension of the piece, not just the size of what is exposed. List the thickness, the width and the length. If a grade suggests itself, list that too. Your drawings should reveal to you whether or not the piece will be exposed to ready view, and thus

whether or not you need a high-quality material.

Continue the list with an accounting of the hardware and miscellany needed. Nails are purchased by the pound, so it is probably a waste of time to count them out. But screws are bought by the piece, so those should be counted out. Hinges usually are packaged with the necessary screws; account for those screws only if you think a size other than what's supplied is necessary. Measure the glass, if any, and the plastic laminate. Calculate the number of tiles needed. Figure in waste.

Review your completed list carefully. Check and recheck. Extra trips and reorders await you if you goof.

The hardware and miscellany list is complete at this point. The wood list must be turned into a purchasable form. To turn your list of pieces into a list of materials to buy is a trial-and-error process. Certainly, you want to limit your purchase to what is absolutely necessary. But you must also allow for cutting loss, for defects, perhaps even for error. It's disheartening to come up short of wood because you chintzed on your materials list.

Plywood is probably the easiest to deal with. Use your graph paper again. Cut out a scale drawing of each plywood piece. Be sure you get the pieces segregated according to thickness and grade. Then sketch out a scale drawing of a 4 by 8 sheet of plywood. Now just arrange and rearrange the pieces on the sheet until you have the most economical cutting layout. Be sure to leave space for saw kerfs **431**

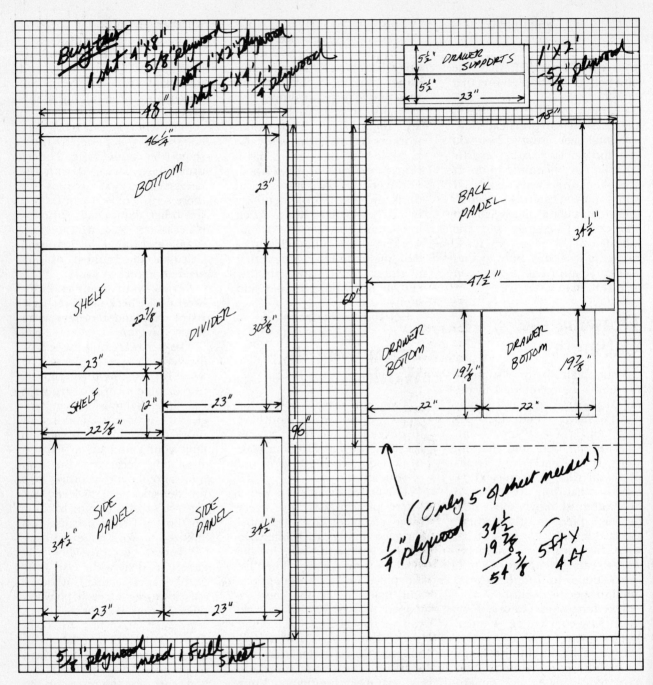

Buy this:
1 sht 4"x8" 5/8" plywood
1 sht 1"x2" plywood
48" 1 sht 5'x4' 1/4" plywood

DRAWER SUPPORTS 5½" 5½" 23" 1'x2' 5/8" plywood

46¼"
BOTTOM 23"
48" 48"

BACK PANEL 34½"

SHELF 22⅞" DIVIDER 30⅜"
23" 23"
SHELF 12" 23"
22⅞" 60"
SIDE PANEL SIDE PANEL 34½"
34½"
96"

47½"

DRAWER BOTTOM 19⅞" DRAWER BOTTOM 19⅞"
22" 22"

(Only 5' of sheet needed)
¼" plywood
34½
19⅞
54⅜ 5 ft x 4 ft

23" 23"

5/8" plywood need 1 Full sheet.

Before buying plywood, work out the most economical layout on graph paper. Clip out a scaled pattern for each piece to be cut, and shuffle them on a scaled pattern of a plywood sheet until the ideal cutting layout is found. Don't buy more plywood than you need simply because you haven't taken the time to finish your planning.

between pieces. It helps to be buying for several cabinets, rather than one, for you seldom need an entire sheet for a single cabinet. You can, however, probably buy a portion of a sheet if it is not a hardwood plywood.

You can follow the same routine with the lumber, although it seems a bit elaborate. If you are using board lumber, you know the standard widths and lengths and can work within those parameters. If you have the tools to rip boards easily, you can often save by laying out narrow pieces side by side on a wide board. Don't be reluctant to combine pieces of different assemblies in one board if it helps to save lumber. In buying boards to be glued up, remember that it's better to glue up narrow boards than wide boards. Think about scraps ripped from glued-up panels. Will they be wide enough and long enough to be used in the cabinet? Will it save on materials to glue up two or three such scraps to get one piece that would otherwise have to be cut from a full-measure board? Keep trying different combinations till you get what seems absolutely to be the most economical list.

Calculating your hardwood needs is more difficult, if only because hardwoods don't come in such handy, uniform boards as softwoods. You have to face random widths and lengths, board feet and a somewhat arcane grading system. If you have no experience with hardwood buying or are unsure of your estimates, you are sim-

ply going to have to play it partly by ear. Be prepared to do some fast figuring at the lumberyard, perhaps be prepared to buy more than you think you need, and perhaps count on the help of an experienced, hopefully understanding salesman or yardman.

Most likely, you'll be allowed to pick and choose your hardwood boards. Take along your list of pieces. Sometimes you can save money by buying a common grade over Firsts and Seconds. A board may be wide enough for your purposes, but too narrow to be graded FAS. Or it may have a knot in the center that devalues it gradewise, but is properly located to allow you to cut two or four needed pieces from the unblemished wood surrounding the knot. The yardman will probably be cooperative, so long as you don't sort through his entire stock, taking the whole afternoon, and selecting only three or four boards. Be reasonable.

The softwood and plywood purchases should go a bit faster. But still you should be selective. This is where your choice of suppliers comes into play. If you go to the local discount house of lumber, you usually get whatever is on top of the pile. The yardman doesn't know and doesn't care. But if you single out a good lumberyard, you'll get knowledgeable guidance, good materials and probably a fair price.

The final task of organization, performed concurrently with the development of your materials list, is planning the

work sequence. As previously noted, it is unwise to cut all the material up as soon as you get it into the shop or kitchen. Work in subassemblies. Cut, fabricate and assemble one, then move to the next.

The work sequence dictates what you do and when you do it. You can probably keep the work sequence in your head, but it doesn't take much effort to jot down notes on paper, to be kept with your drawings. You will discover that the work progresses much more smoothly and efficiently—and happily— when you take the time to work out beforehand just how and when you will do things.

Again, don't be cowed by your friend with the mind for woodworking and the big scrap pile. You do your thinking and planning on paper. You won't regret it.

Putting It to the Wood

From here on out, the work should be a pleasure. You know just what you are going to do. You've drawn your design, selected your materials, amassed your tools and equipment and planned your work knowledgeably. You know what you can do. Perhaps you've planned a few challenges into your project, perhaps not. In any case, you know where you are going, what you are doing.

The sawdust is going to fly, you're going to have a good time, and your cabinets are going to be a source of pride and pleasure for years to come. **433**

Shelves

Up to now, the talk has been all cabinets, all hiding things behind closed doors, all squirreling them away in drawers. But maybe you want to put your kitchen things on display.

If your talent is gardening and canning, why bury your talent deep in the pantry or hide it behind cabinet doors? Put those jars of peas and beans and to-

matoes and peaches and pears out where folks can see and admire them. If you've got beautiful dishes and pottery and pots and pans, why not show them off, always, not just when they are actually being used.

Cabinets won't allow you to show off. Shelves will.

Moreover, shelves will put those important, regularly used items within easy reach of the busy cook. When you need an herb or a trivet or a dish, the one that's on a shelf is easy to put your eye, and your hand, on. The one in a cabinet, behind a door, is not. You may not surrender cabinets completely, but surely you'll have *some* shelves.

There are other reasons for choosing shelves over cabinets.

Tracks and Brackets

There's no easier way to get tiers of shelves in your kitchen than to install commercial shelf hardware to support ordinary pine boards. Although there are slight variations of design, the quintessential hardware is composed of upright supports—the tracks—which have slots in them, and brackets, which have lugs that hook into the slots. You need at least two tracks for any shelf setup. The tracks are attached to the wall with screws. The brackets are hooked into place, and boards are laid across them.

You can get hung up calculating weights and spans to figure out how many tracks you need for the length of shelves you

If your talent is not woodworking, but you *are* committed to redoing your kitchen yourself, cabinets may be your Waterloo. Shelves may be the stratagem that will save you.

If you are pinched for money, shelving surely will save you some. Not only will you save on materials, you will save on time as well. The job is less involved, hence it will go faster.

You can, of course, get involved with shelving and end up spending a lot of both time and money installing attractive and durable shelves. You can build cases for them and get tangled up in complex woodworking joints and wood finishing. Certainly your kitchen will look the better for it. But you can take a plain and simple approach.

want to install. But for a kitchen installation, in which it is quite likely you'll have a substantial load placed on the shelves, skip the arithmetic and install a track at each stud. In houses built in relatively recent years, that will place a track every 16 inches. If you have an old house, you may find the tracks are spaced closer together or farther apart than 16 inches. You may even find they are irregularly spaced. In any case, you need to drive the attachment screws into the studs, not just the wall surface material, to get the support you need.

Finding the studs can sometimes be vexing unless you either have done work that in-

volved removing some or all of the wall surface or are willing to drill or punch some holes in the wall surface. If you've ripped out the walls or done some rewiring or run new plumbing, you undoubtedly have a very good idea where all the studs are. But if all you have before you is unblemished wall—wall that you'd prefer to keep unblemished—you've got a distinct problem.

Some people can thump on a wall and, from the vibrations or reverberations, tell where the studs are. It sounds easy, but it isn't a terribly reliable way to locate the studs, especially if you've never done it before. Another approach is to use a little magnetic device called a stud-finder, which is supposed to detect any steel hidden under the plaster. Presumably the steel is a nail driven into a stud, but it could be armored cable or steel pipe as easily as it could be a steel nail.

The best way to locate the studs for hanging shelf tracks is the same way you locate them for installing new wall boxes or for hanging wall cabinets. Drill a hole at random. Bend a piece of wire, slip it through the hole and twirl it. If you hit an obstruction, it is likely to be a stud (although it *could* be wiring or plumbing or firestopping). Gauge the distance from the hole to the obstruction and bore another test hole. If you experience continued resistance as you drill, and especially if you get little flecks of wood turned out of the hole by the drill bit, you've found a stud. If the drill merely turns out a little plaster **435**

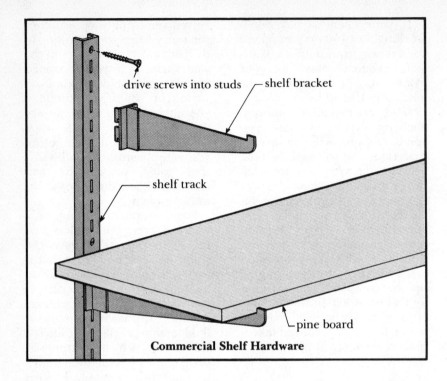

Commercial Shelf Hardware

(drive screws into studs, shelf bracket, shelf track, pine board)

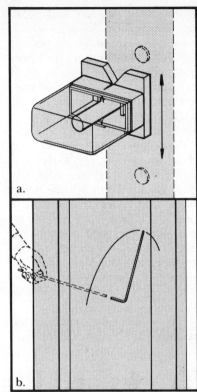

Locating studs: a. Using a magnetic stud-finder to locate nails driven into studs. b. Twisting a length of wire inserted in a test hole.

dust, then breaks through, your obstruction was something other than a stud.

The screws supplied with the tracks should be sufficiently long to get a good purchase in the stud. But if you are skeptical, toss them out and buy longer ones, say 2 to 3 inches. Just be sure the shank will fit the holes in the tracks. Be sure too that you run a screw into every hole in each track. The last thing you'll want is the shelves pulling away from the wall and dumping all your dishes or canned goods on the floor.

What if you have a masonry wall you want to hang tracks on? Your best bet is to use another kind of shelves. The next best bet is to use an electric drill and a masonry drill bit to bore holes into the mortar, then slip lead plugs into the holes. Turn the screws through the tracks into the plugs. You must match the length of the screw to the depth of the plug; if the screw is too long, it will shear off when it hits the bottom of the plug. With such an installation, you should limit the load you put on the shelves.

Cased-In Shelves

The most elaborate shelving installation would be the one in

which the shelf unit resembles the case of a cabinet. Two or

436

Shelf hardware can be hung on masonry walls by driving screws into lead plugs fitted into holes drilled in the mortar.

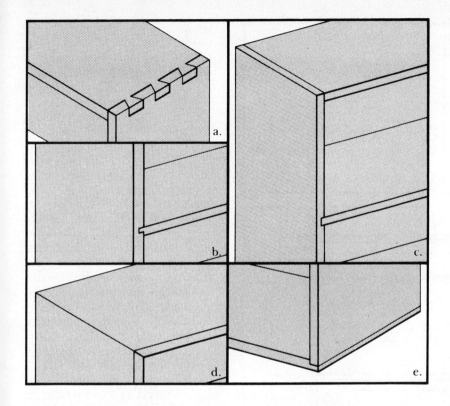

If the unit will be a wall-mounted one, you must incorporate some way of attaching it to the wall. In a wall cabinet, a hanging rail is built into the case. It need be nothing more than a 1 × 4 nailed between the sides, parallel to the back, perpendicular to the top. Screws are then driven through it into the wall studs. While it's most common to think of a wall-mounted unit as being one that "hangs" on the wall, you should, just as with cabinets, attach any substantial shelf unit to the wall. If your shelf unit is a divider—separating work area from dining area, for example—you should attach the unit to the floor. Nothing dogmatic here, it's just the way it is generally done.

As the unit gets more elaborate, more finished, you may

more upright sides and perhaps an intermediate partition or two to support shelves. In a fancy setup, the unit might even have a face frame. What it is is a simple cabinet. No doors, no drawers, just shelves in a case.

As a consequence, construction of such shelves is like construction of a cabinet. Cut two sides and the shelves. Mark the locations of the shelves on the sides and glue and nail the unit together. You can use any of the joints you'd use to join a case: butt joints, dado joints, rabbet joints, dado-and-rabbet joints, even dovetail joints.

Install a hanging rail at the back of cased-in shelves, just beneath the top. Screws are driven through it to attach the unit to the wall.

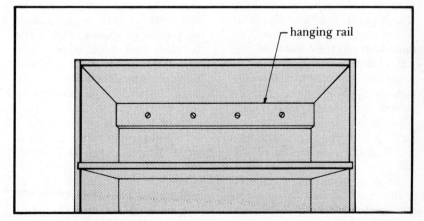

hanging rail

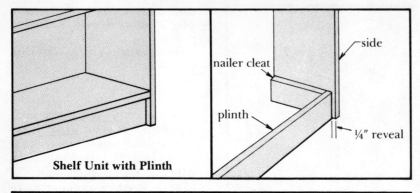

Shelf Unit with Plinth

nailer cleat

plinth

side

¼″ reveal

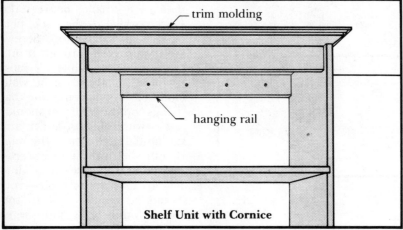

trim molding

hanging rail

Shelf Unit with Cornice

choose to design and build it with a toe space or a plinth at the bottom and with a soffit at the top. If the unit is deep, mimicking a base cabinet, incorporate a toe space (sometimes called a kick space). In this situation, cut a notch into the base of each side piece, about 3 inches wide and 3½ inches high. Nail the plinth, which is the face strip across the base, into this notch during assembly of the unit.

In most instances, shelf units won't have a kick space. The plinth should simply be placed between the sides, beneath the bottom shelf, with a ¼-inch reveal. The easiest way to handle this element is to attach nailers to the sides, flush with their bottoms and back edges. The nailers should be 1 inch shorter than the sides are wide and the same width as the plinth. To install the plinth, just butt it against the ends of the nailers. You'll automatically get the desired ¼-inch reveal. The bottom (or bottom shelf) is fitted between the sides and rests on the nailers and the plinth.

To create a soffit, the same

setup can be turned upside down. The joint between the top of the shelf unit and the ceiling or the soffit and the shelf unit and the soffit and ceiling is concealed by trim molding.

The shelves in such a unit can be glued and nailed in fixed positions, or they can be adjustable. The same techniques used to put adjustable shelves in cabinets are used. Quickest and easiest to install are commercial tracks and clips. These closely resemble the track-and-bracket hardware used to hang shelves on walls. But these tracks have horizontal slots, and the clips are merely tabs upon which the shelf rests. You need four tracks for a shelf unit, with four clips supporting each shelf.

If you are economizing, support the shelves with metal shelf-support pins or bits of dowel thrust in holes drilled in the sides. The holes have to be laid out precisely, with a pair of holes in one side matched by a pair of holes in the facing side. The holes should be drilled about ⅜ inch deep.

Any materials you'd use to construct cabinets you can use to build shelves. For deep shelves, perhaps you'd use plywood or particle board, but for units up to 11 inches deep, use board lumber. A half-dozen #2 pine boards can yield a commodious shelf unit at a relatively low price. The higher the grade of lumber you use, of course, the better the appearance will be (and the more it will cost).

Finishing such a shelf unit is done the same way finishing a cabinet is. Use paint, varnish, oil or other finishing material.

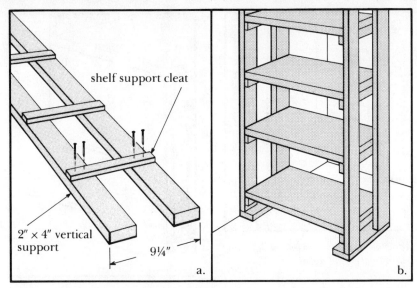

Constructing pantry shelving: a. Make supports by nailing cleats across two 2 x 4 uprights. b. After the supports are erected, drop shelves in place.

Pantry Shelves

Shelves in a pantry are not intrinsically different from shelves in a kitchen. But simply because of the nature of a pantry—or a cold cellar or a root cellar—the shelves you build for that room can in a practical way be different.

They don't need to be attractive. They just need to be sturdy.

The pantry is the place to get some practice if you've never done woodworking, or if you've never built anything on the order of shelves or cabinets. You can use lower-grade—and thus less costly—materials. Your cutting and joining can be rougher. You need not fret over minor mistakes, even if they show. This is the pantry, a prac-

tical place, not a showplace.

It is doubtful that you'd want to use track-and-bracket hardware in the pantry. Your pantry shelves will bear precious stores, so you want to be fully confident of their ability to support the load.

Use framing lumber: 2 × 4s, 2 × 6s, 2 × 10s. You can either construct a framework to sup-

port the shelves, or you can case-in shelves.

Consider, for example, constructing floor-to-ceiling shelves for all your canned goods. Use 2 × 4s in pairs for the vertical supports. For each support, lay out two 2 × 4s cut to a length 1½ inches shy of the distance from floor to ceiling. Cut pieces of furring (usually low-grade 1 × 2 stock) as long as the shelves are wide. Nail them across the 2 × 4s for shelf-support cleats. In spacing them, be sure to account for the thickness of the shelf. When the support assemblies are finished, nail lengths of 2 × 4 to the floor for these supports to be set upon. Stand the supports on end, hoist them onto the 2 × 4s nailed to the floor, which should raise them to the ceiling, and toenail them to both the ceiling and the floor. Cut the shelves to length from 2 × 6, 2 × 8 or 2 × 10 stock, and set them in place.

In such a situation, you should probably limit the shelf span to 24 to 36 inches. A shelf longer than that, loaded up with canning jars—full ones—two or three or four deep may well sag. That's unnerving, especially when those jars represent months of your labor.

Shelving Miscellany

Shelving can meld any of the elements of the three basic varieties already seen: hardware-supported shelves, cased-in shelves, framed-in shelves. You could, for example, fabricate

shelf units by attaching a cleat across each end of the shelf board, then attaching the cleats to vertical supports, like floor-to-ceiling 2 × 4s. In a rough form, the finished shelf setup

439

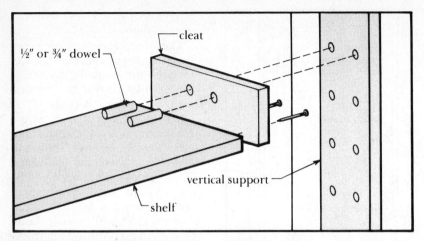

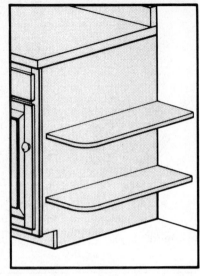

Adjustable shelves can be made using board lumber and dowels.

Finish a run of wall or base cabinets with a tier of open shelves.

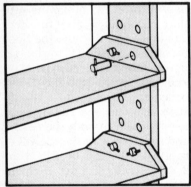

The appearance of homemade adjustable shelves can be refined by mitering the upper corners of the cleats and installing stop pins in the adjusting dowels.

would resemble the pantry shelves. But if made of good-quality materials, carefully crafted and thoughtfully appointed, such a setup would be very attractive.

Similarly, you could convert such a setup into adjustable shelves by boring pairs of holes through each cleat and a series of matching pairs of holes in the vertical supports. A bit of dowel—say ½-inch- or ¾-inch-diameter—stuck through the cleat into the support would hold the shelf, but would permit you to move it.

Shelves don't have to be in multiples. You can spot single shelves here and there about the kitchen, positioning them just where you need them. A shelf by the stove for herbs and spices is a kitchen commonplace. You can use individual stamped-steel brackets, wrought iron brackets, handmade wooden brackets or lengths of rope or chain or metal rod to support such shelves.

You can build a cabinet and case-in shelves atop it, making a hutch or sideboard. You can finish off a run of wall or floor cabinets with a tier of mitered or rounded-edged shelves.

The point is that shelves aren't difficult to make or install. If you've come this far in building your harvest kitchen, don't be put off from creating your own storage space by a perceived but undemonstrated lack of skill. You *can* build at least shelves. You are limited only by your nerve. And your imagination.

440

Prefabricated cabinets are built in a shop, carted to the kitchen, and bolted or screwed in place. The vast majority of kitchens built these days have prefab cabinets.

If you decide, for one reason or another, that you are not going to build your own cabinets, chances are that you'll visit a kitchen cabinet dealer,

Prefab Cabinets

look through his almost-endless variety of wall, floor and corner modules, his selection of door- and drawer-front styles and his wood and finish selections, and pick cabinets to fill your kitchen. If you are better heeled, perhaps just more demanding, you'll visit a custom cabinetmaker and have cabinets designed and built especially for your harvest kitchen.

The custom cabinetmaker may come to your house and build your kitchen cabinets right there in your kitchen. But don't be surprised if he doesn't. He may arrive with a truckload of cabinet modules, ready to be bolted or screwed in place.

Certainly, that's the way your kitchen cabinets from the Kus-tom Kitchen Kreations Kompany's cabinet factory will arrive. In a matter of a day or two, well-practiced installers will have fastened the modules to the walls and to each other. The cabinets will be plumb and level and so tightly joined it'll look as though they were built in place. A counter top will have been installed—even that can be purchased prefabbed—and the sink and any built-in appliances will have been installed too.

And that's the biggest part of making a kitchen a kitchen. Redoing walls and floors, moving windows or doors, and rewiring are all things that could happen in any room-remodeling project. Only the kitchen gets the cabinets, the sink, the stove.

Building Your Own

You don't have to buy cabinets to benefit from the advantages of prefabbing. You can build your own cabinets in the shop, and after they're all finished and the kitchen is ready, you can cart them into the kitchen and bolt or screw them in place. The cabinetmaking is largely confined to the shop, which should be set up for it. The kitchen project can be speeded up, even if it is only by a couple of weeks.

The disadvantage is that you'll undoubtedly use a little more material. The modules have to be made in manageable sizes. If you can't carry the cabinet or get it through the door, you've made trouble, not eliminated it. Each module has to be a complete unit, with side, top and back panels or frames. It's likely you'll end up with double thicknesses of plywood here and there where a single thickness would suffice, because you've made the run of cabinets in two, three or four modules, each with plywood sides. You may install backs where you wouldn't if you were building in place. The difference in materials costs could run to several hundred dollars.

But that expense may be worthwhile. You can spend as much time as you want building cabinets, then do the kitchen itself when they are done. Why spend months operating a kitchen out of boxes in the dining room? Building cabinets in place can have you doing that, especially if you've only got weekends and evenings in which to do the job.

Building in modules requires you to break your cabinet design into basic units. A unit to hold a sink may be 6 feet long, while a space between the stove and a wall may be only a foot wide. While you can make individual units longer or shorter than this, it's doubtful that you'd want to. Cabinet factories make a dozen or more different lengths: 12, 18, 24, 27, 30, 33, 36, 42, 48, 54, 60, 66, 72 and 84 inches, for example. The narrowest ones have a single door and drawer. Others have two doors and one long drawer, or a door and a rank of drawers, or in the longest units, several doors and drawers and accommodation for a sink or rangetop to be installed.

These are the basics for base, or floor, cabinets. But in addition, there are wall cabinets and special tall cabinets to house a wall oven or two, or to make a broom closet or pantry.

The construction routines are the same for each cabinet of its type, though the dimensions of the pieces vary. Most any style of door will work, ranging from a simple-to-make plywood door to a complicated raised-panel door. Drawers can be constructed with simple joints or with handcrafted dovetails. There can be special features, like compartmented drawers for silverware and utensils, or a special holder for a trash can, or bins for vegetables, or drawer-shelves for heavy equipment like mixers or grain mills.

Cabinet Plans

Just how you build the specific cabinets you need is up to you. In the pages following are specific instructions for constructing more than a dozen cabinets. It's pretty doubtful that you'd use one of each in your harvest kitchen, but there should be one of everything you *will* use. You can follow the directions and make them exactly as shown, or you can modify the plans as necessary to suit your needs. You may, for example, want to trim or stretch the size of the basic base or wall cabinets by a few inches to fit the expanse of wall you have for cabinetry.

You may choose to sidestep the somewhat difficult-to-make raised-panel doors, since these are almost impossible to make without a table saw or radial arm saw. But frame doors with a plain panel or plain plywood doors can be made without expensive shop tools.

Materials Lists

All of the cabinets were made with plywood and board lumber. Obviously, they can be made with hardwoods, if you've got the money and the ability and the urge. The materials list with each cabinet itemizes the supplies necessary to build that particular cabinet, including material for a counter top for it alone. If you choose to make more than one of them, you'll probably be able to save here

and there by making necessary parts for one out of the scraps from another.

Review the lists carefully before you buy. The rationale in developing the lists for the cabinets, as well as the lists for the projects in Part V, was to provide a cuttings list and a shopping list. The chart lists a board to be purchased, followed by the pieces it will yield. Every effort was made to minimize purchases, but usually you are faced with a supplier who won't part with anything less than a minimum standard length. If you've got someone who *will* sell you a 2- or 3-foot length of

board lumber, by all means revise the list.

Construction Specifics

After you've made your purchase, follow the construction directions. Since all the cabinets are of the same style, all of the specifics aren't repeated and repeated. The basic floor cabinet, a 36-inch model, has all the specifics. You are referred to that cabinet to find out exactly how to join the doors; how to dowel the face frame; how to laminate the counter top. If you want to change the plans, or substitute a different joining technique for the one specified, do so. "The Cabinetmaker's Craft" may help you.

Installing Prefab Cabinets

Once you've completed your prefab cabinets and all the rough-in work of preparing the kitchen itself, you are ready to install the cabinets. If your kitchen is in fact plumb and square—and it'll be unusual if it is—the cabinet installation shouldn't take too long.

The biggest part of any installation is the plumbing and leveling. You have to secure the cabinets firmly to each other and to the walls, the floor, and sometimes the ceiling of the kitchen. If the walls are bowed or worse, the cabinets will be racked out of shape as you screw them to the walls. The doors won't open, or they won't

close. The drawers won't work right. The edges of individual modules won't meet; the counter top will start your fresh eggs rolling toward the precipice.

To avoid all the woe, you've got to spend whatever time it takes to install your cabinets plumb and level. And secure.

Your first step is to assess the situation and to decide on your work sequence.

Though there is a logical progression, it can start either with the base cabinets or the wall cabinets. If you install the base cabinets first, you can use these cabinets as part of the support for the wall cabinets as they are **443**

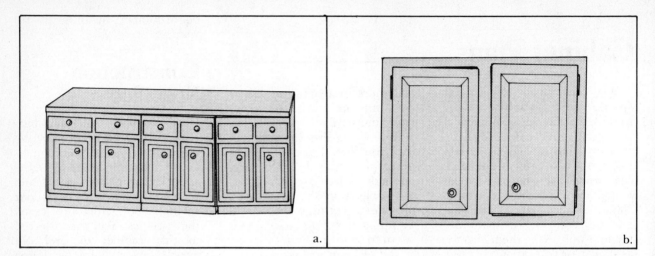

a.

b.

Cabinets must be installed properly to look and work right: a. Gaps between units and crooked counter tops are consequences of failure to level the cabinets. b. Ill-fitting doors that won't stay closed or are difficult to open are a consequence of fastening cabinets tightly to walls that aren't flat.

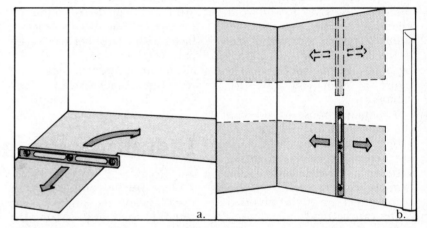

a.

b.

Using a level to check the floor and walls: a. Go over the floor where the base cabinets will be located and check carefully for peaks and valleys; mark the highest and lowest spots. b. Do the same with the walls, checking for plumb and for high spots and low spots.

installed. But using the base cabinets in this way can, if you aren't careful, cause them to get banged up. Even though you have to cobble up a bit more scaffolding to support them during the operation, or punch a few holes in the walls that you'll have to patch, it's usually easiest, and less damaging, to install the wall cabinets first.

A few general rules apply equally to wall, base and floor-to-ceiling cabinet installations. First is always to use screws or lag bolts for this work, never nails. Always secure the cabinets to the studs or joists, not to whatever material sheathes the room. Use a long level to give you the lay of the walls, ceiling **444** and floor; find the low and high

spots before you begin. Mark a plumb line and a level line on the wall. Work from the corner or corners out.

Don't clutter up the kitchen space with cabinets. After you've decided in what order you are going to install the cabinets, carry them into the kitchen in that order. If the wall cabinets go up first, carry them

in, fasten them together, hoist them up onto the wall and screw them fast. Only then go out for the floor cabinets.

Don't make the job harder by trying to work with the drawers and doors installed. Remove the doors, especially from the wall cabinets. They'll add to the weight your helpers must lift, but more important, they'll be

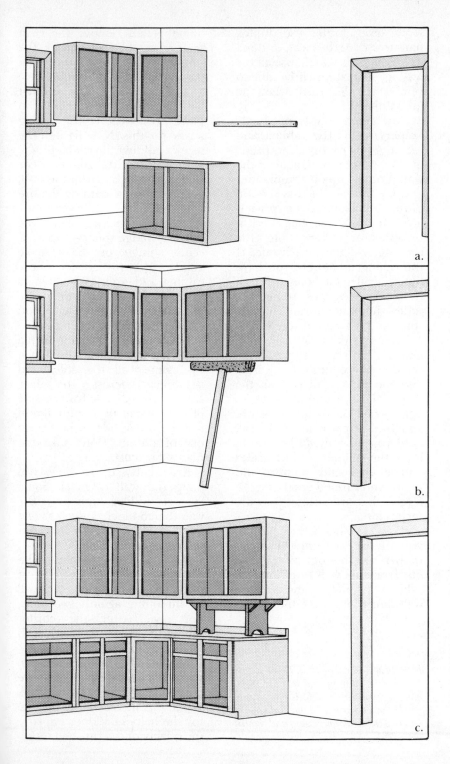

in the way. It won't take long at all to reinstall the doors and drawers after the cabinets are in place.

Wall Cabinets

The big trick in installing a wall cabinet is holding it in position, plumb and level, until you get pilot holes drilled and screws driven. You can't just hoist it up against the wall, then screw it fast. You have to do some jockeying to get the cabinet level, and to get the back properly shimmed from a wall that's surely a little uneven. And *then* you have to *hold* it in that state until the pilot holes are drilled and the screws driven.

The easiest way to do it is to nail a cleat or ledger to the wall and use it as the fulcrum of your support. Obviously, this will put holes in the wall, and if you've got the finish coat of paint or the wallpaper applied, you aren't going to do this. But it is, nevertheless, the most sure approach.

Since wall cabinets are usually installed 54 inches above the floor, nail the cleat to the wall 54 inches above the floor. Measure from the high point of the floor. Be very sure the cleat is per-

Setting up wall cabinets: a. Level and fasten a support cleat to the wall; the cabinet is rested on the cleat while it is being installed. b. Or construct a padded T-shaped support; the device supports the cabinet while it is leveled and installed. c. If base cabinets are in place, use a small benchlike support to hold the wall cabinets during installation.

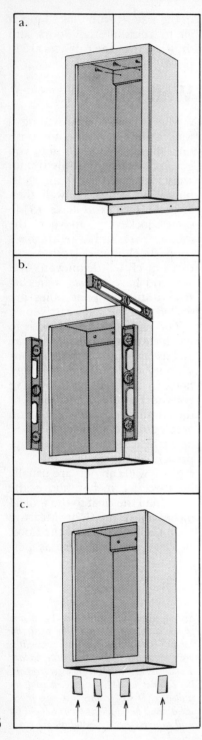

a.

b.

c.

fectly level. Either use duplex nails to secure the cleat, or don't drive the nails you do use all the way in, so that you'll be able to remove the cleat easily when the job's done.

Now get a couple of sturdy helpers to lift the cabinet and rest it gently on the cleat, pressing the cabinet back against the wall. You get up on a stepladder and lay the level across the top of the cabinet, just to be sure it is level. It should be, but check it nonetheless. Then hold the level against the face frame. If the cabinet is plumb, you have but to drill pilot holes through the back crosspiece, sometimes called the hanging rail, into the studs and drive your screws.

Use screws that are long enough. You have to penetrate the crosspiece and cabinet back and the plaster 'til you hit the stud. That can amount to 1½ to 1¾ inches of material before you hit supporting material. And you do want to be able to stack the cabinets full of dishes and glasses and pottery and plants and canned goods. So use screws that are at least 3 to 3½ inches long.

If the cabinet is not plumb, you will have to shim it from the wall. If the bottom must come out from the wall to plumb the cabinet, fasten the cabinet to the wall, but don't drive the screws

Installing wall cabinets: a. Drive screws through the hanging rail into the studs; don't tighten them yet. b. Use a level to check the alignment of the cabinet. c. Insert shims where necessary and tighten the screws.

home. Then remove the cleat and shim the bottom of the cabinet out from the wall enough to make it plumb. Drive a screw through the cabinet back into the shim to hold it in place. You needn't use a long screw for this. Now tighten the screws holding the cabinet.

If the top of the cabinet needs to come out a bit from the wall, you do the shimming before you drill holes and drive screws. While your helpers hold the cabinet, wedge shims—pieces of cedar shingle or shake make good shims—between the cabinet and wall. Your helpers have to apply enough muscle to pin the shims in place until you do get the cabinet secured.

In checking the plumb with a level, check all the angles. Lay it up against all the stiles and diagonally across the face frame. It is possible for one side of the cabinet to be plumb and for the other side to be pulled out of plumb. Don't take too many shortcuts.

Essentially, that's how you hang the wall cabinets. Some cabinets will be higher on the wall than 54 inches, such as one over a sink or refrigerator. But the process is the same.

Start in the corner. The corner cabinet will be the most difficult to hang, since you will be shimming against two walls, not one. After the corner cabinet is fixed, proceed with the rest.

All the other cabinets in a run should be joined before they are hoisted into place and secured. While this increases the burden for the helpers, it does improve the quality of the finished instal-

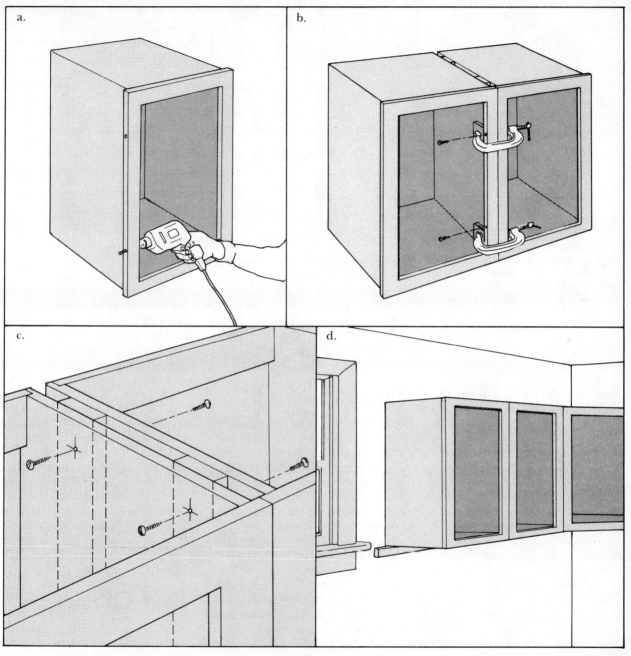

Tying the cabinets in a run together: a. Drill holes through the edges of the outside stiles. b. Clamp the cabinets together and drive screws through one stile into another. c. An alternative is to drive screws through cabinet sides into spacers between the units. d. Short runs can be joined, then installed as a single unit.

lation and makes the process go faster.

The usual way of fastening

447

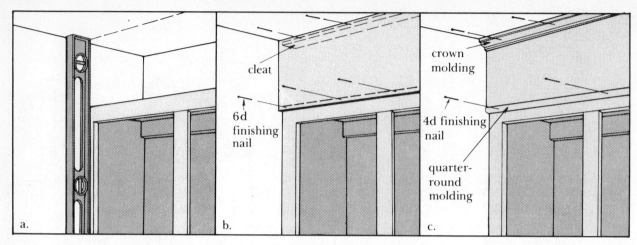

Constructing a soffit: a. Use a level or framing square to transfer cabinet outline to the ceiling. b. Nail a cleat to the ceiling, then attach the soffit to the cleat and the cabinet. c. Install trim to conceal the seams.

the cabinets together is to drive screws through the edge of the face frame stiles of each into the face frame of its neighbors. This requires careful boring and long, slender screws. An easier approach is to drive screws through the cabinet sides into ½-inch spacers placed between the cases. To do this, line up the cabinets on the floor and clamp them together with C clamps. Get the stile edges of adjoining cabinets lined up carefully, so they are flush and in contact along their entire lengths. Slip a spacer between the cabinets against the face frame. Drill a couple holes through both sides of each cabinet into the spaces and drive in 1½-inch screws. The final step is to slip another ½-inch spacer between the case sides near the back and drive screws into it.

After the run of wall cabinets is in place, fasten it to the corner cabinet, if there is one. Remove the cleat and install the cabinet doors and this part of the job is done, unless you plan to install a soffit between the cabinets and the ceiling.

Building a Soffit

Unless you have unusually low ceilings or remarkably tall cabinets, you will have a space of a foot or more high between the top of the wall (or so-called floor-to-ceiling) cabinets and the ceiling. The smart designer plans to use the space for display or near-dead storage. You can put plants, knickknacks, pottery, even cookbooks on top of the cabinets. No sense wasting useful open shelf space.

But it is common to install a soffit, which is essentially a false wall between the cabinet top and the ceiling. Nail cleats to the ceiling that parallel the front and ends of the cabinets. Then fasten boards, paneling or wallboard to the cabinets and

the cleats, covering the gap. Finish the job by nailing molding to trim and thus obscure the joint between the cabinet and the soffit and between the soffit and the ceiling.

An alternative method is to nail cleats to both the top of the cabinet and the ceiling. Set them back from the cabinet edge so that the soffit material, be it wallboard, paneling or pieces of board lumber, will fit flush with the face frame of the cabinet. You will still need some sort of trim to cover the joint between the soffit and the cabinet.

The soffit serves no really useful purpose. In some kitchens, the soffit may hide a ventilation duct, but it is usually purely decorative.

Base Cabinets

After installing the wall cabinets, installing the base cabinets is easy. You do have to shim them to keep them plumb and level, but you don't have to prop or muscle them.

As with the wall cabinets, you

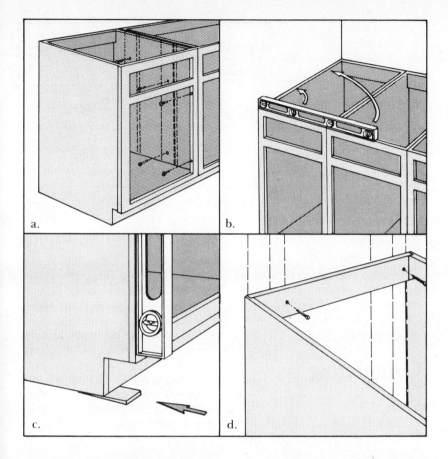

a.

b.

c.

d.

level—a long one is best—along the top of the cabinets, and drive shims under the cabinet sides as necessary to get the entire run straight and level. Check the entire surface area with the level, checking diagonally across the top, from the front edge to the wall and from end to end. Apply the level to the face frames, too. If the top's level at this point, so should the front be plumb. But check it.

Fasten the cabinets to the wall, just as you did the wall cabinets, except that you need not use such long screws. Here, the floor will support the cabinets; the screws hold the cabinets in alignment, but do not support them.

As you do this drilling and driving, check with the level to be sure you aren't racking the cabinets as you secure them to the wall. If there's an obvious gap between the wall and the cabinet, caused by bowing in the wall, wedge a shim in the gap.

So-called floor-to-ceiling cabinets, like one for a wall oven or a broom closet or pantry, are installed with the floor cabinets, but they must also align with any wall cabinets, especially those they adjoin. When they adjoin, they should be fastened together.

should start in a corner and work along the run. Individual units must be fastened to their neighbors. The whole run must be fastened to the wall.

You must shim everything up to the level of the high point of the floor. It won't do to fasten a corner cabinet to the wall, then add a couple more units, only to discover that the third unit rides up on the high spot, throwing the run out of kilter. If at all possible, fasten all the cabinets in a run together, then shim them and secure them to the wall. Failing that, scribe a level line on the wall 34 inches above the floor at the high spot. Shim

up the cabinets until they align with this line, and you should get a level installation.

As you assemble the cabinets into the run, fasten them together using the same approach you used with the wall cabinets. Draw neighboring units together with C clamps, then drive screws through the case sides into ½-inch spacers between the sides of adjoining cabinets. Put screws along the front and the back of both sides of each cabinet. Obviously, you should do this work with the cabinets in position along the wall.

Now start leveling. Lay the

449

The final step in installing the base cabinets is to install the counter top and—if you haven't already done so—the plinth, which is the facing in the toe space. For the best appearance and most utilitarian installation, both should be one-piece elements. In the cabinet projects that follow, specifications are given for individual plinths and counter tops. More than anything else, these specifications will serve you when it comes time to order materials.

The plinth is seldom anything other than a length of 1 × 4, crosscut to fit the run, slipped into place and nailed to the cases of the cabinets. However, if the floor is a rolling one, you may want to go to the trouble of cutting a contour on the bottom edge of the plinth to match the floor. You have to do it before you install the cabinets. To do this, set the plinth on edge, blocked about an inch above the floor, exactly where it will be installed. Shim it until it is level. Then set a compass so that when it is held roughly parallel to the floor, the point will be on the low spot of the floor and the pencil on the very edge of the plinth. Draw the compass along the floor, transforming its dips and swells into a contour line along the plinth. Cut along the line with a saber saw or coping saw.

The counter top can have been prefabricated, but it may be wiser to have the material on hand and fabricate the counter top to suit the actual installation. The details of that enterprise are found elsewhere. Once the counter top is finished, set it in

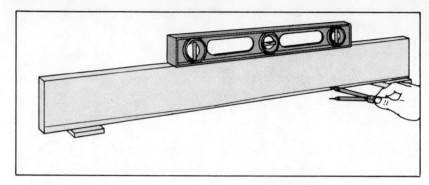

Trace the contour of the floor on the plinth using a compass. The plinth must be shimmed so it is level.

place atop the cabinets, and attach it with 1¾-inch screws driven through the front and rear top crosspieces of each cabinet into the core.

Completing the Job

The last details of the installation are decorative. Any ex-posed cabinet sides should be covered with a piece of ¼-inch hardwood plywood or sheet paneling that harmonizes with the rest of the cabinetry and the rest of the kitchen. Use contact cement for this job.

Then install molding between the walls and cabinets to conceal mismatching caused by uneven walls.

The Basic Base Cabinet

This base cabinet is the model for all the others in this chapter. Once you've built this cabinet, you've dealt with almost all the problems you'll meet in cabinet building.

The cabinet has the standard architectural measurements for a kitchen cabinet. With the counter top in place, it is 36 inches tall, 25 inches deep (the

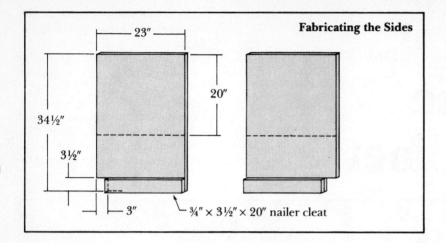

Fabricating the Sides

23"

20"

34½"

3½"

3"

¾" × 3½" × 20" nailer cleat

cabinet itself is 24 inches deep) and 36 inches wide. Of course, it can be freestanding, but it is really designed to be a part of a run of cabinets.

Two raised-panel doors and two drawers are included in the cabinet. Behind the right door is a shallow drawer at shelf height for heavy equipment. An ordinary shelf is behind the left door.

Case Construction

The first step is to build the case. Construction materials for this consist of interior plywood with one good side, 1 × 4 #2 pine and 2 × 6 fir.

a. From ⅝-inch A-C interior plywood, cut two pieces 23 inches by 34½ inches for the side panels, two pieces 23 inches by 34¼ inches for the bottom and the shelf, and three pieces 5½ inches by 23 inches for the drawer supports. From ¼-inch A-C interior plywood, cut a piece 34½ inches by 35½ inches for the back. From 1 × 4 #2

pine, cut two pieces 20 inches long for the nailer cleats, one piece 36 inches long for the plinth and three pieces 34¼ inches long for the top and back crosspieces. From 2 × 6 construction-grade fir, cut one piece 23 inches long for the lower center drawer support and one piece 22¼ inches long for the

upper center drawer support.

b. In one corner of each side panel cut a 3-inch-wide by 3½-inch-high notch for the toe space. Be certain to cut the notches so you have a right and left side panel. Orient the good side of the plywood to the inside of the case. Using 1-inch underlayment nails and glue, attach the nailer cleats to the inside of the panels at the bottom. They should be flush with the bottom edge and with the edge of the toe space.

c. Begin assembly of the case by gluing and nailing the bottom in place, using 6d coated nails. Use corner clamps to hold the side panels and bottom in position until you get the nails driven. Nail through the sides into the edges of the bottom. Install the two top crosspieces next, using corner clamps to position the pieces until you get the nails driven through the sides into the crosspieces. Use

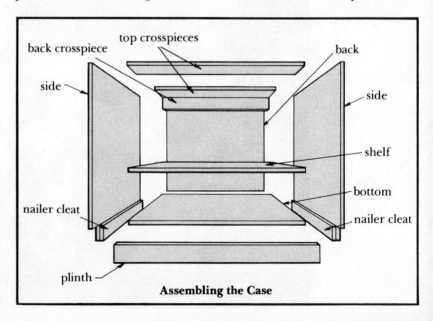

back crosspiece

top crosspieces

back

side

side

shelf

bottom

nailer cleat

nailer cleat

plinth

Assembling the Case

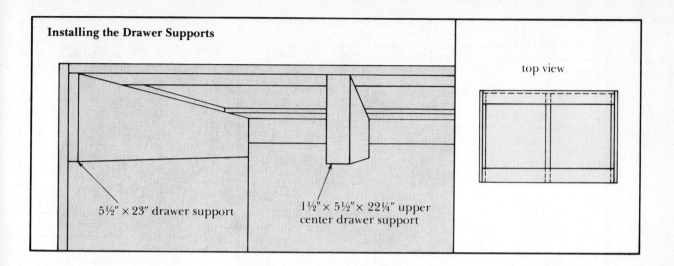

Installing the Drawer Supports

top view

$5\frac{1}{2}'' \times 23''$ drawer support

$1\frac{1}{2}'' \times 5\frac{1}{2}'' \times 22\frac{1}{4}''$ upper center drawer support

glue here too, and in every other joint. One crosspiece should be flush with the front and top edges of the side panels, and one should be flush with the back and top edges. The third crosspiece, for the back, should be glued and nailed between the side panels, against the rear top crosspiece, though at right angles to it. Glue and nail the plinth in place across the case front in the toe space. It should project past each side an equal amount. (If you are constructing several cabinets you probably will want to tie them together with a single-piece plinth, just as you would with a single-piece counter top.) The shelf goes in next. Position it 20 inches from the top edges, holding it in place with corner clamps until the nails are driven. Check the squareness of the cabinet with a framing square and by measuring diagonally from corner to corner (if the diagonals are equal, the cabinet is square). Glue and nail the

back in place, butting it against the edges of the sides and covering the back crosspiece.

d. Next, install the drawer supports. Glue a plywood support on the inside of each side panel, directly below the top crosspieces. Drive some 1-inch underlayment nails through the supports into the sides. Glue and nail the upper center drawer support—the shorter 2 × 6—to the crosspieces, centered 16⅜ inches from each side panel. Glue and nail the lower 2 × 6 center drawer support to the shelf, directly below the upper such support. Glue and nail, with the underlayment nails, the third plywood support on the right side above, but resting upon, the shelf.

Face Frame Construction

The face frame is composed of three uprights, called stiles, joined with ⅜-inch dowels to six

crosspieces, called rails.

a. From 1 × 2 select pine, cut three 31⅞-inch-long stiles and six 15¾-inch-long rails. From ⅜-inch dowel, cut twenty-four pieces, each 1½ inches long.

After cutting and sanding the rails and stiles, lay them face down on the workbench with the rails between the stiles as in the final assembly. Discreetly mark each piece at each joint so you'll always be mating the same pieces at the same places. Place the two intermediate rails 3¾ inches below the upper rails. Mark the positions of the rails on the stiles to aid in drilling for the dowel joints.

b. Mark the hole locations on both the rails and stiles, joint by joint. The idea is to put a mark on a common face of the pieces—either front or back —marking both rail and stile with a single stroke along a square. Set your doweling jig so it will center the hole you drill ⅜ inch from either edge of the piece. Carefully line up the **453**

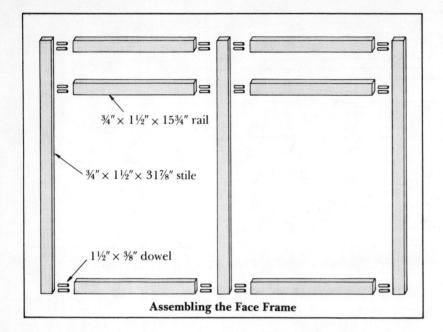

¾″ × 1½″ × 15¾″ rail

¾″ × 1½″ × 31⅞″ stile

1½″ × ⅜″ dowel

Assembling the Face Frame

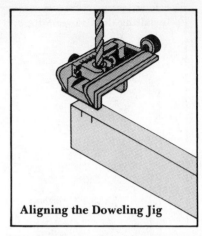

Aligning the Doweling Jig

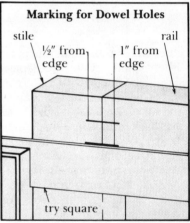

Marking for Dowel Holes

stile   rail

½″ from edge   1″ from edge

try square

alignment mark on the jig with the line you made on the piece. Drill the hole using a drill bit, or better, using a brad-point drill bit. Move the jig to the second mark at the joint and drill that hole. Transfer the jig to the mating piece, line it up and drill. As long as you don't monkey with the hole-center setting of the jig and as long as you always use the marks on the common face of each piece, you should have holes that line up properly.

Each joint must have two dowels, centered from edge to edge, and located ½ inch and 1 inch from the top of the mating area. Take the time required to do this work as precisely as possible. If the holes are the slightest bit off, the rail and the stile won't mate properly. If one hole is off, in fact, it can completely prevent you from as-**454**

sembling the joint.

The holes in the outer stiles should be ever-so-slightly deeper than ¾ inch, but don't drill all the way through. Do drill all the way through the center stile. When you are done, there should be six holes through it from edge to edge, two at each point at which the rails abut it. Drill holes slightly more than ¾ inch deep into the rails, using the same technique you used with the stiles.

c. Dry-fit the dowels into the holes. They should fit tightly, but not so tightly that they have to be pounded into place. The glue will swell them, and if they are tighter than a press fit now, they'll be too tight at final assembly. If the fit is too tight, try to sand down the dowels, rather than trying to enlarge the holes. The best approach is to measure the dowel carefully before you

buy, so you get material that is actually ⅜ inch in diameter; it isn't always so.

Round the ends of each piece slightly with sandpaper or, if you have one, a dowel pointer. Put glue into the holes of each rail and tap the dowels into the holes with a hammer. You don't want to seat the dowels firmly against the hole bottom, but neither do you want to have too much protruding. Let the glue set for about 15 minutes. Join each rail to the stile it adjoins by applying glue to the holes and

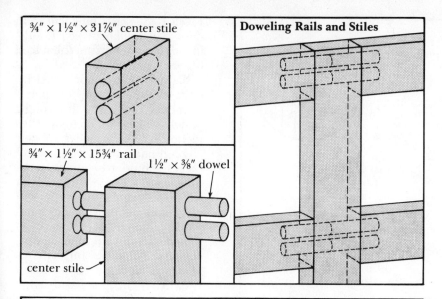

¾" × 1½" × 31⅞" center stile

¾" × 1½" × 15¾" rail

1½" × ⅜" dowel

center stile

Doweling Rails and Stiles

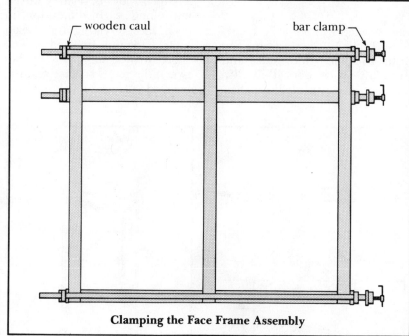

wooden caul

bar clamp

Clamping the Face Frame Assembly

around the outer stiles directly over the top and bottom rails. Protect the stiles with wooden cauls inserted between the stiles and the clamp jaws. Tighten the clamps until glue is forced out of the joints, then measure the diagonals of the frame to be sure it is square. Check its flatness, too. Add a third bar clamp, across the opposite face of the frame from the other two, directly across the two middle rails. After the glue has dried and the clamps have been removed, use a sharp chisel to remove any dried squeeze-out. Then sand any visible markings from the frame.

d. To attach the frame to the case, set the case flat on its back, lay the frame in place and check the fit. The frame should extend ¼ inch beyond the case on either side. The upper edge of the bottom rails should be flush with the top surface of the bottom, and, of course, the top edges of the case and the frame should be flush. Glue the frame to the plywood edges of the cabinet. Drill pilot holes, and fasten the frame with 6d finishing or casing nails. Work along each side stile, following with the center stile and the rails. Set the nails, and fill the nail holes with wood filler, using a color to match the ultimate finish of the cabinet. Sand the face frame for the last time.

Door Construction

The cabinet doors are assembled by joining the door rails and stiles with mortise-and-tenon joints around a raised panel. A table saw or a radial

dowels. Set the stile on edge and work the rail into place, rocking it from side to side, if necessary, and tapping it with a hammer.

Continue assembling the frame in this manner. Set the completed frame across a workbench, and fasten bar clamps

455

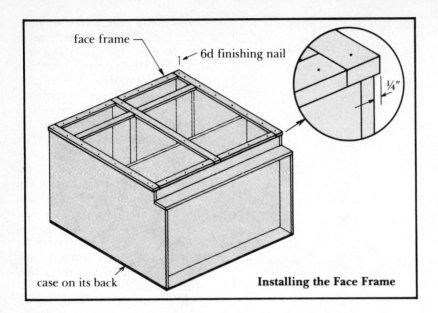

face frame

6d finishing nail

¼"

case on its back

Installing the Face Frame

arm saw is a necessary tool in the construction of these doors. Plain panel doors, in which an ordinary plywood panel replaces the raised panel, can be constructed without a shop saw.

a. From 1 × 3 select pine, cut four 24¼-inch door stiles and four 13¾-inch door rails. Rip them to a width of 2¼ inches.

From 1 × 8 select pine, cut four door panel elements, each 20½ inches long. Then rip them to a 6¼-inch width.

b. Make each door panel by edge-gluing two of the panel elements together; the rough panels will be ¾ inch by 12½ inches by 20½ inches. When edge-gluing, the grain of all pieces should run in the same direction. Arrange the pieces so the growth rings run in opposite directions, to prevent cupping. Apply glue to the edges to be joined, clamp with pipe clamps, check the flatness and squareness, and let dry.

c. After the glue has dried, a 1⅝-inch-wide beveled band is cut along each dimension in each face, creating the raised panel. In the finished panel, there will be a ⅛-inch lip between the panel surface and the beveled surface. The combined

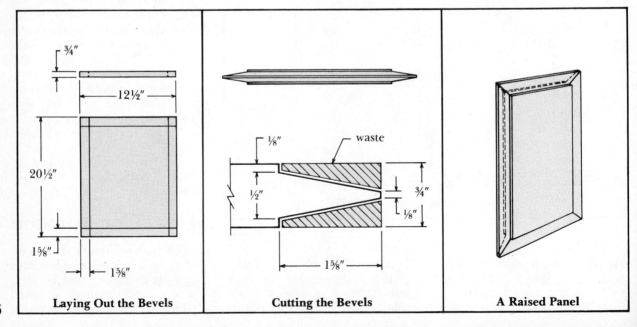

Laying Out the Bevels   **Cutting the Bevels**   **A Raised Panel**

bevels in the faces of the rough panel will taper the thickness of the wood from ½ inch at the base of the lip (1⅝ inches from the edge) to ⅛ inch at the edge.

Cut the bevel on a table saw or radial arm saw.

Using a table saw, set the blade to a cutting depth of ⅛ inch, and position the rip fence 1⅝ inches from the blade. Using the fence as a guide, make a cut along each dimension of each face. You'll have to remove the blade guard and splitter from the saw to do this, so be extra careful. When you've completed both panels, move the fence to the left side of the blade (if necessary), attach a tall auxiliary fence to the fence, and position it ⁷⁄₁₆ inch from the blade. Set the depth of cut to 1⅝ inches, then tilt the blade so that its top is ⅝ inch from the fence. This should give the desired taper, but you may want to test-cut a scrap piece to be sure. When all is ready, bevel each panel by standing it on edge, holding it firmly against the fence and sliding it past the blade.

Using a radial arm saw, make the initial cuts by setting the saw in rip position, 1⅝ inches from the fence, with a ⅛-inch depth of cut. Cut along all dimensions of both faces. Cutting the bevels on a radial arm saw requires setting the blade to a horizontal rip position, then tipping the blade up slightly so that it cuts the bevel. Experiment with specific settings until you get the bevel you need. When the saw is properly set, cut along each dimension of each face, creating a raised panel on both sides.

Sand the finished panel before assembly.

d. The first step in preparing the rails and stiles is to plow a ¼-inch-wide by ⅜-inch-deep groove along the center of one edge of each piece. This will become the inside edge. The panel will fit into this groove when the frame is assembled. The second step is to cut mortises in the stiles; the third, to cut matching tenons on the rail ends.

All of these cuts are most easily made with a dado head in a shop saw. It is possible to do them with a router if you set up the proper jigs. You won't, however, be able to cut the mortises to the same depth, and you'll certainly wear the sharpness out of the bit if you must do more than a dozen doors.

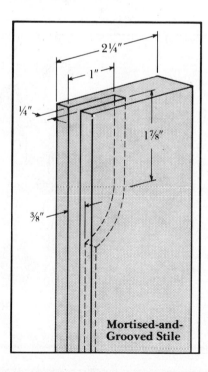

Mortised-and-Grooved Stile

First plow the ¼-inch by ⅜-inch groove from end to end on each piece. Then adjust the blade so that it will cut the same width groove, but to a depth of 1 inch. You now want to replow the ends of the groove in the stiles so that a ¼-inch-thick by 1⅞-inch-wide by 1-inch-long tenon will fit into the groove at the ends. Since the dado blade will create a groove that stops with the bottom arcing to match the diameter of the blade, either you'll have to plow further into the stile than 1⅞ inches, or you'll have to square off the bottom and inner edge of the mortise with a chisel. After determining how far you have to plow, clamp a stop block to the saw fence to expedite the cutting of the remaining mortises. This is especially efficient if you are doing doors for more than one cabinet.

The tenons can be created on the rails by cutting 1-inch-wide by ¼-inch-deep rabbets across both faces of the rail ends with the dado blade, or by using a

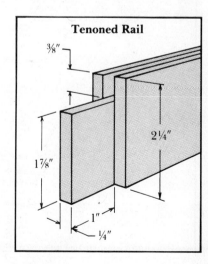

Tenoned Rail

457

tenoning jig in conjunction with the regular saw blade. Whichever way you choose to cut the tenons, cut one first, deliberately making it a mite oversized. Fit it to a mortise, paring an equal amount from each cheek until a snug press fit is attained. With this in mind, it may be a good idea, while you have the dado blade in the saw, to use it to cut the tenons. Set it for a ¼-inch depth of cut. The tenon will be centered in the rail because you'll be cutting away an equal amount of material from each face. One setting of the blade will enable you to cut all the tenons. With the tenoning jig setup, you have to set the saw blade for the shoulder cuts, then reset it for the cheek cuts.

Again, the fit you want at this point is a snug press fit. You shouldn't have to hammer the

tenons into place. The glue will swell the wood and make it impossible to close a joint that's too tight.

With all the grooves, mortises and tenons cut, sand all the stiles and rails.

e. Dry-fit each door to see that everything fits. Test the clamping procedure, if you aren't sure how it'll work. When all is ready, assemble the doors. Use glue only on the mortise-and-tenon joints. Don't glue the panels into the grooves. They should fit tightly enough that they don't rattle in the grooves, and gluing them in place will prevent them from moving as humidity changes swell or shrink the wood. Spread glue on both mortise and tenon, but don't overdo it. Fit first one rail to one stile, then add the second stile. Slip the panel in place and

add the second rail. Place a pipe clamp across each end, parallel to the rail, with the pipe along the edge, rather than the face, of the frame. Use cauls to protect the wood. Then put a C clamp on each stile at the joints to press the mortise firmly against the tenon cheeks. Use cauls here too. Check the squareness and flatness of the door. If the door is at all warped, it won't fit the cabinet properly. Tighten the clamps firmly and set the unit aside to dry.

f. After the glue is dry, make the final router cuts. Cut a ⅜-inch-wide by ⅜-inch-deep rabbet around the perimeter of the inside face. Using a rounding-over bit, break the edges of the perimeter of the outside face of the door.

g. With the cabinet lying on

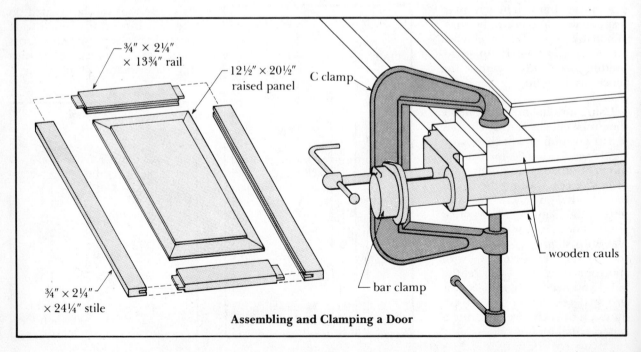

¾" × 2¼" × 13¾" rail

12½" × 20½" raised panel

C clamp

¾" × 2¼" × 24¼" stile

bar clamp

wooden cauls

Assembling and Clamping a Door

its back, set the doors in place. Mark the positions of the hinges and knobs on the doors and on the face frame. The hinges should be the double-offset, semiconcealed, self-closing variety. No mortises are necessary for them. They should be positioned about 2 inches from the top and the bottom of the door, along the outer stiles. The knobs should be centered on the inner door stiles, about 5 inches from the top of the doors. Be sure the two knobs line up, and that the hinges on one door line up with those on the other door.

Drawer Construction

The cabinet has two drawers, with inside dimensions of $3'' \times 13\frac{1}{8} \times 20\frac{7}{8}$, mounted on commercial metal drawer slides.

a. From 1×4 select pine, cut four drawer sides 22 inches long and two drawer backs $13\frac{1}{8}$ inches long. Rip the drawer backs to a $2\frac{3}{4}$-inch width. From 1×6 select pine, cut two drawer fronts $16\frac{3}{8}$ inches long, and rip them to a $4\frac{1}{4}$-inch width. From $\frac{1}{4}$-inch A-C interior plywood, cut two pieces $13\frac{7}{8}$ inches by 22 inches for the drawer bottoms.

b. Plow a $\frac{1}{4}$-inch-wide by $\frac{3}{8}$-inch-deep groove for the drawer bottoms in the inside face of the sides, $\frac{1}{4}$ inch from the bottom edge, and in the fronts, $\frac{5}{8}$ inch from the bottom edge. Plow a $\frac{3}{8}$-inch-wide by $\frac{3}{8}$-inch-deep rabbet along the top and bottom inside edges of the drawer fronts. Cut a $1\frac{5}{8}$-inch-wide by $\frac{3}{8}$-inch-deep rab-

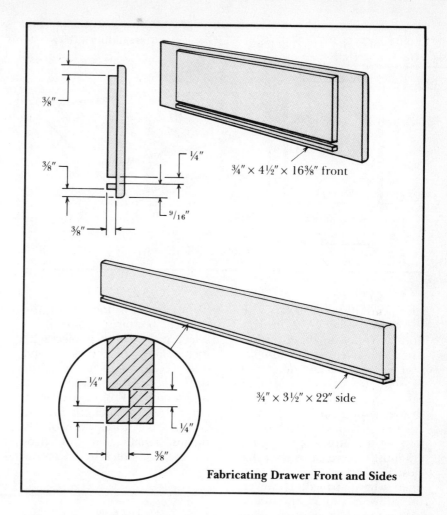

$\frac{3}{4}'' \times 4\frac{1}{2}'' \times 16\frac{3}{8}''$ front

$\frac{3}{4}'' \times 3\frac{1}{2}'' \times 22''$ side

Fabricating Drawer Front and Sides

bet across the inside face of each end of the drawer fronts. Using a rounding-over bit in a router, break the outside edges of the fronts and the two top edges of the sides and backs. Sand all of the pieces.

c. Assemble the drawers with glue and 6d finishing nails. Fit the sides to the front, gluing and nailing them in place. Slip the bottom into its groove without glue, then spread glue on the ends of the back and set it in place, nailing through the sides

into its ends. The back's top edge will be a tad lower than the top edges of the sides. Check the drawer with a try square, then drive several nails through the bottom into the back to secure it. Mount a $1\frac{1}{2}$-inch-diameter wooden knob in the center of each drawer front, that is, $8\frac{3}{16}$ inches from either end and $2\frac{1}{8}$ inches from the top and bottom.

d. To mount the drawer in the cabinet, use 22-inch-long commercial drawer slides. The **459**

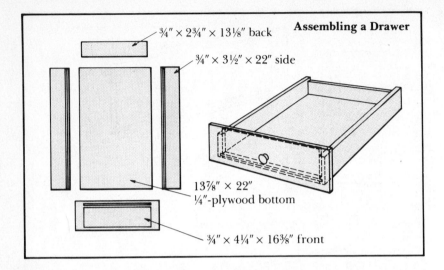

¾" × 2¾" × 13⅛" back

Assembling a Drawer

¾" × 3½" × 22" side

13⅞" × 22"
¼"-plywood bottom

¾" × 4¼" × 16⅜" front

specifics of installation vary with the brand; follow the instructions provided by the manufacturer. In essence, the installation will involve fastening a set of slide tracks to the drawer sides and a mating set to the drawer supports of the cabinet. All designs make accommodation for adjustments; the drawers must be leveled so they stay closed when closed and stay open when opened. However, the drawers should be painted before the slides are fastened to them, as should the inside of the cabinet.

Mixer Drawer Construction

The inside of this special interior drawer measures 3 inches deep, 13¼ inches wide and 21¼ inches long. Its construction is somewhat simpler than that of the cabinet's other two drawers.

a. From ½-inch A-C interior plywood, cut one piece 14

460

inches by 22⅜ inches for the drawer bottom. From 1 × 4 select pine, cut two pieces 22 inches long for the sides, and one piece 13¼ inches long for the back. Rip the back to a width of 2⅜ inches. From 1 × 6 stock, cut a 15⅝-inch length for the front. Rip it to a width of 4¼ inches. Finally, cut two strips measuring ½ inch by 1¼ inches

by 22 inches to serve as lips on the tops of the sides to cover the drawer slides.

b. The bottom, which is thicker than the ordinary bottom because it's expected the contents of this drawer will be heavy, fits into a groove in the sides and front. The back rests atop the bottom. Plow a ½-inch-wide by ⅜-inch-deep groove along the inner face of the sides and front, ¼ inch from the bottom edge. Using a rounding-over bit in a router, break the top edges of the back and of the lips for the sides. Sand the pieces.

c. The drawer is assembled with glue and nails, using simple butt joints. The front butts against the ends of the sides; nails are driven through the front into the ends, countersunk and puttied over. The front should extend beyond the sides by ⅜ inch on each end to hide the slides in the finished installation. Use glue to bond sides and front, but not to bond

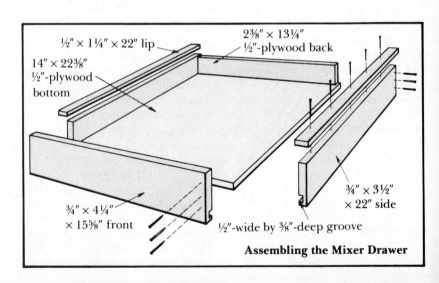

½" × 1¼" × 22" lip

2⅜" × 13¼"
½"-plywood back

14" × 22⅜"
½"-plywood bottom

¾" × 3½"
× 22" side

¾" × 4¼"
× 15⅝" front

½"-wide by ⅜"-deep groove

Assembling the Mixer Drawer

bottom and drawer frame. With the front and sides joined, fit the bottom in place, then glue and nail the back in place. After checking the squareness of the drawer with a try square, drive several nails through the bottom into the back. Finally, glue and nail the lips atop the sides, so they extend over the outsides of the sides. Countersink the nails and putty over them.

d. After painting the drawer according to the directions in the following section, install it in the cabinet using 22-inch-long commercial drawer slides. The approach to use is the same as that used with the other drawers in the cabinet.

Finishing

Finishing should largely be a matter of glue cleanup, touch-up finish-sanding and applying the finish. The face frame, doors and drawers, all critical elements in the finishing process, should have been finish-sanded before assembly, because the right-angle intersections of grain and the corners make them difficult to sand well after assembly. Similarly, the few nail holes that exist should already have been filled with a wood filler to match the final finish.

Complete any detail work that's unfinished. Clean the wood thoroughly, first with a vacuum cleaner, then with a rag dampened with turpentine or mineral spirits or with a tack rag. Get all the dust out of and off the cabinet.

The interior should be painted. Although latex paint isn't a good choice for an exterior finish, it is a reasonable one for the interior. It will wear well, and it is easy to apply. Use at least two coats. After the inside of the cabinets and the drawers are painted, install the drawer slides and put the drawers in the cabinet.

The exterior finish is your choice. The cabinet shown was given several coats of a synthetic finish applied directly to the wood. No stain, filler, sealer or other substance sullies the wood. A coat of wax helps protect the finish.

Counter Top Construction

The counter top can be constructed anytime, but it isn't usually installed until after the cabinet is painted, varnished and installed in the kitchen. The counter top here is sufficiently large to cover the cabinet, with a flush fit on the sides but the usual overhang at the front. It has a backsplash and is covered with plastic laminate. Obviously, you'll build a one-piece counter top that'll cover *all* the cabinets you install side-by-side if you build more than one.

a. From ¾-inch flakeboard (a special, premium-quality particle board), cut two pieces 25 inches by 36 inches for the counter top core. From 1 × 4 #2 pine, cut one 36-inch piece for the backsplash. From standard ¹/₁₆-inch plastic laminate, cut one piece 24½ inches by 36½ inches for the top, one piece 3¾ inches by 36½ inches for the backsplash face, one piece 2 inches by 36½ inches for the front edge, two pieces 2 inches by 25¼ inches for the side edges, one piece 1¼ inches by 36½ inches for the top edge of the backsplash and two pieces 1¼ inches by 3¾ inches for the ends of the backsplash. All the laminate pieces are oversized to allow for trimming during installation.

b. The core for the counter top is created by laminating the two flakeboard panels together to make a single piece 1½ inches thick. Use ordinary white or yellow glue and underlayment nails to bond the two core elements.

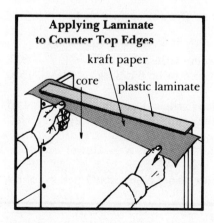

Applying Laminate to Counter Top Edges

kraft paper

core plastic laminate

Trimming the Laminate

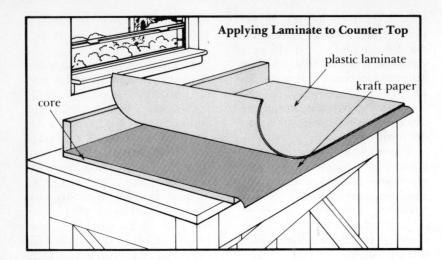

Applying Laminate to Counter Top

plastic laminate

kraft paper

core

Best get a helper for this operation. Lay one panel flat on the workbench or across a couple sawhorses. Spread glue on it. Hold the second panel and line up one edge of it with the matching edge of the other panel. Lower the panel you are holding and carefully lay it on the other panel. Square the edges and clamp the panels while you drive 1- to 1¼-inch underlayment nails through what will be the bottom layer

Materials

Wood

1–4′ × 8′ sht. ⅝″ A-C int. plywood or **Side panels:** 2 pcs. 23″ × 34 ½″
Bottom: 1 pc. 23″ × 34 ¼″
Shelf: 1 pc. 23″ × 34 ¼″
Drawer supports: 3 pcs. 5½″ × 23″

1–4′ × 5′ sht. ¼″ A-C int. plywood or **Back panel:** 1 pc. 34½″ × 35½″
Drawer bottoms: 2 pcs. 13⅞″ × 22″

2 pcs. 1 × 4 × 10′ #2 pine or **Nailer cleats:** 2 pcs. ¾″ × 3½″ × 20″
Plinth: 1 pc. ¾″ × 3½″ × 36″
Crosspieces: 3 pcs. ¾″ × 3½″ × 34¼″
Backsplash: 1 pc. ¾″ × 3½″ × 36″

1 pc. 2 × 6 × 4′ constr.-grade fir or **Drawer supports:** 1 pc. 1½″ × 5½″ × 23″
1 pc. 1½″ × 5½″ × 22¼″

2 pcs. 1 × 2 × 8′ select pine or **Frame stiles:** 3 pcs. ¾″ × 1½″ × 31⅞″
Frame rails: 6 pcs. ¾″ × 1½″ × 15¾″

2 pcs. 1 × 3 × 8′ select pine or **Door stiles:** 4 pcs. ¾″ × 2¼″ × 24¼″
Door rails: 4 pcs. ¾″ × 2¼″ × 13¾″

2 pcs. 36″ × ⅜″ dowel or **Dowels:** 24 pcs. 1½″ × ⅜″ dowel

1 pc. 1 × 8 × 8′ select pine or **Door panel elements:** 4 pcs. ¾″ × 6¼″ × 20½″

2 pcs. 1 × 4 × 8′ select pine or **Drawer sides:** 4 pcs. ¾″ × 3½″ × 22″
Drawer backs: 2 pcs. ¾″ × 2¾″ × 13⅛″
Mixer drawer sides: 2 pcs. ¾″ × 3½″ × 22″
Mixer drawer backs: 1 pc. ¾″ × 2⅜″ × 13¼″

1–2′ sq. sht. ½″ A-C int. plywood or **Mixer drawer bottom:** 1 pc. 14″ × 22⅜″

1 pc. 1 × 6 × 6′ select pine or **Drawer fronts:** 2 pcs. ¾″ × 4¼″ × 16⅜″
Mixer drawer front: 1 pc. ¾″ × 4¼″ × 15⅝″
Mixer drawer lips: 2 pcs. ½″ × 1¼″ × 22″

1–3′ × 5′ sht. ¾″ flakeboard or **Counter top core:** 2 pcs. ¾″ × 25″ × 36″

Hardware
1″ underlayment nails
6d coated box nails
6d finishing nails
4–1 ½″ rnd. wood knobs
2 pr. ⅜″ double-offset, semiconcealed, self-closing hinges
3 pr. 22″ drawer slides
6–3″ #10 screws
12–1¾″ #10 screws

Miscellaneous
Glue
Semigloss latex enamel
Clear varnish
Contact cement
1–38″ × 36″ sht. ¹⁄₁₆″ plastic laminate or **Top:** 1 pc. 24½″ × 36½″
Backsplash: 1 pc. 3¾″ × 36½″
Front edge: 1 pc. 2″ × 36½″
Ends: 2 pcs. 2″ × 25¼″
Backsplash top edge: 1 pc. 1¼″ × 36½″
Backsplash ends: 2 pcs. 1¼″ × 3¾″

into the top layer. Scatter the nails over the whole surface, making sure that complete contact has been made.

Glue and screw the backsplash to the core. Spread glue on the backsplash edge, set it atop the core flush with the back, and clamp it. Turn the core over and drill pilot holes for four to six 3-inch #10 wood screws. Drive the screws, then remove the clamps.

c. The plastic laminate is applied using contact cement. Each piece is applied, then trimmed using a file or a laminate trimming bit in a router. Since the core hasn't been attached to the cabinet, you can tip it up or stand it on end so you are always working with a horizontal surface. You apply the edge pieces first, then the backsplash pieces, and finally the top. Spread the cement, let it dry, then lay kraft paper or newspaper over the core, aligning the laminate atop that. Finally, with extreme care, pull

Completing the Bond

the paper out and bond the laminate to the core. Use a

laminate roller or the mallet-and-block technique to ensure that the bond is complete over the entire surface.

Again, the routine is to apply the side edges and trim them. Then the front edge and trim it. Then the backsplash edges. Followed by the backsplash face. And finally the top.

d. With the plastic laminate all applied and the cabinet installed, it is time to attach the counter top. Do not glue it in place, for you would be unable to remove it, should you ever

want to do that. Only use screws.

In any particle board, the usual-size pilot holes are too big, since the material has no grain structure. So drill pilot holes in stages, rather than with the convenient combination pilot-countersink bits. Drill a shank hole in the cabinet top cross-pieces and countersink them. Then drill fine pilot holes in the counter top. Drive four to six 1¾-inch #10 screws through each crosspiece into the core.

And the job is finished.

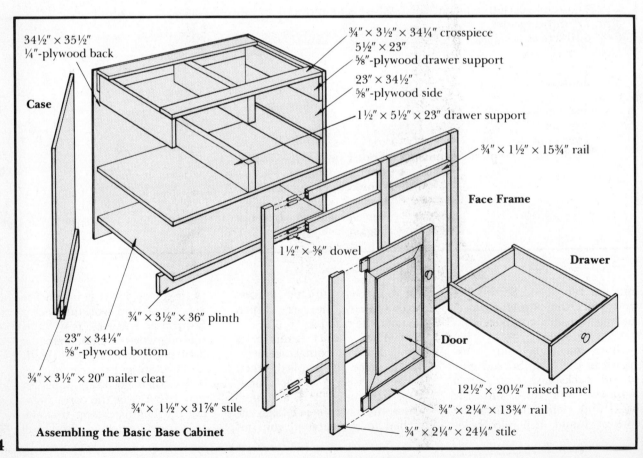

34½″ × 35½″ ¼″-plywood back

Case

¾″ × 3½″ × 34¼″ crosspiece
5½″ × 23″ ⅝″-plywood drawer support
23″ × 34½″ ⅝″-plywood side
1½″ × 5½″ × 23″ drawer support

¾″ × 1½″ × 15¾″ rail

Face Frame

1½″ × ⅜″ dowel

Drawer

¾″ × 3½″ × 36″ plinth

23″ × 34¼″ ⅝″-plywood bottom

¾″ × 3½″ × 20″ nailer cleat

¾″ × 1½″ × 31⅞″ stile

Door

12½″ × 20½″ raised panel

¾″ × 2¼″ × 13¾″ rail

¾″ × 2¼″ × 24¼″ stile

Assembling the Basic Base Cabinet

48-Inch Base Cabinet

Storage space is plentiful in this standard base cabinet. Two drawers, mounted on commercial drawer slides. are ideal for storage of towels, pot holders, and other kitchen linens. The raised-panel doors conceal adjustable shelves for holding those large, hard-to-fit casseroles, pots and pans, or small appliances. This basic cabinet

can be used by itself or as a part of a larger run of cabinets.

Construction

1. Begin by assembling the case, which is constructed of interior plywood, 1 × 4 #2 pine and 2 × 6 fir. Fabrication and assembly details are given in the "Case Construction" section of "The Basic Base Cabinet."

a. From ⅝-inch A-C interior plywood, cut two pieces 23 inches by 34½ inches for cabinet sides, one piece 23 inches by 30⅜ inches for the divider, one piece 23 inches by 46¼ inches for the bottom, one piece 23 inches by 22⅝ inches for a shelf, one piece 12 inches by 22⅝ inches for a shelf and two pieces 5½ inches by 23 inches for drawer supports. From ¼-inch A-C interior plywood, cut one piece 34½ inches by 47½ inches for the back. From 1 × 4 #2 pine, cut three pieces 46¼ inches long for crosspieces, two pieces 20 inches long for nailer cleats and one piece 48 inches long for the plinth. From 2 × 6 construction-grade fir, cut a 23-inch-long drawer support.

b. On the good side of each side panel and both sides of the center divider, lay out and drill ¼-inch-diameter, ⅜-inch-deep holes for the shelf support pins for the adjustable shelves. There should be six sets of holes, each two inches below the last set, beginning 14 inches from the top edge and ending 10½ inches from the bottom edge of each panel. On the right panel and

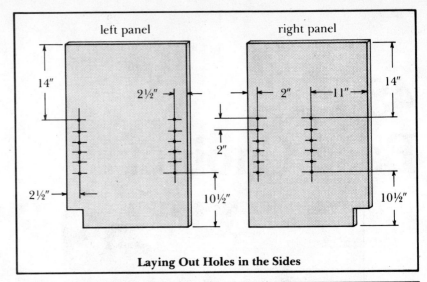

Laying Out Holes in the Sides

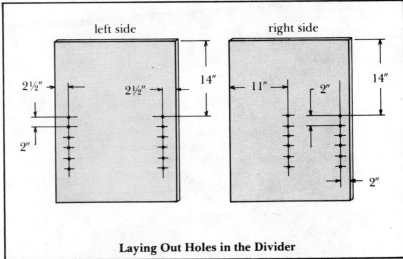

Laying Out Holes in the Divider

the right side of the center divider, one line of holes should be positioned 2 inches from the back edge of the panels and the second line of holes, 11 inches from the front edge of the panels. On the left panel and left side of the center divider, one line of holes should be positioned 2½ inches from the front edge of the panels and the second line 2½ inches from the back edges. Mark the hole locations carefully and drill each hole perpendicularly, so the shelves are sturdy and level. Work carefully to avoid drilling all the way through the side panels.

c. In one corner of each side panel cut a 3-inch-wide by 3½-inch-high notch for the toe space. Using 1-inch underlayment nails, glue and nail the bottom nailer cleats on the inside of the end panels.

d. Begin the actual assembly by gluing and nailing, using 6d coated nails, the side panels to the bottom. Then glue and nail the crosspieces between the side panels. After ensuring that the case is square, glue and nail the back panel and the plinth in place.

e. Glue and nail, using the underlayment nails, a ⅝-inch plywood drawer support on the inside of each end panel, and the center fir drawer support to the crosspieces, 21¾ inches from each side. Finally, glue and nail the divider in place in the center of the case, 22⅞ inches from either side. Nail through the bottom and back into the divider, and carefully toenail through the divider into the center drawer support.

2. The face frame is composed of three upright pieces, called stiles, joined with dowels to six crosspieces, called rails. Fabrication and assembly details are given in the "Face Frame Construction" section of "The Basic Base Cabinet."

a. From 1 × 2 select pine, cut three 31⅞-inch-long frame stiles and six 21¾-inch-long frame rails. From ⅜-inch dowel, cut twenty-four pieces, each 1½ inches long. After cutting the stiles and rails, lay them face down on the workbench with the rails between the upright stiles as in the final assembly. Place the two middle rails 3¾ inches below the upper rails. Mark each board at intersecting points to aid in drilling for the dowel joints.

b. Lay out and drill the holes for the dowels, glue dowels in the rails, then glue and assemble the rails and stiles, forming the face frame.

c. Glue and nail the face frame to the case, using 6d finishing or casing nails. The top of the face frame should be flush with the top edges of the case, while the outer stiles should overhang the case sides by ¼ inch.

3. The cabinet doors are assembled by joining the door rails and stiles around a raised panel. Fabrication and assembly details are given in the "Door Construction" section of "The Basic Base Cabinet."

a. From 1 × 3 select pine, cut four pieces 24¼ inches

Materials

Wood

1–4′ × 8′ sht. ⅝″ A-C int. plywood or **Side panels:** 2 pcs. 23″ × 34½″
  Divider: 1 pc. 23″ × 30⅜″
  Bottom: 1 pc. 23″ × 46¼″
  Shelves: 1 pc. 23″ × 22⅞″
    1 pc. 12″ × 22⅞″

1–1′ × 2′ sht. ⅝″ A-C int. plywood or **Drawer supports:** 2 pcs. 5½″ × 23″

1–5′ × 4′ sht. ¼″ A-C int. plywood or **Back panel:** 1 pc. 34½″ × 47½″
  Drawer bottoms: 2 pcs. 19⅞″ × 22″

2 pcs. 1 × 4 × 12′ #2 pine or **Crosspieces:** 3 pcs. ¾″ × 3½″ × 46¼″
  Nailer cleats: 2 pcs. ¾″ × 3½″ × 20″
  Plinth: 1 pc. ¾″ × 3½″ × 48″
  Backsplash: 1 pc. ¾″ × 3½″ × 48″

[continued on next page]

1 pc. 2 × 6 × 2′ constr.-grade fir or **Drawer support:** 1 pc. 1½″ × 5½″ × 23″

2 pcs. 1 × 2 × 10′ select pine or **Frame stiles:** 3 pcs. ¾″ × 1½″ × 31⅞″
Frame rails: 6 pcs. ¾″ × 1½″ × 21¾″

1 pc. 36″ × ⅜″ dowel or **Dowels:** 24 pcs. 1½″ × ⅜″ dowel

2 pcs. 1 × 3 × 8′ select pine or **Door stiles:** 4 pcs. ¾″ × 2¼″ × 24¼″
Door rails: 4 pcs. ¾″ × 2¼″ × 19¾″

1 pc. 1 × 6 × 10′ select pine or **Door panel elements:** 6 pcs. ¾″ × 5½″ × 20½″
1 pc. 1 × 6 × 8′ select pine   2 pcs. ¾″ × 2″ × 20½″
Drawer fronts: 2 pcs. ¾″ × 4¼″ × 22⅜″
Drawer backs: 2 pcs. ¾″ × 2¾″ × 19⅛″

1 pc. 1 × 4 × 8′ select pine or **Drawer sides:** 4 pcs. ¾″ × 3½″ × 22″

1–4′ × 6′ sht. ¾″ flakeboard or **Counter top core:** 2 pcs. 25″ × 48″

Hardware
1″ underlayment nails
6d coated box nails
6d finishing nails
4–1½″ rnd. wood knobs
2 pt. ⅜″ double-offset, semiconcealed, self-closing hinges
2 pr. 22″ drawer slides
8 shelf support clips
8–3″ #10 screws
16–1¾″ #10 screws

Miscellaneous
Glue
Semigloss latex enamel
Clear varnish
Contact cement
1–36″ × 60″ sht. ¹/₁₆″ plastic laminate or **Top:** 1 pc. 24½″ × 48½″
Front edge: 1 pc. 2″ × 48½″
Ends: 2 pcs. 2″ × 25¼″
Backsplash: 1 pc. 3¾″ × 48½″
Backsplash top edge: 1 pc. 1¼″ × 48½″
Backsplash end edges: 2 pcs. 1¼″ × 3¾″

long for door stiles and four pieces 19¾ inches long for door rails. Rip all to a 2¼-inch width. From 1 × 6 select pine, cut seven pieces 20½ inches long, and rip one of them to two 2-inch widths.
   b. To create the door panels, edge-glue three 5½-inch pieces and one 2-inch piece together; the rough panels will be ¾ inch by 18½

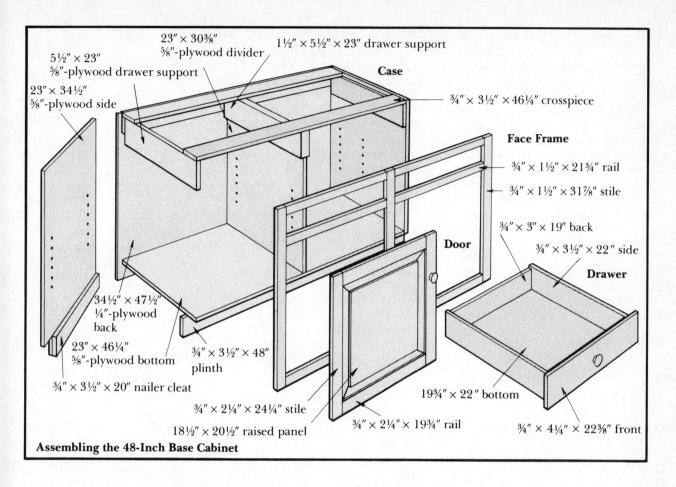

23" × 30⅜"
⅝"-plywood divider

1½" × 5½" × 23" drawer support

5½" × 23"
⅝"-plywood drawer support

Case

23" × 34½"
⅝"-plywood side

¾" × 3½" × 46¼" crosspiece

Face Frame

¾" × 1½" × 21¾" rail

¾" × 1½" × 31⅞" stile

¾" × 3" × 19" back

Door

¾" × 3½" × 22" side

Drawer

34½" × 47½"
¼"-plywood back

23" × 46¼"
⅝"-plywood bottom

¾" × 3½" × 48"
plinth

19¾" × 22" bottom

¾" × 3½" × 20" nailer cleat

¾" × 2¼" × 24¼" stile

18½" × 20½" raised panel

¾" × 2¼" × 19¾" rail

¾" × 4¼" × 22⅜" front

Assembling the 48-Inch Base Cabinet

by 20½ inches. Cut the bevels around both faces, creating the raised panel.

c. Fabricate the rails and stiles, then assemble them around the door panels. Rabbet the perimeter of the inside face, and break the edges of the perimeter of the outside face. Mount the knobs.

d. Install the doors on the cabinet.

4. The cabinet has two drawers, which are constructed with lapped fronts and simple butt joints. Details of construction are given in the "Drawer Construction" section of "The Basic Base Cabinet."

a. From 1 × 6 select pine, cut two pieces 22⅜ inches long and rip them to a 4¼-inch width for the drawer fronts. Cut two pieces 19⅛ inches long and rip them to a 2¾-inch width for the drawer backs. From 1 × 4 select pine, cut four pieces 22 inches long for drawer sides. From ¼-inch A-C interior plywood, cut two pieces 19⅞ inches by 22 inches for drawer bottoms.

b. Groove the sides, and rabbet and groove the front.

Use a rounding-over bit in a router to break the appropriate edges of front, sides and back.

c. Assemble the drawers, using glue and nails. Mount a knob in the center of each drawer front.

d. Install and adjust the drawers, using the commercial drawer slides, after finishing the cabinet.

5. Finish the cabinet inside and out, as detailed in the "Finishing" section of "The Basic Base Cabinet." In brief, the sanding and cleanup should

469

be completed, the inside of the cabinet and drawers painted, and the front of the cabinet finished however you desire.

6. The counter top is installed after the cabinet is fastened in place in the kitchen. Usually, a single counter top will cover all the cabinets. As with the other cabinets, however, you may build a top for this cabinet alone. Details of assembly are given in the "Counter Top Construction" section of "The Basic Base Cabinet."

a. From ¾-inch flakeboard, cut two pieces 25 inches by 48 inches for the cabinet top. From 1 × 4 **#2** pine, cut a piece 48 inches long for the backsplash. From ¹/₁₆-inch plastic laminate, cut one piece 24½ inches by 48½ inches for the top, one piece 2 inches by 48½ inches for the front edge, two pieces 2 inches by 25¼ inches for the ends, one piece 3¾ inches by 48½ inches for the backsplash, one piece 1¼ inches by 48½ inches for the backsplash top edge and two pieces 1¼ inches by 3¾ inches for the backsplash ends.

b. Laminate the core, using glue and underlayment nails. Fasten the backsplash to it with six to eight 3-inch **#10** screws and glue. Then apply the plastic laminate with contact cement. Trim each piece after it is applied and before the next piece is applied.

c. Attach the top to the cabinet with six to eight 1¾-inch **#10** screws driven through each top crosspiece into the top core.

Sink Base Cabinet

471

Every kitchen has a sink, and while some are freestanding, most are set into a counter top installed on a base cabinet especially designed to accommodate the sink and its plumbing.

This 72-inch-long cabinet is so designed. The middle two drawer openings are covered with blanks, creating the space needed for the sink in the center of the unit. On either side are special features that complement any preparation center. On the right is a handy drawer for a waste basket, which allows you to have the container close at hand without having it where it's the center of attention or underfoot. On the left is a deep, divided drawer for storing a couple handfuls of vegetables, enough for a meal or three, but not so much that the vegies will spoil before you use them up.

In addition, there are drawers for utensil storage and the expected under-sink storage space.

Construction

1. Begin by assembling the case, which is constructed of interior plywood and 1 × 4 #2 pine. Fabrication and assembly details are given in the "Case Construction" section of "The Basic Base Cabinet."

a. From ⅝-inch A-C interior plywood, cut two pieces 23 inches by 34½ inches for sides, one piece 23 inches by 70¼ inches for the bottom, two pieces 23 inches by 30⅜ inches for dividers, and two pieces 12 inches by 23 inches for drawer supports. From ¼-inch A-C interior plywood, cut one piece 34½ inches by 71½ inches for the back. From 1 × 4 #2 pine, cut three pieces 70¼ inches for crosspieces, two pieces 20 inches long for nailer cleats, and one piece 72 inches long for the plinth.

b. In one corner of each side panel cut a 3-inch-wide by 3½-inch-high notch for the toe space. Using 1-inch underlayment nails, glue and nail the bottom nailer cleats on the inside of the side panels.

c. Cut two notches ¾ inch deep and 3½ inches wide on the top edge of each divider panel, one at the front and one at the back. At the top of the back edge, cut a notch ¾ inch deep and 3½ inches wide. The three crosspieces will fit into these notches.

d. Begin the actual assembly by gluing and nailing, using 6d coated nails, the side panels to the bottom. Then glue and nail the crosspieces between the side panels. Install the dividers, gluing and nailing them to the bottom and crosspieces, positioning one 16¼ inches from each side panel. After ensuring that the case is square, glue and nail the back panel and nail the plinth in place.

e. Glue and nail, using the

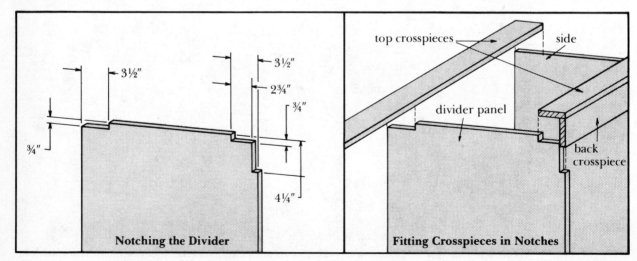

3½"   3½"   2¾"   ¾"   ¾"   4¼"

Notching the Divider

top crosspieces   side   divider panel   back crosspiece

Fitting Crosspieces in Notches

underlayment nails, a ⅝-inch plywood drawer support on the inside of each side panel.

2. The face frame is composed of 5 stiles and 12 rails. It is larger and has more pieces than any of the other face frames, but in essence the assembly process is the same as it is for other cabinets. Fabrication and assembly details are given in the "Face Frame Construction" section of "The Basic Base Cabinet."

a. From 1 × 2 select pine, cut five pieces 31⅞ inches long for frame stiles, six pieces 16½ inches long and six pieces 15¾ inches long for frame rails. From 1 × 6 select pine, cut two 17⅛-inch-long drawer blanks, and rip them to a 4¼-inch width. From 1 × 2 #2 pine, cut four 4½-inch drawer blank hold-ins. From ⅜-inch dowel, cut forty-eight pieces, each 1½ inches long.

b. After cutting the stiles and rails lay them face down on the workbench with the rails between the stiles as in the final assembly. Place the 16½-inch rails in the center of the cabinet for the center doors. Place the row of intermediate rails 3¾ inches below the top rails. Mark each board at intersecting points to aid in drilling for the dowel joints.

c. Lay out and drill the holes for the dowels, glue dowels in the rails, then glue and assemble the rails and stiles, forming the face frame.

d. Glue and nail the face frame to the case, using 6d finishing or casing nails. The top of the face frame should be flush with the top edges of the case, while the outer stiles should overhang the case sides by ¼ inch.

e. Cut a ⅜-inch-wide by ⅜-inch-deep rabbet around what will be the inner edges of the drawer blanks. Then, break the exterior edges. Prepare the hold-ins for the blanks by cutting a ⅜-inch by ⅜-inch rabbet on both ends of each piece. Position the blanks in the two middle drawer openings. Glue two hold-ins behind and into each blank. Drive two 1-inch #8 screws through each hold-in and into the blank. Place the hold-ins 1½ inches from the stiles. This will hold the blanks securely in place.

3. The cabinet doors are assembled by joining the door rails and stiles around a raised panel. Fabrication and assembly details are given in the "Door Construction" section of "The Basic Base Cabinet."

a. From 1 × 3 select pine, cut eight pieces 24¼ inches long for door stiles, four pieces 13¾ inches long and four pieces 14½ inches long for door rails. Rip all to a 2¼-inch width. From 1 × 8 select pine, cut four pieces 20½ inches long and rip them to a 6¼-inch width, and cut four pieces 20½ inches long and rip them to a 6⅝-inch width for door panel elements.

b. To make the door panels, edge-glue two 6¼-inch-wide elements together for each of the left and right doors, forming panels ¾ inch by 12½ inches by 20½ inches.

Installing Drawer Blank

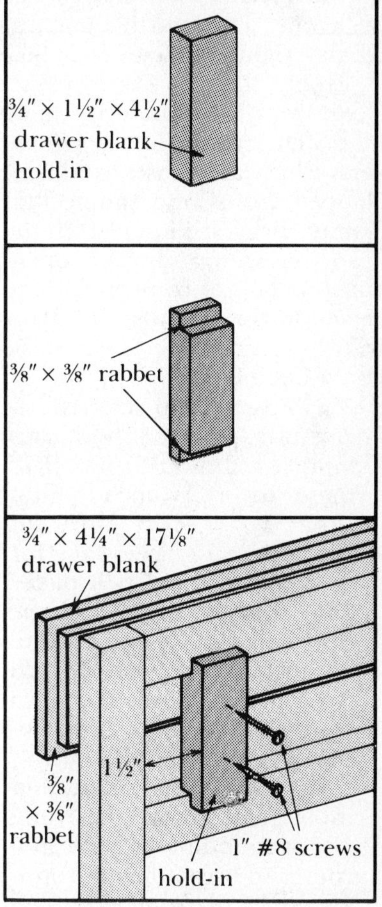
¾″ × 1½″ × 4½″
drawer blank hold-in
⅜″ × ⅜″ rabbet
¾″ × 4¼″ × 17⅛″
drawer blank
1½″
⅜″ × ⅜″ rabbet
1″ #8 screws
hold-in

Edge-glue two 6⅝-inch-wide elements together for each of the center doors, forming panels ¾ inch by 13¼ inches by 20½ inches. Cut the bevels around both faces of each panel, creating the raised panel.

c. Fabricate the rails and stiles, then assemble them around the door panels. Rabbet the perimeter of the inside face, and break the edges of the perimeter of the outside face.

d. Install three doors on the cabinet and mount the knobs. The fourth door, for the right opening, is a fake front for a waste basket drawer. Set it aside for now.

4. The cabinet has two drawers, which are constructed with lapped fronts and simple butt joints. They are installed in the two remaining drawer openings. Details of construction are given in the "Drawer Construction" section of "The Basic Base Cabinet."

a. From 1 × 6 select pine, cut two pieces 16⅜ inches long for drawer fronts. Rip these to a 4¼-inch width. From 1 × 4 select pine, cut four pieces 22 inches long for drawer sides and two pieces 13¼ inches long for the drawer backs. Rip the backs to a 3-inch width. From ¼-inch A-C interior plywood, cut two pieces 14 inches by 22 inches for the drawer bottoms.

b. Groove the sides, and rabbet and groove the front. Use a rounding-over bit in a router to break the appropriate edges of front, sides and back.

c. Assemble each drawer, using glue and nails. Mount a knob in the center of each drawer front.

d. Install and adjust the drawers, using commercial drawer slides, after finishing the cabinet.

5. The door opening on the right is for a large drawer designed to accommodate a waste basket. It uses the fourth door panel as a front.

a. From ⅝-inch A-C interior plywood, cut two pieces

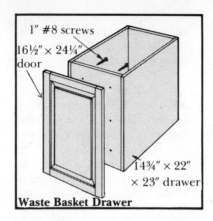

1" #8 screws
16½" × 24¼" door
14¾" × 22" × 23" drawer

Waste Basket Drawer

22 inches by 23 inches for the trash drawer sides, two pieces 13½ inches by 23 inches for the trash drawer front and back, and one piece 13½ inches by 20¾ inches for the trash drawer bottom.

b. Using butt joints, assemble the drawer. The sides butt against the front and

back. The bottom fits inside the frame thus created. Use glue and 6d coated nails to assemble the drawer. Glue the fourth door panel to the front of the drawer and drive six 1-inch #8 screws through the drawer front into the door frame. Mount a wooden door knob on the drawer front in the center of the raised door panel, 6½ inches from the top edge of the door-drawer.

c. Install and adjust the drawer, using 22-inch drawer slides, after finishing the cabinet.

6. The vegetable drawer is hidden behind the left door. The drawer is 8½ inches deep and has a center partition.

a. From ⅝-inch A-C interior plywood, cut two pieces 9 inches by 22 inches for the vegetable drawer sides, one

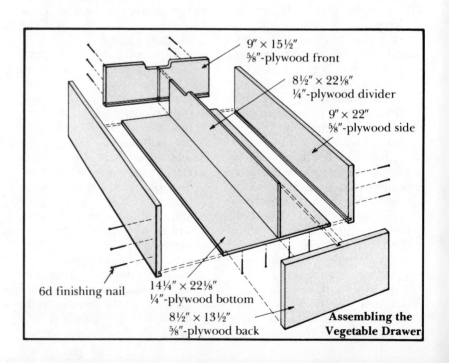

9" × 15½" ⅝"-plywood front
8½" × 22⅛" ¼"-plywood divider
9" × 22" ⅝"-plywood side
6d finishing nail
14¼" × 22⅛" ¼"-plywood bottom
8½" × 13½" ⅝"-plywood back

Assembling the Vegetable Drawer

474

piece 9 inches by 15½ inches for the vegetable drawer front, and one piece 8½ inches by 13½ inches for the vegetable drawer back. From ¼-inch A-C plywood, cut one piece 8½ inches by 22⅛ inches for the vegetable drawer divider and one piece 14¼ inches by 22⅛ inches for the vegetable drawer bottom.

b. Cut a 1-inch-deep by 4-inch-wide notch on what will be the front top edge of the drawer divider. Cut a notch in the center of the top edge of the drawer front, 1 inch deep and 4 inches wide, beginning 5¼ inches from each side edge. Cut a ¼-inch-wide by ⅜-inch-deep groove across the center of the inside face of the drawer front and back to accommodate the drawer divider.

c. Plow a ¼-inch-wide by ⅜-inch-deep groove along the inside face of the sides and the front, ¼ inch from the bottom edge.

d. Assemble the drawer by butting the front against the sides, and the sides against the back. The front must overhang the sides by ⅜ inch on each side. Slide the bottom into its groove and drive several nails through it into the bottom of the back. Glue the divider into its groove.

e. Install and adjust the drawer, using 22-inch commercial drawer slides, after the cabinet has been finished.

7. Finish the cabinet inside

Materials

Wood

2–4′ × 8′ shts. ⅝″ A-C int. plywood or **Side panels:** 2 pcs. 23″ × 34½″
Bottom panel: 1 pc. 23″ × 70¼″
Dividers: 2 pcs. 23″ × 30⅜″
Drawer supports: 2 pcs. 12″ × 23″
Trash drawer sides: 2 pcs. 22″ × 23″
Trash drawer front and back: 2 pcs. 13½″ × 23″
Trash drawer bottom: 1 pc. 13½″ × 20¾″
Vegetable drawer sides: 2 pcs. 9″ × 22″
Vegetable drawer front: 1 pc. 9″ × 15½″
Vegetable drawer back: 1 pc. 8½″ × 13½″

1–4′ × 8′ sht. ¼″ A-C int. plywood or **Back panel:** 1 pc. 34½″ × 71½″
Drawer bottoms: 2 pcs. 14″ × 22″
Vegetable drawer divider: 1 pc. 8½″ × 22⅛″
Vegetable drawer bottom: 1 pc. 14¼″ × 22⅛″

1 pc. 1 × 4 × 10′ #2 pine or **Crosspieces:** 3 pcs. ¾″ × 3½″ × 70¼″
2 pcs. 1 × 4 × 12′ #2 pine **Nailer cleats:** 2 pcs. ¾″ × 3½″ × 20″
Plinth: 1 pc. ¾″ × 3½″ × 72″
Backsplash: 1 pc. ¾″ × 3½″ × 72″

1 pc. 1 × 2 × 8′ select pine or **Frame stiles:** 5 pcs. ¾″ × 1½″ × 31⅞″
2 pcs. 1 × 2 × 12′ select pine **Frame rails:** 6 pcs. ¾″ × 1½″ × 16½″
6 pcs. ¾″ × 1½″ × 15¾″

1 pc. 1 × 6 × 8′ select pine or **Drawer blanks:** 2 pcs. ¾″ × 4¼″ × 17⅛″
Drawer fronts: 2 pcs. ¾″ × 4¼″ × 16⅜″

[continued on next page]

1 pc. 1 × 2 × 2' #2 pine or **Blank hold-ins:** 4 pcs. ¾" × 1½" × 4½"

3 pcs. 36" × ⅜" dowel or **Dowels:** 48 pcs. 1½" × ⅜" dowel

1 pc. 1 × 3 × 8' select pine or **Door stiles:** 8 pcs. ¾" × 2¼" × 24¼"
2 pcs. 1 × 3 × 10' select pine **Door rails:** 4 pcs. ¾" × 2¼" × 13¾"
    4 pcs. ¾" × 2¼" × 14½"

2 pcs. 1 × 8 × 8' select pine or **Door panel elements:** 4 pcs. ¾" × 6¼" × 20½"
    4 pcs. ¾" × 6⅝" × 20½"

1 pc. 1 × 4 × 12' select pine or **Drawer sides:** 4 pcs. ¾" × 3½" × 22"
    Drawer backs: 2 pcs. ¾" × 3" × 13¼"

2–4' × 6' shts. ¾" flakeboard or **Top:** 2 pcs. ¾" × 25" × 72"

Hardware
1" underlayment nails
6d coated box nails
6d finishing nails
6–1½" rnd. wood knobs
3 pr. ⅜" double-offset, semiconcealed, self-closing hinges
4 pr. 22" drawer slides
12–3" #10 screws
24–1¾" #10 screws
14–1" #8 screws

Miscellaneous
Glue
Semigloss latex enamel
Clear varnish
Contact cement
1–45" × 72" sht. ¹⁄₁₆" plastic laminate or **Top:** 1 pc. 24½" × 72½"
    Front edge: 1 pc. 2" × 72½"
    End edges: 2 pcs. 2" × 25¼"
    Backsplash: 1 pc. 3¾" × 72½"
    Backsplash top edge: 1 pc. 1¼" × 72½"
    Backsplash end edge: 2 pcs. 1¼" × 3¾"

and out, as detailed in the "Finishing" section of "The Basic Base Cabinet." In brief, the sanding and cleanup should be completed, the inside of the cabinet and drawers painted and the front of the cabinet finished however you desire.

8. The counter top is installed after the cabinet is fastened in place in the kitchen. Usually, a single counter top will cover all the cabinets. As with the other cabinets, however, you may build a top for this cabinet alone. Details of assembly are given in the "Counter Top Construction" section of "The Basic

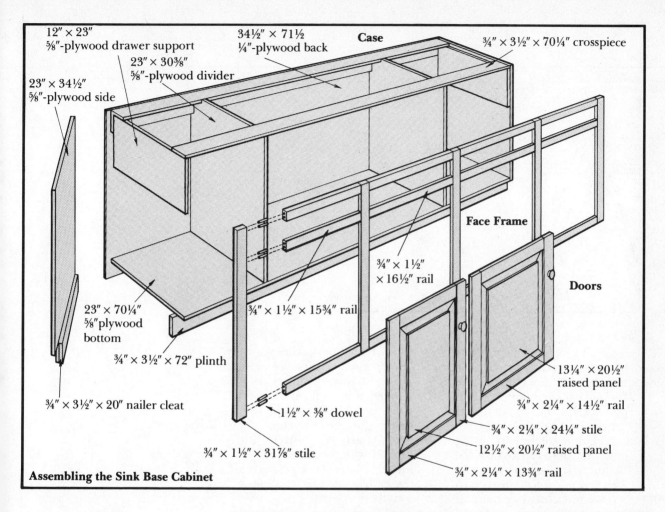

12" × 23"
⅝"-plywood drawer support

34½" × 71½
¼"-plywood back

Case

¾" × 3½" × 70¼" crosspiece

23" × 30⅜"
⅝"-plywood divider

23" × 34½"
⅝"-plywood side

Face Frame

¾" × 1½"
× 16½" rail

¾" × 1½" × 15¾" rail

Doors

23" × 70¼"
⅝"plywood
bottom

¾" × 3½" × 72" plinth

13¼" × 20½"
raised panel

¾" × 3½" × 20" nailer cleat

1½" × ⅜" dowel

¾" × 2¼" × 14½" rail

¾" × 2¼" × 24¼" stile

12½" × 20½" raised panel

¾" × 1½" × 31⅞" stile

¾" × 2¼" × 13¾" rail

Assembling the Sink Base Cabinet

Base Cabinet."

a. From ¾-inch flake-board, cut two pieces 25 inches by 72 inches for the cabinet top. From 1 × 4 **#2** pine, cut a piece 72 inches long for the backsplash. From ¹⁄₁₆-inch plastic laminate, cut one piece 24½ inches by 72½ inches for the top, one piece 2 inches by 72½ inches for the front edge, two pieces 2 inches by 25¼ inches for the end edges, one piece 3¾

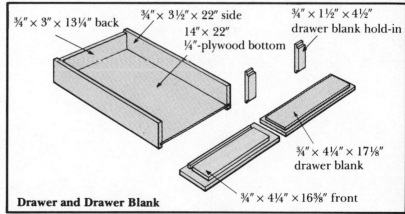

¾" × 3" × 13¼" back

¾" × 3½" × 22" side

14" × 22"
¼"-plywood bottom

¾" × 1½" × 4½"
drawer blank hold-in

¾" × 4¼" × 17⅛"
drawer blank

¾" × 4¼" × 16⅜" front

Drawer and Drawer Blank

477

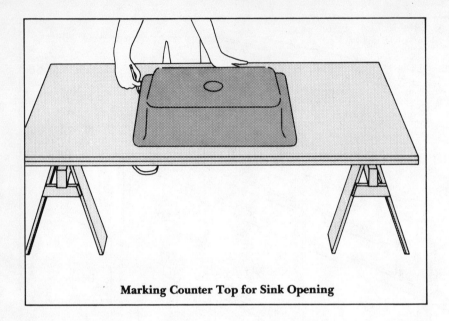

Marking Counter Top for Sink Opening

inches by 72½ inches for the backsplash, one piece 1¼ inches by 72½ inches for the backsplash top edge and two pieces 1¼ inches by 3¾ inches for the backsplash ends.

b. Laminate the core, using glue and underlayment nails. Fasten the backsplash to it with ten to twelve 3-inch #10 screws and glue. Lay out and cut out the opening for the sink. Then apply the plastic laminate with contact cement. Trim each piece after it is applied and before the next piece is applied. Cut the sink opening in the laminate.

c. Attach the top to the cabinet with ten to twelve 1¾-inch #10 screws driven through each top crosspiece into the top core.

Counter Top Range Cabinet

If you have chosen a counter top range unit, this cabinet is what you need. Space for the cooking unit is created by eliminating the drawers. The holes in the face frame are covered with blanks, boards that look like drawer fronts but that don't have knobs and don't open.

Behind the raised-panel

doors are four sliding drawers, perfect for organizing pots, pans and lids. They eliminate the stretching and clatter often associated with storage of pots and pans.

Construction

1. Begin by assembling the case of interior plywood, 1 × 4 #2 pine, and 2 × 6 fir. Fabrication and assembly details are given in the "Case Construction" section of "The Basic Base Cabinet."

a. From ⅝-inch A-C interior plywood, cut two pieces 23 inches by 34½ inches for the sides, one piece 23 inches by 34¼ inches for the bottom and four pieces 5½ inches by 23 inches for the drawer supports. From ¼-inch A-C interior plywood, cut one piece 34½ inches by 35½ inches for the back. From 1 × 4 #2 pine, cut three pieces 34¼ inches for the crosspieces, two pieces 20 inches long for nailer cleats and one piece 36 inches long for the plinth. From 2 × 6 construction-grade fir, cut two pieces 23 inches long for drawer supports.

b. In one corner of each end panel, cut a 3-inch-wide by 3½-inch-high notch for the toe space. Attach the nailer cleats.

c. Assemble the case, using glue and 6d coated nails. Join the sides and bottom first, followed by the three crosspieces, the back and finally the plinth.

d. Glue and nail two ⅝-inch plywood drawer supports on the inside of each side. One rests directly on the bottom; the bottom of the other should be 18½ inches from the side's top edge.

2. The face frame is composed of three stiles and six rails, joined by ⅜-inch dowels. Blanks are installed where drawers ordinarily would be. Fabrication and assembly details are given in the "Face Frame Construction" section of "The Basic Base Cabinet."

a. From 1 × 2 select pine, cut three 31⅞-inch-long frame stiles and six 15¾-inch-long frame rails. From ⅜-inch dowel, cut twenty-four pieces 1½ inches long. From 1 × 6 select pine, cut two pieces 16¼ inches long for drawer blanks. Rip these to a 4¼-inch width. From 1 × 2 #2 pine, cut four pieces 4½ inches long to use as hold-ins for the blanks.

b. Lay out and drill the holes for the dowels, glue dowels in the rails, then glue and assemble the rails and stiles, forming the face frame.

c. Glue and nail the face frame to the case, using 6d finishing or casing nails. The top of the face frame should be flush with the top edges of the case, while the outer stiles should overhang the case sides by ¼ inch.

d. Cut a ⅜-inch-wide by ⅜-inch-deep rabbet around what will be the inner edges of the drawer blanks. Then, break the exterior edges. Prepare the hold-ins for the blanks by cutting a ⅜-inch by ⅜-inch rabbet across both ends of each piece. Glue two

hold-ins behind each blank. Drive two 1-inch #8 screws through each hold-in and into the blank. Place each hold-in 1½ inches from the stiles. This will hold the blanks securely in place.

e. Attach the center drawer supports of 2 × 6 fir by gluing and nailing them to the center frame stile and the cabinet back. The lower drawer support can rest on the cabinet bottom. The upper drawer support's bottom edge should be 18½ inches below the cabinet's top edge.

3. The cabinet doors are assembled by joining the door rails and stiles around a raised panel. Fabrication and assembly details are given in the "Door Construction" section of "The Basic Base Cabinet."

a. From 1 × 3 select pine, cut four pieces 24¼ inches long for door stiles and four pieces 13¾ inches long for door rails. Rip all of these to a 2¼-inch width. From 1 × 8 select pine, cut four pieces 20½ inches long for door panels. Rip these to a 6¼-inch width.

b. To make each door panel, edge-glue two 6¼-inch panels together; the rough panels will be ¾ inch by 12½ inches by 20½ inches. Cut the bevels around both faces, creating the raised panels.

c. Fabricate the rails and stiles, then assemble them around the door panels. Rabbet the perimeter of the inside face of the door, and break the edges of the perimeter of the outside face.

Mount the knobs.

d. Install the doors on the cabinet.

4. This cabinet has four interior drawers, each with an inside measurement of 3 inches by 14 inches by 20⅞ inches and mounted on commercial drawer slides. They can be constructed in much the same manner as the mixer drawer in "The Basic Base Cabinet."

a. From 1 × 4 select pine, cut eight pieces 22 inches long for drawer sides, four pieces 15½ inches long for drawer fronts, and four pieces 14 inches long for drawer backs. Rip the backs to a 3-inch width. From ¼-inch A-C inte-

rior plywood, cut four pieces 14¾ inches by 21⅝ inches for the drawer bottoms.

b. Groove the sides, and rabbet and groove the fronts. Use a rounding-over bit in a router to break the appropriate edges.

c. Assemble the drawers, using glue and nails. Mount knobs on the drawer fronts.

d. Install and adjust the drawers, using commercial drawer slides, after finishing the cabinet.

5. Finish the cabinet inside and out, as detailed in the "Finishing" section of "The Basic Base Cabinet." In brief, the sanding and cleanup should

be completed, the inside of the cabinet and drawers painted, and the front of the cabinet finished however you desire.

6. The counter top is installed after the cabinet is fastened in place in the kitchen. Usually, a single counter top will cover all the cabinets. As with the other cabinets, however, you may build a top for this cabinet alone. In any case, you will have to cut a hole in the counter to accommodate the stovetop unit. Details of assembly are given in the "Counter Top Construction" section of "The Basic Base Cabinet."

a. From ¾-inch flakeboard, cut two pieces 25

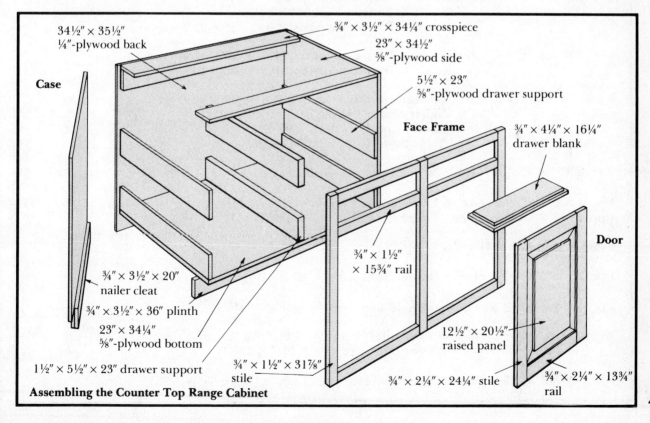

Assembling the Counter Top Range Cabinet

481

inches by 36 inches for the cabinet top. From 1 × 4 #2 pine, cut a piece 36 inches long for the backsplash. From $^1/_{16}$-inch plastic laminate, cut one piece for the top, 24½ inches by 36½ inches, one piece 3¾ inches by 36½ inches for the backsplash, one piece 2 inches by 36½ inches for the front edge, one piece 1¼ inches by 36½ inches for the backsplash top edge, two pieces 1¼ inches by 3¾ inches

for the backsplash and edges, and two pieces 2 inches by 25½ inches for the end edges.

b. Laminate the core, using glue and underlayment nails. Fasten the backsplash to it with six to eight 3-inch #10 screws and glue. Then apply the plastic laminate with contact cement. Trim each piece after it is applied and before the next piece is applied.

c. Attach the top to the cabinet with six to eight 1¾-

inch #10 screws driven through each top crosspiece into the top core.

d. Use the template or dimensions supplied with the stovetop to lay out the necessary opening in the counter top. Drill a hole in each corner of the area to be removed and, using a saber saw, cut the hole for the stovetop. The unit should then be installed according to the manufacturer's instructions.

Materials

Wood

1–4′ × 8′ sht. ⅝″ A-C int. plywood or **Side panels:** 2 pcs. 23″ × 34½″
Bottom: 1 pc. 23″ × 34¼″
Drawer supports: 4 pcs. 5½″ × 23″

1–4′ × 6′ sht. ¼″ A-C int. plywood or **Back panel:** 1 pc. 34½″ × 35½″
Drawer bottoms: 4 pcs. 14¾″ × 21⅝″

2 pcs. 1 × 4 × 8′ #2 pine or **Crosspieces:** 3 pcs. ¾″ × 3½″ × 34¼″
Nailer cleats: 2 pcs. ¾″ × 3½″ × 20″
Plinth: 1 pc. ¾″ × 3½″ × 36″
Backsplash: 1 pc. ¾″ × 3½″ × 36″

1 pc. 2 × 6 × 4′ constr.-grade fir or **Drawer supports:** 2 pcs. 1½″ × 5½″ × 23″

1 pc. 1 × 2 × 8′ select pine or **Frame stiles:** 3 pcs. ¾″ × 1½″ × 31⅞″
1 pc. 1 × 2 × 10′ select pine   **Frame rails:** 6 pcs. ¾″ × 1½″ × 15¾″

2–36″ × ⅜″ dowel or **Dowels:** 24 pcs. 1½″ × ⅜″

1 pc. 1 × 6 × 4′ select pine or **Drawer blanks:** 2 pcs. ¾″ × 4¼″ × 16¼″

1 pc. 1 × 2 × 2′ #2 pine or **Blank hold-ins:** 4 pcs. ¾″ × 1½″ × 4½″

2 pcs. 1 × 3 × 8′ select pine or **Door stiles:** 4 pcs. ¾″ × 2¼″ × 24¼″
Door rails: 4 pcs. ¾″ × 2¼″ × 13¾″

1 pc. 1 × 8 × 8′ select pine or **Door panel elements:** 4 pcs. ¾″ × 6¼″ × 20½″

2 pcs. 1 × 4 × 10′ select pine or **Drawer sides:** 8 pcs. ¾″ × 3½″ × 22″
Drawer fronts: 4 pcs. ¾″ × 3½″ × 15½″
Drawer backs: 4 pcs. ¾″ × 3″ × 14″

1–4′ × 6′ sht. ¾″ flakeboard or **Counter top core:** 2 pcs. ¾″ × 25″ × 36″

Hardware
1″ underlayment nails
6d coated box nails
6d finishing nails
4 pr. 22″ drawer slides
2–1½″ rnd. wood knobs
2 pr. ⅜″ double-offset, semiconcealed, self-closing hinges
8–3″ #10 screws
16–1¾″ #10 screws
8–1″ #8 screws

Miscellaneous
Glue
Semigloss latex enamel
Clear varnish
Contact cement
1–45″ × 36″ sht. ¹/₁₆″ plastic laminate or **Top:** 1 pc. 24½″ × 36½″
Backsplash: 1 pc. 3¾″ × 36½″
Front edge: 1 pc. 2″ × 36½″
Backsplash top edge: 1 pc. 1¼″ × 36½″
Backsplash end edges: 2 pcs. 1¼″ × 3¾″
End edges: 2 pcs. 2″ × 25½″

Drop-In Range Cabinet

A familiar alternative to the freestanding range or the cooktop and separate wall oven is the drop-in range. This is a cooktop-oven unit for which you, rather than the manufacturer, provide the cabinet.

While the usual cabinet for such a range is an open case with a U-shaped face frame, this particular cabinet has a narrow compartment on the right side for cookie sheets and the like.

The cabinet was designed to accommodate the standard 30-inch drop-in range. However, details for fitting and installation vary from brand to brand, so you would be wise to determine the exact requirements for the particular brand and model you intend to use *before* building the cabinet, before, in fact, including it in your cabinetry plans. You'll be awfully frustrated if you build all your cabinets, then discover you've made this cabinet too small for your new stove.

Construction

1. Begin by assembling the case, which is constructed of interior plywood and 1×4 #2 pine. Although this cabinet *seems* different from the others because of its open front, fabrication and assembly details are almost exactly as given in the "Case Construction" section of "The Basic Base Cabinet."

a. From ⅝-inch A-C interior plywood, cut two pieces 23 inches by 34½ inches for sides, one piece 23 inches by 34¼ inches for the bottom, one piece 23 inches by 30⅜ inches for the divider and one piece 5 inches by 23 inches for the shelf. From ¼-inch A-C interior plywood, cut one piece 34½ inches by 35½ inches for the back panel. From 1×4 #2 pine, cut two pieces 34¼ inches long for the crosspieces, one piece 5 inches long for the front top crosspiece, two pieces 20 inches long for nailer cleats and one piece 36 inches long for the plinth.

b. In one corner of each side panel cut a 3-inch-wide by 3½-inch-high notch for the toe space. Using 1-inch underlayment nails, glue and nail the bottom nailer cleats on the inside of the end panels. Cut a ¾-inch-deep by 3½-inch-wide notch on the upper edge of the divider at the back. Then on the back edge at the top, cut a notch ¾ inch wide by 3½ inches deep. The crosspieces fit into these notches.

c. Begin the actual assembly by gluing and nailing, using 6d coated nails, the side panels to the bottom. Then glue and nail the rear crosspiece and the back crosspiece between the side panels. The divider is positioned 5 inches from the right side and glued and nailed in place. The short crosspiece is glued and nailed between the divider and the right side, at the case front. Glue and nail the shelf inside the cabinet door 8 inches down from the top of the end panel and divider panel. After ensuring that the case is square, glue and nail the back panel and nail the plinth in place.

2. The face frame is composed of three stiles, joined with dowels to three rails. Because of the nature of this cabinet, its face frame looks considerably different from those of the other cabinets. But the fabrication and assembly details are much as given in the "Face Frame Construction" section of "The Basic Base Cabinet."

a. From 1×2 select pine, cut 3 pieces 31⅞ inches long

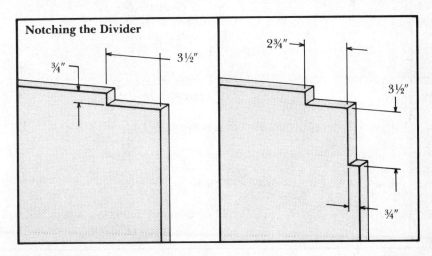

Notching the Divider

for stiles and 2 pieces 4½ inches long for rails. From 1 × 8 select pine, cut 1 piece 27 inches long for the rail beneath the stove. Rip it to a 5¾-inch width. From ⅜-inch dowel, cut 12 pieces, each 1½ inches long.

b. After cutting the stiles and rails, lay them face up on the workbench with the rails and stiles positioned as in the final assembly. Place the 5¾-inch-wide rail between the left stile and the intermediate stile with bottom edges flush. Place the two 4½-inch-long rails between the top and bottom edges of the intermediate stile and the right stile, forming the frame for the door. Mark each board at intersecting points to aid in drilling for the dowel joints.

c. Lay out and drill the holes for the dowels, glue dowels in the rails, then glue and assemble the rails and stiles, forming the face frame.

d. Glue and nail the face frame to the case, using 6d finishing or casing nails. The top of the face frame should be flush with the top edges of the case, while the outer stiles should overhang the case sides by ¼ inch.

3. Only one door is used on this cabinet, and it is not a frame-and-panel door. Instead, it is made from a length of 1 × 6. It covers the tall, narrow opening between the divider and the right side.

a. From 1 × 6 select pine, cut one piece 29½ inches long for the door. Rip it to a 5⅛-inch width.

b. Cut a ⅜-inch-wide by ⅜-inch-deep rabbet around the inside edges of the door.

Materials

Wood

1–4′ × 6′ sht. ⅝″ A-C int. plywood or **Side panels:** 2 pcs. 23″ × 34½″
    Bottom: 1 pc. 23″ × 34¼″
    Divider: 1 pc. 23″ × 30⅜″
    Shelf: 1 pc. 5″ × 23″

1–3′ × 4′ sht. ¼″ A-C int. plywood or **Back panel:** 1 pc. 34½″ × 35½″

2 pcs. 1 × 4 × 8′ #2 pine or **Crosspieces:** 2 pcs. ¾″ × 3½″ × 34¼″
    1 pc. ¾″ × 3½″ × 5″
    Nailer cleats: 2 pcs. ¾″ × 3½″ × 20″
    Plinth: 1 pc. ¾″ × 3½″ × 36″
    Backsplash: 1 pc. ¾″ × 3½″ × 7½″
    1 pc. ¾″ × 3½″ × 1½″

1 pc. 1 × 2 × 10′ select pine or **Frame stiles:** 3 pcs. ¾″ × 1½″ × 31⅞″
    Frame rails: 2 pcs. ¾″ × 1½″ × 4½″

1 pc. 1 × 8 × 3′ select pine or **Frame rail:** 1 pc. ¾″ × 5¾″ × 27″

1 pc. 36″ × ⅜″ dowel or **Dowels:** 12 pcs. 1½″ × ⅜″

1 pc. 1 × 6 × 3′ select pine or **Door panel:** 1 pc. ¾″ × 5⅛″ × 29½″

1 pc. 2′ × 4′ sht. ¾″ flakeboard or **Counter top core:** 2 pcs. 7½″ × 25″
    2 pcs. 1½″ × 25″

Hardware
1″ underlayment nails
6d coated box nails
6d finish nails
1–1½″ rnd. wood knob
1 pr. ⅜″ double-offset, semiconcealed, self-closing hinges
3–3″ #10 screws
5–1¾″ #10 screws

Miscellaneous
Glue
Semigloss latex enamel
Clear varnish
Contact cement
1–3′ × 4′sht. ¹/₁₆″ plastic laminate or

Top: 1 pc. 8″ × 24½″
1 pc. 2″ × 24½″
Backsplash: 1 pc. 3¾″ × 8″
1 pc. 2″ × 3¾″
Backsplash top: 1 pc. 1¼″ × 8″
1 pc. 1¼″ × 2″
Front edge: 1 pc. 2″ × 8″
1 pc. 2″ × 2″
Edges: 4 pcs. 2″ × 25½″
Backsplash end edges: 4 pcs. 1¼″ × 3¾″

Then use a router with a rounding-off bit to break the door's exterior edges. Mount a wooden door knob on the left side of the door panel, 14¾ inches from the top edge. Door hinges should be mounted 2 inches from the top and bottom of the door, and the door installed on the cabinet.

4. Finish the cabinet inside and out, as detailed in the "Finishing" section of "The Basic Base Cabinet." In brief, the sanding and cleanup should be completed, the inside of the cabinet painted and the front of the cabinet finished however you desire.

5. The counter top is in-stalled after the cabinet is fastened in place in the kitchen. Usually, a single counter top will cover all the cabinets. As with the other cabinets, however, you may build a top for this cabinet alone. It will be two very small pieces, one fitted to each side of the stove. The wisdom of building a large counter top to cover several cabinets will become clear as you consider installing these two pieces. Details of assembly are given in the "Counter Top Construction" section of "The Basic Base Cabinet."

a. To minimize the confusion associated with lots of little pieces of wood and plastic laminate, cut and assemble the pieces for one counter top, then do the second. Do the wider section first. From ¾-inch flakeboard, cut two pieces 7½ inches by 25 inches. From 1 × 4 #2 pine, cut a 7½-inch backsplash. From ¹/₁₆-inch plastic laminate, cut an 8-inch by 24½-inch piece for the top, a 3¾-inch by 8-inch piece for the back-splash, a 1¼-inch by 8-inch piece for the backsplash top, a 2-inch by 8-inch piece for the front edge, two 25½-inch by 2-inch pieces for the ends and two 1¼-inch by 3¾-inch pieces for the backsplash ends.

b. Laminate the core, using glue and underlayment **487**

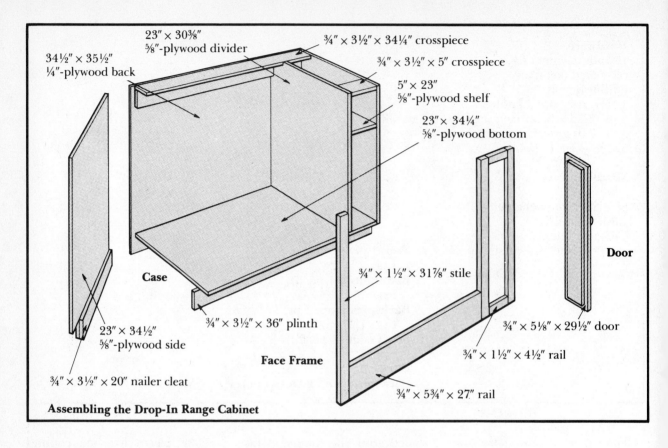

23″ × 30⅜″
⅝″-plywood divider

¾″ × 3½″ × 34¼″ crosspiece

34½″ × 35½″
¼″-plywood back

¾″ × 3½″ × 5″ crosspiece

5″ × 23″
⅝″-plywood shelf

23″ × 34¼″
⅝″-plywood bottom

Door

¾″ × 1½″ × 31⅞″ stile

Case

23″ × 34½″
⅝″-plywood side

¾″ × 3½″ × 36″ plinth

¾″ × 5⅛″ × 29½″ door

¾″ × 3½″ × 20″ nailer cleat

Face Frame

¾″ × 1½″ × 4½″ rail

¾″ × 5¾″ × 27″ rail

Assembling the Drop-In Range Cabinet

nails. Fasten the backsplash to it with two 3-inch #10 screws and glue. Then apply the plastic laminate with contact cement. Trim each piece after it is applied, and before the next piece is applied.

c. Next cut and assemble the second, narrower section. From ¾-inch flakeboard, cut two 1½-inch by 25-inch pieces for the core. From 1 × 4 #2 pine, cut a 1½-inch backsplash. From the plastic laminate, cut a 2-inch by 24½-inch piece for the top, a 2-inch by 3¾-inch piece for the backsplash, a 1¼-inch by 2-inch piece for the backsplash top, a 2-inch-square piece for the

front edge, two 2-inch by 25½-inch pieces for the ends and two 1¼-inch by 3¾-inch pieces for the backsplash ends.

d. Repeat the assembly process.

e. Attach the tops to the cabinet. The wider section will be easy enough to install by driving screws through the top crosspieces into the core. But the narrow section will be difficult, simply because there's only space for a single screw through the top crosspiece at the rear. In this instance, though it's not generally recommended, glue the counter top to the cabinet.

Base Corner Cabinet

A base corner cabinet is used in almost every arrangement of kitchen cabinets. If you are building your cabinets, you thus will have to build at least one.

This particular version is basic. It is not the most easily constructed cabinet, but it does provide a lot of accessible storage space.

Construction

1. Begin by assembling the case, which is constructed of interior plywood, 1 × 4 #2 pine, and 2 × 2 fir. Fabrication and assembly details are much as given in the "Case Construction" section of "The Basic Base Cabinet."

a. From ⅝-inch A-C interior plywood, cut two pieces 23 inches by 34½ inches for the sides and two pieces 36⅞ inches by 36⅞ inches for the top and bottom. From ¼-inch A-C interior plywood, cut one piece 34½ inches by 37¾ inches and one piece 34½ inches by 37½ inches for the back panels. From 1 × 4 #2 pine, cut one 36⅞-inch piece and one 36⅛-inch piece for crosspieces, three 20-inch pieces for the nailer cleats and the floor support and one 21½-inch piece and two 3-inch pieces for the plinth. From 2 × 2 construction-grade fir, cut one 29¾-inch piece for the corner support.

b. In one corner of each side panel, cut a 3-inch-wide by 3½-inch-high notch for the toe space. Using 1-inch underlayment nails, glue and nail the nailer cleats on the inside of the end panels.

c. Measure along the sides of the top and bottom 13⅞ inches from the front corner. Mark this point on both sides. The recess for the face frame should be made by scribing a line ⅞ inches long, perpendicular to the sides, parallel to the cabinet back from these two points. Mark these points

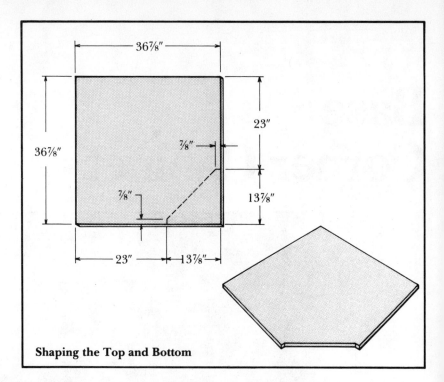

Shaping the Top and Bottom

and join them with a straight line. Cut along these lines with a saber saw, creating the recess.

d. Measure 14 inches from the back corner along each edge of the cabinet bottom, and mark these points. Mount the 20-inch floor support diagonally across the bottom between these two points.

e. The support for the back corner of the case must be rabbeted to accept the crosspieces. Cut 3½-inch-wide by ¾-inch-deep rabbets across two adjoining faces at one end of the support. A stub of wood, ¾ inch by ¾ inch by 3½ inches, will be left projecting from the end of the support.

f. Begin assembling the

case by gluing and nailing the sides to the bottom and top. Then glue and nail the corner support in place at the back corner of the case, between the top and bottom. Be sure the rabbeted end is up, with the rabbets facing out. Glue and nail the rear crosspieces in place. The longer crosspiece will overlap the shorter one at the corner support. After ensuring that the case is square, glue and nail the back panels in place. Again, the longer panel will overlap the shorter one at the corner support.

g. The plinth is made by cutting 45-degree bevels on one end of each of the two shorter plinth pieces. With the case turned upside down,

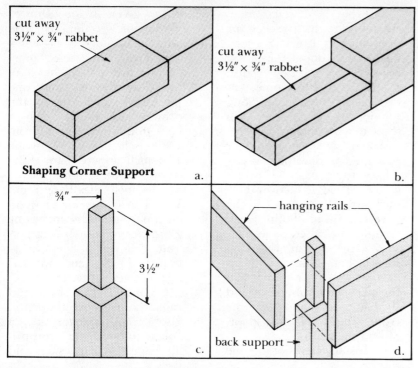

cut away
3½" × ¾" rabbet

cut away
3½" × ¾" rabbet

Shaping Corner Support

a.

b.

¾"

3½"

hanging rails

back support

c.

d.

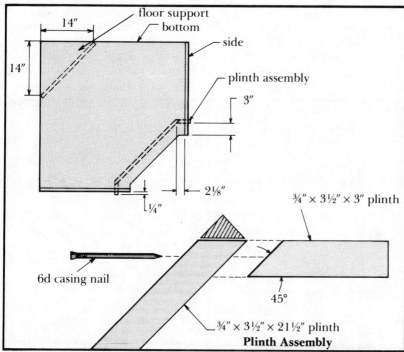

14"

floor support

bottom

side

14"

plinth assembly

3"

2⅛"

¼"

6d casing nail

¾" × 3½" × 3" plinth

45°

¾" × 3½" × 21½" plinth

Plinth Assembly

nail these two pieces into the toe notches, with the bevels facing in and the squared ends overhanging the sides by ¼ inch. Then position the long plinth piece across the beveled ends parallel to the cabinet front, and glue and nail it in place.

2. The face frame of this corner cabinet is somewhat different from those of other cabinets, since it must fit into the recess cut in the front of the case's horizontal members. The frame has four stiles, all with a bevel ripped along one edge. When the pairs of stiles are glued together, they form 135-degree angles. Despite the differences, however, the details of the frame's basic construction are as given in "Face Frame Construction" under "The Basic Base Cabinet."

a. From 1 × 3 select pine, cut four 31⅞-inch pieces for frame stiles and three 14¾-inch pieces for frame rails. From ⅜-inch dowel, cut twelve pieces 1½ inches long. Rip the rails to a 1½-inch width. Then rip a 22½-degree bevel along one edge of each stile. The cut should reduce the width of one face (the exposed one) to exactly 1½ inches and of the opposite face to about 1¾ inches. Put aside two of the stiles, then lay out the others, along with the rails, face down, as they will be in the final assembly. Place the intermediate rail 3¾ inches below the top rail. Mark each board at intersecting points to aid in drilling for the dowel joints.

b. Lay out and drill the **491**

holes for the dowels, glue dowels in the rails, then glue and assemble the rails and stiles forming the face frame. Glue and nail the second set of stiles to the frame, bonding beveled edge to beveled edge, so that the exposed faces of the stiles being glued together are at 135-degree angles to each other. Carefully drive a few finishing nails through the back of the frame into the outermost stiles.

c. Glue and nail the face frame to the case, using 6d finishing or casing nails. The top of the face frame should be flush with the top edges of the case, while the outer stiles should overhang the case sides by ¼ inch.

3. The cabinet door is assembled by joining the door rails and stiles around a raised panel. Fabrication and assembly details are given in the "Door Construction" section of "The Basic Base Cabinet."

a. From 1 × 3 select pine, cut two 24¼-inch pieces for door stiles and two 12¾-inch pieces for door rails. Rip these to a 2¼-inch width. From 1 × 8 select pine, cut two pieces 20½ inches long for door panel elements. Rip these to a 5¾-inch width.

b. To create the door panel, edge-glue the two elements together; the rough panel will be ¾ inch by 11½ inches by 20½ inches. Cut the bevels around both faces, creating the raised panel.

c. Fabricate the rails and stiles, then assemble them around the door panel. Cut the perimeter rabbet around the back edges, and break the front edges of the door. Mount the knob.

d. Install the door on the cabinet.

4. The cabinet has one drawer, which is constructed with a lipped front and simple butt joints. Details of construc-

tion are given in the "Drawer Construction" section of "The Basic Base Cabinet."

a. From 1 × 4 select pine, cut two pieces 22 inches long for drawer sides and one piece 12⅛ inches long for the drawer back. Rip the drawer back to a 3-inch width. From 1 × 6 select pine, cut one 15⅜-inch piece for the drawer front. Rip this piece to a 4¼-inch width. From ¼-inch A-C interior plywood cut one piece 12⅞ inches by 22 inches for the drawer bottom. From 2 × 6 construction-grade fir, cut two 24-inch drawer supports.

b. Groove the sides and rabbet and groove the front. Use a rounding-over bit in a router to break the appropriate edges of front, sides and back.

c. Assemble the drawer, using glue and nails. Mount the knob on the center of the drawer front.

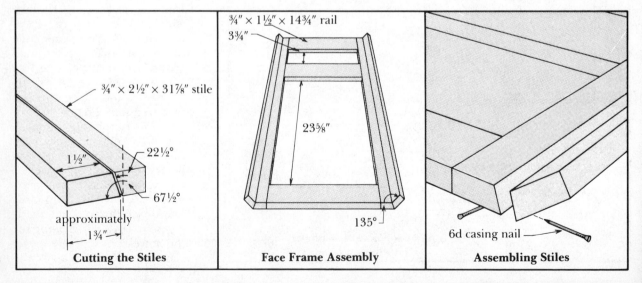

¾" × 2½" × 31⅞" stile
1½"
22½°
67½°
approximately
1¾"

Cutting the Stiles

¾" × 1½" × 14¾" rail
3¾"
23⅝"
135°

Face Frame Assembly

6d casing nail

Assembling Stiles

d. Glue and nail the drawer supports inside the cabinet, with one end joined to the face frame and the top joined to the case top. One support is on each side of the drawer opening, flush with the face frame and perpendicular to it. Install and adjust the drawers, using commercial drawer slides, after finishing the cabinet.

5. Finish the cabinet inside and out, as detailed in the "Finishing" section of "The Basic Base Cabinet." In brief, the sanding and cleanup should be completed, the inside of the cabinet and the drawer painted and the front of the cabinet finished however you desire.

6. The counter top is installed after the cabinet is fastened in place in the kitchen. Usually, a single counter top will cover all the cabinets. As with the other cabinets, however, you may build a top for this cabinet alone. Details of assembly are given in the "Counter Top Construction" section of "The Basic Base Cabinet."

a. From ¾-inch flakeboard, cut two pieces 38 inches by 38 inches for the core. From 1 × 4 #2 pine, cut a 38-inch backsplash and a 37¼-inch backsplash. From 1/16-inch plastic laminate, cut one piece 37½ inches by 37½ inches for the top, one piece 1¼ inches by 38½ inches and one piece 1¼ inches by 37½ inches for the backsplash top edges, two pieces 3¾ inches by 37½ inches for the backsplash, two pieces 1¼ inches by 3¾ inches for the backsplash end edges, one

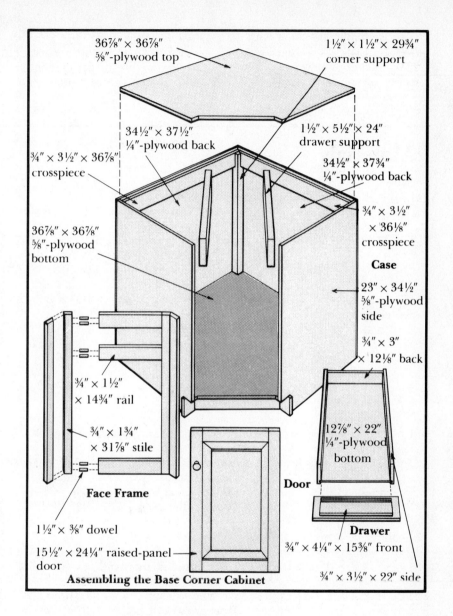

34½″ × 37½″ ¼″-plywood back
36⅞″ × 36⅞″ ⅝″-plywood top
1½″ × 1½″ × 29¾″ corner support
1½″ × 5½″ × 24″ drawer support
34½″ × 37¾″ ¼″-plywood back
¾″ × 3½″ × 36⅞″ crosspiece
¾″ × 3½″ × 36⅛″ crosspiece
36⅞″ × 36⅞″ ⅝″-plywood bottom
Case
23″ × 34½″ ⅝″-plywood side
¾″ × 3″ × 12⅛″ back
¾″ × 1½″ × 14¾″ rail
¾″ × 1¾″ × 31⅞″ stile
12⅞″ × 22″ ¼″-plywood bottom
Door
Face Frame
1½″ × ⅜″ dowel
15½″ × 24¼″ raised-panel door
Drawer
¾″ × 4¼″ × 15⅜″ front
¾″ × 3½″ × 22″ side
Assembling the Base Corner Cabinet

piece 2 inches by 18¾ inches for the front edge and two pieces 2 inches by 25½ inches for the end edges.

b. Trim one corner from each core element and the top laminate so the finished counter top will conform to the shape of the cabinet. From each side corner of the core pieces, measure 25 inches along the side toward the front. Connect these points, then cut along the diagonal thus formed, creating the front edge of the top. **493**

Do essentially the same with the laminate, but measure 25¼ inches instead of 25 inches so you have the requisite overhang.

c. Laminate the core, using glue and underlayment nails. Fasten the backsplashes to it with six to eight 3-inch #10 screws and glue. Then apply the plastic laminate with contact cement. Trim

Materials

Wood

1–4′ × 4′ sht. ⅝″ A-C int. plywood or **Sides:** 2 pcs. 23″ × 34½″
1–4′ × 8′ sht. ⅝″ A-C int. plywood   **Top and bottom:** 2 pcs. 36⅞″ × 36⅞″

1–4′ × 8′ sht. ¼″ A-C int. plywood or **Back panels:** 1 pc. 34½″ × 37¾″
                        1 pc. 34½″ × 37½″
                        Drawer bottom: 1 pc. 12⅞″ × 22″

2 pcs. 1 × 4 × 10′ #2 pine or **Crosspieces:** 1 pc. ¾″ × 3½″ × 36⅞″
                        1 pc. ¾″ × 3½″ × 36⅛″
            Floor support: 1 pc. ¾″ × 3½″ × 20″
            Nailer cleats: 2 pcs. ¾″ × 3½″ × 20″
            Plinth: 1 pc. ¾″ × 3½″ × 21½″
                        2 pcs. ¾″ × 3½″ × 3″
            Backsplash: 1 pc. ¾″ × 3½″ × 38″
                        1 pc. ¾″ × 3½″ × 37¼″

1 pc. 2 × 2 × 4′ constr.-grade fir or **Corner support:** 1 pc. 1½″ × 1½″ × 29¾″

3 pcs. 1 × 3 × 8′ select pine or **Frame stiles:** 4 pcs. ¾″ × 1¾″ × 31⅞″*
            Frame rails: 3 pcs. ¾″ × 1½″ × 14¾″
            Door stiles: 2 pcs. ¾″ × 2¼″ × 24¼″
            Door rails: 2 pcs. ¾″ × 2¼″ × 12¾″

1–36″ × ⅜″ dowel or **Dowels:** 12 pcs. 1½″ × ⅜″ dowel

1 pc. 1 × 8 × 4′ select pine or **Door panel elements:** 2 pcs. ¾″ × 5¾″ × 20½″

1 pc. 1 × 4 × 6′ select pine or **Drawer sides:** 2 pcs. ¾″ × 3½″ × 22″
            Drawer back: 1 pc. ¾″ × 3″ × 12⅛″

1 pc. 1 × 6 × 2′ select pine or **Drawer front:** 1 pc. ¾″ × 4¼″ × 15⅜″

1 pc. 2 × 6 × 4′ constr.-grade fir or **Drawer supports:** 2 pcs. 1½″ × 5½″ × 24″

1–4′ × 8′ sht. ¾″ flakeboard or **Core:** 2 pcs. 38″ × 38″

*In ripping to finished width, one edge must be beveled at a 22½-degree angle.

Hardware
1″ underlayment nails
6d coated box nails
6d finishing nails
2–1½″ rnd. wood knobs
1 pr. ⅜″ double-offset, semiconcealed, self-closing hinges
1 pr. 22″ drawer slides
8–3″ #10 screws
8–1¾″ #10 screws

Miscellaneous
Glue
Semigloss latex enamel
Clear varnish
Contact cement
1–48″ × 60″ sht. ¹⁄₁₆″ plastic laminate or **Top:** 1 pc. 37½″ × 37½″
Backsplash top edges: 1 pc. 1¼″ × 38½″
 1 pc. 1¼″ × 37½″
Backsplash: 2 pcs. 3¾″ × 37½″
End edges: 2 pcs. 1¼″ × 3¾″
Front edge: 1 pc. 2″ × 18¾″
End edges: 2 pcs. 2″ × 25½″

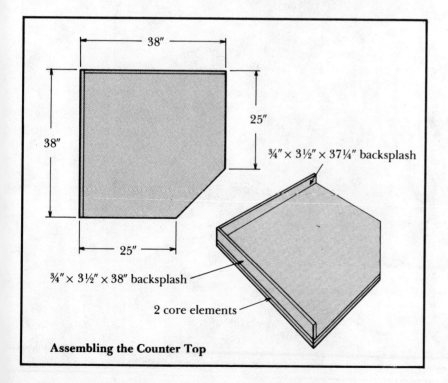

38″

25″

38″

¾″ × 3½″ × 37¼″ backsplash

25″

¾″ × 3½″ × 38″ backsplash

2 core elements

Assembling the Counter Top

each piece after it is applied, and before the next piece is applied.

d. Attach the top to the cabinet with six to eight 1¾-inch #10 screws driven through the top into the top core.

This cabinet is much like the preceding cabinet. It has no drawer, but it does have a lazy Susan.

Three 34-inch-diameter shelves swing past the door, bringing your boxes, bags and cans of food to your fingertips. The secret to successful completion of this cabinet is the use of lazy Susan hardware.

Lazy Susan Corner Cabinet

Construction

1. Begin by assembling the case, which is constructed of interior plywood, 1×4 #2 pine and 2×2 fir. Fabrication and assembly details are given in the "Case Construction" section of "The Basic Base Cabinet."

a. From ⅝-inch A-C interior plywood, cut two pieces 23 inches by 34½ inches for the sides, two pieces 36⅞ inches by 36⅞ inches for the top and bottom and three pieces 34 inches by 34 inches for the shelves. From ¼-inch A-C interior plywood, cut one piece 34½ inches by 37¾ inches and one piece 34½ inches by 37½ inches for the back panels. From 1×4 #2 pine, cut one 36⅞-inch piece and one 36⅛-inch piece for crosspieces, three 20-inch pieces for the nailer cleats and the floor support and one 21½-inch piece and two 3-inch pieces for the plinth. From 2×2 construction-grade fir, cut one 29¾-inch piece for the corner support.

b. In one corner of each side panel, cut a 3-inch-wide by 3½-inch-high notch for the toe space. Using 1-inch underlayment nails, glue and nail the nailer cleats on the inside of the end panels.

c. Measure along the sides of the top and bottom 13⅞ inches from the front corner. Mark this point on both sides. The recess for the face frame should be made by scribing a line ⅞ inch long, perpendicular to the sides, parallel to the cabinet back from these two

points. Mark these points and join them with a straight line. Cut along these lines with a saber saw, creating the recess.

d. Measure 14 inches from the back corner along each edge of the cabinet bottom, and mark these points. Mount the 20-inch floor support diagonally across the bottom between these two points.

e. The support for the back corner of the case must be rabbeted to accept the hanging rails. Cut 3½-inch-wide by ¾-inch-deep rabbets across two adjoining faces at one end of the support. A stub of wood, ¾ inch by ¾ inch by 3½ inches, will be left projecting from the end of the support.

f. Using a makeshift compass—a strip of wood with two appropriately placed nails, for example—scribe a 34-inch-diameter circle on each of the shelf pieces. Using a band saw or saber saw, cut out the shelves. Drill a hole in

the center of each shelf to match the size of the spindle supplied with the lazy Susan hardware. Mount the hardware on the shelves (locate the hardware on the top of the bottom shelf and the bottom of the other two shelves), and mount them on the spindle. Position the middle shelf 11⅛ inches above the bottom shelf, and the top shelf 9¼ inches above the middle shelf. Mount the pivot blocks on the top and bottom pieces. The center should be 17¼ inches from the edge of

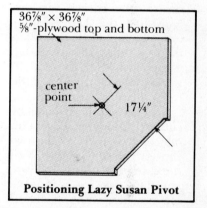

36⅞″ × 36⅞″
⅝″-plywood top and bottom

center point

17¼″

Positioning Lazy Susan Pivot

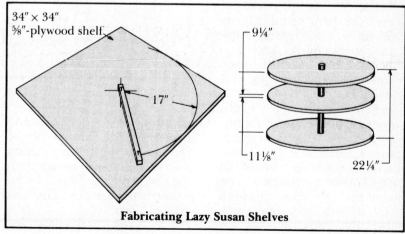

34″ × 34″
⅝″-plywood shelf

17″

9¼″

11⅛″

22¼″

Fabricating Lazy Susan Shelves

the front recess, on a line extended from the center of the recess to the back corner.

g. Begin assembling the case by gluing and nailing the sides to the bottom. Then glue and nail the corner support in place at the back corner of the case. Be sure the rabbeted end is up, with the rabbets facing out. Glue and nail the rear crosspieces in place. The longer crosspiece will overlap the shorter one at the corner support. After ensuring that the case is square, glue and nail the back panels in place. Again, the longer panel will overlap the shorter one at the corner support. Now drop the shelf assembly into position. Finally, position the top, fitting the lazy Susan pivot block over the end of the spindle. Glue and nail the top in place.

h. The plinth is made by cutting 45-degree bevels on one end of each of the two shorter plinth pieces. With the case turned upside down, nail these two pieces into the toe notches, with the bevels facing in and the squared ends overhanging the sides by ¼ inch. Then position the long plinth piece across the beveled ends, parallel to the cabinet front, and glue and nail it in place.

2. The face frame of this corner cabinet is somewhat different from those of other cabinets, since it must fit into the recess cut in the front of the case's horizontal members. The frame has four stiles, all with a bevel ripped along one edge. When the pairs of stiles are

498

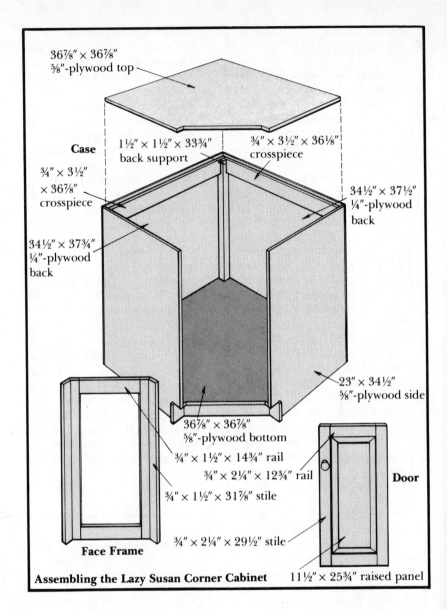

36⅞" × 36⅞"
⅝"-plywood top

Case

¾" × 3½"
× 36⅞"
crosspiece

1½" × 1½" × 33¾"
back support

¾" × 3½" × 36⅛"
crosspiece

34½" × 37½"
¼"-plywood
back

34½" × 37¾"
¼"-plywood
back

23" × 34½"
⅝"-plywood side

36⅞" × 36⅞"
⅝"-plywood bottom

¾" × 1½" × 14¾" rail

¾" × 2¼" × 12¾" rail

¾" × 1½" × 31⅞" stile

¾" × 2¼" × 29½" stile

Face Frame

Door

11½" × 25¾" raised panel

Assembling the Lazy Susan Corner Cabinet

glued together, they form 135-degree angles. Despite the differences, however, the details of the frame's basic construction are as given in "Face Frame Construction" under "The Basic Base Cabinet."

a. From 1 × 3 select pine, cut four 31⅞-inch pieces for frame stiles and two 14¾-inch pieces for frame rails. From ⅜-inch dowel, cut eight pieces 1½ inches long. Rip the rails to a 1½-inch width. Then rip a 22½-degree bevel along one edge of each stile. The cut should reduce the width of one face (the exposed one) to exactly 1½ inches and of the opposite face to about 1¾ inches. Put aside two of the stiles, then lay out the others, face down, along with the rails, as they will be in the final assembly. Mark each board at intersecting points to aid in drilling for the dowel joints.

b. Lay out and drill the holes for the dowels, glue dowels in the rails, then glue and assemble the rails and stiles, forming the face frame. Glue and nail the second set of stiles to the frame, bonding beveled edge to beveled edge, so that the exposed faces of the stiles being glued together are at 135-degree angles to each other. Carefully drive a

few finishing nails through the back of the frame into the outermost stiles.

c. Glue and nail the face frame to the case, using 6d finishing or casing nails. The top of the face should be flush with the top edges of the case, while the outer stiles should overhang the case sides by ¼ inch.

3. The cabinet door is assem-

Materials

Wood

3–4′ × 8′ shts. ⅝″ A-C int. plywood or **Sides:** 2 pcs. 23″ × 34½″
Top and bottom: 2 pcs. 36⅞″ × 36⅞″
Shelves: 3 pcs. 34″ diameter

1–4′ × 8′ sht. ¼″ A-C int. plywood or **Back panels:** 1 pc. 34½″ × 37¾″
1 pc. 34½″ × 37½″

1 pc. 1 × 4 × 8′ #2 pine or **Crosspieces:** 1 pc. ¾″ × 3½″ × 36⅞″
1 pc. 1 × 4 × 12′ #2 pine   1 pc. ¾″ × 3½″ × 36⅛″
Nailer cleats: 2 pcs. ¾″ × 3½″ × 20″
Floor support: 1 pc. ¾″ × 3½″ × 20″
Plinth: 1 pc. ¾″ × 3½″ × 21½″
2 pcs. ¾″ × 3½″ × 3″
Backsplash: 1 pc. ¾″ × 3½″ × 38″
1 pc. ¾″ × 3½″ × 37¼″

1 pc. 2 × 2 × 4′ constr.-grade fir or **Back support:** 1 pc. 1½″ × 1½″ × 33¾″

1 pc. 1 × 3 × 14′ select pine or **Frame stiles:** 4 pcs. ¾″ × 1½″ × 31⅞″
Frame rails: 2 pcs. ¾″ × 1½″ × 14¾″

1–36″ × ⅜″ dowel or **Dowels:** 8 pcs. 1½″ × ⅜″ dowel

1 pc. 1 × 3 × 8′ select pine or **Door stiles:** 2 pcs. ¾″ × 2¼″ × 29½″
Door rails: 2 pcs. ¾″ × 2¼″ × 12¾″

1 pc. 1 × 8 × 6′ select pine or **Door panel elements:** 2 pcs. ¾″ × 5¾″ × 25¾″

1–4′ × 8′ sht. ¾″ flakeboard or **Core:** 2 pcs. 38″ × 38″

[continued on next page]

Hardware
1″ underlayment nails
6d coated box nails
6d finishing nails
Lazy Susan hardware: 1 spindle, 2 pivot blocks and 3 shelf supports
1–1½″ rnd. wood knob
1 pr. ⅜″ double-offset, semiconcealed, self-closing hinges
8–3″ #10 screws
8–1¾″ #10 screws

Miscellaneous
Glue
Semigloss latex enamel
Clear varnish
Contact cement
1–48″ × 60″ sht. ¹⁄₁₆″ plastic laminate or **Top:** 1 pc. 37½″ × 37½″
Backsplash top edge: 1 pc. 1¼″ × 38½″
1 pc. 1¼″ × 37½″
Backsplash: 2 pcs. 3¾″ × 37½″
Backsplash end edges: 2 pcs. 1¼″ × 3¾″
Front edge: 1 pc. 2″ × 18″
End edges: 2 pcs. 2″ × 25½″

bled by joining the door rails and stiles around a raised panel. Fabrication and assembly details are given in the "Door Construction" section of "The Basic Base Cabinet."

a. From 1 × 3 select pine, cut two 29½-inch pieces for door stiles and two 12¾-inch pieces for door rails. Rip these to a 2¼-inch width. From 1 × 8 select pine, cut two pieces 25¾ inches long for door panel elements. Rip these to a 5¾-inch width.

b. To create the door panel, edge-glue the two elements together; the rough panel will be ¾ inch by 11½ inches by 25¾ inches. Cut the bevels around both faces, creating the raised panel.

c. Fabricate the rails and stiles, then assemble them around the door panel. Cut the perimeter rabbet around the back edges of the door, and break the front edges. Mount the knob.

d. Install the door on the cabinet.

4. Finish the cabinet inside and out, as detailed in the "Finishing" section of "The Basic Base Cabinet." In brief, the sanding and cleanup should be completed, the inside of the cabinet painted and the front of the cabinet finished however you desire.

5. The counter top is installed after the cabinet is fastened in place in the kitchen. Usually, a single counter top will cover all the cabinets. As with other cabinets, however, you may build a top for this cabinet alone. Details of assembly are given in the "Counter Top Construction" section of "The Basic Base Cabinet."

a. From ¾-inch flakeboard, cut two pieces 38 inches by 38 inches for the core. From 1 × 4 #2 pine, cut a 38-inch backsplash and a 37¼-inch backsplash. From ¹⁄₁₆-inch plastic laminate, cut one piece 37½ inches by 37½ inches for the top, one piece 1¼ inch by 38½ inches and one piece 1¼ inches by 37½ inches for the backsplash top edges, two pieces 3¾ inches by 37½ inches for the backsplash, two pieces 1¼ inches by 3¾ inches for the backsplash end edges, one piece 2 inches by 18¾ inches for the front edge and two pieces 2 inches by 25½ inches for the end edges.

b. Trim one corner from each core element and the top laminate so the finished counter top will conform to the shape of the cabinet. From each side corner of the core pieces, measure 25 inches along the side toward the front. Connect these points, then cut along the diagonal thus formed, creating the front edge of the top. Do essentially the same with the laminate, but measure 25¼ inches instead of 25 inches so you have the requisite overhang.

c. Laminate the core, using glue and underlayment nails. Fasten the backsplashes to it with six to eight 3-inch #10 screws and glue. Then apply the plastic laminate with contact cement. Trim each piece after it is applied, and before the next piece is applied.

d. Attach the top to the cabinet with six to eight 1¾-inch #10 screws driven through the top into the top core.

Revolving Front Corner Cabinet

This base corner cabinet is significantly different from the preceding two. The front is shaped differently, and the "door" is attached to the lazy Susan shelf unit and revolves with it.

These differences mean not only that the distance between the cabinet front and the back corner is reduced, but also that

the shelf capacity is reduced. There is little difference, however, in the construction of the cabinet. The case is largely plywood, the face frame and door fronts select pine.

Construction

1. Begin by assembling the case, which is constructed of interior plywood, 1×4 #2 pine and 2×2 fir. Fabrication and assembly details are given in the "Case Construction" section of "The Basic Base Cabinet."

a. From ⅝-inch A-C interior plywood, cut two pieces 23 inches by 34½ inches for the sides, two pieces 36⅞ inches by 36⅞ inches for the top and bottom, three 32-inch by 32-inch pieces for the shelves and one 11½-inch by 26½-inch piece and one 12¼-inch by 26½-inch piece for door panel backers. From ¼-inch A-C interior plywood,

cut one piece 34½ inches by 37¾ inches and one piece 34½ inches by 37½ inches for the back panels. From 1×4 #2 pine, cut one 36⅞-inch piece and one 36⅛-inch piece for crosspieces, three 20-inch pieces for the nailer cleats and the floor support and one 17⅜-inch piece and one 17¾-inch piece for the plinth. From 2×2 construction-grade fir, cut one 29¾-inch piece for the corner support.

b. In one corner of each side panel, cut a 3-inch-wide by 3½-inch-high notch for the toe space. Using 1-inch underlayment nails, glue and nail the nailer cleats on the inside of the end panels.

c. Measure along the sides of the top and bottom 13⅞ inches and 17⅜ inches from the front corner. Mark both these points on both sides, then extend a perpendicular from each across each panel.

They should intersect on a diagonal drawn from the front corner to the back corner. Cut along the two 13⅞-inch lines (not the diagonal), forming an inside corner that will be the front of the case. The point where the 17⅜-inch lines intersect is the centerpoint for installing the lazy Susan pivot block. Mount the pivot blocks.

d. Measure 14 inches from the back corner along each edge of the cabinet bottom, and mark these points. Mount the 20-inch floor support diagonally across the bottom between these two points.

e. The support for the back corner of the case must be rabbeted to accept the crosspieces. Cut 3½-inch-wide by ¾-inch-deep rabbets across two adjoining faces at one end of the support. A stub of wood, ¾ inch by ¾ inch by 3½ inches, will be left projecting from the end of the support.

f. Using a makeshift compass—a strip of wood with two appropriately placed nails, for example—scribe a 32-inch-diameter circle on each of the shelf pieces. Then scribe a 13-inch by 13-inch notch into one corner of each shelf panel. The backer panels will fit into these notches in the final assembly. Using a band saw or saber saw, cut out the shelves. Drill a hole in the center of each shelf to match the size of the spindle supplied with the lazy Susan hardware. Mount the hardware on the bottom of the shelves and mount them **503**

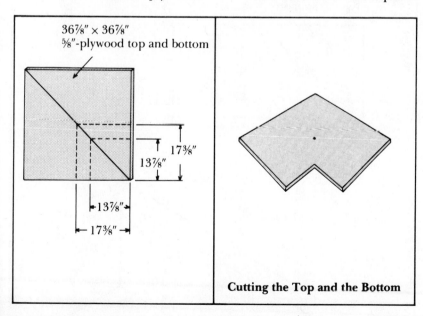

Cutting the Top and the Bottom

36⅞″ × 36⅞″
⅝″-plywood top and bottom

17⅜″
13⅞″
13⅞″
17⅜″

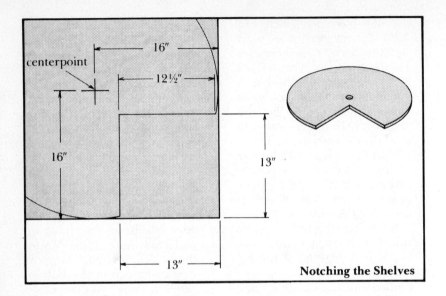

Notching the Shelves

will overlap the shorter one at the corner support. After ensuring that the case is square, glue and nail the back panel in place. Again, the longer panel will overlap the shorter one at the corner support. Now drop the shelf assembly into place. Position the top, fitting the lazy Susan pivot block over the end of the spindle. Glue and nail the top in place. The outer surfaces of the backer panels should be flush with the edges of the top and bottom.

h. The plinth is made by cutting a ¾-inch-wide by ⅜-inch-deep rabbet across one end of the 17¾-inch plinth piece. The shorter plinth piece is glued and nailed in this rabbet. Glue and nail these two pieces into the

on the spindle, aligning the notches. Position the middle shelf 9¼ inches above the bottom shelf and the top shelf 8¼ inches above the middle shelf. Cut ⅝-inch-wide by ¼-inch-deep dadoes across the backer panels for the shelves to fit into. The first dado is 6⅞ inches from the top edge, the second 15¾ inches from the top edge and the third 25⅝ inches from the top edge. Finally, glue and nail the backer panels in the notches in the shelves, with the shelf edges in the dadoes. Install the wider panel first, then install the narrower one, butting one edge of it against the back of the first.

g. Begin assembling the case by gluing and nailing the sides to the bottom and top. Then glue and nail the corner support in place at the back corner of the case, between the top and bottom. Be sure the rabbeted end is up, with the

rabbets facing out. Glue and nail the rear crosspieces in place. The longer crosspiece

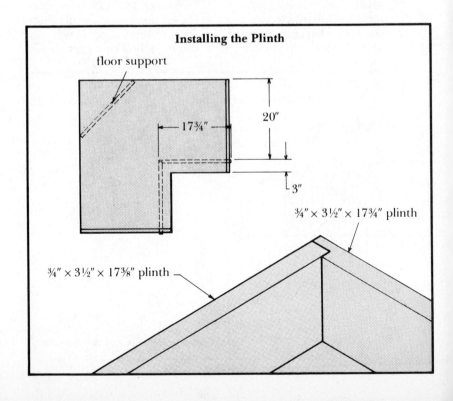

Installing the Plinth

floor support

17¾"

20"

3"

¾" × 3½" × 17¾" plinth

¾" × 3½" × 17⅜" plinth

toe notches, with the ends overhanging the sides by ¼ inch.

2. The face frame of this corner cabinet is somewhat different from those of other cabinets, since it must fit into the notch cut in the front of the case's horizontal members. The frame has two stiles and four rails. The top and bottom rail assemblies are formed by joining two of the rail pieces at right angles to each other with a rabbet joint. Despite the differences, however, the details of the frame's basic construction are as given in "Face Frame Construction" under "The Basic Base Cabinet."

a. From 1 × 2 select pine, cut two 31⅞-inch pieces for frame stiles and two 13½-inch pieces and two 13⅛-inch pieces for frame rails. From ⅜-inch dowel, cut eight pieces 1½ inches long. Rip a 22½-degree bevel along one edge of each stile without reducing the width of the broader face. The 1½-inch face will be the exposed face; the beveled edge will be the inner edge. Crosscut a similar bevel across one end of each rail. The shorter face of each rail will be the exposed face. Two rails should have these faces 13¼ inches long, the other two 12⅞ inches long. Lay out the stiles and the rails face down, as they will be in the final assembly. Mark the intersecting points on each board to aid in drilling for the dowel joints.

b. Cut a ¾-inch-wide by ⅜-inch-deep rabbet across the exposed face of the square end of the two 13¼-inch rails.

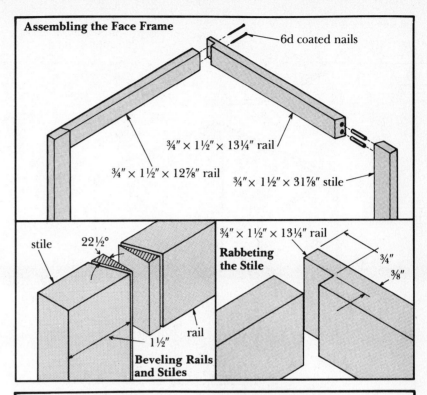

Assembling the Face Frame

6d coated nails

¾" × 1½" × 13¼" rail

¾" × 1½" × 12⅞" rail

¾" × 1½" × 31⅞" stile

stile

22½°

rail

1½"

Beveling Rails and Stiles

¾" × 1½" × 13¼" rail

Rabbeting the Stile

¾"

⅜"

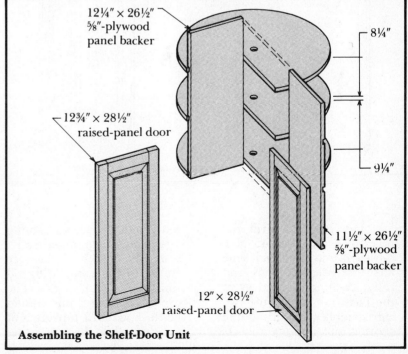

12¼" × 26½" ⅝"-plywood panel backer

8¼"

12¾" × 28½" raised-panel door

9¼"

11½" × 26½" ⅝"-plywood panel backer

12" × 28½" raised-panel door

Assembling the Shelf-Door Unit

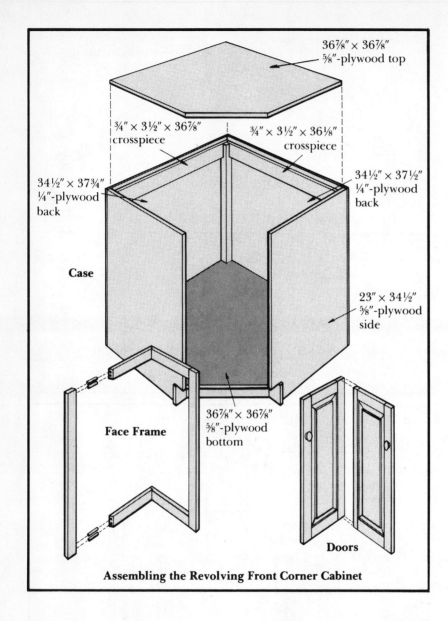

36⅞" × 36⅞"
⅝"-plywood top

¾" × 3½" × 36⅞"
crosspiece

¾" × 3½" × 36⅛"
crosspiece

34½" × 37¾"
¼"-plywood
back

34½" × 37½"
¼"-plywood
back

Case

23" × 34½"
⅝"-plywood
side

Face Frame

36⅞" × 36⅞"
⅝"-plywood
bottom

Doors

Assembling the Revolving Front Corner Cabinet

should overhang the case sides by ¼ inch.

3. The door for this cabinet is actually a two-piece false front. Each piece is assembled by joining door rails and stiles around a raised panel. Fabrication and assembly details are given in the "Door Construction" section of "The Basic Base Cabinet."

a. From 1 × 3 select pine, cut four 28½-inch pieces for door stiles and four 11-inch pieces for door rails. Rip the rails to a 2¼-inch width. Rip two stiles to a 2-inch width. One of the remaining stiles should be ripped to a 1¾-inch width, the other to a 1-inch width. From 1 × 6 select pine, cut four pieces 24¾ inches long for door panel elements. Rip these to a 4⅞-inch width.

b. To create each door panel, edge-glue two elements together; each rough panel will be ¾ inch by 9¾ inches by 24¾ inches. Cut the bevels around both faces of each, creating the raised panels.

c. Fabricate the rails and stiles but do not rabbet their edges. These will not be lipped doors. Then assemble them around the door panels. Break the front edges of the doors. Mount the knobs.

d. Install the doors on the cabinet by gluing them to the backer panels, then driving several 1-inch #6 screws through the backer panels into the frames of the doors. The door with the uniform stiles is installed first, then the other door is installed with the narrow stile butted against the first door. Install a

c. Lay out and drill the holes for the dowels, glue dowels in the rails, then glue and assemble the rails and stiles, creating two halves of the face frame. Join the two subassemblies by fitting the shorter rails into the rabbets in the longer ones and gluing and nailing them together.

d. Glue and nail the face frame to the case, using 6d finishing or casing nails. The top of the face frame should be flush with the top edges of the case, while the outer stiles

roller catch plate on one stile, midway between the top and bottom rails. Position the roller on the adjacent door so that the catch will keep the door from revolving when it is "closed."

4. Finish the cabinet inside and out, as detailed in the "Finishing" section of "The Basic Base Cabinet." In brief, the sanding and cleanup should be completed, the inside of the cabinet painted and the front of the cabinet finished however you desire.

5. The counter top is installed after the cabinet is fastened in place in the kitchen. Usually, a single counter top will cover all the cabinets. As with the other cabinets, however, you may build a top for this cabinet alone. Details of assembly are given in the "Counter Top Construction" section of "The Basic Base Cabinet."

a. From ¾-inch flakeboard, cut two pieces 38 inches by 38 inches for the core. From

Materials

Wood

3–4′ × 8′ shts. ⅝″ A-C int. plywood or **Sides:** 2 pcs. 23″ × 34½″
Top and bottom: 2 pcs. 36⅞″ × 36⅞″
Shelves: 3 pcs. 32″ diameter
Panel backers: 1 pc. 11½″ × 26½″
1 pc. 12¼″ × 26½″

1–4′ × 8′ sht. ¼″ A-C int. plywood or **Back panels:** 1 pc. 34½″ × 37¾″
1 pc. 34½″ × 37½″

1 pc. 1 × 4 × 10′ #2 pine or **Crosspieces:** 1 pc. ¾″ × 3½″ × 36⅞″
1 pc. 1 × 4 × 12′ #2 pine 1 pc. ¾″ × 3½″ × 36⅛″
Nailer cleats: 2 pcs. ¾″ × 3½″ × 20″
Floor support: 1 pc. ¾″ × 3½″ × 20″
Plinth: 1 pc. ¾″ × 3½″ × 17⅜″
1 pc. ¾″ × 3½″ × 17¾″
Backsplash: 1 pc. ¾″ × 3½″ × 38″
1 pc. ¾″ × 3½″ × 37¼″

1 pc. 2 × 2 × 4′ constr.-grade fir or **Back support:** 1 pc. 1½″ × 1½″ × 29¾″

1 pc. 1 × 2 × 12′ select pine or **Frame stiles:** 2 pcs. ¾″ × 1½″ × 31⅞″
Frame rails: 2 pcs. ¾″ × 1½″ × 13½″
2 pcs. ¾″ × 1½″ × 13⅛″

1–36″ × ⅜″ dowels or **Dowels:** 8 pcs. 1½″ × ⅜″

2 pcs. 1 × 3 × 8′ select pine or **Door stiles:** 4 pcs. ¾″ × 2¼″ × 28½″
Door rails: 4 pcs. ¾″ × 2¼″ × 11″

2 pcs. 1 × 6 × 10′ select pine or **Door panel elements:** 4 pcs. ¾″ × 4⅞″ × 24¾″

1–4′ × 8′ sht. ¾″ flakeboard or **Core:** 2 pcs. 38″ × 38″

[continued on next page]

Hardware
1″ underlayment nails
6d coated box nails
6d finishing nails
Lazy Susan hardware: 1 spindle, 2 pivot blocks, 3 shelf supports
2–1½″ rnd. wood knobs
12–1″ #6 screws
8–3″ #10 screws
8–1¾″ #10 screws
1 roller catch unit

Miscellaneous
Glue
Semigloss latex enamel
Clear varnish
Contact cement
1–48″ × 60″ sht. plastic laminate or **Top:** 1 pc. 37½″ × 37½″
Backsplash top edge: 1 pc. 1¼″ × 38½″
    1 pc. 1¼″ × 37½″
Backsplash: 2 pcs. 3¾″ × 37½″
Backsplash end edges: 2 pcs. 1¼″ × 3¾″
Front edges: 2 pcs. 2″ × 13¼″
End edges: 2 pcs. 2″ × 25½″

1 × 4 #2 pine, cut a 38-inch backsplash and a 37¼-inch backsplash. From ¹/₁₆-inch plastic laminate, cut one piece 37½ inches by 37½ inches for the top, one piece 1¼ inches by 38½ inches and one piece 1¼ inches by 37½ inches for the backsplash top edges, two pieces 3¾ inches by 37½ inches for the backsplash, two pieces 1¼ inches by 3¾ inches for the backsplash end edges, two pieces 2 inches by 13¼ inches for the front edge and two pieces 2 inches by 25½ inches for the end edges.

b. Notch one corner of each core element and the top laminate so the finished counter top will conform to the shape of the cabinet. From each side corner of the core pieces, measure 25 inches along the side toward the front. Scribe perpendicular lines across the piece until they intersect. Then cut along these lines, creating the front edge of the top. Do essentially the same with the laminate, but measure 25¼ inches in-stead of 25 inches so you have the requisite overhang.

c. Laminate the core, using glue and underlayment nails. Fasten the backsplashes to it with six to eight 3-inch #10 screws and glue. Then apply the plastic laminate with contact cement. Trim each piece after it is applied, and before the next piece is applied.

d. Attach the top to the cabinet with six to eight 1¾-inch #10 screws driven through the top into the top core.

This is the basic wall cabinet. It is 36 inches wide and has two doors and three adjustable shelves.

If you are going to build wall cabinets at all, this is the prototype of what you will make. It's a simple matter to alter the size. A wider unit, say 48 inches, would simply be stretched, with longer rails, top, bottom and

Wall Cabinet

shelves and a wider back and doors. Anything wider than 48 inches should be created by marrying several basic units during installation. An 18-inch model would have a single door. Anything narrower than that would be made by simply cutting pieces shorter. Likewise, the height of the unit could be increased or cut, according to your needs.

Construction

1. Begin by fabricating the cabinet's case. With the exception of a 1 × 4 hanging rail, the case is made of interior plywood. Fabrication and assembly details follow the pattern set in the "Case Construction" section of "The Basic Base Cabinet."

a. From ⅝-inch A-C interior plywood, cut two pieces 11 inches by 29⅛ inches for the sides, two pieces 11 inches by 34¼ inches for the top and bottom, and three pieces 10⅞ inches by 34¹/₁₆ inches for shelves. Cut a piece of 1 × 4 #2 pine 34¼ inches long for the hanging rail. From ¼-inch A-C interior plywood, cut a piece 29⅛ inches by 35½ inches for the back.

b. On the good side of each side panel, lay out and drill ¼-inch-diameter, ⅜-inch-deep holes for the shelf support pins for the adjustable shelves. There should be nine sets of holes, each 2 inches below the last set, beginning 7⅛ inches from the top edge and ending 6 inches from the bottom edge of each panel.

One line of holes should be positioned 2¼ inches from the front edge of the panel and a second, 2¼ inches from the back edge. Mark the hole locations carefully, and drill each hole perpendicularly, so the shelves are steady and level. Work carefully to avoid drilling all the way through the side panels.

c. To assemble the cabinet case, glue and nail the side panels to the top and bottom with the side panels overlapping the top and bottom in a simple butt joint. Use 6d coated nails. Place the good side of the plywood pieces to the inside. Glue and nail the

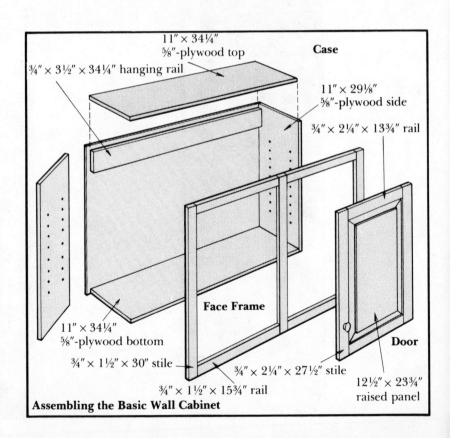

7⅛″

2″

6″

2¼″   2¼″

Laying Out Holes in Side Panels

11″ × 34¼″ ⅝″-plywood top

¾″ × 3½″ × 34¼″ hanging rail

Case

11″ × 29⅛″ ⅝″-plywood side

¾″ × 2¼″ × 13¾″ rail

Face Frame

11″ × 34¼″ ⅝″-plywood bottom

¾″ × 1½″ × 30″ stile

¾″ × 2¼″ × 27½″ stile

¾″ × 1½″ × 15¾″ rail

Door

12½″ × 23¾″ raised panel

Assembling the Basic Wall Cabinet

Materials

Wood

1–4′ × 6′ sht. ⅝″ A-C int. plywood or **Sides:** 2 pcs. 11″ × 29⅛″
Top and bottom: 2 pcs. 11″ × 34¼″
Shelves: 3 pcs. 10⅞″ × 34¹⁄₁₆″

1 pc. 1 × 4 × 3′ #2 pine or **Hanging rail:** 1 pc. ¾″ × 3½″ × 34¼″

1–4′ × 4′ sht. ¼″ A-C int. plywood or **Back:** 1 pc. 29⅛″ × 35½″

2 pcs. 1 × 2 × 8′ select pine or **Frame stiles:** 3 pcs. ¾″ × 1½″ × 30″
Frame rails: 4 pcs. ¾″ × 1½″ × 15¾″

2 pcs. 36″ × ⅜″ dowel or **Dowels:** 16 pcs. 1½″ × ⅜″

2 pcs. 1 × 3 × 8′ select pine or **Door stiles:** 4 pcs. ¾″ × 2¼″ × 27½″
Door rails: 4 pcs. ¾″ × 2¼″ × 13¾″

1 pc. 1 × 8 × 8′ select pine or **Door panels:** 4 pcs. ¾″ × 6¼″ × 23¾″

Hardware

12 shelf support pins
6d coated box nails
6d finishing nails
2–1½″ rnd. wood knobs
2 pr. ⅜″ double-offset, semiconcealed, self-closing hinges

Miscellaneous

Semigloss latex enamel
Glue
Clear varnish

hanging rail between the side panels, snug against the top of the cabinet. Be sure the cabinet case is square. Then glue and nail the back panel to the cabinet, overlapping top, bottom and side panels.

2. The face frame is composed of three stiles, joined by dowels to four rails. Fabrication and assembly details are given in the "Face Frame Construc-

tion" section of "The Basic Base Cabinet."

a. From 1 × 2 select pine, cut three 30-inch-long frame stiles and four 15¾-inch-long frame rails. From ⅜-inch dowel, cut sixteen pieces, each 1½ inches long. After cutting the stiles and rails, lay them face down on the workbench with the rails between the upright stiles as in the final as-

sembly. Mark each board at intersecting points to aid in drilling for the dowel joints.

b. Lay out and drill the holes for the dowels, glue dowels in the rails, then glue and assemble the rails and stiles, forming the face frame.

c. Glue and nail the face frame to the case, using 6d finishing or casing nails. The top of the face frame should be flush with the top edges of the case, while the outer stiles should overhang the case sides by ¼ inch.

3. The cabinet doors are assembled by joining the door rails and stiles around a raised panel. Fabrication and assembly details are given in the "Door Construction" section of "The Basic Base Cabinet."

a. From 1 × 3 select pine, cut four 27½-inch door stiles and four 13¾-inch door rails. Rip them to a 2¼-inch width. The elements glued up to form the door panels are cut from 1 × 8 select pine. Cut four 23¾-inch pieces, then rip them to a 6¼-inch width.

b. To create each door panel, edge-glue two of the elements together; the rough panels will be ¾ inch by 12½ inches by 23¾ inches. Cut the bevels around both faces, creating the raised panel.

c. Fabricate the rails and stiles, then assemble them around the door panels. Cut the perimeter rabbet around the back edges, and break the front edges of the doors. Mount the knobs.

d. Install the doors on the cabinet.

4. Finish the cabinet inside and out, as detailed in the "Finishing" section of "The Basic Base Cabinet." In brief, the sanding and cleanup should be completed, the inside of the cabinet painted and the front of the cabinet finished however you desire.

Wall Corner Cabinet

If your cabinet plans include wall cabinets, it isn't at all unlikely that you'll need to build a corner cabinet.

This one is very similar in construction to the base corner cabinets. The face frame is the most complicated element to construct. There are other ways to turn the corner with a run of cabinets, but this corner cabinet

may be the best. Its design allows the best possible access to all corners of the unit.

Construction

1. The first step is to construct the cabinet case which is made of interior plywood and #2 pine. Fabrication and assembly details are much as given in the "Case Construction" section of "The Basic Base Cabinet."

a. From ⅝-inch A-C interior plywood, cut two pieces 11 inches by 29⅛ inches for the sides and four pieces 22⅞ inches by 22⅞ inches for the top, bottom and two shelves. From ¼-inch A-C interior plywood, cut one piece 29⅛ inches by 23¾ inches for one back panel and one piece 29⅛ inches by 23½ inches for the other. From 1 × 4 #2 pine, cut one 22⅞-inch piece and one 22⅛-inch piece for hanging rails.

b. Begin by cutting the top, bottom and shelves to the correct dimensions. Measure 10¾ inches along adjoining sides of each piece from the front corner. Mark this point on both sides. To form the front recess, scribe a line ¾ inch long, perpendicular to the sides, parallel to the cabinet back. Mark this point on both sides of both sides of each piece, join the lines across the front of each piece and cut along this line, forming the recessed front.

c. Orienting the good side of the plywood to the inside, glue and nail a hanging rail to the upper edge of each back

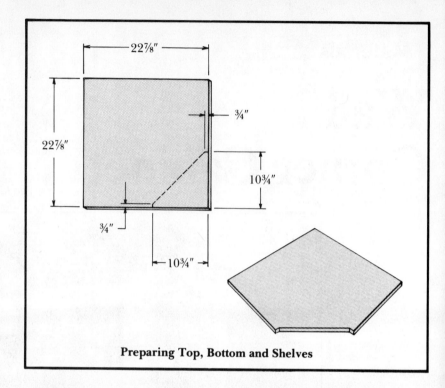

Preparing Top, Bottom and Shelves

panel, joining the hanging rails in a butt edge. Glue and nail the top, bottom, and shelves to the end panels. Be sure the case is square, then glue and nail the back panels to the cabinet case, overlapping all edges.

2. The face frame is composed of two frame stiles joined by dowels to two frame rails. Two additional stiles are glued at an angle along the frame stiles, forming a frame that will fit into the recess cut into the case's horizontal members. Details of the face frame's construction are much as given in the "Face Frame Construction" section of "The Basic Base Cabinet."

a. From 1 × 3 select pine, cut four pieces 30 inches long

for frame stiles and two pieces 12 inches long for frame rails. Rip the rails only to a 1½-inch width. From ⅜-inch dowel cut eight pieces 1½ inches long.

b. Rip a 22½-degree bevel along one edge of each frame stile so that the width of one side will be 1½ inches and the width of the other side 1¾ inches. After cutting the stiles and rails, set two stiles aside, then lay the other pieces face down on the workbench as in the final assembly. The broad faces of the stiles are the backs; the beveled edges are to the outside. Mark each piece at intersecting points to aid in drilling for the dowel joints.

c. Lay out and drill the holes for the dowels, glue

514

Materials

Wood

1–4′ × 6′ sht. ⅝″ A-C int. plywood or **Sides:** 2 pcs. 11″ × 29⅛″

Top and bottom: 2 pcs. 22⅞″ × 22⅞″

Shelves: 2 pcs. 22⅞″ × 22⅞″

1–4′ × 4′ sht. ¼″ A-C int. plywood or **Back panels:** 1 pc. 29⅛″ × 23¾″

1 pc. 29⅛″ × 23½″

1 pc. 1 × 4 × 4′ #2 pine or **Hanging rails:** 1 pc. ¾″ × 3½″ × 22⅞″

1 pc. ¾″ × 3½″ × 22⅛″

1 pc. 1 × 3 × 8′ select pine or **Frame stiles:** 4 pcs. ¾″ × 1¾″ × 30″*
1 pc. 1 × 3 × 14′ select pine   **Frame rails:** 2 pcs. ¾″ × 1½″ × 12″

Door stiles: 2 pcs. ¾″ × 2¼″ × 27½″

Door rails: 2 pcs. ¾″ × 2¼″ × 10″

1–36″ × ⅜″ dowel or **Dowels:** 8 pcs. 1½″ × ⅜″

1 pc. 1 × 10 × 2′ select pine or **Door panel:** 1 pc. ¾″ × 8¾″ × 23¾″

Hardware

1″ underlayment nails
6d coated box nails
6d finishing nails
1–1½″ rnd. wood knob
1 pr. ⅜″ double-offset, semiconcealed, self-closing hinges

Miscellaneous

Glue
Semigloss latex enamel
Clear varnish

*In ripping to finished width, one edge must be beveled at a 22½-degree angle.

dowels in the rails, then glue and assemble the rails and stiles forming the face frame. Glue and nail the second set of stiles to the frame, bonding beveled edge to beveled edge, so that the exposed faces of the stiles being glued together are a 135-degree angle to each other. Carefully drive a few finishing nails through the back of the frame into the outermost stiles.

d. Glue and nail the face frame to the case, using 6d finishing or casing nails. The top of the face frame should be flush with the top edges of the case, while the outer stiles should overhang the case sides by ¼ inch.

3. The cabinet door is assembled by joining the door rails and stiles around a raised panel. Fabrication and assembly details are given in the "Door Construction" section of "The Basic Base Cabinet."

a. From 1 × 3 select pine, cut two pieces 27½ inches **515**

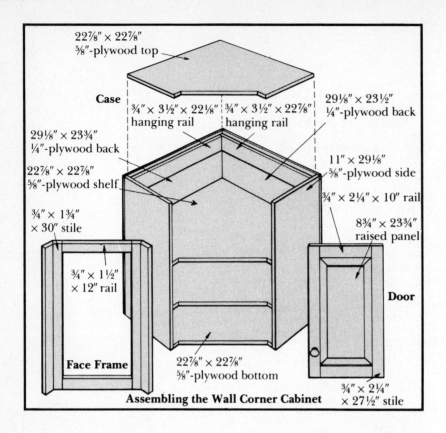

22⅞" × 22⅞"
⅝"-plywood top

Case

¾" × 3½" × 22⅛"
hanging rail

¾" × 3½" × 22⅞"
hanging rail

29⅛" × 23½"
¼"-plywood back

29⅛" × 23¾"
¼"-plywood back

11" × 29⅛"
⅝"-plywood side

22⅞" × 22⅞"
⅝"-plywood shelf

¾" × 2¼" × 10" rail

¾" × 1¾"
× 30" stile

8¾" × 23¾"
raised panel

¾" × 1½"
× 12" rail

Door

Face Frame

22⅞" × 22⅞"
⅝"-plywood bottom

¾" × 2¼"
× 27½" stile

Assembling the Wall Corner Cabinet

long for door stiles and two pieces 10 inches long for door rails. Rip them to a 2¼-inch width. From 1 × 10 select pine, cut one piece 23¾ inches long, ripped to 8¾ inches wide for the door panel.

b. To create the door panel, cut the bevels around both faces of the board.

c. Fabricate the rails and stiles, then assemble them around the door panel. Cut the perimeter rabbet around

the back edge, and break the front edge of the door. Mount the knob.

d. Install the door on the cabinet.

4. Finish the cabinet inside and out, as detailed in the "Finishing" section of "The Basic Base Cabinet." In brief, the sanding and cleanup should be completed, the inside of the cabinet painted and the front of the cabinet finished however you desire.

Wall Oven Cabinet

This cabinet is the mate of the one for the counter top range. In addition to housing a wall oven unit, it provides lots of storage for baking equipment, including pots and pans that can be hung on the sliding rack in the lower compartment.

The wall oven cabinet is the first of several so-called floor-to-ceiling cabinets. The usual

height for them is 84 inches, making it a foot or so shy of today's 8-foot ceilings. The size of the cabinet doesn't markedly change how it's made, however. The general design principles and construction techniques are comparable to those of the other cabinets.

The cabinet is designed to accommodate the typical single-oven unit. The installation procedure will vary according to the brand and model you select. To be on the safe side, it isn't a bad idea to confirm that the oven you will use will, in fact, fit the space allotted for it *before* you build the cabinet.

Construction

1. Begin by assembling the case, which is constructed of interior plywood and 1×4 #2 pine. Fabrication and assembly details are given in the "Case Construction" section of "The Basic Base Cabinet."

a. From ⅝-inch A-C interior plywood, cut two pieces 23 inches by 84 inches for the sides and four pieces 23 inches by 25¼ inches for the top, bottom, and shelves. From ¼-inch A-C interior plywood, cut one piece 26½ inches by 25¼ inches for the back panel. From 1×4 #2 pine, cut one piece 25¼ inches long for the hanging rail, two pieces 20 inches long for nailer cleats and one piece 27 inches long for the plinth.

b. In one corner of each side, cut a 3-inch-wide by 3½-inch-high notch for the toe space. Using 1-inch underlayment nails, glue and nail

the bottom nailer cleats to the inside of the sides.

c. Begin the actual assembly by gluing and nailing, using 6d coated nails, the side panels to the top and bottom. Then glue and nail the top shelf 22 inches from the top of the side panels and the second shelf 29¾ inches below the top shelf bottom. Glue and nail the hanging rail between the end panels directly below the cabinet top. Square the cabinet case, then glue and nail the ¼-inch plywood back and the plinth in place.

2. The face frame is composed of two stiles, joined with

dowels to four rails. Fabrication and assembly details are given in the "Face Frame Construction" section of "The Basic Base Cabinet."

a. From 1×2 select pine, cut 2 pieces 81⅜ inches long for frame stiles and 4 pieces 24 inches long for frame rails. From ⅜-inch dowel cut 16 pieces 1½ inches long. After cutting the stiles and rails, lay them face down on the workbench with the rails between the stiles as in the final assembly. Place the upper intermediate rail 20⅝ inches from the top rail and the lower intermediate rail 28 inches below the second rail. Mark

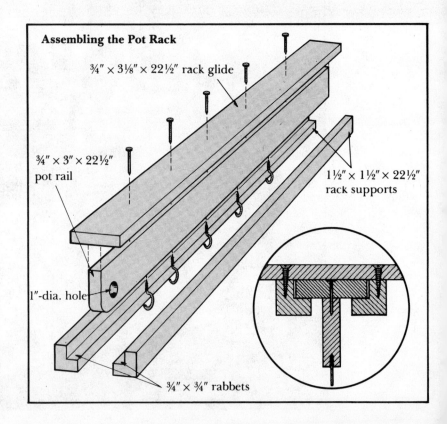

Assembling the Pot Rack

¾" × 3⅛" × 22½" rack glide

¾" × 3" × 22½" pot rail

1"-dia. hole

1½" × 1½" × 22½" rack supports

¾" × ¾" rabbets

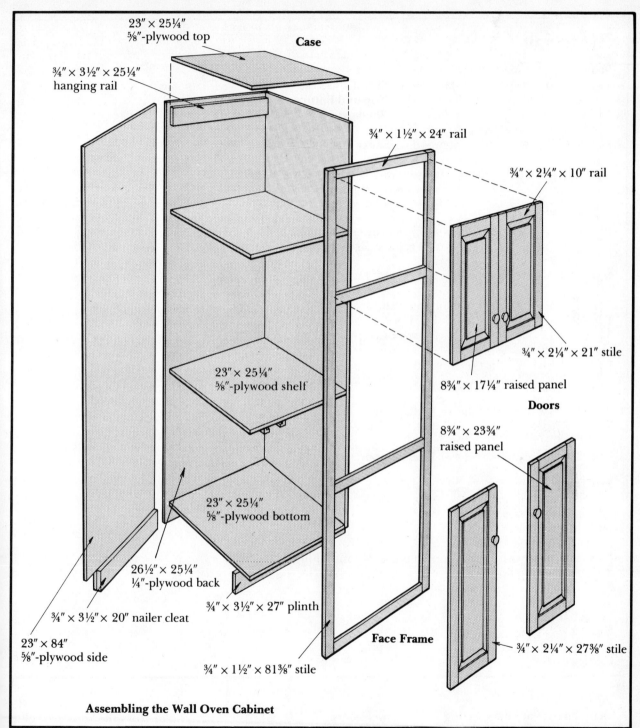

23" × 25¼"
⅝"-plywood top

Case

¾" × 3½" × 25¼"
hanging rail

¾" × 1½" × 24" rail

¾" × 2¼" × 10" rail

¾" × 2¼" × 21" stile

8¾" × 17¼" raised panel

Doors

8¾" × 23¾"
raised panel

23" × 25¼"
⅝"-plywood shelf

23" × 25¼"
⅝"-plywood bottom

26½" × 25¼"
¼"-plywood back

¾" × 3½" × 27" plinth

¾" × 2¼" × 27⅜" stile

¾" × 3½" × 20" nailer cleat

23" × 84"
⅝"-plywood side

Face Frame

¾" × 1½" × 81⅜" stile

Assembling the Wall Oven Cabinet

519

Materials

Wood

2-4′ × 8′ shts. ⅝″ A-C int. plywood or **Sides:** 2 pcs. 23″ × 84″
Top and bottom: 2 pcs. 23″ × 25¼″
Shelves: 2 pcs. 23″ × 25¼″

1–4′ × 4′ sht. ¼″ A-C int. plywood or **Back:** 1 pc. 26½″ × 25¼″

1 pc. 1 × 4 × 8′ #2 pine or **Hanging rail:** 1 pc. ¾″ × 3½″ × 25¼″
Nailer cleats: 2 pcs. ¾″ × 3½″ × 20″
Plinth: 1 pc. ¾″ × 3½″ × 27″

2 pcs. 1 × 2 × 10′ select pine or **Frame stiles:** 2 pcs. ¾″ × 1½″ × 81⅜″
Frame rails: 4 pcs. ¾″ × 1½″ × 24″

3 pcs. 36″ × ⅜″ dowel or **Dowels:** 16 pcs. 1½″ × ⅜″

1 pc. 1 × 3 × 10′ select pine or **Door stiles:** 4 pcs. ¾″ × 2¼″ × 21″
1 pc. 1 × 3 × 14′ select pine   4 pcs. ¾″ × 2¼″ × 27⅜″
Door rails: 8 pcs. ¾″ × 2¼″ × 10″

1 pc. 1 × 10 × 8′ select pine or **Door panels:** 2 pcs. ¾″ × 8¾″ × 17¼″
2 pcs. ¾″ × 8¾″ × 23¾″

1 pc. 1 × 4 × 4′ select pine or **Rack glide:** 1 pc. ¾″ × 3⅛″ × 22½″
Pot rail: 1 pc. ¾″ × 3″ × 22½″

1 pc. 2 × 2 × 4′ select pine or **Rack supports:** 2 pcs. 1½″ × 1½″ × 22½″

Hardware
1″ underlayment nails
6d coated box nails
6d finishing nails
4–1½″ rnd. wood knobs
4 pr. ⅜″ double-offset, semiconcealed, self-closing hinges
5–¾″ × 1½″ cup hooks
8–1¼″ #8 flathead screws

Miscellaneous
Glue
Semigloss latex enamel
Clear varnish

each board at intersecting points to aid in drilling the dowel joints.

b. Lay out and drill the holes for the dowels, glue dowels in the rails, then glue and assemble the rails and stiles, forming the face frame.

c. Glue and nail the face frame to the case, using 6d finishing or casing nails. The top of the face frame should be flush with the top edges of the case, while the outer stiles should overhang the case sides by ¼ inch.

3. The cabinet doors are assembled by joining the door rails and stiles around a raised panel. Fabrication and assembly details are given in the "Door Construction" section of "The Basic Base Cabinet."

a. From 1 × 3 select pine, cut four pieces 21 inches long and four pieces 27⅜ inches long for door stiles and eight pieces 10 inches long for door rails. Rip all the pieces to a 2¼-inch width. From 1 × 10 select pine, cut two pieces 17¼ inches long and two pieces 23¾ inches long for door panels. Rip these to an 8¾-inch width.

b. Cut bevels around both faces of each door panel board, creating the raised panel.

c. Fabricate the rails and stiles, then assemble them around the door panels. Cut the perimeter rabbet around the back edges, and break the front edges of each door. Rip 5/16-inch from what will be the center stile of each door, squaring the edge and reducing the width of the door so it will fit properly. Mount the knobs.

d. Install the doors on the cabinet. The taller pair goes on the bottom.

4. The pot rack is located in the lower compartment for easy access.

a. From 1 × 4 select pine, cut one piece 22½ inches long, ripped to a 3⅛-inch width, for the rack glide and one piece 22½ inches long, ripped to a 3-inch width, for the pot rail. From 2 × 2 select pine, cut two pieces 22½ inches long for rack supports.

b. Plow a ¾-inch-deep by ¾-inch-wide rabbet along the full length of both rack supports. Glue and screw one support on the underside of the second shelf, with the rabbeted side facing the right, 3¾ inches from the left end panel. Mount the second support 8 inches from the left end panel with the rabbeted side facing left. The shoulders of the rabbets should be 3¼ inches apart. Use 1¼-inch #8 screws, driving four through the shelf into each support.

c. Round off the front edge of the pot rail and cut a 1-inch-diameter finger hole ½ inch from the front edge. Space cup hooks along the bottom edge of the pot rail to accommodate your pots. Glue and nail the rack glide to the top edge of the pot rail, centering it $1^9/_{16}$ inches from either edge. Sand the pot rack and insert it into the rack supports. Check for ease of movement.

5. Finish the cabinet inside and out, as detailed in the "Finishing" section of "The Basic Base Cabinet." In brief, the sanding and cleanup should be completed, the inside of the cabinet painted and the front of the cabinet finished however you desire. After the cabinet is installed in the kitchen, the wall oven unit can be installed according to the manufactuer's instructions.

Broom-Utility Cabinet

For a kitchen without a closet, this cabinet provides a place to keep brooms, mops and cleaning supplies handy. A wide ⅝-inch plywood back reinforcement stiffens the cabinet and provides a solid place to put hooks for hanging mops and brooms. Seldom-used items can be stored in the upper section. The cabinet can be transformed

into a pantry by installing shelves, fixed or adjustable.

Construction

1. Begin by assembling the cabinet case. The case is constructed of interior plywood and 1 × 4 #2 pine.

a. From ⅝-inch A-C interior plywood, cut two pieces 23 inches by 84 inches for the side panels and four pieces 23 inches by 22¼ inches for the top, bottom, shelf and back reinforcement. From ¼-inch A-C interior plywood, cut one piece 23½ inches by 84 inches for the back panel. From 1 × 4 #2 pine, cut one piece 22¼ inches long for the back crosspiece, two pieces 20 inches long for the nailer cleats, and one piece 24 inches long for the plinth.

b. In one corner of each side panel, cut a 3-inch-wide by 3½-inch-high notch for the toe space. Be certain to cut the notches so you have a right and left side panel. Place the good face of the plywood on the inside. Using 1-inch underlayment nails, glue and nail the nailer cleats on the inside of the end panels, flush with the bottom edge and level with the cutout for the toe space.

c. Use 6d coated nails to assemble the case. Glue and nail the top and bottom to the side panels, with the sides overlapping the top and bottom. Install the top crosspiece between the sides tight against the top. Glue and nail the shelf 18⅝ inches down from the cabinet top, then in-

stall the ⅝-inch plywood back reinforcement tight against the shelf. Measure the cabinet case diagonally to be sure it is square. Glue and nail the back panel to the cabinet case over the rear hanging rail. Glue and nail the plinth in place at the bottom front of the cabinet, in the notches cut for the toe space.

2. The face frame is composed of two stiles, joined by dowels to three rails.

a. From 1 × 2 select pine, cut 2 pieces 81⅜ inches long for the frame stiles and 3 pieces 21 inches long for the frame rails. Cut 12 pieces of ⅜-inch dowel, each 1½ inches long. After cutting the stiles and rails, lay them face down on the workbench with the rails between the upright stiles as in the final assembly. Place the middle rail 17⅝ inches below the upper rail. Mark each board at intersecting points to aid in drilling for the dowel joints.

b. Lay out and drill the holes for the dowels, glue dowels in the rails, then glue and assemble the rails and stiles, forming the face frame.

c. Glue and nail the face frame to the case, using 6d finishing or casing nails. The top of the face should be flush with the top edges of the case, while the outer stiles should overhang the case sides by ¼ inch.

3. The cabinet doors are assembled by joining the door rails and stiles around a raised panel. The closet door in this cabinet is a bit more difficult to make because it has a middle

rail and two panels. But fabrication and assembly details are essentially as given in the "Door Construction" section of "The Basic Base Cabinet."

a. From 1 × 3 select pine, cut two pieces 18¼ inches long for the upper door stiles, five pieces 19 inches long for door rails and two pieces 59¾ inches long for the closet door stiles. From 1 × 10 select pine, cut two pieces 14⅝ inches long, two pieces 25⅞ inches long and two pieces 28½ inches long for door panel elements. Rip all of these to a 8⅞-inch width.

b. To make the door panels, edge-glue two boards of the same length together to form three door panels. The rough measurements of these panels should be ¾ inch by 17¾ inches by 14⅝ inches, ¾ inch by 17¾ inches by 25⅞ inches and ¾ inch by 17¾ inches by 28½ inches. Cut the bevels around both faces of

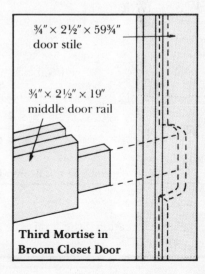

¾" × 2½" × 59¾" door stile

¾" × 2½" × 19" middle door rail

Third Mortise in Broom Closet Door

523

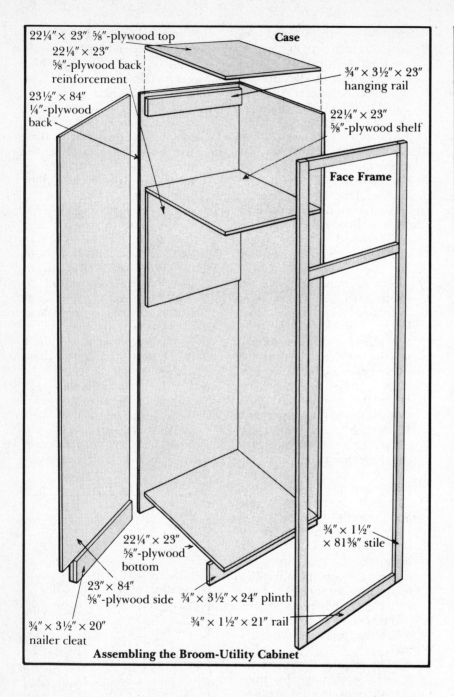

Case

22¼″ × 23″ ⅝″-plywood top

22¼″ × 23″ ⅝″-plywood back reinforcement

23½″ × 84″ ¼″-plywood back

¾″ × 3½″ × 23″ hanging rail

22¼″ × 23″ ⅝″-plywood shelf

Face Frame

22¼″ × 23″ ⅝″-plywood bottom

23″ × 84″ ⅝″-plywood side

¾″ × 3½″ × 20″ nailer cleat

¾″ × 3½″ × 24″ plinth

¾″ × 1½″ × 21″ rail

¾″ × 1½″ × 81⅜″ stile

Assembling the Broom-Utility Cabinet

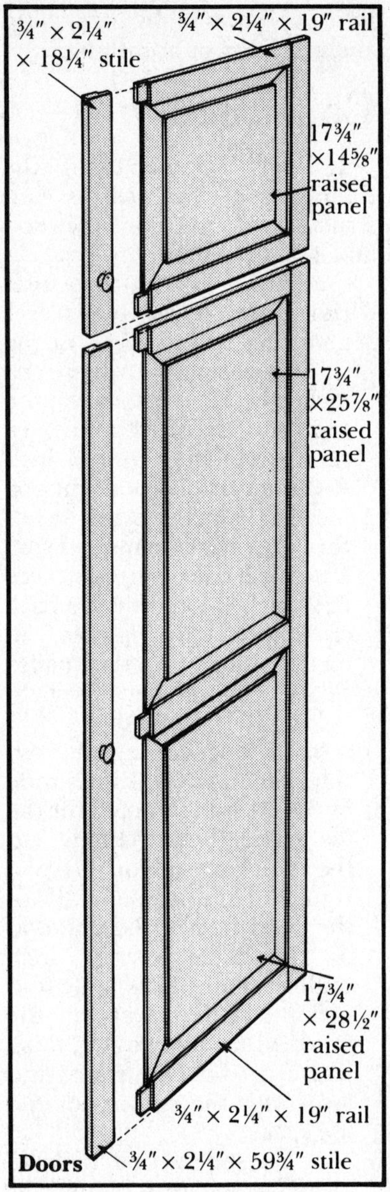

¾″ × 2¼″ × 18¼″ stile

¾″ × 2¼″ × 19″ rail

17¾″ × 14⅝″ raised panel

17¾″ × 25⅞″ raised panel

17¾″ × 28½″ raised panel

¾″ × 2¼″ × 19″ rail

Doors

¾″ × 2¼″ × 59¾″ stile

524 each, creating the raised panels.

c. Fabricate the rails and stiles for the upper door, then assemble them around the 17¾-inch by 14⅝-inch door panel. Two of the rails for the closet door are fabricated as are all the other rails. The

Materials

Wood

1–4′ × 4′ sht. ⅝″ A-C int. plywood or **Sides:** 2 pcs. 23″ × 84″

1–4′ × 8′ sht. ⅝″ A-C int. plywood   **Top, bottom and shelf:** 3 pcs. 22¼″ × 23″
    Back reinforcement: 1 pc. 22¼″ × 23″

1–4′ × 8′ sht. ¼″ A-C int. plywood or **Back:** 1 pc. 23½″ × 84″

1 pc. 1 × 4 × 8′ #2 pine or **Crosspiece:** 1 pc. ¾″ × 3½″ × 22¼″
    Nailer cleats: 2 pcs. ¾″ × 3½″ × 20″
    Plinth: 1 pc. ¾″ × 3½″ × 24″

1 pc. 1 × 2 × 6′ select pine or **Frame stiles:** 2 pcs. ¾″ × 1½″ × 81⅜″
1 pc. 1 × 2 × 14′ select pine   **Frame rails:** 3 pcs. ¾″ × 1½″ × 21″

1 pc. 36″ × ⅜″ dowel or **Dowels:** 12 pcs. 1½″ × ⅜″

1 pc. 1 × 3 × 10′ select pine or **Door stiles:** 2 pcs. ¾″ × 2½″ × 18¼″
1 pc. 1 × 3 × 14′ select pine   2 pcs. ¾″ × 2½″ × 59¾″
    Door rails: 5 pcs. ¾″ × 2½″ × 19″

1 pc. 1 × 10 × 12′ select pine or **Door panel elements:** 2 pcs. ¾″ × 8⅞″ × 14⅝″
    2 pcs. ¾″ × 8⅞″ × 25⅞″
    2 pcs. ¾″ × 8⅞″ × 28½″

Hardware

1″ underlayment nails
6d coated box nails
6d finishing nails
2–1½″ rnd. wood knobs
5–⅜″ double-offset, semiconcealed, self-closing hinges

Miscellaneous

Glue
Semigloss latex enamel
Clear varnish

closet door stiles are grooved and mortised at their ends as are all the rest. But to accommodate the middle rail, a third mortise must be cut into each stile. Mark the top of each stile, being sure that you have a right and a left stile. Then cut the third mortise in each so that the center of the mortise is 28⅝ inches from the top. You need merely to plunge into the existing groove with the dado blade set for the correct depth of cut. If necessary, round the edges of the tenon to complete the fit. Assemble the door with the smaller of the two raised panels at the top. Use an extra bar clamp across the door parallel to the middle rail. Cut the perimeter rabbet around the back edges of the door, and break the front edges. Mount the knob.

d. Install the doors on the cabinet. Use three hinges on the closet door, positioning the third hinge beside the middle rail.

5. Finish the cabinet inside and out, as detailed in the "Finishing" section of "The Basic Base Cabinet." In brief, the sanding and cleanup should be completed, the inside of the cabinet painted and the front of the cabinet finished however you desire.

Pantry

The pantry, used for storage of home-canned goods, traditionally was a room apart from the kitchen. Now you can bring the convenience of pantry storage right into your kitchen with this special cabinet.

The pantry doors are great for storing home-canned fruits and vegetables. Adjustable shelves in the cabinet are ideal

for keeping canning supplies handy. If home food preservation is a priority for you, the extra effort it takes to build this cabinet will be worth it.

Construction

1. Begin by assembling the case, which is constructed of interior plywood and 1 × 4 #2 pine. Fabrication and assembly details are given in the "Case Construction" section of "The Basic Base Cabinet."

a. From ⅝-inch A-C interior plywood, cut two pieces 23 inches by 84 inches for the sides, three pieces 23 inches by 21 inches for the top, bottom and shelf and five pieces 18 inches by 20⅞ inches for the adjustable shelves. From ¼-inch interior plywood, cut one piece 22¼ inches by 84 inches for the back panel. From 1 × 4 #2 pine, cut one 21-inch hanging rail, two 20-inch nailer cleats and one 24-inch plinth. From pine stock, also cut five shelf-lip strips measuring ¼ inch by ⅝ inch by 20⅞ inches.

b. On the inside of each side panel, drill ¼-inch holes to accommodate the adjustable shelves. Beginning 8⅝ inches from the top, 8 inches from the front, and 4¼ inches from the back, drill 11 pairs of holes, with each pair 2 inches below the last pair. Be careful not to drill all the way through the side panels. Measure the hole positions accurately to ensure that the shelves will be steady and level. The same type of ¼-inch holes should be drilled

on the inside of each side panel to accommodate an adjustable shelf in the bottom section. Drill 4 pairs of holes beginning 10¾ inches from the bottom, 8 inches from the front, and 4¼ inches from the back with each pair 2 inches above the last pair.

c. In one corner of each

side panel cut a 3-inch-wide by 3½-inch-high notch for the toe space. Using 1-inch underlayment nails, glue and nail the nailer cleats on the inside of the end panels.

d. Begin the actual assembly by gluing and nailing, using 6d coated nails, the side panels to the top and bottom.

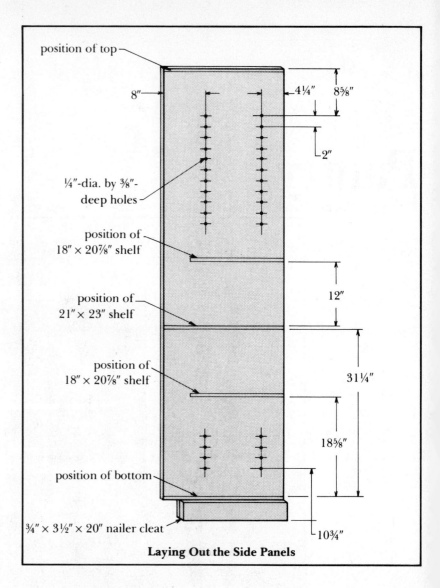

position of top

8″

¼″-dia. by ⅜″-deep holes

position of 18″ × 20⅞″ shelf

position of 21″ × 23″ shelf

position of 18″ × 20⅞″ shelf

position of bottom

¾″ × 3½″ × 20″ nailer cleat

4¼″ 8⅝″

2″

12″

31¼″

18⅝″

10¾″

Laying Out the Side Panels

Then glue and nail the hanging rail between the side panels, against the top. Glue and nail the three stationary shelves in place. The 23-inch by 21-inch shelf is positioned 31¼ inches from the cabinet bottom; one 18-inch by 20⅞-inch shelf 18⅝ inches from the cabinet bottom and another 12 inches above the 23-inch by 21-inch shelf. The remaining shelves are adjustable and can be placed at convenient locations after the cabinet is installed. At some point prior to finishing, glue and nail the ⅝-inch-wide shelf-lip strips to what will be the front edge of each shelf to hide the plywood end grain. Square the cabinet case and glue and nail the back to the case, overlapping all edges. Finally, glue and nail the plinth in place.

2. The face frame is composed of two frame stiles joined by dowels to three frame rails. Details of fabrication and assembly are given in the "Face Frame Construction" section of "The Basic Base Cabinet."

   a. From 1 × 2 select pine, cut three 21-inch frame rails and two 81⅜-inch frame stiles. Cut 12 pieces of ⅜-inch dowel, each 1½ inches long. After cutting the stiles and rails, lay them face down on the workbench with the rails between the stiles as in the final assembly. Place the intermediate rail 46½ inches below the top rail. Mark each board at intersecting points to aid in drilling for the dowel joints.

   b. Lay out and drill the

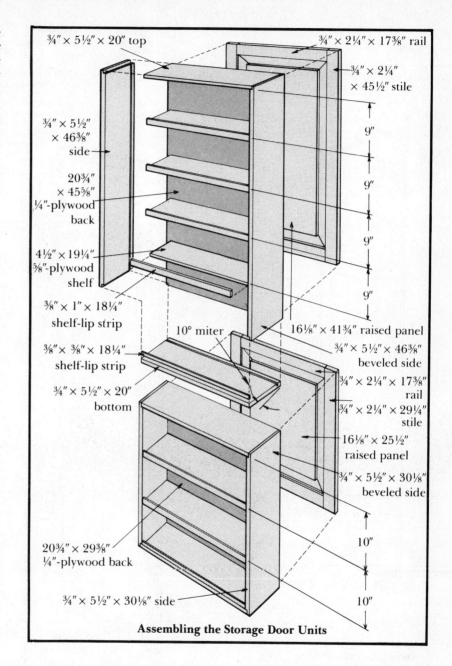

Assembling the Storage Door Units

holes for the dowels, glue dowels in the rails, then glue and assemble the rails and stiles, forming the face frame.

   c. Glue and nail the face frame to the case, using 6d finishing or casing nails. The top of the face frame should be flush with the top edges of the case, while the outer stiles

529

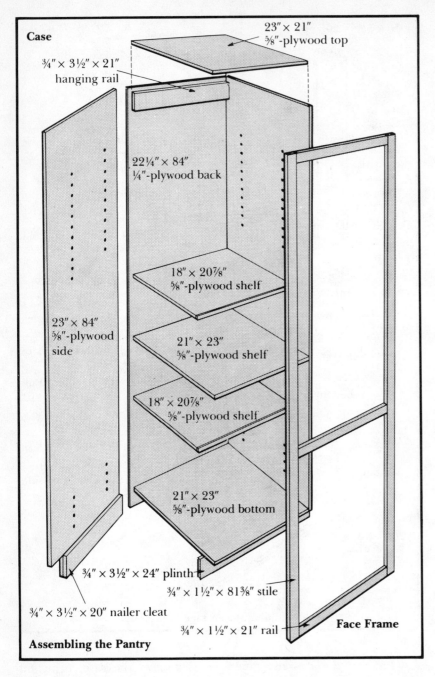

Case

23″ × 21″
⅝″-plywood top

¾″ × 3½″ × 21″
hanging rail

22¼″ × 84″
¼″-plywood back

18″ × 20⅞″
⅝″-plywood shelf

21″ × 23″
⅝″-plywood shelf

23″ × 84″
⅝″-plywood
side

18″ × 20⅞″
⅝″-plywood shelf

21″ × 23″
⅝″-plywood bottom

¾″ × 3½″ × 24″ plinth

¾″ × 1½″ × 81⅜″ stile

¾″ × 3½″ × 20″ nailer cleat

¾″ × 1½″ × 21″ rail

Face Frame

Assembling the Pantry

finished with the installation of a raised panel door in the recess. Construction of the shelf units is a special project, but fabrication and assembly of the door is detailed in the "Door Construction" section of "The Basic Base Cabinet." Build the shelf units first, then the doors.

a. From 1 × 8 select pine, cut one 46⅜-inch and one 30⅛-inch side piece. From 1 × 6 select pine, cut two more side pieces of identical lengths. From the 1 × 6, cut four 20-inch pieces for the tops and bottoms of the two units. From ⅝-inch A-C interior plywood, cut six 4½-inch by 19¼-inch shelves. From ¼-inch A-C interior plywood, cut one 20¾-inch by 45⅝-inch back panel and one 20¾-inch by 29⅜-inch back panel. From 1 × 2 #2 pine, cut eight pieces for lips for the edges of the shelves. Six should measure ⅜ inch by 1 inch by 18¼ inches. Two should measure ⅜ inch by ⅜ inch by 18¼ inches.

b. The catch side of the finished doors must be beveled so that the door will swing open and closed freely. Rip a 10-degree bevel on both edges of the 1 × 8 sides and, in doing so, reduce their finished width to 5½ inches. Plow a ¼-inch-wide by ⅜-inch-deep groove, ⅜ inch from one edge, along each piece. This groove should also be cut at a 10-degree angle parallel to the beveled edges of the pieces. This groove is for the back panel to fit into. Cut a ¾-inch-wide by ⅜-inch-deep rabbet across both ends

should overhang the case sides by ¼ inch.

3. The pantry doors are storage units. A set of shelves with a recessed back must be constructed for each door, then

of each piece, cutting into the same face that's been grooved.

c. To match the tops and bottoms to the angled side in the finished assembly, one end of each must be cut on a 10-degree miter. Plow a ¼-inch-wide by ⅜-inch-deep groove along the inner face of each piece, ⅜ inch from the longer of the two edges.

Do not cut all the same; rather cut two identical tops and two identical bottoms, the bottoms being mirror images of the tops.

d. Cut a ¼-inch-wide by

Materials

Wood

2–4′ × 8′ shts. ⅝″ A-C int. plywood or **Sides:** 2 pcs. 23″ × 84″
Top, bottom and shelf: 3 pcs. 21″ × 23″
Shelves: 5 pcs. 18″ × 20⅞″
6 pcs. 4½″ × 19¼″

1–4′ × 8′ sht. ¼″ A-C int. plywood or **Back panels:** 1 pc. 22¼″ × 84″
1 pc. 20¾″ × 45⅝″
1 pc. 20¾″ × 29⅜″

1 pc. 1 × 4 × 8′ #2 pine or **Hanging rail:** 1 pc. ¾″ × 3½″ × 21″
Nailer cleats: 2 pcs. ¾″ × 3½″ × 20″
Plinth: 1 pc. ¾″ × 3½″ × 24″

2 pcs. 1 × 2 × 6′ select pine or **Frame rails:** 3 pcs. ¾″ × 1½″ × 21″
1 pc. 1 × 2 × 14′ select pine   **Frame stiles:** 2 pcs. ¾″ × 1½″ × 81⅜″

1 pc. 36″ × ⅜″ dowel or **Dowels:** 12 pcs. 1½″ × ⅜″ dowel

1 pc. 1 × 8 × 10′ select pine or **Storage door sides:** 1 pc. ¾″ × 5¾″ × 46⅜″*
1 pc. ¾″ × 5¾″ × 30⅛″*
Shelf-lip strips: 5 pcs. ¼″ × ⅝″ × 20⅞″
6 pcs. ⅜″ × 1″ × 18¼″
2 pcs. ⅜″ × ⅜″ × 18¼″

1 pc. 1 × 6 × 14′ select pine or **Storage door sides:** 1 pc. ¾″ × 5½″ × 46⅜″
1 pc. ¾″ × 5½″ × 30⅛″
Top and bottom door members: 4 pcs. ¾″ × 5½″ × 20″

1 pc. 1 × 3 × 8′ select pine or **Door stiles:** 2 pcs. ¾″ × 2¼″ × 45½″
1 pc. 1 × 3 × 12′ select pine   2 pcs. ¾″ × 2¼″ × 29¼″
Door rails: 4 pcs. ¾″ × 2¼″ × 17⅜″

1 pc. 1 × 10 × 12′ select pine or **Door panel elements:** 2 pcs. ¾″ × 8¹/₁₆″ × 41¾″
2 pcs. ¾″ × 8¹/₁₆″ × 25½″

*In ripping to finished width, both edges must be beveled at a 10-degree angle.

[continued on next page]

Hardware
1" underlayment nails
6d coated box nails
6d finishing nails
2–1½" rnd. wood knobs
1–1½" × 46" piano hinge
1–1½" × 30" piano hinge
10–½" #6 screws

Miscellaneous
Glue
Semigloss latex enamel
Clear varnish

⅜-inch-deep groove along one side of the two remaining side pieces (the 1 × 6s), ⅜ inch from one edge. Cut ¾-inch-wide by ⅜-inch-deep rabbets in both ends of each piece, cutting into the face that's been grooved.

e. Assemble each shelf case, using glue and 6d finishing or casing nails. The back panel fits into the groove, while the sides fit into the rabbets in the top and bottom. Do not glue the back panel in place. Be sure the unit is square.

f. Cut a 10-degree miter on one end of each of the plywood shelves. Glue and nail four of them in the larger shelf case, positioning them 9 inches apart from top of shelf to top of shelf. Glue and nail the remaining two in the smaller unit, positioning them 10 inches apart, from top of shelf. Glue and nail the shelf-lip strips to the shelf edges. The 1-inch-wide strips fit against the edges of the plywood shelves; the ⅜-inch-wide strips fit atop the bottom pieces.

g. Construction of the raised panel doors to face the backs of the shelf units is done according to the instructions given in the "Door Construction" section of "The Basic Base Cabinet." From 1 × 3 select pine, cut two 45½-inch door stiles, two 29¼-inch door stiles and four 17⅜-inch door rails. Rip all to a 2¼-inch width. From 1 × 10 select pine, cut two 41¾-inch door panel elements and two 25½-inch door panel elements. Rip all to an 8¹/₁₆-inch width.

h. To create the top door panel, edge-glue the two 41¾-inch-long boards together; the rough panel will be ¾ inch by 16⅛ inches by 41¾ inches. Glue up the two shorter boards to form the ¾-inch by 16⅛-inch by 25½-inch bottom door panel. Cut the bevels around both faces of each, creating the raised panels. Fabricate the rails and stiles, then assemble them around the door panels.

i. Install the completed doors on the shelf unit backs by spreading a bit of glue in the rabbets around the doors, fitting them into the recesses on the backs of the shelf units and driving several ½-inch #6 screws through the plywood back into the raised area of the door panel.

j. Install the completed storage door units in the cabinet with piano hinges after you have applied the finish to the cabinet.

4. Finish the cabinet inside and out, as detailed in the "Finishing" section of "The Basic Base Cabinet." In brief, the sanding and cleanup should be completed, the inside of the cabinet painted and the front of the cabinet finished however you desire.

Built-In Cabinets

For the home builder, the most economical method of building cabinets is to build them in place. The savings is realized in materials: You simply don't use as much material when you make the cabinet almost an integral part of the room.

If you have an old house, with the original kitchen, you'll

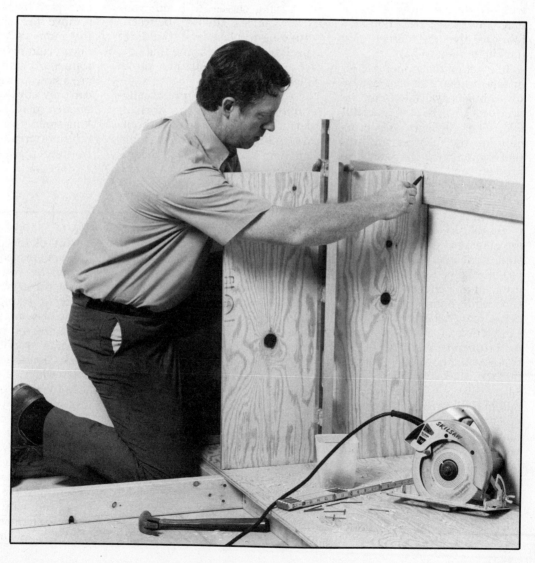

probably have one with cabinets that were built in place. In the old days kitchens didn't have the yards and yards of cabinets that today's kitchens do. Materials and labor weren't as expensive, and industrial woodworking techniques obviously were not as advanced. It was far more efficient in those days for the house builder to have the finish carpenter who was installing the trim—and there was a lot of that in those old houses—fabricate the few cabinets that the kitchen was to have.

The situation is completely different now. The least expensive cabinets available today are products of a factory assembly line. The efficiency and economy of the process and the uniformity of the finished product can't be beat.

Moreover, today's house builder is working with borrowed cash. The longer it takes to get that house built and onto the market, the greater the amount of interest he's going to pay. Prefabbed cabinets can be installed in a kitchen in a day or two, while building cabinets in place may delay the kitchen's completion by a week or more. And that time is money.

For you, the harvest kitchen builder, the situation is somewhat different. You may be building for pride or pleasure as much or more than you are building for economy. Regardless, you face at least one, and perhaps two decisions.

The first is whether or not to build your own cabinets. Obviously you've given the matter a lot of thought, and you probably figure yourself to be capable

of doing it. Whether or not you choose to can involve a lot of criteria, many of them personal. But many a home kitchen builder has discovered he (or she) can *buy* ready-made cabinets cheaper than he can buy the materials for homemade cabinets. For some people, that makes the decision. For others, such information is not persuasive.

Having chosen to build, you then must choose between building-in-place and building prefabs. If you've come this far, you presumably already know about prefabbing.

You know that prefabbing cabinets means you can work at leisure in a workshop without disrupting the use of an existing kitchen. You also know it means

you'll sometimes have two pieces of wood where only one is necessary and one piece of wood where none is necessary. But you can take your time.

Building-in-place means that you construct the cabinets in the kitchen itself. You have to have the floors and walls finished, though not necessarily painted or tiled or otherwise "finished." It means your kitchen will be disrupted from the moment you remove the old cabinets until the moment you get the new onces completed, finished and topped off with counters. If you are a slow woodworker, of if you can only work sporadically, your kitchen may be a shambles a long time.

There really is a distinct trade-off.

How to Do It

Building-in-place involves constructing the case, and sometimes the face frame, in the kitchen, piece by piece. It is really sensible only if you are building a fairly extensive run of cabinets, certainly something more than 4 to 6 feet.

In building-in-place, you don't have the luxury of moving the cabinet around or of tipping it up on end or laying it on its back. Every piece is fastened in its final orientation as you go.

There's a lot of leveling to do. You can't assemble the case, then wrench it into alignment. It has to be in alignment as you set up the individual sides and partitions. It can be a bit tedious, but it isn't all that difficult.

Any of the preceding prefab cabinet projects can be converted by you into build-it-in-place projects. You have to do some adjusting of the dimensions of some pieces, and there are a few you can eliminate.

Since you'll eliminate the back, the sides must be cut ¼ inch wider. This will compensate for the space the back takes up, and give you the same-size cabinet when completed. If you are starting the run of cabinets in a corner, you can eliminate the side that will be against the wall and replace it with nailers screwed to the studs. Then you can eliminate the duplicated sides. Eliminating these sides necessitates the adjustment of the face frame and perhaps the drawer supports.

The sink base cabinet may be the best project to review as you consider this approach. It's a 6-foot-long cabinet, with several partitions. Note especially how the partitions are spaced, flush with one edge of the face frame so that you need to install drawer supports on one side, rather than both. All you need to do is extend it to 8, 10 or 12 feet. Do some sketching. Combine it with a corner cabinet. Figure how you'd combine it

with a tall cabinet like the pantry.

Write down the proper dimensions of each necessary piece, thus creating a new cuttings list. Figure out how much material you'll need for the cabinets. Then compare it with the materials list for the prefabbed versions of the cabinets you propose to meld into one unit. See if the difference is significant enough to make building-in-place worthwhile for you.

Maybe it is worthwhile for you period.

crosspiece attached to the wall and the base frame attached to the floor. If you've chosen not to build a base frame, then it will be helpful to tack position cleats to the floor for the sides to fit against.

Fit the bottom in place next, followed by the partitions, the top crosspieces and the fixed shelves.

At each step, you must check the alignment of the piece being installed. You have to lay your level across all the faces and edges, bridging from piece to piece, to ensure that when finished, the sides will be plumb, the top will be level, the front will be square, flat and plumb.

Getting Down to Work

The first step, after purchasing your materials and cutting the parts for the casework, is to do layouts on the walls and floor. Mark the positions and thicknesses of sides and partitions, crosspieces and nailers.

Start the assembly at one end and work toward the other. Attach the first crosspiece to the wall, driving screws through it into the studs. Be sure it is level, at the correct height and in the proper right-to-left position. This crosspiece should extend from one side to the other. Notch the partitions for this crosspiece.

Very often, a base frame is constructed when cabinets are built in place. This frame com-

bines the nailer cleats and the plinth used in the prefab-cabinet approach with a back member which is shorter than the plinth by the thickness of the two sides, and several crosspieces. If you decide to build such a frame, cut the pieces and nail it together. Then tack it in position on the floor.

The sides are next set into position, fitting against the

You'll have to nail carefully. You won't be free to use coated box nails or common nails in as many places as you might in prefabbing. If you do use them, they'll show. You'll have to learn how to toenail, and how to toenail well. You won't be able to tip the cabinet on its back to drive nails through the bottom into the bottom edges of the partitions. You won't be able to

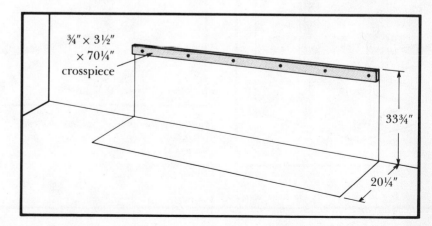

The first step in building cabinets in place is to lay out the cabinet outline on the wall and floor and attach the crosspiece to the wall.

535

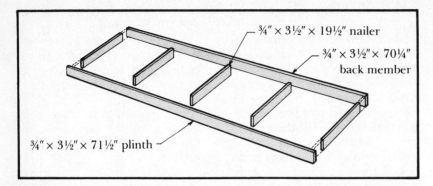

¾" × 3½" × 19½" nailer

¾" × 3½" × 70¼"
back member

¾" × 3½" × 71½" plinth

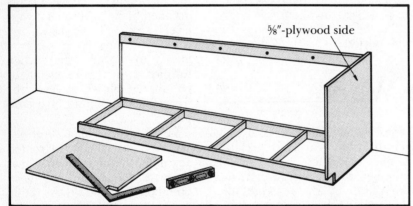

⅝"-plywood side

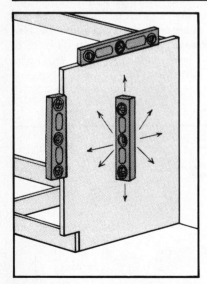

Level each piece as it is added to the growing assembly. Lay the level across all faces and edges, insuring all is plumb and level.

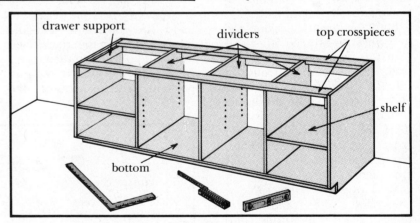

drawer support

dividers

top crosspieces

shelf

bottom

Continue the process, adding bottom, partitions, shelves, crosspieces and drawer supports.

Constructing a base frame is the second step.

nail through the back crosspiece into the partition edges.

At first, with just the back crosspiece, the base frame and the sides in place, the structure may seem rickety. But as you tie together the partitions and top crosspieces, the case will become more and more rigid.

When the case is finished, your next step is to build the face frame. You have two options. You can construct a face frame unit, just as you would in prefabbing. Cut the pieces and dowel them together, then attach it to the front of the case.

With the base frame in place, the sides are set up and attached to the frame and crosspiece.

Or you can cut the pieces and assemble them as you attach them to the case.

In this situation, it will probably be easier to do the latter. Especially if you are working

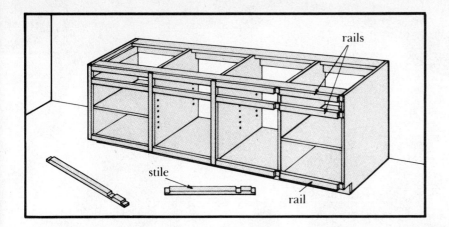

Assembling the face frame in place is easiest if lap joints are used. Align and attach rails, then stiles.

with a 10- to 12-foot frame, attaching a single assembly to the built-in casework will be very difficult, largely because you'll go nuts trying to align it plumb and level and clamp it. Once that's done, nailing it fast is no trouble.

But you will have an easier time of aligning individual rails and stiles. A good approach here may be to use lap joints to join the rails and stiles. Cut all the rails to extend from side to side. Lay out and cut half-laps where appropriate. Then cut the stiles and lap them. Glue and nail the rails to the case, then the stiles.

The drawers and doors are constructed just as they would be were you prefabbing the cabinets. The construction of the counter top too is no different.

Building-in wall cabinets would follow much the same pattern. Attach the hanging rail to the wall and hang the sides on it. You probably will find it helpful to tack a temporary brace to the front edges of the sides to keep them in alignment. Then attach the top, bottom and any fixed shelves. And the face frame.

That's really all there is to building-in cabinets. Whether or not it is the approach for you to take only you can say.

Constructing a wall cabinet in place involves the same basic steps as the base cabinet.

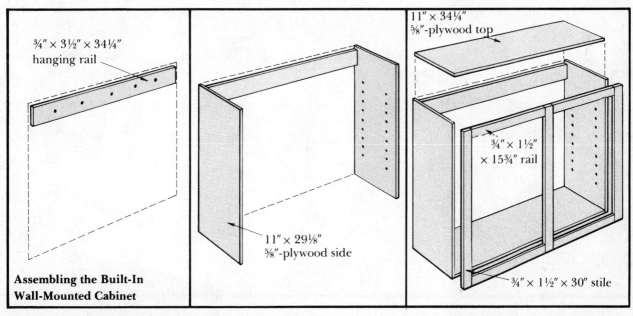

Assembling the Built-In Wall-Mounted Cabinet

537

Part V

Building Projects for the Harvest Kitchen

Cabinetmaking yields, in addition to cabinets, lots of scraps. And new skills. With those woodworking skills, the scraps can be turned into a variety of kitchen gadgets. More elaborate build-it-yourself projects may require materials other than scraps, but they in turn yield scraps. It's an endless cycle that the handy person revels in, gluing up cutting boards and cheese trays, cobbling up racks and containers, crafting tables and chairs. In the harvest kitchen, the potential for building projects almost never ends. Even if the kitchen itself is finished.

Cheese Boards

Here are cheese boards that should get lots of use in your kitchen and dining room, and at parties too. You'll use them to serve cheese and hors d'oeuvres, but they also can be used as cutting boards and they make handy trivets. They can be made from hardwood strips glued edge to edge, or they can be made from single, wider

pieces of wood. White oak was used here, but you also can consider other hardwoods such as maple, walnut or even birch.

These boards have an attractive curved shape. They can be given a warm rubbed finish with vegetable oil. Put these elements together with a couple of hours of your time, and you'll have a better cheese board than you can buy at the department store or even at the chic kitchen boutique.

There are two boards, really just two sizes of the same thing. Your boards can be any length, especially if you work with scrap pieces.

The directions here give you the procedure for making a board with strips of stock glued together. If you use a single board, skip the first two steps.

Construction

1. Rip three 12-inch lengths of wood to 2½-inch widths. (Your wood can be anywhere from ½ inch to 1 inch thick.)

2. The easiest way to glue the strips together is with a couple of bar clamps. After the glue has dried, crosscut both ends of your board on the table saw, removing just enough to even off the ends of your strips.

3. This is where you start if you are using just one wide board. Lay out the curved edges. Locate the center point on the end of the board. Draw a line at least 1 inch long; it will be used later to locate the hole used to hang the board up. Next, measure ¼ inch from each corner along the length of your board, and mark those

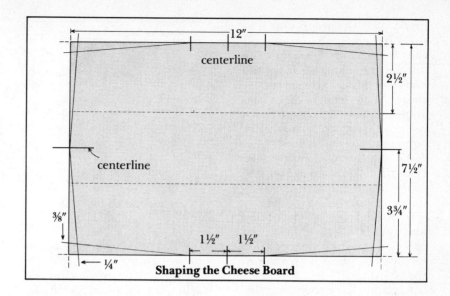

Shaping the Cheese Board

points. Measure ⅜ inch from each corner along the end of the board, and mark those points. Now, locate the centerline across the width of the board, then make a mark 1½ inches to

each side of it on both edges of the board. Use a straightedge to connect each of these marks to the closest ⅜-inch mark. Then, from the center point at each end, draw a line to each ¼-inch

Materials (Large Board)

Wood
1 pc. ⁵/₄ × 3″ × 4′ FAS white oak or **Board:** 3 pcs. 1″ × 2½″ × 12″

Miscellaneous
Waterproof glue
Vegetable oil

Materials (Small Board)

Wood
1 pc. ⁵/₄ × 3″ × 3′ FAS white oak or **Board:** 3 pcs. 1″ × 2½″ × 9¾″

Miscellaneous
Waterproof glue
Vegetable oil

mark. At each corner, sketch or use a french curve to round off the intersecting lines. Smooth out the lines along the sides and ends to make gentle curves, rather than straight lines and angles. Cut out the cheese board using a coping saw or a saber or band saw.

4. Measure ¾ inch down the centerline you drew at one end of the board and drill a ½-inch-diameter hole.

5. Round all of the edges and inside the hole with a router or rasp and sandpaper. Remember to finish both sides of the board.

6. Sand all the edges and surfaces. Finish with a rubbed-in coat of vegetable oil. The oil rub can be repeated from time to

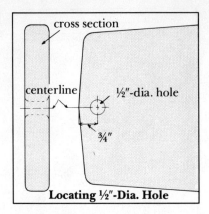

Locating ½"-Dia. Hole

time to keep your cheese board looking new.

Note: If you are making the smaller, 9¾-inch-long board, the procedure is exactly the same, including the measurements setting up your curved sides.

Cutting Boards

Cutting boards get lots of use in the harvest kitchen. They get so much use, in fact, that many self-providers get a butcher block or have counter tops fabricated of butcher block. But a small cutting board is still a necessity.

You can easily make your own cutting boards, regardless of your woodworking skill. Simple

ones can be cut from a single hardwood board. You can add a personal touch by using a coping saw or band saw to cut the board in a shape, maybe the silhouette of a homestead pig. Such a board would be the kin of the cheese boards previously described.

The cutting boards shown here are more advanced projects, but they are good for the woodworker who wants to hone jointing and gluing skills. These cutting boards were made by gluing up strips of maple, walnut and oak to get alternating light and dark stripes. Hardwoods are available at lumberyards, but seldom at home improvement centers. Preparing them for gluing up takes either patience and skill with hand tools, or a planer, a jointer and a power saw. You can buy hardwood that's planed and jointed for you, but you must be willing to pay for it.

One board has a perimeter groove for catching meat juices and the like. Cutting this groove requires some router work, but it is not work that is beyond the realm of possibility for anyone.

Construction (Serving Board)

1. The serving board comprises four 1¼-inch by 1⅛-inch by 22-inch soft maple strips, two 1¼-inch by ¾-inch by 22-inch black walnut strips and three 1¼-inch by 1⅛-inch by 22-inch white oak strips. Preparation of these strips for gluing up is the first step, one which you may have done at the lumberyard

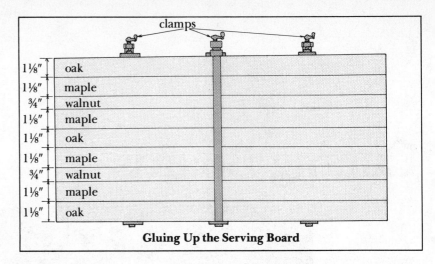

Gluing Up the Serving Board

where you purchase the wood or at a cabinetmaking shop. The routine to follow in doing the prep work yourself is as follows:

a. Select appropriate pieces of rough-sawn hardwood stock and, using a jointer, surface one face and one edge.

b. Run the boards through a planer, surfacing the second face and reducing the thickness to the desired 1¼ inches. The use of a planer will ensure that the second face is parallel to the first face. This operation, often called thicknessing, can be done on a jointer, but you can't ensure that the two faces will be parallel. An alternative method for those not having a planer is to resaw the boards on a band saw or table saw to a thickness slightly in excess of the desired 1¼ inches. Use the jointer to clean up the sawn face.

c. With the thickness of the boards established, rip the wood into strips of the appropriate widths, 1⅛ inches for the maple and oak, ¾ inch for the walnut. Clean up the sawn edges with a pass through the jointer.

d. Crosscut the strips to the desired 22-inch length.

2. Lay out the strips on the workbench, side by side, and play around with the matchings until you find an arrangement that is particularly pleasing. The serving board shown has an alternating arrangement of oak–maple–walnut, maple–oak–maple, walnut–maple–oak, which seems fairly routine and is, except that you will find that blends and contrasts of grain from strip to strip will give you a lot of choices. Apply a waterproof glue to mating surfaces and clamp the strips together with bar or pipe clamps. It's a good idea to use at least three clamps, two on the bottom and one on the top. Use a try square to true up the broad surface of the panel as you clamp it.

3. After the glue has dried, clean up any squeeze-out with a chisel or scraper, then square the ends with a saw, if necessary.

4. Mark and cut out the handle loops. Scribe the centerline of each loop 1½ inches from the end and parallel to it. Measure in along each centerline $3^1/_{16}$ inches from each side; each of these points marks the center of a 1-inch-diameter hole to be drilled. Drill the four holes, two for each handle loop, with a brace and auger bit. Using a coping saw or saber saw, cut out the material between adjoining pairs of holes. Clean up the insides of the loops with a file.

5. The shape of the board is laid out by scribing guidelines with a straightedge, then rounding them off freehand. Start by measuring 1 inch from each corner along the width, then ¼ inch from each corner along the length. Then locate the center of each of the sides and the ends. Next, scribe straight lines from the 1-inch marks to the centers of the sides and from the ¼-inch marks to the centers of the ends. This gives you the rough shape, which you can soften with some freehand work. An alternative is to buy a set of french curves at an art supply store and use these plastic templates to guide your pencil in putting some grace in your cutting board's lines. When the shape is set, cut out the board using a coping saw, saber saw or band saw.

6. Round off all the edges of the board and the inside edges of the handle loops using a ¼-inch rounding-off bit in a router. Carefully sand both

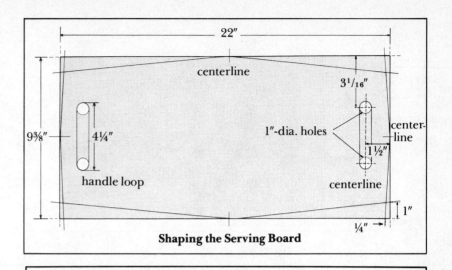

Shaping the Serving Board

Materials (Serving Board)

Wood
1 pc. $^6/_4 \times 6'' \times 2'$ FAS soft maple or **Strips:** 4 pcs. 1¼″ × 1⅛″ × 22″

1 pc. $^6/_4 \times 2'' \times 2'$ FAS black walnut or **Strips:** 2 pcs. 1¼″ × ¾″ × 22″

1 pc. $^6/_4 \times 4'' \times 2'$ FAS white oak or **Strips:** 3 pcs. 1¼″ × 1⅛″ × 22″

Miscellaneous
Waterproof glue
Vegetable oil

faces of the cutting board, clean it well, then finish the board with the same vegetable oil you use for cooking.

Construction (Grooved Board)

1. The grooved cutting board comprises nine 1¼-inch by 1⅛-inch soft maple strips.

These strips must either be purchased already dressed or be jointed and planed by you as explained in the directions for making the serving board. Three of the strips must be cut 18 inches long, the other six 14 inches long.

2. Using a waterproof glue, glue up the strips with the longest three in the center and all flush at one end. The board **545**

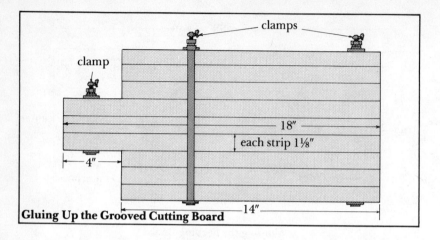

clamps

clamp

clamp

18"

each strip 1⅛"

4"

14"

Gluing Up the Grooved Cutting Board

will be roughly paddle shaped. Use bar or pipe clamps to secure the strips while the glue dries; it would be best to have three on the body of the board and one on the handle extension. Put two on the top and two on the bottom to counter any tendency to cup. Use a try square to true the surface of the cutting board as you tighten the clamps.

3. After the glue has dried, clean up any squeeze-out with a chisel or scraper, then square the ends with a saw, if necessary.

4. Lay out the finished shape of the board.

    a. The handle has a head 3¼ inches wide and 2½ inches long and a neck 1 inch wide and 1½ inches long. Scribe a centerline the length of the board, then lay out the handle on the handle extension using the centerline as a reference point. The corners of the head should be rounded with a ¼-inch

radius, the base of the neck with a ½-inch radius.

    b. To shape the ends of the board's body, measure ¼ inch along the sides from the corner, then draw lines to these points from the centers of the ends. Give each of these straight lines a gentle arc, either freehand or using a french curve as a guide. Round the corners with a ¼-inch radius.

5. Cut out the board, using a coping saw, a saber saw or a band saw. Drill a ½-inch-diameter hole in the center of the handle head, that is, 1¼ inches down the centerline from the edge.

6. The groove around the perimeter of the board is cut with a router with a ½-inch corebox bit. It is ¼ inch deep and its outer edge is ½ inch from the board's edge. There are three ways to rout the groove. Relying upon a steady hand may seem the easiest, but it certainly is the riskiest: one slip and you ruin the piece.

    a. Another method involves the use of a template, which you make from ⅛-inch Masonite or ¼-inch plywood, and a general-purpose template guide, which you must purchase to fit your router. You make the template by scribing the path of the inner edge of the groove on the template material. Cut out the template using a coping saw or saber saw, then clean up the edge with any straight bit in the router. Make the template just a tad undersize, to compensate for the

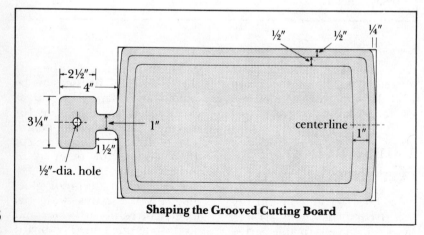

½" ½" ¼"

2½"

4"

3¼" 1"

centerline

1"

1½"

½"-dia. hole

Shaping the Grooved Cutting Board

template guide, which will hold the router bit a fraction of an inch away from the template. To rout the groove, clamp the template in position on the cutting board, attach the template guide to your router, mount the bit in the router, then carefully rout the groove. This method is the best for cutting the basic groove. But it will not work quite as well for routing the reservoir opposite the handle. This reservoir is a full inch wide and 3/8 inch deep.

b. The third method is the easiest for routing the reservoir, and it will work well for routing the groove along the sides, but it won't work well at the handle end. This method involves the use of an edge guide, which is a router accessory that allows you to rout a groove at a fixed though adjustable distance from an edge by using the edge as a

guide. Simply adjust the guide so your bit cuts the groove at the proper place. Then, as you rout, keep the guide firmly against the edge of the cutting board; be especially careful at the corners, so that your groove is a closed loop. To rout the reservoir you'd best make three or more passes, readjusting the guide slightly with each pass, until the reservoir is its proper width. At the handle end of the board, the handle and the edge guide will be in each other's way, so you'll either have to use the template method there or try freehanding it.

7. With the groove cut, all that remains is to break the edges of the board with a 1/4-inch rounding-off bit in your router, including the edges of the hole in the handle, and sand the board well. Finish it with vegetable oil.

Materials (Grooved Board)

Wood
1 pc. 6/4 × 4″ × 4′ FAS soft maple or **Strips:** 6 pcs. 1¼″ × 1⅛″ × 14″
3 pcs. 1¼″ × 1⅛″ × 18″

Miscellaneous
Waterproof glue
Vegetable oil

Ever grate a large piece of ricotta cheese for homemade pizza, and have cheese spilling out over the top and squeezing out from under the grater? Or dice three or four onions on the counter and then have to scoop them up to put them in a pan? Nothing to get upset about, certainly. But a chopping tray will alleviate problems of this nature

Chopping Tray

and keep your counters free for other things.

As you grate or cut, the grated cheese or diced onions may simply be pushed into the tray. When you are ready for the ingredients, just slide them into the bowl or pan. If a larger cutting area is needed for slicing bread or carving meats, the reverse side may also be used.

This chopping tray is a good project for the beginning woodworker. Although cutting and gluing thirty-five 1-inch squares may seem tedious, there are no complicated angles or curves to cut, and the experience of gluing up the tray will be good practice for more complicated projects later on. This is not to say that the tray is no more than practice material. A little care will render a beautiful tool from just a little wood.

Construction

1. From ½-inch stock, cut

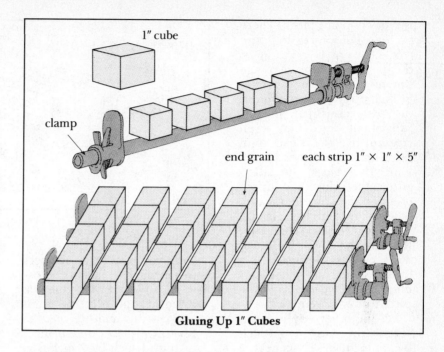

Gluing Up 1″ Cubes

one piece measuring 7 inches by 12 inches for the bottom.

2. From ½-inch stock, cut two pieces measuring 1½ inches by 12 inches for the sides and one piece measuring 1½ inches

by 8 inches for the back. A slight curve may be cut on one end of each piece as shown, or the rectangular shape may be retained.

3. From 1-inch stock, cut thirty-five 1-inch squares to

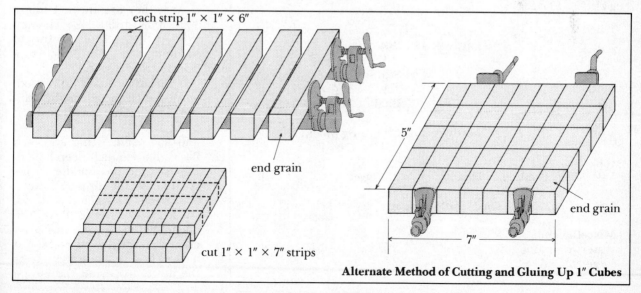

Alternate Method of Cutting and Gluing Up 1″ Cubes

form the chopping block. There are a couple of ways to do this:

a. One way is to cut all of the pieces at once. Arrange the pieces so that the end-grain is up and forms interesting patterns. Break the arrangement down into seven strips of five blocks each and, using glue and a bar clamp, glue the blocks together. After the glue has dried, clean up the squeeze-out and, using glue and bar clamps, glue the seven strips together, forming the 5-inch by 7-inch block. After the glue has dried, scrape off the excess glue and plane and sand the piece to a smooth finish.

b. The other way is to rip seven strips measuring 1 inch by 1 inch by 6 inches as shown. Glue them together using glue and bar clamps to form a piece measuring 6 inches by 7 inches. (If you

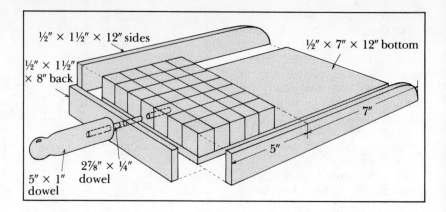

½" × 1½" × 12" sides
½" × 1½" × 8" back
5" × 1" dowel
2⅞" × ¼" dowel
½" × 7" × 12" bottom
7"
5"

wish, you may trim this piece to 5 inches by 7 inches and use it as is.) After the glue has dried, scrape off the excess and cut this built-up piece to form five pieces measuring 1 inch by 1 inch by 7 inches as shown. Turn the pieces so that the end grain is up. Again using glue and bar clamps, glue the pieces together.

After the glue has dried, scrape off the excess glue and plane and sand the piece to a smooth finish.

4. Glue and clamp the chopping block to the bottom piece. After the glue has dried, remove the excess and trim the edges, if necessary, so that they are flush.

5. Glue and clamp the side and back pieces into place. When the glue has dried, remove the excess and trim the edges, if necessary, so that they are flush. Using a ¼-inch bit, drill a 1½-inch-deep hole in the back of the tray to accommodate the dowel support for the handle.

6. From a 1-inch dowel rod, cut a 5-inch piece for the handle. The handle may be turned on a lathe, carved, or sanded and left plain. Using a ¼-inch bit, drill a 1½-inch-deep hole in the base of the handle to accommodate the support dowel.

7. From a ¼-inch dowel rod, cut a 2⅞-inch piece. Bevel the ends slightly to ensure easy entry into the drilled holes. Cut a small groove along the side of the dowel to permit the escape

Materials

Wood

1 pc. ⁴⁄₄ × 8" × 3' FAS hardwood or **Bottom:** 1 pc.
½" × 7" × 12"

Sides: 2 pcs.
½" × 1½" × 12"
Back: 1 pc. ½" × 1½" × 8"

1 pc. ⁵⁄₄ × 6" × 1' FAS hardwood or **Chopping block:** 35 pcs.
1" × 1" × 1"

1 pc. 36" × 1" dowel or **Handle:** 5" × 1" dowel

1 pc. 36" × ¼" dowel or **Handle support:** 2⅞" × ¼" dowel

Miscellaneous
Waterproof glue
Vegetable oil

of air and glue. Using a cotton swab, apply glue to the hole in the handle and to the protruding dowel, and join the handle to the tray.

8. After the glue has dried, a hole may be drilled in the end of the handle to accommodate a thong for hanging. Remove any excess glue, sand the tray to a smooth finish, and apply several coats of vegetable oil.

Knife Rack

Here's a sharp way to store your kitchen knives. The portable rack allows the knives to be moved easily from one kitchen counter to another. At the same time it protects the edges of the blades.

The solid wood construction makes the rack heavy enough so it won't tip over, and the open slots make it easy to clean.

Of course, kitchen knives come in all sizes and shapes, so you should customize the slots in your rack to fit the knives in your collection. This is easy enough to do. Just measure how wide each blade is and cut the slots a little bit deeper or a little bit shallower to accommodate them.

Construction

1. From ¾-inch pine stock rip five pieces that are 2⅝ inches wide and 11 inches long.

2. Coat the faces of the five blocks with glue and clamp them together to form a single block that is 2⅝ inches by 3¾ inches by 11 inches. After the glue has dried, remove the ex-cess, and plane the edges, if necessary, so they are flush.

3. Measure ⅝ inch from the edge of one of the 2⅝-inch faces and cut a ½-inch by ½-inch groove to hold your steel. This groove can be cut with a router, with a series of saw cuts or by making one saw cut on each side and using a small chisel to cut out the center.

4. From ¾-inch pine stock, rip two 3¾-inch by 11-inch strips.

5. Apply glue to the face of one of these blocks and to the larger block that has the ½-inch groove in it. Clamp the two pieces together to form a single block. After the glue dries, re-move the excess and plane the edges, if necessary, so they are flush.

6. Measure how wide the blades of your kitchen knives are and use a saw to cut slots in the block that will fit your knives. Each slot should be a bit more than 5/16 inch wider than the blade it is to hold. The knife rack shown here has an orna-mental slot cut into the groove that holds the steel. This bal-ances the knife-slot on the op-posite side and makes both sides of the rack look alike.

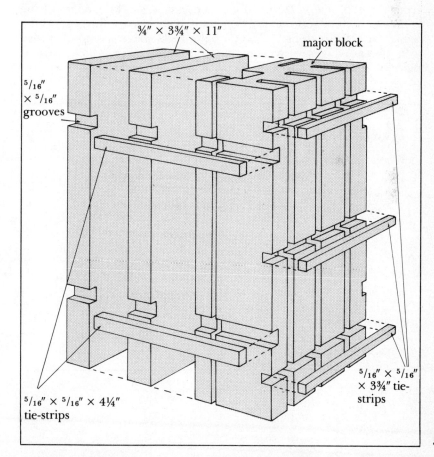

7. Place a ⅛-inch by 3-inch by 11-inch plywood spacer between the second ¾-inch by 3¾-inch by 11-inch block and the first one that you glued to the main block. Clamp these pieces together to form a single block. Use a try square to see that they are clamped flush and square.

8. Cut $5/16$-inch by $5/16$-inch grooves on three sides of the block to hold the tie-strips. Two grooves go across each of the 4¼-inch faces of the block. One of them is 1⅞ inches from the top and one is 2⅜ inches from the bottom on each side. Three grooves go across the slotted 3¾-inch face. One is 1¾ inches from the top, one is 1⅛ inches from the bottom and one is 5⅜ inches from the bottom.

9. Plane or resaw a short piece of ¾-inch stock to a thickness of $5/16$ inch. Rip seven $5/16$-inch-wide strips from the piece. Cut four strips 4¼ inches long and three 3¾ inches long. Glue these tie-strips into the grooves cut for them.

10. When the glue is dry, remove the clamps and the ⅛-inch plywood spacer. The spacer will have created a slot the width of the rack for a large, broad knife. Your rack is now ready for the finishing touches.

11. Saw ⅛ inch off each end of the block squarely. This will make the final block 10¾ inches long.

12. Remove any excess glue around the tie-strips and, if necessary, sand the edges of the strips so they are flush. Sand the entire block to a smooth finish and apply several coats of whatever finish is desired.

Materials

Wood

1 pc. 1 × 12 × 2′ select pine or

Major block: 5 pcs. ¾″ × 2⅝″ × 11″

Minor block: 2 pcs. ¾″ × 3¾″ × 11″

Tie-strips: 4 pcs. $5/16″ × 5/16″ × 4¼″$ 3 pcs. $5/16″ × 5/16″ × 3¾″$

1–1′ sq. sht. ⅛″ B-D int. plywood or **Spacer:** 1 pc. 3″ × 11¼″

Miscellaneous
Glue
Finish

Trivets

When you've got a hot pot you want to set down, it's handy to have a trivet so you won't mar a counter top or scorch a table-cloth. Since pots and pans come in different sizes, so do trivets.

These two trivets are easy to make quickly. They're also good projects for using up scrap wood left over from other projects, because the slats used to

make the trivets are so small.

There's no hard-and-fast rule on what size a trivet should be, and you can change the size of these simply by adding slats to them.

If one design strikes your fancy more than the other, feel free to make a larger version of the small trivet or a smaller version of the large trivet.

Construction (Small Trivet)

1. From ¾-inch stock rip seven 1¼-inch by 11-inch pieces for the slats of the trivet and two pieces the same size for a drilling box. At the same time, cut one 1¼-inch by 3¾-inch piece for the end of the drilling box.

2. From ½-inch particle board, cut six 1¼-inch by 7-inch strips to use as spacers between the slats during assembly, one piece 3¾ inches by 12¼ inches for the bottom of the drilling box, and two pieces 1¼ inches by 11 inches to be used in shaping the ends of the trivet's slats.

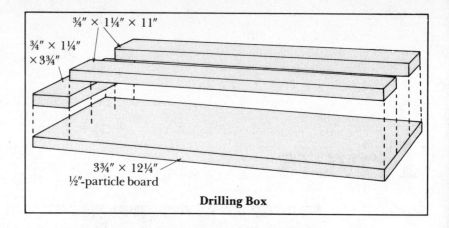

¾″ × 1¼″ × 11″

¾″ × 1¼″ × 3¾″

3¾″ × 12¼″ ½″-particle board

Drilling Box

3. Assemble the drilling box by gluing two 11-inch pieces to the particle-board bottom of the box and the 3¾-inch piece along the end. Be careful to see that the end piece is square with the two side pieces. Also check to see that one of the slats fits snugly in the middle of the drilling box.

4. Take one of the slats and mark points at each end of it that are 1¼ inches from the end and ⅝ inch in from the sides. Place the slat in the drilling box and use a ½-inch bit to drill

holes at these points. You should drill through both the slat and the bottom of the drilling box.

5. Remove the slat with the holes in it from the drilling box and drill uniform ½-inch holes in all the other slats by placing them snugly in the drilling box and using the holes in the bottom of the box as guides for the drill bit. Be very careful in drilling these hoses that you don't split out the wood as the bit breaks through. If you use a

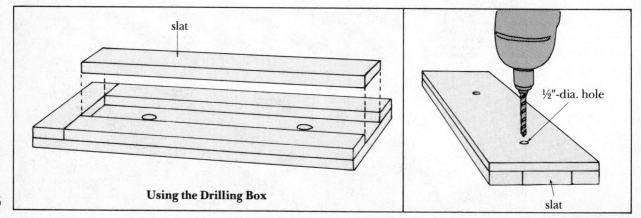

slat

Using the Drilling Box

½″-dia. hole

slat

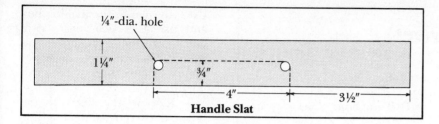

¼"-dia. hole

1¼"

¾"

4"

3½"

Handle Slat

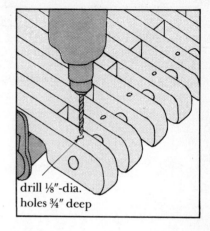

drill ⅛"-dia.
holes ¾" deep

brace and bit, you can stop drilling when the auger screw penetrates the slat, turn the slat over and complete the hole from the second side.

6. Cut handle notches in two slats that will be the sides of the trivet. These notches should be 4 inches long, ¾ inch deep and 3½ inches from each end of the two slats. The inside corners of the notches can be rounded in several ways. You can simply round them with a coping saw or a saber saw, or you can first drill ¼-inch holes in the corners and then cut to the holes. Use a

rat-tail file or a dowel wrapped with sandpaper to finish these inside corners, regardless of how you cut them. The outer edges of the holes also should be filed or sawed round.

7. Clamp the seven slats tightly together with one of the 1¼-inch by 11-inch pieces of particle board on each end. You may now round the edges of the slats with either a router, a file or a plane. The pieces of particle board will keep the end slats from splitting. Round both edges on both ends of the slats to a ½-inch radius. Unclamp the

slats and sand the sides and rounded edges of all the slats.

8. From ½-inch dowel cut two pieces 8¼ inches long. Slide the slats onto the two dowels. Place one of the 1¼-inch by 7-inch particle-board spacers between each slat.

9. Clamp the slats and spacers together. Now use a ⅛-inch bit to drill ¾-inch-deep holes through the top of each slat into each ½-inch dowel. These holes should be drilled 1¼ inches in from the end of each slat and ⅜ inch in from the side.

10. From ⅛-inch dowel cut 14 plugs, each ¾ inch long. Bevel one end of each slightly to ensure easy entry into the holes. Apply glue to each hole and each plug, and stick the plugs in the holes.

11. When the glue has dried, remove any excess glue. Then remove the spacers, sand the trivet smooth and apply whatever finish is desired. Keep in mind that the trivet will be exposed to heat, which could burn off varnish.

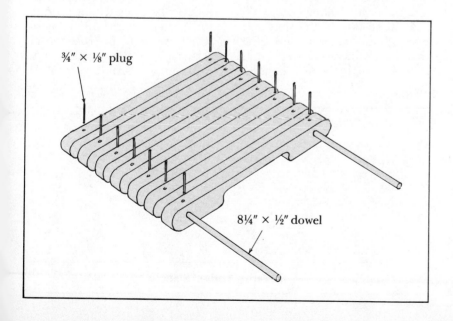

¾" × ⅛" plug

8¼" × ½" dowel

557

Materials (Small Trivet)

Wood
1 pc. 1 × 12 × 2′ select white pine or **Slats:** 7 pcs.
                      ¾″ × 1¼″ × 11″
                      Drilling box: 2 pcs.
                      ¾″ × 1¼″ × 11″
                      1 pc. ¾″ × 1¼″ × 3¾″

1–1′ × 2′ sht. ½″ particle board or **Spacers:** 6 pcs. 1¼″ × 7″
                      Drilling box: 1 pc.
                      3¾″ × 12¼″
                      End buffers: 2 pcs.
                      1¼″ × 11″

1 pc. 36″ × ½″ dowel or **Slat holders:** 2 pcs. 8¼″ × ½″ dowel

1 pc. 36″ × ⅛″ dowel or **Plugs:** 14 pcs. ¾″ × ⅛″ dowel

Miscellaneous
Glue
Finish

Construction (Large Trivet)

1. From ¾-inch stock rip ten 1¼-inch by 12½-inch pieces. Eight of these are slats for the trivet and two are sides for a drilling box. Cut one 1¼-inch by 3¾-inch end for the drilling box from the same stock.

2. From ½-inch particle board cut seven 1¼-inch by 7-inch strips to use as spacers between the slats and one 3¾-inch by 13¾-inch piece for the bottom of the drilling box.

3. Assemble the drilling box by gluing the two 12½-inch pieces along the sides of the particle-board bottom and the 3¾-inch piece along the end. Be careful to see that the end piece is square with the two side pieces. Also check to see that one of the slats fits snugly in the middle of the drilling box.

4. Take one of the slats and mark points at each end of it that are 2¼ inches from the end and ⅝ inch in from the sides.

Place the slat in the drilling box and use a ½-inch bit to drill holes at these points. You should drill through both the slat and the bottom of the drilling box.

5. Remove the slat with the holes in it from the drilling box and drill uniform ½-inch holes in all the other slats by placing them snugly in the drilling box and using the holes in the bottom of the box as guides for the drill bit. Be very careful in drilling these hoses that you don't split out the wood as the bit breaks through. If you use a brace and bit, you can stop drilling when the auger screw penetrates the slat, turn the slat over and complete the hole from the second side.

6. Bevel the ends of each slat. To do this, first find the midpoint of the slat's side, ⅝ inch from the top and bottom. Draw a horizontal line along the midpoint. Measure in 1¼ inches from each end and draw perpendicular lines. Use a protractor to measure the angles along which you will cut from the intersection of these two lines to the outer edges of the slat. Mark

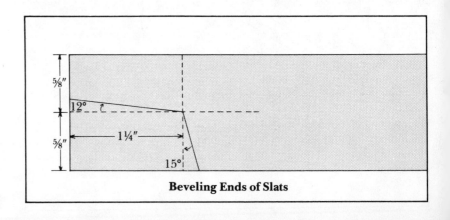

Beveling Ends of Slats

one angle 12 degrees above the horizontal midline. Mark the other angle 15 degrees toward the center of the slat from the perpendicular. If you measure and cut both ends of the first slat correctly, you can then use this slat as a pattern from which to draw the cut-lines on the other slats. After cutting the bevels with a backsaw, sand all the slats thoroughly.

7. From ½-inch dowel cut two 9½-inch pieces. Slide the slats onto the two dowels. Place one of the 7-inch particle-board spacers between each slat.

8. Clamp the slats and spacers together. Use a ⅛-inch bit to drill ¾-inch-deep holes through the top of each slat into each ½-inch dowel. These holes should be drilled 2¼ inches in from the end of each slat and ⅜

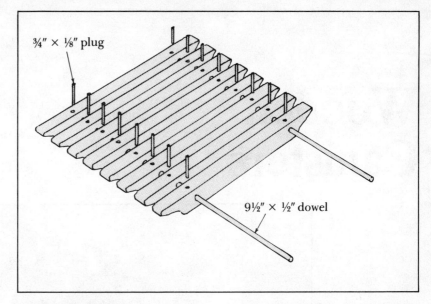

¾″ × ⅛″ plug

9½″ × ½″ dowel

inch in from the side.

9. From ⅛-inch dowel cut 16 plugs, each ¾ inch long. Bevel one end of each plug slightly to

ensure easy entry into the holes. Apply glue to each hole and each plug, and stick the plugs into the holes.

10. When the glue has dried, remove any excess glue. Then remove the spacers, sand the trivet smooth and apply whatever finish is desired. Keep in mind that the trivet will be exposed to heat, which could burn off varnish.

Materials (Large Trivet)

Wood

1 pc. 1 × 12 × 4′ select white pine or **Slats:** 8 pcs. ¾″ × 1¼″ × 12½″
Drilling box: 2 pcs. ¾″ × 1¼″ × 12½″
1 pc. ¾″ × 1¼″ × 3¾″

1–1′ × 2′ sht. ½″ particle board or **Spacers:** 7 pcs. 1¼″ × 7″
Drilling box: 1 pc. 3¾″ × 13¾″

1 pc. 36″ × ½″ dowel or **Slat holders:** 2 pcs. 9½″ × ½″ dowel

1 pc. 36″ × ⅛″ dowel or **Plugs:** 16 pcs. ¾″ × ⅛″ dowel

Miscellaneous
Glue
Finish

Wooden Canisters

What kitchen is without canisters of some sort for keeping flour, tea, coffee, cookies or treats within reach? This set of canisters is easy to build and provides an inexpensive way of avoiding the purchase of the mass-produced canister set, which is generally neither well constructed nor well designed.

Follow the directions and

construct five canisters decreasing in size in 1-inch increments from 8 to 4 inches. Or make five canisters the same size. Or however many you want in whatever size you want. The design leaves plenty of room for individual expression. By simply changing the dimensions, you can make the canisters tall or short, rectangular or square, whatever shape or size fits your particular space or fancy. The canisters may be stained, painted, varnished, decorated, labeled or left plain, and any knob can be used for a handle. White porcelain knobs and varnished canisters may look beautiful in one kitchen, painted canisters may counterpoint the use of unpainted wooden cabinets, walls and floors in another, while paint, varnish and protruding handles may be completely unnecessary in a third kitchen.

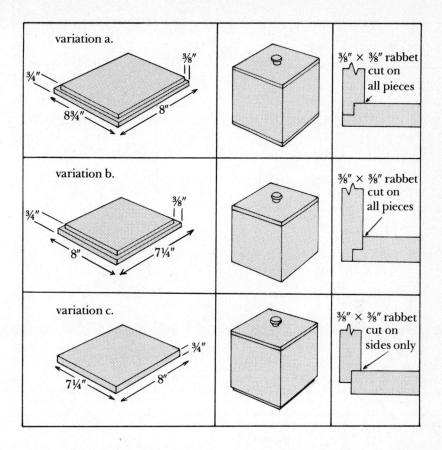

variation a.
variation b.
variation c.

⅜" × ⅜" rabbet cut on all pieces

⅜" × ⅜" rabbet cut on all pieces

⅜" × ⅜" rabbet cut on sides only

Construction

1. Cut a 12-foot length of 1 × 12 white pine into the following lengths: 50 inches, 44 inches and 38 inches.

a. Rip the 50-inch piece into an 8-inch width.

b. Rip the 44-inch piece into one piece 7 inches wide and another 4 inches wide.

c. Rip the 38-inch piece into a 6-inch and a 5-inch width.

2. Cut four side pieces and a top and bottom piece for each of the five canisters:

a. From the 8-inch by 50-inch piece cut four 8-inch by 8-inch pieces and two 8-inch by 8¾-inch pieces.

b. From the 7-inch by 44-inch piece cut four pieces 7 inches long and two pieces 7¾ inches long.

c. From the 6-inch by 38-inch piece cut four pieces 6 inches long and two 6¾ inches long.

d. From the 5-inch by 38-inch piece cut four pieces 5 inches long and two 5¾ inches long.

e. From the 4-inch by 44-inch piece cut four pieces 4 inches long and two 4¾ inches long.

3. At this point you may consider three variations of the canister bottom piece as illustrated in a, b and c. The mea-

surements in these examples are for the 8-inch by 8¾-inch canister; calculate measurements accordingly for other sizes. For example, if variation b or c is desired, cut the 7-inch by 7¾-inch bottom piece to 6¼ inches by 7 inches.

4. Select the best-looking side of each canister piece. Then, using a router, saw or jointer, make a ⅜-inch-wide by ⅜-inch-deep rabbet cut on the four edges of the opposite side of all pieces (unless variation c of the bottom piece was selected, in which case all pieces with the exception of the five bottom pieces would be rabbeted). Any deco-

561

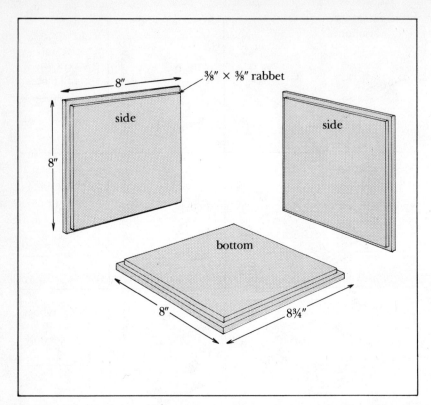

side

8"

8"

⅜" × ⅜" rabbet

side

bottom

8"

8¾"

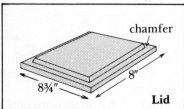

chamfer

8"

8¾"

Lid

countersink the nail heads and fill the holes with wood filler. After the wood filler has dried, sand to a smooth finish.

8. Chamfer the inside edges of the rabbets on the lids.

9. Sand the canisters and lids. Round off all edges and outside corners slightly with medium and then fine sandpaper.

10. If wooden knobs are to be used in either similar or graduating diameters (2½, 2, 1¾, 1¼, 1), attach them at this time. If porcelain, plastic, metal or any other type of handle is to be used, provide pilot holes for the screws or bolts.

11. Apply paint, stain, varnish or whatever type of finish is desired, and attach handles if they have not already been secured to the lid.

rative engraving of designs or labels should be done at this time.

5. Sand all cut edges lightly with medium sandpaper to remove roughness, but do not round off edges or corners.

6. Glue and nail the bottom and side pieces of the five canisters as shown, using 4d finish nails and any glue that is suitable for wood.

562 **7.** After the glue has dried,

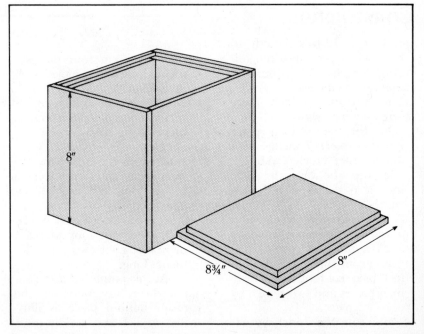

8"

8¾"

8"

Materials

Wood

1 pc. 1 × 12 × 12′ select white pine or **Sides:** 4 pcs. ¾″ × 8″ × 8″
4 pcs. ¾″ × 7″ × 7″
4 pcs. ¾″ × 6″ × 6″
4 pcs. ¾″ × 5″ × 5″
4 pcs. ¾″ × 4″ × 4″

Tops and bottoms:
2 pcs. ¾″ × 8″ × 8¾″
2 pcs. ¾″ × 7″ × 7¾″
2 pcs. ¾″ × 6″ × 6¾″
2 pcs. ¾″ × 5″ × 5¾″
2 pcs. ¾″ × 4″ × 4¾″

Hardware

4d finishing nails
5 knobs

Miscellaneous

Glue
Wood filler
Finish

Spice Cabinet

This spice cabinet is a good project for the woodworker who owns a limited number of tools and aspires to hone his or her skills with hand tools. It is, of course, more easily made using power tools.

The cabinet shown was constructed of cherry. A jointer was used to surface the wood, a router to cut the dadoes and finish

the edges. But the materials list assumes you will use the lumberyard's dimension stock (pine) to make your spice cabinet.

Construction

1. From ¾-inch stock cut two 4-inch by 15¾-inch pieces for the sides and two 4¼-inch by 13¼-inch pieces for the top and bottom.

2. On the inside surface of both the top and bottom pieces, measure 5/16 inch from the front and side edges, and use a router to cut a ¼-inch-deep by ¾-inch-wide stopped dado on both ends of the two pieces as shown. Square off the stopped end of the dado with a chisel.

3. Using a router with a ¼-inch bead cutter, shape the inside front and side edges of the top and bottom pieces, and then sand the top, bottom and side pieces to a smooth finish.

4. From ¾-inch stock, cut one 11-inch by 15¼-inch piece for the door and one 11⅝-inch by 15¾-inch piece for the back. (It may be necessary to glue narrower pieces together to form the required 11-inch and 11⅝-inch widths. If you are using 1 × 12, rip a 15¾-inch length to an 11-inch width and save the waste strip. Trim the piece to 15¼ inches and use it for the door. Glue the waste strip to another 15¾-inch length of the 1 × 12, then rip the glued-up board to an 11⅝-inch width.)

5. On the front of the door, draw an oval measuring about 7¾ inches by 13 inches. If you don't think you can do it freehand, you can make an oval template using a piece of string,

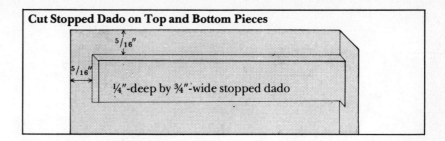

Cut Stopped Dado on Top and Bottom Pieces

5/16″

5/16″

¼″-deep by ¾″-wide stopped dado

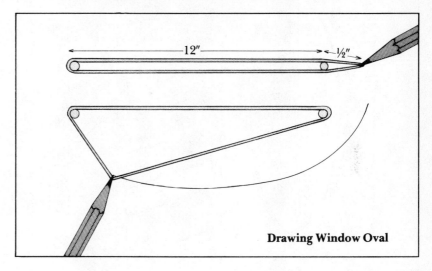

12″   ½″

Drawing Window Oval

two nails, a pencil and a piece of paper. Lay the piece of paper on your workbench or on a piece of scrap plywood, and tack two 3d finishing nails through the paper and into the wood, about 12 inches apart. Loop a piece of string around the nails and tie the string so that it stretches out about ½ inch when pulled away in a straight line with the nails. Scribe the oval with a pencil as shown, and then change the length of the string or the position of the nails, if you wish, until you arrive at a configuration that yields the most pleasing oval for your eye. When you get what you want, slip a clean piece of paper over

the nail heads, draw the oval and then cut it out with scissors. Position this template on the door and draw around it with a pencil to transfer your oval to the door. Cut the oval from the door with a saber saw; use a router with a cove bit to shape the perimeter of the oval; and then sand the door to a smooth finish.

6. Across the inside surface of the back piece, cut two ½-inch-wide by ⅜-inch-deep dadoes with their respective centers 5¼ inches and 10½ inches from the bottom. These are to support the shelves.

7. From ½-inch stock, cut two shelves measuring 2⅜

565

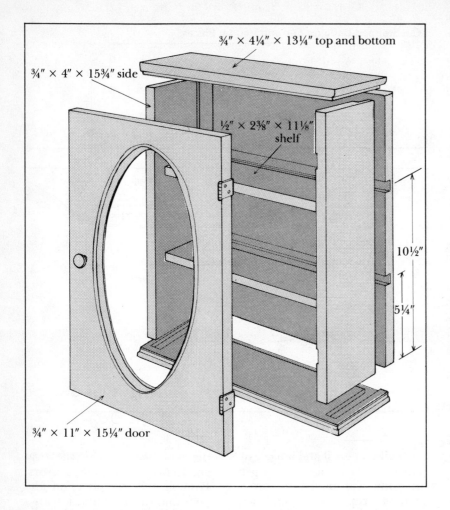

¾″ × 4¼″ × 13¼″ top and bottom

¾″ × 4″ × 15¾″ side

½″ × 2⅜″ × 11⅛″ shelf

10½″

5¼″

¾″ × 11″ × 15¼″ door

modate the back piece.

9. Apply glue and fit the back piece into position. Then drive nails through the top, bottom and side pieces to attach it securely, drilling pilot holes for the nails if hardwood is used.

10. Apply glue and fit the two shelves into the dadoes prepared for them. Ensure that they are level, and drive 3d finishing nails through the sides and back of the cabinet to attach them securely. Again, if hardwood is used, drill pilot holes for the nails.

11. Countersink all nails and apply wood filler in the appropriate color to all holes.

12. Mark the position of the hinges carefully, on both the door and the right side of the cabinet as shown in the photograph, and use a router or chisel to remove enough wood so that the four hinge plates are flush with the surrounding wood. Drill pilot holes, attach the hinges to the cabinet and door, and ensure that the door opens and closes without binding. When a good fit is attained, install a magnetic catch to keep the door closed. After it is properly adjusted, remove the door, the hinges and the catch.

13. To accommodate the

inches by 11⅛ inches, and then sand the two shelves and the back piece to a smooth finish. (For appearance' sake, it's best not to use plywood for the shelves. They are not large and can be hand planed from ¾-inch stock.)

8. Using glue and 3d finishing nails, assemble the side pieces into the dadoes in the top and bottom pieces, drilling pilot holes for the nails if hardwood is used. Then, using a router with a ¼-inch rabbeting bit, cut

a ¾-inch-deep rabbet around the inside perimeter of the back of the cabinet frame to accommodate the back piece to accom-

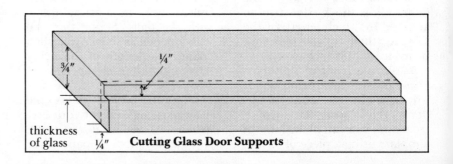

¾″

¼″

thickness of glass   ¼″   **Cutting Glass Door Supports**

knob, drill a hole that is centered from top to bottom, ¾ inch from the left edge of the door.

14. The glass is attached to the door using several ¼-inch-thick strips of wood, rabbeted to accept the glass. The easiest way to cut the rabbets is to do it before ripping the strips from broader stock. So start with ¾-inch stock, a piece at least 13½ inches long, and the rectangle of glass you will use. Measure the thickness of the glass. Cut a rabbet in the edge of the wood that is as deep as the glass is thick and ¼ inch wide. Then rip a ¼-inch-wide strip from the working stock; if the glass is more than ⅛ inch thick, it may be best to rip a strip more than a ¼ inch thick. You will need two 9½-inch-long strips and two 13½-inch-long strips. Sand these pieces and the entire cabinet to a smooth finish.

15. Apply several coats of whatever finish is desired. When the final coat is dry, lay the door facedown on a clean cloth to protect the finish, and center the glass over the window opening. Attach it to the door using the ¼-inch rabbeted strips and ½-inch brads. Be careful driving the brads so you don't crack the glass. Attach the hinges, magnetic catch and the knob. The cabinet should be attached directly to the wall with screws or bolts.

Materials

Wood

1 pc. 1 × 6 × 6′ select pine or **Sides:** 2 pcs. ¾″ × 4″ × 15¾″
Top and bottom: 2 pcs. ¾″ × 4¼″ × 13¼″

1 pc. 1 × 12 × 4′ select pine or **Door:** 1 pc. ¾″ × 11″ × 15¼″
Back: 1 pc. ¾″ × 11⅝″ × 15¾″

1 pc. 1 × 4 × 2′ select pine or **Shelves:** 2 pcs. ½″ × 2⅜″ × 11⅛″
Strips: 2 pcs. ¾″ × ¼″ × 9½″
2 pcs. ¾″ × ¼″ × 13½″

Hardware

3d finishing nails
1 pr. 1″ × 1½″ hinges
1 magnetic catch
½″ brads
1–¾″ knob
Screws or bolts

Miscellaneous

Glue
Wood filler
1 pc. 8½″ × 14″ single-strength window glass
Finish

Paper-Towel Holder

Most paper-towel holders on the market today are made of flimsy plastic. This one was made from ¾-inch cherry, but any kind of hardwood will suffice. Why not purchase a small amount of wood to match your kitchen cabinets, and build a paper-towel holder that you can feel good about? Sturdy and simple, this holder not only ac-

commodates paper towels but doubles as a shelf for spices, knickknacks or whatnot.

Construction

1. Cut the pieces that will form the back and shelf of the towel holder:

a. Cut one piece measuring ¾ inch by 3½ inches by 18½ inches for the back.

b. Cut one piece measuring ¾ inch by 4¼ inches by 17½ inches for the shelf.

c. If a curved, sculptured effect is desired on the back piece, draw curves as shown (or as you wish) and use a saber saw, band saw or coping saw to cut the required configuration. Sand this cut surface to a smooth finish. (You may want to maintain the rectangular shape and decorate the back piece to match the cabinet decorations in the kitchen.)

d. Using a router and the desired bit, cut a curve or bevel along the front edge of the back piece, and along the top edge of the front and sides of the shelf as shown. Then sand both pieces.

2. Drill and countersink pilot holes, and attach the back piece to the shelf using two 1½-inch #10 flathead wood screws.

3. Cut the supports for the towel rod:

a. Cut a piece of wood measuring 4¾ inches by 11 inches.

b. Measure 2¾ inches from each end of the piece, and 2½ inches from one of the side edges, and make two marks.

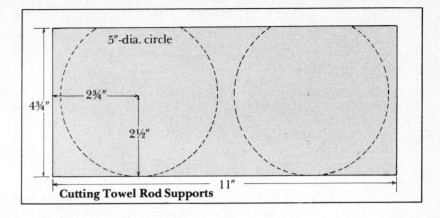

Cutting Towel Rod Supports

c. Place the point of a compass on these two marks and draw two 5-inch circles as shown. This will produce the 2-inch flat surfaces necessary for mounting the rod supports to the underside of the shelf.

d. Drill a 1-inch hole in the center of each circle, and use a saber saw, band saw or coping saw to cut the rod supports from the board. Then sand both pieces.

4. Drill and countersink pilot holes and use two 1½-inch #10 flathead wood screws to attach the rod supports to the underside of the shelf, 2¼ inches from each end.

5. From a 1-inch dowel rod, cut a piece 18½ inches long. Measure 2¾ inches from each end and mark the dowel to indicate the end of the handle area. The handles shown in the illustrations were turned on a lathe, but more personalized

Materials

Wood
1 pc. ⁴/₄ × 5″ × 4′ FAS cherry or **Back:** 1 pc.
¾″ × 3½″ × 18½″
Shelf: 1 pc. ¾″ × 4¼″ × 17½″
Rod supports: 2 pcs. 5″ diameter

1 pc. 36″ × 1″ dowel or **Roll support:** 1 pc. 18½″ × 1″ dowel

Hardware
4–1½″ #10 f.h. wood screws

Miscellaneous
Finish

569

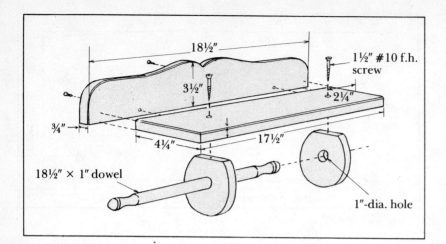

18½"

1½" #10 f.h. screw

3½"

2¼"

¾"

4¼"

17½"

18½" × 1" dowel

1"-dia. hole

handles may easily be fashioned using simple hand tools. After the handles are formed, sand the entire rod.

6. Sand the paper-towel holder and apply several coats of whatever finish is desired.

Waxed-Paper Rack

Waxed paper, aluminum foil and plastic wrap are all handy to have in the kitchen when you've got some sandwiches or leftovers you want to wrap up. But where do you keep these wrapping materials under wraps until they're needed?

This rack is designed to hold boxes of these products and others similar to them. The size

of the cabinet allows it to fit between a hanging wall cabinet and the counter top, but it's attractive enough to be more openly displayed.

The artwork required for the tin panels on the doors may provide an opportunity for the artist in your family to assist the family carpenter on the project. The designs on the panels may be painted, punched or both.

You can use the designs shown here or create your own unique, artistic design. The more self-expression you put into your work, the more enjoyment you'll get out of it.

Construction

1. From ¾-inch stock, cut two pieces 4 inches by 14¾ inches for the top and bottom, and two pieces 4 inches wide by 15 inches for the sides.

2. Rout out a ⅜-inch by ¾-inch rabbet across each end of the sides.

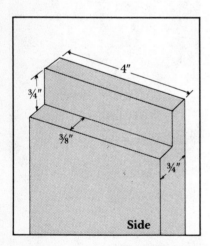

Side

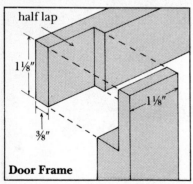

572 | **Door Frame**

Pattern for Punched Tin Door Panels   scale: 1 sq. equals ¼"

3. Cut a ¼-inch rabbet on the back inside edge of the top, the bottom and both sides. When the rack is assembled, the back of the cabinet will fit into this rabbet.

4. Glue the top and bottom to the two sides. Use a framing square to make sure the four pieces are square when you glue them. Use bar clamps to hold them in place. When the glue has dried, drive three 4d finishing nails into each corner. Make sure you countersink the nails deep enough so you won't hit them when you round off the corners.

5. From ¼-inch plywood, cut a piece 14 inches by 14 ½ inches for the back. Glue the back into the ¼-inch by ¼-inch rabbet you cut in the sides and back. When the glue has dried, nail the back in place with ½-inch, 20-gauge brads.

6. From ½-inch stock, cut three pieces 3 inches by 14 inches for the shelves. The shelves should be set 3 inches apart inside the rack. There should be 3¾ inches between the bottom of the bottom shelf and the bottom of the cabinet, and there should be 3¾ inches between the top of the top shelf and the top of the cabinet. After you've made these measurements on both sides of the cabinet, glue the shelves in place. When the glue dries, drive two 4d finishing nails through the sides of the rack into both ends of each shelf.

7. Use a compass to draw a 1-inch circle on a piece of cardboard. Cut out the circle and use it as a template to draw circles on the four corners of

the rack. Saw or plane the corners on these 1-inch-radius lines.

8. Round all exposed edges to a ¼-inch radius. This can be done with a router or you can pull a piece of sandpaper back and forth over each edge until it is rounded to your satisfaction.

9. From ¾-inch stock, cut four pieces 1⅛ inch by 13⁷/₁₆ inches for the side rails of the doors and four pieces 1⅛ inches by 7 inches for the top and bottom rails of the doors.

10. Cut half-lap rabbets in

the ends of the four top and bottom rails and the four side rails. Sound complicated? Not at all. The rails are supposed to overlap where they meet at the corners. Each rail has to be cut halfway through where they meet at the corners. Since each rail is 1⅛ inches wide, that's how wide each rabbet at the end of each rail should be. Since each rail is ¾ inch thick, each rabbet should be cut half that much, or ⅜ inch. Use a straight bit in a router, a dado head in a table or radial arm saw, or a backsaw

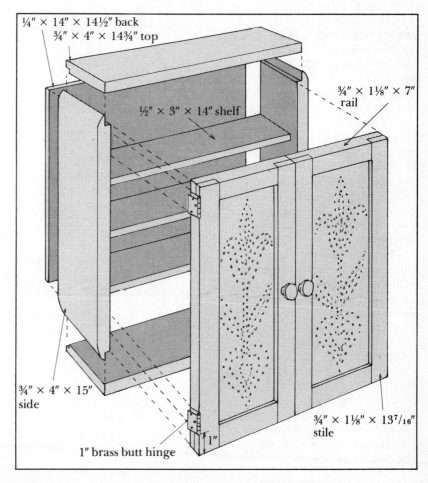

¼″ × 14″ × 14½″ back
¾″ × 4″ × 14¾″ top
½″ × 3″ × 14″ shelf
¾″ × 1⅛″ × 7″ rail
¾″ × 4″ × 15″ side
¾″ × 1⅛″ × 13⁷/₁₆″ stile
1″ brass butt hinge
1″

and chisel to cut the half laps.

11. Cut a ¼-inch by ¼-inch rabbet on the inside edge of all eight door rails.

12. Glue the four rails of each door together carefully, making sure they are square. You don't need clamps to do this, but corner clamps would help. It's important to remember that if you don't do it right the first time, the second time will be much harder.

13. Cut two pieces of tin 5¼ inch by 11⅝ inch for door panels.

14. Decorate the door panels. You can do this by tracing the design shown here, or by making up your own design. Once you have chosen a design you like, you can punch it in the tin, or paint it on the tin. Be as creative and original as you can.

15. From a ¼-inch by ¼-inch strip cut four pieces 5¼ inches long and four pieces 10⅞ inches long. Glue a tin panel into each doorframe. Glue the ¼-inch by ¼-inch strips into the rabbets to hold the tin panels in place on the inner edges of the two doorframes you have assembled.

16. The doors should be hung on four brass hinges, installed 1 inch from the top and 1 inch from the bottom of each side of the cabinet. If necessary, plane the doors to fit.

17. The two 1-inch-diameter knobs should be installed on the doors with the center of each knob 7 inches above the bottom of the cabinet.

18. Two magnetic catches should be installed at the top, in the center of the rack, to hold the two doors closed.

19. Sand all wooden parts of the cabinet and finish the wood with a finish of your choice, being careful not to let any of the wood finish dry on the tin panels.

Materials

Wood

1 pc. 1 × 6 × 6′ select pine or **Top and bottom:** 2 pcs. ¾″ × 4″ × 14¾″

Sides: 2 pcs. ¾″ × 4″ × 15″

1–2′ sq. sht. ¼″ A-C int. plywood or **Back:** 1 pc. 14″ × 14½″

1 pc. 1 × 4 × 4′ select pine or **Shelves:** 3 pcs. ½″ × 3″ × 14″

1 pc. 1 × 2 × 8′ select pine or **Side rails:** 4 pcs.
1 pc. 1 × 2 × 6′ select pine ¾″ × 1⅛″ × 13⁷/₁₆″

Top and bottom rails: 4 pcs. ¾″ × 1⅛″ × 7″

Retainer strips: 4 pcs. ¼″ × ¼″ × 5¼″
4 pcs. ¼″ × ¼″ × 10⅞″

Hardware
4d finishing nails
½″ 20-gauge brads
4–1″ brass butt hinges
2–1″ dia. wood knobs
2 magnetic catches

Miscellaneous
Glue
2 pcs. tin, each 5¼″ × 11⅝
Finish

Every cook has recipe cards. Sometimes they are kept in tin, store-bought file boxes. Sometimes they are tossed in a drawer, and sometimes they are stuck in the pages of cookbooks. There has to be a better way, you say, and indeed there is: this attractive wood recipe file. It has two compartments inside and an acrylic plastic cover on

Recipe File

the lid. The covered lid provides a convenient place to put cards so you can read them while you are working, and protects them from drips and spatter.

The box is designed with a sloped bottom to make the file easier to skim through. The lid also is sloped to better display the cards inside the plastic cover. The partition piece is a parallelogram, so some tricky measuring is involved. And plowing the angled grooves for the bottom make a table saw or radial arm saw pretty much a must; a router can't cut these grooves. The file box measures 12 inches by 4 inches and $5^5/_{16}$ inches tall. It was made mostly with $^3/_4$-inch pine, but other woods can be used. It can be made without the plastic card holder on the lid.

Construction

1. Cut three 12-inch pieces of 1 × 6. Resaw one into two $^1/_4$-inch-thick pieces. One of these will become the top of the file, the other the inside partition. But set these pieces aside for now.

2. To make the front of the box, rip one of the two remaining 12-inch pieces to a $4^1/_8$-inch width. To make the back of the box, rip the other piece to a 5-inch width. Cut a $^3/_4$-inch-wide by $^3/_8$-inch-deep rabbet on both ends of the front and back pieces.

3. For the joint that will later hold the center partition between the front and back pieces, cut a $^1/_4$-inch-wide by $^3/_8$-inch-deep dado following the vertical centers of the front and back.

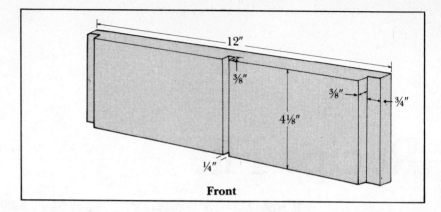

Front

You can use a router, or backsaw and chisel to make the dadoes.

4. Because of the slope of the top and bottom of the file box, a series of cuts must be made with either a radial arm or table saw with the blade set at a 15-degree angle.

a. Bevel the top edges of the front and back pieces to accommodate the slanted top of the file box. Make sure both are bevelled in the proper direction, slanted toward the front of the box.

b. Next, take the front piece (it's $4^1/_8$ inches wide) and plow a $^1/_4$-inch-wide by $^3/_8$-inch-deep groove the length of the piece, up $^1/_4$ inch from the bottom edge. Cut a similar groove on the back piece, but to set up the slanted bottom of the file box, this groove is $^3/_4$ inch up from the bottom. Be sure the grooves have the proper angle to them; the front piece should have the groove angled toward the bottom, the back piece should have the groove angled toward the top.

c. Take the $^1/_4$-inch-thick

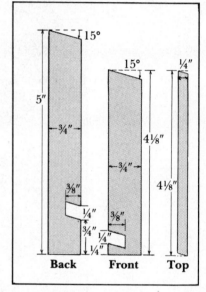

Back   **Front**   **Top**

piece that is the top of the file box, rip it to a 4 $^1/_8$-inch width and bevel both edges. Now you're done with the 15-degree cutting, so set the saw blade back to the square.

5. Cut a $3^1/_4$-inch by $10^1/_2$-inch piece of $^1/_4$-inch mahogany plywood for the bottom of the box.

6. Cut two 3 $^1/_4$-inch by 5-inch ends from the 1 × 6. Miter the top edge of each at a 15-degree slant. The easiest method to lay

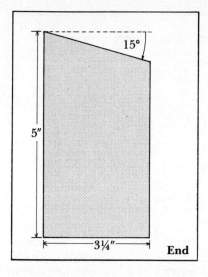

15°

5"

3¼"   **End**

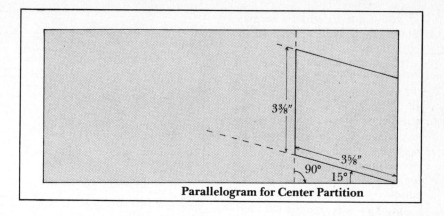

3⅜"

3⅝"

90°   15°

Parallelogram for Center Partition

out this angle is with a protractor.

7. Take the other piece of ¼-inch pine. This will be the center partition and must be laid out as a 15-degree parallelogram. This piece now measures 5½ inches by 12 inches. At the bottom corner of one end, use a protractor to raise a 15-degree angle from the bottom, or long edge. From the same corner, measure 3⅝ inches along this line and make a point. Next, use a try square to draw a line perpendicular to the long edge and passing through the point you just drew. From that intersection, measure 3⅜ inches up on the perpendicular line and make a second point. From this point, draw a line back to the first, or end edge, exactly parallel to the 15-degree line. You should now have a parallelogram. Cut out this piece.

8. Dry-fit your pieces together, cleaning up the inside of the dadoes and grooves if

needed. Glue all the pieces together and clamp the box together. You should now have a closed box with no openings.

9. To cut off the lid, use a band saw or backsaw. Measure 3½ inches up from the bottom edge, and cut straight through.

Sand the fresh cuts. Use a chisel to mortise for two brass butt hinges on the back piece and the back of the top assembly, and then install the hinges.

At this point you could round all the edges with a router, sand and finish a very fine recipe file.

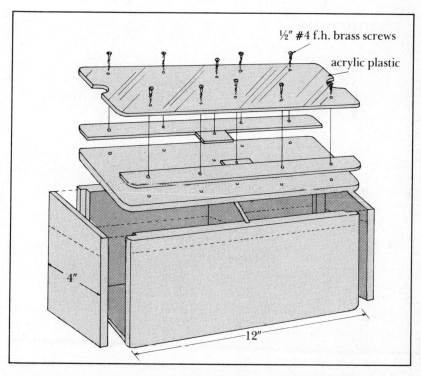

½" #4 f.h. brass screws

acrylic plastic

4"

12"

If you want to add the acrylic plastic card holder, your work continues.

10. From scraps of pine, cut two strips $^3/_{32}$ inch by $^1/_2$ inch by 12 inches and two strips $^3/_{32}$ inch by $^1/_2$ inch by 1¾ inches. Glue the long strips, or spacers, along the edges of the file box top, and center the shorter strips on their inside edges, exactly opposite each other, to act as card stops.

11. Cut a rectangle 4¼ inches by 12 inches from a piece of ⅛-inch acrylic plastic. (You can cut plastic as you would glass, except that you use a knife rather than a glass cutter to scribe the lines along which you want to break the material. Or, use any power saw with a fine-

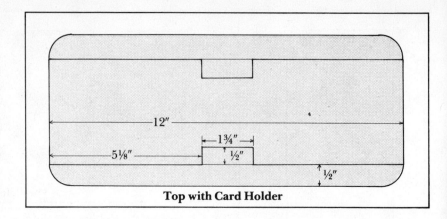

Top with Card Holder

tooth blade.) The plastic will be held to the $^3/_{32}$-inch-thick strips with eight ½-inch #4 flathead brass screws. Space, drill and countersink four holes along each edge of the plastic. Use the low speed on your drill.

To allow you to pull recipe cards out of the holder more easily, cut a ⅓-inch-radius semi-circle centered at each end.

12. Screw the acrylic plastic to your box top. Sand the edges flush with the edges of the box lid. Use very fine sandpaper and clean it up with a buffer.

13. Remove the acrylic plastic and sand and finish the entire box. Finally, remount the plastic cover.

Materials

Wood
1 pc. 1 × 6 × 4' select pine or **Top:** 1 pc. ¼" × 4⅛" × 12"
Partition: 1 pc. ¼" × 3½" × 4" (cut according to instructions)
Front: 1 pc. ¾" × 4⅛" × 12"
Back: 1 pc. ¾" × 5" × 12"
Ends: 2 pcs. ¾" × 3¼" × 5"
Spacers: 2 pcs. $^3/_{32}$" × ½" × 12"
Card stops: 2 pcs. $^3/_{32}$" × ½" × 1¾"

1–1" sq. sht. ¼" mahogany int. plywood or **Bottom:** 1 pc. 3¼" × 10½"

Hardware
2–1½" × ⅞" brass butt hinges
8–½" #4 f.h. brass screws

Miscellaneous
Glue
1–1' sq. sht. ⅛" acrylic plastic or 1 pc. 4¼" × 12"
Finish

Dish Drainer

A dish drainer is an item found in virtually every kitchen, and most often, it is a plastic-coated wire rack. But a unique touch can be added to your harvest kitchen by this easily made wooden dish drainer.

This is the perfect project for the complete novice. Making the drainer requires only common woodworking tools, some

relatively inexpensive materials and an evening's worth of your time.

The drainer shown was made of white pine and finished with a clear, waterproof varnish, but this is the sort of item that could easily be made of a durable, rot-resistant wood like redwood or cedar and left unvarnished.

Construction

1. From 1 × 2 select white pine, cut two 17¾-inch-long side rails and one 8-inch-long center rail. Cut three 8-inch-long stretchers from ½-inch dowel.

2. Lay out and drill holes for the stretchers in the three rails. The easiest way to drill the holes uniformly is to clamp all three pieces in a vise and drill all the holes at the same time. This way, you need only mark one side rail. Mark a center point for one hole at each end of the rail, ¾ inch from the end and ¾ inch from each edge. The center point for the third hole is ¾ inch from each edge and 7¼ inches from one end. Clamp the three pieces together with the center rail outside, not between, the side rails. Drill the three ½-inch-diameter holes. Clamp a scrap of wood with the rails so the drill bit doesn't split the wood as it breaks through.

3. Round all the edges of the rails with a ¼-inch rounding-off bit in a router. Sand the pieces well, including the stretchers, and assemble the drainer's framework. A stretcher is put through each set of holes, with a side rail at each extremity and the center rail midway between them.

4. The framework is locked together with 1-inch-long pins cut from ⅛-inch dowel. Turn the framework bottom up and drill ⅛-inch-diameter holes into the rails and through the stretchers. The holes can be a little more than 1 inch deep, but don't completely penetrate the rail or you'll spoil the appearance of the drainer. Put some glue on each pin and push it into place.

5. You must next lay out and drill holes for the 27 support

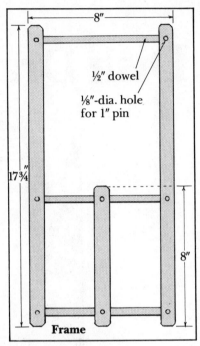

½" dowel

⅛"-dia. hole for 1" pin

Frame

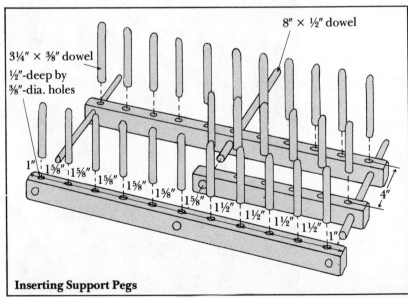

3¼" × ⅜" dowel
½"-deep by ⅜"-dia. holes

8" × ½" dowel

1"   1⅝"   1⅝"   1⅝"   1⅝"   1⅝"   1⅝"   1½"   1½"   1½"   1½"   1"

4"

Inserting Support Pegs

7¼"

½"-dia. hole

¾"   ¾"   ¾"

580   **Rails**

pegs that will hold the dishes. The center rail has five pegs, matched by five pegs in each side rail. These pegs are spaced on 1½-inch centers, beginning 1 inch from the end of the drainer framework. In addition to these pegs, each side rail has six other pegs, spaced on 1⅝-inch centers, beginning 1 inch from the opposite end of the drainer framework. The pegs are located on the centerline of the rails, that is, ⅜ inch from either edge. After marking for each peg hole, drill ½-inch-deep, ⅜-inch-diameter holes.

6. Cut 27 pieces of ⅜-inch dowel, each 3¼ inches long. Bevel the bottom of each peg so it will easily fit its hole, and round the top for appearance sake. Apply a tad of glue to the bottom of each peg and thrust it into place.

7. Finish the drainer with a coat of clear, waterproof varnish.

Materials

Wood

1 pc. 1 × 2 × 4′ select white pine or **Side rails:** 2 pcs. ¾″ × 1½″ × 17¾″
Center rail: 1 pc. ¾″ × 1½″ × 8″

1 pc. 36″ × ½″ dowel or **Stretchers:** 3 pcs. 8″ × ½″ dowel

1 pc. 36″ × ⅛″ dowel or **Frame pins:** 8 pcs. 1″ × ⅛″ dowel

3 pcs. 36″ × ⅜″ dowel or **Support pegs:** 27 pcs. 3¼″ × ⅜″ dowel

Miscellaneous
Waterproof glue
Waterproof varnish

Pot Rack

Here's a crafty way to display your kitchen finery and provide storage space for cookware within convenient reach of a busy cook: make this wooden pot rack.

Easy to build, the rack is designed to combine pots and pans together on the wall with their matching lids, so that if you need one, the other is right

there with it. The whole works will quickly enliven a vacant wall, and would be just the thing for areas with limited cabinet and storage space.

Not a lot of skill is required to make the rack. It's held together by glued lap joints and can be easily mounted using a few nails or wood screws. Several extra pegs have been sunk into the bottom member of the rack for pot holders, or if you like, mixing spoons or utensils.

Select white pine is the recommended material for this project; it's a soft wood, easy to work with, and it accepts staining.

Construction

1. To start with you'll need two pieces of 1 × 3 stock, each 40 inches long, and two more pieces just 18 inches long. The short ones are the sides; the others will be the top and bottom sections.

2. The final piece will be used across the center of the rack and eventually will support the lids. Since not all pots and pans are the same size, this member should be somewhat wider than the rest to accommodate different dowel locations. Use a 1 × 6 for this particular member, cutting it 40 inches long.

3. The only move resembling anything like work in this project is cutting the joints, and half-lap joints are really the simplest kind to cut, particularly where the ends of two members cross to form the corner of the framework. The waste can be removed using a backsaw and

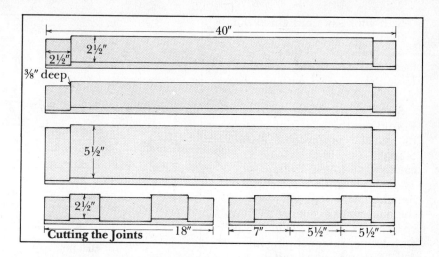

Cutting the Joints

chisel, a router or a circular saw.

a. It works to your advantage that all the pieces of wood are equally thick. Every end will therefore get the same treatment: a cut edge to edge, ⅜ inch deep and 2½ inches long. This is true too for the wider crossbar used across the center. Lay out the measurements and mark cut-lines on the ends of all five members. Take your time and cut carefully. Inac-

curacies, however slight, will weaken the final joint.

b. That brings us to the two T-laps where the center member joins the sides. These will be cut into each of the 18-inch vertical boards. What's most important here is that the cut start exactly 7 inches from the bottom of the rack. Carefully lay out the cutout 5½ inches long, ⅜ inch deep and the width of the board, make the crosscuts

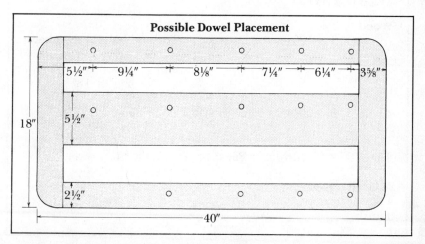

Possible Dowel Placement

583

with your saw, and chisel out the waste.

4. Sand down all the new surfaces and dry-fit the assembly. If you're satisfied with the fit, glue it together.

5. Now for the corners. Rounding them off gives the rack a real professional touch. Start at the inside corner on each of the four corners. Use it as a midpoint for a circle with a 3-inch radius. This will give you the guidelines to cut off all four corners exactly the same way with a saber saw or coping saw.

6. Put a $^5/_{16}$-inch bit in the drill. But before drilling any holes, you'd better fetch the pots, pans and lids you intend to use so you can place the dowels where they will do the most good. The top and middle crossbars each get five holes, all of them $^5/_8$ inch deep. Remember the dowel spacing on the center section must be adjusted so the lids are centered

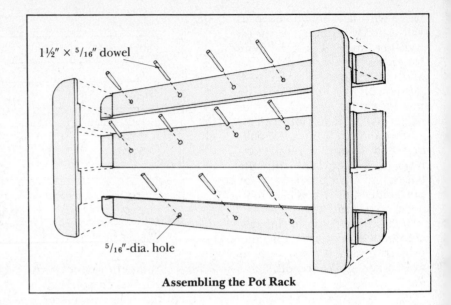

1½″ × $^5/_{16}$″ dowel

$^5/_{16}$″-dia. hole

Assembling the Pot Rack

within the pots covering them. The four dowels along the bottom member are for pot holders.

7. After drilling the holes, cut 14 pieces of $^5/_{16}$-inch dowel 1½ inches long. Round off the

ends of the pegs with sandpaper, then glue one in each hole.

8. After a complete sanding, the rack can be finished with your choice of finish.

Materials

Wood

1 pc. 1 × 3 × 10′ select white pine or **Top and bottom members:**
2 pcs. ¾″ × 2½″ × 40″
Sides: 2 pcs.
¾″ × 2½″ × 18″

1 pc. 1 × 6 × 4′ select white pine or **Center member:** 1 pc.
¾″ × 5½″ × 40″

1 pc. 36″ × $^5/_{16}$″ dowel or **Pegs:** 14 pcs. 1½″ × $^5/_{16}$″ dowel

Miscellaneous
Glue
Finish

Cabinet Drying Rack

When was the last time you saw a folding, wooden drying rack crouched in the middle of somebody's kitchen or laundry room? Not especially interesting or attractive, would you say? But it's pretty handy.

Here is a new design patterned after the old idea; a cabinet-cum-drying rack that doesn't crouch on the floor and

get in the way and looks good either in the bathroom or kitchen. It makes a great towel rack or drying rack for herbs, and the extra cabinet space behind the doors can hold soap or spices or whatever you like.

Cherry was used to make the cabinet, but any kind of wood will suffice. Hardwood is probably the best choice though, unless you are planning to paint the cabinet, simply because it is better looking than pine or fir. Make the rack first, then the cabinet frame and back, and finally the doors.

Construction

1. Cut and prepare the pieces for the collapsible drying rack:

   a. Cut ten 18-inch pieces of ½-inch or ⅜-inch dowel. If ½-inch dowels are selected, use a ¼-inch bit to drill a hole ⅜ inch deep and 1 inch from each end of all ten pieces as shown. If ⅜-inch dowels are selected, use a $^{3}/_{16}$-inch bit to drill a hole ¼ inch deep and ⅞ inch from each end of all ten pieces.

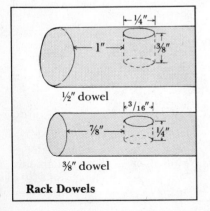

Rack Dowels

(labels: ¼″, 1″, ⅜″, ½″ dowel, $^{3}/_{16}$″, ⅞″, ¼″, ⅜″ dowel)

   b. From ¾-inch hardwood, cut 12 pieces measuring ⅜ inch by 12 inches, and 4 pieces measuring ⅜ inch by 6½ inches for the drying rack frame. If ½-inch dowels are to be used for drying racks, drill $^{9}/_{16}$-inch holes $^{25}/_{36}$ inch from each end of all 16 frame pieces. If ⅜-inch dowels are to be used, drill $^{7}/_{16}$-inch

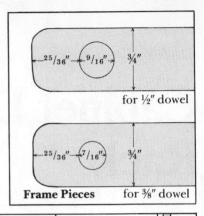

(labels: $^{25}/_{36}$″, $^{9}/_{16}$″, ¾″, for ½″ dowel; $^{25}/_{36}$″, $^{7}/_{16}$″, ¾″)

Frame Pieces   for ⅜″ dowel

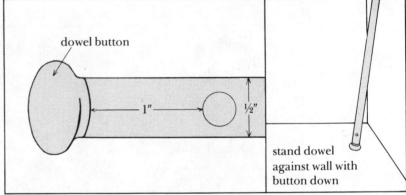

dowel button

1″   ½″

stand dowel against wall with button down

holes. Round off all corners and edges, and sand to a smooth finish.

   c. On one end of each 18-inch dowel, glue a ½-inch or ⅜-inch dowel button as shown. Stand the rods upside down against a wall until the glue has dried. (Brass screws and washers may be substituted, if desired.)

   d. Assemble four of the frame pieces and the ten dowel rods as shown. Then, in the opposite direction, slide four more frame pieces onto the dowel rods at each position indicated by the dotted lines. Slide four more frame

pieces onto the dowels to match the first four installed, then slide the final four on to match the second four installed. Then glue the remaining dowel buttons to the ends of the rods. When the glue has dried, if ½-inch dowels were used, cut twenty ½-inch pieces from a ¼-inch dowel; if ⅜-inch dowels were used, cut twenty ⅜-inch pieces from a $^{3}/_{16}$-inch dowel, and glue them into place as shown to keep the frame sections in position. The holes left vacant are to accommodate the dowel and pins that will secure the rack to the cabinet.

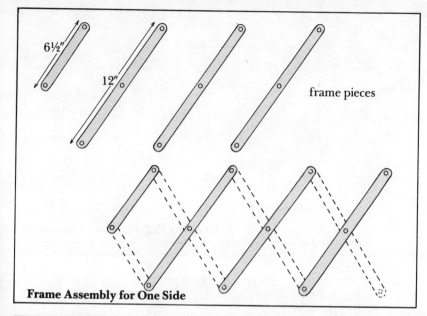

6½"

12"

frame pieces

Frame Assembly for One Side

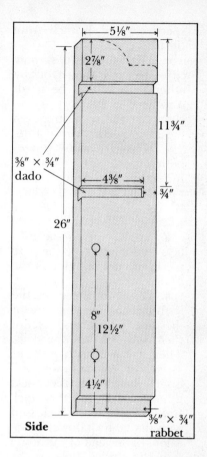

5⅛"

2⅞"

11¾"

⅜" × ¾"
dado

4⅜"

¾"

26"

8"

12½"

4½"

Side

⅜" × ¾"
rabbet

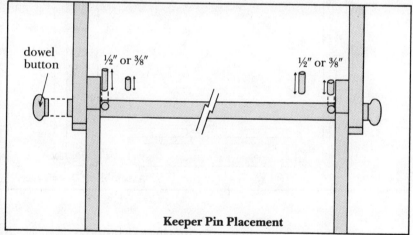

dowel
button

½" or ⅜"

½" or ⅜"

Keeper Pin Placement

2. Cut and prepare the pieces for the sides, top, bottom and shelf:

a. Cut two pieces, each measuring ¾ inch by 5⅛ inches by 26 inches for the sides.

b. Cut two pieces, each measuring ¾ inch by 5⅛ inches by 20 inches for the top and bottom.

c. Cut one piece measuring ¾ inch by 3⅞ inches by 20 inches for the shelf.

d. Sand all pieces to a smooth finish.

3. Prepare both side pieces as follows:

a. Measure 2⅞ inches down from the top and cut a ⅜-inch deep by ¾-inch wide dado from the front to the back edge.

b. Measure 11¾ inches down from the top and cut a ⅜-inch deep by ¾-inch wide blind dado from the back edge to within ⅞ inch of the front edge. Use a chisel to finish the cut to ¾ inch from the front edge.

c. Cut a ⅜-inch deep by ¾-inch wide rabbet from the inside bottom edge.

d. Drill two ½-inch-deep, ½-inch- or ⅜-inch-diameter holes, 4½ inches and 12½ inches from the bottom re- **587**

spectively and 7/8 inch from the back edge.

e. The top edges may either be cut as shown, or any other pattern may be used. Another possibility is to eliminate the projecting top pieces altogether by cutting 2⅞ inches from the top of both side pieces; then cut a ⅜-inch deep by ¾-inch wide rabbet on the top inside edges.

4. Assemble the cabinet frame:

a. Apply glue to the rabbets and dadoes in the side pieces; do not put glue in the drilled holes.

b. Fit the top piece and the shelf into the dadoes in one of the side pieces, and secure them with 4d finishing nails. Then, cut a 20-inch piece of ½-inch or ⅜-inch dowel, and insert it through the back, upper holes in the rack frame. Collapse the rack, and with the 20-inch dowel in position, fit one end of the dowel into the drilled hole in the side piece. Then fit the other side piece into position and secure it to the top piece and shelf with 4d finishing nails.

c. Fit the bottom piece into the prepared rabbets and secure the sides to the bottom piece with 4d finishing nails.

5. Cut two 3-inch pieces of ½-inch dowel to be used as removable pins to position the rack. Simply insert the dowels through the holes in the lower rack members and into the holes in the sides of the cabinet to position the rack for use, or remove the pins to fold the rack into the cabinet.

588 **6.** Using a router and a

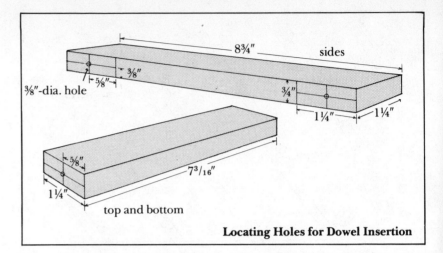

Locating Holes for Dowel Insertion

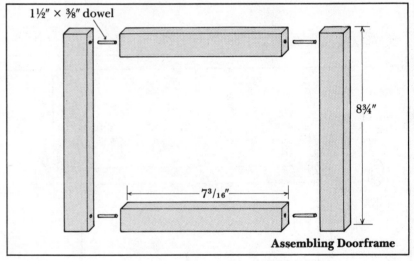

Assembling Doorframe

¼-inch rabbeting bit, cut a ¼-inch-deep by ¼-inch-wide rabbet around the inside perimeter of the back of the cabinet. Square off the corners with a chisel.

7. Cut one piece of mahogany plywood measuring 19¾ inches by 22⅛ inches for the back of the cabinet. Set it into the prepared rabbet and fasten with glue and ¾-inch brads.

8. Cut and prepare the pieces

for the doorframes:

a. Cut four pieces measuring ¾ inch by 1¼ inches by 8¾ inches for sides.

b. Cut four pieces measuring ¾ inch by 1¼ inches by 7³/₁₆ inches for tops and bottoms.

c. Sand all pieces to smooth finish.

d. Mark each joint as shown. Use a doweling jig, if possible, and use a ⅜-inch bit

Materials

Wood

6 pcs. 36″ × ½″ dowel or **Rack:** 10 pcs. 18″ × ½″ dowel
Rack support: 1 pc. 20″ × ½″ dowel
Removable pins: 2 pcs. 3″ × ½″ dowel

1 pc. ⁴/₄ × 4″ × 2′ FAS cherry or **Rack frame:** 12 pcs. ¾″ × ⅜″ × 12″
4 pcs. ¾″ × ⅜″ × 6½″

20 pcs. ½″ dowel buttons or **Dowel end keepers:** 20 pcs. ½″ dowel buttons

1 pc. 36″ × ¼″ dowel or **Keeper pins:** 20 pcs. ½″ × ¼″ dowel

1 pc. ⁴/₄ × 6″ × 8′ FAS cherry or **Sides:** 2 pcs. ¾″ × 5⅛″ × 26″
Top and bottom: 2 pcs. ¾″ × 5⅛″ × 20″

1 pc. ⁴/₄ × 5″ × 4′ FAS cherry or **Shelf:** 1 pc. ¾″ × 3⅞″ × 20″
Door panels: 2 pcs. ¼″ × 6¾″ × 7⅝″

1–2′ sq. sht. ¼″ mahogany int. plywood or **Back:** 1 pc. 19¾″ × 22⅛″

1 pc. ¾″ × 2″ × 6′ cherry or **Doorframes:** 4 pcs. ¾″ × 1¼″ × 8¾″
4 pcs. ¾″ × 1¼″ × 7⅛″

1 pc. 36″ × ⅜″ dowel or **Doorframe supports:** 8 pcs. 1½″ × ⅜″ dowel

Hardware
4d finishing nails
¾″ brads
⅝″ brads
2 pr. 1″ × ¾″ hinges
2–¾″ door pulls
2 magnetic catches

Miscellaneous
Glue
Wood filler
Finish

to drill a hole ⅞ inch deep at each line intersection on all pieces.

e. Cut eight pieces of 1½-inch by ⅜-inch dowel. Glue and dowel each joint and clamp the frames together as shown.

f. After the glue has dried, remove the excess and sand to a smooth finish. Using a router and a ¼-inch rabbeting bit, cut a ¼-inch deep by ¼-inch wide rabbet around the inside perimeter of both doorframes to accommodate the door panels. Square off the corners with a chisel.

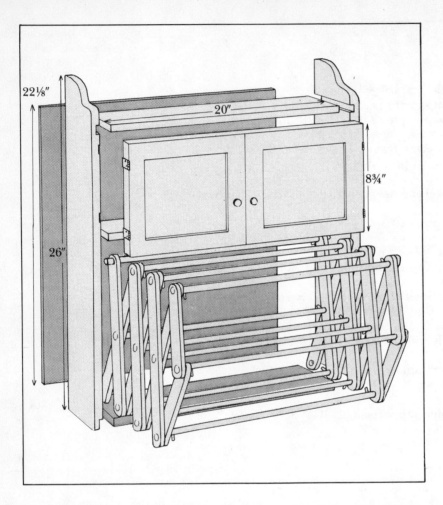

g. Using a router and a quarter-round bit, shape the inside perimeter of the front of both doorframes.

9. Fabricate two pieces measuring ¼ inch by 6¾ inches by 7⅝ inches for door panels. The wood used to make the cabinet may be planed to ¼ inch, then narrow strips of it glued up edge-to-edge to make pieces of the required width. Fasten the panels to the frame with glue and ⅝-inch brads.

10. Mortise the hinges into the doors and the sides of the cabinet so that the hinge plates are flush with the surrounding surface. You may have to plane the edges of the doors to get the desired fit. Countersink all nail heads and fill the holes with wood filler of the appropriate color. Sand the entire unit to a smooth finish and apply several coats of oil, varnish or whatever finish is desired. When the final coat is dry, attach the door pulls and magnetic catches.

Food Dryer

Drying is an increasingly popular way to preserve foods. There are lots of ways to do it, ranging from setting trays of food out in the sun to heating trays of food in a slow oven. There are also many commercial food dryers on the market.

But here's an easily made food dryer that doubles as a yogurt maker-cum-proofing

591

box. And if you've got a wood-burning stove with a 12-inch by 18-inch flat spot on top, you can capture the heat in a special base unit and eliminate the need for electricity to dry your foods.

The system consists of a base unit that either collects or generates the heat, drying racks that stack one atop another and a lid. In the electric model, heat is generated by three light bulbs controlled by an ordinary dimmer switch. By varying the wattage of bulbs used and by adjusting the dimmer, you can control the heat. A probe thermometer can be inserted in the lid to measure the heat actually being generated.

You can stack as many racks atop the base as you like, within reason, of course. It's a good idea to restack the racks periodically during the drying process, rotating them to ensure that the food will dry uniformly.

An accessory for the system is a special box—it fits atop the base and under the lid—that can hold a small bowl of yogurt or dough. The same slow, gentle heat that dries your foods can culture your yogurt or prompt the dough to rise.

The dryer can be constructed with common woodworking tools and common lumberyard materials. The racks have fiberglass screening so foods aren't tainted. It is better not to put a finish on the wood because of the heat the unit runs on.

Construction (Stove-Top Base Unit)

1. The basic parts of the unit are four pieces of 1 × 6. Cut

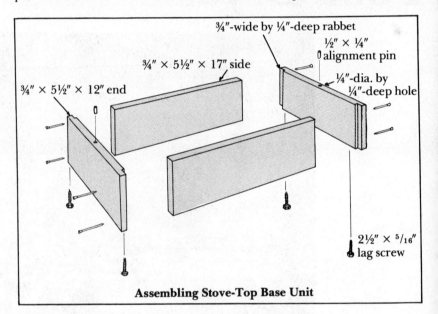

¾"-wide by ¼"-deep rabbet

¾" × 5½" × 17" side

¾" × 5½" × 12" end

½" × ¼" alignment pin

¼"-dia. by ¼"-deep hole

2½" × ⁵⁄₁₆" lag screw

Assembling Stove-Top Base Unit

two 12-inch ends and two 17-inch sides from a length of 1 × 6.

2. Cut a ¾-inch-wide by ¼-inch-deep rabbet each end of both end pieces.

3. Glue and nail the four pieces together.

4. Drill a ¼-inch-diameter, ¼-inch-deep hole for alignment pins centered on the top of each end, ½ inch from the outside edge. Drill a ¼-inch-diameter hole 2 inches deep into the bottom edge at each corner for a

Materials (Stove-Top Base Unit)

Wood
1 pc. 1 × 6 × 6' select pine or **Ends:** 2 pcs. ¾" × 5½" × 12"
Sides: 2 pcs. ¾" × 5½" × 17"

1 pc. 36" × ¼" dowel or **Alignment pins:** 2 pcs. ½" × ¼" dowel

Hardware
6d finishing nails
4–2½" × ⁵⁄₁₆" lag screws

Miscellaneous
Glue

foot screw. Cut two ½-inch
lengths of ¼-inch dowel, round
one end of each and glue one in
each of the holes for the alignment pins with the rounded end
protruding. Turn a 2½-inch by
⁵/₁₆-inch lag screw into each
corner hole. These screws are
the feet; turning them in and
out of their holes adjusts the
unit's height.

Construction (Light Bulb Base Unit)

1. The shell for the light bulb
dryer is constructed from two
12-inch ends and two 17-inch
sides cut from 1 × 6. Cut a
¾-inch-wide by ¼-inch-deep
rabbet across each end of both
end pieces. Then plow a ¼-inch
by ¼-inch rabbet along both top
and bottom inside edges of all
four pieces. The ends will have
all rabbets in the same face.

2. The light dimmer control
is installed in a hole cut in one
end piece. The hole measures
1¾ inches by 3 inches. The top
of this hole is 1½ inches from
the top edge and the vertical centerline is 2¼ inches from the
end. After laying out the hole,
drill a hole in each corner and
cut out the waste wood with a
coping saw or saber saw.

3. Glue and nail the four
pieces together, using 6d finishing nails.

4. Cut an 11-inch by 17-inch
piece of ¼-inch plywood for the
bottom. Lay out a series of
½-inch holes in a grid on the
plywood. Place them on 1½-
inch centers, about 1¹/₁₆ inches

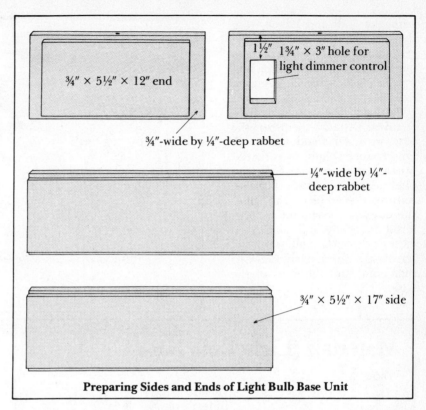

¾" × 5½" × 12" end

1½"   1¾" × 3" hole for light dimmer control

¾"-wide by ¼"-deep rabbet

¼"-wide by ¼"-deep rabbet

¾" × 5½" × 17" side

Preparing Sides and Ends of Light Bulb Base Unit

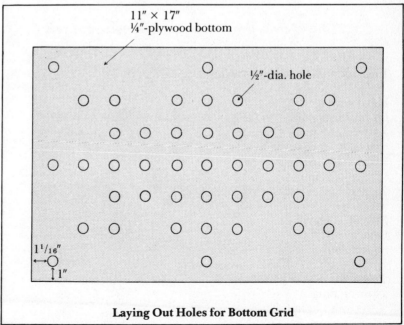

11" × 17" ¼"-plywood bottom

½"-dia. hole

1¹/₁₆"

1"

Laying Out Holes for Bottom Grid

from the ends and 1 inch from the sides. After marking the centers for the holes, drill them out. Then glue and nail the bottom in place, using 2d common nails.

5. Install the porcelain light fixtures. Attach them to the base with #6 wood screws. A lone fixture should be centered horizontally and vertically on one side, while the other two fixtures should be on the opposite side. They should be centered vertically and placed on either side of the point opposite the first bulb, midway between that point and the ends of the base.

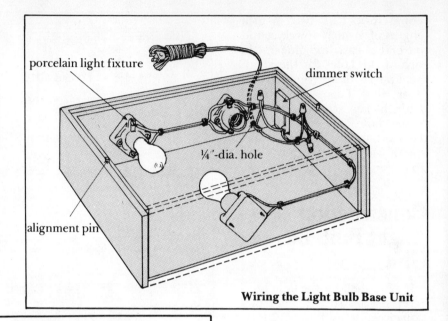

porcelain light fixture

dimmer switch

¼"-dia. hole

alignment pin

Wiring the Light Bulb Base Unit

Materials (Light Bulb Base Unit)

Wood
1 pc. 1 × 6 × 6′ select pine or **Ends:** 2 pcs. ¾″ × 5½″ × 12″
                                            Sides: 2 pcs. ¾″ × 5½″ × 17″

1–1′ × 2′ sht. ¼″ mahogany int. plywood or **Bottom:** 1 pc.
                                             11″ × 17″

1 pc. 36″ × ¼″ dowel or **Alignment pins:** 2 pcs. ½″ × ¼″ dowel

Hardware
6d finishing nails
2d common nails
6–1¼″ #6 screws
Insulated wire staples
½″ dia. tack glides
1 pc. 11″ × 17″ expanded sheet steel

Miscellaneous
Glue
3 porcelain-base light fixtures
1 solid-state on-off dial dimmer switch
12″ #16 two-wire lamp cord
2-prong plug
3–100-watt light bulbs

6. Install the dimmer switch and wire it to the light fixtures as shown. Drill a ¼-inch hole through the side near the dimmer switch for the power cord. Run the cord through the hole and wire it to the dimmer switch.

7. For alignment pins, drill a ¼-inch-diameter, ¼-inch-deep hole in the center of the top edge of each end, ½ inch from the outside edge. Cut two ½-inch pieces of ¼-inch dowel, round one end of each and glue one in each hole with the rounded end protruding.

8. Install a tack glide at each bottom corner.

9. Cut an 11-inch by 17-inch piece of expanded sheet steel for a heat diffuser. After screwing light bulbs into the fixtures, drop the diffuser in its rabbeted recess.

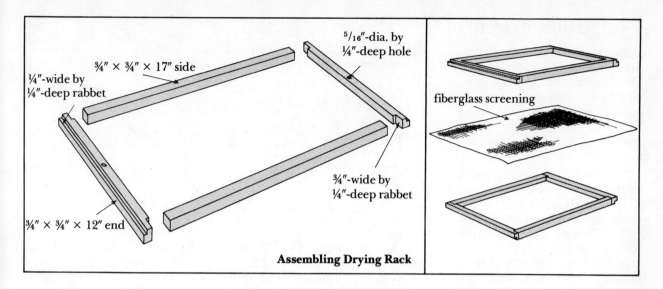

¾" × ¾" × 17" side

⁵⁄₁₆"-dia. by ¼"-deep hole

¼"-wide by ¼"-deep rabbet

¾"-wide by ¼"-deep rabbet

¾" × ¾" × 12" end

fiberglass screening

Assembling Drying Rack

Construction (Drying Rack)

1. The drying rack is constructed by sandwiching a piece of screening between two rectangular frames. The frames are fabricated of ¾-inch by ¾-inch stock. Cut four 12-inch pieces of the material for the ends and four 17-inch pieces for the sides.

2. Cut a ¼-inch by ¼-inch rabbet along one edge of each end piece. Then cut a ¾-inch-wide by ¼-inch-deep rabbet across each end of the end pieces. These rabbets should be perpendicular to the edge rabbet and through the opposite face.

3. Glue and nail the two frame assemblies together. When the glue is dry, lay out one frame with the edge rabbets down and stretch fiberglass screening over it. After stapling the screening fast, lay the sec-ond frame atop the first with edge rabbets up and nail the two together. Finally, trim the screening.

4. Drill a ⁵⁄₁₆-inch-diameter, ¼-inch-deep hole in the center of the bottom edge of each frame end, ½ inch from the outside edge. These are for the alignment pins of the component below to fit into. Turn the frame over and drill a ¼-inch-diameter, ¼-inch-deep hole in the center of the top edge of each end, ½ inch from the outside edge. Cut two ½-inch pieces of ¼-inch dowel, round one end of each, and glue one in each hole, the rounded end protruding. These are the alignment pins for the rack above, or the lid, to fit onto.

Materials (Drying Rack)

Wood
1 pc. 1 × 1 × 10' select pine or **Ends:** 4 pcs. ¾" × ¾" × 12"
Sides: 4 pcs. ¾" × ¾" × 17"

1 pc. 36" × ¼" dowel or **Alignment pins:** 2 pcs. ½" × ¼" dowel

Hardware
3d finishing nails
½" staples

Miscellaneous
Glue
Fiberglass screening

Construction (Lid)

1. The lid is constructed by putting a perforated plywood panel inside a frame made of ¾-inch by 1¼-inch stock. Begin by cutting two 12-inch end pieces and two 17-inch side pieces from the ¾-inch by 1¼-inch material.

2. Take up the two end pieces and mark one face on each piece as being the outside and the opposite face as the inside. Cut a ¼-inch by ¼-inch rabbet along the bottom outside edge of each end. Then cut a ¾-inch-wide by ¼-inch-deep rabbet across the inside end of each end piece. Finally, plow a ¼-inch-wide by ¼-inch-deep groove along the inside face of each end piece, ¼ inch from the top edge.

3. Plow a ¼-inch-wide by ¼-inch-deep groove along one face of each side piece, ¼ inch from the edge. The groove will be on the top inside face of the pieces.

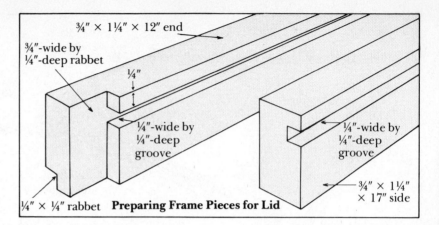

Preparing Frame Pieces for Lid

¾″ × 1¼″ × 12″ end
¾″-wide by ¼″-deep rabbet
¼″
¼″-wide by ¼″-deep groove
¼″ × ¼″ rabbet
¼″-wide by ¼″-deep groove
¾″ × 1¼″ × 17″ side

4. Cut an 11-inch by 17-inch panel from ¼-inch plywood for the top. Lay out a series of ⅜-inch holes in a grid on the plywood. Place them on 1½-inch centers, beginning about 1¹/₁₆ inches from the ends and 1 inch from the sides. Drill the holes.

5. Assemble the lid with glue and nails.

6. Turn the lid upside down, that is, with the edge rabbet up, and drill a ⁵/₁₆-inch-diameter, ¼-inch-deep hole for the alignment pins in the center of the bottom edge of each end, ½ inch from the outside edge.

Optional: Drill a ¼-inch-diameter hole through the center of one side for a probe thermometer to be inserted.

Construction (Yogurt Maker)

1. The yogurt maker is essentially a box made of 1 × 6 with an open top and a series of dowels forming a rack across the bottom. To begin construction, cut two 12-inch ends and two 17-inch sides from 1 × 6.

2. Cut a ¾-inch-wide by ¼-inch-deep rabbet across each end of each end piece. Turn the pieces over and plow a ½-inch-wide by ¼-inch-deep rabbet along one edge, which will be the bottom outside edge.

3. Lay out and drill seven ¼-inch-diameter, ⅜-inch-deep holes on the inside face of each side for the dowels. The holes should be spaced on 2-inch centers beginning at the centerline and on a line ⅜ inch from the bottom edge.

Materials (Lid)

Wood

1 pc. 1 × 2 × 6′ select pine or **Ends:** 2 pcs. ¾″ × 1¼″ × 12″
      Sides: 2 pcs. ¾″ × 1¼″ × 17″

1–1′ × 2′ sht. ¼″ mahogany int. plywood or **Top:** 1 pc. 11″ × 17″

Hardware

4d finishing nails

Miscellaneous

Glue

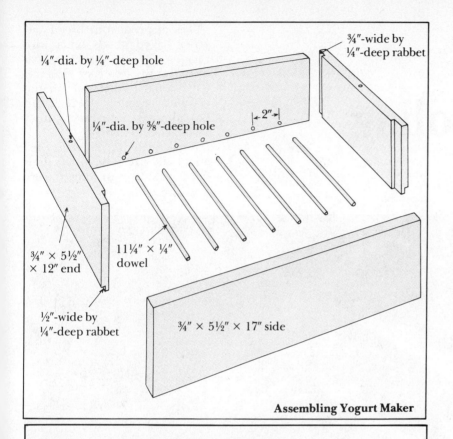

¼"-dia. by ¼"-deep hole

¾"-wide by
¼"-deep rabbet

¼"-dia. by ⅜"-deep hole

|←2"→|

¾" × 5½"
× 12" end

11¼" × ¼"
dowel

½"-wide by
¼"-deep rabbet

¾" × 5½" × 17" side

Assembling Yogurt Maker

4. Cut seven 11¼-inch lengths of ¼-inch dowel for the support rods.

5. Assemble the sides, ends and support rods with glue. Nail the ends to the sides.

6. Drill a ⁵⁄₁₆-inch-diameter, ¼-inch-deep hole in the center of the bottom edge of each end, ½ inch from the outside edge. These are for the alignment pins for the component below to fit into. Turn the box over and drill a ¼-inch-diameter, ¼-inch-deep hole for an alignment pin in the center of the top edge of each end, ½ inch from the outside edge. Cut two ½-inch lengths of ¼-inch dowel, round one end and glue one in each hole with the rounded end protruding.

Materials (Yogurt Maker)

Wood
1 pc. 1 × 6 × 6′ select pine or **Ends:** 2 pcs. ¾" × 5½" × 12"
Sides: 2 pcs. ¾" × 5½" × 17"

3 pcs. 36" × ¼" dowel or **Support rods:** 7 pcs. 11¼" × ¼" dowel
Alignment pins: 2 pcs. ½" × ¼" dowel

Hardware
6d finishing nails

Miscellaneous
Glue

Bread Cooling Rack

You can cool your bread and other baked goods on a wire rack you buy. But here's a beautiful wooden rack that you will want to keep out on the counter, or hang where it can be admired with your other kitchen equipment.

This rack can be made just about any size. The instructions here include a drilling fixture

that you make from scrap wood. It's just a three-sided box that will allow you to drill the holes in both side pieces at the same time and thus get them exactly lined up. Of course, you can measure and drill your holes without it, but once you make the drilling fixture, you will be able to make many side pieces in a short time, so it will be no great amount of additional work to turn out racks for gifts.

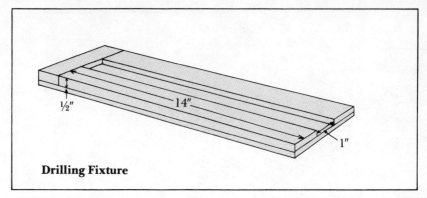

Drilling Fixture

Construction

1. Use any wood to make the drilling fixture. The bottom can be plywood. The sides must be at least ½ inch high. The inside dimensions should be 1 inch by 14 inches. Leave one of the ends open. After gluing the bottom and sides together, mark a centerline the length of the box. Starting at the closed end, make 13 marks at 1-inch intervals, and center-punch each point. Then, drill through the board at each point with a $^5/_{16}$-inch bit. The drilling fixture now is ready for use.

2. Cut two pieces of soft maple ¾ inch by 1 inch by 14 inches for the sides of the rack. Place the drilling fixture over one piece of the maple, making sure it is snug against the closed end. Drill the 13 holes, each $^5/_{16}$ inch in diameter, in the side, making each only ⅜ inch deep. Adjust the depth stop on your drill press, if you have one. If you are using a hand drill, use the depth guide offered as an accessory by manufacturers. Or, if you feel you have a steady hand, make a mark on the bit with paint or nail polish, and be

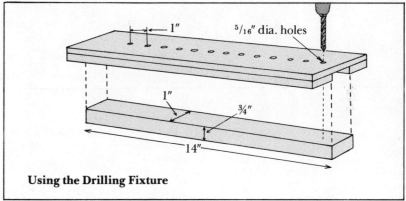

Using the Drilling Fixture

careful. Drill the holes in the second side in the same manner.

3. Rout a ¼-inch radius on all the edges of your side pieces, or, if you prefer, just break the edges with sandpaper.

4. Cut 13 pieces of $^5/_{16}$-inch dowel. You can make them any length you want, but this rack used 8¾-inch lengths.

Materials

Wood

1 pc. $^4/_4$ × 3″ × 2′ FAS soft maple or **Sides:** 2 pcs. ¾″ × 1″ × 14″

4 pcs. 36″ × $^5/_{16}$″ dowel or **Rods:** 13 pcs. 8¾″ × $^5/_{16}$″ dowel

Miscellaneous
Glue
Finish

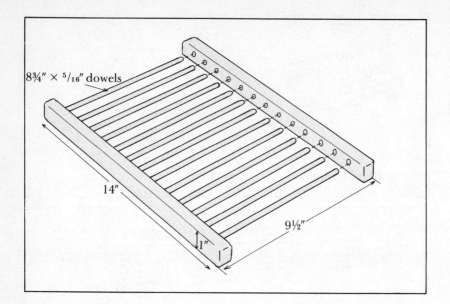

8¾" × ⁵/₁₆" dowels

14"

1"

9½"

5. Sand the dowels and side pieces. Put a drop of glue in each hole and insert the dowels. True-up the assembly on a flat surface and let it dry. Finally, finish your rack with clear Deft or a comparable finish.

Bread Slicing Guide

Everyone who bakes bread has faced the problem: how to slice a nice even slab from the loaf. A sharp knife and a steady hand help, but this bread slicing guide will help even more. You merely put the loaf on the cutting board against the side, slide the adjustable guide against the loaf, drop the knife in the guide slots and saw away.

The result is a straight and even slice every time.

This guide is not available in stores. You can only have one if you make it. And making it is as easy as slicing warm bread.

Construction

1. Begin work by preparing the cutting board base. If you have a single piece of soft maple or other hardwood that measures 1¼ inches by 7¼ inches by 16 inches, the work merely involves dressing the faces and edges and squaring the ends. If you haven't a single piece of suitable size, you'll have to glue up strips of wood edge to edge to make the base. Rip seven 1¼-inch by 1⅛-inch by 16-inch pieces of soft maple. Glue up the strips and clamp them with bar clamps. When dry, crosscut both ends, removing just enough stock to square the panel, and rip it to the 7¼-inch width.

2. To accommodate the movable slicing guide piece, use your router with a dovetail bit to cut a ½-inch-deep by 1¾-inch-wide dovetail groove across the base. The center of the dovetail should be 5⁹⁄₁₆ inches from one end.

3. Use a ½-inch by 3-inch by 7¼-inch piece of soft maple to make the slide. Rough-cut the piece with a saw, trying to approximate, if not duplicate, the angle of the dovetail slot's sides. Using a block plane, carefully trim the slide until it slides smoothly inside the dovetail groove. Don't make it too loose, however. Drill two ⁷⁄₁₆-inch holes, centered 1 inch from one end of the slide and ½ inch

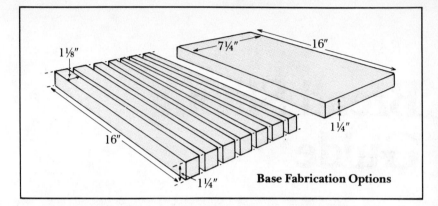

Base Fabrication Options

apart, to accept the guide dowels. Cut two 6-inch pieces of ⁷⁄₁₆-inch dowel, round one end of each and glue them in the holes, rounded ends up.

4. Cut a 6-inch by 15-inch piece from ¾-inch soft maple for the side of the slicing frame. Cut a 1-inch radius on both corners of what will be the top edge. Then, crosscut this piece in two, 5 inches from one end.

5. Glue the two sections of

the side on top of the base. The edges of the side pieces are glued atop the base so that the backs of the side pieces are flush with the edge of the base. Leave a ⅛-inch space between the two, and center this space over the dovetail slide. After the glue dries, strengthen the assembly by drilling four ¼-inch holes, two in each section, through the base and 3 inches deep into the back pieces. Cut four 3-inch

Materials

Wood

1 pc. ⁶⁄₄ × 6″ × 3′ FAS soft maple or **Base:** 7 pcs.
1¼″ × 1⅛″ × 16″

1 pc. ⁴⁄₄ × 6″ × 2′ FAS soft maple or **Slide:** 1 pc. ½″ × 3″ × 7¼″
Side: 1 pc. ¾″ × 6″ × 15″

1 pc. 36″ × ⁷⁄₁₆″ dowel or **Guide dowels:** 2 pcs. 6″ × ⁷⁄₁₆″ dowel

1 pc. 36″ × ¼″ dowel or **Dowels:** 4 pcs. 3″ × ¼″ dowel

Miscellaneous
Glue
Varnish or vegetable oil

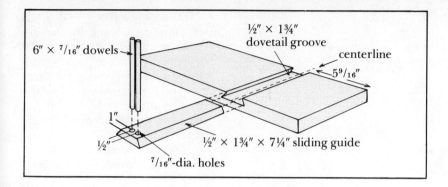

6" × $^7/_{16}$" dowels

$^1/_2$" × 1$^3/_4$" dovetail groove

centerline

5$^9/_{16}$"

1"

$^1/_2$"

$^7/_{16}$"-dia. holes

$^1/_2$" × 1$^3/_4$" × 7$^1/_4$" sliding guide

pieces of $^1/_4$-inch dowel. Put a little glue on each and drive one into each hole.

6. Round all the edges with a rounding-off bit in a router, and sand all the surfaces. Finally, finish with varnish or vegetable oil.

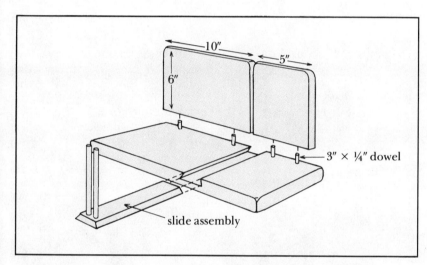

10"

5"

6"

3" × $^1/_4$" dowel

slide assembly

Bread Box

It used to be that one day was set aside each week for baking the bread. The loaves were placed in specially made boxes and stored in a cool place. But there were no preservatives to fool the tongue, and by the middle of the week the bread would begin to get stale.

Today, the coldest place in the house is usually the freezer,

which is also the best place to store loaves of bread that will not be eaten in about three days. People who bake their own bread either bake more than once a week or freeze the extra loaves.

But there is something to be said for the traditional—and there is no doubt something alluring about making a bread box in which to store one's daily bread.

Almost any kind of wood will serve for this counter-top bread box. The materials list calls for common lumberyard pine, but the bread box shown was crafted of cherry. If you do use a hardwood, like cherry, you may have to glue strips of board edge to edge to get the required widths. Do the front, back and sides of the box first (including the lid) and leave the top and bottom till last.

Construction

1. Cut a ¾-inch by 4-inch by 17-inch piece for the lower front piece. Using a router, saw or jointer, cut a 30-degree rabbet in the top edge as shown to act as a stop for the lid.

2. Cut a ¾-inch by 11-inch by 17-inch piece for the back.

3. Cut two ¾-inch by 11-inch by 11½-inch pieces for the sides. Measure 4 inches up from the bottom of the front edge, and cut a 30-degree angle to the top edge of both side pieces as shown.

4. Begin fabrication of the lid by cutting a ¾-inch by 8½-inch by 16¹⁵/₁₆-inch piece for the lid.

a. Cut a ⅜-inch by ⅜-inch rabbet in the inside bottom

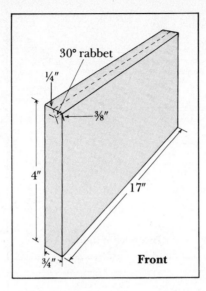

Front

edge as shown.

b. Cut a 30-degree angle from the inside top edge to approximately ¹³/₃₂ inch down from the outside top edge as shown.

c. On each side of the lid, measure ½ inch down from the center of the 30-degree angle and make a small pilot hole; then drill a hole ¼ inch in diameter and ½ inch deep. The upper edge of this hole must be ⅜ inch from the top edge as shown.

d. Cut two ⅞-inch by ¼-inch dowels. Apply glue to one end of each dowel and lightly tap one into each hole.

e. If a window is desired in the lid, center and trace a 5¼-inch by 9¼-inch oval on the lid. If you don't think you can do it freehand, you can make an oval template using a piece of string, two nails, a pencil and a piece of paper. Lay the piece of paper on your workbench or on a piece of scrap

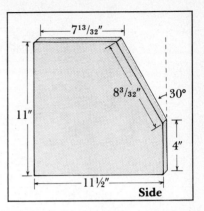

Side

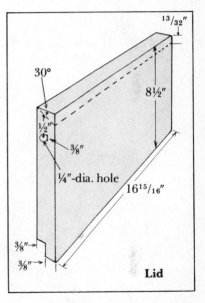

Lid

plywood, and tack two 3d finishing nails through the paper and into the wood, about 7½ inches apart. Loop a piece of string around the nails and tie the string so that it stretches out about ¾ inch when pulled away in a straight line with the nails. Scribe the oval with a pencil as shown, and then change the length of the string or the position of the nails, if you wish, until you arrive at a con-

605

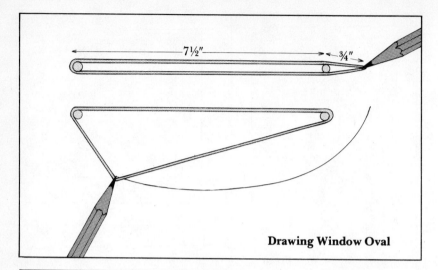

Drawing Window Oval

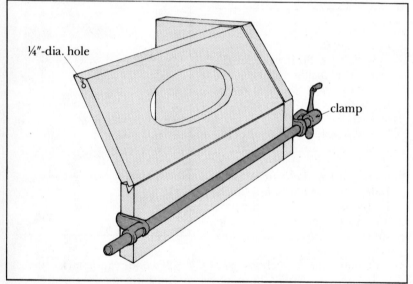

¼"-dia. hole

clamp

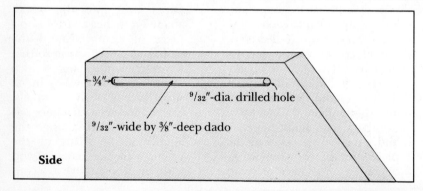

¾"

⁹/₃₂"-dia. drilled hole

⁹/₃₂"-wide by ⅜"-deep dado

Side

figuration that yields the most pleasing oval for your eye. When you get what you want, slip a clean piece of paper over the nail heads, draw the oval, and then cut it out with scissors. Position this template on the door and draw around it with a pencil to transfer your oval to the door. Cut the oval from the door with a saber saw; use a router with a cove bit to shape the perimeter of the oval; and then sand the door to a smooth finish.

f. Below the oval cutout and centered on the lid, make a small pilot hole to receive either a screw or bolt according to the type of knob that is to be used for a handle.

5. Mark the side pieces for the position of the dowel channel:

a. Using bar clamps, clamp one side at a time to the front, and fit the lid into place against the side as shown, holding it at the proper angle.

b. Ensure that the angle of the lid is exactly parallel to the angle of the side piece.

c. Tap the lid lightly to mark the side piece with the dowel.

6. Make a small pilot hole in the center of the dowel mark on each side piece and drill a hole ⁹/₃₂ inch in diameter and ⅜ inch deep. Then, using a router, cut a channel (dado) which is ⅜ inch deep and the same distance from the top as the drilled hole, starting ¾ inch from the back of the piece and extending to the drilled hole as shown.

7. Dry-fit the sides, front, back and lid as shown, and clamp them together with bar

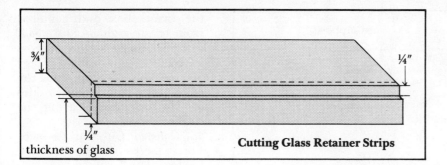

Cutting Glass Retainer Strips

¾″   ¼″   thickness of glass   ¼″

clamps. Ensure that the lid does not bind when it is opened or closed. Correct any problems and recheck until the lid moves easily.

8. If a 6-inch by 10-inch piece of glass is to be installed behind the lid, attach it with ¼-inch-thick strips of wood, rabbeted to accept the glass. Cut the rabbets into ¾-inch-wide stock that is several inches wide, and at least 11 inches long. Cut the rabbet the same depth as the thickness of the glass, and ¼ inch wide, then rip a ¼-inch strip from the stock. If the glass is over ⅛ inch thick, rip the strips slightly wider than ¼ inch. For glass supports, cut two pieces measuring ¼ inch by ¾ inch by 11 inches, and two pieces measuring ¼ inch by ¾ inch by 5½ inches. Sand lightly.

9. Clean the glass and center it on the inside of the lid, over the oval hole, and place the recessed lip of the wooden supports over the glass as shown. Fasten with ½-inch brads.

10. Ensure that the lid is in position. Assemble the bread box using glue and 4d finishing nails. It may be advisable to drill pilot holes for the nails, especially if you are using hardwood.

11. Cut two ¼-inch by ¾-inch by 6½-inch pieces, and cut a

30-degree angle on one end of each piece as shown. Sand lightly. Using ½-inch brads, attach these pieces to the sides, directly below the lid as shown, to act as supports when the lid is in the open position. Before driving the brads all the way in, ensure that the lid opens and closes smoothly.

12. Using a router, cut a ¼-inch by ¼-inch rabbet around the inside perimeter of the bottom of the bread box to accom-

Materials

Wood

1 pc. 1 × 12 × 6′ select pine or **Front:** 1 pc. ¾″ × 4″ × 17″
Back: 1 pc. ¾″ × 11″ × 17″
Sides: 2 pcs. ¾″ × 11″ × 11½″
Glass Supports: 2 pcs. ¼″ × ¾″ × 11″
2 pcs. ¼″ × ¾″ × 5½″
Lid Supports: 2 pcs. ¼″ × ¾″ × 6½″
Legs: 4 pcs. ¾″ × 2⅝″ × 2⅝″

1 pc. 1 × 10 × 4′ select pine or **Lid:** 1 pc. ¾″ × 8½″ × 16¹⁵/₁₆″
Top: 1 pc. ¾″ × 8⅜″ × 19″

1 pc. 36″ × ¼″ dowel or **Hinges:** 2 pcs. ⅞″ × ¼″ dowel

1–1′ × 2′ sht. ¼″ A-C int. plywood or **Bottom:** 1 pc. 10½″ × 17½″

Hardware
½″ brads
4d finishing nails
¾″ brads
1 knob

Miscellaneous
Glue
1 pc. 6″ × 10″ single-strength glass
Wood filler
Finish

607

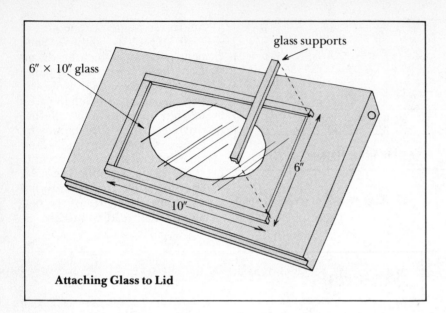

6″ × 10″ glass

glass supports

6″

10″

Attaching Glass to Lid

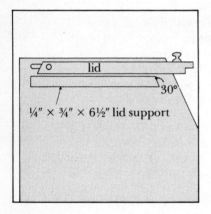

lid

30°

¼″ × ¾″ × 6½″ lid support

the bread box and centered from left to right. Again, drilling pilot holes for the nails is advisable. Then, using a router and ogee bit, cut around the top edge of the front and two sides of the top piece, leaving the back edge as is.

15. *Optional:* Cut four 2⅝-inch-square pieces from ¾-inch stock for legs. Use a router and ogee bit to cut around the four top edges of each piece. Fasten them to the bottom corners of the bread box with glue and 4d finishing nails, driving the nails into the front, back and side pieces

modate the bottom piece.

13. From ¼-inch mahogany (or other) plywood, cut a 10½-inch by 17½-inch piece for the bottom. Fasten the bottom to the bread box with glue and ¾-inch brads.

14. Cut a ¾-inch by 8⅜-inch by 19-inch piece for the top. Fasten the top to the bread box with glue and 4d finishing nails so that the back edge of the top piece is flush with the back of

608

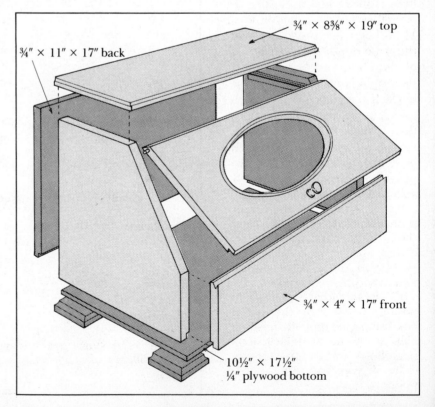

¾″ × 11″ × 17″ back

¾″ × 8⅜″ × 19″ top

¾″ × 4″ × 17″ front

10½″ × 17½″
¼″ plywood bottom

from below. Drill pilot holes for the nails. Avoid nailing into the ¼-inch plywood bottom.

16. Countersink all nailheads and fill the holes with wood filler in the appropriate color. When the wood filler is dry, sand the bread box completely.

17. Apply several coats of whatever finish is desired, and when this has dried completely, attach a knob to the lid.

Pie Safe

The pie safe is an old-time piece of kitchen or dining room furniture you don't often see anymore; it certainly is one you can't buy in the furniture store. The purpose of the pie safe is to provide a ventilated storage place for baked goods that will protect them from the predations of flies, ants and their ilk. Nowadays, folks put pies in the

610

refrigerator or cover them with plastic domes.

Actually, you don't have to use the pie safe for pies or baked goods. It's an attractive place to store all sorts of kitchen items. In fact, the punched tin motif could be adapted to a whole kitchenful of cabinets.

This particular pie safe was made of select pine, crown molding and tin. The pine and the crown molding are standard lumberyard stock, but the tin could be a little hard to find. It is correctly called tin-plated steel, and you'll have to shop among duct fabricators and sheet metal specialty shops for one that both stocks it and is willing to shear a piece off a roll or large sheet for you. If you find a cooperative supplier, you may be able to have the piece sheared into the five exact-size pieces you need.

Into the tin panels is punched a Pennsylvania Dutch flower design, but you could use any design that harmonizes with your kitchen.

The pie safe is a freestanding storage unit, but by eliminating the crown molding on the back, you could make it wall mounted.

Construction

1. From ¾-inch pine stock cut the following: four pieces 2 inches by 18 inches for the front and rear verticals, four pieces 2 inches by 25½ inches for the front and rear horizontals, four pieces 1½ inches by 18 inches for the side verticals, four pieces 2 inches by 12 inches for the side horizontals.

2. Each of the frames is as-

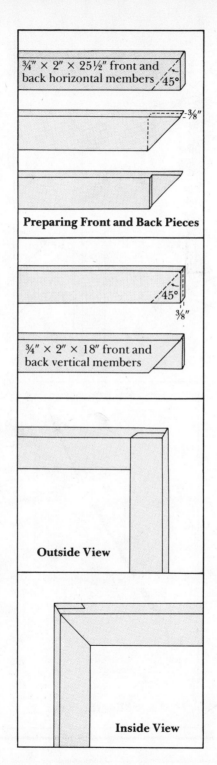

¾″ × 2″ × 25½″ front and back horizontal members 45°

⅜″

Preparing Front and Back Pieces

45°

⅜″

¾″ × 2″ × 18″ front and back vertical members

Outside View

Inside View

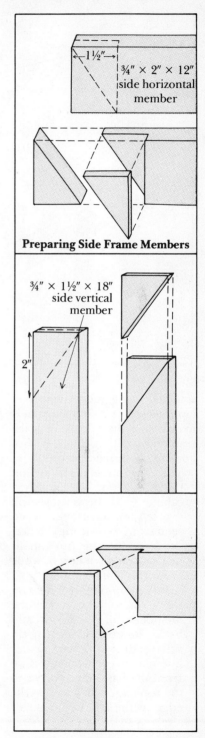

1½″

¾″ × 2″ × 12″ side horizontal member

Preparing Side Frame Members

¾″ × 1½″ × 18″ side vertical member

2″

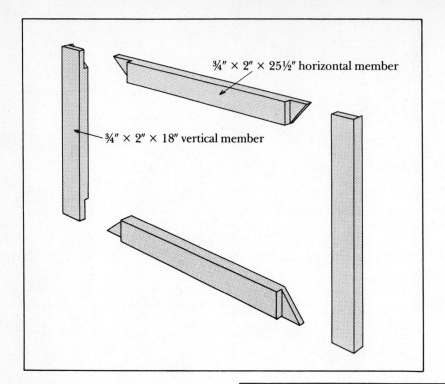

¾" × 2" × 25½" horizontal member

¾" × 2" × 18" vertical member

the thickness of the member outside of this line, a triangular area, using a dado head in a power saw, a router or a chisel. Precision is the key to the strength of this joint, so cut the laps carefully.

c. Using a combination square, draw 45-degree miters on the inside face of each of the vertical members for the front and back frames. DON'T cut these miters. These lines are the edges of the laps. Using the same technique as you did in the previous step, cut the triangular laps.

d. The miters and laps for the side frame members are cut the same way as those for the front and back frame

sembled using miters with end lap joints. The best approach is to lay out the pieces of each frame in position. Then lay out and cut the individual joints.

a. The miters will be on the inside of the finished cabinet, and the verticals will overlap the horizontals when seen from the outside. Hence, the ends of the horizontals will actually be mitered, while the verticals will not.

b. Cut 45-degree miters on the ends of the horizontal members for the front and back frames. Using a try square, draw a perpendicular line across each outside face from the base of the miter to the top edge. This will be the edge of the lap. Remove half

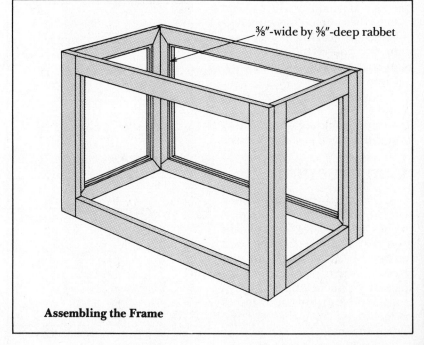

⅜"-wide by ⅜"-deep rabbet

Assembling the Frame

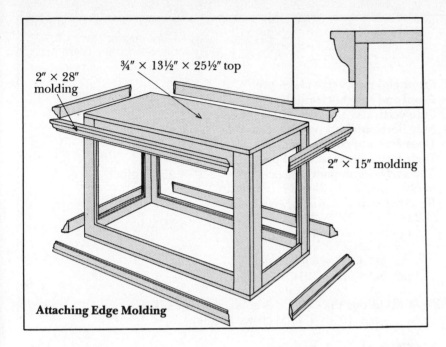

2" × 28" molding

¾" × 13½" × 25½" top

2" × 15" molding

Attaching Edge Molding

members, but since the frames have 2-inch and 1½-inch members, the layout is a bit different. The miters are not 45 degrees. On the horizontal members, measure 1½ inches from each end and scribe a perpendicular across the outside face, which will be the edge of the lap. Next scribe a diagonal from corner to corner that will be the miter. Cut the miters and the laps. On the vertical members, measure 2 inches from each end and scribe a perpendicular across the inside face. Then scribe the diagonal from corner to corner that will be the miter. This miter will be the edge of the lap. Cut the laps.

3. Assemble the front frame using two of the 2-inch-wide horizontal members and two of the matching vertical members. The finished frame should measure 18 inches by 25½ inches.

4. The inside edges of the side and rear frames must be rabbeted to accept the tin inserts. It's easiest to cut the rabbets before assembling the frames. So cut a ⅜-inch by ⅜-inch rabbet along one edge of each of the remaining 12 frame pieces. You can't go wrong if you dry-assemble each frame with the miters up and mark the inside edges for rabbeting. After the rabbets are cut, glue the frames together.

5. The next step is to fabricate and assemble the door frames. Cut four 1¼-inch by 10¾-inch pieces of ¾-inch pine for the door horizontals, and four 1¼-inch by 14-inch pieces for the door verticals. Lay out and cut miters with end laps on the ends of these eight pieces, just as you did with the cabinet frame pieces. Cut a ⅜-inch by ⅜-inch rabbet on the inside edges for the tin panels, as you did with the cabinet frames. Glue and assemble the two door frames. Then, drill a ¼-inch hole in the middle of the appropriate vertical piece on each to accommodate the door knobs. The hole should be centered edge to edge and end to end.

6. Glue and nail the four frames—front, back and two sides—to make a rectangular box with inside dimensions of 12 inches by 24 inches by 18 inches. The front and back frames overlap the side frames. The corners are simple butt joints held with 3d finishing nails. Remember to countersink the nails and fill the holes with wood filler.

7. From the ¾-inch pine stock, cut enough pieces to glue up edge to edge to yield two 13½-inch by 25½-inch panels. These will be the pie safe's top and bottom. Glue the strips, and clamp them with bar clamps.

8. Glue and nail the top and bottom panels to the frame. Then, cut eight pieces of 2-inch crown molding to fit around the outside edges of the top and bottom. The edge of the molding should be flush with the outer surfaces of the top and bottom. Miter the corners and glue and nail with the 6d finishing nails. Countersink the nails and fill the holes with wood filler.

613

Materials

Wood

2 pcs. 1 × 6 × 8' select pine or
2 pcs. 1 × 6 × 10' select pine

Front and rear verticals: 4 pcs. ¾" × 2" × 18"
Front and rear horizontals: 4 pcs. ¾" × 2" × 25½"
Side verticals: 4 pcs. ¾" × 1½" × 18"
Side horizontals: 4 pcs. ¾" × 2" × 12"
Door frame verticals: 4 pcs. ¾" × 1¼" × 14"
Door frame horizontals: 4 pcs. ¾" × 1¼" × 10¾"
Top and bottom panels: 2 pcs. ¾" × 13½" × 25½" (glued up)
Shelf: 1 pc. ¾" × 12" × 24" (glued up)
Retainer strips: 2 pcs. ⅜" × ⅜" × 14¾"
 2 pcs. ⅜" × ⅜" × 21½"
 4 pcs. ⅜" × ⅜" × 9¾"
 4 pcs. ⅜" × ⅜" × 14"
 4 pcs. ⅜" × ⅜" × 8"
 4 pcs. ⅜" × ⅜" × 12¼"

2 pcs. 8' × 2" solid crown molding or **Molding:** 4 pcs. 28" × 2" solid crown molding
 4 pcs. 15" × 2" solid crown molding

1 pc. 36" × ¼" dowel or **Shelf supports:** 4 pcs. ¾" × ¼" dowel

Hardware

4d finishing nails
6d finishing nails
4–1½" brass butt hinges
1 pc. 15" × 60" 28-gauge tin-plated steel or **Door panels:** 2 pcs. 9" × 12¼"
 Side panels: 2 pcs. 9¾" × 14¾"
 Back panel: 1 pc. 14¾" × 22¼"

¾" 16-gauge brads
2–1" hardwood door knobs
2 magnetic catches

Miscellaneous

Glue
Wood filler
Varnish

9. Drill a ¼-inch blind hole on the inside of each vertical side member to hold your shelf supports. DON'T drill all the way through. Be sure all four holes are in the same horizontal plane or the shelf will be loose and tipsy. If you want your shelf to be adjustable, drill several sets of holes. You can use hardwood dowels cut about ⅜ inch longer than the hole is deep to support the shelf, or you can buy a set of metal supports, available at most hardware stores. To make the shelf, cut strips from ¾-inch pine and glue up a panel that matches the measurements inside the pie safe. It should be about 12 inches by 24 inches.

Securing Molding to Frame

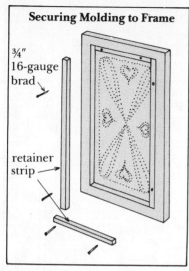

¾″ 16-gauge brad

retainer strip

10. Install the doors with two 1½-inch brass butt hinges on each door. Cut mortises for each hinge in both the door and the cabinet so the hinge plates will be flush with the surface of the wood. Plane doors to fit.

11. Cut ⅜-inch by ⅜-inch strips to be used as molding to hold the tin sheets in the rabbets in the doors and frames. You will need about 21 feet of the strips, cut as follows: two 14¾-inch and two 21½-inch lengths for the back, four 9¾-inch and four 14-inch lengths for the sides, and four 8-inch and four 12¼-inch lengths for the doors.

12. Sand all the edges and surfaces. Then, finish off the pie safe inside and out with varnish.

13. Cut five pieces of 28-gauge tin-plated steel for the sides, back and doors. The door pieces measure 9 inches by 12¼ inches, the sides are 9¾ inches by 14¾ inches, and the back is 14¾ inches by 22¼ inches. If you haven't prepared your perforation design ahead of time, put it on paper now.

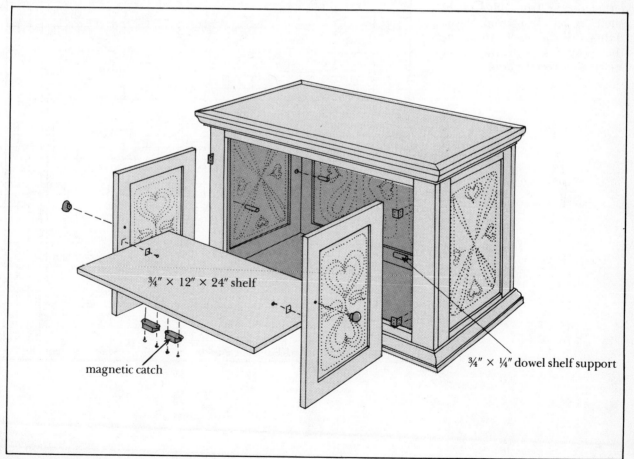

¾″ × 12″ × 24″ shelf

magnetic catch

¾″ × ¼″ dowel shelf support

You can either tape the paper to the tin, or transfer the design directly to the tin. Then, use a sharp punch (a nail will leave irregularly shaped holes), and punch out the design on all your sheets.

14. Drill holes through the ⅜-inch by ⅜-inch strips to accept 16-gauge brads. You can use a brad as a drill bit. Then, using these strips and the ¾-inch 16-gauge brads, mount the tin panels in the cabinet.

15. The last step is to mount the door knobs and the magnetic cabinet door catches. You can place the magnetic catches either on the front edge of the shelf, or on the bottom, if you didn't use the shelf. Match up the positions with the metal strike plates on the doors.

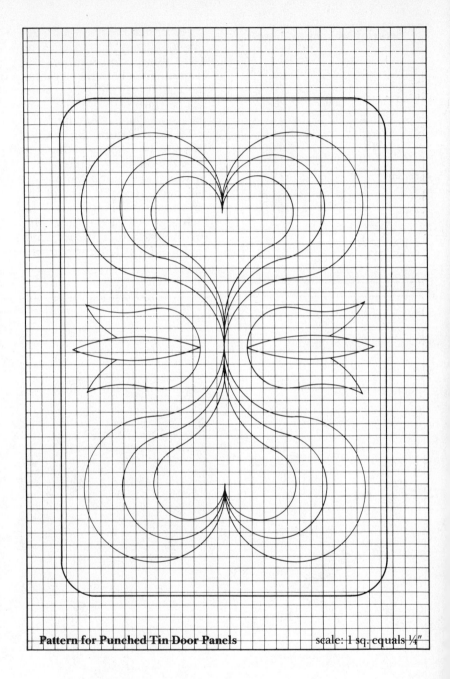

Pattern for Punched Tin Door Panels   scale: 1 sq. equals ¼″

Pattern for Punched Tin Side Panels   scale: 1 sq. equals ¼"

Pastry Center

No avid baker should be without a spot for storing all her or his baking ingredients and equipment. When everything is in one place, the start-up and the cleanup are both faster. You can focus on the baking project itself.

This pastry center can be that single spot. In this cabinet the size of a dishwasher, you can

store all the equipment you use in baking—mixing bowls and spoons, measuring cups and spoons, pans and cookie sheets, rolling pins and sifters—and have room left for many of the special ingredients you use for baking alone. The cabinet's storage space, accessible from two sides, is divided into drawers and deep shelves on one side and a variety of shallow shelves on the other. It is designed to roll under the counter, all but out of sight, thanks to a false front that matches the surrounding cabinets. The unit shown has a false front that looks like a raised-panel door, but you'll want to fabricate and install a panel that will match the cabinets in your kitchen.

The pastry center fits under the standard counter because its working surface is slightly lower than the standard height of 36 inches. This makes it just a little easier to get on top of that mound of bread dough when you're kneading. If your counter tops are lower or higher than the assembly-line kitchen's 36 inches, you'll have to make some adjustments in the design to allow it to fit your kitchen.

The cabinet is constructed mostly of ⅝-inch interior plywood (one sheet with one good side will yield all the plywood pieces you need). It is assembled with glue and nails, using simple butt joints. While you can get by without a shopful of tools, you will need several bar or pipe clamps and corner clamps. The work isn't all that difficult, but the result here—as in every woodworking endeavor—will reflect the care you put into the project.

Construction

1. The first step is to cut the major shelves and partitions from a sheet of ⅝-inch plywood, and all *can* be cut from a single sheet if care is used in laying them out and cutting them. The cabinet is, in essence, an open-sided plywood box with a central partition dividing the space into a shallow left-hand compartment and a deep right-hand compartment. The front and back panels measure 23 inches by 28¾ inches, while the top and bottom measure 21 inches by 23 inches. The central partition is called partition #1 for the purposes of these instructions; it measures 21 inches by 27½ inches. The main partition that divides the right side vertically is called partition #2 and mea-

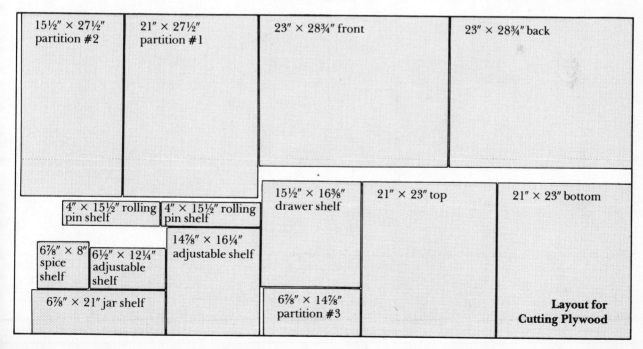

15½″ × 27½″ partition #2

21″ × 27½″ partition #1

23″ × 28¾″ front

23″ × 28¾″ back

4″ × 15½″ rolling pin shelf

4″ × 15½″ rolling pin shelf

15½″ × 16⅜″ drawer shelf

21″ × 23″ top

21″ × 23″ bottom

14⅞″ × 16¼″ adjustable shelf

6⅞″ × 8″ spice shelf

6½″ × 12¼″ adjustable shelf

6⅞″ × 21″ jar shelf

6⅞″ × 14⅞″ partition #3

Layout for Cutting Plywood

619

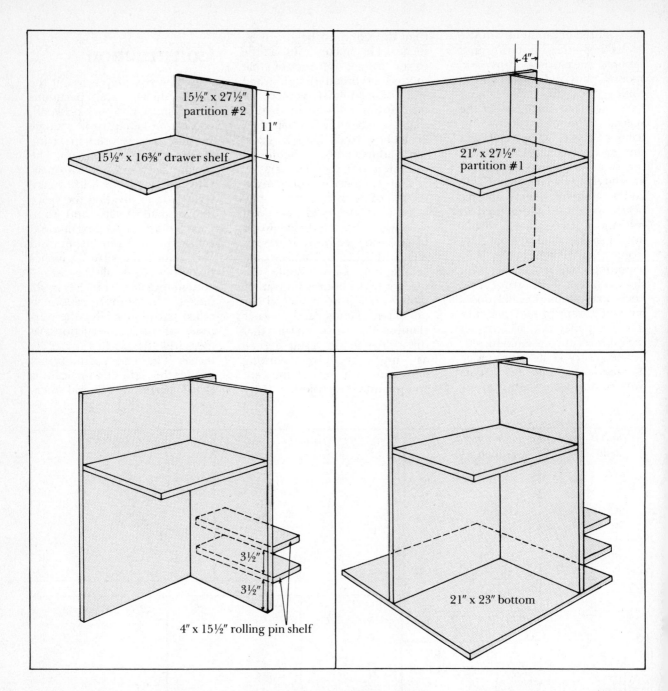

15½" x 27½"
partition #2

11"

15½" x 16⅜" drawer shelf

4"

21" x 27½"
partition #1

3½"

3½"

4" x 15½" rolling pin shelf

21" x 23" bottom

sures 15½ inches by 27½ inches, while the comparable divider for the left side, partition #3, measures 6⅞ inches by 14⅞

620

inches. In addition to cutting these pieces, cut a drawer shelf: 15½ inches by 16⅜ inches; two rolling pin shelves: 4 inches by

15½ inches each; a jar shelf: 6⅞ inches by 21 inches; a spice shelf: 6⅞ inches by 8 inches; a large adjustable shelf: 14⅞

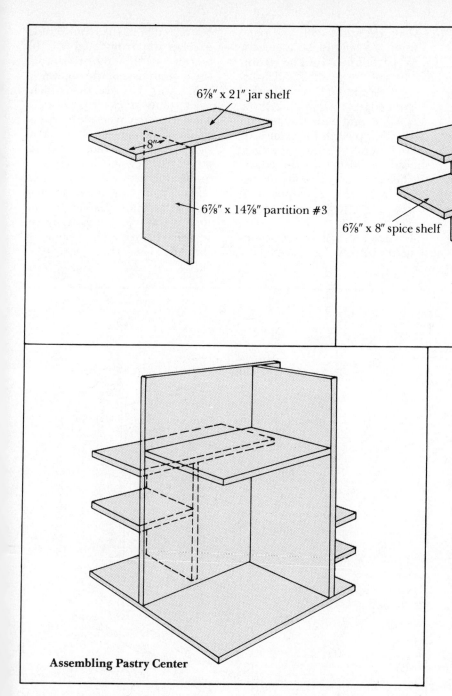

6⅞" x 21" jar shelf

8"

6⅞" x 14⅞" partition #3

5¼"

6⅞" x 8" spice shelf

Assembling Pastry Center

ing the internal partitions together using glue and 4d finishing nails. The chore is eased by the use of corner clamps to secure pieces at right angles to each other while you drive nails. When attaching a shelf to a partition, mark the position of the shelf on both sides of the partition. That way you'll not only position the new part correctly, you'll know where to drive nails so they don't miss their mark and mar your work with needless punctures. Because you are nailing the pieces together in addition to gluing, you won't need to clamp them while the glue dries.

a. Attach the drawer shelf to partition #2 so that the top of the shelf is 11 inches down from the top of the partition.

b. Glue and nail partition #1 to the first two pieces. Par-

inches by 16¼ inches; and a small adjustable shelf: 6½ inches by 12¼ inches.

2. Begin assembly by fasten-

tition #2 should be 4 inches from the back edge of partition #1. Since the first two pieces form a T, it should be easy to stand them on edge, lay partition #1 on them and drive your nails through the back of that partition into the glue-smeared edges of the other two pieces.

c. Next, glue and nail the two 4-inch rolling pin shelves in place. The rolling pin shelves should be 3½ inches apart and the bottom of the bottom shelf should be 3½ inches from the bottom of partitions #1 and #2.

d. Stand the unit upside down and glue and nail the bottom in place. The front and back edges of partition #1 should be flush with the front and back edges of the bottom. At the same time, the edge of partition #2 should be flush with the right edge of the bottom.

e. Fasten the 21-inch jar shelf to partition #3. The partition should join the jar shelf at right angles, 8 inches from one edge, which thus becomes the front edge of the shelf.

f. Glue and nail the spice shelf to partition #3. The spice shelf should join the partition at right angles with the top of the spice shelf 5¼ inches below the bottom of the jar shelf.

g. Now it's time for left to meet right. Glue and nail the smaller unit to the larger unit. The bottom edge of partition #3 should be fastened to the bottom of the cabinet. The inside edges of the jar

shelf, the spice shelf and partition #3 should be attached to partition #1. The front edges of the jar shelf and spice shelf should be flush with the front edge of partition #1.

3. Glue and nail the top in place. This piece is the same size as the bottom, and its edges should be flush with the edges of shelves and partitions in the same way that the bottom's edges are flush with these pieces.

4. Glue and nail the plywood structural front in place. The

bottom edge of the front should overlap the front edge of the bottom and should be flush with the bottom face of the bottom.

5. From a piece of ⅝-inch-thick pine stock, rip ¼-inch-wide strips to cover up the edges of the plywood that show. You need about 30 feet of these strips. (Dimension lumber sold at all lumberyards is ¾ inch thick. You can have such a board thickness-planed by the lumber supplier, or you *can* do it yourself with a hand plane or jointer.) Cut these strips as

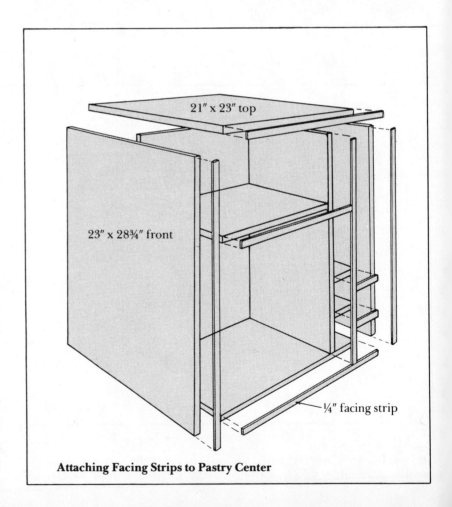

21" x 23" top

23" x 28¾" front

¼" facing strip

Attaching Facing Strips to Pastry Center

needed and glue and nail them to the exposed plywood edges on both sides of the unit. Include the two side edges of the back piece, which is still unattached. You do not have to put any strips on the top or bottom edges of the back and front, since these will be covered or out of sight.

6. From the ⅝-inch stock, rip two pieces ⅞ inch wide to form the facing-cum-lip for each of the adjustable shelves. One piece should be 16¼ inches long and the other should be 12¼ inches long. Glue and nail these pieces over the plywood edges that will show.

7. Use a nail set and hammer to tap all the nails out of sight, then fill the nail holes with wood filler. Then sand and finish the entire unit, the two adjustable shelves and the back.

8. Glue and nail the back to the unit. The bottom edge of the back should overlap the back edge of the bottom and should be flush with the bottom face of the bottom. Once the glue has dried, set the nails, apply wood filler and touch up the finish.

9. Drill ¼-inch-diameter, ¼-inch-deep holes for the shelf-support pins for the two adjustable shelves. Each adjustable shelf will be supported by four pins. The more sets of holes you drill for these pins, the more adjustable the shelves will be. In most cases, three levels are sufficient. This requires 12 holes for each adjustable shelf. The holes for the small adjustable shelf should be 2 inches in from the front and back of the shelf. The

holes for the large adjustable shelf should be 3 inches in from the front and back of the shelf. You can tailor their locations up and down to fit your canisters and mixing bowls. One way to position these holes is to put one set of four in the vertical center of the space where the shelf will hang, then place other sets 3 inches above and 3 inches below these centered holes. The main thing to watch, when drilling these holes, is that the holes are level and in the same plane, so the shelf won't be tipped at an angle or loose and tipsy. Take your time in laying out the holes; use a level. Drill carefully to get the holes perpendicular, and don't drill all the way through.

10. Turn the unit upside down and place two flat plate swivel casters with 3-inch hard rubber wheels in the front corners of the bottom and two fixed casters with 3-inch hard rubber wheels in the back cor-

---

Applying Facing Strip to Shelf

14⅞" x 16¼" shelf

⅝" x ⅞" x 16¼" facing strip

6½" x 12¼" shelf

⅝" x ⅞" x 12¼" facing strip

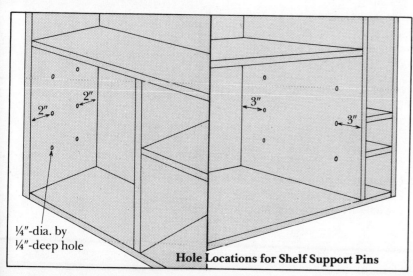

¼"-dia. by ¼"-deep hole

2" 2" 2"

3" 3"

Hole Locations for Shelf Support Pins

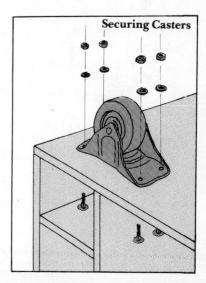

Securing Casters

Materials

Wood

1 sht. ⅝" A-C fir plywood or **Structural front and back:** 2 pcs. 23" × 28¾"

Top and bottom: 2 pcs. 21" × 23"

Partition #1: 1 pc. 21" × 27½"

Partition #2: 1 pc. 15½" × 27½"

Partition #3: 1 pc. 6⅞" × 14⅞"

Drawer shelf: 1 pc. 15½" × 16⅜"

Rolling pin shelves: 2 pcs. 4" × 15½"

Jar shelf: 1 pc. 6⅞" × 21"

Spice shelf: 1 pc. 6⅞" × 8"

Adjustable shelf: 1 pc. 14⅞" × 16¼"

Adjustable shelf: 1 pc. 6½" × 12¼"

1 pc. 1 × 4 × 8' select pine or **Facing strips:** ¼" × ⅝" × various lengths as needed

Facing strip: 1 pc. ⅝" × ⅞" × 16¼"

Facing strip: 1 pc. ⅝" × ⅞" × 12¼"

Drawer fronts: 3 pcs. ¾" × 3½" × 16⅛"

1 pc. 1 × 4 × 12' select pine or **Drawer sides:** 6 pcs. ½" × 3½" × 15⅛"

Drawer backs: 3 pcs. ½" × 3" × 14⅜"

1–2' × 4' sht. ¼" mahogany int. plywood or **Drawer bottoms:** 3 pcs. 14⅞" × 15"

1–2' sq. sht. 1½" particle board or **Finished top:** 1 pc. 22¼" × 23½"

Hardware

4d finishing nails

8–¼" dia. shelf-support pins

2 flat plate swivel casters w/3" hard rubber wheels

2 fixed casters w/3" hard rubber wheels

16–1" × ¼" carriage bolts w/lock washers and nuts

3 prs. 14" drawer slides

4–1¼" #10 f.h. wood screws

6–1" #10 f.h. wood screws

Miscellaneous

Glue

Wood filler

Finish

1–2' × 4' sht. plastic laminate or **Finished top surface:** 1 pc. 22¼" × 23½"

Finished top edging: 2 pcs. 1½" × 22¼"

Finished top edging: 1 pc. 1½" × 23½"

Contact cement

Semigloss enamel paint

ners. These should be placed 2 inches in from the front and back and 2 inches in from the sides. Hold each caster and wheel in place and draw circles through the bolt holes. Remove the casters and wheels and drill four ¼-inch holes for each of them. Attach the casters and wheels, using 1-inch by ¼-inch carriage bolts with lock washers and nuts.

11. From ½-inch pine stock, cut six drawer sides, each measuring 3½ inches by 15⅛ inches. Plow a ¼-inch by ¼-inch groove along the length of each side piece, ¼ inch up from the bottom edge, for the drawer bottoms.

12. From 1 × 4, cut three drawer fronts each 16⅛ inches long. Drill a 1-inch-diameter hole in each for a drawer pull. The hole should be centered 1½ inches from the top and 8¹/₁₆ inches in from either end. Rout a ¼-inch radius around the inside and outside edges of each hole. Then cut a ⅞-inch-wide by ⅜-inch-deep rabbet across the inside ends of each drawer front. Plow a ¼-inch by ¼-inch groove along the inside of each drawer front, ¼ inch from the bottom edge.

13. From ½-inch stock, cut three 3-inch by 14⅜-inch drawer backs.

14. From ¼-inch mahogany plywood, cut three drawer bottoms, each measuring 14⅞ inches by 15 inches.

15. Assemble the drawers with glue and nails. You'll find this easier if you glue and nail each piece as you go, rather than waiting until you have all five pieces together before you start to drive nails. First attach

one side to the front. Then glue in the bottom and tack in a couple of nails to hold it. Next add the other side, and finish up by gluing and nailing the back. Use corner clamps.

16. Mount three sets of 14-inch drawer glides to support the drawers. These come with their own screws and instruc-

tions, and are installed quite easily. The main thing is to see that they are level so the drawers slide in and out easily.

17. From 1½-inch particle board, cut a piece that measures 22¼ inches by 23½ inches. Use contact cement to fasten a piece of plastic laminate the same size on the top of it. Cut and glue

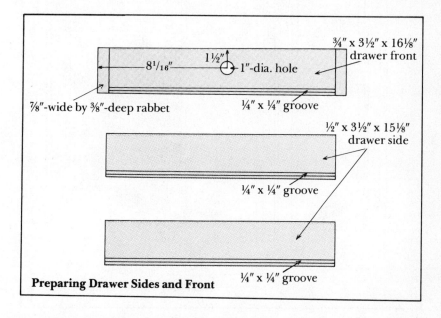

Preparing Drawer Sides and Front

¾" x 3½" x 16⅛" drawer front
8¹/₁₆" 1½" 1"-dia. hole
⅞"-wide by ⅜"-deep rabbet   ¼" x ¼" groove
½" x 3½" x 15⅛" drawer side
¼" x ¼" groove
¼" x ¼" groove

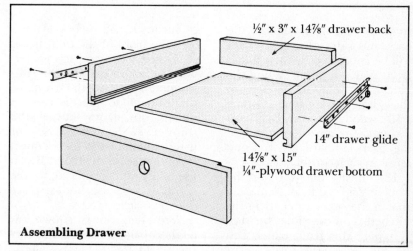

Assembling Drawer

½" x 3" x 14⅞" drawer back
14" drawer glide
14⅞" x 15" ¼"-plywood drawer bottom

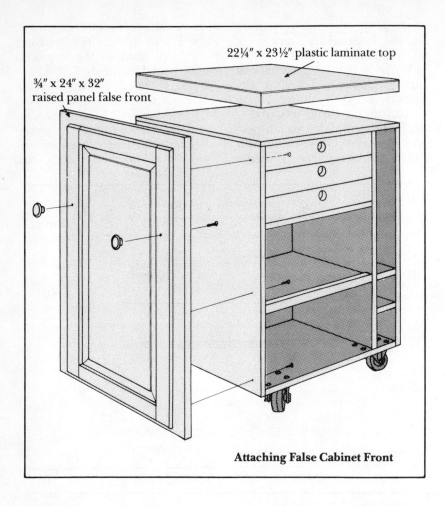

22¼" x 23½" plastic laminate top

¾" x 24" x 32"
raised panel false front

Attaching False Cabinet Front

construction has been detailed in Part IV. The essence of the panel is that it *looks* like a cabinet frame and door. The 24-inch by 32-inch frame is assembled from two 32-inch and two 21-inch pieces of 1 × 2. Construction details for raised-panel doors are given in "The Cabinetmaker's Craft" in Part IV. Construct a door that measures 29⅝ inches by 21⅝ inches. Glue it into the frame, then attach the unit to the pastry cabinet front as described above.

strips of the laminate on the back and sides of it. The front will be concealed by the cabinet front you will install. When the glue dries, mount this top on the cabinet, using four 1¼-inch #10 wood screws. Drill up through the plywood top into the particle-board top for one screw in each corner.

18. Finish the cabinet by applying a false front to make it match the other cabinets in the kitchen. You can either build or purchase this front panel. Just be sure it measures ¾ inch by 24 inches by 32 inches. Attach it to the front of the unit, using six 1-inch #10 wood screws. Attach either a handle or two wooden knobs to the front of the cabinet so that it can be pulled out from under the counter easily. The knobs or handle should be 12 inches down from the top of the front. If you use a handle, center it in the front. If you use knobs, place one near each side.

Note: The cabinet shown has a raised-panel front that matches the style of cabinets whose

Home Baking Center

Every harvest kitchen *needs* a baking center, but the baking center is often the work area that gets squeezed out. There's only so much room, you know.

But here's a solution: a kitchen island that's a working center and a storage cabinet for all the baker's equipment and raw materials, from grain mill to measuring spoons to mixing bowl, from spices to honey to freshly ground flour.

The core of this home baking center is a cavernous cabinet divided lengthwise into a shallow side and a deep side. Shelved doors open on adjustable shelves for foodstuffs storage on the shallow side and there are drawers for equipment on the other. There's a proofing box, albeit a small one. The butcher-block work surface is a few inches lower than normal, making it ideal for kneading and rolling dough. An outlet provides a convenient place to plug in electric appliances— mixer or mill, for example. And casters increase the center's usefulness by allowing you to move it around.

Accommodation is the keynote of the center. The shelves of the food storage side of the unit are adjustable, so you can create a space suited to the size of containers you must deal with. The shelves have retainer lips, so nothing should slip or roll off when the center is moved. The storage doors have spaces for cookie sheets, waxed paper, spice cans and jars, long-handled whips, eggbeaters and other hard-to-store items. On the equipment storage side, shallow, shelflike drawers

spaced apart offer efficient, accessible accommodations for heavy mixing bowls. One drawer designed to hold a mixer has a high back and side so that attachments can be hung for easy, organized access. The top is designed with substantial overhang so a grain mill can be clamped to it.

The proofing box—a heated compartment for raising yeasted doughs—is an insulated, aluminum-lined space with a drop-hinged door. An ordinary light bulb, adjusted by a dimmer switch, is the heat source. As designed, the box works well, but it is too small for raising more than a couple or three loaves of bread at a time. If your baking routine demands a bigger proofing box, and you're willing to yield some storage space, convert one of the other spaces in the cabinet into the proofing box. A natural alternative: Instead of installing the proofing box where we did, put two drawers there and install the proofing box in the space immediately below.

The design is flexible too. You can add shelves or alter their locations and sizes. You can add or eliminate drawers. You don't even *have* to use the unit as a baking center. Just use it as an island.

The top is butcher block. Unless you have a very elaborate woodworking shop and lots of experience, you are probably better off purchasing the top as a piece. If you don't think the butcher block is what you want, you can replace it with a top covered with plastic laminate. An alternative that's very much

in keeping with the use of the unit as a baking center would be a counter with a marble insert; marble is considered to be the ideal surface for rolling pastry and cookie dough and pasta.

This is not an easy or inexpensive project. The materials will cost several hundred dollars. And you'll not knock it together in a couple of evenings. It'll take several weeks of deliberate work, cutting the pieces, then gluing a few together at a time. Your cabinet-making skills will be tested in making drawers and doors, as well as in constructing a case. You'll have to work with sheet metal and do some wiring.

In sum, the baking center is a useful piece for the harvest kitchen, and if you joy in challenge, it's one you certainly should tackle as your skills develop. In itself, the home baking center can transform your kitchen.

Construction

1. Begin the project by cutting the major panels that compose the cabinet. Cut a 22½-inch by 42½-inch bottom from a sheet of ¾-inch A/C interior plywood. From a sheet of ¾-inch A/C birch interior plywood, cut two 22½-inch by 30-inch end panels. From ⅝-inch A/C interior plywood, cut a 27¾-inch by 42½-inch middle divider, and a 14⅜-inch by 27¾-inch deep-side divider. From ½-inch B/D interior plywood, cut a 7½-inch by 42½-inch subtop, a 14⅜-inch by 20⅜-inch subtop and two 14⅜-inch by 21½-inch pieces

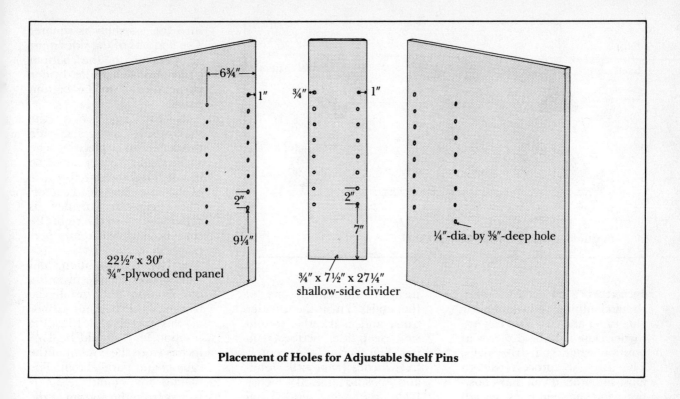

6¾"
1"
¾"
1"
2"
2"
9¼"
7"
22½" x 30"
¾"-plywood end panel
¾" x 7½" x 27¼"
shallow-side divider
¼"-dia. by ⅜"-deep hole

Placement of Holes for Adjustable Shelf Pins

for the top and bottom of the proofing box. Cut a 27¼-inch length of 1 × 10 and rip it to a 7½-inch width for the shallow-side divider.

2. Lay out and drill ¼-inch-diameter by ⅜-inch-deep holes for adjustable shelf pins in the end panels and the shallow-side divider. Do the divider first. The holes in it can completely penetrate the wood. Scribe a line the length of the divider 1 inch from one edge and a second line ¾ inch from the other edge. Center points for the holes should be marked on these lines. The bottom holes should be 7 inches from the bottom end of the divider, and the remaining holes should be 2 inches apart, center to center.

There are eight sets of holes. Drill the holes in this divider all the way through the board, but be absolutely sure they are perpendicular to the face of the board. The sides, or end panels, should have matching holes. Several cautions: Be sure to drill only ⅜ inch deep; drill on what will be the inside faces; be sure you lay out the holes in the sides in mirror images, not in duplicate. Scribe a line 1 inch from the edge, and a second line 6¾ inches from the same edge. The bottom holes are 9¼ inches from the bottom edge of the side, with the remaining holes on 2-inch centers. Drill the holes.

3. Position and mount the casters on the bottom panel. The two fixed casters are lo-

cated at one end of the panel and each is flush with a corner. The two swivel casters are located at the opposite end and each is positioned ⅞ inch from the side and end edges. Place the casters in position on the panel, mark the locations of the bolt holes, then drill ¼-inch holes through the panel. Mount the casters using 1½-inch by ¼-inch carriage bolts.

4. Assemble the basic cabinet. This is a major step. You should do some layout work, then proceed piece by piece to glue and nail, using 6d finishing nails, bottom, dividers, sides and sub-tops one to another. Since you will be nailing the pieces together, you can move through the entire assembly process at

629

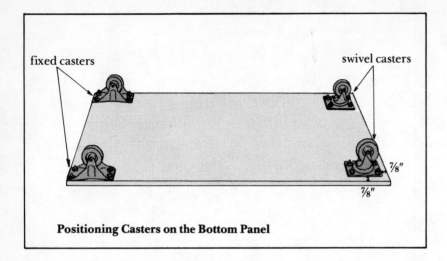

fixed casters

swivel casters

7/8"

7/8"

Positioning Casters on the Bottom Panel

once; there's no need to worry about clamping and waiting for glue to set and dry. You can use corner clamps to hold pieces in position while you drive nails. The assembly process will go most smoothly if you mark position and nailing lines in advance.

a. With the bottom panel sitting on its casters, scribe a line the length of the piece 7½ inches from one long edge. Turn the panel casters-up and scribe a nailing line $7^{13}/_{16}$ inches from the same edge. Lay out the side panels with the holes down and scribe a nailing line $7^{13}/_{16}$ inches from the edge closest to and parallel with the holes. Scribe another line, perpendicular to the first and $1^{13}/_{16}$ inches from the bottom edge. Now lay out the middle divider. Mark the surface facing you "shallow side" and scribe a nailing line parallel to the short dimension and $20^{11}/_{16}$ inches from one end. Scribe a position line 21⅝

inches from either one of the ends. Turn the divider over, and mark the second side "deep side." Scribe a nailing line across the center, 21¼ inches from either end, and a position line 20⅜ inches from the same end from which you measured to locate the nailing line on the other side of the divider.

b. Begin assembly by gluing and nailing the middle divider and the bottom panel together. The shallow side should be 7½ inches from one edge of the bottom. The nailing line on that side should be off center to the left; this is important.

c. Glue and nail the sides in place. The holes in the sides for the adjustable shelves should be on the shallow side of the cabinet and should face the inside of the cabinet. The tops should be flush with the top edges of the divider while the bottoms should overhang the bottom panel by 1½ inches. Make

sure the assembly is square: The bottoms of the sides must be parallel to the bottom panel and the middle divider perpendicular to the bottom panel.

d. Glue and nail the shallow-side and deep-side dividers in place. The shallow-side divider must be installed right end up because of the holes, and dead center. The deep-side divider is offset slightly to the right. Be sure both dividers are perpendicular.

e. Lay out position and nailing lines for the proofing box bottom and install the bottom. The bottom surface of this piece, and thus the position line, should be 17⅛ inches from the bottom of the cabinet and parallel to it. The nailing line should be $17^{7}/_{16}$ inches from the bottom of the cabinet ($19^{11}/_{16}$ inches from the bottom of the side). The lines should be marked on the appropriate faces of the side, middle divider and deep-side divider. The top and bottom of the proofing box will only fit in the space to the left of the deep-side divider. After gluing and nailing the bottom in place, glue and nail the top in place. The top should be flush with the top edges of the sides and dividers. In installing these panels, clamp a hand screw to the side and another to the divider flush with the position line; the hand screws will hold the panels in position whilst you drive the nails home.

f. Glue and nail the shallow-side subtop in place.

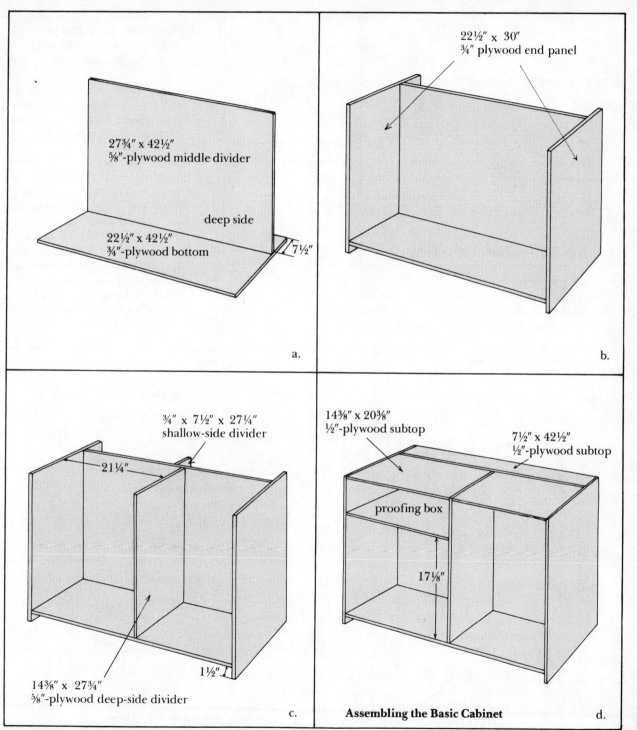

27¾" x 42½"
⅝"-plywood middle divider

deep side

22½" x 42½"
¾"-plywood bottom

7½"

a.

22½" x 30"
¾" plywood end panel

b.

¾" x 7½" x 27¼"
shallow-side divider

21¼"

1½"

14⅜" x 27¾"
⅝"-plywood deep-side divider

c.

14⅜" x 20⅜"
½"-plywood subtop

7½" x 42½"
½"-plywood subtop

proofing box

17⅛"

Assembling the Basic Cabinet

d.

631

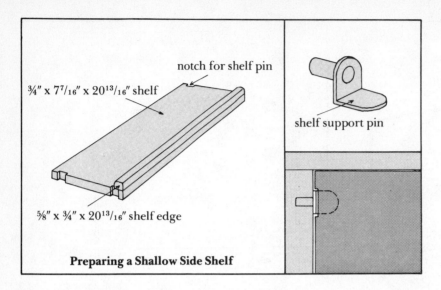

notch for shelf pin

¾" x 7⁷/₁₆" x 20¹³/₁₆" shelf

shelf support pin

⅝" x ¾" x 20¹³/₁₆" shelf edge

Preparing a Shallow Side Shelf

This piece extends from side to side, passing atop the

shallow-side divider; it is flush with the top edges of the sides

and middle divider. Again, hand screws clamped to the sides can be used to hold the piece in position while you nail.

g. Finally, glue and nail the deep-side subtop in place. You will have to toenail through the dividers into this piece; be careful.

5. Cut four 20¹³/₁₆-inch-long shelves for the shallow side from 1 × 10 pine. Rip the shelves so they are 7⁷/₁₆ inches wide. Rip four ⅝-inch-wide strips from a piece of ¾-inch stock; each strip should be 20¹³/₁₆ inches long. Glue a strip to the face of each shelf at the front edge, forming a retainer lip on the shelf. Using a rounding-off bit in a router,

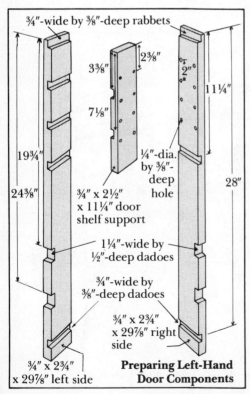

Preparing Left-Hand Door Components

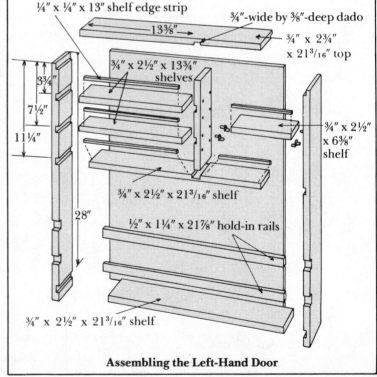

Assembling the Left-Hand Door

break the two edges of the retainer lip. Put shelf pins in the holes drilled for them in the shallow side of the cabinet and test-fit the shelves. It may be necessary to cut shallow notches in the ends of the shelves to accommodate the shelf pins so that the shelves will fit.

6. Storage doors for the shallow side of the cabinet are the next elements to be constructed. Begin by cutting the various pieces composing the doors. From ¾-inch pine stock, cut two 2¾-inch by 21³/₁₆-inch tops, four 2¾-inch by 29⅞-inch sides, four 2½-inch by 21³/₁₆-inch shelves, two 2½-inch by 13¾-inch shelves, one 2½-inch by 11¼-inch shelf support and one

2½-inch by 6⅜-inch adjustable shelf. From ½-inch stock, cut three 1¼-inch by 21⅞-inch strips. Two of these are for hold-in rails for cookie sheets. The third strip, to be a hold-in rail for the spice shelf, is re-ripped or planed to a ¼-inch thickness (so it will measure ¼ inch by 1¼ inches by 21⅞ inches). Cut two 21³/₁₆-inch by 29½-inch door panels from ¼-inch A-C birch interior plywood.

7. Plow a ⅜-inch-wide by ¼-inch-deep rabbet along one long edge of each of the top and side pieces. The rabbet will accommodate the door panel. The rabbeted edge will be the outside edge of each piece, while the rabbeted face will be the

inside face of each of the pieces.

8. The left-hand door is more complicated than the right. Select the pieces that have to be worked on—two of the sides, a top, one 21³/₁₆-inch-long shelf and the shelf support—for the left-hand door.

a. The side that is on your left when the door is open, or the left side, is fabricated as follows: Cut a ¾-inch-wide by ⅜-inch-deep rabbet across the inside face at the top. Cut four ¾-inch-wide by ⅜-inch-deep dadoes across the inside face; their upper edges will be 3¾ inches, 7½ inches, 11¼ inches and 28 inches from the top. Finally, cut two 1¼-inch-wide by ½-inch-deep

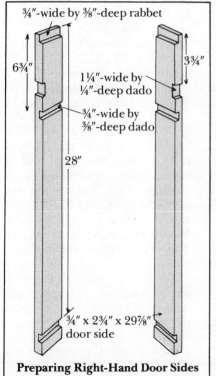

Preparing Right-Hand Door Sides

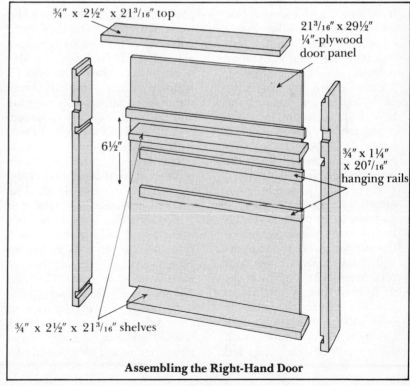

Assembling the Right-Hand Door

dadoes across the inside edges; the top edges of the dadoes are 19¾ inches and 24⅜ inches from the top.

b. The right side for the door is fabricated as follows: Cut a ¾-inch-wide by ⅜-inch-deep rabbet across the inside face at the top. Cut two ¾-inch-wide by ⅜-inch-deep dadoes across the inside face, one with its top edge 11¼ inches from the top, the other with its top edge 28 inches from the top. Cut two 1¼-inch-wide by ½-inch-deep dadoes across the inside edge of the sides, with their top edges 19¾ inches and 24⅜ inches from the top of the side. In the space between the rabbet and the first dado, lay out a series of holes for adjustable shelf pins. Scribe one line ¼ inch and a second line 2¼ inches from the inside edge of the side. Mark a center point for each of four holes on each line, beginning 2 inches down from the edge of the rabbet and locating the holes on 2-inch centers. Use a try square to line up pairs of holes. Drill ¼-inch holes ⅜ inch deep; *don't* drill all the way through the side.

c. Lay out a matching set of holes in the shelf support. Lay out the top two holes 2⅜ inches from the top edge of the support, since the support will fit into a dado in the door top. After laying out the holes, drill them, just as you did in the side. Turn the support over and cut two ¾-inch-wide by ⅜-inch-deep dadoes, with their top edges 3⅜ inches and

7⅛ inches from the top respectively.

d. Cut a ¾-inch-wide by ⅜-inch-deep dado across the inside face of the top, 13⅜ inches from what will be the left end of the top. Lay this out carefully; when the top is laid out with its inside face up and the rabbeted edge away from you, the edge of the dado should be 13⅜ inches from the right end of the top.

e. Cut a similar dado in one of the 21³⁄₁₆-inch shelves. It should be ¾ inch wide and ⅜ inch deep and 13⅜ inches from one end.

9. Assemble the left-hand door, using glue and 6d finishing nails. This door will use the pieces you've just specially fabricated for it, as well as a 21³⁄₁₆-inch-long shelf, the two 13¾-inch-long shelves and the two ½-inch-thick hold-in rails. Ultimately, the 6⅜-inch adjustable shelf is included in this door, too. After the door's framework is assembled, install the door panel, again using glue and 6d finishing nails. Countersink all the nails and cover them with wood filler.

10. The remaining door pieces are used to construct the right-hand storage door. The side pieces must be rabbeted and dadoed to accept the top, shelves and hold-in rail. Cut a ¾-inch-wide by ⅜-inch-deep rabbet across the inside face of each side at the top. Cut two ¾-inch-wide by ⅜-inch-deep dadoes across the inside face of each side, with their top edges 6¾ inches and 28 inches from the top. Cut a 1¼-inch-wide by

¼-inch-deep dado across the inside edge of each side, 3¾ inches from the top.

11. Assemble the door using glue and 6d finishing nails. Countersink the nails and cover them with wood filler.

12. Cut two 1¼-inch by 20⁷⁄₁₆-inch hanging rails from ¾-inch stock. These are glued into the right-hand door, below the spice shelf. The top edge of one is 2 inches below the shelf bottom, the other 6½ inches below the shelf bottom. Ultimately, you can turn screw hooks into these rails to hang odd-shaped baking utensils on.

13. Rip about 4½ feet of ¼-inch by ¼-inch strips. Cut three 13-inch lengths and two 6¾-inch lengths of the strips. Glue the strips to the shelves in the upper portion of the left-hand door. The strips serve as retainer lips; they prevent items from toppling off the shelves when the door is opened or the baking center is moved.

14. Hang the storage doors on the cabinet using two pairs of ¾-inch offset hinges. Lay out and drill holes for the door knobs. Each knob should be 5 inches from the top and 2 inches from the center edge of its door. Use 1½-inch wooden knobs. Finally, install magnetic catches to hold the doors closed. Mount the strike plate on the door, then mount the catch on the divider.

15. Now turn your attention to the deep side of the cabinet. You must construct a variety of drawers for this side, as well as the proofing box. But first you must construct the face frame.

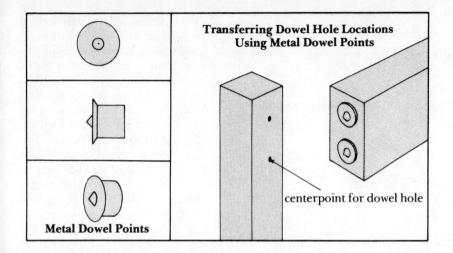

Transferring Dowel Hole Locations Using Metal Dowel Points

Metal Dowel Points

centerpoint for dowel hole

drill press or a hand drill with a doweling jig to ensure that the holes are perpendicular. In either device, use a brad-point drill bit.

d. Use metal dowel points inserted in the holes in each rail to transfer the hole locations to the stiles. Having done that, use the same drilling setup to drill ⅜-inch holes for dowels in the stiles. Be sure not to drill too deeply; if the bit breaks through the side stiles, the piece is ruined. Make the holes in the side stiles no more than ½ inch deep, and those in the center stile no more than ⅝ inch deep.

e. Cut 24 pieces of ⅜-inch dowel (measure it to be sure it's ⅜ inch in diameter; actual sizes do vary slightly), each 1¾ inches long. Bevel the edges slightly and file or cut a groove or two extending from end to end to act as a glue channel. (Pregrooved dowels

a. From ¾-inch pine stock, cut the following pieces: a 1⅝-inch by 30-inch center stile, two ¾-inch by 30-inch side stiles, four 1½-inch by 20⁷/₁₆-inch rails and two 2½-inch by 20⁷/₁₆-inch rails.

b. Lay out the pieces. With the three stiles abutting each other edge to edge, designate one end to be the top and mark points 9 inches down from it on both sides of each stile. Slide the stiles apart and lay the rails in place, with the 2½-inch-wide pieces flush with the bottoms of the stiles, two 1½-inch-wide pieces flush with the tops and the remaining pieces lined up with their tops on a line with the 9-inch marks. The face frame must be assembled using dowel joints, with two dowels in each joint.

c. Lay out two ⅜-inch holes for the dowel joints in the butt end of each rail

Scribe the vertical centerline between the end edges on the butt end. Then measure ⁷/₁₆ inch along the line from each edge, and mark those spots as the centers of the holes for the dowels. Drill a ⅜-inch hole at each spot, making it about 1½ inches deep. Use a

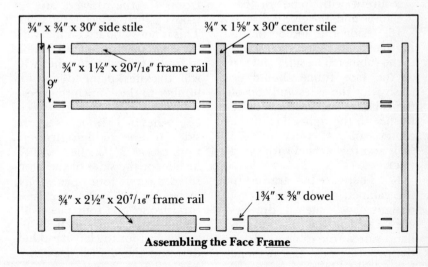

¾" x ¾" x 30" side stile   ¾" x 1⅝" x 30" center stile

¾" x 1½" x 20⁷/₁₆" frame rail

9"

¾" x 2½" x 20⁷/₁₆" frame rail   1¾" x ⅜" dowel

Assembling the Face Frame

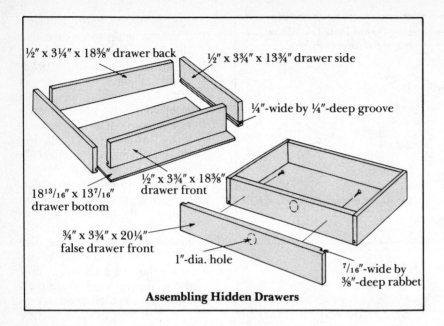

½" x 3¼" x 18⅜" drawer back

½" x 3¾" x 13¾" drawer side

¼"-wide by ¼"-deep groove

18¹³/₁₆" x 13⁷/₁₆" drawer bottom

½" x 3¾" x 18⅜" drawer front

¾" x 3¾" x 20¼" false drawer front

1"-dia. hole

⁷/₁₆"-wide by ⅜"-deep rabbet

Assembling Hidden Drawers

are available from some lumberyards and many woodworking specialty houses.

f. As you assemble the face frame, smear glue on each dowel as you insert it in its hole. Be sure the face frame is square and flat, then clamp it securely with pipe or bar clamps until the glue is dry.

16. Using glue and 6d finishing nails, attach the face frame to the cabinet. The sides and top of the face frame should be flush with the sides and top of the cabinet; the divider will be flush with the right edge of the center stile. Countersink the nails and cover them with wood filler.

17. There are five drawers in the cabinet, of three different designs. Two utensil drawers are located in the upper right-hand side of the cabinet, beside the proofing box. Below them, behind the door, is a special

drawer for a mixer or food processor with accessories or attachments. Beside this drawer, behind the left-hand door, are two drawers of the third design. Begin the process of making the drawers by cutting the parts. The sides, backs and structural fronts for the drawers are cut from ½-inch select pine stock. This is not standard lumberyard material, but you should be able to find a millwork supplier who will thickness-plane dimension lumber to the ½-inch thickness. From this stock, cut five pieces 3¾ inches by 13¾ inches for the sides of the hidden drawers, four pieces 3¾ inches by 14⅜ inches for the sides of the utensil drawers, four pieces 3¾ inches by 18⅜ inches for structural fronts and four pieces 3¼ inches by 18⅜ inches for backs—all for the left-hand hidden and the utensil drawers— and one piece 3¾ inches by

18¼ inches for a structural front for the mixer drawer. From ⅝-inch A-C interior plywood cut a 13½-inch by 18¾-inch back and a 14-inch by 13¾-inch side for the mixer drawer. From ¼-inch A-C interior plywood, cut three 18¹³/₁₆-inch by 13⁷/₁₆-inch bottom panels for the hidden drawers and two 18¹³/₁₆-inch by 14¹/₁₆-inch bottom panels for the utensil drawers. From ¾-inch select pine, cut three 3¾-inch by 20¼-inch false fronts for the hidden drawers and two 4-inch by 21-inch false fronts for the utensil drawers.

18. Assemble the two left-hand hidden drawers first. Select four of the 13¾-inch-long sides, two backs and two structural fronts. Plow a ¼-inch-wide by ¼-inch-deep groove along the inside face of each of the sides and fronts, ¼ inch from the bottom edge. Glue and nail, using 6d finishing nails, the sides, front and back together. The sides overlap the ends of the front and back in simple butt joints. All four pieces should be flush along their top edges. Select two of the bottom panels and slide them into the grooves plowed for them. Drive several 6d finishing nails through the back of the panel into the bottom edge of the back. Select two of the 20¼-inch false fronts and cut a ⁷/₁₆-inch wide by ⅜-inch-deep rabbet across each end of both. Glue this front to the structural fronts of the drawers, then drive six 1-inch #6 screws through the structural front into the false front of each drawer. Drill a 1-inch diameter hole completely through the

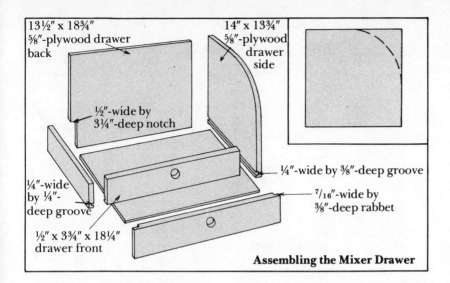

13½" x 18¾"
⅝"-plywood drawer
back

14" x 13¾"
⅝"-plywood
drawer
side

½"-wide by
3¼"-deep notch

¼"-wide by ⅜"-deep groove

¼"-wide
by ¼"-
deep groove

⁷/₁₆"-wide by
⅜"-deep rabbet

½" x 3¾" x 18¼"
drawer front

Assembling the Mixer Drawer

front of the drawer, and drive six 1-inch #6 screws through the structural front into this front. Drill and finish a finger hole as you did in the previously assembled drawers.

20. The utensil drawers are the final ones to be assembled. You'll obviously use the remaining pieces. Plow a ¼-inch-wide by ¼-inch-deep groove along the inside of each side and front, ¼ inch from the bottom edge. Glue and nail the sides, fronts and backs together, using simple butt joints. The pieces are flush along their top edges. Slide the bottom panels in place and nail them to the back. Take the two 4-inch by 21-inch drawer fronts and cut a ⅜-inch-wide by ⅜-inch-deep rabbet across both ends and along one side of each. Glue and screw these fronts to the structural fronts, making sure the side rabbet overhangs the top edge of one drawer and

front of each drawer so you will be able to pull it open. The hole should be centered from left to right and 1½ inches from the top edge. Use a ¼-inch rounding-off bit in a router to break the exterior edge of the hole.

19. Now assemble the special mixer drawer. This drawer is composed of the remaining 13¾-inch side, the plywood back and side and the 18¼-inch structural front. Plow a ¼-inch-wide by ¼-inch-deep groove in the pine side and front, ¼ inch from the bottom edge of each. Plow a ¼-inch-wide by ⅜-inch-deep groove in the plywood side, ¼ inch from the bottom edge. Using a compass set for a 7½-inch radius, scribe a line to round off the top front corner of the plywood side. Cut along the line. Notch out the lower back corner of the plywood back to fit over the pine side; the notch should be ½ inch wide and 3¼ inches deep. Glue and nail the sides, front and back together, using butt joints. Slide

a bottom panel into the grooves plowed for it and drive several nails through the bottom into the bottom edge of the back. Take the remaining 20¼-inch front and cut a ⁷/₁₆-inch-wide by ⅜-inch-deep rabbet across each end. Then glue it to the

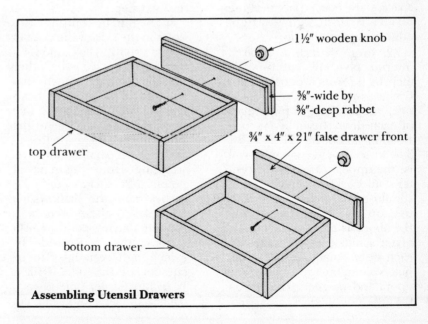

1½" wooden knob

⅜"-wide by
⅜"-deep rabbet

¾" x 4" x 21" false drawer front

top drawer

bottom drawer

Assembling Utensil Drawers

the bottom edge of the other. Locate and mark the center of each drawer front, left to right and top to bottom, and mount a 1½-inch wooden knob there.

21. Attach drawer slide assemblies to the drawers and to the cabinet. Information packaged with the assemblies will detail how to position the hardware on the drawers and cabinets and how to adjust them. The two utensil drawers go in the upper right-hand space in the deep side. The mixer drawer is positioned in the lower right space so that it just clears the cabinet bottom. One of the remaining two drawers is similarly positioned in the left lower space, with the second drawer positioned so that there is a 3⅝-inch space between them. Before you can install the slide hardware for the latter two drawers, you'll have to attach two 1-inch by 3¼-inch by 14⅜-inch spacers to the divider. The spacers are needed because the divider is flush with the right edge of the center stile.

22. From ¾-inch A/C birch interior plywood, cut two 21-inch by 17¾-inch door panels. Cut a ⅜-inch-wide by ⅜-inch-deep rabbet along all four edges of each door. Install a 1½-inch wooden knob on each door. The knob should go in what will be the upper corner at the center stile. The center point should be 1¾ inches from both the top and side edges. Hang the doors using a pair of double offset semiconcealed hinges on each one. Finally, install strike plates along the top edges of the doors and magnetic catches on the adjacent rails.

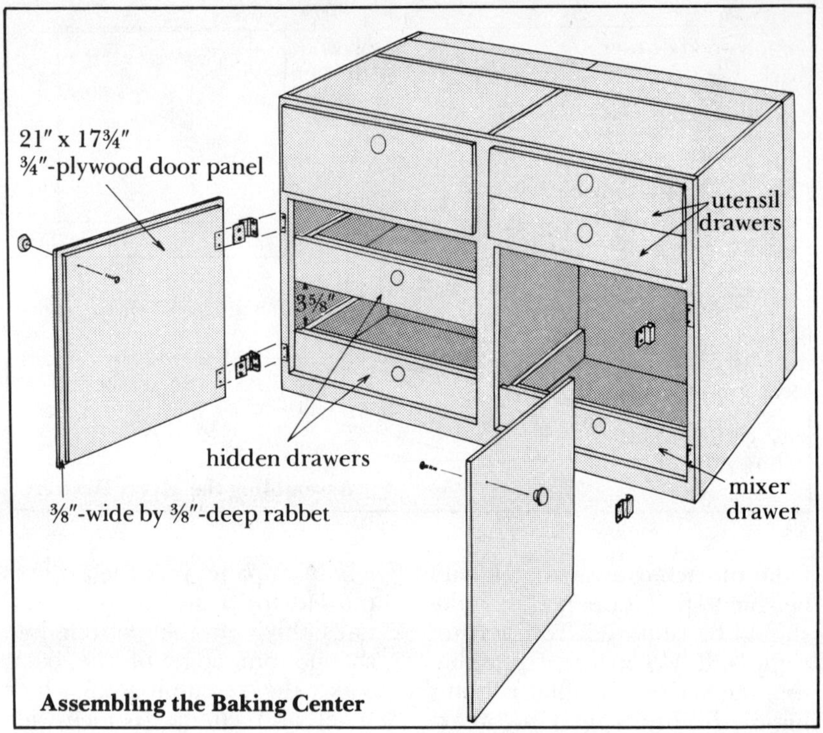
21" x 17¾"
¾"-plywood door panel
utensil drawers
3⅝"
hidden drawers
⅜"-wide by ⅜"-deep rabbet
mixer drawer
Assembling the Baking Center

23. The wiring of the center is the next step.

a. Begin by cutting two holes in the side of the cabinet by the proofing box, one for a duplex receptacle, the other for the dimmer switch that will control the proofing box's heating light. Scribe a line parallel to the top edge of the side and 4½ inches below it. Scribe perpendiculars descending from this line at points 5⅜ inches and 9⅛ inches from the shallow-side edge. Using these corners as top left starting points, finish scribing two 2-inch-wide by 3-inch-high rectangles to be cut out of the side. Drill a ¼-inch or larger hole in each corner of each box and cut out the box with a keyhole saw or saber saw.

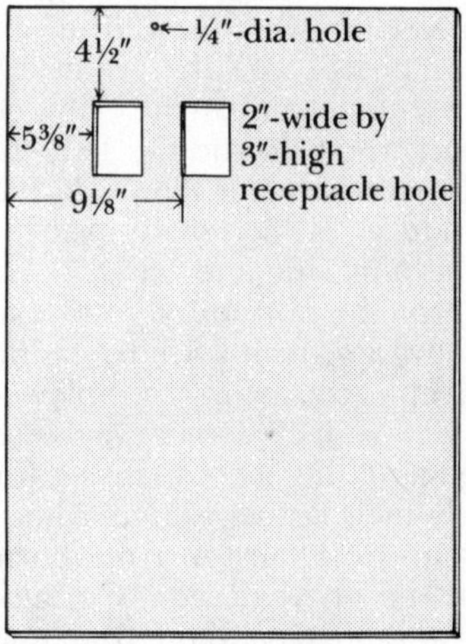
¼"-dia. hole
4½"
5⅜"
9⅛"
2"-wide by
3"-high
receptacle hole
Placement of Receptacle Holes

b. Drill a ¼-inch to ⅜-inch

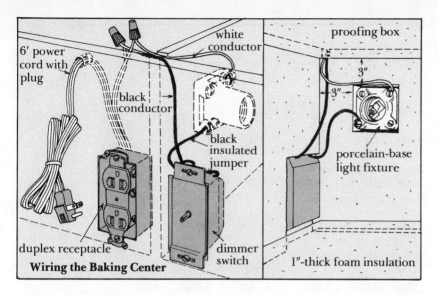

c. Remove two knockouts from a wall box. Install the box in the left-hand hole, then install connectors in the knockout holes. Fish the power cord through one of them, and a short piece of 14/2 nonmetallic cable through the other. Wire a duplex receptacle to the power cord and the cable as diagrammed, then install the receptacle in the box. Mount a wall plate over the receptacle.

d. Install a porcelain light fixture inside the proofing box. The fixture should be attached to the back wall of the box on a center point approximately 3 inches below the top and to the left side of the cabinet. Wire the fixture and a dimmer switch into the circuit. The dimmer switch will go in the second

hole in the cabinet side for the power cord. Position the hole just to the left of the two rectangular holes and just below the top edge. Drill a similar-size hole through the middle divider adjacent to the holes in the cabinet side. Install a plug on one end of the power cord, then fish the free end through the hole you've drilled in the cabinet side.

Materials

Wood

1–2' × 4' sht. ¾" A-C int. plywood or **Bottom:** 1 pc. 22½" × 42½"

1–4' sq. sht. ¾" birch int. plywood or **Ends:** 2 pcs. 22½" × 30"
    Doors: 2 pcs. 21" × 17¾"

1–4' × 6' sht. ⅝" A-C int. plywood or **Middle Divider:** 1 pc. 27¾" × 42½"
    Deep-side divider: 1 pc. 14⅜" × 27¾"
    Drawer back: 1 pc. 13½" × 18¾"
    Drawer side: 1 pc. 14" × 13¾"

1–2' × 4' sht. ½" B-D int. plywood or **Subtop:** 1 pc. 7½" × 42½"
    Subtop: 1 pc. 14⅜" × 20⅜"
    Proofing box top and bottom: 2 pcs. 14⅜" × 21½"

1 pc. 1 × 10 × 10' select pine or **Shallow-side divider:** 1 pc. ¾" × 7½" × 27¼"
    Adjustable shelves: 4 pcs. ¾" × 7⁷⁄₁₆" × 20¹³⁄₁₆"
    Shelf edges: 4 pcs. ⅝" × ¾" × 20¹³⁄₁₆"

[continued on next page]

1 pc. 1 × 4 × 8′ select pine or **Door tops:** 2 pcs. ¾″ × 2¾″ × 21³/₁₆″
Hanging rails: 2 pcs. ¾″ × 1¼″ × 20⁷/₁₆″
Center stile: 1 pc. ¾″ × 1⅝″ × 30″

1 pc. 1 × 4 × 10′ select pine or **Door sides:** 4 pcs. ¾″ × 2¾″ × 29⅞″

2 pcs. 1 × 3 × 8′ select pine or **Door shelves:** 4 pcs. ¾″ × 2½″ × 21³/₁₆″
Door shelves: 2 pcs. ¾″ × 2½″ × 13¾″
Door shelf support: 1 pc. ¾″ × 2½″ × 11¼″
Door shelf: 1 pc. ¾″ × 2½″ × 6⅜″
Face frame bottom rails: 2 pcs. ¾″ × 2½″ × 20⁷/₁₆″

1 pc. 1 × 10 × 10′ select pine or **Door hold-ins:** 2 pcs. ½″ × 1¼″ × 21⅞″
Hold-in: 1 pc. ¼″ × 1¼″ × 21⅞″
Shelf edge strips: 3 pcs. ¼″ × ¼″ × 13″
2 pcs. ¼″ × ¼″ × 6¾″
Drawer sides: 5 pcs. ½″ × 3¾″ × 13¾″
4 pcs. ½″ × 3¾″ × 14⅜″
Drawer fronts: 4 pcs. ½″ × 3¾″ × 18⅜″
1 pc. ½″ × 3¾″ × 18¼″

1–4′ sq. sht. ¼″ birch int. plywood or **Door panels:** 2 pcs. 21³/₁₆″ × 29½″

1 pc. 1 × 4 × 8′ select pine or **Drawer backs:** 4 pcs. ½″ × 3¼″ × 18⅜″

1 pc. 1 × 10 × 8′ select pine or **Face frame side stiles:** 2 pcs. ¾″ × ¾″ × 30″
False drawer fronts: 3 pcs. ¾″ × 3¾″ × 20¼″
False drawer fronts: 2 pcs. ¾″ × 4″ × 21″
Proofing box door: 3 pcs. ¾″ × 2¾″ × 21″ (glue up)

1 pc. 1 × 2 × 8′ select pine or **Face frame rails:** 4 pcs. ¾″ × 1½″ × 20⁷/₁₆″

1–4′ sq. sht. ¼″ A-C int. plywood or **Drawer bottoms:** 3 pcs. 18¹³/₁₆″ × 13⁷/₁₆″
2 pcs. 18¹³/₁₆″ × 14¹/₁₆″

2 pcs. 36″ × ⅜″ dowel or **Dowels:** 24 pcs. 1¾″ × ⅜″ dowel

1 pc. ⁵/₄ × 8 × 2′ #2 pine or **Spacers:** 2 pcs. 1″ × 3¼″ × 14⅜″

1 pc. 1¾″ × 30″ × 48″ maple butcher block

Hardware
2 fixed casters w/3″ wheels
2 swivel casters w/3″ wheels
16–1½″ × ¼″ carriage bolts w/nuts and lock washers
6d finishing nails
20 shelf support pins

2 pr.–¾″ offset hinges
7–1½″ wooden knobs
4 magnetic catches
30–1″ #6 f.h. screws
3 pr. 12″ drawer slides
2 pr. 14″ drawer slides
2 pr. double offset semiconcealed hinges
1–3′ sq. sht. aluminum
10 pop rivets
9–1″ #6 r.h. screws
1–10½″ × 11″ pc. ¼″ sq. mesh hardware cloth
3–¾″ #8 sheet-metal screws
1 pr. double offset semiconcealed self-closing hinges
1 friction lid support
6–1½″ #10 f.h. screws

Miscellaneous
Glue
Wood filler
6′ 14/2 type SJT power cord w/plug
1 wall box
2′ 14/2 nonmetallic cable
3 wire nuts
1 duplex receptacle
1 receptacle plate
1 porcelain-base light fixture
1 dimmer switch
1 switch plate
1 light bulb
1 sht. 1″ Styrofoam insulation
Contact cement
Nontoxic semigloss enamel paint

hole that's been cut into the cabinet, so keep that in mind as you work. In essence, you will be running both the white and black insulated conductors to the light fixture, then putting the switch in the hot, or black, side of the circuit. So run the white conductor to the fixture and wire it to a terminal. Wire the black conductor from the cable to the switch, then run a short, black insulated jumper from the switch to the fixture. Neither the switch nor the fixture has a ground terminal, so the ground wire ends at the receptacle. After testing the circuit, install the dimmer switch in the cabinet, without a wall box, and cover it with a switch plate.

24. From a 1-inch-thick panel of Styrofoam or comparable insulation, cut pieces for the top, bottom, back and sides of the proofing box. Glue them in place with contact cement. The pieces should measure approximately 14⅜ inches by 21½ inches for the top and bottom, 7⅝ inches by 14⅜ inches for the sides and 19½ inches by 7⅝ inches for the back. Better to cut the pieces slightly oversize and trim than to cut them too small. The fit should be snug. The back piece will have to be cut out to accom-

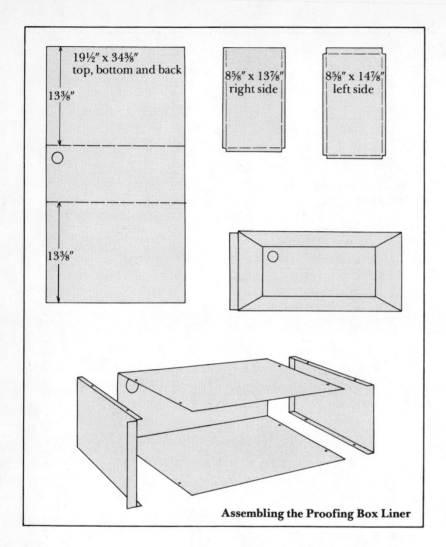

19½" x 34⅜"
top, bottom and back

13⅜"

13⅜"

8⅝" x 13⅞"
right side

8⅝" x 14⅞"
left side

Assembling the Proofing Box Liner

while the three ½-inch tabs are bent up.

c. The second piece is scribed and bent in the same way, except that there is no 1-inch tab; the piece has only three tabs.

d. The third piece is bent along its 19½-inch dimension at points 13⅜ inches from each end. Dry-fit this piece in the proofing box and mark the location of the light fixture on the metal. Remove the piece and cut away the aluminum for the fixture.

e. Dry-fit the three pieces together, forming an open-ended box. The pieces are

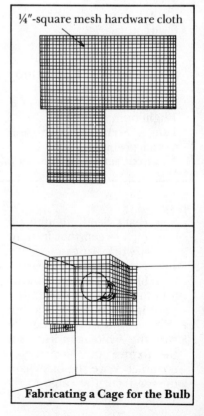

¼"-square mesh hardware cloth

Fabricating a Cage for the Bulb

modate the heating-light fixture.

25. Fabricate the aluminum liner for the proofing box.

a. Cut three pieces from a 3-foot-square sheet of aluminum. One measures 14⅞ inches by 8⅝ inches and is for the left side of the proofing box. The second, for the right side, is 13⅞ inches by 8⅝ inches. The third piece, for the bottom, back and top, is

34 ⅜ inches by 19½ inches.

b. Take the first piece. Measure in ½ inch from each side and scribe a line parallel to the side. Do the same at one end. At the other end, measure in 1 inch and scribe a line parallel to the end. Using tin snips, cut away the metal where the lines intersect, thus notching the corners. Bend the aluminum along the lines; the 1-inch tab is bent down,

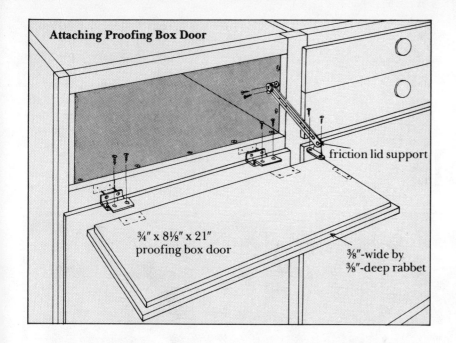

Attaching Proofing Box Door

friction lid support

¾" x 8⅛" x 21" proofing box door

⅜"-wide by ⅜"-deep rabbet

of the door and the proofing box. Attach a 1½-inch wooden knob 2 inches below the top edge and 10½ inches from either end of the door.

29. Paint the entire cabinet with two coats of semigloss enamel paint or some other finish of your choice.

30. The top is a 1¾-inch-thick maple butcher block measuring 30 inches by 48 inches. It's advisable that you purchase this item rather than construct it in the home workshop. Position the top on the cabinet and fasten it by driving six or more 1½-inch #10 screws through the subtops into the butcher block.

fastened together with 10 pop rivets. Drill holes of the appropriate size for the pop rivets you are using through the tabs and the liner proper and complete the assembly.

26. Slide the liner into the proofing box. Drill holes through the liner and into the stile and rail edges for 1-inch #6 roundhead screws. Put five along the top, two in the right side and two in the bottom.

27. Install a light bulb in the fixture. Then fabricate a cage for around the bulb from ¼-inch-square mesh hardware cloth. Start with a 10½-inch by 11-inch piece of the wire mesh. Cut a 5½-inch square from one corner. Bend the resulting L-shaped piece into a three-sided cage. Counterbend ½-inch-wide tabs on each side of the cage and trim the ½-inch-wide excess strip from what is the

bottom of the cage. Hold the cage over the bulb with the tabs against the proofing box liner. The cage will be fastened in place with a sheet-metal screw in each tab. Mark the locations of the screws, drill holes in the liner and fasten the cage in place.

28. The proofing box door can be fashioned from a single broad board, like a 1 × 10. Or, to make more efficient use of materials, it can be glued up from three pieces measuring ¾ inch by 2 ¾ inches by 21 inches. In either case, trim the door to ¾ inch by 8⅛ inches by 21 inches, then cut a ⅜-inch-wide by ⅜-inch-deep rabbet along each edge of the door. Hang the door using a pair of double offset semiconcealed self-closing hinges along the bottom edge. The self-closing hinges keep the door closed. Install a friction lid support between the right side

643

There is a time to dine and a time to snack. And this tray table can be handy to have at either time.

For dining, you want everything right: from soup to nuts, from candlelight to linen napkins. Keeping it all together, handy but not obtrusive, is a job for this tray table.

But when the time for snack-

Tray Table

644

ing rolls around, the tray table is in its true metier. It will serve as a place to set out dishes of snacks for a party or social get-together just as well as it will replace those shoddily made metal tv tables.

The tray table is sturdy, attractive, and not all that difficult to make. The principal pieces can be cut from a length of 1 × 2 and a small piece of plywood, both of which are available at every lumberyard. The required tools can be found in the shop of almost every woodworker: a saw, router, drill and some clamps.

Construction

1. There are two basic components to the tray table: the tray and the stand. The tray is constructed first. From 1 × 2 stock, cut two 15⅝-inch pieces for the tray ends and two 24⅜-inch pieces for the tray sides.

2. Cut a ¾-inch-wide by ⅜-inch-deep rabbet across both ends of each end piece. The rabbeted face will be the inside. Plow a ⁵/₁₆-inch-wide by ⅜-inch-deep groove on the inside face of each side and end, ¼ inch below the top edge. This is for the tray bottom to fit into.

3. From ¼-inch plywood, cut a piece measuring 14⅞ inches by 24⅜ inches for the tray bottom. Cut a piece of plastic laminate the same size and glue it to the bottom with contact cement.

4. Glue the sides and ends to the tray bottom, clamping the unit with bar or pipe clamps.

5. From 1 × 2 stock, cut four 32½-inch table legs. Use a compass set for a ¾-inch radius and

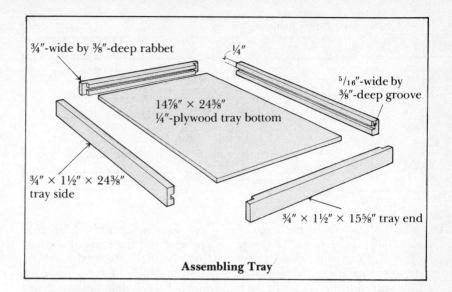

¾"-wide by ⅜"-deep rabbet

¼"

⁵/₁₆"-wide by ⅜"-deep groove

14⅞" × 24⅜" ¼"-plywood tray bottom

¾" × 1½" × 24⅜" tray side

¾" × 1½" × 15⅝" tray end

Assembling Tray

Materials

Wood
2 pcs. 1 × 2 × 10′ select pine or **Tray ends:** 2 pcs.
ㅤㅤㅤㅤㅤ¾" × 1½" × 15⅝"
ㅤㅤㅤㅤㅤ**Tray sides:** 2 pcs.
ㅤㅤㅤㅤㅤ¾" × 1½" × 24⅜"
ㅤㅤㅤㅤㅤ**Legs:** 4 pcs.
ㅤㅤㅤㅤㅤ¾" × 1½" × 32½"

1–2′ × 4′ sht. ¼" A-C int. plywood or **Tray bottom:** 1 pc.
ㅤㅤㅤㅤㅤ14⅞" × 24⅜"

3 pcs. 36" × ½" dowel or **Cross-members:** 3 pcs.
ㅤㅤㅤㅤㅤ14" × ½" dowel
ㅤㅤㅤㅤㅤ**Cross-members:** 2 pcs.
ㅤㅤㅤㅤㅤ12½" × ½" dowel

Hardware
2–¾" #6 screw eyes
24" brass jack chain

Miscellaneous
1–2′ × 4′ sht. plastic laminate or **Tray surface:** 1 pc.
ㅤㅤㅤㅤㅤ14⅞" × 24⅜"

Contact cement
Glue
Varnish

645

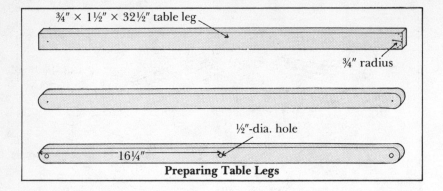

¾″ × 1½″ × 32½″ table leg

¾″ radius

½″-dia. hole

16¼″

Preparing Table Legs

draw a semicircle on each end of each table leg. Use a coping saw or a rasp to round the legs on these radius lines. Drill a ½-inch hole through the center of each

leg. The holes should be 16¼ inches from the ends of the legs and ¾ inch from the edges. Also drill a ½-inch hole in each end of each leg, at the point

used to radius the ends.

6. Use a rounding-off bit in a router to break all the edges, on both the tray and all the legs.

7. Cut three 14-inch cross-members and two 12½-inch cross-members from ½-inch dowel.

8. Glue the ends of the two 12½-inch dowels into the holes in the ends of two legs which will be the inside legs. Use a try square to make sure the legs and dowels are square.

9. When the glue has dried, insert a 14-inch dowel through the center holes of the legs that are glued to the 12½-inch dowels. Don't glue the 14-inch dowel to these legs. Rather, glue the ends of this center dowel into the center holes of the other two legs. When the glue dries, glue the other two 14-inch dowels into the end holes of the two outside legs.

10. After sanding and finishing all wood surfaces, install the retainer chain. Turn a screw eye into the center of each upper cross-member with the eye on the inner side of the member and so that the eye will be parallel to the floor when the stand is open. Extend a length of brass jack chain between the eyes to hold the stand in the appropriate open position.

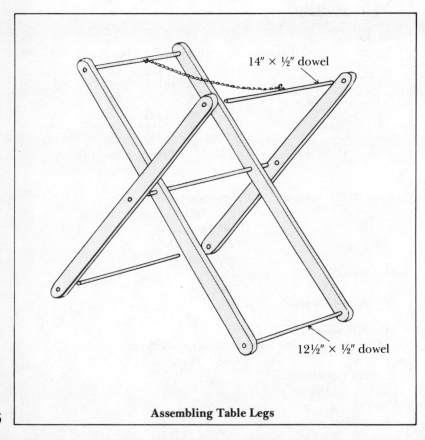

14″ × ½″ dowel

12½″ × ½″ dowel

Assembling Table Legs

Bed Tray Table

Breakfast in bed! It can be a soothing, intimate, relaxing way to begin the day, either for yourself or for someone you love.

But breakfast in bed can also ruin the day if you bring it in on a regular tray. Ever have a lapful of hot coffee and scrambled eggs in bed just because you shifted your

knees? If so, you'll appreciate this handy little bed tray table. The table sits on folding legs that rest on the mattress on either side of the lap. It has a raised lip all around it to prevent cups and plates from sliding around, either on the way to the bedroom or after the tray table has been placed in position on the bed. When breakfast is over, this light tray table can be easily removed, cleaned and, with the legs folded in flat, stored out of sight in a closet or cabinet.

It probably won't stay out of sight for long, for this versatile little table will find many uses in your home. Perhaps you will find that you use it for reading or doing homework in bed. Or the kids will use it for a game of checkers or a picture puzzle in front of the fire on a rainy afternoon. Or the plant-lover in the family will whisk it off to hold the cactus collection so that the plants can be moved around the house to get the advantage of light from various windows as the winter sun shifts in the sky.

The 14-inch by 24-inch bed tray table is not difficult to make, but it does require some precise measuring and cutting. It is particularly important that the legs be set in as outlined below, or else the table may be either too low to comfortably clear the lap or too wobbly.

Keep in mind that you can make your own adjustments to the basic design. For example, if you do not like the look or feel of plastic laminate for the top of the tray, you might have

an old breadboard you will want to cut down. And instead of dowels, you may want to use flat stock for the legs. Half the fun of building is designing, so adapt the design to your own needs and collection of scrap wood.

Construction

1. From ¾-inch wood, cut two pieces 1¾ inches by 23¼ inches for the sides, and two more 1¾ inches by 14 inches for the ends.

2. Using a router with the proper-size bit or a table or radial arm saw, plow a groove in all four of these pieces to receive the top panel. The groove should be 5/16 inch wide and ⅜ inch deep. It should begin ¼ inch from the top edge.

3. While you have your router or saw set for a ⅜-inch-deep cut, machine a ¾-inch rabbet in both ends of both 14-inch end pieces. Note that the rabbet must be cut out of the side with the groove in it, so that the outside of the piece is unmarked.

4. The next step is to cut the handholes in both of those same two end pieces. These

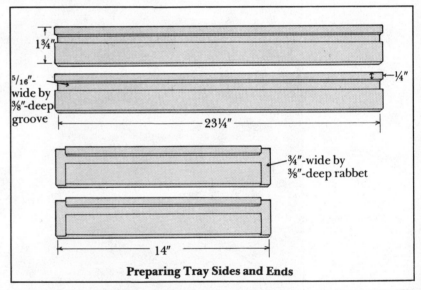

5/16″-wide by ⅜″-deep groove

1¾″

¼″

23¼″

¾″-wide by ⅜″-deep rabbet

14″

Preparing Tray Sides and Ends

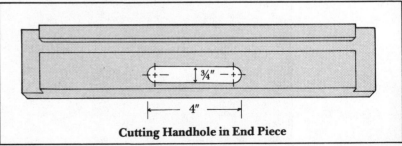

¾″

4″

Cutting Handhole in End Piece

handholes are not absolutely essential, but they will make carrying the tray table much easier. All you need for the job is a drill and a ¾-inch bit. After laying out a ¾-inch by 4-inch flat oval in the center of each end piece (keeping at least ¼ inch from the bottom edge), carefully drill five or six holes in each oval and then chisel the inside excess wood out with a sharp chisel. A wood rasp and a piece of sandpaper will permit you to smooth out the handholes.

5. While you have the ¾-inch drill bit in your drill, drill two holes on the inside of each side piece to accept the pivot dowels. To find the center for the hole, measure ¾ inch in from the ends on the inside (the side with the groove cut into it) of the two side pieces, and ½ inch from the bottom of the groove. Where those measurements intersect, punch a small guide-hole with a nail or an awl. Set the point of the drill in the guide hole and drill

down 5/16 inch. To ensure that the hole does not get too deep, it is best to try to mark the drill or to purchase a depth gauge that clamps to the bit. In any case, drill carefully and stop to measure each hole as you go.

6. Now it's time to work on the dowels that make up the leg structure. You might as well do all the cutting at once:

two pivot dowels, 13 inches by ¾ inch;
two base dowels, 12¼ inches by 1 inch;
four leg dowels, 9½ inches by ½ inch.

7. Now drill ½-inch holes in the pivot dowels and the base dowels. Drilling into round stock can be tricky, but if you take care you will do all right. The primary problem will be to keep the dowels from rolling as you drill. Perhaps you will want to make yourself a little grooved V-block for your drill press by ripping two 45-degree intersecting cuts in a piece of scrap

wood. To find where to drill the holes, measure 1 inch in from both ends of the ¾-inch pivot dowels, and ⅝ inch in from both ends of the base dowels. Check your marks by making sure they are exactly 11 inches apart on all four dowels. Now drill the eight holes with your ½-inch drill bit, making sure that both holes on each of the four dowels are parallel. The holes in the pivot dowels should be ⅜ inch deep; the holes in the base dowels should be ½ inch deep.

8. After sanding the ends of all the dowels, you are ready to assemble and glue the leg units. It is best if you have on hand a half-dozen strong rubber bands that will stretch out to around 10 inches. These will act as clamps to hold the joints tight as the glue dries. After applying the glue to the ends of the leg dowels, push them into the holes in the pivot and base dowels, twist

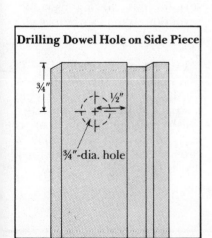

Drilling Dowel Hole on Side Piece

¾"
½"
¾"-dia. hole

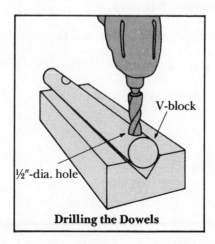

½"-dia. hole

V-block

Drilling the Dowels

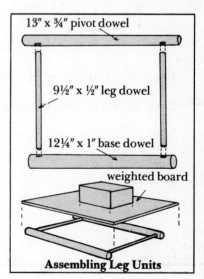

13" x ¾" pivot dowel

9½" x ½" leg dowel

12¼" x 1" base dowel

weighted board

Assembling Leg Units

649

them slightly to ensure an even distribution of the glue, and snap the rubber bands around the pivot and base dowels. Then lay both sets of leg structures on a flat surface and lay over them a weighted flat board to make sure that the structures will be perfectly straight as the glue dries.

9. As the glue on the leg assemblies dries, work on the table top. For this you will need a piece of ¼-inch plywood and a piece of plastic laminate, both cut to 13¼ inches by 23¼ inches. Cement the laminate to the plywood using a contact adhesive.

10. Now you are ready for the most exciting part, final assembly of the complete unit. If all your work has been

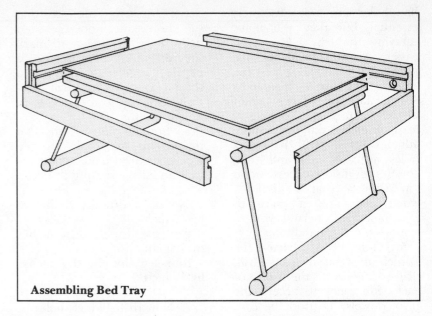

Assembling Bed Tray

careful and accurate, all the pieces will fit together. Put them together dry to make sure everything does fit, then apply glue to the side and end pieces—to the groove for the table top, and to the ends which will be joined together. (Make sure not to get any glue in the holes that will receive the pivot dowels.) Now slip the pieces together and clamp with furniture clamps, making sure to put the leg assembly pivot dowels in place before you clamp. Wipe off all excess glue.

11. When all the glue is dry, sand all the edges and finish the unit with a couple of coats of Deft or some other finish coating. When that is dry, go to bed and enjoy a cup of coffee on your new bed tray table.

Materials

Wood
1 pc. 1 × 3 × 8′ select pine or **Sides:** 2 pcs. ¾″ × 1¾″ × 23¼″
Ends: 2 pcs. ¾″ × 1¾″ × 14″

1 pc. 36″ × ¾″ dowel or **Pivot dowels:** 2 pcs. 13″ × ¾″ dowel

1 pc. 36″ × 1″ dowel or **Base dowels:** 2 pcs. 12¼″ × 1″ dowel

2 pcs. 36″ × ½″ dowel or **Leg dowels:** 4 pcs. 9½″ × ½″ dowel

1–2′ sq. sht. ¼″ int. plywood or **Table top base:** 1 pc. 13¼″ × 23¼″

Miscellaneous
Glue
1–2′ sq. sht. ¹/₁₆″ plastic laminate or **Table top:** 1 pc. 13¼″ × 23¼″

Contact cement
Finish

Step Stool

It is a rare kitchen that would not be enhanced by this dandy little step stool. Use it to get out the canning lids for another season. Or to fetch the special dishes for Thanksgiving dinner. Carry it to another part of the house to ease the stretch of changing a light bulb or . . . well, you'll find dozens of uses for this

651

handsome portable step stool.

Building the stool will be interesting and challenging. If you are a beginning woodworker, you will have a relatively simple piece to practice on, yet at the same time a piece that will introduce you to many of the techniques you will need to know about to tackle some of the larger projects in this book.

When you are finished you will have not merely a useful tool but a beautiful piece of furniture as well, one that would not look out of place as a plant stand or a footstool in most living rooms. You could find—or devise—less complicated designs for a step stool, but it would be difficult to find one that yields a product of such simple elegance, a product of which you will be proud to say, "I made it from scratch."

The basic pieces of the step stool—the sides, the steps and the stretcher—are all constructed from what is called "five-quarter" stock. That means the lumber is cut at the sawmill to be $5/4$ inches, or $1\frac{1}{4}$

inches thick. By the time it emerges from the planing mill, it is more like $1\frac{1}{8}$ inches thick. If you go to the lumberyard and ask for an 8-foot-long piece of 8-inch-wide five-quarter white pine, you will have enough for this project. The only other wood you will need is a piece of $5/16$-inch dowel—but you can whittle out your own dowel if you want to.

Construction

1. The first step is to glue

together the two pieces that will make each side. For this you will need to cut two 15-inch pieces of the five-quarter pine and two $7\frac{1}{2}$-inch pieces. Glue one of the short pieces to the side edge of each of the long pieces, using bar clamps to hold the material while it is drying. Keep the two pieces flush at one end.

2. While the glue on the side pieces is drying, cut the two steps, also out of the five-quarter pine. Each step should be $6\frac{3}{4}$ inches by $15\frac{3}{4}$ inches.

3. In one of the two steps, lay

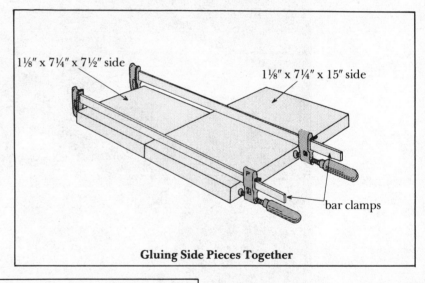

$1\frac{1}{8}"$ x $7\frac{1}{4}"$ x $7\frac{1}{2}"$ side

$1\frac{1}{8}"$ x $7\frac{1}{4}"$ x $15"$ side

bar clamps

Gluing Side Pieces Together

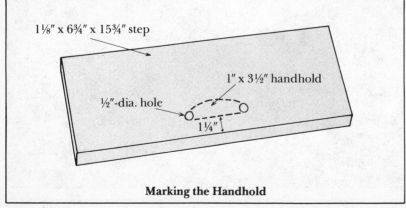

$1\frac{1}{8}"$ x $6\frac{3}{4}"$ x $15\frac{3}{4}"$ step

$1"$ x $3\frac{1}{2}"$ handhold

$\frac{1}{2}"$-dia. hole

$1\frac{1}{4}"$

Marking the Handhold

out and cut the handhold. On ours we made a half-moon shape, but a simple oval would be adequate. It should, in any case, be centered between the two ends of the top step, begin about $1\frac{1}{4}$ inches from the front edge and be about 1 inch by $3\frac{1}{2}$ inches. To cut the handhold, drill two $\frac{1}{2}$-inch-diameter holes, one at each end. Then, using a coping saw or a saber saw, cut out the plug from between the two holes. Use a wood rasp and sandpaper to smooth out the edges of the hole so that it will be comfortable to grip.

4. Mark out and cut the dovetail in each end of each step. Begin by marking the exact center of each end. On the top side of the step, measure out 1¼ inches on each side of the mark. On the bottom side, measure ⅞ inch on each side of the mark. Now connect the marks you have just made on the top and bottom edges. Doing so should give you a wedge-shaped mark 2½ inches at the top and 1¾ inches at the bottom. Take your square and mark back 1⅛ inches on the face of the board at each point where the wedge marks meet the edge. Then square off the ends of those marks and you are ready to begin cutting. Cutting the dovetail out requires care and precision, but it can be done easily enough with a backsaw and a sharp chisel. Begin by sawing along the marks you have made. All you have left to do now in this operation is chiseling out the wedges. It is essential that your chisel be *very* sharp, for you will be cutting against the grain, and you must have a smooth, straight cut when you are finished. To avoid splitting out either the top or the bottom of the step, you should chisel half the wedge out from the top and the other half out from the bottom. If you have measured accurately and held your chisel vertically as you cut, the two cuts will meet perfectly in the middle. Repeat this procedure on both ends of both steps.

5. When the glue on the side

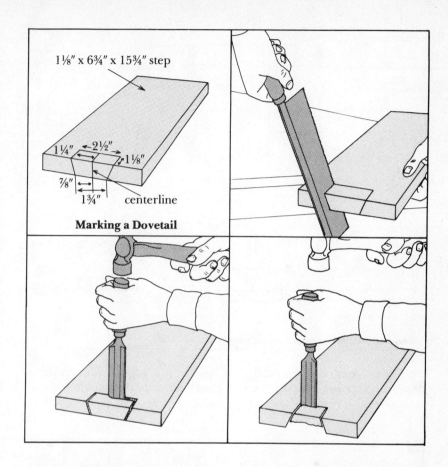

Marking a Dovetail

pieces has dried, you can mark out and cut the 5-degree tapers on the front and back edges of both of the side pieces. Before doing so, make sure that the bottoms of the side pieces are 14½ inches long. The easiest way to lay out the cuts is to use a protractor. Place the flat part of the protractor even with the horizontal part of the back of the side piece, with the center of it even with the vertical part. Then make a mark at the 5-degree point—that is, at the spot on the protractor marked 85 degrees. Remove the protractor and scribe along a straightedge, connecting the corner with the mark you have

just made, extending the line to the end of the side piece. Repeat the procedure on the two short vertical edges on the step side of the piece. After sawing out the 5-degree tapers, use the first side piece to mark an identical pattern on the second side piece, and cut it also.

6. Now mark out the dovetail joint on the side pieces to match the ones on the two steps you have already cut out. The simplest way to do this is to lay out the side on the bench top, hold the step piece perpendicular to it, and trace on the side piece the edges you have on the end of the step. Before you make your marks, be sure that **653**

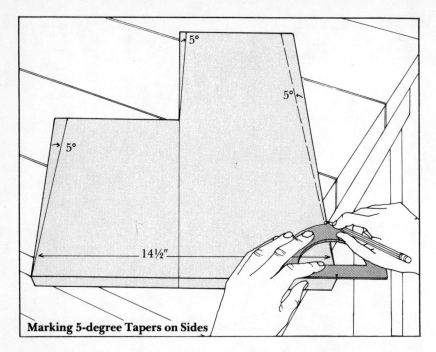

Marking 5-degree Tapers on Sides

have made slight variations in your cuts on the steps. When you mark the lower step cut on the side piece, mark also the 5-degree taper on the back edge of the step so that, when you cut the edge off at that angle, it will fit neatly against the back of the tapered riser. Make the cuts carefully with a sharp backsaw. Chiseling is not necessary in the dovetail joints on the side pieces, *except* to remove the back block on the lower step.

7. Now it is time to prepare the holes that will receive the stretcher that is designed to provide additional strength to your step stool. Begin by cutting the rectangular holes, or mortises, in both side pieces. These should be 1⅛ inches wide and 2 inches high, and should be positioned 5 inches from the bottom and 3 inches from the back of the side piece. Be sure you

the side piece is centered on the step, with an equal extension on each side of the top of the side piece. It is a good idea to mark each dovetail to match the one that will receive it, in case you

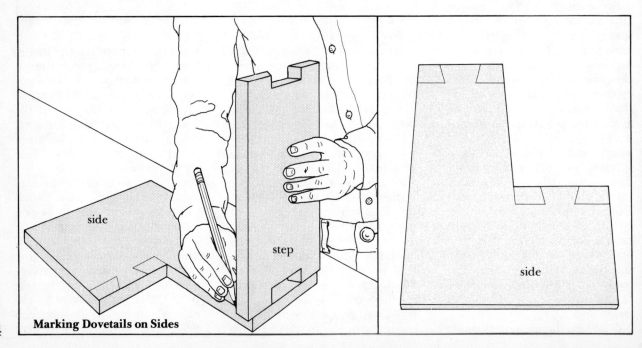

side

step

Marking Dovetails on Sides

side

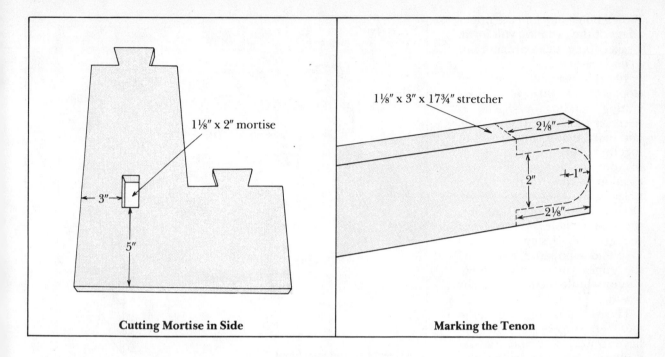

Cutting Mortise in Side

1⅛″ x 2″ mortise

3″

5″

1⅛″ x 3″ x 17¾″ stretcher

2⅛″

2″

1″

2⅛″

Marking the Tenon

use both edges to align the mortises, rather than the front or back edges, otherwise the mortises will be cocked at a 5-degree angle. The simplest way to cut the mortises is with a very sharp chisel. Again, chisel in from both sides to avoid splitting out one side. It will be easier if you drill two 1-inch holes first.

8. To make the stretcher, cut a piece of the five-quarter pine 3 inches wide by 17¾ inches long. To cut the tenon—the tongue that goes into the mortise you have just cut—measure 2⅛ inches back from both ends. Using a square, make a mark all around the piece. If your measurements and markings have been accurate, the two marks should be 13½ inches apart— the distance between the insides of the two side pieces. Mark a point 1 inch from the ends of the stretcher and exactly mid-

way between the two sides. Set a compass for exactly a 1-inch radius and, putting the needle at the point you have just marked, make a half-circle on each end of the stretcher. After marking back parallel from the two sides of the half-circle to the mark you made earlier 2⅛ inches from the ends, you are ready to cut out the tenon. A

coping, saber or band saw will do the job.

9. There remains one last cut in the side pieces—a notch along the bottom to form the legs. The notch should be 1 inch high by about 8½ inches long, leaving feet about 3 inches long. Using the same compass setting you used to round off the end of the tenon, mark the ends of

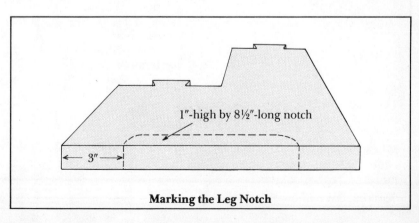

1″-high by 8½″-long notch

3″

Marking the Leg Notch

655

the leg notch and join the upper edges of the two radii you form. Use a coping, saber or band saw to make the cut.

10. Dry-assemble the step stool, doing whatever minor cutting, sanding or shaving is necessary to make the dovetail and mortise-and-tenon joints fit together. When everything fits to your satisfaction, mark the location of the $5/16$-inch dowel holes in the ends of the tenon. Disassemble the stool and drill the $5/16$-inch holes in each end of the stretcher. Using a plane, a rasp and sandpaper, round off the edges you want rounded. Cut or whittle the two 2-inch by $5/16$-inch dowels.

11. Now it is time to glue the members together. You will have to work fast, and you will want to have your bar clamps handy. When the various pieces are all clamped tight, wipe off the excess glue.

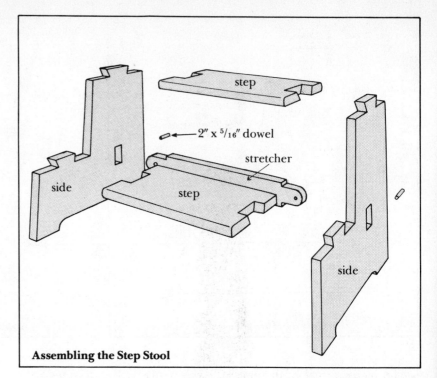

Assembling the Step Stool

12. When the glue has dried overnight, sand down the step stool. If your dovetail joints have not met up perfectly, rectify the situation with sanding, so that the side pieces and step tops are perfectly smooth at the dovetails.

13. Finish the stool with clear Deft or some other finish. You have just executed a lovely piece of furniture, and in doing so you have made dovetail and mortise-and-tenon joints, joints which challenge the abilities of the very best craftsmen.

Materials

Wood
1 pc. $5/4 \times 8 \times 8'$ select white pine or **Sides:** 2 pcs.
  $1\frac{1}{8}" \times 7\frac{1}{4}" \times 15"$
  2 pcs.
  $1\frac{1}{8}" \times 7\frac{1}{4}" \times 7\frac{1}{2}"$
Steps: 2 pcs.
  $1\frac{1}{8}" \times 6\frac{3}{4}" \times 15\frac{3}{4}"$
Stretcher: 1 pc.
  $1\frac{1}{8}" \times 3" \times 17\frac{3}{4}"$

1 pc. $36" \times 5/16"$ dowel or **Stretcher pins:** 2 pcs.
  $2" \times 5/16"$ dowel

Miscellaneous
Glue
Finish

Folding A-Type Stepladder

Stepladders are designed to be underfoot when they are in use. But some are underfoot when you don't want them to be. You find yourself tripping over them, or moving them to the basement or attic just to get them out of your way. This little folding ladder is light and handy and strong, yet folds up in a second to be tucked into a

cabinet or placed on a shelf or hung in a closet.

It has its limitations, of course. It is not designed to hold more than 200 pounds, and it won't get you more than 2 feet off the ground, but for household use it will pay for itself in beauty and convenience. It will do fine for getting the good dishes or the canner down from the top shelf in the cupboard.

This is not a difficult project. The lumber will cost you relatively little—even at today's prices. Chances are you'll have scraps left over from another project that you can use. And it takes no special skill to make the cuts you will need to make, al-though you will have to be careful and precise as you make the various angles and rabbets and grooves. The only power tool you'll really need is a circular saw—and even that is not crucial, if you have some skill and patience with a handsaw and a chisel.

Construction

1. Out of relatively clear (that is, without large knots) 1 × 4 stock, cut four pieces 25¾ inches long for the ladder sides. At each end of each of the four boards, cut a 70-degree angle. To determine this angle, hold the flat side of a protractor parallel with one side, with the

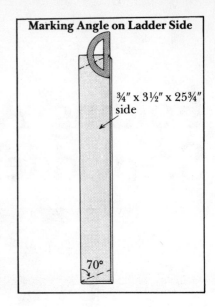
Marking Angle on Ladder Side

¾" x 3½" x 25¾" side

70°

center of the protractor at the corner. Make a mark at the 70-degree spot, remove the protractor and scribe along a straightedge, connecting that mark with the corner. Once you get one cut, you can use it as a pattern to mark the other seven cuts.

2. Cut a 20-degree taper on one end of each of the four side pieces. To do this, put a try

Materials

Wood

1 pc. 1 × 4 × 14′ select pine or **Sides:** 4 pcs. ¾″ × 3½″ × 25¾″
Braces: 4 pcs. ¾″ × 3½″ × 14½″

1 pc. 1 × 6 × 8′ select pine or **Steps:** 4 pcs. ¾″ × 5½″ × 15¼″
(rip and bevel as specified in text)
Top step: 1 pc. ¾″ × 5½″ × 16″
(rip and bevel as specified in text)

Hardware
Finishing nails
8–1½″ #12 f.h. wood screws
1–1½″ × 14½″ piano hinge
2–¾″ #6 screw eyes
12″ steel jack chain

Miscellaneous
Glue
Wood filler
Finish

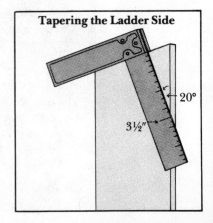
Tapering the Ladder Side

20°

3½″

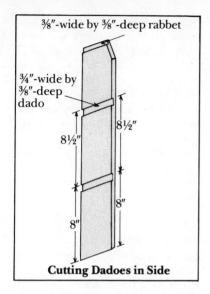

⅜"-wide by ⅜"-deep rabbet

¾"-wide by ⅜"-deep dado

8½"

8½"

8"

8"

Cutting Dadoes in Side

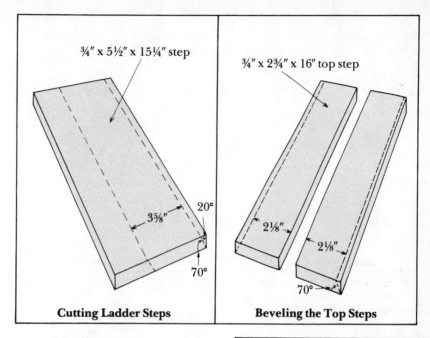

¾" x 5½" x 15¼" step

3⅝"

20°

70°

Cutting Ladder Steps

¾" x 2¾" x 16" top step

2⅛"

2⅛"

70°

Beveling the Top Steps

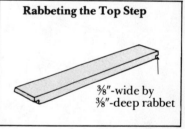

Rabbeting the Top Step

⅜"-wide by ⅜"-deep rabbet

square on the 70-degree cut you have just made and make a mark on the side where the 3½-inch mark on the tool's blade intersects with it. Then draw a line along the blade. Check the line with a protractor held against the side edge. If the line is 20 degrees away from the edge, your measuring has been correct and you can make the saw cut—and three more like it, one on each of the other side pieces.

3. Cut two dadoes in each side piece to receive the steps. These should be cut at a 70-degree angle, ⅜ inch deep and ¾ inch wide. The top of the lower dado should be 8 inches from the bottom edge and the top of the second dado should be 8½ inches from the top of the first. The top rabbet can be cut at this time also, for this will receive the top step. It is ⅜ inch deep by ⅜ inch wide. You can use one of the sides as a pattern to lay out the dadoes, or you can

use a sliding T bevel set to the proper angle. If you do not have a router or a set of dado blades, you can cut the sides of the grooves with a circular saw or a handsaw, then chisel the grooves out. Your grooves and rabbets will not be quite as neat, but if you are careful, they will serve.

4. After rounding off the bottom corners and the edges of the side pieces, you are ready to make the steps. For the steps cut four 15¼-inch pieces out of 1 × 6 stock. Bevel both edges at 20 degrees with a power saw or a plane. The edges must be parallel. There should be 3⅝ inches of tread area on each step.

5. For the top step, cut a 16-inch piece of 1 × 6. Now rip it in two and bevel one edge of each piece at 20 degrees. That should leave 2⅛ inches on the

top of each piece. Rabbet the ends of each piece ⅜ inch by ⅜ inch to fit into the rabbets you have already cut in the tops of the side pieces. The rabbets must be in the broader face of each piece.

6. Cut four braces out of 1 × 4 material. Each piece should be 14½ inches long. Glue one to the bottom of each of the top step pieces, flush with the inside edge. Glue the other 1½ inches in from the outer edge on the bottom of each bottom step. The braces should be **659**

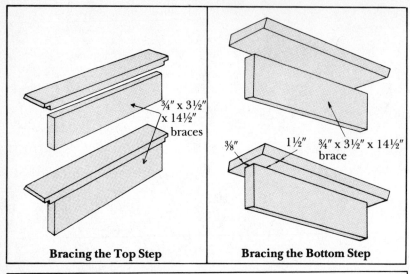

¾" x 3½" x 14½" braces

Bracing the Top Step

⅜" 1½" ¾" x 3½" x 14½" brace

Bracing the Bottom Step

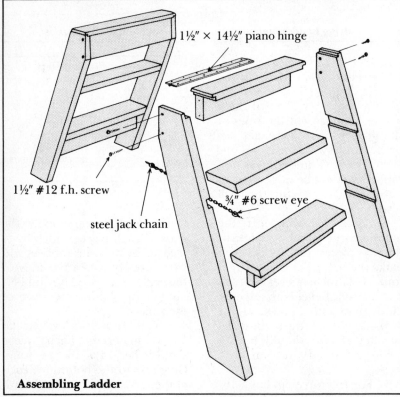

1½" × 14½" piano hinge

1½" #12 f.h. screw

steel jack chain

¾" #6 screw eye

Assembling Ladder

perpendicular to the steps and centered so that there will be ⅜ inch of step at each end to fit into the dadoes. Round off the bottom edges of the braces and sand the top, sides and steps.

7. Glue and assemble the two halves of the ladder, making sure as you clamp them together that they are both square. Small finishing nails driven through the side pieces into the steps will strengthen the structure. Before the glue dries, drill and countersink for two 1½-inch #12 wood screws in each end of each of the top step braces. Drive the screws in and fill or plug the holes.

8. After final sanding of both halves of the ladder, apply whatever finish you like— varnish, lacquer or polyure- thane.

9. When the finish is dry, you can join the two halves. To do this fasten a 1½-inch by 14½- inch piano hinge to the bottom of the upper step braces. Then insert a screw eye into each bot- tom step brace to hold the safety chain. Attach a piece of steel jack chain to both screw eyes, adjusting the length so that the chain is taut just when the two halves of the top step are tight together.

Folding Stepladder

This stepladder looks a bit different from the one described previously, but it works in just about the same way. It is, in other words, a boon for folks with storage in high places or with short people around the house who need—for another year or two anyway—a boost to reach the sink or the glass cupboard.

The nice thing about this folding stepladder is that it will hunker right up next to the wall or cabinet, rendering all the contents of a cabinet or closet safely within arm's reach. It will also double as a convenient stool. The ladder folds into its box easily and will neatly hang on the wall or in a closet when not in use.

The ladder does have limits, however. If you're over 200 pounds, be warned that it wasn't designed to support you. You'll either have to lose weight or construct the ladder from a stout hardwood like oak or ash and reinforce the joints with screws.

As constructed, the ladder is fabricated using carefully fitted and securely glued joints. No nails or screws are used. If you feel uneasy about it, drive a couple of screws through the side pieces into each step. And in any case, be sure to use the safety chains.

Construction

1. The sides of the ladder are cut from 1 × 4 stock. Cut two 27½-inch pieces. Use a compass to draw a 1¾-inch-radius semicircle on what will be the top end of each side piece. After cutting the rounded ends, drill a ¾-inch hole centered at the compass point. This hole is for the pivot that attaches the ladder to the box.

2. The bottom ends of the sides must be cut on an angle, as must the dadoes for the steps, so that the unit will be stable and the steps level when the ladder is opened for use. You can mark

the initial cut with a protractor, then set a sliding T bevel to the angle and use it to lay out the other cuts. Lay the protractor on the bottom corner of one side and mark the angle 25 degrees up from the end, 65 degrees down from the side. To position the dadoes for the steps, use a framing square and measure perpendicularly 8 inches up from the line for the bottom cut. Then measure perpendicularly another 8 inches up from that point to the top of the dado for the second step. Lay out these dadoes so that they are parallel to the angle scribed for the bottom. Cut the bottoms of the sides and, using a router with the appropriate bit or a dado head in a power saw,

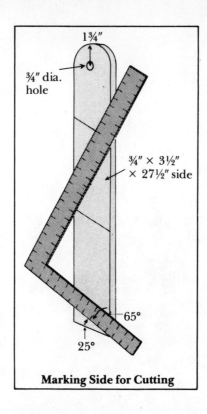

Marking Side for Cutting

1¾"

¾" dia. hole

¾" × 3½" × 27½" side

65°

25°

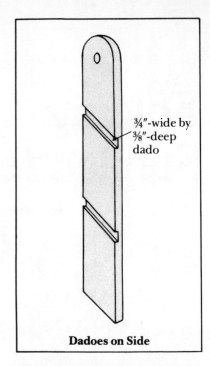

¾"-wide by ⅜"-deep dado

Dadoes on Side

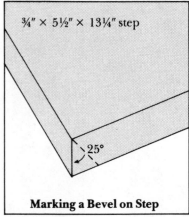

¾" × 5½" × 13¼" step

25°

Marking a Bevel on Step

cut the dadoes ¾ inch wide and ⅜ inch deep.

3. Finish the sides by cutting ½-inch radii on the two bottom corners, then use a rounding-off bit in a router to break all the edges. Sand the sides well.

4. From 1 × 6 stock, cut two 13¼-inch steps. Cut a bevel 25

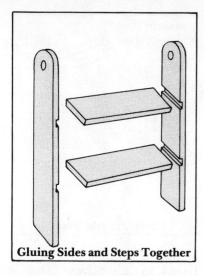

Gluing Sides and Steps Together

degrees from vertical on the back edge of each. Break the front edges of the steps with a rounding-off bit in a router, then sand the steps.

5. Glue the sides and steps together, clamping them with bar or pipe clamps until the glue

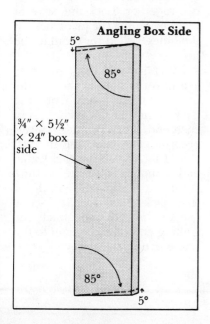

Angling Box Side

5°

85°

¾" × 5½"
× 24" box
side

85°

5°

is dry. The steps should be flush with the sides along the back, but the front edges of the steps should protrude.

6. The box into which the ladder folds has two sides and a top, all cut from 1 × 6 stock, and a plywood back. Cut two 24-inch sides and a 16-inch top.

7. The ends of the box sides must be cut on a slight angle, so that the finished unit will be stable and level when opened for use. Lay out one cut with a protractor and use a sliding T bevel set to the angle to lay out the other three cuts. Place the protractor on a corner and measure 5 degrees up from the end, 85 degrees down from the side.

In laying out the cuts, be sure that the tops and bottoms will be parallel. Saw off the tops and bottoms as marked.

8. Drill a ¾-inch hole in each box side, centered 2¾ inches from the top and 2 inches from the front edge. Then plow a ¼-inch-wide by ⅜-inch-deep groove the length of the inside face of each side, ¼ inch from the back edge. This will hold the plywood back. Round off the two bottom corners on a ½-inch radius, then break all the edges of the box sides with a rounding-off bit in a router.

9. Cut a ¾-inch-wide by ⅜-inch-deep rabbet across each end of the top. Then plow a

Materials

Wood
1 pc. 1 × 4 × 6′ select pine or **Sides:** 2 pcs. ¾′ × 3½″ × 27½″

1 pc. 1 × 6 × 8′ select pine or **Steps:** 2 pcs. ¾″ × 5½″ × 13¼″
Box sides: 2 pcs.
¾″ × 5½″ × 24″
Top step: 1 pc.
¾″ × 5½″ × 16″

1–2′ sq. sht. ¼″ mahogany int. plywood or **Box back:** 1 pc.
15¼″ × 23″

1 pc. 36″ × ¾″ dowel or **Pivot:** 1 pc. 16″ × ¾″ dowel

1 pc. 36″ × ³/₁₆″ dowel or **Pivot locks:** 2 pcs. 1½″ × ³/₁₆″ dowel

Hardware
3–¾″ #6 screw eyes
2 pcs. 12½″ steel jack chain

Miscellaneous
Glue
Finish

¼-inch-wide by ⅜-inch-deep groove in the same face, ¼ inch from the back edge. Before you cut it, be sure this groove will match the grooves in the sides when the box is assembled. Break the edges of the top as you did those on the other pieces, and sand the box pieces.

10. Cut a 15¼-inch by 23-inch piece of ¼-inch mahogany plywood for the back of the box. Sand the piece and, if you choose to have this panel contrast with the natural finish of the other elements of the ladder, paint it, as in the model shown.

11. Cut a 16-inch length of

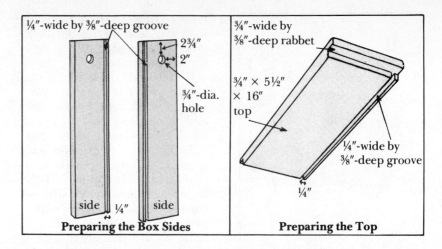

¼"-wide by ⅜"-deep groove

2¾"

2"

¾"-dia. hole

side   ¼"   side

Preparing the Box Sides

¾"-wide by ⅜"-deep rabbet

¾" × 5½" × 16" top

¼"-wide by ⅜"-deep groove

¼"

Preparing the Top

¾-inch dowel for the pivot and two 1½-inch lengths of ³/₁₆-inch

dowel for pivot locks. Drill a ³/₁₆-inch hole ⅞ inch from each end of the pivot dowel.

12. Apply the finish of your choice to the ladder, the box top and sides, the pivot and pivot locks. When it's dry, glue up the box, clamping it securely until the glue is dry. Then slide the pivot through the holes in the box and the ladder to join the two together. Lock the pivot in place by gluing the pivot locks in the holes drilled for them in the pivot.

13. Turn a ¾-inch #6 screw eye into the bottom face of the bottom step, 1 inch from the back edge and 6¼ inches from each end. Turn two more screw eyes into the box, one in each side, 1 inch from the back panel and 7 inches from the bottom. Attach a 12½-inch length of steel jack chain to each screw eye in the box and attach the trailing end of each chain to the screw eye in the step.

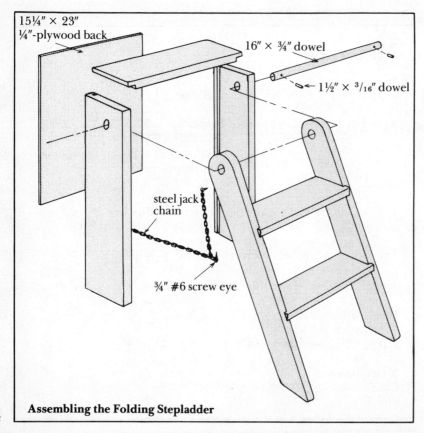

15¼" × 23" ¼"-plywood back

16" × ¾" dowel

1½" × ³/₁₆" dowel

steel jack chain

¾" #6 screw eye

Assembling the Folding Stepladder

Serving Cart

Once you build this serving cart, you'll wonder how you got along without it.

It is designed primarily, as its name suggests, to be used in serving. The cook in your household will find it a useful right-hand helper when it is time to transport food and serving utensils from the kitchen to the dining room or patio. Once

there, it becomes a useful supplementary table or buffet, if that seems desirable. If not, just wheel it into the hallway or kitchen and bring it back when it is time to clear the table and take the dirty dishes back to the kitchen.

Most folks will find other uses for the serving cart. It becomes, for example, an ideal plant stand, one that can be easily moved around the room or the house to give your plants the advantage of dawn-to-dusk sunlight. It could even double as a movable stand for a small television set.

The beauty of this particular serving cart is that it is made entirely of wood, and so has more strength and grace than its plastic and stamped-metal sisters. It has two trays—one fixed in place, the other removable. This last will prove to be particularly attractive to the proud owner of the cart, for it can be lifted off and carried around with drinks or snacks for guests, or used to carry food up and down stairs.

This serving cart is not extremely difficult to build, yet it will provide sufficient challenge to most woodworkers.

There are three basic components to the serving cart: the wheeled frame, the removable upper tray and the fixed lower tray.

Construction

1. Cut four pieces of ¾-inch pine 2½ inches wide and 43⅜ inches long. These four are the crosspieces of the cart and must hold most of the weight, so you

should select pieces that are clear and without large knots that might weaken the structure. With a compass set for a 1¼-inch radius, mark semicircles on both ends of all four pieces. Cut the corners off with a band, saber or coping saw.

2. Lay out and drill three dowel holes in each of the four crosspieces. Two of the holes are centered in the points you have already used to mark the radius on the ends of the crosspieces. Of these, one is to be a 1-inch-diameter hole and the other a ¾-inch-diameter hole. A second ¾-inch-diameter hole is to be drilled 5½ inches below the 1-inch-diameter hole.

3. Lay out cross laps in each piece. To do this, measure 22¼ inches from the top end of the crosspiece (the end with the 1-inch-diameter hole in it). After squaring this mark off across the piece, make a second mark

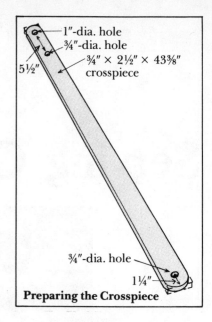

Preparing the Crosspiece

1″-dia. hole
¾″-dia. hole
¾″ × 2½″ × 43⅜″ crosspiece
5½″
¾″-dia. hole
1¼″

2½ inches below that mark and square that one off also. If you have measured everything correctly, you should have a length of 18⅝ inches from that second

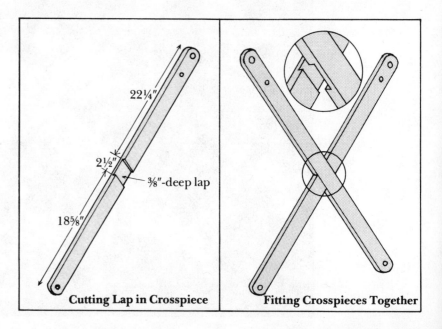

Cutting Lap in Crosspiece

22¼″
2½″
⅜″-deep lap
18⅝″

Fitting Crosspieces Together

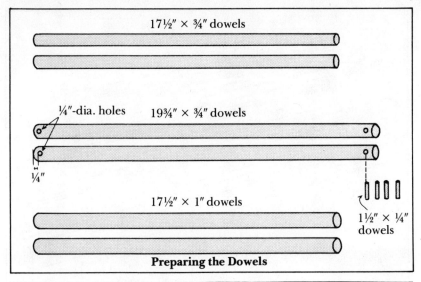

17½″ × ¾″ dowels

¼″-dia. holes

19¾″ × ¾″ dowels

¼″

17½″ × 1″ dowels

1½″ × ¼″ dowels

Preparing the Dowels

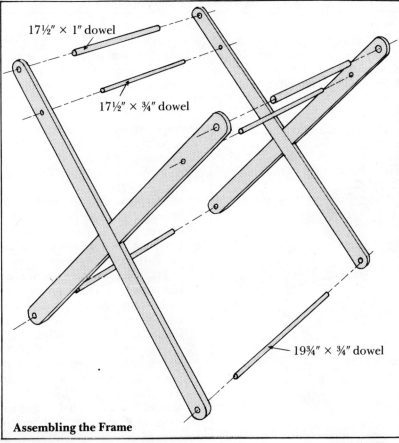

17½″ × 1″ dowel

17½″ × ¾″ dowel

19¾″ × ¾″ dowel

Assembling the Frame

mark to the bottom end of the piece. Now cut out a ⅜-inch-deep lap in each crosspiece, using a router, a dado head in a power saw, or saw and chisel. Try to keep your laps a touch small rather than a touch large, and test them by trying to fit another side piece into the lap you are cutting. Glue the two sets of crosspieces together at the laps you have just made. If you have made your laps accurately, the sides will be flush. Clamp them until the glue dries.

4. Now cut the dowels. You will need two 1-inch and two ¾-inch dowels cut 17½ inches long. And you will need two ¾-inch dowels cut to a 19¾-inch length. In each end of each of the two longer dowels, drill a ¼-inch hole through the dowel's side, ¼ inch in from the end. Glue the six dowels into the crosspieces, taking care to use the longer dowels at the bottom. These must stick through the crosspieces 1⅛ inches on each side to receive the wheels. The distance between the crosspieces must be 16 inches at all points.

5. To make the wheels, lay out four 3¾-inch-diameter circles (1⅞-inch radius) in ¾-inch pine, and then cut them out with a band, saber or coping saw. Then drill a ²⁵/₃₂-inch or ¹³/₁₆-inch hole in the center of each wheel. If the wheel is too tight on its ¾-inch axle, sand the axle down until the wheel spins freely. Then cut four 1½-inch lengths of ¼-inch dowel. Put the wheels on and glue in the ¼-inch pegs to hold them in place.

6. Break the edges with a rounding-off bit in a router and

667

sand all the exposed edges of the frame and wheels to give the frame a smooth, finished appearance. Now go on with the removable upper tray.

7. From a piece of ¼-inch mahogany plywood, cut a 26¼-inch by 15¼-inch panel. Cut a piece of plastic laminate exactly the same size, and with contact cement, glue the two pieces together.

8. From ¾-inch pine, cut two pieces 1¾ inches by 15¹⁵/₁₆ inches for the tray ends and two 1¾ inches by 26¼ inches for the sides. Using a router or a table saw, plow a ⁵/₁₆-inch-wide and ⅜-inch-deep groove ¼ inch down from the top rim of each of these four pieces. To prepare the two end pieces for assembly, cut a ¾-inch-wide by ⅜-inch-deep rabbet in both ends of each piece. Lay out a ¾-inch high by 4¼-inch-long

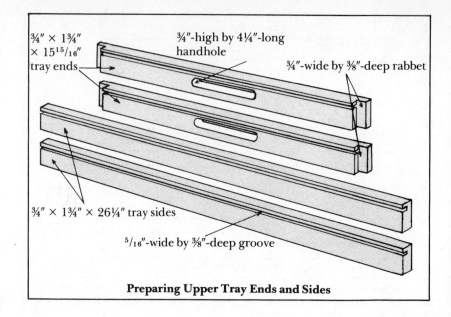

¾" × 1¾" × 15¹⁵/₁₆" tray ends

¾"-high by 4¼"-long handhole

¾"-wide by ⅜"-deep rabbet

¾" × 1¾" × 26¼" tray sides

⁵/₁₆"-wide by ⅜"-deep groove

Preparing Upper Tray Ends and Sides

handhole in each end piece. The hole should be equidistant from each end and its top should be ⅝ inch below the top

edge of the piece. A series of ¾-inch holes and a saber saw, coping saw or chisel will work well in cutting the handholes.

9. Glue and assemble the tray. Clamp the ends and sides together after fitting the plastic laminate and plywood into the groove. As the glue dries, get going on the fixed lower tray.

10. From ¼-inch mahogany plywood, cut a piece 15¼ inches square. Cut a piece of plastic laminate the same size, and cement the two together.

11. From ¾-inch pine, cut two pieces 1¾ inches by 15¼ inches for the tray ends, and two pieces 1¾ inches by 16 inches for the tray sides. As in the upper tray, plow a ⁵/₁₆-inch by ⅜-inch groove in all four pieces to receive the tray top. The top edge of the groove should be ¼ inch below the top edge of the piece. Rabbet the ends of the side pieces ⅜ inch by ¾ inch, as in the upper tray.

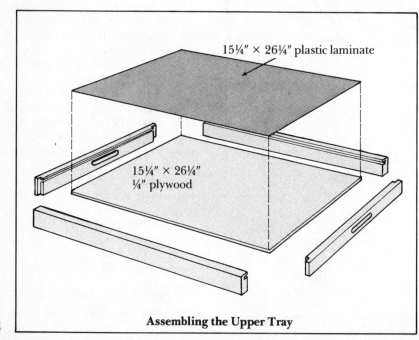

15¼" × 26¼" plastic laminate

15¼" × 26¼" ¼" plywood

Assembling the Upper Tray

Materials

Wood

2 pcs. 1 × 3 × 8′ select pine or **Crosspieces:** 4 pcs. ¾″ × 2½″ × 43⅜″

1 pc. 36″ × 1″ dowel or **Handles:** 2 pcs. 17½″ × 1″ dowel

3 pcs. 36″ × ¾″ dowel or **Tray supports:** 2 pcs. 17½″ × ¾″ dowel
Axles: 2 pcs. 19¾″ × ¾″ dowel

1 pc. 36″ × ¼″ dowel or **Wheel retainers:** 4 pcs. 1½″ × ¼″ dowel

1 pc. 1 × 6 × 8′ select pine or **Wheels:** 4 pcs. ¾″ × 3¾″ dia.
Upper tray ends: 2 pcs. ¾″ × 1¾″ × 15¹⁵/₁₆″
Upper tray sides: 2 pcs. ¾″ × 1¾″ × 26¼″
Lower tray ends: 2 pcs. ¾″ × 1¾″ × 15¼″
Lower tray sides: 2 pcs. ¾″ × 1¾″ × 16″

1–2′ × 4′ sht. ¼″ mahogany int. plywood or **Upper tray top:** 1 pc. 26¼″ × 15¼″
Lower tray top: 1 pc. 15¼″ sq.

Hardware

4–1¼″ #8 f.h. wood screws

Miscellaneous

Glue
1–2′ × 4′ sht. plastic laminate or **Upper tray top:** 1 pc. 26¼″ × 15¼″
Lower tray top: 1 pc. 15¼″ sq.

Contact cement
Varnish

Note, however, that no hand-holes are necessary in this lower tray.

12. Glue and assemble the tray, as in the upper tray. Then drill and countersink two holes under the top in each side for #8 wood screws. The holes should be 1¾ inches from the center, one to the right and the other to the left, and ¼ inch from the bottom edge. They should penetrate from the inside out.

13. Place the upper tray in

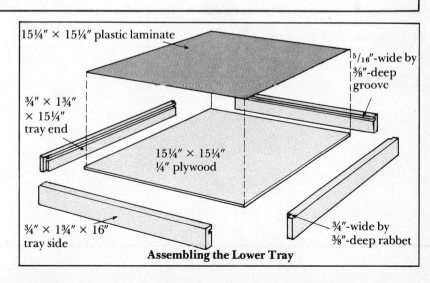

15¼″ × 15¼″ plastic laminate

⁵/₁₆″-wide by ⅜″-deep groove

¾″ × 1¾″ × 15¼″ tray end

15¼″ × 15¼″ ¼″ plywood

¾″ × 1¾″ × 16″ tray side

¾″-wide by ⅜″-deep rabbet

Assembling the Lower Tray

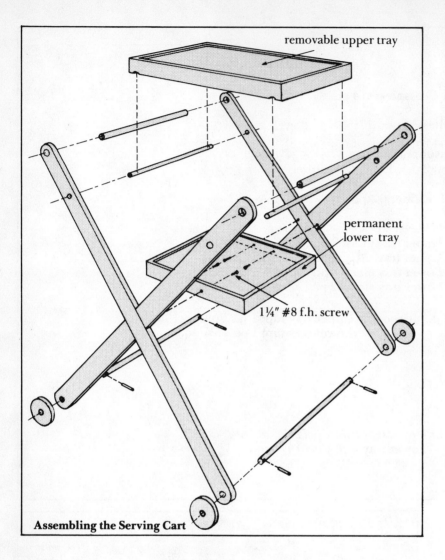

removable upper tray

permanent lower tray

1¼″ #8 f.h. screw

Assembling the Serving Cart

position and mark on the tray the places where the tray rests on the upper ¾-inch dowels. Using these as the centers, cut ¾-inch semicircles in the bottom of each side piece with a half-round rasp so that the tray will fit down over the dowels and not slide when the cart is in motion.

14. Round off all the edges with a rounding-off bit in a router and sand all the exposed edges of the trays in preparation for the finish.

15. Position the permanent tray in the frame 12 inches below the removable upper tray and attach it with a little glue and four 1¼-inch #8 wood screws.

16. Finish all the wooden parts of the cart and the trays with varnish or whatever finish you desire.

Butcher-Block Worktable

Counter space is a necessity in a harvest kitchen. Any kitchen that's short of counter space is miserable, but this worktable can ease, if not eliminate altogether, such kitchen misery. With its butcher-block top, the table provides a solid working surface for all sorts of kitchen chores. The shelf beneath the table not only provides more space but

braces the legs, and this gives an extremely stable work surface. Casters mounted in the bottoms of the legs make moving the table a simple task; when additional counter space is needed anywhere in the kitchen, the table is simply rolled into position. The table was made from 1¾-inch hard maple, the wood used traditionally for butcher blocks, but any hardwood may be substituted.

Construction

1. From 1¾-inch milled stock, cut the pieces that will form the top of the table:

a. Cut 19 pieces, each measuring 1½ inches by 17 inches. Joint and glue up the pieces, narrow face to narrow face, to form one piece measuring 1½ inches by 17 inches by 33¼ inches. After the glue has dried, remove the excess and trim the edges so that they are true and the piece measures 16¾ inches by 33 inches. Then sand the piece to a smooth finish.

b. From 1¾-inch by 4½-inch stock, cut four 9½-inch pieces. Joint and glue them up, edge to edge, to form one piece measuring 1¾ inches by 9½ inches by 18 inches. After the glue has dried, remove the excess, and sand to a smooth finish. Then, from this piece, cut two pieces which measure 1¾ inches by 4 inches by 16¾ inches, and sand the cut edges to a smooth finish.

c. From 1¾-inch by 4½-inch stock, cut two pieces which measure 1¾ inches by 4 inches by 36½ inches, and sand these to a smooth finish.

2. Glue and clamp the 16¾-inch-long and 36½-inch-long pieces to the perimeter of the top piece as shown. After the glue has dried, remove the excess and round off all edges and corners slightly. Then sand the unit to a smooth finish.

3. From 1¾-inch stock, cut and glue up two 3⅛-inch by 34⅛-inch pieces for each leg. After the glue has dried, remove the excess. Then plane the sides and square each end to form four 34-inch legs that measure 3 inches by 3 inches.

4. *Optional:* If turned legs are desired, use a saw to cut the four corners of each leg on a 45-degree angle, then mark and turn the legs as shown.

5. From the top of each leg, cut two 1-inch by 2¼-inch notches on the sides that will

face out when assembled to the table top. Then, from the opposite sides, 14¾ inches from the top edge, cut two ¾-inch by ¾-inch by 2¼-inch blind dadoes to accommodate the shelf as shown. Then sand the legs to a smooth finish.

6. Cut enough 35⅜-inch-long pieces of ¾-inch stock to form a 19⅛-inch-wide shelf. Joint and glue up the pieces. After the glue has dried, remove the excess and trim the edges so that they are true and the piece measures 18¾ inches by 35 inches. Then notch each corner as shown and sand the piece to a smooth finish.

7. With the table upside down, secure the legs against the inside corners, and drill pilot holes for each leg to accommodate the 3½-inch by ⅜-inch lag screws as shown. Use a ⅜-inch bit to drill a hole as

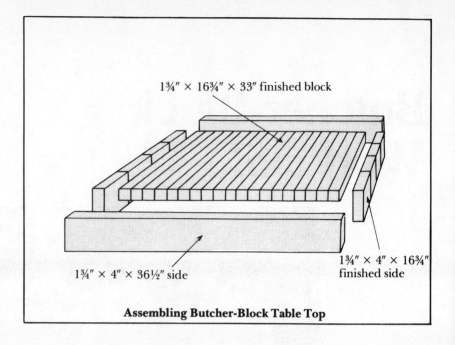

1¾″ × 16¾″ × 33″ finished block

1¾″ × 4″ × 36½″ side

1¾″ × 4″ × 16¾″ finished side

Assembling Butcher-Block Table Top

672

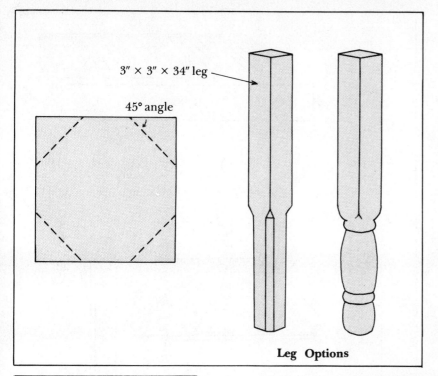

3" × 3" × 34" leg

45° angle

Leg Options

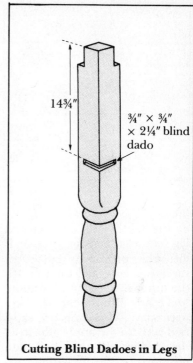

14¾"

¾" × ¾" × 2¼" blind dado

Cutting Blind Dadoes in Legs

Cutting Notches in Legs

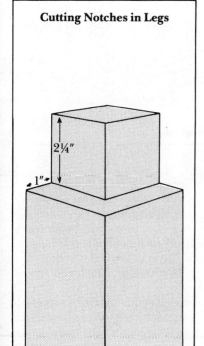

2¼"

1"

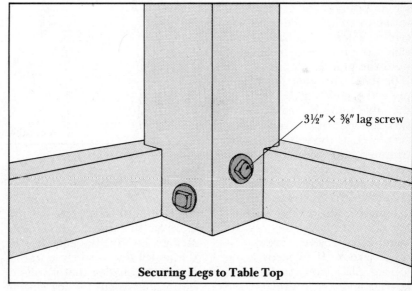

3½" × ⅜" lag screw

Securing Legs to Table Top

deep as the smooth shank of the lag screw, and then use a ⁵/₁₆-inch bit for the second part of the hole.

8. After the holes are drilled, fasten two of the legs to one side **673**

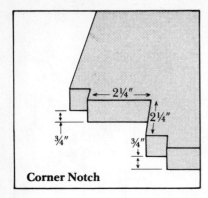

Corner Notch

of the table with washers and lag screws. Dry-fit the shelf into the prepared dadoes in these two legs, and then dry-fit the other two legs into position. Make any adjustments that are necessary. When you are satisfied with the fit, apply glue to all the dadoes, fit the shelf into position, fit the remaining two legs in position and fasten them to the top with washers and lag screws. Then, using bar clamps, clamp the four legs to the shelf until the glue is dry.

9. After the glue has dried, place the table on the floor. If the table rocks it means one of two things: either your floor isn't level, or the legs need to be trimmed. So check the floor with a level, first. If the table doesn't rock, there is the remote possibility that two legs may be off on one side, making it stable but out of square. So check the table with a level, even if it doesn't rock. If it needs to be leveled, place it on a surface that is true and lay a level on the table top in all directions. Under the legs that need to be shored up, put pennies, toothpicks or

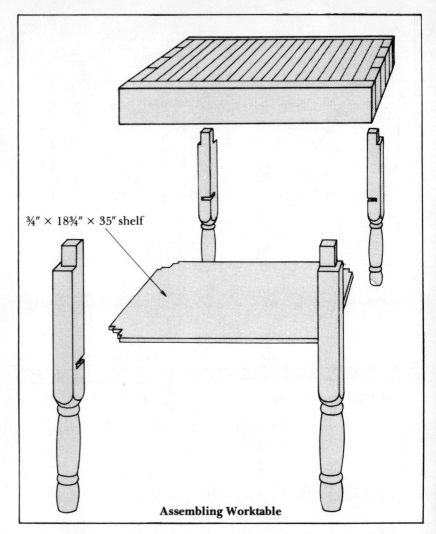

¾″ × 18¾″ × 35″ shelf

Assembling Worktable

whatever it takes to make the table top level. When the table top is level, sharpen a pencil, lay it on its side on the floor and scribe a line around each leg. If the pencil line is so close to the bottom of any leg that it will be impossible to cut the leg with a handsaw, put a piece of cardboard or two under the pencil and scribe new lines

higher up on all legs. Use a handsaw to trim the legs off at this line. Check the table for trueness, then drill holes of the appropriate size in the bottoms of the legs for the casters.

10. Ensure that the entire table is sanded to a smooth finish. Apply several coats of oil, varnish or whatever finish is desired.

Materials

Wood

1 pc. $^8/_4 \times 5\frac{1}{2}" \times 6'$ FAS hard maple or **Top:** 19 pcs.
1 pc. $^8/_4 \times 5\frac{1}{2}" \times 5'$ FAS hard maple $\quad 1\frac{3}{4}" \times 1\frac{1}{2}" \times 17'$

1 pc. $^8/_4 \times 4\frac{1}{2}" \times 10'$ FAS hard maple or **Sides:** 4 pcs.
$\quad\quad\quad\quad\quad\quad\quad\quad\quad\quad\quad\quad 1\frac{3}{4}" \times 4\frac{1}{2}" \times 9\frac{1}{2}"$
$\quad\quad\quad\quad\quad\quad\quad\quad\quad\quad\quad\quad$ 2 pcs.
$\quad\quad\quad\quad\quad\quad\quad\quad\quad\quad\quad\quad 1\frac{3}{4}" \times 4" \times 36\frac{1}{2}"$

4 pcs. $^8/_4 \times 3\frac{1}{2}" \times 6'$ FAS hard maple or **Legs:** 8 pcs.
$\quad\quad\quad\quad\quad\quad\quad\quad\quad\quad\quad\quad 1\frac{3}{4}" \times 3\frac{1}{8}" \times 34\frac{1}{8}"$

5 pcs. $^4/_4 \times 4" \times 3'$ FAS hard maple or **Shelf:** 1 pc.
$\quad\quad\quad\quad\quad\quad\quad\quad\quad\quad\quad\quad \frac{3}{4}" \times 19\frac{1}{8}" \times 35\frac{3}{8}"$

Hardware
8–$\frac{3}{8}"$ washers
8–$3\frac{1}{2}" \times \frac{3}{8}"$ lag screws
4 casters

Miscellaneous
Glue
Finish

This is stupid! The guy builds this wonderful Butcher Block and how does he cut his tomatoes? on a cutting board!
Ron

Butcher Block

Butcher blocks are friendly. Their wood is warm and sensual and reaches out to soothe the eye. Beautiful anywhere, they really glow in the kitchen, and if you've ever seen one for yourself in someone else's kitchen, you've probably thought about getting one of your own. Now you can make one.

Genuine, professional chop-

ping blocks are made of laminated hard maple, 12 inches thick. They are not only expensive but are very heavy. For normal kitchen use, a 12-inch-thick, solid maple butcher block is not necessary, and although maple is the traditional wood, birch, oak or ash may be substituted.

The butcher block in the photograph was made from maple and looks as if it is 9 inches thick. In fact, it is only 2. But this good-looking table sacrifices nothing for the sake of economy and provides an excellent cutting and chopping surface.

This is not a project for the novice or the underequipped woodworker. The eminently practical would tell you to avoid the project altogether, because cutting, ripping and surfacing the amount of hardwood necessary to build the butcher block is more trouble than it's worth. The less practical will tackle the project anyway, figuring that the work can be spread over weeks or months, or farmed out to a millwork firm, but figuring that there's nothing like the satisfaction of saying, "I built it myself."

Construction

1. From 2-inch stock, cut the pieces that will form the top of the table:

a. Cut 12 pieces measuring 1¾ inches by 2 inches by 21¼ inches. Joint and glue the pieces as described in "The Cabinetmaker's Craft" in Part IV, to form one piece measuring 2 inches by 21 inches by

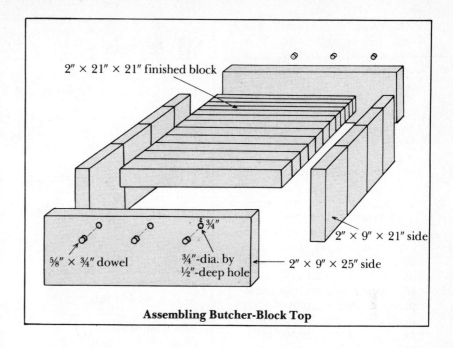

2″ × 21″ × 21″ finished block

⅝″ × ¾″ dowel

¾″-dia. by ½″-deep hole

¾″

2″ × 9″ × 21″ side

2″ × 9″ × 25″ side

Assembling Butcher-Block Top

21¼ inches. After the glue has dried, remove the excess and trim the edges so that the piece becomes a perfect 21-inch square. Then sand the piece to a smooth finish.

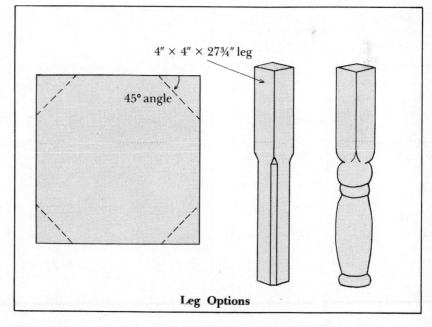

4″ × 4″ × 27¾″ leg

45° angle

Leg Options

b. From 2-inch stock, cut four pieces measuring 5⁵/₁₆ inches by 18½ inches. Joint and glue them to form one piece measuring 18½ inches by 21¼ inches. After the glue has dried, remove the excess and sand to a smooth finish. Then, from this piece, cut two pieces that measure 9 inches by 21 inches. These are for two opposite sides. Sand the cut edges to a smooth finish.

c. From 2-inch stock, cut two pieces for the other two sides that measure 9 inches by 25 inches. For an ornamental touch, drill three, evenly spaced holes in both of these pieces, ½ inch deep by ¾ inch in diameter. The holes should be ¾ inch from the top edge on the side that you want to be the outside. Then, from a ¾-inch dowel rod, cut six ⅝-inch pieces and glue these into the holes. After the glue has dried, plane and sand the dowels to a smooth finish, level with the surrounding wood.

Materials

Wood

1 pc. ⁸/₄ × 8″ × 6′ FAS maple or **Top:** 12 pcs. 1¾″ × 2″ × 21¼″

1 pc. ¹⁰/₄ × 6″ × 7′ FAS maple or **Sides:** 4 pcs. 2″ × 5⁵/₁₆″ × 18½″

1 pc. ¹⁰/₄ × 9″ × 5′ FAS maple or **Sides:** 2 pcs. 2″ × 9″ × 25″

1 pc. 36″ × ¾″ dowel or **Plugs:** 6 pcs. ⅝″ × ¾″ dowel

3 pcs. ¹⁰/₄ × 4″ × 8′ FAS maple or **Legs:** 8 pcs. 2″ × 4″ × 30″

Hardware
8–⅜″ washers
8–4″ × ⅜″ lag screws

Miscellaneous
Glue
Vegetable oil

2. Glue and clamp the 21-inch and 25-inch pieces to the perimeter of the top piece as shown. After the glue has dried,

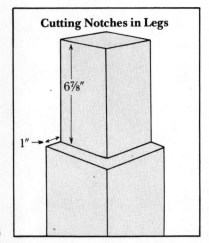

Cutting Notches in Legs

6⅞″

1″

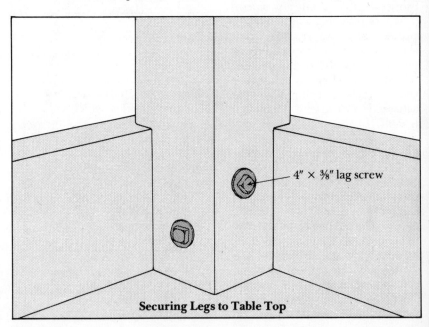

4″ × ⅜″ lag screw

Securing Legs to Table Top

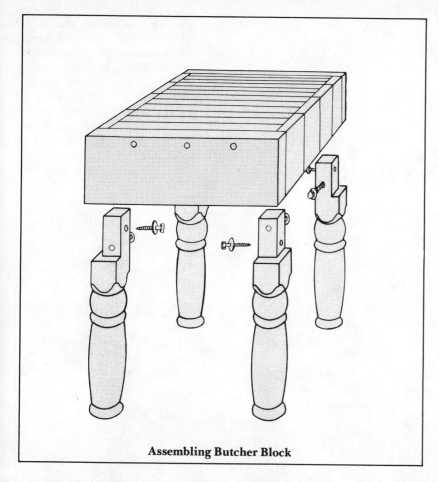

Assembling Butcher Block

remove the excess and round off all edges and corners slightly. Then sand the unit to a smooth finish.

3. From 2-inch stock, cut and glue two 4-inch by 30-inch pieces for each leg. After the glue has dried, remove the excess. Then square and trim the ends of each leg to form four 27¾-inch legs that measure 4 inches square.

4. *Optional:* If turned legs are desired, use a saw to cut the four corners of each leg on a 45-degree angle, then mark and turn the legs as shown.

5. From the top of each leg cut two 1-inch by 6⅞-inch notches on the sides which will face out when assembled to the table top. Sand to a smooth finish.

6. With the table upside down, secure the legs against the inside corners, and drill two holes for each leg. Fasten the legs with washers and 4-inch by ⅜-inch lag screws as shown.

7. Ensure that the entire table is sanded to a smooth finish, then rub several coats of vegetable oil into the top. The legs may be varnished, oiled or left unfinished.

Counter Stools

No harvest kitchen should be without a stool or two. Nothing's more wearying than standing by the sink all day, snapping beans, shelling peas, getting garden produce ready for canning or freezing. With a stool of the right height, you can take a load off your feet and still get the work done.

These stools serve just that

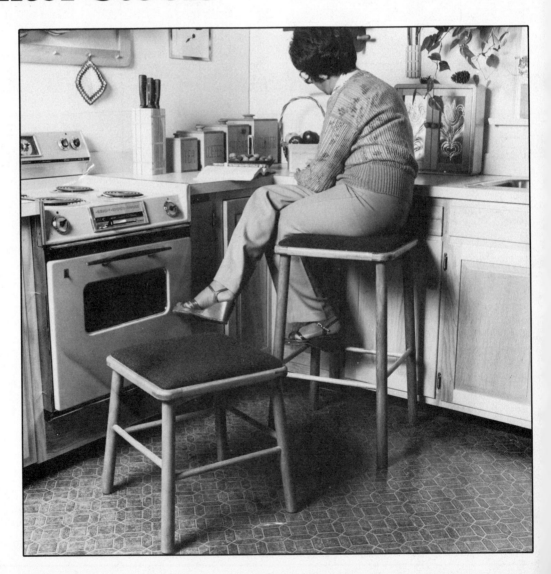

purpose, and a multitude of others besides. They'll hold you up while you talk on the telephone or plan the day's menu. They'll provide seating for meals served at a counter.

There are two stools shown. They are the same but for the length of the legs. One stool stands 19 inches high, the other 30 inches high. Both have up-holstered seats.

The stools are made from fairly readily available materials. The seat frame is fabricated of 5/4 stock, while the legs are lengths of full-round molding. These materials must be shaped and assembled with consider-able skill and care if the stool is to be sound and stable. The challenge lies in boring the holes for the legs and the stretchers. An easily made drill-ing jig can ease the difficulty, and a drill press can eliminate it altogether.

Construction

1. The seat frame is the first part of the stool to construct. It is fabricated from 5/4 stock using open mortise-and-tenon joints. Begin by cutting four pieces of 5/4 stock 2½ inches wide and 17 inches long. Two of the pieces will have open mor-tises cut on both ends, while the other two will have tenons cut on both ends. The easiest way to cut both mortises and tenons is with a dado head in a table saw, but you can cut them with a backsaw and chisel. In any case, each mortise is ⅜ inch wide, extends from edge to edge and is 2½ inches long, measured from the end. It is centered in

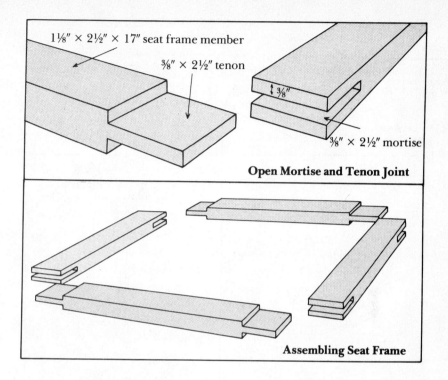

1⅛″ × 2½″ × 17″ seat frame member

⅜″ × 2½″ tenon

⅜″

⅜″ × 2½″ mortise

Open Mortise and Tenon Joint

Assembling Seat Frame

the thickness of the wood. Most dressed 5/4 stock is 1⅛ inches thick, so the mortise will be bounded by two tongues of wood ⅜ inch thick. In turn, each tenon is a tongue of wood ⅜ inch thick, 2½ inches long and 2½ inches wide, created by cutting a ⅜-inch-deep lap into each face of the wood. If your 5/4 stock measures anything less than 1⅛ inches thick, and it could, adjust the sizes of the mortise and the tenon accord-ingly. Lay out and make the cuts carefully, then glue the frame together.

2. Using a compass set for a 1½-inch radius, mark each corner of the frame to be rounded off. Using a punch or awl, mark the center point of each corner's radius; this will be the center of the hole to be

drilled for the leg. Round off the corners with a saw or rasp, then break the edges of the frame with a ½-inch rounding-off bit in a router.

3. The holes for the legs must be counterbored and must be drilled at an angle. This is a critical element in the project; the angle must be duplicated when holes are drilled in the legs for the stretchers. For the tall stool, the angle is 3 degrees from vertical. For the short stool it is 5 degrees. Drilling the holes is relatively easy with a drill press, somewhat more difficult with a hand drill. The initial hole is 1½ inches in diameter and ½ inch deep. The second hole, bored using the center point of the first hole, is 1 inch in diameter and completely penetrates the wood. To get the **681**

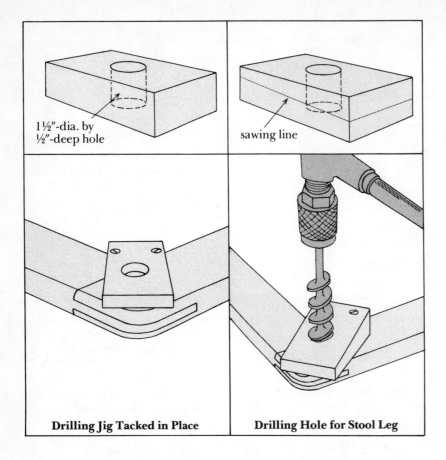

1½"-dia. by ½"-deep hole

sawing line

Drilling Jig Tacked in Place

Drilling Hole for Stool Leg

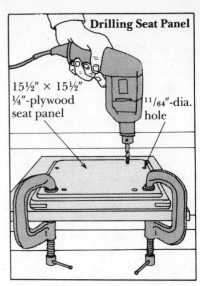

Drilling Seat Panel

15½" × 15½"
¼"-plywood
seat panel

$^{11}/_{64}$"-dia.
hole

correct angle, make two drilling jigs for each stool, one for the 1½-inch holes, one for the 1-inch holes. In each case, drill a hole of the correct size perpendicularly through a scrap of thick wood. Then, using a protractor, scribe a line across the block at the desired angle and saw the block in two along this line. When the sawn face is placed on the work, the hole should be at the correct angle. Tack the jig to the work and use it to guide the bit as you drill. In boring the holes for the legs, be sure the angle is aligned with the corner, so that the legs, when installed, will splay uniformly from the seat frame. The face of the frame into which you drill will be the bottom. Be sure to clamp a piece of scrap to the top as you drill so that you don't splinter the wood around the holes when the bit penetrates.

4. The seat panel is a 15½-inch-square piece of ¼-inch interior plywood. After cutting a ⅞-inch radius on each corner of the panel, center it on top of the seat frame and tack it in place. Drill eight $^{11}/_{64}$-inch-diameter holes through the panel and frame, two evenly spaced along each side. Again, a scrap of wood clamped to the frame bottom will prevent the wood from splintering when the bit penetrates. Mark the seat and frame so they can be re-aligned for easy reassembly, then remove the panel from the frame. From the bottom, countersink the holes in the frame. Install a ⅛-inch by 32 T-nut in the top of each hole in the panel.

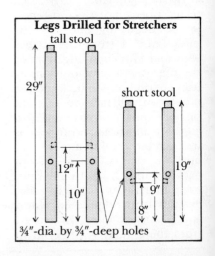

Legs Drilled for Stretchers

tall stool

short stool

29"

12"

10"

19"

9"

8"

¾"-dia. by ¾"-deep holes

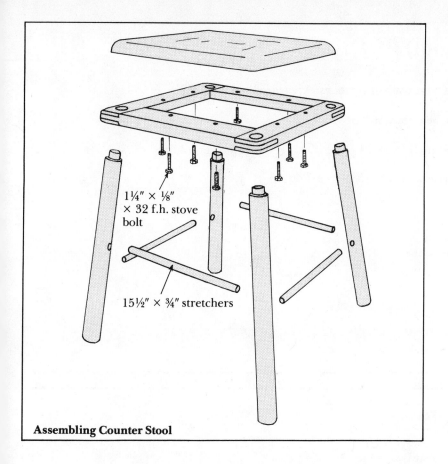

1¼" × ⅛" × 32 f.h. stove bolt

15½" × ¾" stretchers

Assembling Counter Stool

5. The seat panel is upholstered with a 1-inch-thick slab of foam rubber. Cut a piece of foam the size of the seat panel and glue it to the top of the plywood with contact cement. Cut a piece of fabric large enough to cover the seat; a 20-inch square should be big enough. Stretch the fabric over the seat and staple the ends to the bottom of the panel making sure that you don't cover the holes. Trim off any excess.

6. Cut four legs for the stool from 1½-inch full-round molding. For the tall stool the legs are 29 inches long; for the short stool they are 19 inches long. One end of each leg, to be the top, must be turned down to a 1-inch diameter, forming a round tenon, so that it will properly fit the counterbored holes in the frame. The turning can be done on a table saw if care is used. Use the fence as a stop, set so that ⅝ inch of the leg is turned. Clamp the miter gauge in position so that only ¼ inch of material will be removed all the way around. With the saw running, hold the round in the miter gauge and slowly, carefully turn it, cutting the tenon.

7. The legs must be drilled for the stretchers. Each leg is drilled in two spots, but not all are exactly the same; they must be laid out and drilled in pairs. All the holes are ¾ inch in diameter and ¾ inch deep. For angle, make a homemade drilling jig, as previously described, second hole should be 10 inches from the bottom. On two legs, the second hole must be at right angles to the first hole on the left. On two other legs, the second hole should be at right angles to the first hole on the right. For the short stool, the holes are 9 and 8 inches from the bottom, positioned in the same manner as for the tall stool. The holes must be at an angle to the length of the leg. For the tall stool, the angle is 3 degrees; for the short stool, the angle is 5 degrees. Plow a deep V-groove in a scrap of wood and lay the round in the groove so it doesn't roll around while you're trying to drill the holes. To ensure the holes are at the correct angle, make a homemade drilling jig, as previously described, but for a ¾-inch-diameter hole. Scribing the bottom of the leg with intersecting lines can help get the holes perpendicular to each other.

8. Cut four 15½-inch stretchers from ¾-inch dowel.

9. Assemble the stool. You may need to get someone to help for this step. A fixture to hold the legs on 17-inch centers may also be helpful. Cut a 20-inch square of plywood and drill a 1½-inch hole in each corner, so that the holes are 17 inches apart, center to center. Clamping the stool until the glue dries can be a challenge. Use a band

Materials (Tall Stool)

Wood

1 pc. 5/4 × 3 × 6′ select pine or **Seat frame members:** 4 pcs. 1⅛″ × 2½″ × 17″

1–2′ sq. sht. ¼″ int. plywood or **Seat panel:** 1 pc. 15½″ sq.

1 pc. 10′ × 1½″ full-round molding or **Legs:** 4 pcs. 29″ × 1½″ full-round molding

2 pcs. 36″ × ¾″ dowel or **Stretchers:** 4 pcs. 15½″ × ¾″ dowel

Hardware

8–⅛″ × 32 T-nuts
⁵/₁₆″ staples
8–1¼″ × ⅛″ × 32 f.h. stove bolts

Miscellaneous

Glue
1 pc. 1″ × 15½″ sq. foam rubber
Contact cement
1 pc. 20″ sq. fabric
Varnish

Materials (Short Stool)

Wood

1 pc. 5/4 × 3 × 6′ select pine or **Seat frame members:** 4 pcs. 1⅛″ × 2½″ × 17″

1–2′ sq. sht. ¼″ int. plywood or **Seat panel:** 1 pc. 15½″ sq.

1 pc. 8′ × 1½″ full-round molding or **Legs:** 4 pcs. 19″ × 1½″ full-round molding

2 pcs. 36″ × ¾″ dowel or **Stretchers:** 4 pcs. 15½″ × ¾″ dowel

Hardware

8–⅛″ × 32 T-nuts
⁵/₁₆″ staples
8–1¼″ × ⅛″ × 32 f.h. stove bolts

Miscellaneous

Glue
1 pc. 1″ × 15½″ sq. foam rubber
Contact cement
1 pc. 20″ sq. fabric
Varnish

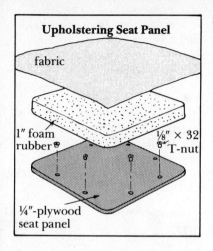

Upholstering Seat Panel

fabric

1" foam
rubber

⅛" × 32
T-nut

¼"-plywood
seat panel

clamp around the legs to secure the stretchers and a bar or pipe clamp extending from each stretcher to the seat frame.

10. After the glue is dry, sand and finish the stool. Then install the seat, lining up the marks you made in step 4 and turning a 1¼-inch × ⅛-inch by 32 flathead stove bolt into each T-nut.

Trestle Table

A sturdy table is a necessity in any harvest kitchen. Not only is it a good place to eat, it's a good place to work.

This attractive trestle table is compatible with almost any style of kitchen, It was designed to be used with benches (the following project). It will comfortably seat six to eight people.

The table is composed of legs,

stretcher and table top, all held together with two wedges and four pegs. By removing the wedges and pegs, you can quickly and easily disassemble the table for moving or storage.

The table is constructed of 5/4 and 8/4 pine stock. The 5/4 material is quite commonly available, although the 8/4 stock may be a little harder to come by. With the exception of the pegs used to hold the top and the leg assembly together, the table can be constructed using common power tools. The pegs are turned on a lathe, but an ingenious woodworker should be able to improvise an alternative method of fabricating them.

Construction

1. The table top is constructed first. It is glued up of four 74-inch lengths of 5/4 stock. Each edge-to-edge joint is reinforced with a thin plywood spline.

a. Cut two 74-inch lengths each of 5/4 × 8 and 5/4 × 10. Five-quarter stock is like other dimension lumber in that the given dimensions are nominal dimensions; its actual thickness ranges from 1 inch to $1\frac{1}{8}$ inches, while board widths follow the pattern of 1-by lumber. Thus, the boards you cut will measure $1\frac{1}{8}$ inches by $7\frac{1}{4}$ inches by 74 inches and $1\frac{1}{8}$ inches by $9\frac{1}{4}$ inches by 74 inches.

b. The edges of the boards should be jointed to true them up for gluing. This operation is most easily done on a jointer, but a long-soled jointer plane can be used. Or you can have the edges

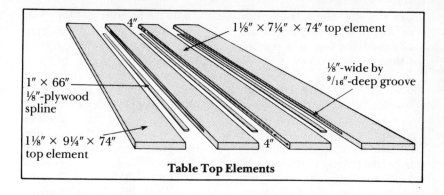

Table Top Elements

1⅛" × 7¼" × 74" top element

⅛"-wide by ⁹/₁₆"-deep groove

1" × 66" ⅛"-plywood spline

1⅛" × 9¼" × 74" top element

4"

jointed by a millwork supplier. After they are jointed, plow a ⅛-inch-wide by ⁹/₁₆-inch-deep groove in the center of each mating edge. The two outside boards, in other words, will have a groove in only one edge, while the two inner boards will have grooves in both edges. These grooves are to hold the splines for the edge-to-edge joints. Each groove is stopped 4 inches from each end of the board. You can use a power saw or a router to plow the grooves.

c. Cut 1-inch-wide strips of ⅛-inch **B-C** interior plywood. The spline for each joint can be made up of a series of pieces. There are three joints, and each requires no more than 66 inches of spline.

d. After dry-assembly to ensure a proper fit, glue up the boards. Use a framing square to true up the top as the clamps are tightened. To eliminate cupping, you should alternate pipe or bar clamps from top to bottom to top. Use a minimum of five clamps for the operation.

e. After the glue has dried,

remove the clamps and scrape off the dried excess glue. Square up the ends of the top by sawing about an inch from each end, bringing the top to a finished length of 72 inches. Then carefully sand the en-

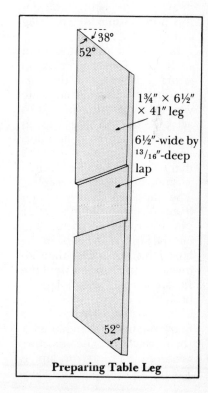

Preparing Table Leg

38°

52°

1¾" × 6½" × 41" leg

6½"-wide by ¹³/₁₆"-deep lap

52°

tire piece. Using a rounding-off bit in a router, break the edges of the top as a part of the sanding process.

2. The legs are next to be fabricated. They are cut from 8/4 stock, which is not quite so commonly available as 5/4 stock. Eight-quarter stock measures 2 inches thick as it comes from the saw. After drying and dressing, it will naturally measure less than 2 inches. You will doubtless have to shop around for 8/4 pine and will have to buy it as you would hardwoods. If possible, have the supplier dress the edges and faces, giving you boards measuring 1¾ inches by 6½ inches.

a. From the 8/4 stock, cut four 41-inch legs. Then crosscut the legs at a 52-degree angle, being sure the top and bottom of each leg are parallel.

b. Lay out and cut a lap in each leg for the cross-lap joints that will join the legs into pairs. The most accurate way to lay out the laps is to actually lay out the legs in pairs, one leg atop another. Use the top leg as a pattern to mark the bottom, then switch positions to mark the top leg. The laps will be $^{13}/_{16}$ inch deep. A dado head in a power saw or a router can be used to cut the laps. It's best to cut the laps a bit undersize, then alternately trim and fit until the fit is correct. Cut the laps in both pairs of legs.

c. Pair up the legs and mark them for the mortise for the stretcher. The mortise, centered in the cross lap, is 1¾ inches wide and 3 inches

high. Its bottom is 11 inches from the baseline of the legs. The easiest way to cut the mortise is to drill out the bulk of the waste material, then clean up the four sides with a chisel. Keep the legs clamped in pairs as you cut the mortise. In drilling, be careful not to splinter the wood as the drill or auger bit breaks through; it's a good idea to drill from both sides to avoid such splintering.

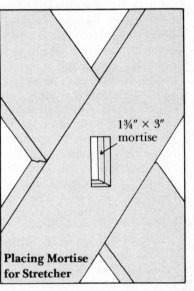

Placing Mortise for Stretcher

1¾″ × 3″ mortise

d. Drill a ⅝-inch-diameter hole through each leg, 1½ inches down from the top and 4⅛ inches in from the outer edge of the top. The holes in each pair of legs should be 18¾ inches apart. These holes are for the pegs that will

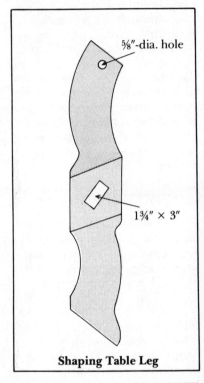

⅝″-dia. hole

1¾″ × 3″

Shaping Table Leg

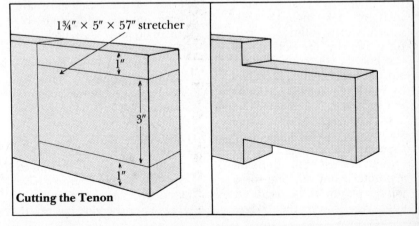

1¾″ × 5″ × 57″ stretcher

1″

3″

1″

Cutting the Tenon

secure the top to the legs.

e. Lay out the final shape of each pair of legs. Unclamp the legs and cut out the legs as marked using a band saw, saber saw or bow saw. After sanding the sawn edges, pair the legs up again and break the exposed edges using a rounding-off bit in a router. Then give the legs a final sanding.

3. Fabricate the stretcher next. Cut from 8/4 stock a piece 5 inches wide and 57 inches long.

a. Lay out a tenon on each end; it is 3 inches high and 1¾ inches wide and is formed by cutting 1-inch-deep shoulders on the top and bottom of the stretcher. Scribe a line all the way around the stretcher 5½ inches from the butt end. Measure down 1 inch from the top and 1 inch up from the bottom and scribe lines parallel to the top and bottom on both sides and the butt end. Cut away the waste material with a backsaw. Cut the tenon slightly oversize and trim it to fit the mortise prepared for it; a snug fit is important.

b. Lay out and cut a mortise through each tenon for the wedges that will hold the entire leg assembly together. Each of these mortises tapers from a ½-inch by 2-inch opening on the top to a ½-inch by 1½-inch opening on the bottom. The mortise is about 1¾ inches from the tenon shoulder and centered from side to side. The wedge must be snug against the legs so the distance from the tenon shoulder to the mortise must be no more than the thickness of the leg. After laying out the mortise outlines on the tenon top and bottom, drill three vertical ½-inch holes, overlapping them slightly, beginning closest to the tenon shoulder and moving toward the butt end. Don't make the rough slot created by the drilled holes longer than 1½ inches. Chisel out the remaining waste ma-

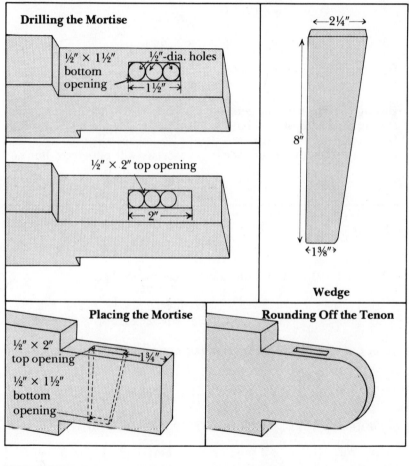

Drilling the Mortise

½″ × 1½″ bottom opening   ½″-dia. holes   1½″

½″ × 2″ top opening   2″

←2¼″→   8″   ←1⅜″→

Wedge

Placing the Mortise

½″ × 2″ top opening   1¾″
½″ × 1½″ bottom opening

Rounding Off the Tenon

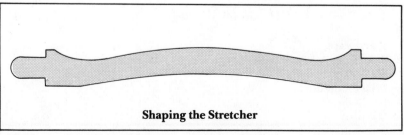

Shaping the Stretcher

terial, tapering the mortise in the process.

c. Mark the end of each tenon to be rounded off. To do this, set a compass to a 1½-inch radius and scribe a semicircle on each side of the tenon tangent to its edges. Also mark the body of the stretcher to be shaped. Cut the stretcher as laid out, as you did the legs. Then sand the sawn edges, break all the exposed edges with a rounding-off bit in a router and give the stretcher a final sanding.

4. Cut out the two wedges; they measure ½ inch by 2¼ inches by 8 inches each. Taper the width from 2¼ inches at one end to 1⅜ inch at the other. Round off the corners and break the edges. Then sand the wedges carefully.

5. From 5/4 × 8 stock, cut two 3-inch-wide by 31-inch-long battens. The battens will be attached to the bottom of the table top and will be used to secure the top to the leg assembly.

a. Turn the table top bottom-up. Assemble the legs and stretcher, using the wedges to lock them together. Turn the assembly upside down and center it on the bottom surface of the top. Position the battens outside the legs and use the legs as patterns to mark the batten ends for shaping and to mark the locations of the peg holes. Also mark the batten locations on the table top.

b. Drill the ⅝-inch-diameter peg holes in the battens, and cut the end shapes. Then drill four holes vertically

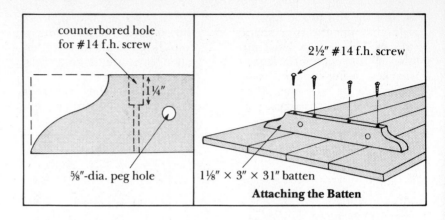

counterbored hole for #14 f.h. screw

1¼"

⅝"-dia. peg hole

2½" #14 f.h. screw

1⅛" × 3" × 31" batten

Attaching the Batten

through each batten, penetrating the width of the board from edge to edge, for 2½-inch #14 screws to secure the battens to the top. Counterbore each hole no more than 1¼ inches deep so that the screws will penetrate but not

Materials

Wood

2 pcs. 5/4 × 8 × 10' #2 pine or **Top elements:** 2 pcs. 1⅛" × 7¼" × 74"
Wedges: 2 pcs. ½" × 2¼" × 8"
Battens: 2 pcs. 1⅛" × 3" × 31"

2 pcs. 5/4 × 10 × 8' #2 pine or **Top elements:** 2 pcs. 1⅛" × 9¼" × 74"

1–1' × 2' sht. ⅛" B-C int. plywood or **Splines:** 18 pcs. 1" × 12"

2 pcs. 8/4 × 8 × 8' #2 pine or **Legs:** 4 pcs. 1¾" × 6½" × 41"

1 pc. 8/4 × 6 × 6' #2 pine or **Stretcher:** 1 pc. 1¾" × 5" × 57"

1 pc. 36" × 1⅛" fir dowel or **Pegs:** 4 pcs. 6" × 1⅛" dowel

Hardware
8–2½" #14 f.h. screws

Miscellaneous
Glue
Varnish

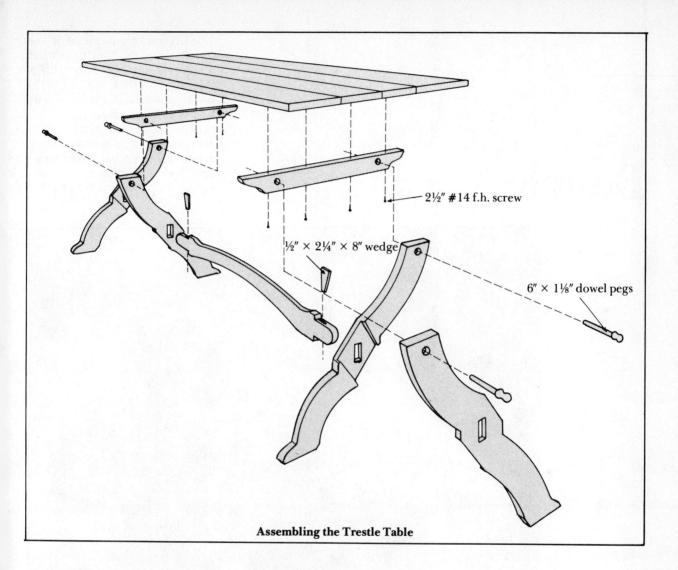

2½" #14 f.h. screw

½" × 2¼" × 8" wedge

6" × 1⅛" dowel pegs

Assembling the Trestle Table

break through the table top. Sand the sawn edges of the battens, break the exposed edges with a rounding-off bit in a router and give the battens a final sanding. Then attach them to the table top with glue and the screws.

6. Fabricate four pegs for securing the top to the leg as-sembly. Each peg can be turned on a lathe from a 6-inch length of 1⅛-inch fir dowel, with a 3-inch section turned down to a ⁹/₁₆-inch diameter and the remainder shaped into a knob.

7. Varnish each component of the table as a separate entity. When the finish is dry, assemble the table.

Designed to complement the trestle table, the bench provides a maximum of seating with a minimum of fuss. With or without the table, it is a natural part of the harvest kitchen.

Construction is simple and economical. The bench is composed of three basic elements: seat, legs and stretcher. All are made from 5/4 stock. The 5/4

Bench

stock from which this bench was made was 1⅛ inches thick. If the stock you use varies from that thickness, and it could, adjust the width of dadoes and mortises accordingly.

Construction

1. The seat panel is glued up of two pieces of 5/4 × 6 pine.

a. Cut two 74-inch lengths of the material and glue them edge to edge. Use bar or pipe clamps to clamp the panel while the glue dries. Alternate the clamps from bottom to top to bottom to avoid any tendency to cup. Use at least five clamps for the panel.

b. After the glue dries, scrape off the excess and rough-sand the panel. Crosscut each end of the panel to square the ends and trim the overall length to 72 inches.

2. Each leg is glued up of two pieces of 5/4 × 6 pine.

a. Cut four 19-inch lengths. Glue up two edge to edge for each leg, clamping each leg with three bar or pipe clamps, alternated from bottom to top to bottom.

b. After the glue dries, scrape off any excess and rough-sand the legs. Square up the legs by crosscutting both ends, shortening each leg to 18 inches.

c. Lay out the two tenons for the seat panel and the notch for the stretcher on each leg. Scribe a line across each face of the leg, 1⅛ inches from the top edge. Scribe perpendicular lines from the top edge to the line 2 inches and 4¾ inches from

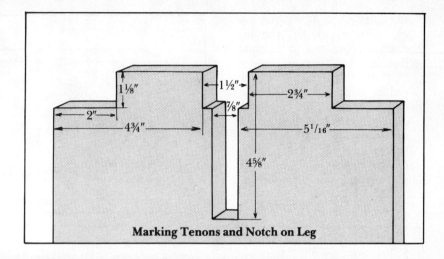

Marking Tenons and Notch on Leg

each side. These lines delineate the tenons and their shoulders; the tenons are 2¾ inches long and have outside shoulders 2 inches long and a common central shoulder 1½ inches long. The notch for the stretcher is cut into the central shoulder. It is 3½ inches deep and ⅞ inches wide; that is, the notch bottom is 4⅝ inches from the top edge of the leg and its sides are 5¹/₁₆ inches from the side edges of the leg. After marking the leg, cut out the tenons and the notch.

d. Mark the finished shape of the leg on the panels and cut them out using a band saw, saber saw or bow saw.

e. With a rounding-off bit in a router, break all the exposed edges of the legs. Do not break the top edges or those of the tenons and the stretcher notch. Finish-sand the legs.

3. Cut a 70-inch length of 5/4 × 4 pine for the stretcher.

a. Cut a 1⅛-inch-wide by

⅛-inch-deep dado on each side at each end; there are four dadoes in all. The outside edge of each dado should be 3 inches from the end. To get a snug fit of stretcher to leg, it's a good idea to cut the dadoes a bit shallow and alternately pare and fit until the appropriate fit is achieved. A loose fit is no good.

b. Cut off the ends of the

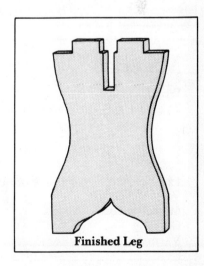

Finished Leg

stretcher on a 30-degree angle, pitched toward the leg dadoes from top to bottom. Round off the bottom corners of the stretcher on a 1-inch radius with a saber saw or rasp. Break the exposed edges of the stretcher with a rounding-off bit in a router. Finish-sand the piece.

4. Dry-fit the stretcher to the legs. Turn the seat panel upside

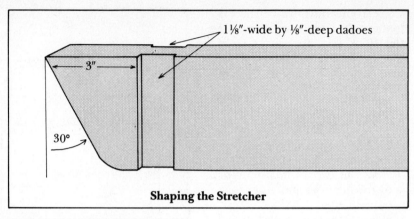

Shaping the Stretcher

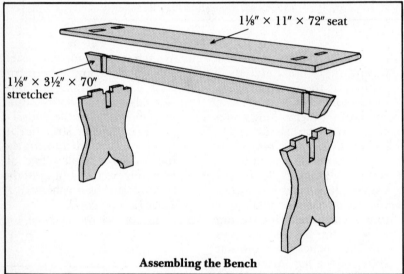

1⅛" × 11" × 72" seat

1⅛" × 3½" × 70" stretcher

Assembling the Bench

down and set the leg assembly atop it to transfer the tenon positions to the seat panel. Scribe the positions and cut mortises for the tenons in the seat. You can drill out the bulk of the waste material and clean up the mortise with a chisel, or you can use a chisel alone to excavate the mortise. In either case, cut the mortise a bit undersize and alternately fit and pare until the correct snug fit is achieved.

5. Round off the corners of the seat on a 1-inch radius. Break the exposed edges as on other pieces, then finish-sand the seat.

6. After gluing the legs, stretcher and seat together, complete the project by finishing the bench with a coat or more of varnish.

Materials

Wood
2 pcs. 5/4 × 6 × 10' #2 pine or **Seat panel:** 2 pcs. 1⅛" × 5½" × 74"
Legs: 4 pcs. 1⅛" × 5½" × 19"

1 pc. 5/4 × 4 × 6' #2 pine or **Stretcher:** 1 pc. 1⅛" × 3½" × 70"

Miscellaneous
Glue
Varnish

Chair

Chair construction is a challenge for the home woodworker. It isn't easy to design a chair that's comfortable and attractive, and that's easy to build in the bargain.

But if you are building your own harvest kitchen, you may want to build your chairs along with everything else.

Here's the solution. This

chair is not difficult to build, even if you have no shop tools. Yet it *is* comfortable. It is attractive. And it will complement the round table or the trestle table, which you can build.

The basic structure is $5/4$ pine, which will vary in actual thickness from 1 inch to $1\frac{1}{8}$ inches. (The following construction directions assume that you'll use 1-inch-thick material. If you use thicker stock, compensate where necessary, by cutting longer dowels for the doweled joint, for example.) You will also use some nominal l-by stock and a small plywood panel.

The trickiest part of the project is making the back pieces. The back is the element that stymies most home woodworkers; the curvature necessary for comfort is difficult to achieve. The approach here, in essence, is to cut a thin, curved piece from a wide block of wood. You can use a bow or frame saw if you're a hand tool devotee, but a saber saw makes the task less laborious, and the band saw is the best tool of all for the job.

The construction sequence leads you through the building of a single chair. The materials list too is for a single chair, but the block you glue up to make the back pieces yields enough backs for four chairs. You can save the extra backs for spare parts, but more likely you'll want to use them to make a quartet of chairs.

Construction

1. Fabricate the seat frame. Cut two 18-inch lengths of

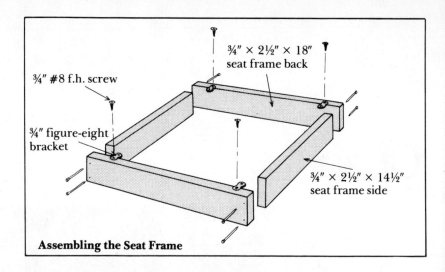

Assembling the Seat Frame

$\frac{3}{4}" \times 2\frac{1}{2}" \times 18"$ seat frame back

$\frac{3}{4}"$ #8 f.h. screw

$\frac{3}{4}"$ figure-eight bracket

$\frac{3}{4}" \times 2\frac{1}{2}" \times 14\frac{1}{2}"$ seat frame side

1×3 for the front and back pieces and two $14\frac{1}{2}$-inch lengths of 1×3 for the sides. Glue and nail the four pieces together in simple butt joints, the front and back overlapping the sides. Countersink the nails and cover them with wood filler. Position a $\frac{3}{4}$-inch figure-eight along the top inside edge of the front and back near each corner—four of these brackets in all—and counterbore the frame to accept them. One loop is attached to the frame and the other overhangs the edge to accept a screw for the seat panel. Use $\frac{3}{4}$-inch #8 screws to attach the figure-eights to the frame. Finally, break the bottom edges of the frame with a rounding-off bit in a router.

2. Prepare the legs and arms for assembly. All are fabricated from $5/4 \times 3$ stock. Arms for one chair can be cut from the $5/4 \times 8$ board used to make the backs; cut a 17-inch length and rip two $2\frac{1}{2}$-inch-wide pieces from it. If you make more than

one chair—a likelihood—then buy $5/4 \times 3$ stock for the arms.

a. Cut two 32-inch back legs. The top ends of these

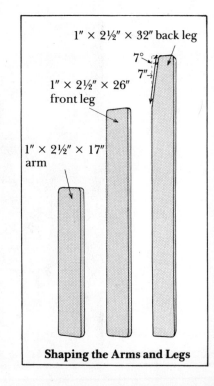

$1" \times 2\frac{1}{2}" \times 32"$ back leg

$7°$

$7"$

$1" \times 2\frac{1}{2}" \times 26"$ front leg

$1" \times 2\frac{1}{2}" \times 17"$ arm

Shaping the Arms and Legs

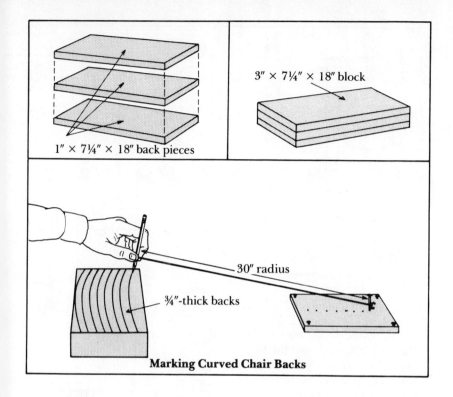

$1'' \times 7\frac{1}{4}'' \times 18''$ back pieces

$3'' \times 7\frac{1}{4}'' \times 18''$ block

30" radius

¾"-thick backs

Marking Curved Chair Backs

legs are tapered slightly. Measure 1¾ inches from what will

be the back edge along the top. Scribe a line from this

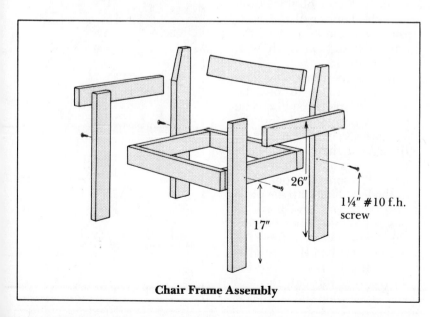

26"

1¼" #10 f.h. screw

17"

Chair Frame Assembly

point at a 7-degree angle toward the front edge. The line should be approximately 7 inches long. Cut along the line. Round off the bottom corners of the legs on a ½-inch radius. Break the edges of the legs with a rounding-off bit in a router.

b. Cut two 26-inch-long front legs. Round off the bottom corners on a ½-inch radius, and break the edges of the pieces.

c. Cut two 17-inch pieces for arms. Break all the edges of the arms with a rounding-off bit in a router.

3. The curved backs are cut from a substantial block of wood with a band saw or a saber saw with a special long blade. Backs for four chairs can be cut from a single block.

a. Cut three 18-inch lengths of $^5/_4 \times 8$ pine. Face-glue the pieces to form a single block measuring approximately 3 inches by 7¼ inches by 18 inches.

b. After the glue has dried, lay out eight ¾-inch-thick by 3-inch-wide backs using a 30-inch radius as shown. Use a scrap strip of wood, or a pencil on a long string, as a makeshift compass to scribe the requisite arcs.

c. Saw out the backs and carefully sand them. Break the top and bottom edges of the backs with a rounding-off bit in a router.

4. Assemble the basic chair frame.

a. Glue the legs to the seat frame and drive a 1¼-inch #10 screw through the frame into each leg. The bottom

697

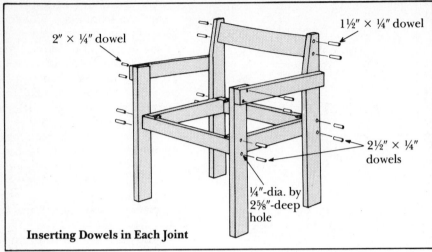

2" × ¼" dowel

1½" × ¼" dowel

2½" × ¼" dowels

¼"-dia. by 2⅝"-deep hole

Inserting Dowels in Each Joint

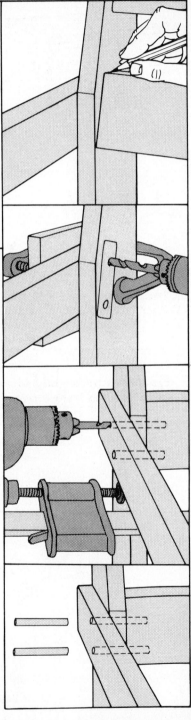

edge of the frame is 17 inches from the bottom of the legs. The front legs extend ½ inch beyond the seat frame, while the back legs extend ¾ inch beyond the seat frame. Glue and clamp each leg in position, then drill a pilot hole and drive the screw. After the screw is in place, the clamp can be removed.

b. Glue and clamp the arms in place. The arm is flush with the top of the front leg and parallel to the seat frame. Its top edge will be 26 inches from the floor.

c. Glue and clamp the upper back piece in place. Its upper edge is ⅜ inch below the top of the legs and its front face is ½ inch from the front edges of the legs. Use a bar or pipe clamp to secure the piece in position until the glue dries.

5. After the glue has set, remove the clamps and install ¼-inch dowels in each joint.

a. Do the leg-to-frame joints first. Cut twelve 2½-inch lengths of the ¼-inch dowel. Drill two 2⅝-inch-deep, ¼-inch-diameter holes through each leg into the butt end of the frame piece. Drive a glue-smeared dowel into each hole. Don't drive the dowel too far into the hole; there should be a gap between the end of the dowel and the bottom of the hole, and the opposite end of the dowel should be flush with the leg surface.

b. Use the remaining four pieces of dowel to pin the lower back piece in place. The piece is positioned below the upper back; its bottom edge is flush with the bottom edges of the arms and its front face is ½ inch from the front edges of the legs. First, slip the piece into the frame and mark its position on the inner faces of the legs. Then, within the marks, drill two ¼-inch holes on each side, from the inside all the way through the legs and arms. Glue and clamp the

698

lower back piece in place, then, using the holes through the arms and sides as guides, drill into the back piece. Do it carefully, so you don't make the existing holes too big. Drive a glue-smeared dowel into each hole. Don't drill too deeply into the back piece, and don't drive the dowels too deep.

c. Cut four 1½-inch lengths of dowel. Drill two holes through the rear leg into each end of the upper back piece. The holes must not break through the back piece, so drill carefully. Drive a glue-smeared dowel into each hole.

d. Cut four 2-inch-plus lengths of dowel. Drill two holes through each arm and leg joint. Clamp a scrap of wood to the joint so that you don't splinter the wood as the drill bit emerges. Drive a glue-smeared dowel into each hole. Cut or sand the dowel flush on both sides of the joint.

6. Carefully sand the entire chair assembly, then apply a coat or more of the finish of your choice.

7. Cut a 17-inch by 17⅞-inch piece of ½-inch B-C interior plywood for the seat panel. Round off all four corners on a ½-inch radius. Cut a 17½-inch by 18½-inch piece of 1-inch-thick foam rubber for the cushion. Using contact cement, glue the foam rubber to the seat panel. Be sure you center the cushion on the panel; it is larger than the panel and should overhang the plywood on all sides equally. Cut a 22-inch

square of fabric and cover the cushion and seat panel. Staple one end of the cloth to the bottom of the seat, then stretch the opposite end over the foam and staple it to the seat bottom. Then pull the remaining ends tight and staple them to the seat bottom. Position the seat on the frame; it should extend about ¼

Materials

Wood

1 pc. 1 × 3 × 6′ select pine or **Seat frame front and back:** 2 pcs. ¾″ × 2½″ × 18″

Seat frame sides: 2 pcs. ¾″ × 2½″ × 14½″

1 pc. ⁵/₄ × 3 × 10′ #2 pine or **Back legs:** 2 pcs. 1″ × 2½″ × 32″
Front legs: 2 pcs. 1″ × 2½″ × 26″

1 pc. ⁵/₄ × 8 × 6′ #2 pine or **Arms:** 2 pcs. 1″ × 2½″ × 17″
Backs: 3 pcs. 1″ × 7¼″ × 18″*

2 pcs. 36″ × ¼″ maple dowel or **Leg and lower back dowels:** 12 pcs. 2½″ × ¼″ dowel
Upper back dowels: 4 pcs. 1½″ × ¼″ dowel
Arm dowels: 4 pcs. 2″ × ¼″ dowel

1–2′ sq. sht. ½″ B-C int. plywood or **Seat panel:** 1 pc. 17″ × 17⅞″

Hardware

5d finishing nails
4–¾″ figure-eights
4–¾″ #8 f.h. screws
4–1¼″ #10 f.h. screws
¼″ staples
4–½″ #6 f.h. screws

Miscellaneous

Glue
Wood filler
Varnish
1 pc. 1″ × 17½″ × 18½″ foam rubber
Contact cement
1 pc. 22″ sq. cloth

*Backs for four chairs are cut from a block glued up from these pieces.

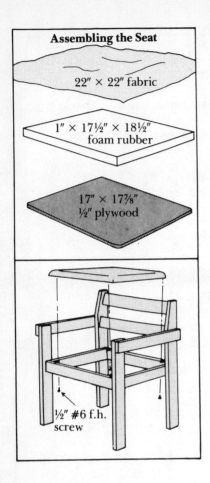

Assembling the Seat

22″ × 22″ fabric

1″ × 17½″ × 18½″
foam rubber

17″ × 17⅞″
½″ plywood

½″ #6 f.h.
screw

inch beyond both front and rear
legs. Secure it to the chair with
½-inch #6 screws driven
through the figure-eights into
the seat bottom.

A small table may have a place in your harvest kitchen. If it does, this round table is for you.

As a table, it is sturdy and attractive. It will seat four. It was designed to be complemented by the chairs previously described.

As a project, it is challenging. The materials are not difficult to find, nor are they outrage-

Round Table

701

ously expensive. The tools required are common to home workshops. Stationary shop tools—as always—will speed the work, but hand tools and portable power tools are sufficient to get the table built.

The table has a circular top cut from a glued-up panel of $^5/_4$ stock. It will be between 1 inch and $1^1/_8$ inches thick. The pedestal has a support for the top, called a spider, and a base, both made from $^8/_4$ stock, and a hollow column fabricated from 1×3s. If anything will be hard to find, it'll be the $^8/_4$ stock. An alternative would be to face-glue pieces of nominal 1-inch and $^5/_4$ stock, to get a piece $1^3/_4$ inches thick. This alternative requires lots of clamps, but it eliminates the need for thicknessing and jointing rough-sawn stock.

For the woodworker with some experience, the round table should be a pleasure to build and use.

Construction

1. The table top is the first element to construct. It is cut from a broad panel glued up of $^5/_4 \times 8$ stock.

a. From $^5/_4 \times 8$ stock, cut two 34-inch pieces, two 42-inch pieces and two 44-inch pieces. Glue up these six boards edge to edge so that the two longest boards are in the center, flanked by two 42-inch boards, which are in turn flanked by the two 34-inch boards. The ends of the boards should be stepped so that a 42-inch circle can be scribed on the resulting

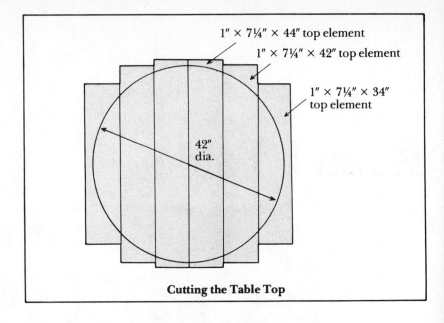

1″ × 7¼″ × 44″ top element
1″ × 7¼″ × 42″ top element
1″ × 7¼″ × 34″ top element
42″ dia.

Cutting the Table Top

panel. Use at least five bar or pipe clamps, alternating them from bottom to top to bottom, to counteract any tendency to cup.

b. After the glue has dried, remove the clamps and scrape up any glue that's squeezed out of the joints and dried. Then, using a scrap strip of wood and a pencil, or a pencil on a string as a makeshift compass, scribe a 42-inch-diameter circle on the glued-up panel. Cut out the circle using a band saw or a saber saw.

c. Rough-sand the sawn edges of the table top. Then break the edges with a ¼-inch rounding-off bit in a router. Finally, finish-sand the top.

2. The spider, the top part of the support pedestal formed by two cross-lapped members, is fabricated next. The spider pieces are made from $^8/_4$ stock,

which is not available in every lumberyard and is usually dealt with as a hardwood. As a consequence, you'll have to either be prepared to surface the faces and joint the edges yourself or pay the lumberyard or a millwork supplier to do it for you. Have the wood dressed to a $1^3/_4$-inch thickness.

a. Cut two pieces $1^3/_4$

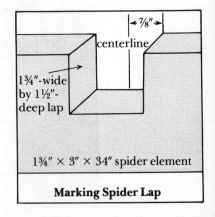

⅞″
centerline
1¾″-wide by 1½″-deep lap
1¾″ × 3″ × 34″ spider element

Marking Spider Lap

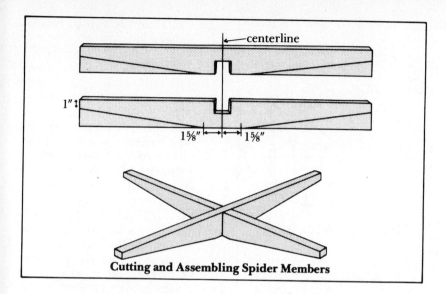

Cutting and Assembling Spider Members

d. Rough-sand the sawn surfaces. Then, using a ½-inch rounding-off bit in a router, break the exposed edges of the spider members. Do not break the edges of the surfaces that will lie against the table top, the edges of the laps or the edges of the untapered midsection of each member. Finish-sand the pieces.

e. Glue the two members together.

3. The base of the pedestal is much like the spider.

a. Cut two 1¾-inch by 3¾-inch by 26-inch base members.

b. Lay out and cut 1¾-inch-wide by 1⅞-inch-deep laps in the middle of each piece, as you did with the spider members.

inches by 3 inches by 34 inches.

b. Lay out and cut a lap in the center of each piece. The laps are 1¾ inches wide and 1½ inches deep. Measure 17 inches from one end and scribe a line across one edge at that point. This is the midline, and the lap is laid out ⅞ inch on both sides of it. Cut the lap with a backsaw and chisel, a router or a dado head in a power saw. Cut both laps slightly undersize and alternately pare and fit until the proper snug fit is obtained.

c. The spider members taper from a short midsection toward the ends. One member has its lapped edge tapered, while the other has its unlapped edge tapered. Don't make both members the same. The taper starts at points 1⅝ inches on both sides of the midline and narrows the member from full

width at those points to a 1-inch width at the ends. After scribing the taper lines, cut the members.

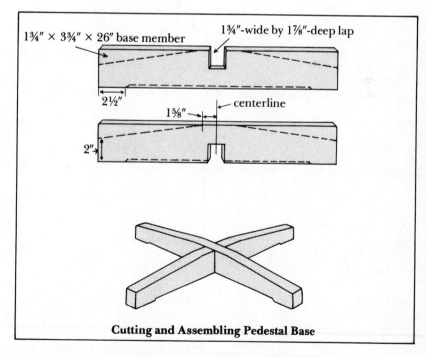

Cutting and Assembling Pedestal Base

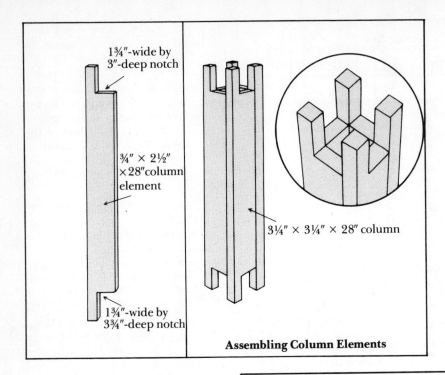

1¾"-wide by 3"-deep notch

¾" × 2½" ×28"column element

1¾"-wide by 3¾"-deep notch

3¼" × 3¼" × 28" column

Assembling Column Elements

e. Glue the two pieces together.

4. The column is composed of four identical boards glued together into a box.

a. Cut four 28-inch pieces of 1 × 3.

b. Cut a 1¾-inch-wide by 3-inch-deep notch into a top corner of each board and a 1¾-inch-wide by 3¾-inch-deep notch into a bottom corner. Cut the notches on the same side of the board. You may want to clamp the four boards together and notch all at the same time. It is wise to cut the notches a tad undersize, so that they can be pared to fit after the column is glued together.

c. Much as you did with the spider members, taper the base pieces from full width at points 1⅝ inches from the midline to a 2-inch width at the ends. Taper the lapped edge of one member and the unlapped edge of the other.

d. Rough-sand the sawn edges. Then using a ½-inch rounding-off bit on a router, break the exposed edges of the base pieces. Do not break the edges of the laps or the full-width midsection of each piece. To create feet, leave 2½ inches of unbroken edge at both ends of both flat bottoms. Measure in and mark points 2½ inches from each end of each member, then rout the edges from mark to mark. Finish-sand the pieces.

Materials

Wood

2 pcs. ⁵/₄ × 8 × 12' #2 pine or **Top elements:** 2 pcs.
1" × 7¼" × 34"
2 pcs. 1" × 7¼" × 42"
2 pcs. 1" × 7¼" × 44"

1 pc. ⁸/₄ × 8 × 6' #2 pine or **Spider elements:** 2 pcs.
1¾" × 3" × 34"
Base elements: 2 pcs.
1¾" × 3¾" × 26"

1 pc. 1 × 3 × 10' #2 pine or **Column elements:** 4 pcs.
¾" × 2½" × 28"

Hardware
4–1½" #14 r.h. screws
4–3" #14 r.h. screws

Miscellaneous
Glue
Varnish

c. With the notches cut, glue the four boards together with each board overlapping a neighbor. The finished column is 3¼ inches square. You may also nail the boards together, but this isn't necessary. If you have only a limited number of clamps, glue the column together in stages. The projecting fingers of the boards, when the column is assembled, form U-shaped channels into which the spider and base fit.

d. Rough-sand the column, then break the four long edges with a ½-inch rounding-off bit in a router. Finish-sand the piece.

5. Fit the spider into the notches at the top of the column. Pare the notches with a chisel to get the spider to settle into place. The fit should be snug. Do the same with the base. Then glue the base and spider to the column.

6. Drill eight ⁹/₃₂-inch-diameter holes in the spider for the #14 roundhead screws that will secure the top to the pedestal. Drill one hole 2 inches and a second 11 inches from the end of each arm of the spider. Counterbore the holes no more than ¼ inch; if you counterbore too deeply, the screws could break through the table top.

7. After applying your choice of finish to the top and pedestal,

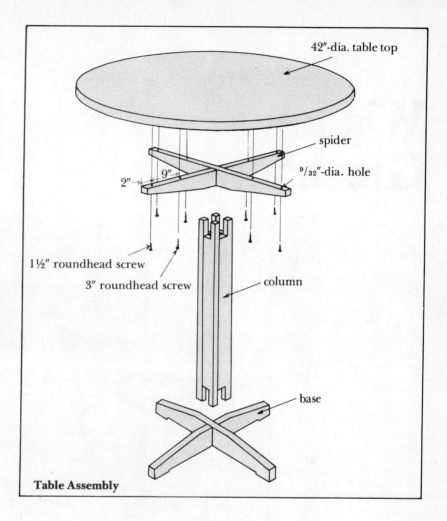

Table Assembly

42″-dia. table top

spider

⁹/₃₂″-dia. hole

1½″ roundhead screw

3″ roundhead screw

column

base

attach the top to the pedestal. Drive a 1½-inch #14 roundhead screw into each of the four outer holes and a 3-inch #14 roundhead screw into each of the other four holes.

Window Greenhouse

No harvest kitchen could be complete without *some* plants. The dream of many a gardener is to have a kitchen with a built-in greenhouse with space for houseplants, herbs and salad plants year-round.

For the gardener with the dream but not the greenhouse, here's a dandy window greenhouse. It's a natural for

the harvest kitchen. The unit is attached to the exterior of the house, over a window. Access is gained by opening the window.

This window greenhouse was designed with three requirements in mind: It had to collect as much light as possible; it had to be easy to build; and it had to look good. The design is successful on all counts.

Acrylic plastic is a key. Its flexibility allows it to be bent over framing bows. The result is a rigid structure with a minimum of shade-producing framework. Moreover, acrylic plastic is a good material for weekend woodworkers, since it doesn't break nearly as easily as glass. The most familiar brand of acrylic plastic is Plexiglas.

Another key is the basement window well cover. The design simply wouldn't work without this acrylic plastic bubble. It is the critical element in the structure, and your greenhouse's size will be limited by the size of the bubble that you are able to buy.

Acrylic plastic does have drawbacks. The first will hit you during construction: The material, according to suppliers' literature, should not be drilled. A check with the manufacturer of the bubble used in this particular greenhouse (Dilworth Manufacturing Company, Box 158, Honey Brook, PA 19344) revealed that while acrylic plastic *should* not be drilled, it *can* be if proper care is exercised. Proper care means using a sharp drill bit, a moderate drilling speed and a solid backup under the plastic. The caveat here is that once you stab the bubble with

your drill, you are on your own as far as the manufacturer is concerned.

But we did it, and you can too.

A second drawback to acrylic plastic is that its surface is susceptible to scratching. This shouldn't be a problem in normal situations; the acrylic plastic should last for years.

The size of the window greenhouse is flexible. This particular greenhouse will fit a window that is, cased in, 40¼ inches wide by 45¼ inches high or smaller. The unit can easily be made taller by constructing a third (or fourth or more) bow frame, extending the sides and using two or more acrylic plastic sheets, overlapped at the bow frames. The width and depth of the unit, however, will be limited by the sizes of bubbles available.

The unit is not difficult to

build. More than great skill, it takes some nerve and a steady hand.

Construction

Note: The plastic bubble is the critical item in constructing the greenhouse. The bow frames for the acrylic plastic, and the main frame, have to be built to accommodate the bubble. The bubble used here is 11¼ inches high and 43¼ inches wide at the flange and projects to a depth of 16¾ inches. If your bubble is some other size, you will have to modify all dimensions that follow for your construction project to be a success.

1. The first step is to map the contour of the bubble. Lay out a large piece of paper, a length of kraft paper, for example, and set the bubble upright atop it. Set a compass for an ⅛-inch

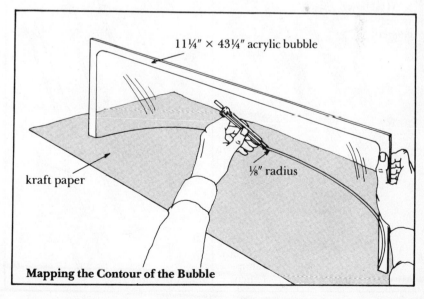

11¼" × 43¼" acrylic bubble

kraft paper

⅛" radius

Mapping the Contour of the Bubble

707

radius and, holding the compass like a divider with the point touching the inside of the bubble, move the compass around the bubble to draw a contour offset by ⅛ inch. The reason for creating a ⅛-inch disparity between the actual contour and the traced contour is that the acrylic plastic will fit between the bow frame and the bubble, and it is ⅛ inch thick.

2. The upper bow frame is constructed next. It is formed of 2 × 4s and 2 × 2s, forming an angular U shape. The tracing is transferred to this frame and the frame is cut to the contour of the bubble.

a. Cut one 31½-inch length and two 18-inch lengths of 2 × 4. The two short pieces are jointed to the ends of the long piece at 45-degree angles and with end-

lap joints. Cut a 45-degree miter on each end of each piece. Lay out the pieces and use one to mark the locations of the shoulders of the laps on the others. Cut a lap on each end of the long piece, but only on one end of each of the short pieces. The lap should be ¾ inch deep.

b. Cut two 17½-inch lengths of 2 × 2. Joining these pieces to the ends of the 18-inch lengths of 2 × 4 at 45-degree angles, using end-lap joints, completes the rough bow frame. Cut a 45-degree miter on one end of the 2 × 2. Use a 2 × 2 to lay out the end laps on the two 2 × 4s, and use a 2 × 4 to lay out the end laps on the 2 × 2s. Cut the laps ¾ inch deep on all four pieces.

c. Dry-assemble the frame,

then carefully trace the bubble contour onto the frame. Ideally, the contour line will be tangent to the outer edges of the 2 × 2s and the center 2 × 4, and will end 5½ inches shy of the 2 × 2s' ends. In the completed assembly, the latter section of the 2 × 2s will be inside the main frame of the greenhouse, while the bubble will abut the main frame's edges. Using a waterproof glue like resorcinol glue (use it throughout the project), glue the five pieces together, clamping them to a table or bench top as the glue dries to assure that the completed frame will be flat. Put a piece of waxed paper between the table top and the frame at each joint to prevent the glue squeeze-out from gluing the frame to the

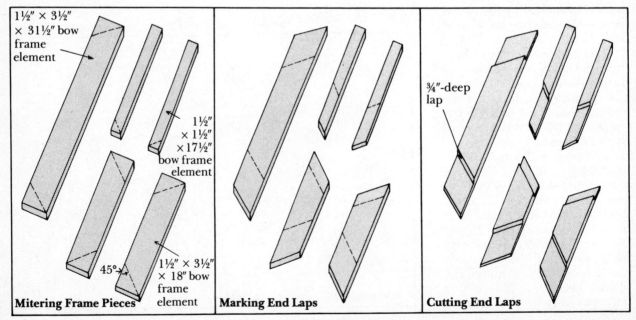

1½" × 3½" × 31½" bow frame element

1½" × 1½" × 17½" bow frame element

45°

1½" × 3½" × 18" bow frame element

Mitering Frame Pieces

Marking End Laps

¾"-deep lap

Cutting End Laps

table. Drive two 1¼-inch #12 screws into each joint, inside the contour line.

d. After the glue dries, unclamp the frame. Check to

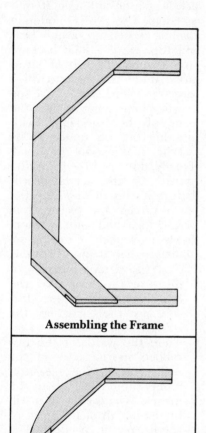

Assembling the Frame

Shaping the Frame Contour

ensure that the traced contour line is accurately laid out, then cut along the line with a band saw or saber saw.

3. Repeat the entire process to create the bottom bow frame. Then cut a 23-inch by 40¼-inch panel from ½-inch exterior plywood. Trace the contour of the bow frame onto the panel, cut it out, then glue and nail the panel to the bottom bow frame.

4. Construct the main frame of the greenhouse.

   a. Cut a 43¼-inch piece of 2 × 6 for the top and two 45¾-inch pieces of 2 × 6 for the sides.

   b. Plow a 1-inch-wide by ⅛-inch-deep rabbet along the inside front edge of each side. The acrylic plastic sheet will fit into this rabbet.

   c. Cut two 4-inch-diameter

holes in each side piece for the vents. One hole should be centered about 5 inches from the top and the second about 10 inches below the first. Use a keyhole saw or saber saw to cut the holes after drilling a starter hole inside and tangent to the edge of the vent hole.

   d. Assemble the frame using resorcinol glue and 2½-inch #12 screws, three in each joint. The top is set across the top ends of the sides. The bottom bow frame is positioned inside the sides, flush with the bottom ends and the back edges. The top of the upper bow frame is positioned 36 inches from the bottom ends of the sides, again inside the sides.

5. Cut and attach the mount-

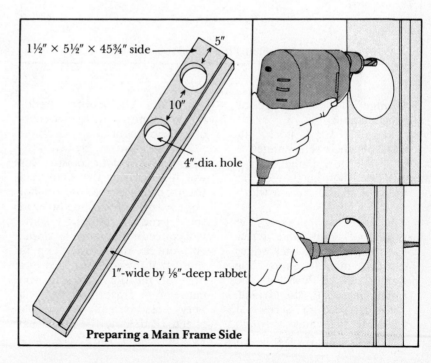

1½" × 5½" × 45¾" side

5"

10"

4"-dia. hole

1"-wide by ⅛"-deep rabbet

Preparing a Main Frame Side

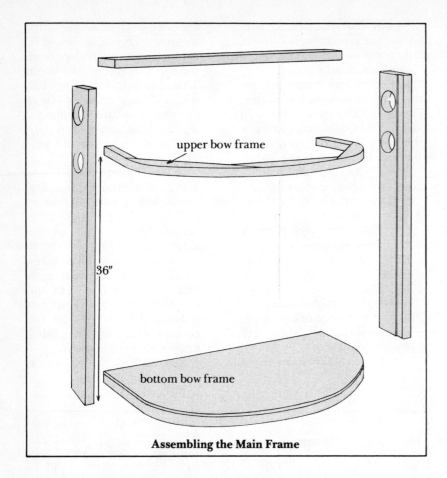

upper bow frame

36″

bottom bow frame

Assembling the Main Frame

bit. If you are capable of regrinding a drill bit, alter the included angle from the usual 85 degrees to 45 degrees. This will make it easier to drill the acrylic plastic although it isn't essential. Use a very moderate drilling speed to avoid heat buildup. Have a solid backup, like a good-size slab of scrap wood, under the area into which you are drilling. Don't have the acrylic plastic hanging over the edge of the workbench with nothing but air under it; it's acrylic plastic, not plywood. Finally, don't tear the protective paper off the acrylic plastic before it's installed. The paper is to protect the plastic from scratching, and you're more likely to scratch it during installation than at any other time.

a. Use a tape measure to measure the length of the bow frames' contours. Measure just the curve, not the straight ends. Be sure to include the width of the two rabbets in the sides of the main frame. The measurement should be about 60 inches. Whatever it is, it will be the length of the sheet of acrylic plastic needed. The height of the sheet is 36 inches. Lay out the dimensions on the acrylic plastic and cut it to size.

b. Install the acrylic plastic by slipping one end into a rabbet, then carefully bending the sheet over the bow frames and slipping the other end into the other rabbet. Bend the sheet gently, gradually; don't overstress it by bending too sharply at any one spot. Work the acrylic

ing flanges to the back edges of the main frame.

a. From 1 × 3 stock, cut two 48¼-inch side flanges, a 40¼-inch top flange and a 40¼-inch bottom flange. Rip the bottom flange to a width of 1½ inches.

b. Glue—again using the resorcinol glue—and screw the flanges to the back edges of the main frame. The flanges will be flush with the inner faces of the frame. Drive 1¼-inch #12 screws, at least four per flange, through the flanges into the frame.

6. Paint the entire greenhouse assembly with two coats of exterior paint.

7. Now's the touchy work: installing the acrylic plastic. It's worth reiterating that manufacturers of acrylic plastic do not approve of your drilling holes in their product, although some will concede that it can be done. As you do the work, keep in mind that overstressing any one area of the acrylic plastic will cause it to craze, and this will very possibly ruin the whole sheet. In drilling the holes that you must drill, use a very sharp

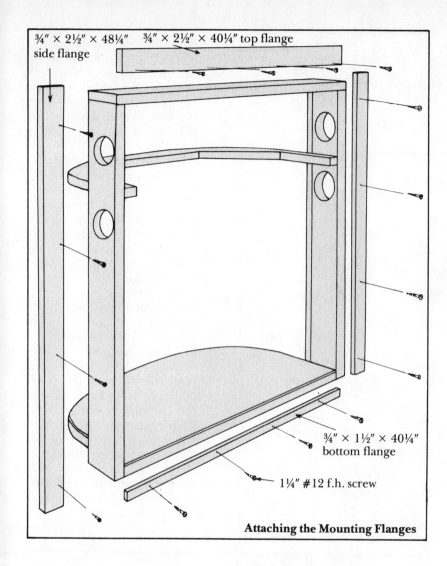

¾″ × 2½″ × 48¼″   ¾″ × 2½″ × 40¼″ top flange
side flange

¾″ × 1½″ × 40¼″
bottom flange

1¼″ #12 f.h. screw

Attaching the Mounting Flanges

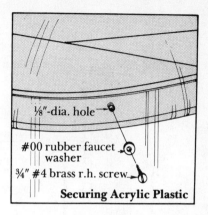

⅛″-dia. hole

#00 rubber faucet
washer

¾″ #4 brass r.h. screw

Securing Acrylic Plastic

the main framework. Do it CAREFULLY. Fasten the bubble in place with the ¾-inch #4 brass roundhead screws with the #00 rubber faucet washers on them. Then CAREFULLY drill more holes, this time through the bubble and the acrylic plastic into the upper bow frame. Complete the installation using the same brass screws and faucet washers. Be gentle.

8. The shelf is the next element to be fabricated and installed. It is suspended from the framework with lightweight chain.

a. From ⅝-inch exterior plywood, cut a 20½-inch by 35¼-inch panel for the shelf. It must be shaped so that it will be flush with the back of the greenhouse and 2½ inches shy of the inner surface of the acrylic plastic. Use the paper pattern you made of the bubble's contour. Cut it out and lay it inside the greenhouse. Set a compass for a 2½-inch radius and, holding the compass like a

plastic into the two rabbets until it fits tightly against the bow frames.

c. CAREFULLY drill ⅛-inch holes through the acrylic plastic into the bottom bow frame. Evenly space seven or more holes along the length of the bottom. Turn a ¾-inch #4 brass roundhead screw with a #00 rubber faucet

washer on it into each hole. The faucet washer will cushion the acrylic plastic and minimize stress on the material. Don't overtighten the screws.

d. Put the bubble in place. It should already have mounting holes drilled in its flanges, but if it doesn't, drill ⅛-inch holes through them and into

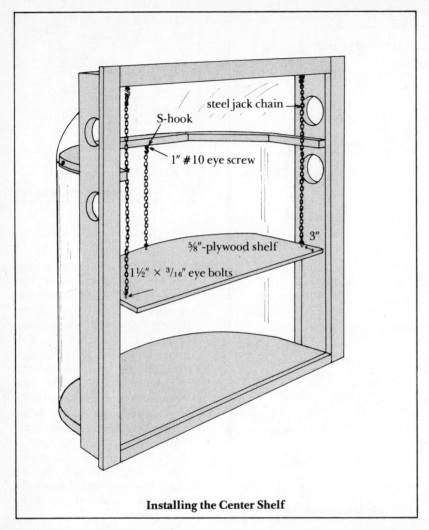

Installing the Center Shelf

steel jack chain

S-hook

1" #10 eye screw

⅝"-plywood shelf

3"

1½" × ³/₁₆" eye bolts

toured edge. The other two holes are similarly close to the contoured edge of the shelf, one on each side, 3 inches from the back edge. Put an eye bolt in each hole, with a flat washer and nut holding it in place.

b. Turn a 1-inch #10 eye screw into the bottom of the upper bow frame. Position it in the middle of the frame, 3 inches from the inner surface of the acrylic plastic. Then turn two eye screws into the main frame top, 3 inches from the back and 3 inches in from each side.

c. Cut three lengths of steel jack chain and put S-hooks on the ends of them. Hook a chain to each eye screw and hang the shelf in place by hooking the lower ends of each chain through the appropriate eye bolts. Position and level the shelf by adjusting the length of the chain; modest adjustments of the shelf can be made by turning the nuts on the eye bolts.

9. The vents are the final element to be completed.

divider as before, trace the offset contour of the greenhouse on the paper, creating a new contour line, the one for the shelf. Transfer the line to the shelf panel and cut the shelf out. Drill three ¼-inch holes in the shelf for 1½-inch by ³/₁₆-inch eye bolts. One hole is located in the middle of the shelf, about ½ inch from the con-

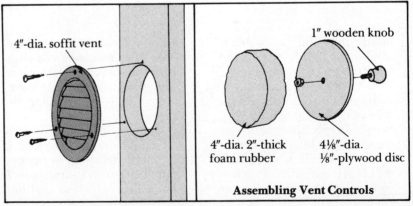

4"-dia. soffit vent

1" wooden knob

4"-dia. 2"-thick foam rubber

4⅛"-dia. ⅛"-plywood disc

Assembling Vent Controls

Materials

Wood

2 pcs. 2 × 4 × 8' #2 pine or **Bow frame element:** 2 pcs. 1½" × 3½ × 31½"
Bow frame element: 4 pcs. 1½" × 3½" × 18"
Bow frame element: 4 pcs. 1½" × 1½" × 17½"

1–2' × 4' sht. ½" A-C ext. plywood or **Bottom:** 1 pc. 23" × 40¼"

1 pc. 2 × 6 × 12' #2 pine or **Top:** 1 pc. 1½" × 5½" × 43¼"
Sides: 2 pcs. 1½" × 5½" × 45 ¾"

2 pcs. 1 × 3 × 8' #2 pine or **Side flanges:** 2 pcs. ¾" × 2½" × 48¼"
Top flange: 1 pc. ¾" × 2½" × 40¼"
Bottom flange: 1 pc. ¾" × 1½" × 40¼"

1–2' × 4' sht. ⅝" A-C ext. plywood or **Shelf:** 1 pc. 20½" × 35¼"

1–1' sq. sht. ⅛" A-C ext. plywood or **Vent controls:** 4 pcs. 4⅛" dia.

Hardware

32–1¼" #12 f.h. screws
4d nails
18–2½" #12 f.h. screws
23–¾" #4 brass r.h. screws
23–#00 rubber faucet washers
3–1½" × ³/₁₆" eye bolts w/washers and nuts
3–1" #10 eye screws
6' steel jack chain
6 S-hooks
4–4" dia. soffit vents
4–1" wooden knobs

Miscellaneous

Resorcinol glue
Exterior paint
1 pc. ⅛" × 36" × 60" acrylic plastic
1 acrylic plastic basement window well cover
1–1' sq. pc. 2" foam rubber
Contact cement
Silicone rubber caulk

a. Install a 4-inch-diameter soffit vent over the outside of each of the vent holes you cut in the frame sides.

b. The vent controls are made by cementing foam rubber discs to plywood discs. After cutting four 4⅛-inch-diameter discs from ⅛-inch plywood, drill a ¼-inch hole in the center of each and attach a 1-inch wooden knob.

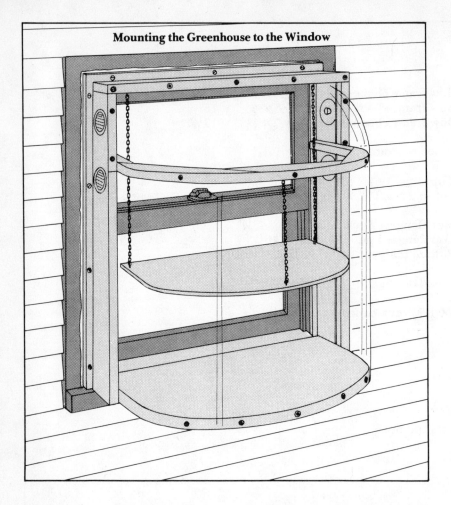

Mounting the Greenhouse to the Window

Then paint the discs. When the paint's dry, cement a 4-inch-diameter disc of 2-inch foam rubber to each plywood disc and put one assembly in each vent hole.

10. Mount the greenhouse to its window by driving screws or lag bolts through the flanges into the siding of the house or the window casing. After the unit is mounted, use silicone rubber caulk to seal the joint between greenhouse and house, and between the bubble and the acrylic plastic and the acrylic plastic and the greenhouse frame.

Part VI A Portfolio of Harvest Kitchens

The finished product is where all the planning, sweating and spending come together. It's the appearance and utility of the finished product that make it all worthwhile.

When the garden yields up its vegetables, when it's time to bake more bread, when a holiday meal is consumed and the dishes are awaiting the cleanup, those are times when the eighth revision of the floor plan, the sore thumbs, the weeks or months spent working in a makeshift kitchen become curiously pleasant reminiscences. The satisfaction in knowing that you really did do it yourself is its own special reward. And this reward will be experienced each time you work or play in your harvest kitchen.

When Johann Siegfried completed his native stone farmhouse in 1803, he didn't envision electricity, central heating or indoor plumbing, so he could not prepare for them. When later owners of Siegfried's Berks County, Pennsylvania, home added a kitchen wing around the turn of the century, they probably regarded such conveniences as citified extravagance, and did not foresee the

Blending the New with the Restored

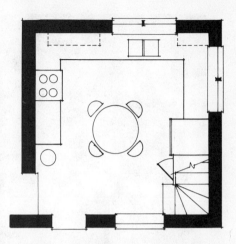

The old and the new share space in the Andrews' kitchen. An ancient chestnut lintel just above the modern electric range serves as a pot rack. And a coal-burning stove that's older than the range but newer than the lintel heats the kitchen in winter.

day when isolated farmhouses would have them as a matter of course. Later owners did modernize as their tastes and budgets permitted, but without any concern for preserving the colonial ambience. The house wasn't ruined by modernization as so many fine old homes have been, but neither was it greatly improved. When Ted and Amy Andrews, the present owners, bought the house, they had to take it as it was, and of course they found what anyone who buys an old house finds: Plumbing and wiring are run where it was convenient to put them; there is little coherence of design or allowance for later modification; and things are seldom found level or plumb. Amy Andrews has a simple approach to these difficulties: "Don't fight it, just go along with what you find."

"Going along," in this case, meant not disturbing the rough stone walls, even though they caused many decorating headaches. Choosing a counter-top material, for instance, wasn't easy. The usual materials, such as plastic laminates, could not be cut to fit snugly against the uneven stone walls. Not wanting unsightly and unsanitary gaps, Ted Andrews hit upon the idea of using ceramic tile to cover the counter tops. The grout surrounding individual tiles is molded tightly to the wall. The appearance in no way conflicts with the overall scheme of the kitchen.

Such choices are always presented in old houses, Andrews says, because "unless it's been furred out and evened up, you're always going to have to deal with exposed pipes or wires. That's part of the challenge, though. It's easy to make a place look like a 90-foot trailer by framing everything out."

With its exposed beams, rough walls, wide plank floors and natural wood doors and **719**

trim, the Andrews' house in no way resembles a house trailer. The challenge of incorporating modern appliances into the traditional decor without threatening it was great, however. The refrigerator, for instance: What do you do with a 5-foot-high, 3-foot-wide, 3-foot-deep white metal box in a colonial-era kitchen? Hide it, obviously, but where? Amy Andrews was pondering that very question one day while watching workmen frame out her counters. Inspiration struck.

"I just looked at the old pantry closet, and then at the refrigerator, and then back again," she recalls. "They were just finishing up, and I said 'Hey, can you take your saw and . . .'" She traces the outline of the now-hidden re-

Economy, ease and compatibility were combined in the Andrews' solution to the problem of kitchen storage. They purchased antique cupboards that were inexpensive because the bottoms were unrestorable, then used only the tops. Hung on the wall, they add to the kitchen's colonial flavor. Their contents are open to view, but then much of the kitchen's ambience is derived from the display/storage—plates in the cupboards, grain jars and baskets on the windowsills, crocks and canisters on the counter top.

frigerator, which was simply shoved into the previously shelved space. "There was some room left over on this side, so Ted just cut doors and put on hardware, and I have this nice little built-in cabinet."

Building contractors, conditioned by "ideal kitchen" concepts, seldom see such possibilities, yet just such simple touches as this give the kitchen its integrated feel. Just another example of how past builders' work is modified for the future. The entire kitchen, Amy laughs, "just sort of grew."

"This is what we did 'Until we can do the kitchen,'" she laughs. The existing plumbing dictated the location of the sink, and the existing wiring limited where they could put the refrigerator and stove. The final design is U-shaped, with the sink midway between the stove and refrigerator and lots of counter space between them. "It just happened to work out into a good, workable kitchen," she says.

Old wood is everywhere in the Andrews house, so it was a natural to use it in the kitchen, too. The beams are exposed, as

721

The light fixtures and the tile counter tops are novel solutions to typical problems with special twists. The Andrews wanted both to harmonize with the rest of the kitchen and knew that conventional solutions wouldn't work. The lights they made, the counters they tiled.

is a massive lintel that forms part of the framework for a walk-in fireplace in the neighboring room. The cupboards are the tops of old drysinks bought at flea markets and auctions. "We got the ones that had bad bottoms, rotted out or cracked," she recalls. "No one else wanted them."

But where others saw only junk, they saw treasure: The good tops were cut off, refinished, and hung as cupboards. They blend into the kitchen decor as no modern reproduction could. Old barn wood was refinished to match and made into cabinet doors.

Lighting fixtures are often a problem for renovators concerned with authenticity. No "period pieces" exist, and the few converted antique lanterns are scarce and very expensive. Modern reproductions are seldom cheap either. Andrews

decided to try his previously inexperienced hand at tinsmithing, and after a few trials and errors, produced a trio of handsome copper hanging lanterns. Working from three-dimensional cardboard models, Andrews traced the pattern on copper sheets and had a local sheet metal shop cut and bend them to shape. He then soldered the pieces together, and installed common lighting fixtures and frosted glass. The resulting pieces are attractive, interesting and authentic-looking. They are also a source of pride for the builders. Best of all, they cost much less than any compatible alternative.

Tile counters that flow into the walls, a "built-in" refrigerator, drysink cupboards, homemade lighting fixtures—all bespeak a commitment to taste and authenticity that can only be achieved through a maximum personal effort. As Amy Andrews says: "Just money won't do it."

A No-Frills Kitchen

Sue Wanner would rather not have a lavish kitchen or a costly stove. It's not the money. She and her husband, Jim, just like to live simply. Her idea of a worthy stove is one that is durable and doesn't waste energy—like her Magic Chef gas range. It's the only economy model she could find with an automatic starter instead of a gas-guzzling pilot light.

Naturally, this approach sometimes runs her afoul of businesspeople pursuing the "more is better" ideal. "I had an awful time getting anyone to show us a 14-foot refrigerator," Sue says. Once they learned that she was buying for a family of four, the salespeople insisted that a 14-cubic-foot model was too small. Finally, to get the reluctant clerks to show her the size she wanted, Sue began saying that there were only two people in the family.

The kitchen she, Jim and their sons Cliff and Mark built when they erected their own home in 1978—on 13½ acres beside Lake Champlain—is well crafted and efficient but not showy. And because not even simplicity comes easy, the Wanners planned each aspect in painful detail. "We planned everything so carefully—we even measured a wine glass to be sure the shelves would fit them," says Sue. Jim spent three years after they bought the building site studying all he could about construction. Sue made over 100 drawings of possible kitchens before she settled on one.

Everything in the kitchen is as open and accessible as possible. "I don't like shutting everything behind doors," says Sue. Pots and pans hang from the ceiling within easy reach. Utensils hang from a section of pegboard and from a wood strip above the counter top. Dishes, jars of food and spices rest on open shelves where the cook can reach them.

The refrigerator and stove stand against one wall of the kitchen. The counters opposite them form an island that separates the kitchen from the di-

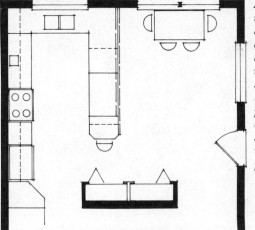

A great deal of planning went into the Wanner's kitchen. For example, Jim and Sue considered the desire for a view from the sink, the height of the person most likely to be working at the sink and the need for natural light in deciding on the size and placement of the window. Similarly, in planning the storage space, dishes, mugs and glasses were measured and just the proper space allocated for them.

ning area. A large bamboo shade can be unrolled from the ceiling to cover the island, shutting off the kitchen on formal occasions. But the informal times are much more common for the Wanners. Jim's favorite chair is in the dining area next to the island. After he comes home from work, Jim settles into the chair, and he and Sue chat while she works in the kitchen.

The kitchen counters form a U with the island as one side and the refrigerator/stove as the other. At the bottom of the U, a double sink under a window gives the cook a view of the woods outside. A single cabinet between the refrigerator and stove offers some place to set down things from the refrigerator. The rest of the counter top between the stove and the sink is butcher block. That's where much of the food preparation is done. The other counter surfaces are plastic laminate.

The counter top at the end of the island is lower than the others. Sue does a lot of baking and the height was planned to give her a good working height for kneading dough. She'd rather have a butcher-block surface for kneading, but tight finances dictated the laminate.

Facing the island is the utensil-laden pegboard that extends from the counter surface to the ceiling. The pegboard was tacked onto the back of a small desk unit built against the end of the island. The desk is a convenient place for planning meals and family business, but not quite large enough for a **725**

Open shelves keep oft-used items close at hand, allowing Sue to work efficiently. The butcher-block work surface between the stove and sink has a small cutting board at its center, which serves as the cover for the garbage drop to the Clivus Multrum composting toilet. Kitchen scraps tossed into it are composted along with body wastes.

typewriter. So when she's working on articles, stories or the many letters she writes, Sue has to go elsewhere.

Opposite the desk—along the passageway between the kitchen and dining area—is a shallow pantry closet. It's over 8 feet wide, with floor-to-ceiling shelves. The pantry holds portable appliances, large pots, extra jars and quantities of flour and honey in large covered buckets. Sue stores additional flour in containers on the large shelf beneath the kneading counter, keeping all the baking materials close at hand.

726 A garbage drop in the

Details reveal the care that went into the planning. The waste basket fits neatly into its own space, just to the right of the sink. Pots and pans hang from the ceiling within easy reach. A large bamboo shade can be unrolled over the divider-counter between kitchen and dining areas.

butcher-block counter leads to a Clivus Multrum composting toilet. The Wanners like the Clivus because it requires no water—all wastes are decomposed in the unit, producing an end product of odorless, sterile soil. A metal bowl fits snugly over the drop with a cutting board on top of that. The Wanners left a gap in the shelf above the cutting board with just enough room to permit the board to be stood on edge, flat against the wall. It's the sort of small but essential detail that consumed much of their planning time.

One detail that didn't work out as well was the choice of floor tile. While the Wanners don't believe in extravagance, they certainly want quality materials. The inexpensive asbestos floor tiles they purchased don't measure up, and they wish they'd gotten better ones. Other than that, the careful planning paid off in a functional, trouble-free kitchen.

Most of the walls in the house are made of tongue-and-groove pine boards. The boards, which the Wanners got through a local

Sue loves to bake. To make it easier to knead dough, a section of the divider-counter is lower than the basic counter height. Beneath the kneading surface is storage for flour canisters and other baking supplies. Overhead are pots and pans; to one side, on a pegboard backing a small desk, are utensils.

lumberyard, were sawn in neighboring upstate New York and air-dried. They were inexpensive. For the kitchen walls, Sue found a wallpaper-covered wallboard that works well. Since the wallpaper wraps around the entire sheet, front and back, there is no rough edge as long as the sheet is not cut. Where two sheets butt together only a small seam is visible. This made everyone happy because Sue wanted walls she could clean while Jim hates to tape and spackle joints.

Making fun of the fact that

Storage space could have been a problem, but the Wanners left room opposite the desk and the dining area windows for a pantry closet. It's shallow, but very wide. Floor-to-ceiling shelves provide plenty of room, and louvered bifold doors close off the pantry from view.

everything is so open and easy to reach, Sue says: "The whole kitchen is designed for a lazy homemaker who likes to cook."

But it's really planned to eliminate waste: wasted energy, wasted steps, wasted effort. Sue describes the kind of building she admires as "solid, simple and, in an austere way, elegant," and this is a perfect description of her own kitchen. A lot of care and effort went into making a kitchen that would function well—gracefully, perhaps, but without frills.

How could Doug and Ann Cowie build their kitchen, let alone the whole house? Not only did they lack building experience, they both work full time. Their teenage kids—a possible source of labor—all had plans for the summer.

With no real solution in mind, the Cowies (Doug's a mathematician and Ann's a super-

A Kitchen the Kids Built

Trailing vines and lots of natural wood help to create an open and relaxed atmosphere in Doug and Ann Cowie's kitchen. There are no walls between the kitchen and the living room, but a peninsular counter helps define the areas. The unit provides plenty of storage and houses the sink as well.

visor for retarded adults) went ahead and took a housebuilding course at the Shelter Institute in Bath, Maine. By the time they were done, they had convinced their three sons, Joe, Jeffrey, and David, and their daughter, Ellen (all teenagers at the time) to drop their summer plans and help build the house—in return for the amount of money they would have earned.

The Cowies finished the Shelter Institute course in the spring of 1975, started work at their Dresden, Maine, building site in June, and moved into the shell of the house (no glass, no doors, no plumbing, no electricity) in

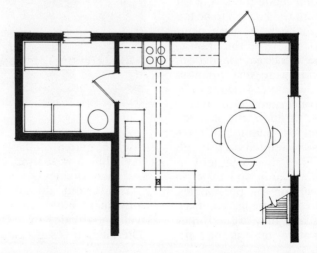

731

October. "It was a horrendous schedule," says Ann.

Consequently, the kitchen plan was laid in only a couple of evenings around the kitchen table of the old farmhouse they were renting. Ann took rough measurements of the farmhouse kitchen as a starting place, then made the layout. "I didn't want the kitchen to be too large," she says. As with plans for the rest of the house, everyone criticized the design. ("The kids were very opinionated," she notes.) Doug was more concerned with traffic patterns through the kitchen than detailed planning of work centers—he wanted no through traffic. They moved paper cutouts around on graph paper to get a feel for the possibilities, trying to keep things compact. They talked, they argued, they thought about moving the stair-

case. Eventually, they agreed that while it wasn't perfect, they had their kitchen.

The layout doesn't fit any convenient mold, since it's not really a corridor or a U shape. The kitchen is segregated from

Pots and pans hang from ceiling beams and on the pine walls. Open shelves hold frequently used spices and seasonings. Surprisingly, the room doesn't seem cluttered, yet everything is within easy reach. Between the stove and the sink is a door to the pantry-laundry room, which houses the refrigerator and a freezer.

the largely open first floor of the house by a peninsular counter, which houses the sink. Opposite it, on the house's east wall, are the stove and more cabinets. Between the two is the entrance to the pantry-laundry room, which is the home of the refrigerator. Large south-facing windows flood the area with natural light.

"The refrigerator is in the pantry because we really didn't have any alternative," says Doug. "We didn't want it in the living area." The Cowies haven't found the location inconvenient. They do some food preparation in the pantry, at a long counter next to the refrigerator—especially bread and pie making. The counter is also a convenient place to set things coming out of or going into the refrigerator.

The rough-sawn cabinets beside the stove were the last major element built in the kitchen. Although other cabinets in the kitchen are made of dressed pine, there's no clash. The rough texture adds visual interest to a room dominated by wood tones and textures.

The stove is just outside the pantry door, against the same wall as the refrigerator. Thus the refrigerator is convenient to the stove—in effect there's a long counter between them, broken only by the pantry wall. A small floor cabinet between the stove and the pantry wall serves as an additional preparation space. Narrow shelves above it are filled with spices and condiments. To the right of the stove are attractive floor and wall cabinets made of rough-sawn pine.

These cabinets were made by their oldest son, Joe, late in the fall as the last major element of the kitchen. Before it was done, Ann had been certain that cabinets made of rough-sawn boards would look awful. So the sink and island cabinets—built earlier by Marty Flaherty, a friend of Joe's—are made of dressed pine. After they were done, Ann saw some beautiful rough-sawn cabinets and re-lented. Both kinds of cabinets are finished with polyurethane, but the rough pine doesn't have a glossy sheen. On it, the finish merely serves to seal and protect the wood.

All the counter tops are of tongue-and-groove pine boards finished with polyurethane. Although the finish has held up well, the pine was intended to be temporary, and the Cowies have purchased hardwood to make butcher-block counters. They expect the work to be straight-forward except that the sink will have to be a little higher to accommodate the thicker butcher block.

Often-used utensils are stored within easy reach in the kitchen; colanders, ladles, pots and strainers hang from the plank wall and from a ceiling beam, along with potted plants and trailing philodendron vines. Ad-justable lamps attached to the wall provide task light for the sink and stove areas. The effect is relaxed and informal, but utilitarian, and the Cowies feel this reflects their own style of living.

The kitchen works for them. Everything in it—the grain stored in glass jars, the all-wood decor, even the hanging greenery—all emphasize the overall mood. And despite the kitchen's compact dimensions, there's plenty of room for friends to gather without interfering with the cook.

Through traffic is not a problem thanks to Doug's concern during the designing phase. The pantry could be larger, notes Ann, and they've got to refinish the floor—the polyurethane has begun to wear from the soft pine floors at well-used spots. But they pretty

South-facing windows flood the dining area with light and help warm the house in winter. A stained-glass lamp hangs from the open beams, adding to the rustic quality of the room.

taken a vocational carpentry course in high school. He helped to work out the construction details, often on a day-to-day basis. Each day when Doug and Ann got home from work, they would sit down with their crew and work out *what* they wanted done the next day. Then Joe would work out *how* to get it done.

Naturally, with the whole family working on the project, there were some tense moments. "It's a wonder we were still speaking to each other," says Ann. "There were very, very bad times—and some really good times when we would have an incredible feeling of accomplishment." And they all gained considerable confidence in their own simple manual skill. "I believe any of those kids could build their own house."

much got the kitchen they wanted. "It works well," says Doug. "I guess we were lucky."

While their parents got a new house and kitchen, the Cowie children earned some cash for the summer and—much more important—learned skills that each of them continues to use.

The only one of the kids who went into the project with any building skill was Joe, who had

More Than Just a Hole in the Ground

"Build a kitchen underground? No thanks! Only a bona fide crazy would want a kitchen in the dank, cold, dark earth. Be good for a root cellar, but not for the whole kitchen."

That's what the neighbors thought when Don and Ellie Pruess started excavating for their underground home. "The neighbors thought we were

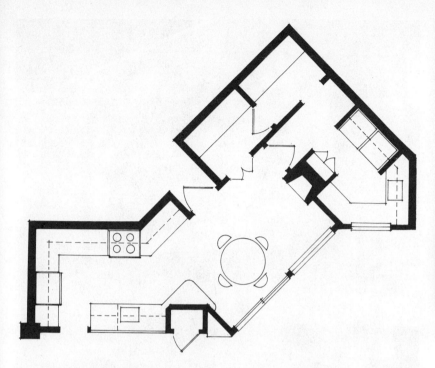

Natural light keeps the kitchen bright during the day without help from the recessed ceiling fixtures. It shines through the south-facing windows in the adjacent dining area and enters the kitchen through the door and the open space between the ceiling-hung cabinets and the counter top.

building a bomb shelter or a bunker," says Don. "Once they heard it was to be our house, they were sure only crazy people would want to live in a stone and concrete vault."

But the Pruess's underground home in no way resembles the cold, dank place their neighbors envisioned. And the kitchen—though set well into the hillside—in no way resembles a root cellar. It's brightened by the daylight that floods through floor-to-ceiling sliding glass doors along the entire

southern exposure. From the kitchen, Ellie can look out through these glass doors onto the surrounding Virginia countryside.

There is, of course, a root cellar built into the house. It would be unthinkable to build an underground harvest kitchen without one. And the Pruess's is ideal. It is combined with a pantry and a summer kitchen-laundry room. Located along the back wall, it is buried in the hillside. The walls have no insulation. Instead, the insulation is between the pantry-root cellar and the rest of the house, keeping the storage area close to 55°F. throughout the year.

When harvest season arrives, the laundry room doubles as a summer kitchen. It's equipped with a stainless steel sink, a hot plate, a convection oven and a

dehydrator. Since this area is close to the pantry and root cellar, the entire process of preserving and storing food can be done efficiently and without interfering with work in the kitchen.

A back door between the pantry-root cellar and the laundry leads through the garage out to the garden. Ellie brings the vegetables in that way and does the rough scrubbing at the laundry sink. Frozen produce such as beans, broccoli and peaches goes to a freezer in the garage. Applesauce, tomatoes, okra and extra beans are canned and stored in the pantry along with dried fruits and vegetables, and grains. Ellie keeps winter squash, potatoes, and less frequently used items in the root cellar. There's even a wine rack whose vintage bottles share the cool air with roots and vegetables. Because it isn't opened

737

as often, the root cellar stays cooler than the pantry.

Across the breakfast room from this food processing center is the kitchen itself.

Ellie wanted the layout of the kitchen to be as compact as possible, so as to save steps, but she didn't want to sacrifice counter space. A narrow, U-shaped design keeps things close together while providing ample working surfaces. Ellie also wanted to be involved in nearby activity and to have a view from the sink. A doorway leads to the dining room through a break in the U shape. The top of the U opens onto the breakfast area. This arrangement prevents the kitchen from being isolated while minimizing traffic through it.

The kitchen cabinets are made of plywood with a beautiful knotty pine veneer. The Pruesses had the carpenter who built them cut a V-shaped groove at random widths to make the cabinets resemble tongue-and-groove boards. Red oak floors add to the warm tones of the room, set off by the white counter tops and appliances.

Ellie dries herbs by hanging them from rods set atop facing wall cabinets. After they dry, it's easy to lift off the rods and slide the bunches of herbs onto a counter top. Ellie usually leaves a few bunches "hanging around" for decoration and for their pleasant scent.

To get some of the light into the kitchen and to further open it to the dining room, the space between the sink and the overhead cabinets was left open.

This opening is arranged so that the person at the sink has a view of the dining room and the hills beyond, but guests will not see stacks of dirty dishes when they look into the kitchen. The overhead cabinets have doors in

Instead of a wall, the Pruesses had cabinets installed to separate the kitchen and dining room areas. The base cabinets have paneling attached to their backs. The ceiling-hung cabinets open from both sides, easing the transfer of dishes from the table to the sink to storage and back to the table for a meal.

Storage space was planned with care. Bowls just fit on the closely spaced shelves of the overhead cabinet, a waste basket fits snugly in a drawer next to the sink, and towels and place mats fit into wide drawers. And all the storage is placed for efficient use.

both the kitchen and the dining room, easing the transfer of dishes between these rooms. The breakfast area is also bright. Its glass doors adjoin a

greenhouse-sunporch filled with ferns. The light from the dining room and breakfast area keeps the kitchen well supplied with natural light.

Because it's well lighted, the kitchen is also well heated, for the sun's warmth provides all the heat necessary for the house—in part because the earth that encloses it on three sides does such a good job of holding in the warmth. A fireplace provides the only backup source of heat. The earth keeps the house cool in summer.

Ellie's brother-in-law, archi-

tect N. N. Culin, designed the earth-sheltered home, and Ellie acted as the contractor.

It didn't take the local craftsmen long to get used to working for a woman, but they did have trouble accepting the passive solar design. "The plumber wanted to install extra pipes and the electrician wanted to install lines for electric heat because they didn't believe our home would be warm enough without a backup heat source," says Ellie.

The Pruesses are pleased with their kitchen. Oh, it may be just a hole in the ground, but you'd have to be crazy not to like it.

The Pruesses studied plans and looked at homes of the type they wanted to build. They researched and planned their design intensively. Ellie thought through the steps she would **739**

The breakfast area (oriented to the southeast, a different angle than the kitchen) receives the morning sunlight through a porch greenhouse to brighten up the first meal of the day. A small message center—with counter, bulletin board and telephone—between the breakfast area and kitchen helps Ellie organize household business.

make cooking and preserving food and mapped the arrangement out accordingly. They paid attention to details—right down to the best size for drawers to hold the tablecloths, hand towels and place mats. The Pruesses got the kitchen they wanted, because they did their planning before the builders got started.

Jars of every description line the shelves of the pantry and the root cellar. The root cellar, the inner chamber, is visited infrequently and thus maintains a lower temperature than the pantry. Ellie's routine is to fill a cart with provisions from the root cellar and pantry, then roll it to the kitchen for restocking of shelves there.

741

A Little Kitchen
That Does Big Work

Beatrice Trum Hunter is not someone who likes to do a lot of socializing in her kitchen. "That I know is contrary to how some people feel," she says, "but when I was trying to get food on the table for guests, I was held up by people trying to talk to me. And I was brought up where there were doors in homes and much more privacy."

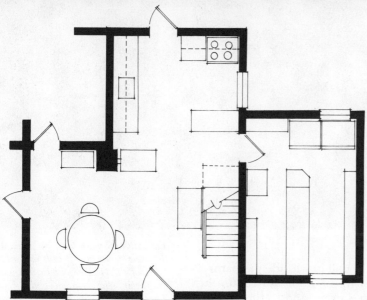

Bea Hunter's is a small and efficient kitchen, in which extra steps and searches for foods and utensils are eliminated. A magnetic strip by the sink holds an assortment of knives ready for use. Herbs and spices are kept in jars by the stove, also ready for use. A low island counter is perfect for kneading dough and doubles as a serving table or a way station between the pantry and the kitchen work areas.

For more than a decade, Bea—the author of many books on nutrition and natural cooking—and her husband John ran a summer guesthouse for individuals who wanted to vacation on a New Hampshire farm. They took in as many as a dozen guests at a time, so there was a lot of cooking to do. But Bea did all the cooking then in the same small kitchen she uses today for family cooking and food preserving.

"You mean you prepare food for all these people in here?" asked one of the guests after taking a look at the kitchen. The secret is a well-organized cook, who transforms the modest facility into a productive center. She cleans up as she goes and relies on a large pantry to keep the kitchen uncluttered.

The pantry is actually larger than the kitchen—with plenty of room for supplies, vegetables from the garden, even a refrigerator and freezer. The refrigerator had been located at the spot where the Hunters broke through the wall to reach the pantry when they remodeled the kitchen. With that wall space gone, the pantry seemed the only reasonable place for the refrigerator.

A shelf by the refrigerator permits easy loading and unloading of quantities of food. Use of a tray and good mealtime planning keep the trips between the kitchen and pantry to a **743**

minimum, so Bea feels the arrangement is quite workable. In winter, the pantry is kept at about 45°F. and serves as a large cool-room. The refrigerator and freezer don't run as often in the chilly pantry as they would in the warm kitchen, saving electricity.

Most of the pantry space not taken up by the refrigerator and freezer is devoted to shelves for storage of grains, food purchased in bulk, produce, stacks of dishes—even an enormous collection of cookbooks. A large

grain mill just inside the pantry, next to the door, is close to the stored grain and to the kitchen island beside the pantry door where Bea kneads the dough.

The island also serves as a buffet table for informal dinner parties—it's easy to transfer food from the stove or oven to the island. The serving dishes don't clutter up the dining table, yet guests readily come back to the island for seconds.

The kitchen island is a recycled wall cabinet. During the remodeling, four legs and a

The cabinets were built in place using the same knotty pine boards used in other parts of the Hunter's house by the same carpenter who renovated those parts. They are relatively plain, but certainly durable.

plastic laminate counter top were added, turning it into a useful work surface. It's set lower than other counter tops—perfect for bread making and other jobs that are done best at a low working height.

The original kitchen was located in the same room as the

The pantry entrance is just past the kitchen island. The island was made by fastening a counter top and legs to an old wall cabinet. A closet under the stairs harbors household cleaning supplies, while decorative items are displayed on shelves just above it.

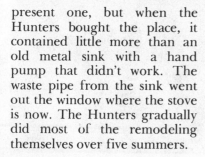

present one, but when the Hunters bought the place, it contained little more than an old metal sink with a hand pump that didn't work. The waste pipe from the sink went out the window where the stove is now. The Hunters gradually did most of the remodeling themselves over five summers.

Working slowly gave them the opportunity to do a good deal of planning during the winter months, and the result is an efficient, step-saving design. Expenditures were made in small lumps that did not require heavy borrowing or undue sacrifice. Because the financial burden was tolerable, the Hunt-

ers bought the best-quality materials and equipment they could find, feeling that these would last best. They also chose natural materials wherever possible—preferably those requiring the least upkeep. The wood paneling for example, is more durable than paint or wallpaper, and—finished to match the cabinets—gives the kitchen a warm, cozy look.

Originally the paneling was to cover the underside of the stairs, but Bea saw potential and insisted that the spaces formed by the stairs be transformed into decorative shelves. The rest of **745**

The pantry is the heart of this truly productive kitchen. Floor-to-ceiling shelves hold not only crocks and jars of foods purchased in bulk, but also extra dishes, canned fruits and vegetables, the refrigerator and freezer, even a library of cookbooks.

the space under the stairwell forms a small catch-all that Bea call her "Fibber McGee" closet—a great place to store paper bags, empty egg cartons and brooms.

Most of the food preparation is done next to the sink or the stove. Knives, colanders and other utensils hang on the wall between the counter top and the wall cabinets to the left of the sink. The deep sink has enough space under the faucet for large bowls or canning pots.

A dishwasher next to the stove is covered with butcher block and is a useful place for

746

The wood stove, in addition to heating the house in winter, serves year-round to separate the kitchen from the dining area. The table is sufficiently large for the meals Bea cooks today, but in years gone by, she served a dozen or more summer guests on the screened-in porch just beyond the door.

final preparations prior to cooking. The spices are within easy reach. The spices—many grown in Bea's garden—are kept in interesting bottles with glass or wooden stoppers.

Although the kitchen and pantry function well, a view from the sink was sacrificed for convenience. The bathroom is on the other side of the wall from the kitchen sink. Rather than extend the pipes from the bathroom under the kitchen, up at the window and locating the sink there, the Hunters placed the sink next to the existing plumbing. Bea now says if they had built from scratch she would have preferred to put the sink by the window, overlooking the rural view.

The Riteway wood stove that heats the house separates the kitchen from the dining area. This creates a relaxed, open look—though it also encouraged the summer guests to chat while Bea was trying to get the food out on the table.

Bea is quite satisfied with her compact kitchen. "I wouldn't like a big old kitchen with a couch and lots of space," she says. She finds that she can get her work done without many unnecessary steps. The small space serves both her efficient style of working and her need for privacy.

747

A Kitchen the Cook Built Herself

Pam Kenyon built her own kitchen. It's not that her husband David isn't handy. It's just that he has a thriving law practice to attend to and not much free time. So when Pam got tired of wiping the dust from dishes stored on the open shelves of her temporary kitchen, she and a friend refurbished the whole thing.

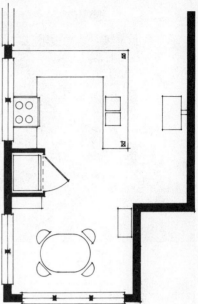

Pam and David Kenyon's house is open, bright and airy, and the kitchen is the heart of it. The kitchen counters form a U in the middle of the house, between the living room and the dining area, separating the entire area into distinct spaces. The absence of wall- or ceiling-hung cabinets contributes to the open feeling.

Pam doesn't believe in renovating little by little. "If you'd like to get it all squared away", she says, "you have to treat it as a real job." That's exactly what she did. She got baby-sitters for the kids, ordered materials well in advance and knocked off the whole project in two weeks.

The frame of the counters was left, but the plywood shelves and the counter top of tongue-and-groove pine boards were ripped out. After squaring the frame, Pam added new shelves, facing, drawers and doors. The counter top is hardwood flooring finished with pure tung oil (not the thinned kind, which contains petroleum distillates). The counter tops are reminiscent of butcher block, but were a lot less expensive to make.

After two and a half years of looking at the refrigerator, Pam was irritated by the sight of it. Its white exterior stood out harshly against the all-wood walls and ceilings, and it loomed ominously over the dining room

table. So when Pam remodeled in May, 1979, she enclosed the refrigerator in a small pine closet. No one seems to mind opening two doors to get to the food, and the closet is a good place to store brooms and mops. There's also storage space above the closet with separate doors.

Pam and David built the original, temporary kitchen when they constructed their house during the summer of 1976—after studying housebuilding at the Shelter Institute in nearby Bath, Maine. The basic layout of the new kitchen remains unchanged, a testament to the initial design. "It was, really, a very acceptable kitchen," says Pam.

By the time Pam remodeled her kitchen, she had solid experience, having built much of her own house and having helped friends build theirs. But when she and her husband started the house, neither of them had done any carpentry to speak of. They decided to build their own home only after tak-

ing the course. David took off work for several weeks to help start the project. He and Pam worked with two helpers to erect the frame and install the roof in those first few weeks. After that, David worked on weekends while Pam labored full time with the two helpers. Friends dropped by occasionally

The kitchen is warmed by the sunlight that pours through the huge south-facing windows, and by the natural hues of the wood used throughout. Even the white of the refrigerator was too cold for Pam, so she enclosed it in a pine closet. Pam did the cabinetry herself, building in all the cabinets and constructing counter tops of oak flooring.

to help. The Kenyons moved into the partially finished home in October, 1976.

The Shelter Institute's co-founder Pat Hennen helped things go smoothly by offering regular technical advice. "I think that's a lot of what helped," says Pam. "Before I started each stage, I would go through it with Pat." As a result, Pam wasn't overwhelmed by the work. "I suppose it never really got to be more than I could handle. It all proceeded step by step."

One notion stressed repeatedly at the Shelter Institute is that a house should reflect the lifestyle of the people who will **751** live in it. Pam and David wouldn't have given much thought to the location of their kitchen, but prompted by this idea, they decided to make it central to the house and open to it. They located the kitchen in the middle of the house, between the living and dining areas. The counters form a U whose open end is toward the dining area. This permits easy transfer of food to the table, while eliminating through traffic. (To get from the dining area to the living area, you walk outside the kitchen U, between the sink counter and the north wall of the house.) Pam located the sink away from the wall because she had always lived where the sink faced a blank wall and wanted something different.

The Kenyons weren't interested in entertaining lots of people at once, especially in formal settings. So they designed small living and dining areas—perfect for relaxed gatherings of a few friends and comfortable for day-to-day living.

During the day, there's plenty of light in the kitchen from the windows in the dining and living areas and from the south-facing window over the stove. At night, one overhead fixture and two strips of five lights each keep the kitchen brightly lighted. The strips each run along a ceiling joist. Pam boxed in the sides to make them as inconspicuous as possible.

One problem with the open kitchen design that Pam didn't foresee is that it is not close to the pantry. The pantry is a large

13-foot by 20-foot room at the back of the house. Pam keeps the canning equipment there and has to haul it out to the kitchen during canning season. She is intrigued by the idea of setting up a temporary summer kitchen in the pantry, but for now the arrangement remains somewhat inconvenient.

The pantry is also a temporary home to the workshop. When the Kenyons build the barn they are planning, they will move the workshop there. The pantry will remain where it is. To the freezer and wall-length shelves that now hold jars and

Both the dining table and the stove have a southern view of a ravine that falls away to a river. In summer, breezes continually move up the ravine, cooling the house. Since the windows were owner-fabricated and don't open, screened openings beneath them are uncovered to ventilate the house. Insulation-backed panels, such as that lying on the stove, cover the ventilation openings in cool weather.

containers of preserved food, the Kenyons will add another set of shelves, doubling the storage space.

Pam also wants to build shelves above the sink counter. She may even put in a dish rack right over the sink. Racks of the kind she wants are popular in Scandinavian countries. The dishes drip-dry and don't have to be put away—the rack is the storage place. Since the sink faces the wood stove and a windowless part of the north wall, shelves won't reduce the view. The kitchen will still be open to the dining and living areas.

Pam considers planning ahead a very important part of building. "Don't assume that by the time you get to the finishing it will fall into place," she warns. Even when the plan is good, all the details take time. "The kitchen proper went fine," says Pam, "but we still haven't done all the finish work. When you are living in it, it's easy to get distracted. If you really want to build your kitchen and know you want to do it, you can. But you have to be careful of thinking of it as glamorous."

753

A Harvest Kitchen for the Age of Energy Efficiency

House designer Michael Jantzen, combines self-sufficiency with space-age technology in the kitchen he and his wife, Ellen, designed and built. Recycling bins and ample pantries blend harmoniously with solar collectors and a unique ventilating system—while a ubiquitous computer monitors household functions.

The Jantzens' basic intent was

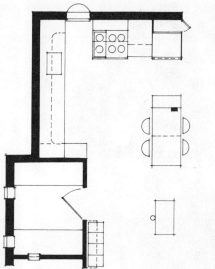

Looking tidy as a ship's galley, the Jantzen's meticulous but constantly evolving kitchen has such features as foldaway stools that resemble cardboard cutouts and insulating window panels that fold down in cold weather to conserve heat.

to ignore traditional aesthetics and build a home that would be in tune with the world around it. They grow 70 to 80 percent of the food they eat, and have made the preservation and storage of it fundamental to the house.

"We put a great deal of emphasis on food storage," says Michael, "because it is very energy intensive to try to grow food in greenhouses in the winter in Illinois. We prefer to put out energy into food storage rather than production—and we emphasize growing sprouts in winter since that doesn't take a lot of energy. You can grow them on your windowsill."

While the Jantzens don't use their greenhouse for winter food production, it is an important part of the gardening plans. Ellen—who up until now has done the bulk of gardening and preserving—uses the greenhouse to start the seedlings for her large garden. And for the last five years she has sold seedlings from it to local gardeners.

Michael sees no point in holding bulk-stored food at room temperature, having it waste valuable heated space, so he stores grains and other food that won't be damaged by heat or cold outside the house. This outside pantry is located on the cool north side where it also serves to buffer the house. It provides an extra layer of insulation. About once a month, Ellen goes out and loads up on the items she needs, storing them in smaller containers in a pantry next to the kitchen.

The inside pantry (also against the north wall) holds not only these batches of bulk food, but all of the canned and frozen food the Jantzens eat throughout the year: quarts of beans, peppers, tomatoes, jelly and jam, and a freezer full of garden produce. There's also plenty of applesauce because 8 of their 17 acres comprise an old but still productive apple orchard.

755

The kitchen island serves a variety of purposes. It's a preparation center and a site for informal dining. But it is also the laundry, as it houses the washer and dryer. Continuing the multifunction theme, water for the washer can be preheated by either solar collectors or the heating stove. The "Fireball" stovepipe stove that Mike designed can also be used to heat the house.

A vent at the top and bottom of the pantry's outside wall keeps the room between 35° and 40°F. during the winter, making the pantry a perfect cool-room for fresh produce and other perishables. Should the temperature drop close to freezing, Ellen or Michael sticks insulated plugs in the vents to retain more heat. In summer, the slightest breeze will pull cool air up through the bottom vent from the crawl space beneath the house. (There are more of these vents throughout the living area for summer cooling.) Because of the low temperature in the pantry, the Amana freezer there doesn't have to work as hard, requiring less than its normally stingy 75 watts.

The layout of the kitchen proper is pretty standard, but there are features not found in the ordinary kitchen. The stove

Storage space was designed carefully. Open shelves over the sink hold a variety of attractive bowls, crocks and baskets. The hodgepodge of jars, bottles and packages that clutter every kitchen are hidden in cabinets. The cabinet face frames and doors were fabricated of single sheets or hardwood plywood; a saber saw was used to cut the doors into the panels. The flush fit and rounded door corners emphasize the clean, modern look of the kitchen.

and refrigerator—separated by a single cabinet—both have energy-saving features. The refrigerator, like the freezer, uses no more electricity than a typical light bulb. The stove operates with either gas or wood— and with acres of trees outside, there is plenty of the latter.

Because they are diligent recyclers, the Jantzens have designed a special recycling center into their kitchen. Scraps from the table go into a bowl under the sink, then out to the compost pile. Next to the pantry, four bins hold aluminum, steel, plastic and paper for recycling or disposal. Since many plastics are not biodegradable and produce poisons when they burn, the Jantzens try to avoid them as

757

much as possible. They also try to buy things in reusable containers.

Michael wants his designs to be flexible and multifunctional. He would like to increase the number of ways a person can do any job and increase the number of jobs an item in the house can do, too.

Take the kitchen island for example. It stands outside the L formed by the refrigerator and stove on one side and the sink on the other. Thus it is a very useful preparation area outside the normal area. It's also next to the wood stove. The island and stove divide the kitchen from the living area.

Until last year, the island had an open space under it where a cart holding wood for the stove was kept. Now, Michael has installed a washer and dryer where the cart once went, making it a laundry.

Michael's also added a back to the island. Sawn out of it like paper cutouts are two stools that can open easily or fold out of the way, flush with the back. Thus, the island also serves as an informal dining place.

Then there's the computer. As originally conceived, it was to monitor temperature, humidity and air movement throughout the house, providing a central "brain" to integrate the different systems and to process the data for future improvements. But Michael wants to use the computer as well to store recipes, inventories of supplies, nutritional information and records of gardening efforts. The latter should be helpful in planning the vegetable garden each year, and might enable Ellen to make her seedling business more profitable.

Michael's philosophy is that arrangements should be fluid.

Even the pantry is tidy, with jars, vegetables, utensils and equipment all neatly arranged. As jars of garden vegetables are emptied the glassware is cleaned and returned to its place on the shelf. The capacity of the pantry is increased by relegating bulk foods like grains to an unheated outside closet located on the north wall of the house. In keeping with the hallmark of the Jantzen home, even the trash containers are tidy. Numbered bins just outside the pantry hold metal and glass for recycling.

"I try to design it so that it allows a freedom of choice in the future. As your life-style changes, the design should be able to flex with it. For instance," he said, "since your photographer was here taking pictures, the appearance of the kitchen has changed completely. You wouldn't recognize it now." Why? Well, the blond wood cabinets were nice, but he and Ellen weren't happy with the

wood finish. The varnish started to yellow and the cabinets didn't look like natural wood anymore. So they painted them an off-white. This has brightened the kitchen considerably, but not so much as to produce unpleasant glare, says Michael. Most of the kitchen illumination is task lighting, and the counter tops are a warm terra-cotta color, so the cook is seldom looking directly at the white.

There have been times, admits Michael, when he has had to rip out things that didn't work out. "That's a chance you take," he says, "but there's a certain freedom to this approach. It keeps a much more fluid design." In fact, when Michael and Ellen started building in 1977 (and they are obviously still at it), they had only a floor plan and a rough scale model. They not only allowed accidents to give them cues and help shape their thinking, they sought them out.

This is contrary to the careful-planning approach most builders follow, but the Jantzens believe it works for them. Michael has been building and making things since he was 11. He's an inveterate tinkerer. For a time he was a sculptor—before he discovered the joy and challenge of sculpting buildings into changing, integrated living space, what he calls conceptual art. Ellen moves easily within this changing environment, making it a functional, warm and productive place.

Naturally they have plenty of plans for the future, and—given their style—they will probably do some things they haven't thought of yet. Michael does plan to get more involved with the gardening, preserving and cooking. He's been feeling left out of that side of things except when there's a heavy load of compost to haul.

There's also a summer kitchen in the works and a methane gas generator (powered by chicken droppings) to run the stove. The Jantzens have just gotten two baby goats who are slated to produce garden fertilizer and, when they get bigger, milk. In other words, things are perking along normally at the Jantzens': lots of change, plenty of ideas and a productive household.

A Country Kitchen in Grand Style

"All the simple things my grandmother did are gourmet things today," says Shirley Cavallo, whose large country home on the banks of the Delaware River contains a kitchen most women—and many men—would give their eyeteeth for. The Cavallo kitchen is large, luxurious, fully equipped and decorated with style, but it

Shirley Cavallo had been using her big gas restaurant range for nearly 10 years when she and her husband designed a grand new kitchen, with the stove as the heart. With six burners, two ovens, a griddle and a broiler, it was up to any meal Shirley wanted to prepare, whether lunch for 2 or dinner for 60. Nine years later, the range is still in mint condition, still the heart of a grand kitchen.

is above all a working kitchen, where Shirley can do "simple things that are gourmet today." She and her husband, Dr. John Cavallo, an Easton, Pennsylvania chiropractor, designed the kitchen nine years ago to better serve the needs of their growing family. With five children, numerous kinfolk and in-laws, and a wide circle of friends and acquaintances dropping by, the Cavallos find that a simple weekday lunch can suddenly turn into a sit-down meal for 12 or 20. They've prepared for such circumstances, and Shirley now says with pride: "I can have 25, 50, even 100 people here, and they'll all feel at home. They usually all end up in the kitchen!"

The kitchen and dining area are one large room, but an island separates the preparation area from the rest of the room. The preparation area is L-shaped, with the island set into the angle, a rather common design that the Cavallos have improved upon: The island is itself L-shaped, with the extension nearest the stove lower than the other. This allows the cook to work on one part and serve from another—in effect, there are two islands, each topped with butcher block. The higher arm holds a deep stainless steel sink (separate from the kitchen's main sink, which is located on the same wall as the stove), a warming drawer for bread, and plenty of storage for linen and tableware. But most important, the island is designed to allow the cook to perform most of her tasks while facing the dining area, a big **761**

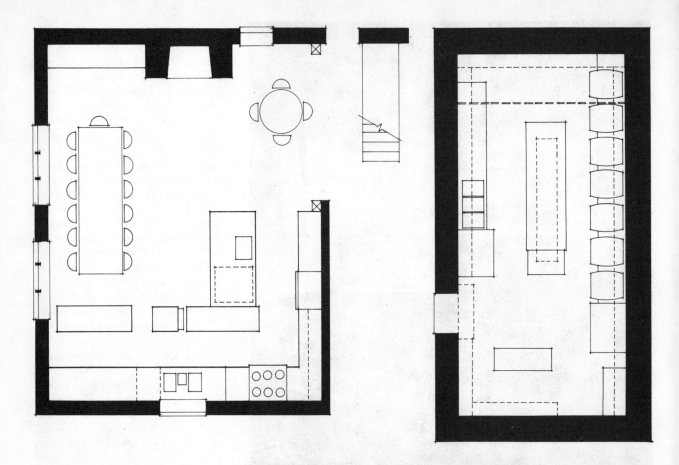

advantage for entertaining.

"I don't like to work up against walls," Shirley says, "especially when we're entertaining. I like to face people, and it gives me a good feeling not to be shut out of the conversation with my back to them. And no one even notices if I haven't finished doing something beforehand. I can hand them a spoon and bowl and say 'Here, you do it,' and it's perfectly natural. It draws them into the cooking process."

The island's storage space allows the table to be set without the cook being disturbed, and it

762

Size is the feature of the Cavallo's kitchen that's most striking initially. It's a huge room. It's got a table for 4 by the fireplace, and a table for 14 by the windows. An enormous island is the principal work area, with a sink built in and the refrigerator and most cooking utensils and equipment close at hand. Its position allows the cook to work without hindrance, yet be a part of any kitchen social activity.

can be used as a buffet table for hors d'oeuvres or make-your-own salads.

Above the island—and indeed above the entire preparation area—hang pots, pans, skillets, tools and utensils of shapes familiar and exotic. The area resembles a hanging garden, in which the flora has been replaced by copper and cast iron, stainless steel and wood. Strings of drying peppers from the garden bounce their hues off shiny copper colanders, and glass and crockery containers of herbs, spices, grains, pasta and other colorful foodstuffs line shelves along the walls. It seems chaotic, but everything is within easy reach of the working cook. "People think I'm crazy having everything sitting out," Shirley laughs, "but I like to be able to

Sensory overload hits in the preparation center. Shirley Cavallo seems to have at least one of every imaginable cooking tool—all at her fingertips. The counter between the stove and the refrigerator (above) is brimming with spice jars, utensils and equipment. Copper-clad pots and pans hang over the island, itself laden with food and equipment. All is within easy reach for Shirley as she works at the stove. It helps that she knows where everything is.

see it and have it within reach. To me, that's beauty."

The preparation area is dominated by an 18-year-old Garland gas restaurant range with griddle and warming oven. The stove is a good example of the Cavallos' philosophy: They prefer to buy commercial-quality items rather than standard consumer items. "It's better to invest in one good thing that will last," Shirley says. "You can hand good things down from generation to generation."

Before the present kitchen

was built, the Cavallo home had a much smaller kitchen, yet the oversize stove was there. "My whole kitchen was centered around it," Shirley adds.

It still forms the center of the preparation area, and is the focal point of the kitchen. Above it, a large exhaust hood provides a handy, out-of-the-way space for drying herbs from the garden.

Dinner for 5, 15 or 50 requires a lot of planning, but it also requires a lot of food. Near the kitchen proper, the Cavallos

765

A big, extended family, the Cavallos do everything on a big scale, including raising and storing food. It's all kept in the cantina, a magnificent walk-in refrigerator that's bigger than most people's kitchens. In it are hundreds of quarts of home canned vegetables, a half-ton or more of grain, meats butchered and processed by the family, and hundreds of gallons of homemade wine. And the equipment to do it— a three-compartment stainless steel utility sink, scales, canning equipment, a sausage stuffer—is kept there too.

have built a large walk-in cold room, which is actually dug into the hillside that is against the rear wall of the kitchen wing. This spacious wine cellar/root cellar/refrigerator/meat locker permits the cook to store all the produce of the home place, to buy in bulk, take advantage of seasonal availability, and prepare some dishes in advance. The Cavallos use it to store everything from eggs to flowers to homemade wine. The *cantina*—cellar—is an integral part of the food preparation system of most Italian country houses, says John. "Every home should be built on a hillside so that it can have an old-fashioned *cantina*. It's energy efficient, too: easy to cool in summer, and it stays cold all winter by itself."

Does the kitchen that has everything lack anything? "Not really," says Shirley, though she admits that a "second separate preparation area would be helpful for large projects."

Through all the planning and building of their kitchen, one thought was uppermost in the Cavallos' minds: The kitchen must work. And it does. Form follows function, and this spacious country kitchen, with its jumble of hanging pots and cluttered shelves, is oddly orderly: It is a working kitchen. As Shirley says with conviction, "I may have all these gadgets around, but I'm a cook who starts with her hands."

Building a Metric Harvest Kitchen

Measurements are a vital, yet routine, part of any building project, including the building of a kitchen. You measure materials to calculate their cost. You measure pieces of materials to ensure they'll fit. Almost every step of every project involves measuring in some way. It's so routine, it's taken for granted.

Yet for many readers of this book, the measurements can be a distinct problem, for the world is metric and the United States (along with Brunei, Burma and Yemen) is not. *Build Your Harvest Kitchen,* being an American book, follows the American system of measurement, called the English system.

For the American reader, there's no problem, although a working knowledge of metrics can be worthwhile. Imported goods, including plywoods, are sized in metrics. And while there's been no mandatory changeover legislated in the U.S., voluntary conversion is planned, and some manufacturers are converting. You ought to know about both systems and be able to convert from one to the other.

For the reader outside the U.S., there probably won't be a problem. Your materials will be metric, as will be your rulers and your thinking. Some conversion may be necessary in following specific directions like for the prefab cabinets in Part IV or for the projects in Part V. But if you live in a metric country, just work as you ordinarily would.

The metric system is based on seven base units from which additional units are developed by using multiples of ten. In building, the most important units are the meter (length), the kilogram (mass or weight), the degree Celsius (temperature), and the liter (liquid volume).

The meter (m) is used to measure length. A meter is about 3⅓ inches longer than the yardstick. It is divided into 100 equal parts called centimeters (cm). Each centimeter is divided into 10 equal parts called millimeters (mm). The millimeter is a little smaller than 1/16 inch. Measurements in woodworking are made to the nearest millimeter. Using metric measurements eliminates fractions, which can often be a source of confusion in woodworking.

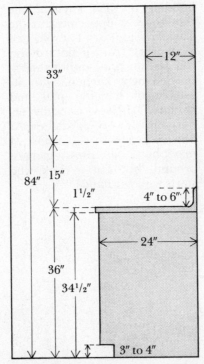
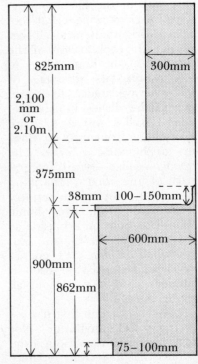

Standard cabinet measurements in English and metric terms.

Metric Conversion of Dimension Lumber
(For purchase, the sizes are rounded off to the nearest millimeter.)

English System (inches)		Metric System (millimeters)	
Nominal Size	*Actual Size*	*Nominal Size*	*Actual Size*
1 x 2	¾ x 1½	25 x 50	19 x 38
1 x 3	¾ x 2½	25 x 75	19 x 63
1 x 4	¾ x 3½	25 x 100	19 x 90
1 x 6	¾ x 5½	25 x 150	19 x 140
1 x 8	¾ x 7¼	25 x 200	19 x 184
1 x 10	¾ x 9¼	25 x 250	19 x 235
1 x 12	¾ x 11¼	25 x 300	19 x 286
2 x 2	1½ x 1½	50 x 50	38 x 38
2 x 3	1½ x 2½	50 x 75	38 x 63
2 x 4	1½ x 3½	50 x 100	38 x 90
2 x 6	1½ x 5½	50 x 150	38 x 140
2 x 8	1½ x 7¼	50 x 200	38 x 184
2 x 10	1½ x 9¼	50 x 250	38 x 235
2 x 12	1½ x 11¼	50 x 300	38 x 286
3 x 4	2½ x 3½	75 x 100	63 x 90
4 x 4	3½ x 3½	100 x 100	90 x 90

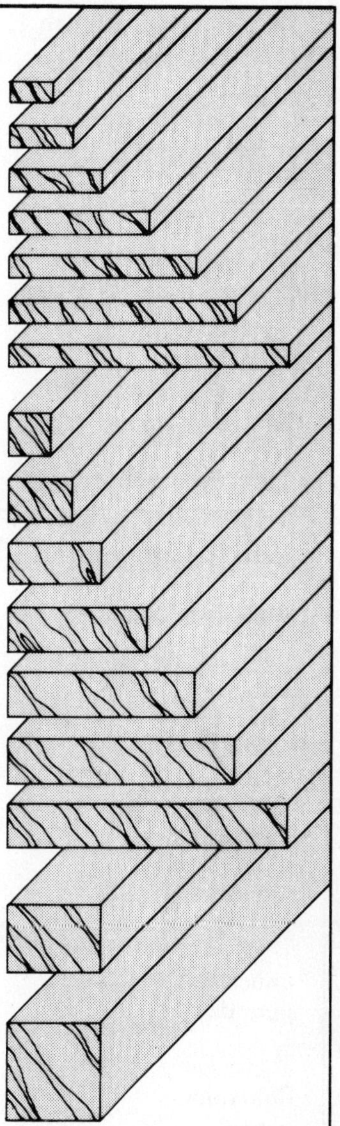

The metric unit used to measure weight is the kilogram (kg), which is equal to about 2.2 pounds. Smaller weights are shown in grams (g). One thousand grams equal one kilogram.

Liquid capacity, for such things as paints, oils and other finishing materials, is measured in liters (L). The liter is slightly larger than the quart and a half-liter (500 milliliters) would be used in place of the pint. Since the liter and half-liter are **769**

Plywood

	English	Metric
	4′ x 8′ sheet	1.22m x 2.44m or 1,220mm x 2,440mm

Actual Thickness

inches	rounded millimeters
¼″	6mm
⅜″	10mm
½″	13mm
⅝″	16mm
¾″	19mm
⅞″	22mm
1″	25mm

Metric Conversion Chart

When You Know	Multiply By	To Find
	length	
inches	25.4	millimeters (mm)
feet	30	centimeters (cm)
yards	.9	meters (m)
	area	
square inches	6.5	square centimeters
square feet	.09	square meters
square yards	.8	square meters
	weight	
ounces	28	grams (g)
pounds	.45	kilograms (kg)
	volume	
fluid ounces	30	milliliters (mL)
pints	.47	milliliters (mL)
quarts	.95	liters (L)
gallons	3.8	liters (L)

a little larger than the pint and quart, expect metric containers to cover a larger area.

The metric measurement for temperature is shown in degrees Celsius (°C). The freezing point and boiling point on this scale are 0° and 100° respectively. Body temperature is 37°C.

Refer to the chart for conversion of dimension lumber from English to metric sizes and vice versa. The metric measurements are rounded off to the nearest millimeter for the actual sizes and to the nearest number ending in 0 or 5 for nominal sizes. Since the millimeter is a bit smaller than $1/16$ inch, metric measurements are very close to English measurements.

In metric countries, dimensions in woodworking are given in millimeters. Although centimeters could be used, it is less confusing if all dimensions are stated in one unit, and the chosen unit is the millimeter. Lengths of dimension lumber start at 1.8 meters (6 feet) and increase in 300-millimeter increments to 6.3 meters (20 feet).

It's probably easiest to forget conversion and just think and work in one system or the other. This may sound difficult, but that's only because it's unfamiliar. If you use an English ruler and figure all your work in English measure, your materials, tools and kitchen won't know the difference. Neither will they notice if you use a metric ruler and do your planning in metrics.

Index